National Playwrights Directory.

SECOND EDITION

EDITED BY PHYLLIS JOHNSON KAYE

A Project of the

Eugene O'Neill Theater Center

305 Great Neck Road
Waterford, Connecticut 06385

Library of Congress Cataloging in Publication Data

Kaye, Phyllis Johnson.
   National playwrights directory.

   Includes index.
   1. Dramatists, American — 20th century — Directories.
2. American drama — 20th century — Bio-biobliography.
I. Title.
PS129.K3   1981   812'.0025'73   81-14097
ISBN 0-9605160-0-X   AACR2

INTRODUCTION

We think we know what people look like, don't we. Don't we?

Weren't most 19th century French painters short, heavy men with lots of face hair, and didn't they wear slobbered-on vests and baggy trousers? Aren't most contemporary ballerinas borderline anorexics, straight of mouth, haunt-eyed (doubtless from the pain of the pulled-back hair)? Is there a living poet ever sunbathes? Has anyone ever seen a drama critic up on all fours? Are not all living composers poor of posture? Is there a tenor not wider than he is tall?

We think we know what people look like, don't we. Don't we?

All playwrights, after all. . . .

Well, take a look at the photos in this book. What a curious lot we are! We are young and old, beautiful and less than plain, fat, thin, tall, short, diagonal, male, female, white, black, Oriental, hetero, homo and bi---; we look like businessmen, housewives, ax murderers, painters, ballerinas, poets, drama critics, composers and tenors. We look like . . . well, we look like playwrights.

Knowing what a creative artist looks like tells us nothing — or next to it. That New England businessman, the one with the carefully trimmed beard . . . was that *really* Charles Ives? That bald hod-carrier with the cigarette still in his face . . . truly Jackson Pollack?

For every W.B. Yeats — professional with the velvet and the poet's tie — there is the cherub gone fat and far to seed, drunk and willful — initial D.T. Stand Nabokov next to Marcel Proust, Stein to Woolf, O'Neill to Ionesco. It all tells us nothing. The artist is container for the art.

Indeed, I used to fear meeting creative people — this back when I was a pup, or less — for I knew I should thereafter have to relate the person to the art, the art to the person. I grew up soon enough, and saw that half the charmers were charlatans, and a portion of the swine had changed the shape of art.

I have friends who practice the arts, of course — poets, novelists, painters, even playwrights, but I have found that if their work is good enough the experiencing of it dissolves their personal image. (If sculptor X has fashioned a great work, I am not troubled by her cooking; if poet Y has attempted the impossible and damn near succeeded, I can forgive his bowling.)

All the above said, it is good to have the photos, biographies, and lists and availablities of works of so many playwrights gathered here in this volume. Our photos are sometimes startling — "My God, does he look like *that!?*" Our biographies are often revealing — "How old!?" (And isn't it interesting how some of us seem to have forgotten when we were born.) And the lists of our works bring to mind treasures and torments we had forgotten.

Above all, this volume reminds us that we are a community of playwrights, all allied by that splendid perversity, and all of us as different as we can possibly be.

Edward Albee
May, 1981
New York City

EDITOR'S NOTES

In 1977, the first edition of the National Playwrights Directory was published as a project of the O'Neill Theater Center. The need for the book evolved out of my work with the Center and with the National Playwrights Conference. I have been with both projects since 1965. In 1967, the Center produced a Playwrights Catalogue which listed only playwrights who had participated in its National Playwrights Conference. The response to the original Catalogue and to the two ensuing versions, which I edited in 1969 and 1971, convinced us of the need for a publication of broader scope. From this background, the National Playwrights Directory took its shape.

The purpose of this Directory is to provide detailed information on the works of the playwrights and a greater exposure for their body of work. The response to the first edition, on both a national and international basis, was immediate and positive. It is my hope that this new, up-dated volume will continue to be a major reference source for producers, regional theaters, college and university drama departments, libraries and community theater groups in their search for plays and playwrights.

Many of the new entries listed were selected as a result of recommendations by Artistic Directors and Literary Managers throughout the United States. They have my deep thanks and appreciation for their help. They are, Lach Adair, Andre Bishop, Alfred Brooks, Anne Cattaneo, John Dillon, Ed Hastings, Linda Koulisis, Eleanor Lindsay, Gail Merrifield, Kathleen Norris, Wendy Rosen, Louis Scheeder, Cynthia Sherman, Morgan Sloan, Richard Thomsen, William Turner, Russell Vandenbrouke and Doug Wager.

Toward my stated goal, the entries contain a contact for the playwright, either their address of their agent's address and information on their plays, and whether they have been published or are in manuscript form. If they have been published by several publishers, only one has been listed. This is usually the acting version. If a publisher has printed more than one play in an entry, the address is listed the first time and only the name is given in subsequent entries. The productions listed are for the first two places the works were done. Many of these were in a reading or a staged reading form. Many of the plays have been done hundreds of times all over the world. No attempt has been made to list the varied performances. I have only shown where they were first done.

A word about the synopses. In the effort to showcase their work, the playwrights are given the option of including synopses for up to three of their plays. If the playwright exercises the option to include synopses, editing is kept to a minimum to enable the flavor of the playwrights words to come through. Some editing has been done to clarify and shorten certain synopses.

In the quest for accuracy, all entries have been updated by the playwrights, since the original questionnaires were received, and are up to date at press time. Each playwright has confirmed the validity of the included information. A few playwrights works were researched, these are noted by an identifying mark after their names.

For the first time, you will find a designation for the plays that can be found in the Lincoln Center Theatre on Film and Tape Collection. These are available for screening to valid theater people by contacting that department at Lincoln Center. There is also an alphabetical index of all the plays in every entry. The asterisks indicate the plays that have synopses contained in the Directory. Although basically this has been a one person project, there are many people who have extended themselves to help me. Given the vastness of the undertaking, my gratitude goes to Edward Albee, Arthur Birsh, ElizaBeth King, F. Andrew Leslie, David LeVine and The Dramatists Guild, Hugh Southern and the Theatre Development Fund, the National Endowment for the Arts, William Talbott, and my special thanks to George C. White, President of the O'Neill Theater Center, for his loyalty and encouragement over the years.

And always and forever, my personal thanks to Bob, Steve and Amy Kaye.

Phyllis J. Kaye
1981

PHOTO CREDITS

Merritt Abrash
Louis C. Adelman
Edward Albee
Woody Allen
D. R. Andersen
Robert Anderson
Herbert Appleman
M. H. Appleman
Ray Aranha
Kenneth Arnold
Robert Auletta
Neville Aurelius

Thomas Babe
Frederick Bailey
James Baldwin
Imamu Amiri Baraka
Benjamin R. Barber
Anna Marie Barlow
Nathan N. Barrett
Bob Barry
Norman Beim
Barry Berg
Mark Berman
Albert Bermel
Kenneth Bernard
David Adams Berry
Sandra Bertrand
Kathleen Betsko
Sallie Bingham
Conrad Bishop
Neal Black
Michael Blankfort
Murray Teigh Bloom
Sam Bobrick
Lucile Bogue
Ludmilla Bollow
Allen Boretz
Bill Bozzone
Benjamin Bradford
Oscar Brand
Johnny Brandon
Anna Brennen
Townsend Brewster
Jay Broad
Kenneth H. Brown
Lennox Brown
William F. Brown
Cynthia Buchanan
Ed Bullins
Louisa Burns-Bisogno
Abe Burrows

June Calender

Lonnie Carter
Steve Carter
Jane Chambers
Susan Charlotte
Michael J. Chepiga
James Childs
John Chodes
Jerome Chodorov
Ron Clark
David U. Clarke
Edward J. Clinton
D. L. Coburn
David Cohen
Edward M. Cohen
Michael Colby
Anne Commire
Peter Copani
Ron Cowen
J. J. Coyle
Michael Cristofer
Mart Crowley
Neil Cuthbert

Wallace Dace
Anthony Damato
Allen Davis III
Luther Davis
Ossie Davis
Dot DeCamp
Peter Dee
Ramon Delgado
Donna de Matteo
Elaine G. Denholtz
Priscilla B. Dewey
Elizabeth Diggs
Stanley Disney
Felix Doherty
Martin Bauml Duberman
Helen Duberstein
Rochelle Holt Dubois
Thomas G. Dunn
Christopher Durang
Susan Dworkin

Charles Eastman
Gus Edwards
Mark Edwards
Mark Eichman
Robert Eisele
Sam Eisenstein
Mark Eisman
James Elward
Joel Ensana
Ken Eulo

Albert Evans
Don Evans
Tom Eyen

Lee Falk
Jules Feiffer
Ernest Ferlita
Barbara Field
John Finch
Mike Firth
B. Fisher
Rolf Fjelde
Lanny Flaherty
Don Flynn
Thomas M. Fontana
Frank B. Ford
Joe Taylor Ford
Richard Foreman
Marie Irene Fornes
Paul Foster
Ray Errol Fox
Terry Curtis Fox
Richard France
J. e. Franklin
Mario Fratti
George Freek
David Freeman
Bruce Jay Friedman
Charles Frink
Martha Ayers Fuentes
Charles Fuller
George Furth

Frank Gagliano
Mary Gallagher
Herb Gardner
Louis Garfinkle
Barbara Garson
Jack Gelber
Clark Gesner
William Gibson
Henry Gilfond
Jack C. Gilhooley
Frank D. Gilroy
Maxwell Glanville
Joanna McClelland Glass
Seth Glassman
Lloyd Gold
Rose Leiman Goldemberg
Jolene Goldenthal
A.E.O. Goldman
James Goldman
Lee Goldsmith
Patricia Goldstone

Gloria Gonzalez
Robert Gordon
Ruth Gordon
Charles Gordone
Philip Kan Gotanda
Joseph Gath Gottfried
Barbara Graham
Percy Granger
Harry Granick
Amlin Gray
William Green
Roma Greth
Susan Griffin
Tom Griffin
William Griffin
Antoni Gronowicz
Theodore Gross
John Guare
A. R. Gurney
Jack Raphael Guss

Oliver Hailey
William Hairston
Martin Halpern
Kelly Hamilton
Wallace Hamilton
George Hammer
Valerie Harris
Joseph Hart
Lezley Havard
Sam Havens
Alan Havis
David Kerry Heefner
Harold Heifetz
Jack Heifner
Lillian Hellman
Nancy Henderson
Beth Henley
Richard Henrickson
Venable Herndon
Mars Hill
Vernon Hinkle
J. Kline Hobbs
Charles Horine
Israel Horovitz
Tina Howe
Lee Hunkins
F. V. Hunt
Frederic Hunter
Paul Hunter
Kathy Hurley
David Henry Hwang

McCrae Imbrie
Robert E. Ingham
Albert Innaurato
Anthony Inneo

Corinne Jacker
R. Eugene Jackson

Jim Jacobs
Michael Jacobs
Arthur Jasspe
John Jiler
C. Robert Jones
Silas Jones
Ernest Joselovitz
Robert Farras Joseph
Joseph Julian

Diane Kagan
Bernard M. Kahn
Gus Kaikkonen
Lee Kalcheim
Garson Kanin
Jack A. Kaplan
Jerome Kass
Michael Kassin
C. H. Keeney
Shannon Keith Kelley
Tim Kelly
Shepard Kerman
E. K. Kerr
Jean Kerr
Larry Ketron
Faizul B. Khan
Jeffrey Kindley
John W. Kirk
James Kirkwood
Warren Kliewer
Norman Kline
Joanne Koch
Arthur Kopit
Robert Kornfield
Charlotte Kraft
Gail Kriegel
Helen Kromer

Stan Lachow
Myrna Lamb
Diane Lampert
James Lapine
Crispin Larangeira
Carl Larsen
Jack Larson
Louis LaRusso II
Arthur Laurents
Shirley Mezvinsky Lauro
Eddie Lawrence
Jerome Lawrence
Lance Lee
Leslie Lee
Robert E. Lee
Richard Lees
Mark Leib
Charles Leipart
Harding Lemay
Stephen Levi
Ira Levin
Jonathan Levy

David Lifson
Paul Stephen Lim
Romulus Linney
Daniel Lipman
Joseph Lizardi
Roy London
Larry Loonin
Eric Merdith Lord
Robert Lord
Tobi Louis
Charles Ludlam

Jerome McDonough
Eugene McKinney
John McLiam
Terrence McNally
Janet McReynolds

Edward H. Mabley
E. Macer-Story
Franklyn MacGregor
C. K. Mack
Wendy Mac Laughlin
Ross MacLean
David Mamet
Joe Manchester
Willard Manus
Robert Wesley Martin
Sharon Stockard Martin
James Paul Marvin
Mark Medoff
Leonard Melfi
Steve Metcalfe
Arthur Miller
Jason Miller
Susan Miller
T. C. Miller
David Scott Milton
Barbara & Carlton Molette
Robert Montgomery
Edward J. Moore
Honor Moore
Judith Morley
Aldyth Morris
Edmund Morris
Frank Moffett Mosier
Paul Mroczka
Lynda Myles

N. Richard Nash
Elyse Nass
John Nassivera
Janet L. Neipris
Stanley Nelson
James Nicholson
Jean Nuchtern

John Olive
Richard Olson
Kevin O'Morrison
Sally Ordway

Owa
Daniel W. Owens
Rochelle Owens
OyamO

William Packard
William Parchment
Stephen Davis Parks
Peter Parnell
Robert Patrick
Sybille Pearson
China Clark Pendarvis
James D. Pendleton
Leonard L. Perlmutter
Avra Petrides
Howard Pflanzer
Louis Phillips
Peggy Phillips
John Pielmeier
Drury Pifer
Robert Pine
Joseph T. Pintauro
Raymond Platt
Abe Polsky
Victor Power
Toni Press
James Prideaux
John Pyros

David Rabe
Frederick A. Raborg, Jr.
Peter Ramsey
Bob Randall
Dennis Reardon
Jean Reavey
Sylvia Regan
Richard Reich
Sy Reiter
Ronald Ribman
Howard Richardson
Robert Riche
Jean Riley
Jonathan Ringkamp
Louis Rivers
Susan Rivers
Lanie Robertson
Betsy Julia Robinson
S. Garrett Robinson
Mary Rohde
Alan Roland
Sheldon Rosen
James Rosenberg
Robert S. Ross
Enid Rudd
Robert Wallace Russell
Leo Rutman

Bernard Sabath

Howard Sackler
Fred Saidy
Arthur Sainer
Edward Sakamoto
Frank Salisbury
Gertrude Samuels
Herb Schapiro
Edan Schappert
Joan Schenkar
James Schevill
Murray Schisgal
Barbara Schneider
Richard Schotter
Joseph Schrank
Sandra Scoppettone
John Scott
Anthony Scully
John Sedlak
Richard Seff
Linda Segal
Neil R. Selden
Bruce Serlen
Ntozake Shange
Adele Edling Shank
Jack Sharkey
Wallace Shawn
Marsha Sheiness
Samuel Shem
Sam Shepard
Martin Sherman
Larry Shue
Michael Shurtleff
Seymour Simckes
Lydia Simmons
Neil Simon
Bernard Slade
Earl Hobson Smith
Glenn Allen Smith
Marc P. Smith
Robert Kimmel Smith
Steven Somkin
Jerry Spindel
Frances H. Stanton
Barrie Stavis
Daniel A. Stein
Joseph Stein
Mark Stein
Herschel Steinhardt
Allen Sternfield
Milan Stitt
Richard Stockton
Samuel Sussman
Jeffrey Sweet
Peter Swet

Brian Taggert
Stanley Taikeff

Ted Tally
Jules Tasca
Ronald Tavel
Hiram Taylor
Howard M. Teichman
Megan Terry
Steve Tesich
Thom Thomas
Fredi Towbin
David Trainer
Clifford Turknett
Dennis Turner
Knox Turner

Yale Udoff
Robert Unger

Jean-Claude van Itallie
W. Edwin Ver Becke
Vincent Viaggio
Gore Vidal
Paula A. Vogel
John von Hartz
Kurt Vonnegut, Jr.

Jeff Wanshel
Brendon Noel Ward
Dale Wasserman
Wendy Wasserstein
Gordon R. Watkins
John Weidman
Leslie Weiner
Michael Weller
Richard Errol Wesley
Hugh Wheeler
Ron Whyte
Sally Dixon Wiener
C. E. Wilkinson
June Vanleer Williams
Tennessee Williams
Doric Wilson
Lanford Wilson
Shimon Wincelberg
Aubrey Wisberg
Ruth Wolff
Herman Wouk
Elizabeth Wray
Elizabeth Wyatt

Wakako Yamauchi
Susan Yankowitz

Saul Zachary
Marc Alan Zagoren
Curtis Zahn
John Randolph Zapor
Dick Zigun
Paul Zindel

MERRITT ABRASH

Born 1930. Ph.D. from Columbia University in Public Law and Government. Has published articles on diplomatic history, art history and utopian literature. Professor of History at Rensselaer Polytechnic Institute, teaching mainly cultural history. Played lead in own play **Postscript** during 1970 run at Berkshire Theater Festival.

Address: Box 237, R.D.1, Stephentown, NY 12168
(518) 733-5586

Agent: Lois Berman, 250 West 57th St., New York, NY 10019 (212) 581-0670/1

TITLE • AVAILABILITY • PRODUCTIONS

Postscript: manuscript*; Berkshire Theater Festival, Stockbridge, MA; Library of the Performing Arts, Lincoln Center, NY

Postscript (one act): manuscript*; Yale Drama Festival; various college and community theater productions

The Film Club: manuscript*; O'Neill Theater Center's National Playwrights Conference, CT

The Outbreak of World War I: manuscript*
*contact author

SYNOPSES

Postscript: Henry thinks he is the sole survivor of the nuclear war and has taken psychological refuge in grotesque and bitter humor about the idiocy of mankind. When Susan appears, mourning the dead with conventional sentiments, Henry's merciless black humor almost drives her away, but one more survivor appears: Paul, once boss of a small company who now interprets the destruction of mankind as a judgment by the biggest boss of all. What a boss says goes, and therefore, decrees Paul, the accidental survivors are not meant to upset the judgment by producing new human life. To Susan this is inhuman and to Henry dogmatic nonsense, but Henry's inability to emerge from behind his mockery and scorn leads to a tragic conclusion at once unexpected and inevitable.

Full length, two acts. Setting: a few standard pieces of furniture, easily adaptable to performance in the round. 2 males, 1 female.

The Film Club: Four young middle-class couples hold a periodic meeting of their film club. This time the films are eight unidentified reels purchased at a junk shop. When the films are shown [note: no actual films or projection equipment are necessary] they prove to be supernatural depictions of the club members' secret realities (adultery, living a lie about a servile job, etc.) and future disasters (a violent fight between two members, the breakdown of the most respected, etc.) By the end of the evening, which had begun with so much seeming warmth and humor, the members' lives and relationships are shattered and there is only one hope left for comfort.

One act. Setting: livingroom. No special equipment necessary. 4 males, 4 females, 1 unseen narrator.

The Outbreak of World War I: An absurdist treatment of the underlying causes of World War I and the events from the assassination of Archduke Franz Ferdinand to the early days of the war. Everything is firmly based on actual history, but replete with farcical twists and unorthodox motivations which impart the hypocrisy, blindness and plain stupidity of many of the attitudes held and decisions made by the diplomats and generals. One-liners and sight gags are woven into the actual development of events, bringing out the inherent absurdity of a catastrophic war arising from human foolishness and thoughtlessness; some brief changes of tone near the end of the play make it plain that there was really nothing funny about it at all.

Full length. Setting: many settings, but should be done with stylized combinations of simple furniture. 8 males, 4 females with maximum doubling.

A

LOUIS C. ADELMAN

Carnegie Tech., B.F.A.; Hunter College, M.A.; TV credits include scripts for CBS, NBC, Plautus Productions; play doctor for Off Broadway musical **Riverwind;** New Dramatists Committee. Actor's Studio playwriting seminar under Clifford Odets; Playwriting Teacher at Marymount Manhattan College. Articles for **The Dramatists Guild Quarterly**. Recipient: Grant, Arts of the Theater Playwriting Competition; Grant-in-Aid from National Institute of Arts and Letters; Fellowship at MacDowell Colony, P.E.N. Grant.

Address: 484 West 43rd St., New York, NY 10036
(212) 736-6931

TITLE • AVAILABILITY • PRODUCTIONS

Corner of God: manuscript*; Carnegie Tech; New Dramatists, NYC

The Man with the Golden Arm (adaptation): manuscript*

The Tall Green Grass: manuscript*

Dressed in Clean Clothes: manuscript*

The Riverside Drive: manuscript*

Touch Light: manuscript*

A Warm Afternoon in Nebraska: manuscript*; Reading, South Street Theatre, NYC

Locking Piece: manuscript*

Night Fishing in Beverly Hills: manuscript*; Reading, No Smoking Playhouse, NYC

Witnesses: manuscript*
    *contact author

SYNOPSIS

A Warm Afternoon in Nebraska: Dixie Milford, a TV make-up man who specializes in creating rubber scars for the stars, put his dreams of being a serious painter behind him years ago. With a paying profession, a Reichian analyst, and an uptown mistress, he has made a good adjustment to life. While he is able to see eye to eye with most people on most things, this is never the case with Bix Milford, his seventeen-year-old son who has already been married four times.

Full length. Setting: A studio apartment in a MacDougal Alley carriage house, located in Greenwich Village. 4 males, 3 females.

EDWARD ALBEE

Born in Washington, DC on March 12, 1928. Educated at Lawrenceville School; Valley Forge Military Academy; Choate; Trinity College. Producer with Richard Barr and Clinton Wilder, New Playwrights Unit Workshop. Recipient: Berlin Festival Award, 1959, 1961; Vernon Rice Award; Obie Award; Argentine Critics Award; Lila D'Arnunzio Award; New York Drama Critics Circle Award; Outer Circle Award; Tony Award; Pulitzer Prize.

Address: 14 Harrison St., New York, NY 10013 (212) 226-2020

Agent: Esther Sherman, c/o William Morris Agency, 1350 Avenue of the Americas, New York, NY 10019 (212) 586-5100

TITLE • AVAILABILITY • PRODUCTIONS

†**The Zoo Story:** Dramatists Play Service, 440 Park Ave. South, New York, NY 10016, $2.50; Berlin; Provincetown Playhouse, NYC

The Death of Bessie Smith: Dramatists Play Service, $2.50; Berlin; York Playhouse, NYC

†**The Sand Box:** with **The Zoo Story;** Jazz Gallery

†**Fam & Yam:** with **The Death of Bessie Smith;** White Barn, CT

†**The American Dream:** with **The Death of Bessie Smith;** York Playhouse, NYC

Who's Afraid of Virginia Woolf?: Dramatists Play Service, $2.50; Broadway

The Ballad of the Sad Cafe (adaptation): Dramatists Play Service, $2.50; Broadway

Tiny Alice: Dramatists Play Service, $2.50; Broadway

Malcolm (adaptation): Dramatists Play Service, $2.50; Broadway

A Delicate Balance: Samuel French, 25 West 45th St., New York, NY 10036, $2.50; Broadway

Everything in the Garden (adaptation): Dramatists Play Service, $2.50; Broadway

Box/Quotations from Chairman Mao Tse-Tung†: Dramatists Play Service, $2.50; Broadway

†**All Over:** Samuel Frénch, $2.50; Broadway

Seascape: Dramatists Play Service, $2.50; Broadway

Counting the Ways and **Listening**†: Dramatists Play Service, $2.50; B.B.C. Radio; Hartford Stage Company, CT

The Lady from Dubuque: Dramatists Play Service, $2.50; Broadway

Lolita (adaptation)*: Broadway
  †Lincoln Center, Theatre on Film & Tape
  *contact agent

A

WOODY ALLEN‡

Born in Brooklyn, NY on December 1, 1935. Attended City College of New York and New York University. Actor, director and filmmaker. Films: **What's New Pussycat; Take the Money and Run; Bananas; Sleeper; Love and Death; Annie Hall; Interiors; Manhattan; Stardust Memories.** Books: **Getting Even; Without Feathers; Side Effects.**

Agent: Jack Rollins, Rollins-Joffe, 130 West 57th St., New York, NY 10019 (212) 582-1940

TITLE • AVAILABILITY • PRODUCTIONS

From A To Z (revue sketches): not available; Off Broadway

Don't Drink the Water: Samuel French, 25 West 45th St., New York, NY 10036, $2.50; Broadway

†**Play It Again, Sam:** Samuel French, $2.50; Broadway

The Floating Lightbulb; manuscript*; Lincoln Center, NYC
    †Lincoln Center, Theatre on Film & Tape
    *contact agent

D. R. ANDERSEN

Born in Harlan, IO on February 15, 1947. Educated at Amherst College; Uppsala University (Sweden). Andersen writes for television and films in addition to the theater. His TV credits include his work as staff writer for **How to Survive a Marriage** and **Jackpot.** He is the editor-author of **Book of Slang** published in 1975; has taught in the English Department at Queens College for three years and writes for national magazines.

Address: 401 East 74th St., 4R, New York, NY 10021 (212) 472-3397

TITLE • AVAILABILITY • PRODUCTIONS

Marry Me! Marry Me!: manuscript*; Albee-Barr-Wilder Workshop, NYC; Clark Center, NYC

The Girls Most Likely to Succeed: manuscript*; Clark Center, NYC

Jenny and the Revolution: manuscript*; Joseph Jefferson Theatre, NYC

Unicorns at Two: manuscript*; Playwrights Horizons, NYC

I Remember the House Where I Was Born: manuscript*; Queens Playhouse, NY

The Castaways [co-author]: manuscript*; John Drew Theatre, NY

My Name is Sybil Ludington: not available

Thirteen Ways of Looking at a Blackbird: not available

A Bistro Car on the CNR (co-author): manuscript*; The Playhouse, NY

Raggedy Andy: manuscript*

Cafe Society: manuscript and tape*
    *contact author

SYNOPSES

The Girls Most Likely to Succeed: A romantic comedy that takes place on reunion day at Smith College. The interlocking stories of four women (classes of '75, '61, '47, and '12) offer proof that everything and nothing changes over the years when it comes to love. "Andersen is an exciting

discovery, and he should be nourished. He has attempted something rare and difficult — a rather gentle tragicomedy about the aging process. This seems rather an unlikely subject for a play, and yet it somehow works. For Mr. Andersen is a poet who finds the common denominator in all the generations. Dennis Andersen is a playwright to watch." —Emory Lewis.
Two acts. Setting: a college dormitory room. 6 males, 7 females.

Raggedy Andy: A romantic comedy about Andy Robbins, a children's author, who finds life turned upside down by his pregnant ex-wife, mother-in-law, agent and a sexy admirer.
Two acts. Setting: livingroom of an Upper Westside New York apartment. 2 males, 3 females.

Cafe Society: A light, sprightly "new" 1930's musical — all about the shenanigans that take place when a rich young couple lose their money, when a wealthy debutante decides she can only love a pauper, when a bellboy disguises himself as a wealthy French count, and when a gossip columnist dishes the dirt about cafe society.
Full length. Setting: unit set — various locales at the Plaza Hotel. 4 males, 4 females.

ROBERT ANDERSON

Born in New York City on April 28, 1917. Educated at Phillips Exeter Academy, Harvard (magna cum laude). Author of novels, **After** and **Getting Up and Going Home.** Films, **The Sand Pebbles, The Nun's Story, Tea and Sympathy, Until They Sail** and **I Never Sang for My Father** plus TV and radio plays. Founder-member of New Dramatists Committee, Member, Playwrights company, 1953–60. President, Dramatists Guild, 1971–73. Vice-President, Authors League. Recipient: **Variety** Poll of NY Drama Critics; National Theater Conference Award for Best Play Written By a W.W. II Serviceman Overseas; Rockefeller Fellowship; Writers Guild of America Award for screenplay; Theater Hall of Fame, 1981.

Agent: Audrey Wood, I.C.M., 40 W. 57th St., New York, NY 10019 (212) 556-5722

TITLE • AVAILABILITY • PRODUCTIONS

Come Marching Home: not available; Blackfriars Guild, NYC

The Eden Rose: not avaliable; Richfield Community Theatre, CT

Love Revisited: not available; Westport Country Playhouse, CT

All Summer Long: Samuel French, 25 W. 45th St., New York, NY 10036, $2.50; Arena Stage, Wash., DC; Broadway

Tea & Sympathy: Samuel French, $2.50; New Haven, CT; Broadway

Silent Night, Lonely Night: Samuel French, $2.50; New Haven, CT; Broadway

The Days Between: Samuel French, $2.50; Dallas Theatre Center, TX; Park Royal Theatre, Off Broadway, NYC

You Know I Can't Hear You When the Water's Running: Dramatists Play Service, 440 Park Ave. South, New York, NY 10016, $2.50; Broadway

I Never Sang for My Father: Dramatists Play Service, $2.50; Philadelphia; Broadway

Solitaire/Double Solitaire: Dramatists Play Service, $2.50; Long Wharf Theatre, CT; Broadway

Free and Clear: under option at publication time

A

HERBERT APPLEMAN

Born in Brooklyn, NY on December 9, 1933.
Educated at Harvard, B.A.; Columbia, M.A.; Yale
University School of Drama. Credits: **When Two
Become Three,** a humorous memoir; more than
twenty television plays and documentaries, in-
cluding **A Different Drummer** (Cowan Citation), **A
Simple Case** (New York Film and TV Festival
Silver Medal), and **... And Suddenly You're Alone**
(Emmy Award). Herb is now Associate Professor
of English at Oakland University in Rochester,
Michigan. He continues to write for the theater,
films, and television. Recipient: American
Playwright's Theater Award, Emmy Award, In-
vitation to Yaddo, Invitation to O'Neill
Playwrights Conference, Election to New
Dramatists, Cowan Citation, New York Film and
TV Festival Silver Medal.

Address: c/o English Department, Oakland University, Rochester, MI 48063 (313) 377-2250

TITLE • AVAILABILITY • PRODUCTIONS

A Perfect Gentleman: manuscript*; O'Neill Theater Center's Playwrights Conference, CT;
   various colleges

A Terrible Saint: manuscript*; New Dramatists, NYC

Heyday (book, lyrics, music, based on Ring Lardner story): manuscript*, New Dramatists, NYC

Unfair to Goliath : (book and lyrics based on work of Israeli humorist Ephraim Kishon):
   manuscript*; Cherry Lane Theater, NYC; Off Broadway; Ohalim Theater, Tel Aviv
   *contact author

SYNOPSES

A Perfect Gentleman: A classic story of the generation gap between a famous Establishment
father, Lord Chesterfield (former statesman, now retired), and his illegitimate son, Philip. Lord
Chesterfield intrigues to have Philip made an ambassador, but Philip manages to sabotage these
arrangements; risking disinheritance, he becomes his own man. Ultimately, because the father
and son are both civilized and loving, the gap between them is bridged with humor and poignancy.
A contemporary play in the tradition of English high comedy.

Full length. Setting: England 1755; the library of Chesterfield House, and the sitting room of a
London inn. 6 males, 3 females.

A Terrible Saint: The noble yet profoundly comic efforts of Count Lev Tolstoy to transform himself
into an ascetic idealist lead to unexpected results: when he is a healthy sinner, his marriage and
family life are serene; when he becomes a saint, everyone suffers.

Full length. Setting: Russia 1879; the garden/verandah of the Tolstoy country estate in Yasnaya
Polyana and the drawing room of the Tolstoy town house in Moscow. 15 males (but 3 can double),
6 females (including 1 child).

M. H. APPLEMAN

Born in Indiana. B.A., Northwestern University;
M.A., Indiana University; Degre Superieur, Sor-
bonne, University of Paris. Assistant Professor
of English (Playwriting), New York University.
Published poet. Recipient: Hartford Foundation
Fellowship; Karolyi Foundation Fellowship.

Address: 411 East 10th St., #21A, New York, NY
10009 (212) 677-4544

Agent: Flora Roberts, 65 East 55th St., New York,
   NY 10022 (212)355-4165

M. H. Appleman (cont'd)

TITLE • AVAILABILITY • PRODUCTIONS

Seduction Duet: manuscript*; Circle Repertory Theater, NYC

Afterglow: manuscript*; Theatre of the Riverside Church, NYC

The Bedroom: manuscript*; St. Clement's, NYC; Impossible Ragtime Theatre, NYC

Penelope's Odyssey: manuscript*; Open Space Theatre, NYC

The Best Is Yet to Be: manuscript*; Manhattan Theatre Club, NYC

Nice Place You Have Here: manuscript*; Omni Theatre, NYC

Calliope: manuscript*

On The Brink: manuscript*
   *contact author

SYNOPSES

Afterglow: Tumultuous and comic events in the neighborhood around them, mirror Irma's and Marvin's private tumult, as they tease and argue with each other in the front yard of Irma's house, and, in the course of one day, discover many secrets about their former spouses, about each other, and themselves.
Full length. Setting: front yard near a bay on Long Island; two chairs and a table. 1 male, 1 female, both over 60.

Seduction Duet: After an office party, Matt takes Cynthia home where they have a wild party of their own, replete with tequila, Mexican music and dance. While trying to turn the tables on each other, they surprise themselves.
One act. Setting: livingroom. 1 male, 1 female.

Penelope's Odyssey: Penelope, her husband, five friends and three students gather to plan a political campaign. They all become intricately involved with each other.
Full length. Setting: the library-game room of a suburban home. 5 males, 5 females.

RAY ARANHA

Bachelor of Arts, Florida A and M University. Studied Professional Theater Acting at the American Academy of Dramatic Arts, New York. Teacher of Drama on young adult and adult levels. Conducted workshops on acting and writing in school and community situations with children, young adults, and adults. Has been a professional actor for ten years and still active. Recipient: Drama Desk Award for Outstanding New Playwright, 1974; Rockefeller Playwright-in-Residence grant, 1975.

Address: GPO Box 1743, New York, NY 10001
   Service (212) 586-6300

TITLE • AVAILABILITY • PRODUCTIONS

My Sister; My Sister: Samuel French, 25 West 45th St., New York, NY 10036, $2.50; Hartford Stage Company, CT; Broadway

The Clowns' Corner Concert [a play for children and adults]: manuscript*; Hartford Stage Company, CT; Center Stage, Baltimore, MD

Way Back When . . . (a play for children and adults): manuscript*; Hartford Stage Co., CT

The Estate: manuscript*; Hartford Stage Co., CT

Ray Aranha (cont'd)

Akosula of the First and Final Day: manuscript*

Willie C, Your'n fer the Axin: manuscript*

Fugue on a Funny House: manuscript*

Snow Pressings: manuscript*; O'Neill Theater Center's National Playwrights Conference, CT; Virginia Tech. University, VA

Remington: manuscript*; Actor's Theatre of Louisville, KY

The Nature of Violence: manuscript*

Creedmore: manuscript*

Sons and Fathers of Sons; manuscript*; O'Neill Theater Center's National Playwrights Conference, CT
 *contact author

SYNOPSES

The Estate: A probing drama of the many-layered and diverse masks which men wear to conceal their disturbing passions from themselves and from their most intimate family and friends. Rooted in history, the thematic conflicts are represented through the personal struggles of Thomas Jefferson, Sally Hemmings, Martha Patsy Jefferson, Benjamin Banneker, Abigail Adams, all of whom lived, whose struggles were real etchings in the fabric of our American past. The cumulative struggles of the characters finally accumulate to represent an even wider focus: the many-layered and diverse masks which America wears as a nation to conceal disturbing truths from itself. "There is enough material and red-hot passion for five plays. **The Estate** is a big play — in terms of the issues it deals with, the style in which it is written, and the emotional opportunities it offers actors." —Mel Gussow, **New York Times.**

Three acts. Setting: a multiple set of steps and levels to represent the estate of Thomas Jefferson in Monticello, Virginia, and the farm of Benjamin Banneker in Baltimore, Maryland. 7 males, 5 females.

My Sister; My Sister: A drama of the nightmares of a young woman in the South, whose love is so innocent and single-minded that she cannot divorce herself from the fanatic holy faith of her mother, the intense sexuality of her sister and the almost childlike love for living of her father. She loves all three and embraces all three, and when Sister, Mother, Father rip each other and their home apart, so is the young woman ripped apart. "An absorbing play. It bears the stamp of truth, with implications beyond its local or ethnic setting." —Harold Clurman, **The Nation.** "The author has a gift for evocative imagery." —Walter Kerr, **New York Times.**

Two acts. Setting: Interior of a house in the South; 1950's. 2 males, 3 females, 5 extras.

KENNETH ARNOLD

Born in Washington, DC on March 29, 1944. B.A. in English, magna cum laude, Lynchburg College; M.A., English Writing, Johns Hopkins University. Poetry published in **Poetry Northwest, Perspective, Southern Poetry Review, American Poetry Review,** the **Little Magazine.** Recipient: Woodrow Wilson Fellow, Johns Hopkins University Writing Seminars.

Address: 6363 Germantown Avenue, Philadelphia, PA 19144 (215) 844-1892

Agent: Lucy Kroll Agency, 390 West End Avenue, New York, NY 10024 (212) 877-0556

TITLE • AVAILABILITY • PRODUCTIONS

Pope Joan: A Play in 14 Episodes; manuscript*; Philadelphia Company, PA; Lynchburg College

The House of Bedlam: manuscript*; New Playwrights Theater, Washington, DC

Kenneth Arnold (cont'd)

She Also Dances: manuscript*; O'Neill Theater Center's National Playwrights Conference, CT
*contact agent

SYNOPSES

The House of Bedlam: Based on the last days of the poet Ezra Pound in Rapallo, Italy. Escaping from the retreating German army, Pound takes his wife to the apartment of his mistress, Olga Rudge, where they are joined by the natural daughter Olga bore him. The resulting conflict brings to a head the domestic and political troubles that Pound had been creating for himself as a collaborator with the Mussolini regime. His arrest by the American army lands him in a cage, where his black guard, Whiteside, gives him a painful education in humility and humanity.

Full length. Setting: room in an apartment and the cage in which Pound was held prisoner. 2 males, 1 of them black; 3 females.

She Also Dances: An exploration of the relationship between a woman confined to a wheelchair and the young man hired to push her around the campus of the college they attend. He is a gymnast who realizes that he wants to be a dancer. Together they make a dance in which they both see the possibility of liberation.

Full length. Setting: open stage. A choreographer is necessary. 1 male, 1 female.

ROBERT AULETTA

Born in New York City on March 5, 1940. B.A., in English Literature, Queens College; M.F.A., in Playwriting, Yale School of Drama. Has written poetry, short stories and articles and directed. Has taught at the Yale School of Drama, University of Illinois, Southern Connecticut State College and the O'Neill Theater Center. Playwright-in-residence, Yale Divinity School, 1975. Presently teaching theater at the School of Visual Arts, NYC. Recipient: Mollie Kazan Award; Rockefeller Grant through the Office of Advanced Drama Research; CBS Grant; John Golden Fellowship; Hazen Foundation Grant.

Address: 161 Prince St., #12, New York, NY 10012
(212) 475-7825

Agent: Helen Merrill, 337 West 22nd St., New York, NY 10011 (212) 924-6314

TITLE • AVAILABILITY • PRODUCTIONS

The National Guard: Yale Theatre, Vol. 1, Box 854, Meriden, CT 06450, $1.50; Yale School of Drama, CT; Boston Free Theatre, MA

Red Mountain High: Yale Theatre, Vol. 2, #3, $2.00; Yale School of Drama, CT; University of Illinois

Coocooshay: manuscript*; New York Shakespeare Festival, NYC

Stops: Playwrights for Tomorrow, University of Minnesota Press, Minneapolis, MN, $3.45; Yale Repertory Theatre, CT; Edinburgh Festival

Foreplay-Doorplay: Yale Theatre, Vol. 6, #3, $2.00; Yale Cabaret, CT; St. Peter's Church, NYC

Walk the Dog, Willie: Yale Theatre, Vol. 6, #1, $2.00; Yale Repertory Theatre, CT

Wednesday Sharp: manuscript*; Yale Cabaret, CT

Guess Work: manuscript*; Yale Repertory Theatre, CT

Expo 99: manuscript*; Earth's Eye Foundation; Yale Cabaret, CT

Joe: A Dramatic Idiocy: manuscript*; Theatre for the New City, NYC

Hage, The Sexual History: manuscript*; O'Neill Theater Center's National Playwrights Conference, CT
*contact author

A

Robert Auletta (cont'd)

SYNOPSES

Walk the Dog, Willie: This is a gothic midwesterner, composed of symbolic, humorous and hallucinatory elements. A strangely eccentric family awaits the return of the long gone but not easily forgotten Willie. When he finally returns, he disappoints none of us with his bizarre brand of confrontational politics. The ending is both violent and ritualistic. Definitely not for the squeamish.

Full length. Setting: back yard and exterior of a house and interior of a veterinarian hospital. 4 males, 3 females.

Guess Work: A man in the middle of nowhere suddenly comes face to face with an audience that forces him to confront the terror and the pain of the past that is hunting and haunting him. A play of lonely poetry and a strong piece for a fearless actor.

One act. Setting: simple set consisting of a pile of wood, an axe and a bucket of water. 1 male.

Hage, The Sexual History: Three men sit down, play poker, drink beer and begin to confront the "essential" female mystique. This is not a realistic play though it tells a "real" story. Events and characters tumble all about the stage. Music, masks and giant figures play a part in the action. The story it tells is satirical-tragic-comic. Hage, the central character must confront death and loss before he can come to witness the bright, burning blue of the sky.

Full length. Setting; open flexible space where props can be moved in and out. 4 males, 9 females.

NEVILLE AURELIUS

Educated in London, England; Clark's College. Served five years in the R.A.F. Trained as an actor with the London School of Dramatic Arts and the Doreen Cannon Theatre Workshop, London. Co-founder of Action Theatre, Paris, France, 1968. Acting Credits include, for stage: **The Boys in the Band, The Black MacBeth, Slow Dance on the Killing Ground**; on TV: **In White America, Special Branch, Softly Softly**; film: **The National Health.**

Address: c/o M. Nase, 32 West 82nd St., #2D, New York, NY 10024

Agent: New York; Dolores Sancetta, DMI Talent Associates, 250 West 57th St., New York, NY 10019 (212) 246-4650: London: Tod Joseph, Joseph & Wagg, 78 New Bond St., London, England 629-1048

TITLE • AVAILABILITY • PRODUCTIONS

Mr. Whittington: manuscript*

With Intent to Commit a Crime: manuscript*; Off Off Broadway; National Arts Theatre, NYC

A Long Night's Dying: manuscript*; Frank Silvera's Writers Workshop, NYC

Yesterday, Once More (with Alice Spivak): manuscript*; Frank Silvera's Writers Workshop, NYC

In Memoriam: manuscript*; Frank Silvera's Writers Workshop, NYC

Hansel And Gretel: unavailable
*contact author or agents

SYNOPSES

Yesterday Once More: The devastating effect that a young black drifter has on the lives of two

Neville Aurelius (cont'd)

older women who live in an isolated region in the south. Each woman uses him as an opportunity to escape her barren existence.

2 males (black), 2 females (1 black, 1 white).

In Memoriam: A successful black British TV personality must deal with his disintegrating interracial marriage and the intrusion of an old antagonist who could destroy his successful career. Setting: a London home. 2 males (1 black), 1 female.

THOMAS BABE

Born in Buffalo, NY on March 13, 1941. B.A. from Harvard and St. Catharine's College, Cambridge; J.D. from Yale Law School, CT. Also writes poetry. With Timothy S. Mayer, founded and was co-artistic director of the Summer Players in Agassiz Theater, Cambridge. Has directed plays and written four film scripts. **Rebel Women** and **A Prayer for My Daughter** were chosen for the Burns Mantel ten best plays book. **Hot Dogs & Soda Pop** recorded for National Public Radio. Panelist for the 1980 CAPS Grants. Recipient: CBS Fellowship, Yale Drama School; Guggenheim Grant; Rockefeller Grant.

Address: 103 Hoyt St., Darien, CT 06820 (203) 325-1487

Agent: The Lantz Office, 114 East 55th St., New York, NY 10022 (212) 751-2107

TITLE • AVAILABILITY • PRODUCTIONS

Kid Champion: Dramatists Play Service, 440 Park Ave. South, New York, NY 10016, $2.50; NY Shakespeare Festival, NYC

Rebel Women: Dramatists Play Service, $2.50; NY Shakespeare Festival, NYC

Billy Irish: manuscript*; Manhattan Theatre Club, NYC

Fathers & Sons: Dramatists Play Service, $2.50; NY Shakespeare Festival, NYC

Mojo Candy: manuscript*; Yale Summer Cabaret, CT

Taken in Marriage: Dramatists Play Service, $2.50; NY Shakespeare Festival, NYC

Planet Fires: not available

Salt Lake City Skyline: Dramatists Play Service, $2.50; NY Shakespeare Festival, NYC

A Prayer for My Daughter: Samuel French, 25 W. 45th St., New York, NY 10036, $2.50; O'Neill Theater Center's National Playwrights Conference, CT; NY Shakespeare Festival, NYC

Great Solo Town: manuscript*; Yale Summer Cabaret, CT; San Francisco Playwrights Festival

When We Were Very Young: Twyla Tharp Foundation, 38 Walker, New York, NY 10013; Twyla Tharp, The Wintergarden, NYC

Daniel Boone: manuscript*; Performing Arts Repertory Theater tour

Home Again Kathleen: manuscript*; Neighborhood Playhouse, NYC; Reading, Center Stage, Baltimore, MD
  *contact agent

SYNOPSIS

Great Solo Town: A play for young actors about coming-of-age on the night Robert Kennedy is killed. The comedy involves a discovery of sex and death.

Full length. Setting: two simple sets. 5 males, 5 females.

B

FREDERICK BAILEY

Born in Dallas, TX on November 7, 1946.
B.F.A. in directing and playwriting from
Southern Methodist University, 1967. He has
directed nearly 100 plays, working Off Off Broadway, in summer stock, regional, resident and
university theaters. For two years, he served as
Managing Director of the Warehouse Theatre in
Oklahoma City under an NEA grant in devel-
opmental theater. He has made short films and
recently published his first two short stories.
Recipient: Wurlitzer Foundation, 1978–79; Commissions from South Coast Repertory, Actors
Theatre of Louisville (three times); Co-winner,
New Play Festival, Actors Theatre of Louisville,
1977.

Address: 926 Old Topanga Canyon Road, Topanga, CA 90290 (213) 455-1438

TITLE • AVAILABILITY • PRODUCTIONS

Set It down with Gold: The Scene, Vol. 1, The Smith, 5 Beekman St., New York, NY 10038,
$2.50; Charles Playhouse, MA; The Playbox, NYC

The Hooded Gnome: The Scene, Vol. III, $4.00; The Playbox, NYC

The Bridgehead: manuscript*; Margo Jones Experimental Theatre, S.M.U., TX; Actors Theatre
of Louisville, KY

Gringo Planet: manuscript*; Warehouse Theatre, OK; La Mama, Los Angeles, CA

Rio Pork: manuscript*; Warehouse Theatre, OK; Manhattan Clearing House, Dallas, TX

Putting on the Dog: manuscript*; Krannert Center, University of Illinois; Back Alley Theatre,
Los Angeles, CA

Midnight in Topanga: manuscript*

A Bitter Exchange: manuscript*; Actors Theatre of Louisville, KY

Coyote Hotel: manuscript*

The Opposite End of the Couch: manuscript*; Warehouse Theatre, OK

An Unscheduled Appearance: manuscript*; New York Theatre Ensemble, NYC; Warehouse
Theatre, OK
    *contact author

SYNOPSIS

Putting on the Dog: A romantic comedy of contemporary life in small town, New Mexico. An old
woman runs a boarding house with a nest of poor but happy tenants. The local sheriff and his
deputy, who is also one of her tenants, must tell her that her driving is becoming a hazard to
others. This plot thread is interwoven with a budding romance between two other tenants.

Full length. Setting: multiple settings. 7 males, 2 females, one small dog.

B

JAMES BALDWIN‡

Born in New York City on August 2, 1924. After
high school, he did odd jobs until moving to
Paris. Author of **Go Tell It on the Mountain,
Notes of a Native Son, Giovanni's Room,
Nobody Knows My Name, The Fire Next Time,
Tell Me How Long the Train's Been Gone, A Rap
on Race, If Beale Street Could Talk, No Name in
the Streets, One Day, When I Was Lost, Up
Above My Head.** Recipient: Eugene F. Saxton
Memorial Trust Award; Rosenwald Fellowship;
Guggenheim Fellowship; National Institute of
Arts and Letters Award; Ford Foundation Grant;
Outstanding Book, American Library Associa-
tion; Certificate of Honor, National Conference
of Christians and Jews.

Address: c/o Dramatists Guild, 234 West 44th Street, New York, NY 10036 (212) 398-9366

TITLE • AVAILABILITY • PRODUCTIONS

The Amen Corner: Samuel French, 25 West 45th St., New York, NY 10036, $5.95; Howard
   University, Washington, DC; Los Angeles, CA

Blues for Mr. Charlie: Samuel French, $1.50; ANTA Theatre, NYC

A Deed from the King of Spain: manuscript*; American Center for Stanislavski Theatre Art
   *contact author

IMAMU AMIRI BARAKA
LeRoi Jones

Born in Newark, NJ on October 7, 1934. Attended
Rutgers University; Howard University, B.A.;
New School for Social Research; Columbia University, M.A. Taught poetry at the New School;
drama at Columbia; literature at Buffalo and
New York University. Visiting Professor at San
Francisco State University. Founder of the Black
Arts Repertory Theater School; Spirit House. Active in Black Rights and Culture. Author of many
books of poetry and essays. Recipient: Whitney
Fellowship, 1961; Obie Award, 1964; Guggenheim Fellowship, 1965; Dakar Festival Prize,
1966; National Endowment for the Arts Grant,
1966.

Address: 808 South 10th St., Newark, NJ 07108

Agent: Joan Brandt, c/o Sterling Lord Agency, 660 Madison Avenue, New York, NY 10021 (212)
   751-2533

TITLE • AVAILABILITY • PRODUCTIONS

A Good Girl Is Hard to Find: not available; Montclair, NJ

Dante (The 8th Ditch): Grove Press, 196 W. Houston St., New York, NY, $4.95; New Bowery
   Theatre, NYC

Dutchman: Samuel French, 25 W. 45th St., New York, NY 10036, $2.50; Playwrights Unit, NYC

The Slave: with **The Dutchman**; St. Mark's Playhouse, NYC

The Baptism: Grove Press, $3.45; Writers Stage, NYC

The Toilet: with **The Baptism**; St. Mark's Playhouse, NYC

B

Imamu Amiri Baraka [LeRoi Jones] (cont'd)

Jello: Third World Press, 7524 S. Cottage Grove, Chicago, Il 60019; Black Arts Group, NYC

Experimental Death Unit 1:Four Black Revolutionary Plays, Bobbs Merrill, 4300 W. 62nd St., Indianapolis, IN 46468; St. Mark's Playhouse, NYC

Black Mass: with **Experimental Death Unit 1**; Proctor's Theatre, Newark, NJ

Arm Yourself and Harm Yourself: manuscript*; Spirit House, Newark, NJ

Madheart: with **Experimental Death Unit 1**; San Francisco, CA

Slave Ship: manuscript*; Newark; Chelsea Theatre Center, NY

Home on the Range: manuscript*; Newark, NJ; NYC

Police: manuscript*; NYC

Great Goodness of Life (A Coon Show): with **Experimental Death Unit 1**; Tambellini's Gate, NYC

Junkies Are Full of Shh . . . : **Black Drama Anthology**, New American Library, 1633 Broadway, New York, NY 10019; Newark, NJ

Bloodrites: with **Junkies Are Full of Shh . . .** ; Newark, NJ

Ba-Ra-Ka: in **Spontaneous Combustion**

A Recent Killing: manuscript*; New Federal Theatre, NYC

Sidnee Poet Heroical: manuscript*; New Federal Theatre, NYC

The Death of Malcolm X: **New Plays from the Black Theatre**; Spirit House, Newark, NJ

Black Power Chant: manuscript*

Board of Education: manuscript*; Spirit House, Newark, NJ

Columbia, Gem of the Ocean: manuscript*; Spirit House Movers, Newark, NJ; Howard University, DC

The Coronation of the Black Queen: not available

Insurrection: manuscript*

S-1: manuscript*; Afro-American Studio, NYC

The Motion of History: **The Motion of History & Other Plays**, William Morrow, 105 Madison Avenue, New York, NY 10016, $3.95; New York Theatre Ensemble, NYC

What Was the Relationship of the Lone Ranger to the Means of Production: manuscript*; Nyoma Poet's Theater; Ladies Fort, NYC

Money (A Jazz Opera): manuscript*

Vomit & The Jungle Bunnies: manuscript*

Boy & Tarzan Appear in a Clearing: manuscript*
    *contact agent

BENJAMIN R. BARBER

Certificates from London School of Economics and Albert Schweitzer College (Switzerland); B.A., honors, Grinnell College; M.A. and Ph.D. (Dept. of Government), Harvard University. Present position: Professor of Political Science, Rutgers University. Editor of **Political Theory: An International Journal of Political Philosophy.** Author of **Liberating Feminism, Superman and Common Men: Freedom, Anarchy and the Revolution,** and a novel, **Marriage Voices.** Articles and reviews have appeared in **Harper's Magazine, The Progressive, Dissent, Modern Occasions, Worldview, Political Studies, The American Political Science Review, The New Republic,** and many other journals. Guest lecturer at Yale Drama School and Dartmouth College's Hopkins Center. Recipient: American Council of Learned Societies Fellowship, 1980–81; Guggenheim Fellowship, 1980–81; Visiting Fellowship, New York Institute for the Humanities, 1980–81; Fulbright Senior Research Fellowship, 1976–77; Rutgers University Research Council Grant, 1972–73; Danforth Graduate Fellowship, 1960–65. Cited as one of eight "Young Builders of America" in cover story in February 9, 1976 issue of **U.S. News and World Report.**

Address: 924 West End Ave., New York, NY 10025

Agent: Charlotte Sheedy, Hoffman and Sheedy, 145 West 86th St., New York, NY 10024 (212) 724-4768

TITLE • AVAILABILITY • PRODUCTIONS

The People's Heart: manuscript*; Theater 3, Off Off Broadway

The Bust: manuscript*; Equity Showcase, NYC; Manhattan Theatre Club, NYC

Delly's Oracle: manuscript*; Berkshire Theater Festival

Doors: manuscript*; Equity Showcase, NYC; Riverside Theater Workshop, NYC

Winning (musical; music by John Duffy): manuscript and tape*; Equity Showcase, NYC; Gene Frankel Theater Workshop

Journeys: A Musical Myth (in collaboration with Martin Best), recorded as **Knight on the Road,** EMI Records, London: manuscript and videotape*; Hopkins Center, Dartmouth College, NH

Home and the River (opera/music theater, music by George Quincy): manuscript*
    *contact agent

SYNOPSES

Winning: A musical comi-tragedy with music by John Duffy based on the college days of an American loser/winner who will one day become President of the United States. An exploration of the darker side of "making it" in America. Set in the Depression, on a small college campus, the play focuses on football, student politics and winning — a mirror of America.

Full length; eighteen songs. Setting: flexible college campus setting. 3 young males, 2 females, 1 mature male (football coach); chorus of 4 to 12.

Journeys: A Musical Myth: A musical allegory using an ensemble of 8 to 12 to suggest in music, dance and narrative the human journey from village innocence to urban anarchy . . . and back again.

Uninterrupted one act (60 minutes) for a mixed (variable) ensemble of 8 to 12; ensemble can include instrumentalists. Simple, austere, flexible set. Videotape available.

Doors: Two one-acters and a curtain-raiser (the one-acters can be done separately) treating with ironies of fear and death in a New York apartment besieged more by hysteria than real adver-

B

Benjamin R. Barber (cont'd)

saries (**Front Door**) and in a slightly demented purgatory where present waiting is shadowed by past history for several characters who seem unready for either Paradise or Hades (**Peter's Door**).

Settings: **Front Door**, a cluttered New York livingroom; **Peter's Door**, a sparse, abstract purgatory — the Door dominates both sets. 5 males, 1 female.

ANNA MARIE BARLOW

Born in Albuquerque, N.M. Lived in California and Louisiana. B.A. from LSU, Speech and Journalism. Came to New York, worked on magazines while studying acting with Stella Adler and Harold Clurman. Acted on Broadway and in summer stock. Wrote first one-act play, became a member of the New Dramatists and Actors Studio. First play, **Ferryboat** won national one-act play contest; second play, **Out of Track** also won contest, and began a playwriting career which has included Broadway, Off Broadway and regional theater. Has directed many of her own plays and also written for all major tv networks. Recipient: University of Delaware Playwriting Contest; John Golden Playwrights Award; Ford Foundation Grant; National Endowment for the Arts Award, 1976–77.

Address: 430 East 63rd St., New York, NY 10021

Agent: Harold Cohen, Kohner-Levy Agency, 9169 Sunset Blvd., Los Angeles, CA 90069 (213) 550-1060

TITLE • AVAILABILITY • PRODUCTIONS

Ferryboat: Dramatists Play Service, 440 Park Ave., South, New York, NY 10016, $1.25; ANTA Matinee Series, NYC; Theatre de Lys, NYC

The Frizzly Hen: manuscript*; ANTA Matinee Series, NYC; Theatre de Lys, NYC

Mr. Biggs: New American Playwrights, Hill & Wang, 19 Union Square, New York, NY 10003; summer stock, Long Island; many regional theatres

Out of Track: manuscript*; Stanford University, CA

On Cobweb Twine: manuscript*; Sea Cliff, L.I.

Cold Christmas: manuscript*; Dallas, TX; Wilmington, DE

Half Past Wednesday (musical): manuscript*; Off Broadway, Orpheum, NYC

Taffy: manuscript*; New Dramatists, NYC

Where the Music Is: manuscript*; Southwest Theater Conference, Baton Rouge, LA

Cruising Speed 500 MPH: manuscript*; New Dramatists, NYC

Spit in the Ocean/The Artists: manuscript*; New Dramatists, NYC

Limb of Snow/The Meeting: Dramatists Play Service, $2.50; ANTA Matinee Series, NYC; Theatre de Lys, NYC

The Bicycle Riders: Best Short Plays of1980, Chilton Press, Chilton Way, Radnor, PA 19089, $10.50; New Dramatists, NYC; Actors Studio, NYC

Glory! Hallelujah!: manuscript*; American Conservatory Theatre, San Francisco, CA; Also NET-TV

Ambassador: manuscript*; Broadway

Other Voices Other Rooms (Dramatization of Capote novel): manuscript*; Buffalo Studio Arena, NY

The Meeting: manuscript*
    *contact agent

SYNOPSES

Glory! Hallelujah!: Play spans the Civil War . . . deals with the nature of wars and not the specific issues of that war. Deals with "the bitch glory" . . . conviction of each side that God's on our side. Takes place with a family in Louisiana and Lee's Army. Stylistically done. The realities of war, done with small intimate scenes (not large battles), is always in juxtaposition to the naive pursuits of glory.
Stylized set pieces against a cyclorama. 18 males, 4 females.

The Artists: Group of people (mid-twenties) writers, sculptors, etc., unable to react to fact one of their group is dying anyway but by "ripping it off" and turning it into some "kind of art."
Setting: Greenwich Village apartment. 4 males, 3 females.

Cruising Speed 500 MPH: Ex-husband and wife, actors, seated side by side on crowded airliner. Primarily comical, sarcastic, bitter. Biting but poignant as we see two people who couldn't grow up.
Setting: Two airplane seats. 1 male, 1 female.

NATHAN NOBLE BARRETT

Born New York City, deposited in Jamaica, West Indies, for ten years, educated and re-educated in New York. Twenty-five years getting B.A. from Brooklyn College. Student teaching at Hunter College, state certification as English teacher. Playwright and novelist (novel: **Bars of Adamant**, Fleet, 1966); gave up writing poetry at twenty (**Floating World: Poems**, Mandrill, 1962). Lives alone with a nutmeg tree. Recipient: Huntington Hartford Fellowship; John Hay Whitney Opportunity Fellowship.

Address: 35 East First St., New York, NY 10003
    (212) 674-7356

TITLE • AVAILABILITY • PRODUCTIONS

Room of Roses: manuscript*; IASTA

Engagement in San Domingue: manuscript*

Yacht-It: manuscript*

Square Roots of Mother: manuscript*

Aunts of Antioch City: manuscript*; Negro Ensemble Company, NYC; National Arts Theatre

Baker-Maker: manuscript*; Playwrights Horizons, NYC

Cut Ups & Cut Outs: manuscript*

Why Lilly Won't Spin: manuscript*; Greenwich Mews, NYC

Itchy Britches: manuscript*; Theater for the New City, NYC
    *contact author

SYNOPSES

Aunts of Antioch City: A black grandmother's determination to advance the interests of her biracial granddaughter with her white aunts. The exploration of her education as she bridges the gap, and fulfills her role most admirably.
Full-length evolutionary comedy; 4 scenes. Single set. 5 females (2 black, 2 white, 1 in-between).

B

Nathan Noble Barrett (cont'd)

Itchy Britches: The rise and fall of one rock singer to the presidency of the United States only to be trapped by his tapes.

Full length. A modern satire with music. 7 males, 3 female, all in "red" face.

Cut-Ups & Cut Outs: Sixteen ex-heroes of World War II live out the dregs of their lives and die in a forgotten, deserted home by the sea. Their deaths are cumulative.

Two acts; morality/black comedy. 16 males (10 white, 6 black).

BOB BARRY

Born in Chicago, IL. Came to New York at 17 to become an actor. He formed a nightclub act with Bobo Lewis and they played such cafes as the Blue Angel. He co-starred on the **Aldrich Family** as Homer Brown for NBC and did most of the top shows during the golden age of television. He was an apprentice agent for two years and then opened his own agency in 1960. He has been writing since 1972.

Address: 249 East 48th St., New York, NY 10036

Agent: The Barry Agency, 165 West 46th St., New York, NY 10036 (212) 869-9310

TITLE • AVAILABILITY • PRODUCTIONS

Murder Among Friends: Samuel French, 25 West 45th St., New York, NY 10036, $2.50; Biltmore Theatre, Broadway

Its Murder in the Hamptons: manuscript*

Lovers and Madmen: manuscript*

Getting It on in Hollywood: manuscript*
    *contact agent

SYNOPSIS

Murder Among Friends: The rich wife of a Broadway matinee idol and her lover, who is her husband's agent, are planning to murder the husband on New Year's Eve. The agent is also the husband's lover, and they are planning to murder the wife on the same night, with the same plan. The agent is murdered. The wife and husband try to outwit each other and shift the blame to the actual murderer.

Full length. Setting: one interior. 4 males, 2 females.

NORMAN BEIM

Attended Ohio State University, Hedgerow Theatre School, and Institute of Contemporary Art. Has worked professionally in the theatre as an actor and director for over twenty years, and has also taught acting, speech, and English. Appeared on Broadway in **Inherit the Wind**. Toured nationally as an actor. Recipient: Second Prize, National Theater Conference for **Inside**; Winner, Metropolitan Short Play Contest (**The Deserter**).

Address: 425 West 57th St., New York, NY 10019
    (212) CO 5-6284 or (212) JU 2-4240 (service)

B

TITLE • AVAILABILITY • PRODUCTIONS

Inside (one act): manuscript*; Columbia University, NYC; Provincetown Playhouse, NYC

David and Jonathan: manuscript*; Off Off Broadway

Battle of Valor: manuscript*; Off Off Broadway

Guess Who's Not Coming to Dinner: manuscript*; Off Off Broadway

The Haircut: manuscript*

3 Black Comedies (one acts): manuscript*; Troupe Theatre, NYC

The Establishment: manuscript*

Success: manuscript*; currently under option

Ida the Indomitable: manuscript*

The Disintegration of Della Longstreet: manuscript*

The Liberation of Linda Dworkin: manuscript*

The Dark Corner of an Empty Room: manuscript*

Pygmalion and Galatea: manuscript*; Staged reading, Off Off Broadway

I Went to a Marvelous Party: manuscript*; Troupe Theatre, NYC

Kingdom by the Sea: manuscript*; Reading, St. Clements, NYC

The World of Dracula: manuscript*; Troupe Theatre, NYC

The First Mistake: manuscript*

The Tyranny of Love: manuscript*

Pickled Peppers: manuscript*

The Deserter: Samuel French, 25 W. 45th St., New York, NY 10036, $2.50; Troupe Theatre, NYC; Circle Repertory Co., NYC

A Marriage of Convenience: manuscript*; Troupe Theatre, NYC

The Professor Graduates: manuscript*; Troupe Theatre, NYC

Women Are Women: manuscript*; Troupe Theatre, NYC

Dreams: manuscript*

Archie's Comeback: manuscript*

Chessman: manuscript*; Reading, Victory Gardens Theatre, Chicago, IL

Second Chance: manuscript*

The Costume Ball: manuscript*

Lonely Places: manuscript*
    *contact author

SYNOPSES

The Battle of Valor: The play deals with a tragic set of circumstances that cause a young NYC soldier's dishonorable discharge from the army on the charge of homosexuality. The subsequent betrayal by the girl he loves and the feigned sympathy of an opportunistic bi-sexual eventually determine the soldier's destiny.

Full length. Setting: bare stage broken into various playing areas, preferably with platforms. 3 males, 3 females.

Pygmalion and Galatea: A famous plastic surgeon, who is somewhat of a "man about town," transforms an unattractive, social young wife into a beauty. The woman eventually divorces her husband, who's much older than she, and marries the surgeon. The doctor discovers, to his chagrin, that the change in his Galatea has been more than skin deep.

Full length. Setting: two interiors — doctor's office and a fashionable sitting room. 2 males, 2 females.

The Deserter: In the darkened room of a deserted French chateau during World War II, Private Eddie Slovik awaits execution. "Written with great perception and sensitivity . . . the author ranks with the best in America today" . . . WHBI Radio.

One act. Setting: one interior. 3 males.

B

BARRY BERG

Born in Brooklyn, NY in 1942. Educated at Brandeis University, B.A.; Yale Drama School, M.F.A. Taught Theatre at Fairleigh Dickinson University, Speech at Manhattan Community College. Has written extensively for film and TV (**Another World**). Recipient: C. Brooks Fry Award by Theatre Americana for Best Play of Season (1972–73); S.U.N.Y. Playwriting Prize (1975).

Address: 28 West 70th St., New York, NY 10023/ Monhegan, ME 04852

TITLE • AVAILABILITY • PRODUCTIONS

The Horror Show: manuscript*; New Theatre Workshop

Toussaint: manuscript*; New Dramatists, NYC

A Quiet Evening at Home with the Human Race: not available; Fairleigh Dickinson University, NJ

I'd Rather Sit Alone on a Pumpkin: manuscript*; Neighborhood Playhouse, NYC; Theatre Americana, CA

Kindly Observe the People: Modern International Drama, 1975*; New Dramatists, NYC

Hello, I Love You: manuscript*; New Dramatists, NYC; Actors Community Theatre, Miami, FL

Nightlight: manuscript*; New Dramatists, NYC

The Man Who Drew Circles: manuscript*; New Dramatists, NYC

The Adversary: manuscript*

Musical Chairs (with Ken Donnelly and Tom Savage); manuscript*; Broadway
      *contact author

SYNOPSES

Nightlight: Four people in a New York hotel (periodontist from Cleveland, his wife, his old college roommate, and an actress turned porn queen) find their lives, for an evening, interwoven. The Cleveland couple, frustrated by the limitations of their lives are fascinated by the New York pair, and are seduced and repelled in turn. The sophisticated couple play superior to Middle American values, but only to cover the thin hold on their own brittle lives. This is a bitter comedy that feeds on the sparks generated when two opposing life-styles clash. The final confrontations are fierce, with neither side emerging victorious.

Full length. Setting: the bar and two hotel rooms of a New York hotel. 3 males, 2 females.

The Man Who Drew Circles: The father of three children died twenty years ago under mysterious circumstances, and now his son Harold is on the verge of suicide. Harold's family, including his own son Ted, gather to deal with Harold's problem, The theme of fathers manipulating sons is explored both in the past (exactly how did the old man die?) and in the present (will Harold succeed in manipulating Ted as his father manipulated him?). This is a taut psychological drama, filled with gallows humor, that snaps when the stories of the past and present merge for Harold in an almost fatal moment of truth.

Full length. Setting: livingroom of an expensive New York City high rise apartment. 3 males, 3 females.

The Adversary: A rational and brilliant scientist is confounded and terrorized as people close to him die by what appears to be spontaneous combustion. A psychotic cult leader presents himself to the scientist, admits responsiblity for the burnings (which can never be attributed to him — indeed what clues there are point to the scientist as murderer) and means to bring the scientist into his cult. This play is a battle between the powers of the rational and irrational, with the scientist forced to delve into his own darker side to finally defeat his adversary.

Full length. Setting: unit set. 3 males, 2 females. Many walk-ons. Some dancers. Special effects with fire required.

MARK BERMAN

Former merchant seaman, FM radio announcer, auto worker. Was playwright-actor with the Guthrie Theatre Company. Served as playwright-in-residence at Pennsylvania and Florida State Universities; Director, Playwrights Theatre, Tallahassee, FL; 5 O'Clock Theatre, Pennsylvania. Married, one son. Recipient: McKnight Fellowship in Playwriting; Office of Advanced Drama Research award; Playwriting award, Sausalito Little Theatre and Birmingham Festival of the Arts.

Address: 10631 Montrose Ave., #203, Bethesda, MD 20014 (301) 493-4778

Agent: Ellen Neuwald, 905 West End Ave., New York, NY 10025 (212) 663-1586

TITLE • AVAILABILITY • PRODUCTIONS

Old Folks at Home: manuscript*; Sausalito Little Theatre, CA; KVOM Radio, Minn, MN.

Please Keep off the Grass: manuscript*; Second Story Players, NYC; West Broadway Workshop, NYC.

I Had 3 Balls But I Lost: manuscript*; Thirteenth Street Theatre, NYC; University of Minnesota

Wake Up in the Morning: manuscript*; University of Minnesota

Pictures at an Inhibition: manuscript*; Harlequin Players, WI; Birmingham-Southern College, AL

A Saxophone for America: manuscript*; Guthrie Theatre, MN

Trips: manuscript*; Cricket Theatre, MN; Purdue University, IN

Train Time: manuscript*; Dallas Theatre Centre, TX; Berkshire Theatre Festival, MA

Route 66: manuscript*; American Conservatory Theatre, CA; Alliance Theatre Company, Atlanta, GA

Caged: manuscript*; Alliance Theatre Company, Atlanta, GA; University of Missouri

The Day the Marching Bands Went Wild: manuscript*; Hartman Theatre, CT; Wisconsin Summer Repertory Theatre

Tall Stories from the Butcher's Block: manuscript*; Alliance Theatre Company, GA

Lady of the Diamond: manuscript*; North Light Repertory, IL; Studio Arena Theatre, Buffalo, NY

Popitch Loves Puccini: manuscript*

Svelte Anna: manuscript*; Commission, Actors Theatre of Louisville, KY
　　*contact author

SYNOPSES

The Day the Marching Bands Went Wild: This play focuses on seven members of the Potowatomi Trust Marching Band, smallest and poorest of the bands entered in a mid-western 47th Annual State Marching Band competition.

Full length comedy-drama. Setting: one set. 6 male, 4 female.

B

Mark Berman (cont'd)

Lady of the Diamond: The story of Connie Weaver, the first major league woman baseball player; how she breaks into the major legues as a pitcher for a Chicago team and what happens after she does.

Full length. Setting: unit set. 8 males, 2 females.

Popitch Loves Puccini: A love affair between a middle-aged used bookstore owner who is threatened with loss of his store and a recently retired opera star who is attempting a comeback.

Full length. Setting: unit set. 3 males, 2 females.

ALBERT BERMEL

Born in London, England on December 20, 1927. Has lived in and around New York City since 1955. Has taught playwriting, theatre criticism, theatre history, play analysis, and more specialized topics, undergraduate to doctoral courses, at Columbia University, Juilliard School, Rutgers University, Lehman College, and Graduate Center of C.U.N.Y. Theatre critic for **The New Leader,** 1964-68, 1972-73. Has written criticism — film, books, theatre — for many other publications; screenplay for feature film **Run;** translations of French plays (all published) by Moliere, Corneille, Courteline, Adamov, Cocteau, Beaumarchais, Labiche. Recipient: Guggenheim Fellowship in Playwriting, 1965; George Jean Nathan Award for Theatre Criticism, 1973-74.

Address: 5 Pershing Ave., New Rochelle, NY 10801 (914) 636-2131.

TITLE • AVAILABILITY • PRODUCTIONS

One Leg Over the Wrong Wall: Drama & Theatre, Vol. 8, No. 3, Spring 1970, The State University College at Fredonia, NY 14063, $1.50; Royal Court, London; The Questors, London

The Workout: Arts in Society, Vol. 5, No. 1, 1968, University Extension, University of Wisconsin, Madison, WI 53706, $2.00; productions in London, New York, Tokyo, Montreal and others

The Adjustment: manuscript*; Spoleto Festival; London; New York; various other productions

Herod First: manuscript*; Saville Theatre, London; UCLA, CA

The Recovery: manuscript*; Edinburgh; London; New Theatre Workshop, NYC

The Mountain Chorus: Best Short Plays of 1968, Chilton Book Company, 201 King of Prussia Rd., Radnor, PA 19089, $6.95; London, New York, various other productions

The Seizure: manuscript*; New York

A Web: manuscript*; Triangle, NYC; Public Theater, NYC

Thrombo: manuscript*; Columbia Summer Theatre, NYC

Family Weather: manuscript*; House Theatre, NYC

Whose Play?: manuscript*
    *contact author

SYNOPSES

The Workout: Les, an average sort of middle-aged citizen, lands in a New York gymnasium where a sexy young woman, Marge, tries to sell him a course that will tone up his spiritual muscles. But Les is himself a salesman and thinks he has better ideas about how to push a high-priced product like God.

Albert Bermel (cont'd)

One act (40 minutes). Setting: a corner of a health gym, with weights, barbells, and an altar. 1 male, 1 female.

The Recovery: A patient has just undergone heavy surgery in a hospital, where he is not given a chance to rest peacefully. He attempts to break out when he discovers the doctors are engineers, the nurses robots, the surgeon was a machine, and something peculiar has happened to his metabolism. One actor plays three roles; so does the actress. The patient tries to play himself. One act (45 minutes). Setting: a hospital bed and adjoining space. 2 males, 1 female.

Family Weather: A mother, father, two sons, and a daughter play out a series of domestic relationships, including love, hate, jealousy, persuasion, and intimidation. But they also go out of — and back into — their family roles. For example, in one episode the father turns into a captain, the older son a sergeant, and younger son a recruit, and the mother and daughter are camp followers; in another episode, one son and the mother become a social worker and a welfare recipient; in a third, the father becomes a sugar daddy and the daughter a woman he has picked up in a Syrian luncheonette. There are many brief scenes, which call for multiple "transformations" on the part of each performer.

Three acts (2¼ hours). Setting: an open stage, a few props and scenic elements; preferably an environmental set with levels. Songs and movement. 3 males, 2 females.

KENNETH BERNARD

Married, three children, living in New York City. Teaches at Long Island University. Has published fiction, poetry, criticism in **Harper's, Paris Review, Viva, Tri-Quarterly Review**, etc. Exhibition of Collages, 1980 at Long Island University, NY and Teachers College, Columbia University. Recipient: OADR Grant, 1971; Guggenheim, 1972 –73; CAPS in Playwriting, 1973; Rockefeller, 1975; CAPS in Fiction, 1976, N.E.A. Grant for Fiction, 1978; Arvon Foundation Prize for Poetry, (England), 1981.

Address: 788 Riverside Dr., New York, NY 10032

TITLE • AVAILABILITY • PRODUCTIONS

Mary Jane: Night Club and Other Plays, available at Drama Book Specialists, 150 West 52nd St., New York, NY 10019, $2.95 (paperback); New York [In one volume with:]

The Giants in the Earth, The Moke-Eater, The Lovers, The Monkeys of the Organ Grinder, Night Club, Mary Jane

The Unknown Chinaman: Playwrights for Tomorrow, Vol. X, University of Minnesota Press, 2307 University Ave. SE, Minneapolis, MN 55414, $3.45 (paperback); Magic Theater, Omaha, NB

Markos: A Vegetarian Fantasy: Massachusetts Review, Summer, 1969*

Goodbye, Dan Bailey: Drama & Theater, Spring, 1971, SUNY at Fredonia, NY 14063, $1.50; Chelsea Theater Center, NYC

The Magic Show of Dr. Ma-Gico: Performing Arts Journal, Playscript Series, #1, P.O. Box 858, Peter Stuyvesant Station, New York, NY 10009, $4.95; New York; Holland; Harvard University, MA

How We Danced While We Burned: manuscript*; Antioch College, OH

King Humpy: manuscript*; New York Theater Strategy; Gate Theater, NYC

The Sixty Minute Queer Show: manuscript*; La Mama, NYC; Holland

La Justice: manuscript*; Theater for the New City, NYC
    *contact author

B

Kenneth Bernard (cont'd)

SYNOPSIS

King Humpy: "Ostensibly about the short unhappy life, gruesome death and final ironic triumph of a hunchback, the play really deals allegorically with any group that is first outcast, scorned and abused and finally vindicated by turns of events. It, therefore, could easily be about Jews, homosexuals, blacks or any component of society which has been singled out this way,"
—Sy Syna, **Wisdoms Child.**

Setting: a make believe renaissance court; multi-level acting area that is now a balcony, now a bedroom, now a town square or ballroom.

DAVID ADAMS BERRY

Born in Denver, CO on July 8, 1943. B.A Wesley-an U., History and Theater; Certificate, Harvard U. Institute in Arts Administration. U.S. Army, Vietnam Veteran. National Theatre Institute, O'Neill Theatre Center, 1971–74. Theatre Consul-tant and Theatre Specialist, RI State Council on the Arts, 1975–76. Playwright-in-Residence, Worcester Consortium for Higher Education (Assumption College and Worcester Polytech-nic, 1977–78). Faculty playwright, Writers' Con-ference, U. of RI, 1980. Recipient: NEA, Creative Writing Fellowship, 1978; Obie Award for **G.R. Point,** 1977; Drama Desk Nomination, **G. R. Point**, 1977.

Address: East Beach Townhouse, #1, R.F.D.,
   Bradford, RI 02808
Agent: Audrey Wood, I.C.M., 40 West 57th St., New York, NY 10019 (212) 556-5722

TITLE • AVAILABILITY • PRODUCTIONS

G.R. Point: Dramatists Play Service, 440 Park Ave. South, New York, NY 10016, $2.50; O'Neill
   Theater Center's National Playwrights Conference, CT; Phoenix Theatre, NYC

The Whales of August: manuscript*; Center Stage, MD; Trinity Square Repertory Company,
   Providence, RI
   *contact agent

SYNOPSES

G.R. Point: The first major American play to be entirely set in Vietnam (in and around an Army Graves Registration unit in South Vietnam in 1969), through the literal and metaphorical journey of the main character it addresses the following themes: the ensemble nature of survival; the common validity of human beings regardless of surface varieties; the power of love and humor to overcome the worst mankind deals itself; and the power of tragedy and conflict to bring positive lessons for "knowing thyself." Without polemic, blame-placing, or gore, the play underscores the American need to heal the wounds of Vietnam.

Full length. Setting: one set, three major playing areas. 8 young males: 3 black, 1 Hispanic, 4 white. 1 female: Oriental.

The Whales of August: A gentle, kind, warm and humorous play which endorses vibrant old age, with characters who in no way caricature old age. Though filled with reminiscence, the play centers on tough life choices in the present tense and on the nature of survival even when life's ends are predictably close; and it suggests that senility is all too often in the eye of the beholder.

Full length. Setting: one set, two major areas. 3 elderly females, 1 elderly male.

SANDRA BERTRAND

Born in Bakersfield, CA on March 19, 1943. Attended Bakersfield College and Stella Adler Theatre Studio. Original member of the New York Theatre Strategy Playwriting Workshop with Maria Irene Fornes. As a journalist, she was New York editor for **Places, A Journal of Theatre**; book reviewer for **West Scene**, and freelance book and play reviewer for **Our Town**. TV writing credits include **The Guiding Light** and **The Big Blue Marble**. Her TV play, **Chameleon**, done at O'Neill Theater Center's National Playwrights Conference.

Address: 220 East 85th Street, New York, NY 10028 (212) 879-1742/(212) 582-4240

TITLE • AVAILABILITY • PRODUCTIONS

Something about the Albatross: manuscript*

The Sentry and the Laughing Ladies: manuscript*; New Play Festival, Off Broadway; Direct Theatre, NYC

Manikin: manuscript*; Staged reading, Manhattan Theatre Club, NYC

A Death in the Rose Arbor: manuscript*; Samuel French Play Festival, NYC; LaMama, Hollywood, CA

The Transformation of Aura Rhanes: manuscript*; Viridian Gallery, NYC

Days & Nights of an Ice Cream Princess: manuscript*; Viridian Gallery, NYC
  *contact author

SYNOPSES

The Transformation of Aura Rhanes: A young girl's identity crisis in the confused and challenging period of the late 50's. Set in a small California town amidst fears of the Cold War, UFO's, earthquakes and adolescent sexuality, the transformation of one teenager becomes a lesson in awareness to us all.
Full length. Setting: platforms with minimum set pieces. 2 males, 5 females.

Manikin: An overweight junk man brings a department store dummy home one night and sets into motion a carnival of suppressed desires. Ironically, a lifeless manikin becomes the catalyst that enables him to touch the lives of those closest to him.
Setting: split set. 4 males, 3 females.

B

KATHLEEN BETSKO

Born in Coventry, England on May 6, 1939. B.A., University of New Hampshire, summa cum laude, Creative Communications. Has studied playwriting with David Magidson, Ed Bullins, Herbert Berghof and Donna de Matteo. As an actress, she has appeared in regional theater, dinner theater, Off Off Broadway and Off Broadway. On Broadway and the road tour, she was in **Equus.** Has had poetry published, finished a screenplay for TV and is at work on a novel. Recipient: Commission, Actors Theatre of Louisville.

Address: 345 West 86th St., New York, NY 10024
    (212) 580-2010

Agent: Esther Sherman, William Morris Agency,
    1350 Avenue of the Americas, New York, NY
    10019 (212) 586-5100

TITLE • AVAILABILITY • PRODUCTIONS

Beggar's Choice: manuscript*; O'Neill Theater Center's National Playwrights Conference, CT; **Earplay**

Johnny Bull: manuscript*; O'Neill Theater Center's National Playwrights Conference, CT

Stitchers and Starlight Talkers: manuscript*
    *contact agent

SYNOPSES

Beggar's Choice: A working-class English girl, tired of her drab existence, fantasizes about escaping to America.
One act. Setting: ladies room of an N.C.O. club. 3 females.

Johnny Bull: The son of an Appalachian coal miner returns from overseas bringing a foreign bride. The new wife disrupts her husband's family and uncovers a dark secret.
Full length. Setting: kitchen. 2 males, 3 females.

Stitchers and Starlight Talkers: A factory stitcher enters a drawing competition and wins a semester of art classes. She meets a cynical male professor who is contemptuous of her social status. In spite of himself, the 'eacher becomes interested in the spirit and talent of his student. A relationship emerges which results in an education for both of them.
Long one act. Setting: 3 areas, an assembly line, kitchen, classroom. 4 males, 3 females.

SALLIE BINGHAM

Born in Louisville, KY on January 22, 1937. B.A., Radcliffe College, magna cum laude. Has taught English and Creative Writing at University of Louisville. Books: **After Such Knowledge; The Touching Hand; The Way It Is Now; Straight Man.** Her works appear in many collections and magazines. Recipient: Dana Reed Award, Harvard, 1958 (first time the prize was awarded to a woman); Yaddo Colony Fellowship, 1980; Mac-Dowell Colony Fellowship, 1979.

Address: 3715 Glen Bluff Road, Louisville, KY
    40222 (502) 425-2851

Agent: Peter Matson, 32 West 40th St., New
    York, NY 10018 (212) 944-1160

Sally Bingham (cont'd)

TITLE • AVAILABILITY • PRODUCTIONS

Family: manuscript*

Country Boy: manuscript*

Milk of Paradise: manuscript*; Women's Project, American Place Theater, NYC

In the Yurt: manuscript**; Actors Theatre of Louisville, KY

The Act: manuscript**; Actors Theatre of Louisville, KY

No Time: manuscript**; Actors Theatre of Louisville, KY

Paducah: manuscript**; Actors Theatre of Louisville, KY
    *contact author
    **contact Actors Theatre of Louisville, 316–320 W. Main St., Louisville, KY 40202

CONRAD BISHOP

Born in Denver, CO on October 8, 1941. B.S. in Speech and Drama, Northwestern University; M.A. in Drama, Northwestern; Ph.D. in Dramatic Literature, Stanford University. Assistant Professor of English, University of South Carolina, 1966–68; Assistant Professor of Theatre Arts, University of Wisconsin/Milwaukee; 1968–71; Company Manager and performer, Theatre X, Milwaukee, 1969–74; Artistic Director, The Independent Eye, 1974–. Recipient: Best of Festival Award, American Personnel and Guidance Film Festival; Silver Gavel Award, American Bar Association.

Address: 409 Fairway Drive, Lancaster, PA 17603
    (717) 393-9088

TITLE • AVAILABILITY • PRODUCTIONS

Marvels: manuscript*; Independent Eye, PA

Wanna: manuscript*; O'Neill Theater Center's National Playwrights Conference, CT

Families: manuscript*; Independent Eye, PA, WUHY-FM

Lifesaver: manuscript*; Independent Eye, PA

Who's There: manuscript*; University of Delaware

Black Dog: manuscript*; Independent Eye, PA

Dreambelly: manuscript*; Independent Eye, PA; Theatre X, WI; Baltimore, MD and the Netherlands

Dessie: manuscript*; Independent Eye, PA; WHA-TV

Knock Knock: not available; University of Delaware

Sunshine Blues: manuscript*; Independent Eye, PA

Song Stories: not available; Independent Eye, PA

I Wanna Go Home: not available; Illinois Status Offenders Services

Goners: not available; The Body Politic, Chicago, IL

The Money Show: not available; Independent Eye, PA

Sunday Morning: not available; Theatre X, WI

Meet: not available; Theatre X, WI

Alice Wake Up: not available; Theatre X, WI

B

Conrad Bishop (cont'd)

Alice in Wonder: not available; Theatre X, WI

Mister Punch: not available; Theatre X, WI

Halfway to Somewhere: not available; Human Education, Inc., Madison, WI; Complete Channel TV, Madison, WI

The Wizard of Spring: not available; Theatre X, WI

The Whiteskin Game: not available; Theatre X, WI

The People vs. the People: not available; Theatre X, WI

My Wife Dies at Stonehenge: not available; Theatre X, WI

Giveaway: not available; Theatre X, WI

X Communication: not available; Theatre X, WI

The Bitch of Kynossema: not available; University of South Carolina

The Silk Block: not available; Stanford Unviersity, CA

Songs of Passersby: not available; Shakerag Players, WI
*contact The Independent Eye, 115 N. Arch St., Lancaster, PA 17603

SYNOPSES

Wanna: An alcoholic drifter comes to his ex-wife's funeral after a 20 year absence and meets his retarded daughter. Their mutual needs lead to violence and reconciliation with uncertain results.
Full length. Setting: realistic interior. 2 males, 3 females.

Dreambelly: A substitute teacher emerges from the trauma of his mother's lingering death to seek a mythical, "super-hero" identity. At last he tries suicide but, bedeviled by his comic survival instinct, fails.
Short full length. Setting: Unit set — locations suggested by chairs and cardboard boxes. 1 male, 1 female (who plays 5 roles).

Marvels: A free adaptation of Gozzi's commedia **The Kind Stag**. A king seeks truth and love in an enchanted forest, the prime minister's daughter lusts for a postal clerk, and a waitress pursues a suicidal custodian in a plot tangle of magic, song and dark melodrama.
Full length. Setting: 3 sets or unit set changeable to castle and enchanted forest locations. Musical score. 6 males, 3 females, 3 clowns.

NEAL BLACK

Born in Akron, OH. A.B. and Sc. B. from Brown University. After four years in Navy settled in New York. Now working in Chicago. Recipient: WTTW (Chicago Educational Television) award in national contest; Charles MacArthur Award of the Chicago Drama Critic League; Drama Club of Evanston Award.

Address: 9436 Pleasant Ave., Chicago, IL 60620
(312) 779-6882

TITLE • AVAILABILITY • PRODUCTIONS

Love in a Tutu: manuscript*; Margo Jones Theatre, Dallas, TX

Love in the Fifth Position: manuscript*; Playwright's Center, Chicago, IL

Eddie in the Doorway: manuscript*; Playwright's Center, Chicago, IL

Love on a Dark Night: manuscript*; Playwright's Center; Theatre First, Chicago, IL; Equity Library Theatre, NYC
    *contact author

SYNOPSIS

Love in the Fifth Position: Arriving in New York for a weekend, Lucy hopes to rekindle a romance with Skate, who is now a promising classical dancer. To block this, Skate's possessive mentor, Cobb, lends Lucy his apartment and calls in as a counterlure Kravchinska, famous and voracious ballerina. But Kravchinska, badly mistaken, thinks Lucy is Cobb's mistress, and so she too wants Cobb. Lucy carefully maneuvers Skate to the apartment, and is startled to have him quickly reestablish himself in her bed. Crowing too proudly the next morning, Skate irritates both Lucy and Cobb. After a fight he bolts, leaving them to cry on each other's shoulders. . . . After enchanting Lucy, Cobb announces that he will marry her unless Skate will take her place in his life. Rejecting these terms, Skate tricks Lucy into a confrontation and wins her back. The youngsters go off, leaving Cobb to Kravchinska who is waiting to devour him.

Full length. Setting: apartment livingroom. 2 males, 2 females.

MICHAEL BLANKFORT

University of Pennsylvania B.A.; Princeton U. M.A.; instructor of Psychology, Bowdoin College, Princeton; playwriting, N.Y.U. Extension; Psychologist, New Jersey State Prison (Rahway); President, Writers Guild of America; Vice-President, Academy of Motion Picture Arts and Sciences; Trustee, Los Angeles County Museum of Art; Board of Directors, Brandeis Institute, Santa Susana, CA.; published twelve novels, one biography; several plays. Author of fifteen screenplays, some with other writers: Among them: **Broken Arrow, Caine Mutiny, The Vintage, Texas, My Six Convicts, Blind Alley, Lydia Bailey, The Juggler, Halls of Montezuma.** Also films for TV: **See How They Run** (from his  novel **The Widow Makers**), **The Other Man, The Plainsman.** Recipient: Samuel Daroff Award (1953) for novel, **The Juggler**; Commonwealth Club Gold Medal for novel, **Behold the Fire**; Academy nomination for screenplay, **Broken Arrow**; Writers Guild Award for **Broken Arrow**; Valentine Davies Award from Writers Guild; Hebrew University, S.Y. Agon Gold Medal for Literature.

Address: 1636 Comstock Ave., Los Angeles, CA 90024 (213) 553-5468 or 273-6807

Agent: Scott Meredith, 845 Third Ave., New York, NY 10022 (212) 245-5500

TITLE • AVAILABILITY • PRODUCTIONS

The Crime: manuscript*; Workers Lab Theatre

Battle Hymn: manuscript*; Federal Theatre, NYC; Chicago, IL

Monique (with Dorothy Blankfort): Samuel French, 25 West 45th St., New York, NY 10036, $2.50; Broadway; London

Goodbye, I Guess: manuscript*; Broadway; London; Baltimore

Karl and Arthur (with Bernard Wolfe): manuscript*
    *contact author

B

Michael Blankfort (cont'd)

SYNOPSIS

Karl and Arthur: Karl Marx, at sixty-one, troubled by lack of recognition, burdened by poverty, a sick wife, a daughter who wants to be an actress — a profession he condemns as useless — guilty over his long relationship with a mistress (a menage a trois) is confronted with the possibility of working out his theories in Ethiopia brought to him by the quintessential bohemian, Arthur Rimbaud. Marx's temptation after the death of his wife to pursue Rimbaud's offer, to make peace with his mistress and daughter, and mostly himself, and to accept his daughter's relationship with the wild, drug-addicted poet is at the core of the play. Rimbaud is as important in the play as Marx. The domestic situation of the Marx family is factual; the meeting with Rimbaud is not.

Full length. Setting: One set — Marx's livingroom, London, 1881. 7 males, including 1 black, 4 females.

MURRAY TEIGH BLOOM

B.A., Columbia College; M.S., Graduate School of Journalism, Columbia. Author of more than six hundred magazine articles and the following books: **Money of Their Own** (Scribner); **The Man Who Stole Portugal** (Scribner); **The Trouble with Lawyers** (Simon & Schuster); **Rogues to Riches** (Putnam); **The 13th Man** (MacMillan), filmed as **Last Embrace.**

Address: 40 Hemlock Drive, Great Neck, NY 11024 (516) 487-8528

Agent: Julian Bach, Jr., 747 Third Ave., New York, NY 10017 (212) 753-2605

TITLE • AVAILABILITY • PRODUCTIONS

Leonora (The White Crow): manuscript*; Dallas, TX; SMU University Theater
   *contact author

SYNOPSIS

Leonora (The White Crow): Call it an egghead melodrama. About 1900, William James was professor of philosophy at Harvard and also the first president of the American Society of Psychic Research. In the latter role, he encounters a young, pretty Boston widow, Leonora Piper, who was a medium. James had several sessions with her and was impressed enough to do a report for the parent society in London. There they read the report and decide poor Will was being taken in by a young and pretty faker. So they decide to send their most experienced psychic investigator, Dr. Richard Hodgson, a handsome Cambridge University don, to Boston to expose Mrs. Piper, as he had already exposed Mme. Blavatsky and Eusapio Palladino, and put the American society on its feet, properly. The play opens in the library in the James' home in Cambridge, Mass., when Hodgson has come for his first seance with Mrs. Piper.

Full length, 3 acts. Setting: livingroom-library of William James home, Cambridge, Mass., turn of the century. 6 males, 3 females.

SAM BOBRICK

Born in Chicago, IL on July 24, 1932. B.S., University of Illinois, 1955. Has written numerous TV shows such as **Smothers Brothers Show, Alan King Special, Kraft Music Hall.** Recipient: Writers Guild of America TV Award (three times) — **Andy Griffith Show, Get Smart, Kraft Music Hall.**

Agent: Creative Artists Agency, 1888 Century Park East, Los Angeles, CA 90067 (213) 277-4545

TITLE • AVAILABILITY • PRODUCTIONS

Norman, Is That You? (with Ron Clark): Samuel French, 25 West 45th St., New York, NY 10036, $2.50; Broadway; Paris, France

No Hard Feelings (with Ron Clark): Samuel French, $2.50; Boston, MA; Broadway

Murder at the Howard Johnson's (with Ron Clark): Samuel French, $2.50; Boston, MA; Broadway

Wally's Cafe (with Ron Clark): manuscript*; Broadway
   *contact agent

LUCILE BOGUE

Born in Salt Lake City, UT. A.A., Colorado College; B.A., University of Northern Colorado; M.A., San Francisco State University. Postgraduate study at Sophia University, Tokyo; Colege Internationale, Cannes; Instituto de San Miguel de Allende; University of California. Three volumes of poetry, **Typhoon! Typhoon!; Eye of the Candor** and **Bloodstones/Lines from a Marriage.** Novel, **Westward the Storm** (Pinnacle Books); biography, **Dancers on Horseback.** Recipient: Colorado Poet of the Year; Browning Society of San Francisco Award; World of Poetry Prize; All Nations Poetry Contest; Stephen Vincent Benet Award; National Writers Club Award.

Address: 2611 Brooks, El Cerrito, CA 94530 (415) 232-0346

Agent: Helen McGrath, 1406 Idaho Court, Concord, CA 94521 (415) 232-0346

TITLE • AVAILABILITY • PRODUCTIONS

Make a Joyful Noise: Contemporary Drama Service, Box 457-HF, Downers Grove, IL 60515, $14.75; Numerous productions

The Lucky Ones: manuscript*;Steamboat Springs, CO

Citizen Number One: manuscript*; Berkeley, CA; San Francisco, CA

Drums Carry a Far Distance: manuscript*

Private Moments in the Life of an Ordinary Woman: manuscript*; Berkeley, CA

Fedra of the Canyon: manuscript*

Freedom Trail!: manuscript*; Steamboat Springs, CO; Denver, CO

The Supper: manuscript*

I . . . As in Identity: manuscript*; Berkeley, CA

Casa Rosa: manuscript*

B

Lucille Bogue (cont'd)

King Katherine I: manuscript*

Moondog: manuscript*
  *contact author

SYNOPSES

Drums Carry a Far Distance: A haunting story of a beautiful African of royal descent, purchased by a young plantation owner in Louisiana in 1857, and of their growing love as she learns American ways. Powerful, delicate, yet violent.
Full length. Setting: bare stage with only a few props. 2 males, 1 female, minor parts — 10-20 men or women, depending upon desirability of doubling parts.

Casa Rosa: Contemporary story set in the home of the American Consul in Ecuador, seeking the fine line dividing the love and the hate between a man and wife. Reveals the disintegration of the mind of a man who attempts to possess, without success, his wife as he would an inanimate object.
Full length. Setting: livingroom in the consul's home. 2 males, 3 females.

King Katherine I: A spoof on American politics, a comedy-fantasy telling of the breakdown of the democratic system and of the nation's decision to become an absolute monarchy. In the final election, a king is elected, a woman! Her "edicts" are issued in torrents, shaking the world to its roots, with hilarious and beneficent results.
Full length. Setting: bare stage, blank wall for projection, only furnishings are a set of steps and a large table with chairs. 3 males, 7 females plus extras.

LUDMILLA BOLLOW

Born in Manitowoc, WI on April 24. Taught: Playwriting, Rhinelander School of Arts, adult creative writing, creative writing for children (Government funded arts program), lectures and workshops on playwriting and acting. Articles, short stories, poetry published in U.S., India and England, teen-age anthology books. Edited **Theatre USA (National Theatre Magazine)**. Reporter and theatre reviewer. Actress: numerous roles, misc. groups including Milwaukee Repertory Theater. Member: Dramatists Guild; Wisconsin Council for Writers; Wisconsin Regional Writers; Wisconsin Theatre Assoc.; Women in the Arts. Judge: American College Theatre Festival. Recipient: Southeastern Theatre Conference New Play for 1976; Russell Sharpe Drama Award; Wisconsin Council for  Writers Playwriting Award (twice) (Johnson Foundation Award); Wisconsin Regional Writers Playwriting Award (twice); Theatre Americana Play Selection; Midwest Playwrights Fellowship, 1978; Wisconsin Women in the Arts Playwrights Award. Best Actress Award, Wisconsin Theatre Association.

Address: 314 W. Sugar Lane, Glendale, WI 53217 (414) 352-8370

TITLE • AVAILABILITY • PRODUCTIONS

In the Rest Room at Rosenblooms: manuscript*; Longwood College; Southeastern Theatre Conference

The Beach Club: Literary Half Yearly of India (U. of Mysore, India)*; Alliance Theatre Co.; University of Wisconsin, Oshkosh; Wisconsin Theatre Conference

Martha's Boy: manuscript*; Theatre Guild of Webster Grove; WI; Idea Theatre; University of Wisconsin

Ludmilla Bollow (cont'd)

Late/Late . . . Computer Date!: manuscript*; Village Church; Berea College

Where Have All the Flowers Gone?: manuscript*; Nicolet Theatre

The Smile on the Kewpie Doll: manuscript*; Gard Theatre

Between the Dark and the Daylight: manuscript*; (Readings)

Harper's Bizarre!: manuscript*; Performing Arts Center

St. Francis: manuscript*; (Readings)

The Silvery Spangly Summer: manuscript*

King of the Beach: manuscript*

Dr. Zastro's Sanatorium for the Ailments of Women — Mental, Physical & Sexual: manuscript*

The Golden Gate Bridge: manuscript; Midwest Playwrights Conference, WI
  *contact author

SYNOPSES

In the Rest Room at Rosenblooms: The story of three elderly ladies who spark their lonely lives by meeting daily in the rest room lounge of a dated downtown department store, and the crazy-touching events that occur the day one of them is supposedly threatened. . . . There is Winifred and her birds, Violet and her doll, Myrah, with a gusto for living her ailing body can't quite keep up with. All stirred up by Olga, an asylum matron, bent on "saving unfortunates." The characters are real, the plot fast moving, and the laughter built in.

Three acts. Setting: one simple set, lounge of downtown department   store. 4 females, 1 nonspeaking.

The Golden Gate Bridge: Samsara, a young girl is restlessly searching for some meaning in life. Martin, a former astronaut, has given up on life. They meet on a cross-country bicycle trip, an outward journey that gently moves inward. Inventive use of three background figures, plus unusual technical aspects, give a magical quality to this unique contemporary drama. A play that hovers between reality and fantasy.

Full length. Setting: bare stage, raised platform with curtain. 2 males, 3 females.

Dr. Zastro's Sanatorium for the Ailments of Women — Mental, Physical & Sexual: It is the 1880's. Dr. Zastro's unique hypnotic powers and electrical/magnetic apparatus make his sanatorium a mecca for afflicted women. Each spring he case studies six diverse women. A first-time love affair with Yana, a gypsy/artist patient, results in domino tragedies, disintegrating his power structure, destroying his inner invincibility. Authentic insight illuminates this most unusual drama.

Full length. Setting: three simple sets/or insets. 2 males, 6 females.

ALLEN BORETZ

Born in New York City. Educated at City College School of Journalism. Songwriter for revues. Published short stories in **Blue Book, Argosy**; epigrams in **Smart Set**; articles in **Variety Green Edition, Hollywood Reporter, New York Times** theatre page, etc. Fifteen major screenplays. Semi-pro ballplayer, tennis, golf, violinist, composer of two unproduced musicals. Blacklisted in 1951 and worked in films in Spain under assumed names. Recipient: Blue Ribbon, Film of the Month for **Where There's Life.**

Address: 15 Vandam St., New York, NY 10013
  (212) 242-2519

Agent: Bertha Case, 345 West 58th St., New York, NY 10019 (212) 541-9451/Audrey Wood, ICM, 40 West 57th St., New York, NY 10019 (212) 556-5722

B

Allen Boretz (cont'd)

TITLE • AVAILABILITY • PRODUCTIONS

The Flying Elephant: manuscript*

Loner: manuscript*

Room Service: Dramatists Play Service, 440 Park Ave. South, New York, NY 10016, $2.50; Broadway

School Teacher: not available; Provincetown Playhouse, MA

Off to Buffalo: not available; Broadway

The Hard Way: not available; Shubert, Boston, MA

As the Twig: not available

The Hot Corner: not available

A Can of Peas: manuscript*; Berliner Allee Theatre, Dusseldorf

Here Come the Butterflies: manuscript*; Barn Theater, MI

A Girl in the Window: not available

The Continued and Repeated Murder of George: not available

Conversation: manuscript*

Marx & Angela: manuscript*

Gaming: manuscript*
    *contact Bertha Case
    **contact Audrey Wood

BILL BOZZONE

Born Brooklyn, NY on November 25, 1947, B.A., Marist College and M.F.A. in Writing, Goddard College. Playwright-in-residence, Collingwood Repertory Co. in Poughkeepsie, NY. Member, Ensemble Studio Theatre, NY. Has given lectures and workshops at U. of Hartford, CT, Community College of Philadelphia and Downstate Correctional Facility, Beacon, NY. Recipient: CAPS Fellowship in Playwriting.

Address: 173 Union St., #A2, Poughkeepsie, NY 12601 (914) 452-5843

TITLE • AVAILABILITY • PRODUCTIONS

Lackland: manuscript*; West-Park Theatre, NYC

Boxing Day: manuscript*; Reading, Ensemble Studio Theatre, NYC

Touch Black: manuscript*; Ensemble Studio Theatre, NYC

American Chestnut: manuscript*; Collingwood Repertory Co.

Only Still Life: manuscript*; Reading, The Night Kitchen, Peekskill, NY

Stuck in the Pictures on a Sunday Afternoon: manuscript*; Ensemble Studio Theatre, NYC
    *contact author

SYNOPSES

Touch Black: The trade is simple. The use of Bernie's apartment in exchange for part of Robbins' 1950 rock n' roll record collection. After the deal is made and Bernie plays a few snatches of the old "goldies," Robbins quickly changes his mind and attempts to call the deal off. Yet Bernie has a personal reason for wanting these records — a reason for refusing to trade back no matter what the price. "Wonderfully rich" . . . Jeffrey Borak, **Poughkeepsie Journal.**

One Act. Setting: an executive men's washroom. 3 males.

Bill Bozzone (cont'd)

American Chestnut: When Warren Engleman loses his job with Chase Manhattan for embezzling funds, he and his wife, Fern move from mid-town to up-state. The relocation, an effort to salvage some semblance of self-esteem, becomes a welcome change for Warren but a cold and desolate existence for Fern. When her brother, Ronnie, a would-be comic moves in, Fern decides that her only alternative is to bring her best friend up; the beginning attempt to "move Manhattan north." Full length. Setting: a rustic cabin. 2 males, 3 females.

Only Still Life: John and Leo are security guards at a primarily all-girls college. In anticipation of the Easter break, the students have cleared the campus. Together at their security station in the early morning hours, the two men have little to occupy their time other than card tricks, push-ups contests, and waiting for John's wife, Vicky, to bring them sandwiches. But there is another person on campus — a mysterious visitor who will cause unexpected turmoil and unbelievable fear. One act. Setting: the security station. 2 males, 1 female.

BENJAMIN BRADFORD

Born, Alexandria, LA on October 28, 1925. Educated Northwestern Louisiana University; Mississippi College; Graduate, L.S.U. School of Medicine, 1948. Playwright-in-residence, University of Kentucky. Member Kentucky Arts Commission Board of Governors, Kentucky Center for the Arts. Recipient: Golden Windmill Award, Radio Nederland, 1971; Citation, Best Play, Best Playwright, **Daily Variety**, LA, 1974; Winner, Kent Messenger Drama Festival, Bar Harbor Drama Festival; runnerup, 1969, '70, '71, John Gassner Memorial Award; Donovan Rhysinger Award, U. of Missouri.

Address: P.O. Box 1542, #11, Mora-Mi, Paducah, Kentucky 42001 (502)443-7357

Agent: Donald B. Hayes City-County Arts Council, Paducah, KY 42001

TITLE • AVAILABILITY • PRODUCTIONS

Game: manuscript*; Los Angeles; various others

Megalith: manuscript*

Circumstance: manuscript*

A Matter of Time: manuscript*

Parabus Objective: manuscript*; Clarion St. College, PA

Concentric Circles: The Scene/I, 5 Beekman St., New York, NY 10038; Louisiana tour; Old Reliable, NYC

The Anthropoligists: manuscript*; Stagelights II, NYC

Where Are You Going, Hollis Jay: Samuel French, 25 W. 45th St., New York, NY 10036, $2.50; U. of Kent, OH; Canterbury, England; various others

The Ideal State: manuscript*; Stagelights II, NYC; Toucan Theatre, NY; various others

Geometric Progression: manuscript*; Theatre 13, NYC

A Game of Kings and Queens: manuscript*

Instructions for a Sandcastle: manuscript*

A High Structure Falls Further: manuscript*; Old Reliable, NYC

Lunch: manuscript*; Jefferson Community College, KY; Staircase, LA

Rendezvous: manuscript*; Jefferson Community College, KY; Staircase, LA

B

Benjamin Bradford (cont'd)

Post Mortem: manuscript*; Lexington, KY; various others

Segments of a Contemporary Morning: manuscript*; Old Reliable, NYC; Staircase Co., LA, CA

Life and Death in a Public Place: manuscript*; Staircase Co., LA, CA

Charcoals and Pastels: manuscript*; Clarion, PA

The Goats: Performance Publishing Co. Elgin, IL 60120, 90¢; Gulfport, MS

Look Away, Look Away: manuscript*; Unicorn Productions, NYC

Princess: Performance Publishing Co., 90¢; Staircase Co., LA, CA; Gulfpark College, MS

Loving Kindness: Performance Publishing Co., 90¢

Spartans: manuscript*

Bugs (with Hal Hoster, Danny Apolinar): manuscript*

Sing Your Song, America (with Hal Hoster, Danny Apolinar): manuscript*

Scoring (with Dexter Freeman): manuscript*; Arts Council Dinner Theatre, KY

Love (with Dexter Freeman): manuscript*; Bucks County Playhouse, PA

Birds of Passage: manuscript*; Unicorn, NYC

A Double Fraktur L: manuscript*, Unicorn, NYC

The Rabbit: manuscript*

Doillies: manuscript*; Gulfport, MS

To Make a Man (with Blatz Harrington): manuscript*; U. of Kentucky; Gulfport Little Theatre, MS; Fort Knox, KY

The Moon Bridge: manuscript*; Broadway Theatre Guild, NYC

The New Woman: manuscript*

The Cowboy and the Legend (with Hal Hester and Chandler Warren): manuscript*; Burt Reynold's Dinner Theater, Jupiter, FL

The Adorable Dodo (with Hal Hester): manuscript*

Balloons and Other Ironies (collection of short plays): manuscript; U. of Kentucky

Helping Hands (with Blatz Harrington): manuscript*; Kentucky State Hospital Assoc.

Plotters: manuscript*

Touch and Go: manuscript*; S.E.T.C., Lexington, KY

Code 99: manuscript*; Earplay

A Small Act of Violence: manuscript*

Rainbow: manuscript*

The Boa Constrictor: manuscript*

The Fence War: manuscript*

The Princess Reluctant: manuscript*

Losing Things: manuscript*; Guignol Theatre, U of Kentucky

Conversation Piece: manuscript*; Staircase Co., LA, CA

The Sack of Oak Park: manuscript*

Good Days, Bad Days: manuscript*; Earplay

Pitfall for a Rational Man: manuscript*; Clarion, PA; Gulfport, MS
  *contact agent

SYNOPSES

Scoring: A young man has moved from Georgia to San Francisco and finds he is terribly lonely. He rehearses the seduction of a young woman he has met. A friend attempts to teach him the newest means of "making out." The girl arrives, and the seduction attempt is a disastrous failure,

Benjamin Bradford (cont'd)

for Clifton can only make out with a girl he loves. The girl, who turns out to be a hooker, is drawn in his fantasies to her own near destruction.

Two acts. Setting: an interior, Clifton's room or efficiency apartment in San Francisco. 2 males, 1 female.

To Make a Man: A musical. The script deals lightly with Benjamin Franklin, Victoria Woodhull, bits and pieces of American History, and a couple of All American people, one of each sex, and young. Franklin bums a ride with Joe in his Chevy van and their journey takes them not only through the great American west and mid-west, but through various times in history as well. The play is happily irreverent and pokes holes in the image of the founding fathers as saints.

Two acts. Fifteen musical numbers. Setting: multiple fragments. 3 males, 2 females.

OSCAR BRAND

Born in Winnipeg, Canada on February 7, 1920. Graduated, Brooklyn College, 1942. In 1945, having won the war (Army), he became coordinator of Folk Music for radio station WNYC. He has written many industrial shows, scripted ballets and many documentary specials for NBC and NET. He is Vice-President of the Songwriters "Hall of Fame" and author of ten best-selling books and manuals of music. He is currently on the faculty of Hofstra University and the New School. Recipient: Every award from Ohio State, Freedoms Foundation, Emmy, Golden Reel, **Scholastic**, etc. (except for the Oscar).

Address: 141 Baker Hill, Great Neck, NY 11023
   (516) 487-5979

Agent: Harold Freedman, Brandt and Brandt, 1501 Broadway, New York, NY 10036 (212) 840-5760

TITLE • AVAILABILITY • PRODUCTIONS

In White America (music): Samuel French, 25 W. 45th St., New York, NY 10036, $2.50; Sheridan Square Playhouse, NYC, numerous productions

How to Steal an Election (music and lyrics with John Gerstad): manuscript*; Pocket Theater, NYC

Thunder Rock (music and lyrics with John Gerstad): manuscript*

Sing America Sing: manuscript*; Kennedy Center, Wash., D.C.

A Joyful Noise (music and lyrics with Paul Nassau); Broadway

The Education of Hyman Kaplan (music and lyrics with Paul Nassau); Dramatic Publishing Co., 4150 N. Milwaukee Ave., Chicago, IL 60641, $2.00; Broadway

The Second Scroll: manuscript*

The Bridge: manuscript*; Greenwich Mews Theatre, NYC
   *contact author

SYNOPSES

Sing America Sing: The Story of America as told by its people in letters, manuscripts and songs. Produced at Kennedy Center 1975, televised 1976 by PBS Network, 6 females, 6 males.

Thunder Rock: Musical version of Robert Ardrey's prize winning 1939 play about a man living in a world of ghosts because the real world is too frightening. 6 males, 2 females.

B

JOHNNY BRANDON

Born in London, England (pre-World War II).
Started professional life at eleven as a song and
dance man in British Variety. Educated at Lawrence House; Brentwood College. Sergeant,
Variety Dept., British Forces Network, Germany.
Singer and song writer. In top ten with **Tomorrow**
and **Don't Worry.** Has published over six hundred
songs. Has written extensively for TV and motion pictures. Owns Grenadier Music (publishing
company). Member: Council of the American
Guild of Authors and Composers; Broadcast
Music, Inc. Recipient: Ivor Novello Award.

Address: 200 East 17th St., New York, NY 10003

Agent: Robert Youdelman, 424 Madison Avenue,
New York, NY 10017 (212) 755-1568

TITLE • AVAILABILITY • PRODUCTIONS

Maid to Measure (lyrics): manuscript*; Cambridge Theatre, London

Love! Love! Love!: not available; Astor Place Theatre, NYC

Cindy (book, Joe Sauter & Mike Sawyer): Tams-Witmark, Inc. 757 Third Ave., New York, NY
10017; Gate Theatre, NYC; Orpheum Theatre, NYC

Billy Noname (book, William W. Mackey): R. E. Richardson Productions, 200 East 17th St., New
York, NY 10003; Truck & Warehouse, NYC; various productions

Sing Me Sunshine: R. E. Richardson Productions

Helen (book, Lucia Victor): manuscript*; AMAS Repertory Theatre, NYC

Ain't Doin' Nothin' but Singin' my Song: R. E. Richardson Productions; Theatre Off Park, NYC

Eubie (co-lyricist): Ashton Springer, 240 W. 44th St., New York, NY 10036; Broadway; national
tour

Suddenly the Music Starts: R. E. Richardson Productions; AMAS Repertory Theatre, NYC;
Academy of Music Cabaret Theatre, PA

The More You Get the More You Want (book, Dan Owens): manuscript*; Black Theatre
Alliance, NYC

That's What's Happening, Baby (book, Guy Bolton, P. G. Wodehouse); not available

Benedictus: not available
*contact author

SYNOPSES

Billy Noname: "Dynamic" musical play has a "vividly exultant vitality and a varied and delightful
score by Johnny Brandon that make it genuinely exciting to watch" —Richard Watts, **New York
Post**. It is the odyssey of a now successful black American writer who, having found his own
place in the sun, is deeply troubled that his voice is perhaps not clearly heard with those of his
brothers who demand "Freedom now!" To find out where he should go from here he retraces his
life from the day of his conception in a street rape in Bay Alley, a southern ghetto, on the night
Joe Louis became heavyweight champ of the world in 1937. "Most of the joy — and there is plenty
of it — is in the good and powerful songs. This all-black musical is so buoyant that its effect lasts
several hours after the house lights come up." —Edith Oliver, **New Yorker**.
Setting: one abstract multi-level set. 8 males, 7 females (larger chorus may be added).

Helen: Concerns Helen of Troy and what might have happened to her when she could no longer
launch a thousand ships, and her laid-back husband, King Menelaus, who much to her an-
noyance, has decided that his duelling days are over. She becomes involved with a subversive
band of young Trojans who are to kidnap Menelaus and hold him for ransom as reparations for
the sacking of Troy.
Full length musical comedy. Setting: a basic unit set with movable pieces, plus a staircase. To be
performed by an interracial cast. Minimum 8 males, 5 females.

Johnny Brandon (cont'd)

Sing Me Sunshine: Based on **Peg o' My Heart** by J. Hartley Manners. Updated to the 1930s. Peg, the originally Irish-American heroine who upsets a snobbish upper-class British family, in this musical version is portrayed as an Afro-American, with rather more pungent but equally satisfying romantic results.

Full length musical comedy. Three basic sets: Manor House Reception Room, Assembly Rooms Church Hall, Village Square. 7 principals and 2 utility people. (Singing and dancing chorus may be added.)

ANNA BRENNEN

Born in Elko, NV on June 27. B.A. from U. of California, Berkeley. Trained in Theater at Carnegie Institute of Technology (Carnegie Mellon), also with Peter Brook, Theatre of Cruelty, Laurence Olivier, Wynn Handman and Lloyd Richards. Five years a professional actress in NYC. Top Xerox sales rep in NYC and Tampa. Writer and editor for NYC High School Equivalency programs and for Columbia U. Fund raising Chairman, Alice People Theatre, Tampa, FL. Recipient: Florida State Fine Arts Council Fellowship.

Address: 120 Adriatic Avenue, Tampa, FL 33606
(813) 251-8984

TITLE • AVAILABILITY • PRODUCTIONS

Sleepless Dancer: manuscript*; N.E.T.W.O.R.K. Theatre, NY; Lenja Productions, NY

Snow-Still: manuscript*; Co-produced: Alice People Theatre & Hillsborough Community College, Tampa, FL
*contact author

TOWNSEND BREWSTER

Born in Glen Cove, NY on July 23, 1924. B.A., Queens College in Greek and Latin; M.A., Columbia in French. Playwright, librettist, poet, lyricist, translator, lecturer, critic, educator. Translations for NBC Television Opera. Two broadcasts on Black Theatre for Danmarks Radio in Copenhagen. Commission from Israeli Music Publications for libretto. Adaptation of **Egmont** for Goethe Festival at Tanglewood. Translation of the **Cid** "Controversy Papers" in **Dramatic Theory and Criticism: Greeks to Grotowski**. Poems in various periodicals and in the anthology **Today's Negro Voices**. Articles for the Metropolitan Opera Program. Critic for **Show Business, The Commonweal, Players, The Denver Quarterly, The Amsterdam News, Routes, Big Red** and **The Harlem Cultural**

Review. He has taught in the Theatre Department of City College. Recipient: National Theatre Conference Playwrights' Fellowship; Koussevitzky Foundation Scholarship in Libretto Writing; William Morris Playwriting Scholarship at the American Theatre Wing; Ford Foundation Librettists' Grant; Louise Bogan Memorial Prize in Poetry; C.U.N.Y. Research Grant; Harlem Cultural Council Grant; Award from **Story Magazine**; Jonathan Swift Award; NEA Librettist Grant.

Address: 171-29 103 Road, Jamaica, NY 11433

Agent: Ronelda Roberts, 1214 Ridge Blvd., Brooklyn, NY 11209 (212)745-0826

B

Townsend Brewster (cont'd)

TITLE • AVAILABILITY • PRODUCTIONS

The Choreography of Love (libretto): manuscript*; Broadcast over WNYC

Rough and Ready (musical): manuscript*

Look Eastward (musical): manuscript*

Andromeda (lyric comedy): manuscript*

Arrangement in Rose and Silver: manuscript*

Little Girl, Big Town: manuscript*; Queens College, NY

Oh, What a Beautiful City!: manuscript*; New Dramatists, NYC

Singapore Sling: manuscript*; Queens Community Theatre, NY

The Tower: Boosey & Hawkes, 30 West 57th St., New York, NY 10019, $2.00; Santa Fe Opera, NM

The Cocktail Sip (one-act opera): manuscript*

The Complete Works of Kalkbrenner: manuscript*; Thirteenth Street Theatre, NYC

How the West Was Fun: manuscript*; University of Denver, CO

Mowgli: manuscript*; University of Denver, CO

Chief Rathebe: manuscript*; University of Denver, CO

What Are Friends For?: manuscript*

Please Don't Cry and Say "No": manuscript*; Circle-in-the-Square, NYC; Armstrong State College

Pinter's Revue Sketches (lyrics): manuscript*; Weathervane Theatre

Harlequinades for Mourners (lyrics): manuscript*; New Theatre

Lady Plum Blossom (lyrics): Modern Theatre for Youth, Inc., 2366 Grandview Terrace, Manhattan, KS 66502, $2.00; Oregon State University, OR

The Main-Chance Rag: manuscript*

Black-Belt Bertram: manuscript*; Frank Silvera Workshop; Double Image Theatre, NYC

Amator, Amator: manuscript*; Trent Gough's Workshop

To See the World in a Drop of Brine: manuscript*

Waiting for Godzilla: manuscript*; Trent Gough's Workshop

The Washerwoman: (children's play): manuscript*

The Ecologists (radio play): manuscript*

Chocolat Volatil (trilogy of one-act lyric comedies): manuscript*

Though It's Been Said Many Times, Many Ways: manuscript*; Frank Silvera's Workshop, NY; Harlem Performance Center, NY

Arthur Ashe and I: manuscript*; Frank Silvera Workshop; Theatre of Riverside Church, NYC

Ebur and Ebony: manuscript*

Thirteen Ways of Looking at Merle: manuscript*

Mascara and Confetti: manuscript*

Idomeneus: manuscript*

The Anonymous Lover: manuscript*; Symphony Space, NYC

O My Pretty Quintroon: manuscript*

A Threnody for the Newly Born (libretto): manuscript*

Mood Indigo: manuscript*; Frank Silvera Workshop, NYC

à: manuscript*

The Palm-Leaf Boogie: manuscript*

The Jade Funerary Suit: manuscript*

Johnny Renaissance: manuscript*

No Place for a Lady: manuscript*

The Girl beneath the Tulip Tree: manuscript*

Sight Unseen: manuscript*

Ananias, Jr.: manuscript*

Praise Song: manuscript*
    *contact author

SYNOPSES

Please Don't Cry and Say "No": A bill of three one-act high comedies by black authors, two of which (Victor Sejour's **The Brown Overcoat** and Machado de Assis's **The Botany Lesson**) were translated by Mr. Brewster and the third of which (**Please Don't Cry and Say "No"**) was written by him. Synopsis of title play: Adina Burroughs, a basically happy young wife, is sufficiently dissatisfied with the position of women in society to burst into irrational tears when her husband, Jed, reports that a promotion that should have gone to a woman, has gone to a man. When her worldly friend, Godiva, advises her to seek solace in an affair, Adina says that her only possible comfort would lie in finding something that a woman may do, but that a man may not. In Central Park, fifteen-year-old Mike, who has been playing handball, finds the courage to speak. At a park concert that night, Jed, in a pique, flirts with Mike's big sister, Chloe. A sudden storm. Jed rushes off with Chloe. Mike and Adina leave in a cab for a brief, delightful sexual interlude. Later, Jed comes home, apologetic, but denying any infidelity — there couldn't be, he explains; Chloe was only seventeen. Adina then relaizes, with unbounded ecstasy, that there *is* something that a woman may do that a man may not, and they all live happily ever after.

One act, five scenes. Four songs between the scenes and a bossa nova at the concert. Setting: the Burroughs apartment, Central Park, and Godiva's apartment. 7 males (6 teen-agers), 3 females (1 teen-ager), persons at park concert (optional).

Oh, What a Beautiful City!: The Angel Gabriel announces to Mayor Crampton Griswold of New York City that he is to select a committee to take an examination that, if passed, will win Heaven for all mankind immediately without waiting for Judgment Day. The Mayor, who cannot see past the next election, chooses party stalwarts though, by a fluke, there is one qualified person appointed, the teacher, Ruth McLinden. While on Earth, Gabriel, for old time's sake, announces the forthcoming birth of her child to April, the wife of the Mayor's chief clerk, Leslie Parry. Not wishing to leave anyone behind who might leak news of the enterprise before the deal is all sewed up, the Mayor takes the Parrys and Branch Mayson, a black clerk and friend of Leslie, along on the expedition. The examination consists of recognizing Heaven when you see it. Ruth, the Parrys, and Branch are able to do so, but only Ruth has a say, and the Mayor and his friends easily outvote her, and, as usual, humanity misses out.

Two acts, in verse. Setting: City Hall, the Parry home, a television studio, a street, Necropolis Airport, and Heaven. 12 males, 4 females.

Vignettes from Worlds I and III (A bill of three one-act comedies):

    Waiting for Godzilla: Dracula, the Wolf Man, the Frankenstein Monster, and company, guests in the haunted mansion of the Ghost of Fanny Kemble in Georgia, find themselves outdone in fiendishness by some solid citizens from whose murderous clutches they rescue a little black boy. Setting: library of a haunted house. 9 males, 3 females.

    To See the World in a Drop of Brine: The kings of the Atlantic and Pacific Oceans threaten to engulf the Earth in their territorial disputes. In verse. Setting: Neptune's throne room. 9 males, 3 females.

    Arthur Ashe and I: A young black teacher, almost browbeaten into letting his colleagues take advantage of a black student, rises to the occasion when Arthur wins at Wimbledon. Setting: a New York apartment. 5 males.

B

JAY BROAD

Attended Westminster College and Penn State. Artistic Director of Theatre Atlanta, 1965–69. Producer/Artistic Director, PAF Playhouse, 1975–80. President, National Theatre Conference, 1977–78. Recipient: Straw Hat Award, 1972.

Address: 100 Riverside Drive, 12E, New York, NY 10024

Agent: Brett Adams, 36 East 61st St., New York, NY 10021 (212) 752-7864

TITLE • AVAILABILITY • PRODUCTIONS

Red, White and Maddox: manuscript*; Theatre Atlanta, GA; Broadway

Conflict of Interest: Samuel French, 25 W. 45th St., New York, NY 10036, $2.50; Arena Stage, Wash, D.C.; Westport Playhouse, CT

Great Big Coca Cola Swamp in the Sky: manuscript*; Westport Playhouse, CT; Paramus Playhouse, NJ

The Killdeer: Samuel French, $2.50; New York Shakespeare Festival, NY

White Pelicans: manuscript*; PAF Playhouse, NY; Theatre de Lys, NYC

Uncle Eddy: manuscript*; PAF/MacDonald Youth Theatre, NY

Events from the Life of Ted Snyder: manuscript*; PAF PLayhouse, NY; Urgent Theatre, NY
   *contact agent

KENNETH H. BROWN

Novel: **The Narrows** (Dial Press). Teaching: Resident Playwright, Yale Drama School; Visiting Lecturer in Improvisational Theatre, Hollins College; History of Theatre, Hunter College; Play Production, University of Iowa. Poetry published in **Yale/Theatre Magazine, Kulchur, City Lights Journal**. Stories and articles published in **Evergreen, The New York Times, Arts Magazine, TDR, Plays and Players** (London). Recipient: Guggenheim Fellowship; Rockefeller Grant; ABC/Yale Fellowship; National Endowment Grant; CAPS Grant.

Address: 150 74th St., Brooklyn, NY 11209

Agent: Ellen Neuwald, 905 West End Ave., New York, NY 10025 (212) 663-1586

TITLE • AVAILABILITY • PRODUCTIONS

The Brig: Hill & Wang, 19 Union Square, New York, NY 10003, $1.50; The Living Theatre, NYC; over one hundred international amateur and professional productions

The Happy Bar: manuscript*; Actors Studio, NYC

Night Light: Samuel French, 25 West 45th St., New York, NY 10036, $2.50; Hartford Stage Company, CT

Blakes Design (one act): **Best Short Plays of 1968**, Chilton Book Co., 201 King of Prussia Rd., Radnor, PA 19089, $6.95; Yale Drama School, CT; Theatre for the New City, NYC

Devices (one act): manuscript*; Actors Studio, NYC; Judson Poets Theatre, NYC; Yale Drama School, CT

Kenneth H. Brown (cont'd)

The Green Room: manuscript**; University of Iowa

The Cretan Bull (one act): manuscript*; O'Neill Theater Center's National Playwrights Conference, CT; Drake University, IA
    *contact agent
    **contact author

SYNOPSIS

The Happy Bar: The play deals with the last weeks that U.S. Marines spent in Japan after the Korean War. It takes place in a brothel and examines relationships of Marines and prostitutes. Full length. Setting: a brothel. 12 males, 12 females.

LENNOX BROWN

Born in Trinidad, he received a Senior Cambridge Certificate at St. Mary's College, a B.A. from the University of Western Ontario, an M.A. from the University of Toronto, Ph.D. in English Literature, University of London, England. He has written about forty plays, most of which fall into three separate cycles. He has written for stage, television, and radio in the Caribbean, Canada, Holland, and the United States. He has published poetry, has been a journalist, a news editor for the C.B.C., and a University lecturer at the University of Hartford and the City University of New York. He is the first playwright to have won the Canadian National Playwriting Competition four times in a row. Recipient: Canada Council; CAPS Grant; National Endowment for the Arts; Arts Council of Great Britain.

Address: 110 West 94th St., #6D, New York, NY 10025

Agent: Emily Jane Goodman, 501 Madison Avenue, New York, NY 10019 (212) 787-6785

TITLE • AVAILABILITY • PRODUCTIONS

A Ballet Behind the Bridge: manuscript*; Negro Ensemble Company, NYC; Canadian Broadcasting Corporation

A Ballet in a Bear Pit: manuscript*

The Blues Smile: manuscript*

The Burning Sky: manuscript*

A Clean Sweep: manuscript*; Trinidad and Tobago TV

A Communion in Dark Sun: manuscript*

The Conversion: manuscript*; Reading, New York Shakespeare Festival, NYC

Devil Mas': Kuntu Drama, edited by P.C. Harrison, Grove Press Inc., 196 W. Houston St., New York, NY 10014, $4.95; Karamu House Theatre, Cleveland, OH; Western State University, IL

Fog Drifts in the Spring: The Twilight Dinner and Other Plays, Talon Books, 201/1019 East Cordova, Vancouver, British Columbia, V6A 1M8, Canada, $5.95; Trinidad Theatre Workshop; Caribbean-American Repertory Theatre

The Gold Coast of Times Square: manuscript*

I Have to Call My Father: Drama and Theatre, Vol. 8, No. 2, 1969–70, State University of New York at Fredonia (also entitled:) **Jour Ouvert**: in catalogue*

Home Is a Long Way: manuscript*; Trinidad & Tobago TV

B

Lennox Brown (cont'd)

The Journey Tonight: manuscript*

A Last Dance in the Sun: manuscript*; Trinidad and Tobago Television

The Meeting: in catalogue*; Canadian Broadcasting Corporation; Ontario Drama Festival

Moon in the Mirror: manuscript*

The Night Class: manuscript*

Night Sun: manuscript*

A Processional from La Basse: manuscript*

Prodigal in Black Stone: manuscript*; O'Neill Theater Center's National Playwrights Conference, CT

The Sisterhood of a Spring Night: manuscript*; Queens College Theatre, NY

Summer Screen: Prism International, Winter 1980, Vol. 19, #2, University of British Columbia, Vancouver, B.C. V6T 1W5, Canada; Frank Silvera's Writers Workshop, NYC

This Scent of Incense: manuscript*; Canadian Broadcasting Corporation

Song of the Spear: manuscript*; Canadian Broadcasting Corporation; Trinidad Theatre Workshop

The Throne in an Autumn Room: manuscript and phonograph record*; Canadian Broadcasting Corporation; Trinidad Theatre Workshop

The Trinity of Four: Caribbean Rhythms, edited by J. Livingston, Simon & Schuster Inc., 1 West 39th St., New York, NY 10018 (Washington Square Press) $1.95; IRT Theatre, NYC; Billie Holiday Theatre, NYC

The Twilight Dinner: Talon Books; Harlem Performing Arts Center, New York; Frank Silvera Writers Workshop; Reading, IRT Theatre, New York

Three Colours of a Dream Quartet: manuscript*

The Winti Train: manuscript*; University of Hartford, CT; Billie Holiday Theatre, NY

Winter is Coming: manuscript*

Wine in Winter: manuscript*; Trinidad Theatre Workshop

The Blood Promise of a Shopping Plaza: with **The Twilight Dinner**

The Basement: manuscript*

Becoming Persons: manuscript*

The Philosophy of a Fast Half-Back: manuscript*

Sunday: manuscript*

The Governor's House: manuscript*

The Team: manuscript*
   *contact agent

SYNOPSES

The Blues Smile: A former black American radical has carved an international reputation for himself in the Third World. He returns to the U.S., is pardoned by Washington, and appointed to head an important office in New York. He falls in love and marries the daughter of an upper class black family. His job places him in charge of black Ivy League graduates. Their upper-class background threatens him. He unknowingly slights one of these graduates, who devises a terrible plan for his downfall. Character and environment ignite.

Full length. Setting: office, bedroom, a street in the Lower East Side of New York. 6 black males, 3 black females.

A Ballet in a Bear Pit: A contemporary tragi-comedy set in North America. Selwyn, a twenty-eight-year-old Caribbean immigrant and university drop-out, tries to make himself a success according to White Protestant ethics. A forest of obstacles grows in his path. He marries a domestic from the Caribbean, but becomes romantically involved with two white women. His wife, meanwhile has started to smell success for her own life. Both Selwyn and his wife climb to the pinnacle of North American success, but at a terrible price to themselves and their marriage.

Lennox Brown (cont'd)

Full length. Setting: livingroom, store interior, and parts of a bare stage. 4 males (2 blacks, 2 whites); 4 females (2 blacks, 2 whites).

Fog Drifts in the Spring: A contemporary tragi-comedy dealing with the black experience set in Paris. A black American sailor, haunted by an irrational sense of guilt resulting from a childhood incident, meets a Caribbean taxi driver. The sailor is apparently doomed to sail the seas forever. He is compelled to tell his story to strangers with a strange obsession. The taxi driver is in Paris for his personal pleasure only — the symbolic journey into whiteness by blacks born outside of Africa. A new meaning of black identity emerges from the meeting, although it is tragic.

One act. Setting: a park, a bench, a tree. 2 males, 1 female, all black.

WILLIAM F. BROWN

Born in Jersey City, NJ. B.A., Princeton University. Worked for **Look Magazine**, MCA, BBDO. Freelance writer/artist since 1962. TV credits include **Love American Style, That Was the Week that Was, The Jackie Gleason Show, Max Liebman CBS Specials, Silents Please**, special material for all major variety and late-night shows. Sketch writer and lyric writer for eight Julius Monk shows from 1960–69. Industrial show writer and lyricist. Freelance magazine gag cartoonist for ten years, selling to all national magazines. Since 1972, co-writer and co-artist (with Mel Casson) of nationally syndicated comic strip **Boomer**. Member of the Dramatists Guild, Writers Guild of America East, ASCAP, National Cartoonists Society. Sketch and continuity writer for **New Faces of 1968**. Author-artist of **Beat Beat Beat** (New American Library), **The Girl in the Freudian Slip** (N.A.L.), **The Abominable Snowman** (N.A.L.), **The World Is My Yo-Yo** (Pocket Books). Recipient: 1975, Tony nomination for Best Book for a Musical (**The Wiz**); 1975 Drama Desk Award for Best Book for a Musical (**The Wiz**).

Address: 164 Newtown Turnpike, Westport, CT 06880 (203) 226-6949

TITLE • AVAILABILITY • PRODUCTIONS

New Faces of 1968 (sketch & continuity writer): manuscript*; Broadway

The Girl in the Freudian Slip: Samuel French, 25 W. 45th St., New York, NY 10036, $2.50; Broadway; stock productions

The Wiz: Samuel French, $2.50 (book); $7.50 (vocals); Broadway; national company; foreign productions

A Single Thing in Common: Samuel French, $2.50; Stock productions

How to Steal an Election: manuscript*; Off Broadway; stock

Wilbur & Me: contact Robert Brittan, 360 W. 55th St., New York, NY 10019

Damon's Song: manuscript*; Rodale Theater, Allentown, PA

Tallulah: manuscript*

Straight up with a Twist: manuscript*; Pheasant Run Playhouse, Chicago, IL
*contact author

SYNOPSES

Damon's Song: A pop-Elizabethan musical. Music and Lyrics by George Robertson. A today musical although the action takes place in 1610. It involves Lady Beth, a hopeless romantic and

B

William F. Brown (cont'd)

three men in her life: Michael, a professional jock of the period: Shala Hadra, a rhinestone cowboy devil; and Damon, a shy but lovable minstrel.

Full length. 5 males, 3 females, 8 in the chorus.

Tallulah: Lyrics by Mae Richard, music by Ted Simons. A highly-stylized musical entertainment about certain events in the life and loves of Tallulah Bankhead; her triumphs and failures; her quest to be loved at all costs. A tour de force for the starring role.

Full length. "Tallulah," plus 3 males, 3 females.

Straight up with a Twist: Words and music by Lesley Davison and Michael Brown. A contemporary revue running the gamut of today's foibles from the joy of sex to the agony of media events. About six sketches and sixteen musical numbers.

Full length. 2 (3) males, 2 (3) females.

CYNTHIA BUCHANAN

Born in Des Moines, IA on October 23, 1942. B.A. Arizona Statue U; M.A., University of the Americas, Mexico. **Maiden,** a novel; **Cock Walk in Exile,** novel-in-progress; **My Mother's Gigolo,** screenplay, Rose Gregorio, co-author. Other: **The New York Times** Op-Ed page, **The New York Times Book Review, The Washington Post Book Review, Newsweek, Oui, Antaeus, Transatlantic Review, The Harvard Advocate, Epoch, South and West, Trace, The Writer, Mexico Quarterly Review, American Women Poets,** etc. Anthologies: **The Indignant Years: Selections from the Op-Ed Page,** edited by Harrison Salisbury; **Best Short Fiction from the Little Magazines 1970,** edited by Curt Johnson. Has worked extensively for Lily Tomlin. Recipient: CAPS grant, 1976; Fulbright Scholar (in creative writing) 1968–70; MacDowell Colony Fellow 1970; Outstanding Young Women of America 1972; **Mademoiselle "Mlle" Award,** 1972; **Maiden** listed in **Encyclopedia Britannica Yearbook,** 1973; **NY Times** noteworthy fiction list, 1972; American Library Association **20 Notable Titles,** 1972.

Address: P.O. 520 (312 S. 17th St.), Cottonwood, AZ 86326 (602) 634-7171

Agent: Lynn Nesbit, International Creative Management, 40 West 57th St., New York, NY 10019 (212) 556-5600

TITLE • AVAILABILITY • PRODUCTIONS

Cabrona: manuscript*; The Arena Stage Workshop, Wash. DC; Hippodrome Theatre, FL
   *contact author or agent

SYNOPSIS

Cabrona: A desperate woman is trapped on a ranch in the Arizona desert. She is at war. Obsessed and enraged (and highly unaware of any of her neuroses), Opal Massey's highest ambition is to appear "educated," "pleasant," and ". . . fair, aren't I always fair?" While forging on with her Panzer-division style; her mission is to break the will of her two worst enemies: who are her only two friends in life — her mother and her brother. The old pioneer mother is bent on death, but first on revenge; the brother, an hysterical Good Old Boy in a deep depression, for salvation is bent on marriage to the town's honky tonk whore. All this against our Opal's design, and without her knowledge. Three over-lapping love triangles in the story tend to obscure, for Opal, "the facts."

Full length. Setting: a ranch-house; time, 1976. 2 males, 3 females. Production note: Cabrona would require minimal or expressionistic staging, to counteract the seeming "naturalism" of the script. And to encourage any of its para-farcicalness.

ED BULLINS

Born in Philadelphia, PA on July 2, 1935. Has taught Writing and English at many colleges. Recently completed a screenplay of **The Electronic Nigger**. Working on a version of **The Lower Depths** for Joseph Papp and also his masterwork, a cycle of twenty plays called **The Twentieth Century Cycle**; also working on the book of a new musical **Satchmo**. He is on the staff of the New York Shakespeare Festival, where he coordinates a playwrights' workshop and works in the Publicity and Press Department. Recipient: New York Drama Critics Circle Award; two Obies; two Guggenheim Fellowships; three Rockefeller Playwriting Grants; CAPS Grant; National Endowment on the Arts Grant; Honorary Doctorate of Letters, Columbia College, Chicago.

Address: 932 East 212th St., Bronx, NY 10469

Agent: Helen Merrill, 337 West 22nd St., New York, NY 10011 (212) 924-6314

TITLE • AVAILABILITY • PRODUCTIONS

Dialect Determinism (or **The Rally**): **Theme Is Blackness**, Samuel French, 25 West 45th St., New York, NY 10036, $7.95; San Francisco Drama Circle, CA; Firehouse Repertory, San Francisco, CA

Clara's Ole Man: Five Plays by Ed Bullins, Samuel French, $7.50; San Francisco Drama Circle, CA; Firehouse Repertory, San Francisco, CA

A Son, Come Home: in **Five Plays**; American Place Theatre, NYC

The Electronic Nigger: in **Five Plays**; American Place Theatre, NYC; St. Clement's Church, NYC

It Has No Choice: in **Theme Is Blackness**; Black Arts West Repertory Theatre School, San Francisco, CA

How Do You Do: Black Fire, Samuel French, $5.95; San Francisco Drama Circle, CA; Firehouse Repertory, San Francisco, CA

Goin' a Buffalo: in **Five Plays**; Rehearsed reading, American Place Theatre, NYC

The Theme Is Blackness: in **Theme Is Blackness**; Black Arts West, CA; New Lafayette Theatre, NYC

A Minor Scene: in **Theme Is Blackness**; Black Arts West Repertory Theatre, San Francisco, CA

In New England Winter: Henry St. Playhouse, NYC

House Party: American Place Theatre, NYC

Do-Wah

In the Wine Time: in **Five Plays**; New Lafayette, NYC

The Man Who Dug Fish: in **Theme Is Blackness**; New Dramatists, NYC

The Corner: in **Theme is Blackness**; New York Shakespeare Festival, NYC; Theatre Company of Boston, MA

The Gentleman Caller: in **Black Quartet**, Mentor, New American Library, 1633 Broadway, New York, NY 10019 $1.50; Chelsea Theater, Brooklyn, NY; Tambellini's Gate, NYC

The Helper: in **Theme Is Blackness**; New Dramatists, NYC

The Pig Pen: Four Dynamite Plays, Samuel French, $2.95; American Place Theatre, NYC

You Gonna Let Me Take You Out Tonight, Baby?: Samuel French, manuscript; New York Shakespeare Festival, NYC

State Office Building Curse: in **Theme Is Blackness**

Night of the Beast: in **Four Dynamite Plays**

B

Ed Bullins (cont'd)

The American Flag Ritual: in **Theme Is Blackness**

The Duplex: A Black Love Fable: Samuel French, $5.95; New Lafayette Theatre, NYC

It Bees Dat Way: in **Four Dynamite Plays**; Ambiance Lunch-Hour Theatre, London

A Short Play for a Small Theatre: in **Theme Is Blackness**

Street Sounds: in **Theme Is Blackness**; La Mama, E.T.C., NYC

The Play of the Play: in **Theme Is Blackness**

Deathlist: in **Four Dynamite Plays**; Theatre Black, NYC

The Fabulous Miss Marie: in **The New Lafayette Presents**, Doubleday; New Lafayette Theatre, NYC

Malcolm: '71: Black World*

Home Boy: manuscript*; Perry Street Theater, NYC

Next Time: manuscript*; Bronx Community College, NY

The Mystery of Phillis Wheatley: manuscript*; New Federal Theatre, NYC

The Taking of Miss Janie: Samuel French, $6.50; manuscript; New Federal Theatre, NYC

I Am Lucy Terry: manuscript*; American Place Theatre, NYC

Jo Anne!: manuscript*; Riverside Church Theatre, NYC

Daddy: manuscript*; New Federal Theatre, NYC

Sepia Star (music & lyrics, Mildred Kayden): manuscript*; Stage 73, NYC

Storyville (music & lyrics, Mildred Kayden): manuscript*; University of California
  *contact agent

LOUISA BURNS-BISOGNO

Born in Brooklyn, NY on September 23, 1936. B.A. in Political Science from Lehman College, graduate work at Hunter College and screenwriting at the New School. She has been a high school teacher, College lecturer in Cultural Anthropology and freelance journalist. Has written screenplays. Recipient: Bicentennial Grant for **Emma Ponafidine**; Commendation from Channel 13 for student adaptation of **One Day in the Life of Ivan Denisovich**.

Address: Ice Pond Road, Brewster, NY 10509
  (914) 279-3481

Agent: Leo Bookman Esther Sherman, William Morris Agency, 1350 Avenue of the Americas, New York, NY 10019 (212) 586-5100

TITLE • AVAILABILITY • PRODUCTIONS

Emma Ponafidine: manuscript*; Brewster School District, NY

The Lilac Season†: manuscript*; O'Neill Theater Center's National Playwrights Conference, CT

Waking: manuscript*
  *contact agent
  †Lincoln Center, Theatre on Film & Tape

ABE BURROWS

Born in New York City on December 18, 1910. Attended City College, NY. Worked in radio, wrote **Rudy Vallee Program, Duffy's Tavern** etc. Writer and director. Panelist on **This Is Show Business, We Take Your Word**. Has often been called a show doctor or Mr. Fixit. Recipient: Drama Critics Circle Award; Tony Award; Pulitzer Prize.

Agent: William Morris Agency, 1350 Avenue of the Americas, New York, NY 10019 (212) 586-5100

TITLE • AVAILABILITY • PRODUCTIONS

Guys and Dolls (with Jo Swerling): Music Theatre International, 119 West 57th St., New York, NY 10019; Broadway

Can-Can: Tams-Witmark, 757 Third Ave., New York, NY 10017; Broadway

Three Wishes for Jamie (with Charles O'Neal): Samuel French, 25 W. 45th St., New York, NY 10036; Broadway

Silk Stockings (with George S. Kaufman and Laureen McGrath): Tams-Witmark; Broadway

Say, Darling (with Richard and Marian Bissell): Tams-Witmark; Broadway

First Impressions: Samuel French, $2.50; Broadway

How to Succeed in Business without Really Trying: Music Theatre International; Broadway

Four on a Garden: Samuel French, $2.50; Broadway

Cactus Flower: Samuel French, $2.50; Broadway

JUNE CALENDER

Born in Versailles, IN on June 7, 1938. A.B. in English/Creative Writing, Indiana University, some graduate work at Indiana University School of Letters. Freelance writing for **Dramatists Guild Quarterly, The Writer** and **Writer's Yearbook, Better Homes and Gardens, Performing Arts Review, Volunteer Leadership** magazine. Consultant work on use of volunteers in the performing arts. Script reader for major regional theatre. Has published poetry, drama criticism and theater newsletters. Recipient: Three times "best work in process," Indiana University Writer's Conference; Poetry Award, P.E.N. Women.

Address: 1 Ledyard Avenue, Cazenovia, NY 13035 (315) 655-9579

TITLE • AVAILABILITY • PRODUCTIONS

Three Part Invention: manuscript*; under option at present time

Sweet Dreams/Wild Dreams: manuscript*

Challah and Raspberries: manuscript*; reading, Spectrum Theatre

Cinnamon Rolls: manuscript*

C

June Calender (cont'd)

The End Of The Teflon-Coated Life: manuscript*; O'Neill Theater Center's National Playwrights Conference, CT

Kinder, Kirche, Kuchen: manuscript*

Dianna Paxton, Dancer: manuscript*

New Years Day: manuscript*
*contact author

SYNOPSES

Kinder, Kirche, Kuchen: Four plays exploring the ways women of two generations relate to one another. It includes **Challah and Raspberries**, women of two ethnic groups related through a child; **Cinnamon Rolls**, mother and daughter love-independence struggle; **Fluffernutters Extraordinaire**; the rituals of motherhood; **Pure Papaya Puree**, business partners-friends and the problems of aging, beauty and need for love.

One act. Setting: one set for each. 2 females for each.

The End Of The Teflon-Coated Life: A woman, dealing with the shock of learning she probably has cancer, seeks perspective from friends and strangers as her mother, husband and son worry about where she has disappeared to. A final confrontation with her husband shows that her comfortable, familiar way of life has ended whether or not she has cancer.

Full length. Setting: fluid set. 4 males, 6 females.

New Years Day: Desiring only to be alone and practice the piano on New Years Day, Sonya finds her daughter and live-in boyfriend bringing their battles to her living room, her almost-ex-husband begging to return to avoid the complications of divorce and the new man in her life expects sexual favors at his convenience rather than hers. Sonya finds a way to play everyone's needs off against each other so that she finally has time to herself.

Full length comedy. Setting: one set. 3 males, 3 females.

LONNIE CARTER

Born October 25, 1942 in Chicago, IL. B.A., Marquette University (Milwaukee, WI), 1964; M.A., Marquette University, 1966; M.F.A., Yale School of Drama, 1969. Teaching: English Composition, Marquette University; Playwriting, Yale School of Drama. Recipient: Molly Kazan Award for Best Original Play, 1967, Yale Drama School; Shubert Fellowships in Playwriting, 1968–69; Peg Santvoord Fellowships in Playwriting, 1970, 1971, 1973, Yale Repertory Theatre; Berkshire Theatre Festival Playwriting Contest, 1971; John Simon Guggenheim Fellowship in Playwriting, 1971–72; National Endowment for the Arts Grant in Writing, 1974; CBS Foundation Grant in Playwriting, 1974–75, Yale Repertory Theatre; Connecticut Commission on the Arts Grant in Playwriting, 1975–76; Open Circle Theatre Award, Goucher College, 1978.

Address: Cream Hill Road, West Cornwall, Ct. 06796

TITLE • AVAILABILITY • PRODUCTIONS

Adam: manuscript*; Marquette University, WI

Another Quiet Evening at Home: manuscript*; Yale Drama School, Yale Cabaret, CT

Holzmann: manuscript*; Yale Drama School, CT

Lonnie Carter (cont'd)

More War in Store with Peace as Chief of Police: manuscript*; Yale Cabaret, Old Reliable Theatre, NYC

Beauty/Truth: manuscript*; Yale Cabaret, CT

Workday: manuscript*; Yale Repertory Theatre Sunday Series, CT

Izzy: Scripts Magazine*; Yale Repertory Theatre, CT; Manhattan Theatre Club, NYC; various other productions

Time/Space: manuscript*; Old Reliable Theatre, NYC; Berkshire Theatre Winter Festival, Stockbridge, MA

Plumb Loco: manuscript*; Berkshire Theatre Winter Festival, MA; WBAI, NY

The Big House: manuscript*; Yale Repertory Theatre, CT

Perdiddle: manuscript*; Yale Repertory Theatre Sunday Series, CT

Smoky Links: manuscript*; American Place Theatre, NYC

Bicicletta: Tri-Quarterly Magazine, Northwestern U., Evanston, IL 60201; Staged reading, New York Shakespeare Festival, NYC

Watergate Classics: Yale/Theatre, 1973–74*; Yale Repertory Theatre, CT

Cream Cheese: manuscript*; American Place Theatre, NYC

Trade-Offs: manuscript*; Yale Repertory Theatre Sunday Series, CT; Playwrights Horizons, NY

Victoria Fellows: manuscript*; Goucher College, MD

The Biograph: manuscript*

The Blinking Heart: manuscript*

The Odd Women (adaptation): manuscript*

Sirens: manuscript*; Staged reading, New York Shakespeare Festival, NYC

Late City Edition (Sarah): manuscript*; Symphony Space Theatre, NYC
    *contact author

SYNOPSES

Iz She Izzy or Iz He Ain'tzy or Is They Both: "This is an uncommonly clever and sophisticated version of the vintage 'courtroom drama' burlesque skit. A wild conglomeration of puns, ditsy dames, and loony lawyers, it features a murder trial so outrageous it would give Perry Mason a nervous breakdown." —Marilyn Stasio, **Cue Magazine**.
Setting: a simple courtroom easily convertible to an office. 4 males, 2 females.

Trade-Offs: A comic response to the Book of Daniel.
Setting: a simple courtroom easily convertible to a fiery furnace. 4 males, 1 female.

Bicicletta, or **The Agony of the Pomegranates in the Garden**: The last inhabitants of an enormous nunnery at the direction of Rome try to determine through courtroom tactics whether one of them is a saint.
Setting: a simple chapel in a nunnery easily convertible into a nun's bedroom. 1 male, 4 females.

C

STEVE CARTER

Born in New York City on November 7, 1929.
Graduated the High School of Music and Art.
Directed **Bread** by Mustapha Matura at Young
Vic Theatre, London. Wrote first three episodes
of **The Courage and the Grace** for CPTV. Set
Designer and Costume Designer for American
Community Theatre; Costume Designer for **The
Sty of the Blind Pig**; Artistic Director and Set
Designer for the Negro Ensemble's Season-
Within-A-Season series. He also runs the Play-
wrights Workshop. Recipient: John Gassner-
Outer Critics Circle Award; National Endowment
for the Arts Creative Writing Fellowship;
Rockefeller Foundation Creative Writing
Fellowship; NYSCA Dramaturgy Grant.

Address: Negro Ensemble Company, 165 West 46th St., Suite 1015, New York, NY 10036
(212) 575-5860

TITLE • AVAILABILITY • PRODUCTIONS

As You Can See: manuscript*; American Community Theatre; Old Reliable Theatre Tavern,
NYC

The Terraced Apartment: manuscript*; American Community Theatre; Old Reliable Theatre
Tavern, NYC

One Last Look: manuscript*; Old Reliable Theatre Tavern, NYC; Negro Ensemble Company,
NYC, WABC-TV

Terraces: manuscript*; Negro Ensemble Company, NYC

Eden: Samuel French, 25 W. 45th St., New York, NY 10036, $2.50; Negro Ensemble Company,
NYC; Karamu House; Keskidee Theatre, London

Nevis Mountain Dew: Dramatists Play Service, 440 Park Ave. South, New York, NY 10016,
$2.50; Negro Ensemble Company, NYC; Arena Stage, Wash. DC

Dame Lorraine: manuscript*; Victory Gardens Theatre, Chicago, IL
*contact Negro Ensemble Company

SYNOPSES

Eden: The plight of Caribbean immigrants to this country just after World War I and what happens
when they are lumped together with their Black American counterparts who have migrated to the
north. How youth finds it difficult to live within the political confines of their parents.

Full length. Setting: apartment with livingroom/kitchen. Hallway with door of apartment across
the hall. 4 males (two teen-aged), 4 females (two teen-aged).

Nevis Mountain Dew: A man challenges his family for his right to self-termination in order to
free them from the imprisonment his totally paralyzing illness has demanded.

Full length. Setting: two-level set, with upstairs master bedroom and iron lung. Downstairs liv-
ing/dining room area. 4 males, 3 females.

Dame Lorraine: A Caribbean family, living in Harlem, awaits the arrival of their oldest and only
surviving son after twenty-seven years in prison. The waiting unravels layers of buried love and
hatred.

Full length. 2 males, 3 females.

All three plays are to be thought of as **The Caribbean Trilogy**.

JANE CHAMBERS

Born in Columbia, SC. Educated at Rollins College, Pasadena Playhouse, University of Maine, and Goddard College. Jane has written for educational and network television, has written feature articles for many publications including **The New York Times** and **Harper's Magazine**. She has also taught creative writing on high school and university levels and has acted, directed and produced both in the theatre and for television. Her first novel, **The Burning**, was published by Jove Press, 1978. Recipient: 1977 CAPS Grant; 1973 Writer's Guild Award (television drama).

Address: 433 West 46th St., New York, NY 10036

Agent: Horen-Allen Management, 850 Seventh Ave., New York, NY 10036 (212) 581-4270

TITLE • AVAILABILITY • PRODUCTIONS

Tales of the Revolution and Other American Fables: manuscript*; O'Neill Theater Center's National Playwrights Conference, CT

Random Violence: manuscript*; Interart Theatre, NYC

One Short Day at the Jamboree (one act): manuscript*; Town Hall (Playwrights Festival), NYC; WNYC-TV (New Plays)

Curfew!: manuscript*; WNYC-TV (New Plays)

Mine!: manuscript*; Interart Theatre, NYC

The Wife (one act): manuscript*; Interart Theatre, NYC

A Late Snow: Gay Plays, The First Collection, Avon Books, 224 West 57th St., New York, NY 10019, $3.50; Clark Center for the Performing Arts, NYC

Common Garden Variety: manuscript*; Mark Taper Forum, Laboratory Theatre, CA

Eye of the Gull: manuscript*

Deadly Nightshade: manuscript*

Last Summer at Bluefish Cove: manuscript*; The Glines, NYC

My Blue Heaven: manuscript*

Kudzu: manuscript*
*contact agent

SYNOPSES

Mine! and **The Wife**: A pair of one-acts to be played together or separately. **Mine!** is the cry of an old woman who stakes out a traffic circle and sets up housekeeping there. The old woman has had enough of feeding and tending others and is determined in her last days of life that something, this traffic circle, will be exclusively "Mine!". **The Wife** is fifty, uneducated, has devoted her life to raising a family, none of whom turned out as she had hoped.

One acts. **Mine!**: bare stage with set pieces. 1 female, 1 male. **The Wife**: housing project living room, kitchenette. 2 females, 2 males.

Common Garden Variety: Grandma, a strong-willed southern woman, has lived on a remote hilltop in North Georgia all her life. She watched her parents and her brother slaughtered by the Indians, her husband lynched by "townies," her daughter Rachel run away to seek a better life. Grandma's only contact with Rachel now is the illegitimate child that she sent back for Grandma to raise. Sari, fourteen, is hungry for the world outside. Rachel returns to reclaim her daughter and three strong women, who love each other, are set against each other, each fighting for their lives, destroying each other's dreams and hopes.

Full length. Setting: the dilapidated porch of a wood shack in the North Georgia hills in 1932. 3 females, 1 girl (14), 1 boy (14).

C

Jane Chambers (cont'd)

Deadly Nightshade: The richest men in the world are drowned in a yachting accident. Their wives, suddenly unexpectedly in charge of the world economy, are being murdered one by one. Who stands to gain by their deaths? Only the sheriff knows — or does she? A merry murderous chase. Full length. Setting: one set. 10 females ranging from 17–70.

SUSAN CHARLOTTE

Born in Brooklyn, NY on July 21, 1954. B.A., Creative Writing/Sociology, State University of New York, Purchase; working towards Masters in Theatre Arts at Columbia University. Has worked in prison reform using drama as a means of communication. Counselor, Women's House of Detention, Riker's Island. Taught drama and poetry at Spofford Juvenile Center and Baychester Diagnostic Center. Supervised the Youth Drama Workshop for Theatre For the Forgotten. Member: Dramatists Guild; The Editorial Freelancers Association. Recipient: Joseph Kesselring Award; Richard Rodgers Scholarship in Theatre Arts.

Address: 355 West 85th St., #39, New York, NY 10024 (212)362-2560

Agent: Helen Harvey, 410 West 24th St., New York, NY 10011 (212) 675-7445

TITLE • AVAILABILITY • PRODUCTIONS

Prism Blues: Proscenium Press, **Journal of Irish LIterature, George Spelvin's Theatre Book**, P.O. Box 361, Newark, DE 19711.** Horace Mann Theatre, NYC; Pratt Institute Theatre, NYC

Is It Raining or Just My Desire?: manuscript*; Gene Frankel Theatre, Workshop reading, NYC

Mythical-Merry-Go-Round: manuscript*; Tour, Theatre For the Forgotten, NY

The Phoenix Flies: manuscript*

Response to a Serpent's Tongue: manuscript*
   *contact author
   **contact agent

MICHAEL J. CHEPIGA

Born in New York City on January 14, 1948. B.A., cum laude, Fordham U.; Ph.D. NY University in English Literature; J.D. Yale U. Taught high school and college English in NYC. Published: **The Wholesome Madness of an Hour** (critical essay on Tennyson's **Idylls of the King**); **Politics and the Uses of Language in Shakespeare's English History Plays**, (doctoral dissertation). He is a member of the New York State Bar.

Address: 411 E. 83rd St., New York, NY 10028 (212) 628-7460

Agent: Jeannine Edmonds, J. Michael Bloom, 400 Madison Ave., New York, NY 10017 (212) 421-4200

Michael J. Chepiga (cont'd)

TITLE • AVAILABILITY • PRODUCTIONS

Stuffed Crocodiles: manuscript*; Off Off Broadway

All Honorable Men: manuscript**; O'Neill Theater Center's National Playwrights Conference, CT; St. Nicholas Theater, Chicago IL

The Meeting of the Creditors of J. Matthew Spengler: manuscript**; O'Neill Theater Center's National Playwrights Conference, CT
   *contact author
   **contact agent

SYNOPSIS

Stuffed Crocodiles: Biographical play about Alfred Jarry, eccentric author of **Ubi Roi**.
Full length. Setting: France in the 1890's. One simple, fluid setting. 7 males, 2 or 3 females.

All Honorable Men: Story of the court martial of the only black cadet at the United States Military Academy at West Point in 1880, who was accused of staging his own brutal beating one night in order to avoid having to take and possibly fail his final exams.
Full length. Setting: one set. 6 males.

The Meeting of the Creditors of J. Matthew Spengler: Comedy about a hapless entrepreneur who gathers his creditors together in order to persuade them not to press him into bankruptcy.
Full length. Setting: one st. 5 males, 3 females.

JAMES CHILDS

Born in Hyannis, MA on March 31, 1939. B.A., M.A., from Southern Connecticut State College. Has been a film and book critic for national and international magazines and newspapers, **New York Times Book Review, Film Comment, Sight and Sound, Michigan Quarterly, Village Voice** and others. Has published poems and a short story. One film script, **The Hunter.** Recipient: National Endowment for the Humanities Grant, 1972.

Address: 186 South Main Street, Middletown, CT 06457 (203) 347-1012

Agent: Joyce Ketay, 320 West 90th St., #2-F, New York, NY 10024 (212) 799-2398

TITLE • AVAILABILITY • PRODUCTIONS

The Bough Break: manuscript*; University of New Haven, CT

The Puppet: manuscript*

A Voice and Nothing More: manuscript*; Readings

All Runners, Come: manuscript*; Terri Schreiber Studio, NYC

The Glory of a Name: manuscript*

Helen: manuscript*

Chieftains: manuscript*; Theatre of St. Clement's, NYC

Darkness, Fierce Winds: manuscript*; American Folk Theater, NYC

Pilgrims: manuscript*
   *contact agent

C

James Childs (cont'd)

SYNOPSES

Chieftains: Edward and Dewey Marker, brother and sister in their eighties, live in Central Massachusetts. Throughout the play, as their lives fail, they uncover some of the past they had never known, as well as their love for one another.
Full length. Setting: livingroom of a large old house. 1 male, 1 female.

A Voice and Nothing More: Jessie Walker dwells on the peculiarities of her life and of those who die about her, as she attempts to maintain a grip on her sanity.
Full length. Setting: livingroom of a modern house. 1 male, 2 females.

Darkness, Fierce Winds: An author attempts to discover how it is a woman can live a life that will eventually lead up to her murder.
Full length. Setting: Kitchen and study. 3 males, 2 females.

JOHN CHODES

Born in New York City on February 23, 1939. Attended Hunter College. He is a commercial photographer, certificate, Germain School of Photography. Non-fiction: **The Myth of America's Military Power,** Branden Press, 1972; **Corbitt,** Tafnews Press, 1974; **Bruce Jenner,** Grosset and Dunlap, 1977. Technical advisor to Dustin Hoffman for **Marathon Man.** Recipient: Journalistic Excellence Award, Amateur Athletic Union for **Corbitt,** 1974.

Address: 411 East 10th St., New York, NY 10009
(212) 677-4917

Agent: Charles Ryweck, 67-48 212 St., Bayside, NY 11364 (212) 224-5373; David Gordon Productions, 405 Strand, London WC2, England 836-2613

TITLE • AVAILABILITY • PRODUCTIONS

Avenue A Anthology: manuscript*; Henry Street Playhouse, NYC; WPA Theatre, NYC

Molineaux: manuscript*; Playwrights Horizons, NYC
    *contact agent

SYNOPSES

Avenue A Anthology: This play is a modern version of **Spoon River Anthology.** The living and dead occupants of a century-old tenement describe their lives in monologue form, directly to the audience.
Full length. Setting: lighting can be used to suggest the frequent time and character changes. 60 character studies, 45 men and 15 women (played by 6 males, 2 females).

Molineaux: The time is 1809 and Tom Molineaux, a recently freed black slave from America, has come to England to be a great fighter. He becomes the most sensational sports figure in England but is swindled out of the boxing championship. His downfall and death occur because Molineaux cannot cope with being a free man.
Full length. Setting: three locations: a pub, interior of a barn and an armory. 6 males, 1 female.

JEROME CHODOROV

Born in New York City on August 10, 1911. Educated in New York schools. Screenwriter of **Louisianna Purchase: My Sister Eileen: Junior Miss.** His plays have been included on the ten best lists at least seven times. Recipient: New York Drama Critics Award; Outer Critic's Circle Award.

Agent: Audrey Wood, c/o International Creative Management, 40 West 57th St., New York, NY 10019 (212) 556-5722

TITLE • AVAILABILITY • PRODUCTIONS

Schoolhouse on the Lot: manuscript*; Broadway

My Sister Eileen: Dramatists Play Service, 440 Park Ave. South, New York, NY 10016, $2.50; Broadway

Junior Miss: Dramatists Play Service, $2.50; Broadway

The French Touch (with Joseph Fields): Dramatists Play Service, $2.75; Broadway

Pretty Penny: manuscript*; Bucks County Playhouse, PA

Wonderful Town: Tams-Witmark, 757 Third Ave., New York, NY 10017; Broadway

The Girl in Pink Tights: manuscript*; Broadway

Anniversary Waltz: Dramatists Play Service, $2.50; Broadway

The Ponder Heart (with Joseph Fields): Samuel French, 25 W. 45th St., New York, NY 10036, $2.50; Broadway

The Happiest Man Alive: manuscript*; Falmouth Playhouse, MA

I Had a Ball: manuscript*; Broadway

Three Bags Full: Samuel French, $2.50; Broadway

Great Waltz: Tams-Witmark; Music Center, Los Angeles, CA

Student Prince: manuscript*; Chandler Pavillion, Los Angeles, CA

Dumas & Son: manuscript*; Chandler Pavillion, Los Angeles, CA

Community of Two: Samuel French, $2.50; Washington, DC

The Bats of Portobello: manuscript*

A Talent for Murder: manuscript*
    *contact agent

C

RON CLARK

Born in Montreal, Canada on July 25, 1933. Attended McGill University. Several screenplays including two Mel Brooks' films, **Silent Movie** and **High Anxiety**; also **Revenge of the Pink Panther** and **Norman, Is That You?**

Agent: Creative Artists Agency, Inc. 1888 Century Park East, Los Angeles, CA 90067 (212) 277-4545

TITLE • AVAILABILITY • PRODUCTIONS

Norman, Is That You? (with Sam Bobrick): Samuel French, 25 W. 45th St., New York, NY 10036, $2.50; Broadway; Paris, France

No Hard Feelings (with Sam Bobrick): Samuel French, $2.50; Boston, MA; Broadway

Murder at the Howard Johnson's (with Sam Bobrick): Samuel French, $2.50; Boston, MA; Broadway

Wally's Cafe: manuscript*; Boston, MA; Broadway
    *contact agent

DAVID ULYSSES CLARKE

Born in Chicago, IL, August 30, 1908. Attended Butler University, IN. As an actor he has appeared in fourteen Broadway plays and fifty films. He played Uncle Tiso on **Ryan's Hope**-ABC-TV. Member S.A.G., Dramatists Guild, New Dramatists, Actors Equity. Recipient: National Endowment for the Arts Grant, 1978–79.

Address: 225 Central Park West, No. 115, New York, NY 10024 (212) 362-1807/TR3-7300

Agent: Henderson-Hogan, 200 West 57th St., New York, NY 10019 (212) 765-5190

TITLE • AVAILABILITY • PRODUCTIONS

Never a Snug Harbor: manuscript*; Milwaukee Repertory Theatre, WI

Matrix: manuscript*

Mrs. Fiske: manuscript*

The Snailer's Smug Larder: manuscript*

Remarkable Anna: manuscript*
    *contact New Dramatists, 424 W. 44th St., New York, NY 10036 (212) PL7-6960

David Ulysses Clarke (cont'd)

SYNOPSIS

Never a Snug Harbor: Story of the early life of a merchant sea captain in Bangor, North Wales, at the turn of the century — the disintegration of his family caused, in part, by his running away to sea. Based on the early life of Captain Harry Lewis, Master Mariner.

Setting: kitchen of a poor family. 7 males, 2 females.

EDWARD CLINTON

Born in Evanston, IL on September 23, 1948. Educated at New York University School of the Arts as an actor. Screenplay, **Honky-Tonk Freeway,** directed by John Schlesinger. Currently working on screenplays for Richard Lester and Anthony Harvey. Recipient: Earplay Award.

Address: "Windy Hill," Cramer Rd. Poughkeepsie, NY 12603 (914) 473-4291

Agent: Janet Roberts, William Morris Agency, 1350 Avenue of the Americas, New York, NY 10019 (212) 586-5100

TITLE • AVAILABILITY • PRODUCTIONS

The Lady Who Cried Fox!: Samuel French, 25 W. 45th St., New York, NY 10036, $2.50; Various dinner theaters and summer stock

Benefit of a Doubt: manuscript*; O'Neill Theater Center's National Playwrights Conference, CT; Cincinnati Playhouse, OH

You'll Love My Wife: Samuel French, $2.50; Various dinner theaters and summer stock

Ten Years Later: manuscript*; Actors Theatre of Louisville, KY

The Bogey Man: manuscript*
    *contact agent

D. L. COBURN

Born in Baltimore, MD on August 4, 1938. Has worked in advertising and was a consultant to several corporations before becoming a playwright. Served with the United States Naval Reserves. Member: Dramatists Guild; Author League of America; Soaring Society of America. Recipient: Pulitzer Prize, 1978.

Agent: Flora Roberts, 65 East 55th St., New York, NY 10022 (212) 355-4165

C

D. L. Coburn (cont'd)

TITLE • AVAILABILITY • PRODUCTIONS

The Gin Game†: Samuel French, 25 W. 45th St., New York, NY 10036, $2.50; Broadway

The Confession: manuscript*
   *contact agent
   †Lincoln Center, Theater on Film & Tape

DAVID COHEN

Born in Boston, MA on October 2, 1952, David was educated at the University of Mass, graduating magna cum laude. Also attended U of Manchester, England. His M.F.A. is in Playwriting from Brandeis U. Playwright-in-residence: U of Montana, U of South Carolina, George Mason U. Has been a staff writer for CBS, director in stock and university theater, written documentary film, **The Incredible Dream.** He is a member of the Dramatists Guild and WGW-East. Currently Co-director and Play-wright-in-Residence at Hampshire College Theatre, Amherst, MA. Recipient: Shubert Fellowship in Playwriting; NEH Grant, American Playwrights; Award of Excellence, American College Theatre Festival 1971 and '73.

Address: Box 810, Amherst, MA 01004 (413) 549-3585

Agent: Mary Dolan, c/o Gloria Safier, Inc. 667 Madison Ave., New York, NY 10021 (212) 838-4868

TITLE • AVAILABILITY • PRODUCTIONS

Tanglewood: manuscript*; Cubiculo Theatre, NYC; Brandeis U

Friends Indeed!: manuscript; Cubiculo Theatre, NYC; Brandeis U

Piaf — A Remembrance: manuscript; Broadway

Where Credit Is Due: manuscript; George Mason U, VA
   *contact author

SYNOPSES

Piaf — A Remembrance: Musical drama based on the tragic life of French singer, Edith Piaf, as seen through the eyes of the four most important men in her life. Includes sixteen songs made famous by Piaf; several translated and adapted by the author.
Full length. Setting: flexible unit. 5 males, 1 female.

Where Credit Is Due: Musical examining credit-card abuse. The play follows the romance between a young Washington accountant and a mysterious, naive mid-western girl. At times comic, ultimately serious, the couple are hounded by a coolly sinister duo of creditors — and haunted by a series of expressionistic nightmares — as they search for happiness through plastic.
Full length. Setting: three simultaneous areas: the apartment, the credit offices, and the dream area. 5 males, 3 females.

Tanglewood: Drama of friendship and loyalty involving three young men: Paul, an aspiring sculptor; Spinelli, his high-school wrestling pal; and Norman, a young musician. Set at the summer home of the Boston Symphony Orchestra, Paul becomes an unwilling victim of a contest between Spinelli and Norman which finally erupts into violence.
One-act (one hour). Setting: unit depicting Paul's room and the surrounding trees. Extremely suitable for college actors. 3 males.

EDWARD M. COHEN

Ed's novel, **$250,000,** was published by G. P. Put-
nam's Sons in the U.S. and by Arthur Barker Ltd.
in London. His stories have appeared in **Ever-
green Review** and **Carleton Miscellany.** He is
also a director who has worked at the New York
Shakespeare Festival, Theatre at St. Clements,
Theatre Genesis, Cubiculo, Playwrights Hor-
izons, Queens Playhouse, and Clark Center.
Member, New Dramatists Committee; past
chairman, O'Neill Playwrights; four-time Fellow,
William Flanagan Memorial Center, Montauk,
Long Island; 1975 Playwright-in-Residence,
Playwrights Horizons, New York City. Recipient:
John Golden Award, **Cakes with the Wine,** 1976.

Address: 949 West End Ave., New York, NY 10025 (212) UN4-5861

Agent: Harriet Wasserman, Russell & Volkening, Inc., 551 Fifth Ave., New York, NY 10017 (212)
682-5340

TITLE • AVAILABILITY • PRODUCTIONS

Breeding Ground: manuscript*; Albee-Barr Playwrights Unit

The Complaint Department Closes at Five: manuscript*; O'Neill Theater Center's National
Playwrights Conference, CT; Mercer Arts Center, NYC

Cakes with the Wine: manuscript*; Albee-Barr Playwrights Unit; New Dramatists Committee,
NYC

Two Girls and a Sailor: manuscript*; Theatre at St. Clements, NYC

A Gorgeous Piece: manuscript*; Actors Studio Playwrights Unit, NYC

The Nearest I'll Get to Heaven: manuscript*; Sarah Lawrence College

The Last Stage of Labor: manuscript*; New Dramatists, NYC; Playwrights Horizons, NYC
*contact author

SYNOPSES

The Complaint Department Closes at Five: Technology destroys the middle class. An ambitious
young executive visits an obsolete employee's home; reveals sordid secrets of his past, seduces
his son, leaves in triumph.
Full length. Setting: livingroom and bedroom of a New York apartment. 3 males, 2 females, 1
teenage boy.

Cakes with the Wine: An unloved woman steals a fortune from the man she adores.
Full length. Two sets, 6 males, 3 females.

The Last Stage of Labor: A comic look at failure and loss. A failed writer and his ex-wife, a failed
political activist, are forced into confrontation when their son starts failing in school because he
has fallen in love with his French teacher.
Full length. Setting: suburban livingroom. 1 male, 2 females, 1 12-year-old boy.

C

MICHAEL COLBY

Born in New York City on October 29, 1951. B.A. in English Literature, Northwestern University; M.A. in Drama, New York University; Special Degree in Journalism, School Press Institute, Syracuse University. Founding member of the Ostrow Foundation/St. Clement's Musical Theatre Lab. Researcher for Dorothy Hart's **Thou Swell, Thou Witty.** Musical comedy consultant to the Berkshire Theatre Festival. Recipient: ASCAP Awards as lyricist; Show Business Award for Best Production of the Year.

Address: 59 West 44th St., New York, NY 10036
(212) 840-6800

TITLE • AVAILABILITY • PRODUCTIONS

Olmsted! (musical): manuscript*; c/o Jeffrey Wachtel, 130 West 71st St., New York, NY 10023; St. Clement's, NYC; West Park Theatre

North Atlantic (musical, with Jim Fradrich): manuscript*; Gene Frankel Media Center, NYC

Androcles and the Lion (children's musical): manuscript, Lee Frank, 251 W. 89th St., #6B, New York, NY 10024; Hartley House, NYC 1978 and 1979

Harlequin and Company (children's musical): manuscript, Lee Frank; Hartley House, NYC, 1979 and 1980

Another Time (adaptation): manuscript*; Lyric Theatre of New York

Ludlow Ladd (mock Christmas opera, with Jerry Markoe): manuscript*, Record available; Lyric Theatre of New York; WBAI-FM

C&W (musical): manuscript, James Jennings ATA, 314 W. 54th St., New York, N.Y. 10019; American Theatre of Actors

Golden Dreams (musical): manuscript*

Passing Fancy (ragtime musical): manuscript*

The Richest Kid in Town (adaptation with Thomas Meehan & Jack Urbont): manuscript*

Charlotte Sweet (mock opera/sequel to **Ludlow Ladd**): manuscript*
*contact author

SYNOPSES

North Atlantic: A spoof of classic American musicals with an Eskimo setting. Honey Snodgrass, the quintessential ingenue and her sassy sidekick, Melanie Fong arrive in the North Atlantic to give an all-American education to illiterate Eskimo children. In the process, the ladies are educated on romance, heartbreak, the strange ways of the North Atlantic people and nearly every other cliche found in Broadway musicals of the 40s and 50s.

Full length. Setting: one unit set with props to suggest scene changes. 3 males, 4 females, 4 male dancers, 2 female dancers.

Ludlow Ladd: An all-sung Christmas satire. On Christmas Eve, in Dickensian Liverpool, the orphan boy, Ludlow Ladd wanders the chilly streets. It is the night of his birth and a mediocre couple, the Grimbles, agree to take him home with them. Once at the Grimble hearth, Ludlow makes a nuisance of himself. Enraged, the Grimbles sentence Ludlow to a supper-less evening. Ludlow dozes and has a splediferous Christmas dream whereby the Christmas tree is transformed into the magical Missus Pinecones. He is whisked to the merry Land of Yuletide Cheer and helped to find the key to his happiness. As Ludlow wakes, his dream has revealed a way to find true happiness with the Grimbles, who are awed by his miraculous experience and accept him as their own son.

Michael Colby (cont'd)

One act, one hour. Setting: one basic set folding out (like a Christmas/Advent card) to three scenes — Liverpool Street, Grimble home, Land of Yuletide Cheer. 4 males, 4 females.

ANNE COMMIRE

B.S., Eastern Michigan University, also attended Wayne State University, University of Birmingham, England, New York University. She is the editor of **Something About the Author** and **Yesterday's Authors** series. With her brother, Ron Shedd, she wrote the screenplay **Hayward's** for a movie starring James Garner and Mariette Hartley, spring 1982; Screenplay of **I'm Dancing as Fast as I Can,** for Paramount; **Rebel for God,** CBS. Recipient: CAPS Grant, 1975; Rockefeller Grant, 1979.

Address: 274 West 95th St., New York, NY 10025 (212) 663-4787 and 81R Oswegatchie Rd., Waterford, CT 06385 (203) 442-6010

Agent: Esther Sherman, William Morris Agency, 1350 Avenue of the Americas, New York, NY 10019 (212) 586-5100

TITLE • AVAILABILITY • PRODUCTIONS

Matinee Ladies: manuscript*; Columbia University, NYC

Shay: Samuel French, 25 W. 45th St., New York, NY 10036, $2.50; O'Neill Theater Center's National Playwrights Conference, CT; University of North Carolina

Transatlantic Bridge: manuscript*; Reading, Playwrights Horizons, NYC

Volunteers for America: manuscript*; Columbia University, NYC

†**Put Them All Together:** Samuel French, $2.50; O'Neill Theater Center's National Playwrights Conference, CT; McCarter Theatre, NJ

Sunday's Red: manuscript*
*contact agent
†Lincoln Center, Theatre on Film & Tape

SYNOPSES

Shay: A comedy-drama about a woman who is afraid to go out of the house.
Full length. Setting: livingroom and kitchen of a small house in Michigan. 4 males, 4 females.

Put Them All Together: A woman's rage builds to the bursting point as she struggles to be the ideal wife and mother.
Full length. Setting: livingroom. 3 males, 4 females.

PETER COPANI

Born September 2, 1942. Educated at Syracuse University, The New School and mainly self. Founder and administrative director of the People Performing Co., Inc. Organization development aimed at cultural change. Combined creative and administrative abilities to produce socially significant theater arts experiences involving the community as well as professionals. Arranged and incorporated education, recreational and therapeutic arts programs geared for the mildly retarded; also minority groups. As Playwright, Director, Producer, Composer Lyricist, Peter created seventeen one-act plays, nine full length plays, ten musicals, two books and hundreds of poems and songs. All (except two) have been produced either Off Broadway, Off Off Broadway or in community street theater. Among them are **The Blind Junkie** and Street Jesus both of which are considered street theater classics. Included in The American Biographical Institute's **Notable Americans of the Bicentennial Era;** Marquis' **Who's Who in the East** "for contributing significantly to the betterment of contemporary society"; **Men of Achievement;** City of New York Certificate of Appreciation presented by Mayor Beame; Washington Square Outdoor Art Exhibit 1975 "for translating the dreams and fears of Urban Youth into beautiful and moving street plays." Recipient; CAPS Grants, 1972, 1974.

Address: 59 Carmine St., New York, NY 10014

TITLE • AVAILABILITY • PRODUCTIONS

Street Jesus (musical): manuscript*; Greenwich Mews Theater, NYC; Provincetown Playhouse, NYC; Lincoln Center Festival, NYC

†**The Blind Junkie** (musical): Lincoln Center Festival (presented by two separate production companies); Thirteenth Street Theater, NYC

Where People Gather: manuscript*; Gramercy Arts Theater, NYC

Bliss or a Psycho-Bedellic Attack: manuscript*; Extension Theater Club, NYC

The Star Is Always Loved: manuscript*; Playbox Theater, NYC

What's the Game Now?: manuscript*; Playbox Theater, NYC

Scream Revolution: manuscript*; New York Theater Ensemble, NYC

Naughty Naughty: manuscript*; Old Reliable Theater Tavern, NYC

The Land I Love: manuscript*; Playbox Theater, NYC

The First Day of Us (musical): Twin Rivers Theatre

†**Choices** (musical): manuscript*; Lincoln Center Festival, NYC

Nowhere to Run (play with music): manuscript*; Playbox Theatre, NYC

Power (musical): manuscript*; Lincoln Center, Outdoors, NYC

America & Its People (musical): manuscript*; Theater Festival

The Great American Succer Family (musical): manuscript*
    *contact author
    †Lincoln Center, Theatre on Film & Tape

SYNOPSIS

Street Jesus: Musical. The show deals with various minority groups and their struggle for unity and understanding of one another. It is epic theater at its fullest.

The sets are simple to no set at all. The show is flexible enough to perform indoors or out of doors. The show has been performed with as few as nine or as many as twenty-five. Inter-racial cast is a must.

RON COWEN

Born in Cincinnati, OH. B.A., English, University of California. Also attended the Annenberg School of Communications, University of Pennsylvania. He has written for TV (**Saturday Adoption,** CBS Playhouse; **Book of Murder,** ABC); for **American Short Stories on Film,** PBS-TV; episodes for **Family** (with Daniel Lipman). Screenplay, **Firefly.** Recipient: Wesleyan Fellowship; Vernon Rice Drama Desk Award, **Summertree.**

Agent: Audrey Wood, International Creative Management, 40 West 57th St., New York, NY 10019 (212) 556-5722

TITLE • AVAILABILITY • PRODUCTIONS

Summertree: Dramatists Play Service, 440 Park Ave. South, New York, NY 10016, $2.50; O'Neill Theater Center's National Playwrights Conference, CT; Lincoln Center, NYC

Redemption Center: not available; O'Neill Theater Center's National Playwrights Conference, CT

Inside Lulu: not available; Section Ten Theatre Co., NYC; Waverly Theatre, NYC

Valentine's Day: not available; Manhattan Theatre Club, NYC

Saturday Adoption: Dramatists Play Service, $2.50; CBS Playhouse

The Book of Murder: Dramatists Play Service, $2.50; ABC Mystery Theater

Porcelain Time: manuscript*; O'Neill Theater Center's National Playwrights Conference, CT; Berkshire Theatre Festival, Stockbridge, MA

Gene & Jean (with Danny Lipman): not available; Stockbridge, MA
    *contact agent

SYNOPSIS

Porcelain Time: A family gathers after their mother's funeral to clear out possessions from the large old house she occupied until her death. The youngest son, the black sheep, has come home, saying everything she owned has been left to him. He will trade the fortune, however, if, in exchange, his oldest sister agrees to destroy all of her mother's cherished possessions, and if his older brother agrees to give him his wife. To help the fun and games along, the younger brother has brought with him a transvestite.

Full length. Setting: a grand old livingroom. 2½ males, 2½ females.

C

J. J. COYLE

Born in Gloucester, MA on May 27, 1928. Attended Tufts University, B.A. in Drama, 1950. Graduate work at Hunter College, NYC.

Address: 437 West 44th St., New York, NY 10036
(212) 586-7357

TITLE • AVAILABILITY • PRODUCTIONS

Down at Maggie Macomber's: manuscript*

Hotel Eros: manuscript*

Toot: manuscript*

The Ninety-Day Mistress: Samuel French, 25 W. 45th St., New York, NY 10036, $2.50; Biltmore Theater, NYC

Land Where Our Fathers Died: manuscript*; Lincoln Center Workshop (one act, titled **Too Bad About Sparrow**), NYC

Inventory: manuscript*

Boston Proper: manuscript*

Patagonia: manuscript*; New Players Company, Baltimore, MD
   *contact author

SYNOPSES

Down at Maggie Macomber's: A comedy-farce set in a Massachusetts fishing town during Prohibition. Maggie Macomber, a Liverpool emigrant, runs a boarding house, bootlegs booze and bribes cops. When her orphaned granddaughter falls in love with an Irish patrolman, Maggie uses all the wiles and guile of a self-supporting widow to see that the romance does not blossom into marriage. Several subplots amplify the action and make Maggie first of all an ensemble, character piece.

Full length. Setting: interior showing kitchen and parlor. 9 males, 4 females.

Toot: Toot is a movie. Patrick Grimes, a 60s liberal, can't quite get his life together. He is about to face his wife after losing another acting job. Terence O'Hara is a black bisexual. He is about to go to Boston to deal with his dying father and possessive mother. Patrick and Terence meet in Jimmy Ray's bar and decide to delay their respective confrontations by going on a toot. In the course of the evening we explore their lives and psyches on a tour of the seamier bars of Manhattan. Rich in flashback and fantasy. Ulysses and Tiresias '65.

Setting: 14 interiors (6 of them bars), 8 exteriors. 2 males, 2 females (principals); 23 bits: extras.

Patagonia: On the coast of the Patagonian desert overlooking a whale sanctuary, a patriarchal figure enacts a painful ritual for the sins of his father. To this barren shore comes Tom Adamson who has lost his son in Vietnam and perhaps his faith as well. With him are his two young sons and his German-born wife. She has arranged to meet her father for the first time, a Nazi biochemist who functioned under Mengele. He in turn is being pursued by Isaac Levy whose parents died at Buchenwald and Auschwitz.

Full length. Setting: one set. 5 males, 2 young boys, 1 female.

MICHAEL CRISTOFER‡

Born in New Jersey in 1945. Playwright and actor. As an actor, he has played major roles at the Mark Taper Forum. Repertory credits include Arena Stage; ACT in Seattle; Theatre of the Living Arts in Philadelphia; Beirut Repertory, Lebanon; Long Wharf Theatre. On TV, he has appeared in **Sandburg's Lincoln, The Entertainer** and **The Last of Mrs. Lincoln.** Recipient: Tony Award, 1977; Pulitzer Prize, 1977.

Agent: Janet Roberts, William Morris Agency, 1350 Avenue of the Americas, New York, NY 10019 (212) 586-5100.

TITLE • AVAILABILITY • PRODUCTIONS

Plot Counter Plot: not available; St. Clements Theatre, NYC

The Mandala: not available; Theatre of the Living Arts, Philadelphia, PA

Americommedia: not available; Street theatre, East Coast

The Shadow Box†: Samuel French, 25 W. 45th St., New York, NY 10036, $2.50; Mark Taper Forum, Los Angeles, CA; Broadway

Ice: manuscript*; Mark Taper Forum, Los Angeles, CA; Manhattan Theatre Club, NYC

Black Angel: manuscript*; Mark Taper Forum, Los Angeles, CA

C. C. Pyle and the Bunyon Derby: manuscript*, under option; Kenyon College, OH

The Lady and the Clarinet: manuscript, under option; Mark Taper Forum, Los Angeles, CA
    *contact agent
    †Lincoln Center, Theatre on Film & Tape

MART CROWLEY

Born in Vicksburg, MS on August 21, 1935. Attended The Catholic University of America, Washington, DC (B.A., 1957).

Address: c/o Paul Wolfowitz, Suite 22, 59 East 54th St., New York, NY 10022

Agent: Audrey Wood, International Creative Management, 40 West 57th St., New York, NY (212) 556-5722

TITLE • AVAILABILITY • PRODUCTIONS

The Boys in the Band: Samuel French, 25 W. 45th St., New York, NY 10036, $2.50; Playwright's Unit, Vandam Theatre, NYC; Theatre Four, NYC

Remote Asylum: manuscript*; Center Theatre Group, Los Angeles, CA

A Tale at Both Ends: manuscript*

C

Mart Crowley (cont'd)

A Breeze from the Gulf: Samuel French, $2.50; Bucks County Playhouse, New Hope, PA,
   Eastside Playhouse, NYC
   *contact agent

NEIL CUTHBERT

Born in Montclair, NJ on May 5, 1951. Educated
at Rutgers University; B.A., English. Playwright-
in-Residence at Rutgers University. Literary
Manager at Ensemble Studio Theatre in New
York. Recipient: 1974 Winner American College
Theater Festival Award for Best New Play, **The
Soft Touch;** Guest Artist at Edward Albee's
Playwright's Foundation.

Address: 484 West 43rd St., #36H, New York, NY
   10036 (212) 564-7972

Agent: George Lane, William Morris Agency,
   1350 Avenue of the Americas, New York, NY
   10019 (212) 586-5100

TITLE • AVAILABILITY • PRODUCTIONS

The Soft Touch: Samuel French, 25 West 45th St., New York, NY 10036, $2.50; Rutgers Univer-
   sity Theater; Wilbur Theater, Boston, MA

Snapping People: manuscript*; Rutgers University Theater, NJ

Buddy Pals: manuscript*; Rutgers University, NJ; Ensemble Studio Theatre, NYC

First Thirty: manuscript*; Ensemble Studio Theatre, NYC

The Perfect Stranger: manuscript*; Ensemble Studio Theatre, NYC

The Smash: manuscript*; Ensemble Studio Theatre, NYC

The Home Planet: manuscript*
   *contact author

SYNOPSES

The Soft Touch: A farce about American sexual madness. Blinky, a young man who desires only
to examine his pornographic magazine and go to sleep, is attacked by an assortment of lunatics;
the Likk Brothers — a schizophrenic who murders anyone named Phil, a housewife changed to a
sexual tigress by the moon, a sadistic landlord obsessed with avenging his great great grandfather's death in the Civil War, and others. Nasty and funny. An attempt to revive commedia in our
theater.
Full length. Setting: a dingy one-room apartment. 6 males and 2 females.

Buddy Pals: Three seventeen-year-old boys meet in a playroom for their regular Friday night
"tube" session. Their boyhood friendship is destroyed and then restored in a re-creation of their
already lost childhood games. A funny and very real play.
One act, 35 minutes. Setting: a playroom. 3 males, 1 offstage woman's voice.

The Perfect Stranger: An unhappy housewife, her husband and the water meter man find
themselves trapped in an unusual but classic triangle on a hot June day. A comedy drama about
love, escape and loneliness.
Two acts. Setting: a playroom. 2 males, 1 female.

WALLACE DACE

Born in Rome, NY. Attended Rice University, Illinois Wesleyan University, B.A., Yale Drama School, MFA; University of Denver, Ph.D. Has taught at Mount Holyoke College, Russell Sage College, Sweet Briar College and is presently Director of Graduate Studies in Theater at Kansas State University. Author of various articles in the **Educational Theater Journal;** with his wife, Letitia Dace: **The Theatre Student: Modern Theatre and Drama** (New York: The Richards Rosen Press, Inc., 1973); **Subsidies for the Theater: A Study of the Central European System of Financing Drama, Opera and Ballet** (Manhattan: The AG Press, 1972); and **Elements of Dramatic Structure** (Manhattan: AG Press, 1972). **Proposal for a National Theater,** (Richard Rosen Press, 1978); **National Theaters in the Larger German and Austrian Cities,** R. Rosen Press. Recipient: National Playwriting Competitions First Prizes for the following plays: **Flight,** Arkansas Chapter of the National Collegiate Players; **October Festival,** Des Plaines Theatre Guild, Arcadia Community Theatre, Des Moines Community Playhouse; **Journey in July,** Richmond Professional Institute, Richmond, Va.; **The Flag-Bearer,** Theatre Department, University of Baylor.

Address: 2217 Stone Post Road, Manhattan, KS 66502 (913) 539-5152

Agent: Ann Elmo Agency, 60 East 42nd St., New York, NY 10017 (212) 661-2880/81

TITLE • AVAILABILITY • PRODUCTIONS

October Festival and **The Sorcerer's Apprentice:** Published as **Two Plays by Wallace Dace,** Whitehall Drama Books, 367 Markham St., Toronto, Ontario, Canada M6G 2K8, $2.00; Des Plaines Theatre Guild; Arcadia Community Theatre

We Commit This Body: Published in **Best Short Plays of 1960,** Beacon Press, 25 Beacon St., Boston, MA 02108

Flight: manuscript*; University of Arkansas Theatre Department

Journey in July: manuscript*; Richmond Professional Institute

The Flag-Bearer: manuscript*; Seattle Repertory Theater

The House on Prince Edward Street: manuscript*; Kansas State Univ. Theater Dept.

A Pledge of Allegiance: manuscript*

Fate, Fortune and Final Solutions: manuscript*

Hitler in Landsberg: manuscript*

Nothing Is Worth Fighting For: manuscript*
  *contact author

SYNOPSIS

Hitler in Landsberg: A turning point in Hitler's life was the thirteen months he spent in Landsberg Prison in Bavaria after the failure of his Putsch against the government in November, 1923. As we see him dictating excerpts from **Mein Kampf** to a young secretary, Ulrich Schwartz, we begin to sense the strange power he was later able to exert over the German people. Flashback scenes concern his youth in Linz, the death of his mother of cancer, his experience in World War I in which he is blinded by gas and a prophetic scene with Bert Brecht in a Munich beer hall. At the end, his prison term ends and his rise to power begins.

Full length. Setting: prison cell with a flexible area. 8 males, 2 females, a few extras who can be doubled.

D

ANTHONY DAMATO

Born in Syracuse, NY on July 12. Educated at Queens College, New York; Alliance Francaise and the Sorbonne in Paris; New York University. Studied painting three years each at Cooper Union and the Art Student's League. Currently member of BMI Musical Theater Workshop led by Lehman Engel; also, member of playwriting workshop conducted by John Guare. Recipient: Art Student's League Travelling Fellowship to Paris (the McDowell); resident fellowship to the Edward MacDowell Art Colony in Peterborough, N H .

Address: 231 East 76th St., New York, NY 10021

Agent: Robert Freedman, Brandt & Brandt, Dramatic Dept., 1501 Broadway, New York, NY 10036 (212) 840-5760

TITLE • AVAILABILITY • PRODUCTIONS

Before the Rain: manuscript*; Thirtieth Street Theatre, NYC; Theatre Genesis, NYC

The Flounder Complex: Dramatists Play Service, 440 Park Ave. South, New York, NY 10016, $1.25; The Old Reliable, NYC; The Playbox, NYC

Me, Myself and You (musical): manuscript*

Manhattan Trilogy: manuscript*

Bibi Robinson: manuscript*

The Sacrifice: manuscript*

Snow and Sand: manuscript*

Banners: manuscript*

Paradise of Glass: manuscript*
    *contact author

SYNOPSES

The Flounder Complex: "A paranoid, nearly blind old woman interviews a young girl who answers her ad for a servant. During the process, the old woman's fear of the outside world shows itself bit by bit, partly through the slightly-veiled hostility of her questions, partly through her revelations about herself. When the girl realizes just how far gone her potential employer is, she decides she doesn't want the job after all; but the old woman, terrified because the girl — who now knows all about her — poses a threat to her safety, shoots her. The author draws from this confrontation a gripping tension, and the old woman is a remarkable creation, as blind and dangerous to herself as she is, symbolically, to the outside world." — **Village Voice.** "Easily one of the most exciting plays to reach the Off Off Broadway circuit." — **Backstage.**

One act (45 minutes). Setting: simple interior. 2 females.

Banners: Al Tuba, a night club entertainer, is always doing what other people want because he's convinced that he doesn't really know who he is and therefore, doesn't know what he himself wants. After suffering a nearly fatal heart attack, he is "reborn" and adopts as his own, his stage identity — namely, a woman. In a series of surrealistic scenes, he is attacked on all sides by everyone who comes in contact with him. His wife leaves him. He's arrested and held for psychiatric observation. When he goes to Bloomingdale's to buy a woman's wig, he's thrown out by the management after it receives numerous complaints that Al Tuba uses the men's room. Finally, in a searing confrontation with his mother, brother and sister, his feminine clothes are ripped off his person and with his wife who comes back to him finally after having undergone changes of her own and now accepts and understands his needs, the play ends with both of them exchanging articles of clothing, each wearing a melange of men's and women's dress, to suggest a partial new beginning.

Anthony Damato (cont'd)

Eight scences (1 hour, 10 minutes). Settings: suggested, rather than depicted. 1 male, 1 female; 14 other characters, many of which can be played by the same actors.

Snow and Sand: With this play the author tries to prove that our outer actions are not related to our interior motives. A young couple with their infant son go on an outing in a forest. The two of them go through experiences that reveal their individual repressed sexual desires, hatred, murderous instincts, greed and dishonesty. At the surprising ending of the play the characters are shattered inwardly, but their outside behavior remains the same, and in a normal fashion, they pick up their belongings and leave.

One act. Setting: a clearing in the forest. 6 males, 2 females.

ALLEN DAVIS III

Born in Cincinnati, OH on March 9, 1929. Educated at Syracuse University, B.A. cum laude; Yale Drama School, MFA in directing. Theatre Administrator/General Manager: Playhouse in the Park, Cincinnati, OH; Santa Fe Theatre Company, New Mexico; Puerto Rican Traveling Theatre, New York City. Writer-in-residence, University of Alaska, Anchorage, 1975. Teaches playwriting at the Puerto Rican Traveling Theatre. Also a stage director. Recipient: Dramatists Guild financial grant; two grants each from The MacDowell Colony, The Helene Wurlitzer Foundation, Yaddo and The Ossabow Island Project; NEA Grant, 1978; CAPS Grant, 1980.

Address: 484 West 43rd St., #20F, New York; NY 10036 (212) 695-1990

Agent: Rosenstone/Wender, 3 East 48th St., New York, NY 10017 (212) 832-8330

TITLE • AVAILABILITY • PRODUCTIONS

Montezuma's Revenge: manuscript*; staged reading, Theatre at St. Clements, NYC

The Head of Hair: manuscript**; Milwaukee Repertory Theater, WI; New Theater Workshop, NYC

Where the Green Bananas Grow: manuscript**; H.B. Playwrights Foundation, NYC

The Rag Doll: manuscript**; U. of Texas; New Dramatists, NYC

Bull Fight Cow: manuscript**; New Dramatists, NYC

Rocco, The Rolling Stone; Samuel French, 25 West 45th St., New York, NY 10036, $2.00; Various productions worldwide

Leroy and the Ark; Samuel French, $2.00; Various productions worldwide

Hook & I's: manuscript**

I Will Be Launched: manuscript**
    *contact agent
    **contact author

SYNOPSES

Montezuma's Revenge: A comedy-drama about the Marine Corps during the Korean War, 1951. An intellectual recruit is drafted. He hates the Marine Corps, but his drill instructor feels he will make a first rate marine. As the drill instructor forces the draftee to shape up, the draftee begins to en-

D

Allen Davis, III (cont'd)

joy his new-found role. Then a death occurs that wrecks the relationship and pits the draftee against his drill instructor in an angry and bitter conclusion.

Full length. Setting: Marine Corps training barracks, interior and exterior, a unit set. 14 males, 3 females.

Where the Green Bananas Grow: A social comedy that takes place on the eve of the Second World War. A black maid stands firm against her wealthy employer who accuses her of stealing three bananas. The maid is innocent, the employer is disturbed by her own feelings of guilt over allowing her son to be raised by the maid. A knockdown, dragout battle occurs with the woman hurling accusation after accusation at her long time maid. The maid up and quits, but not before giving a surprise sendoff to her employer. . .

Full Length. Setting: Master bedroom of an expensive home. 1 male, 4 females.

The Rag Doll: A drama that starts with the loss of a woman's six-year-old twin son. The remaining brother chooses to replace him with a life size doll. The mother is soon drawn to the doll as the father tries to bring his wife and his son back to reality. The situation worsens and it reaches a climax as the rag doll "dies." The life cycle of the doll has run its course, and the parents begin to pick up the pieces of their lives.

Short full length. Setting: a unit set including the interior of a large home and open space that doubles for other locales. 4 males (including a child), 8 females (including a child).

LUTHER DAVIS

B.A. Yale 1938, Walter Pritchard Eaton Playwriting Course. U.S. Air Corps World War II. Screenplays: **The Hucksters** (MGM), **B F's Daughter** (MGM), **Black Hand** (MGM), **A Lion Is in the Streets** (WB), **Lady in a Cage** (Paramount), **Across 110th Street** (UA). Recipient: Antoinette Perry Award (with Charles Lederer) for book of **Kismet**, 1953–54; Charles Derwent Award 1945 for best new American play, **Kiss Them for Me;** Mystery Writers of America Edgar Allan Poe award 1964 for TV play, **The End of the World Baby** and 1970 for TV "Movie of the Week" **The Old Man Who Cried Wolf;** Fame Award 1964 for Best Original Screenplay, **Lady in a Cage;** Writers Guild of America nomination for Best Teleplay 1967, adaptation **Arsenic and Old Lace.**

Address: 18 West 55th St., New York, NY 10019 (212) 757-3514

TITLE • AVAILABILITY • PRODUCTIONS

Kiss Them for Me: manuscript*; Belasco Theater, Fulton Theater, Broadway

At the Grand (book): manuscript*; Los Angeles Civic Light Opera, Los Angeles, CA; San Francisco Civic Light Opera, CA

Kismet: Music Theater Inc., 119 West 57th St., New York, NY 10019; Los Angeles Civic Light Opera, LA, CA; Ziegfeld Theater, Broadway; numerous productions

They Voted Yes!: manuscript*;
*contact author

SYNOPSES

Kiss Them for Me: Based on Frederic Wakeman's novel **Shore Leave,** the play tells of three World War II naval aviators who come to San Francisco fresh from combat and meet the civilian world of black marketing and "Victory girls" and business as usual and war profiteering; tone of play is farce-comedy with some heavy moments.

Luther Davis (cont'd)

Setting: hotel suite and hospital ward. 19 speaking parts of which 6 are females.

At the Grand: Musical comedy version of Vicki Baum's **Grand Hotel,** set in Rome post-World War II instead of Berlin post-World War I, and the old man Kringelein has been made the focus of the action. In the musical he is an old scullery worker who, learning he hasn't long to live, takes his life savings and moves upstairs "where the halls are full of music"; singing requirements for this role are modest but female lead (an opera star) must sing well; good singers required for part of the Baron and the semi-prostitute.

Setting: very grand hotel; three different rooms and the lobby and corridors.

They Voted Yes! A tragic drama about the early days of the Nazi party in Germany in 1932. At rise a typical German family derides the "street hoodlums" but at final curtain it has joined the Nazis.

Setting: tenement living room. 3 males, 4 females.

OSSIE DAVIS

Born in Cogdell, GA on December 18, 1917. Attended Howard University and Columbia University. Has acted in film, TV and on stage. Notable roles include **Green Pastures, Anna Lucasta, Raisin in the Sun** and **Purlie Victorius.** Contributed written works to **New York Times, Amsterdam News, Negro History Bulletin, Washington Post** and **Philadelphia Bulletin.** Recipient: Coretta Scott King Award for **Escape to Freedom;** Jane Adams Award; Honorary Doctorates from Howard University, University of Massachusetts, Wilberforce University, Virginia State University.

Address: 44 Cortland Avenue, New Rochelle, NY 10801 (914) 235-6867

Agent: Clifford Stevens, 888 Seventh Avenue, New York, NY 10019 (212) 246-1030

TITLE • AVAILABILITY • PRODUCTIONS

Point Blank; not available

They Seek a City; not available

The Mayor of Harlem; not available

The Last Dance for Sybil; manuscript*

Clay's Rebellion; not available

Alice in Wonder; not available; Elks Community Theatre, NY

The Big Deal; not available; New Playwrights Theatre, NYC

What Can You Say to Mississippi?; not available

Montgomery Footprints; not available

Purlie Victorious; Samuel French, 25 West 45th St., New York, NY, $2.50; Broadway

Purlie (music, Gary Geld, lyrics, Peter Udell); Samuel French, $2.50; Broadway

Escape to Freedom; Viking Press, 625 Madison Avenue, New York, NY 10021, $7.95

Alexis Is Fallen; not available

Curtain Call, Mr. Aldridge Sir: manuscript*; University of California
   *contact author or agent

D

DOT DECAMP

Born in Philadelphia, PA, on January 13, 1920 and raised in Washington, DC. A.B., Beaver College, Glenside, PA. A former newspaper reporter and columnist and book reviewer. Author of Oak Ridge guide book, **From Secret City to Science City.** She is married to a nuclear engineer, Sam DeCamp, and has one daughter. She is a member of the Dramatists Guild and is presently Information Representative for the Oak Ridge Public Libary. Recipient: Etheridge Award sponsored by Dramatists Alliance, Stanford, CA. First Prize National Collegiate Players Play Contest sponsored by U. of Arkansas; Showcase Award sponsored by Arcadia Community Theatre, Arcadia, CA; First Prize One Act Play Contest (nation-wide) sponsored by Lambuth College, Jackson, TN.

Address: 106 Middlebury Rd., Oak Ridge, TN 37830

TITLE • AVAILABILITY • PRODUCTIONS

The Mad Hatter's Psychiatrist (one-act): manuscript*; Carousel Theatre, Knoxville, TN

Bed of Rose's (one act): manuscript*; Carousel Theatre, TN

The Solitary in the House (three act); Beth El Center, Oak Ridge, TN

Patty O'Brien and the Tallest Leprechaun (two-act): manuscript*; Student Players, Oak Ridge, TN and Birmingham Youth Players, Birmingham MI

Star Spangled Manor (three act): manuscript*; Arcadia Community Theatre, Arcadia, CA

Make Haste to Be Kind: manuscript*; Beth El Center, TN

S.O.B. (three act): manuscript*; Pioneer Playhouse, Danville KY (produced under the title **The Unbelievable Mr. B).**

Bone of Contention (one act): manuscript*; Lambuth College drama dept., Jackson, TN.
　　*contact author

PETER DEE

Born in Winchester, MA on April 11, 1939. B.A. in English from Boston College. Associate of Occupational Studies from the American Academy of Dramatic Arts. Member of New Dramatists: The Playwrights Workshop of the Circle Repertory Co.

Address: 341 West 88th St., New York, NY 10024
　　(212)799-6617

Agent: Elisabeth Marton, 96 Fifth Avenue, New York, NY 10011 (212) 255-1908

TITLE • AVAILABILITY • PRODUCTIONS

A Sea of White Horses: Samuel French, 25 W. 45th St., New York, NY 10036, $2.50; Courtyard Playhouse, NYC; Walden Theater, NYC

Filigree People: manuscript*, Charles Mann 117 E. 77th St., New York, NY 10021; The New Dramatists, NYC

Quartet: manuscript*

Morés: manuscript*; State College Theater Dept., New Paltz, NY; Circle Repertory Co., NYC

Martinique: manuscript*

Peter Dee (cont'd)

One More Waltz with Molly O'Flynn: Baker's Plays, 100 Chauncy St., Boston, MA 02111, $1.25; numerous productions

Devil in the Grass: Baker's Plays, $1.25; Numerous productions

Daughter of a Traveling Lady: Samuel French, $1.25; Numerous productions

The Man Who Stayed by His Negative: Samuel French, $1.25; Numerous productions

No One Wants to Know: Samuel French, $1.25; Numerous productions
  *contact agent

SYNOPSES

A Sea of White Horses: A father runs away from his children. For two years since the death of his wife, Ed Shaw, has lived in a seaside shack working at a gas station and fishing to forget his painful past and his responsibilities. One by one his children descend on him. First Connie, a young black woman, he never knew he fathered, then Stephen, full of contempt for his father and forced to come to him against his will, and finally, Janice his youngest child, trying desperately to survive with the family's natural gift of strength and humor but sinking rapidly into a helplessly lost state.

Full length. Setting: one set. 2 males, 2 females.

Filigree People: A playwright (Tom) meets a talented older actress (Lorraine) who's the last of a famous theatrical family. He writes a play especially for her, based on a lot of biographical stories she told him when they met. However, by the time he gets the script to her, she has lapsed back into drinking, bitterness and is too frightened to work anymore. She would rather have him as a lover than a playwright but this is impossible since he already has a lover (Kevin). The situation complicates itself when Tom makes love to Lorraine after bringing her his script. She then thinks she has a chance to win him if she does his play, even though facing the ghosts of her dead family may do her in during rehearsals.

Full length. Setting: one set. 2 males, 2 females.

Quartet: Vincent and Kate become acquainted in a hospital where he was a patient and she is a nurse. They are drawn to each other though both have their guard up due to past life experiences. Previous to his meeting Kate, Vincent has befriended a fifteen-year-old girl, Rebecca, who has moved into the building where Vincent lives to get away from her father who beats her. These three people develop a trust and growing love for each other that nearly has them on the way to becoming a family when Rebecca's father gives them a disastrous setback. Kate and Vincent are left with the choice of continuing what has begun.

Full length. Setting: one set. 2 males, 2 females.

RAMON LOUIS DELGADO

Born in Tampa, FL on December 16, 1937. B.A., Stetson University; M.A., Dallas Theatre Center; M.F.A., Yale School of Drama; Ph.D., Southern Illinois University. Educator at Chipola Junior College, Kentucky Wesleyan College, Hardin-Simmons University, St. Cloud State University, Montclair State College. Honors in national play contests: Samuel French; **Story Magazine;** University of Missouri; Peoria Players; Earplay; Baylor University; Theta Alpha Phi; American College Theatre Festival, David Library. Listed in **Outstanding Educators of America; Contemporary Authors; International Authors & Writers Who's Who.** Editor, **The Best Short Plays,** 1981.

Address: c/o Speech-Theatre Dept., Montclair State College, Upper Montclair, NJ 07043 (201) 893-4217

Agent: Philip Minges, Curtis Brown, Ltd., 575 Madison Avenue, New York, NY 10022 (212) 755-4200

D

Ramon Louis Delgado (cont'd)

TITLE • AVAILABILITY • PRODUCTIONS

Waiting for the Bus: Baker's Plays, 100 Chauncy, Boston, MA 02111, $1.25; Florida Theatre Festival; Stetson University

Once Below a Lighthouse: Best Short Plays of 1972, Chilton Press, Chilton Way, Radnor, PA 19089, $7.95; Southern Illinois University; The Glines, NYC

The Youngest Child of Pablos Peco: Stetson Review, Deland, FL 32720

Sparrows of the Field: Baker's Plays, $1.25; Southern Illinois University

The Little Toy Dog: Baker's Plays, $1.25; Southern Illinois University

Omega's Ninth: Stage Magic, Schulenburg, TX 78956, $1.00; Yale School of Drama, CT

The Knight-Mare's Nest: Stage Magic, $1.50; University of Missouri

Nest Among the Stars: manuscript*; Florida Theatre Festival

Hedge of Serpents: manuscript*; American College Theatre Festival; Kentucky Wesleyan College

Brambles on the Sheepskin: manuscript*; American College Theatre Festival; Kentucky Wesleyan College

Brother of Dragons: manuscript*; American College Theatre Festival; Hardin-Simmons University

Flight of the Dodo: manuscript*; Southern Illinois University; University of Missouri

Listen, My Children: manuscript*; American College Theatre Festival; Stetson University

The Fabulous Jeromes: manuscript*

A Little Holy Water: manuscript*; American College Theatre Festival; St. Cloud State University, MN

The Jerusalem Thorn: manuscript*; Whole Theatre Company, NJ; Shandol Theatre

The Fabulous Jennie (musical): manuscript*
    *contact agent

SYNOPSES

The Fabulous Jeromes: Defying the conservative mores of her mother, unconventional Jennie Jerome (future mother of Winston Churchill) follows in the footsteps of her liberal father, Leonard. She secures Leonard's permission only to face dealing with the revelation of Randolph's syphilis. " . . . a very stageworthy play. The characterizations are delicately wrought and roundly dimensional . . . The dialogue literate and lively." Dr. Christian Moe, Southern Illinois University.

Full length. Setting: six minimal sets. 6 males, 8 females.

The Jerusalem Thorn: An aging gay artist and a sensitive young art teacher struggle with self-acceptance on a day of crisis. ". . . a word-fabric of astonishing strength and delicacy . . . power and poignancy . . . laughter and pain." Dale Wasserman

Full length. Setting: an artist's studio. 2 males.

A Little Holy Water: Mercedes Hernandez, wife of a Cuban-American cigar worker opposed to the violence advocated by her husband, a leader in a Cuban Union strike during the depression, eventually succumbs to the pressures around her and joins in her husband's struggle. ". . . an interesting and amusing piece." Ezra Stone.

Full length. Setting: kitchen and porch of the Hernandez home. 5 males, 6 females.

DONNA de MATTEO

Born in New York City, June 24, 1941. Educated at Marymount College and New York University. A graduate of the N.Y.U. school of film. Donna teaches playwriting at the HB Studio in Manhattan, and has taught at the Contemporary Theatre at the College of New Rochelle. She is also a member of the Italian-American Playwrights Forum.

Address: 15 East 88th St., New York, NY 10028
(212) 831-3533

Agent: Esther Sherman, William Morris Agency, 1350 Ave. of the Americas, New York, NY 10019 (212) 586-5100

TITLE • AVAILABILITY • PRODUCTIONS

The Barbecue Pit: manuscript*; Theatre East, NYC

Almost on a Runway: manuscript*; HB Playwrights Foundation, NYC

The Expatriate: manuscript*; HB Playwrights Foundation, NYC; Westchester Playhouse, NY

The Paradise Kid: manuscript*; HB Playwrights Foundation, NYC

Dear Mr. Giordano: manuscript*; HB Playwrights Foundation, NYC; Roundabout Theatre, NYC

Playing with Strindberg's Fire: manuscript*;

There She Is, Ms. America: manuscript*

Animal Lovers: manuscript*; HB Playwrights Foundation, NYC

A Horse Story: manuscript*; HB Playwrights Foundation, NYC

Rocky Road: manuscript*;
   *contact agent

SYNOPSES

There She Is, Ms. America: Four women, one by one, enter a hospital room in New York. They represent a cross section of American life, but they are all there for the same reason, to get an abortion. All have conflicting ideas about their situation. Add to this combination a black nurse, a Japanese lady gynecologist, an hysterical mother of one of the patients, and due to hospital inefficiency, an eighty-year-old woman who enters the room accidentally. One of the patients, instead of having an abortion, has a baby, and this brings about a lot of internal and external conflict amongst the rest of the patients.

Full length. Setting: hospital room with four beds. 8 females.

Rocky Road: The story about a thirty-eight-year-old housewife who suffers a nervous breakdown after her husband of seventeen years falls in love with a younger woman. The play takes place in the suburban familyroom of Lynn and Michael and it involves their twin teenaged daughters and Lynn's sister and brother-in-law (a polyester suit manufacturer). Subject matter is dealt with comedically.

D

ELAINE G. DENHOLTZ

B.A. from Bucknell U., Phi Beta Kappa. M.A. from
Seaton Hall U. Author of published short fiction,
articles, and books; also radio play, educational
and documentary films; television and screen-
plays. Presently on English Faculty of Fairleigh
Dickinson U. Recipient: Doris Bell Paiss Drama
Award; Fenimore Players Playwriting Contest;
Courtyard Playhouse Drama Prize; Russell A.
Sharp Drama Prize; MacArthur Playwriting Con-
test, NEA and Shubert Grants; New Jersey State
Council on the Arts — Playwriting; Dubuque
Fine Arts Society Playwriting Contest.

Address: 13 Birchwood Drive, Livingston, NJ
07039 (201) 992-5480

Agent: Maria Carvainis, 235 West End Ave., New
York, NY 10023 (212) 580-1559

TITLE • AVAILABILITY • PRODUCTIONS

Judge Not: manuscript*

Frozen: manuscript*; Clark Center for Performing Arts, NYC

The Dungmen Are Coming: manuscript*; Cocktail Theatre, Bucknell University, PA

Hey Out There, Is Anyone Out There?: manuscript*; New York Theatre Ensemble, NYC

Some Men Are Good at That: manuscript*; The Assembly, NYC; Courtyard Playhouse, NYC

An Even Exchange: manuscript*

The Highchairs: Dramatic Publishing Co., 4150 N. Milwaukee Ave., Chicago, IL 60641, $1.75;
Conkle Workshop, U. of TX; Actor's Cafe Theatre, NJ

Love Games: manuscript*
   *contact author

SYNOPSES

Some Men Are Good at That: A comedy in which a repairman is brought in by the landlady to fix a
leak in a cheap Philadelphia apartment which is rented by a girl who is in bed with the flu. The
repairman not only fixes the leak, but manages — with a little cooperation from the girl — to cure
her, too.

One Act. Setting: one set, bedroom. 1 male, 2 females.

The Highchairs: The love-guilt relationships between married people, who have children of their
own and their elderly parents. The ironic role reversal is comic but the deeper question of
euthanasia explores the tender bonds between generations.

Full length. Setting: one set, kitchen. 2 males, 3 females.

Love Games: A recently divorced woman, on a single day, finds strength to put her life in order. A
comedy about the sexual and social politics between men and women.

Full length. Setting. one set, living room/kitchen. 1 male, 4 females (inter-racial cast).

PRISCILLA B. DEWEY

Born in Boston, MA on October 16, 1924. Pine
Manor College, School of the Museum of Fine
Arts; M.A. in Theater Arts, Goddard College.
Author of The Charles River Creative Arts Program Handbook (Charles River Creative Arts
Press, 1979); Publicity Guide (NEA grant); author
of poems appearing in **New York Times Sunday
Arts and Leisure, Boston Globe, Christian Science Monitor** etc. Arts Consultant National
Episcopal Bicentennial Committee. Director,
Charles River Creative Arts Program and consultant for their affiliates in twelve states. Member
of the Board of Directors, Religious Community
and the Arts. Trustee Middlesex School. Active
member of Dramatists Guild. Lyricist, BMI. Fa-
cilitator for National Endowment for the Arts
City Spirit Program.

Address: 307 Orchard St., Millis, MA 02054
(617)376-8893 or (617) 785-0068

TITLE • AVAILABILITY • PRODUCTIONS

Two If by Sea (book and lyrics): manuscript*; Fenway Theater, Boston; Theater by the Sea,
Matunuck, RI; Circle in the Square, NYC

The Mouse in the White House (book and lyrics): manuscript*; Charles River Festival Theater;
Theatre by the Sea Matunick, RI.

Prime Time (book and lyrics): manuscript*; Festival Theater, Dover

King Arthur's Knights & Days (book and lyrics): manuscript*; Theater by the Sea, Matunick, RI;
Festival Theatre, Dover

The Pied Piper (book and lyrics): Baker's Plays, 100 Chauncey St., Boston, MA 20111, Script,
$3.00; Score, $10.00; Theater by the Sea, Boston Theatres and Schools

Rip's New Wrinkle: manuscript*; Charles River Festival; Channel 5, WCVB-TV

Young Country: Baker's Plays, Script $3.00, Score $10.00; Jordan Marsh, Boston 200, Middlesex School, Newton City Hall, Charles River Playhouse, Boston: White House,
Washington, DC

Dearo Family (with David Downing); manuscript*; Boston Theaters and schools

To Find a Rose. Baker's Plays, Script, $3.00
*contact author

SYNOPSES

Young Country: Paul and Rachel Revere, Sam Adams, John Hancock, Dolly Quincy and others
representing in song, dance and scenes, activities in Boston from the Tea Party to the night of the
eighteenth of April in '75.

Simple single set: 3 platforms, projections. 7 males, 3 females, 1 boy, 1 girl, extras.

To Find a Rose: Based on the traditional story of Beauty and the Beast. Beauty and her spirit of
sacrifice and love carry us through this tale of her father's changing fortunes and her sisters' dis-
dain. The play explores the nature of beauty and juxtaposes the pursuit of material wealth
against the possiblities of the spirit as expressed in the arts and in human relationships.

Large flexible cast.

The Pied Piper: This familiar story deals with music as magic. The mayor of Hamlin and his coun-
cilors bring great sorrow to their town by their arrogance and greed. The play focuses on the importance of children and the warmth and joy they bring.

Large, flexible cast.

D

ELIZABETH DIGGS

Born in Tulsa, OK on August 6, 1939. B.A., Brown University; M.A., Ph.D., Columbia University, Literature. Taught Writing, Literature, Women's Studies at Queens College, C.U.N.Y. and Jersey City State College. Member of the Ensemble Studio Theatre.

Address: 48 Prospect Place, Brooklyn, NY 11217

Agent: George Lane, William Morris Agency, 1350 Avenue of the Americas, New York, NY 10019 (212) 586-5100

TITLE • AVAILABILITY • PRODUCTIONS

Close Ties: manuscript*; Long Wharf Theatre, New Haven, CT; Lexington Conservatory Theatre, NY

Goodbye Freddy: manuscript*; Lexington Conservatory Theatre, NY

Scapegoat (one act): manuscript*

Daddy's Girl (one act): manuscript*

Dumping Ground: manuscript*; Ensemble Studio Theatre, NYC
    *contact agent

SYNOPSES

Close Ties: Three generations of the Frye family come together on an August weekend at their summer home in the Berkshires, where they must share a critical decision as their 84-year-old matriarch faces the anguish of encroaching old age. As the reunion gathers momentum, some members' long-smoldering resentments ignite into open hostility, while others experience a moving affirmation of enduring love and loyalty.
Full length. Setting: a large country kitchen. 3 males, 5 females.

Goodbye Freddy: Six friends who grew up together in Kansas City are reunited at the funeral of their dear friend, Freddy, who has died unexpectedly and alone. His friends confront their mortality as well as the passionate, funny and sometimes bitter tangle of their love and friendship for each other.
Full length. Setting: an elegant sunporch. 3 males, 3 females.

STANLEY DISNEY

Born in Muskogee, OK on August 10, 1910. L.L.B., George Washington University; A.B., Oklahoma University. Practiced law until 1976. Served in the Army for five years; four years with the State Department in Germany. Specialized in anti-trust law with United States Department of Justice. Recipient: Russell Sharp Drama Award.

Address: P.O. Box 2006, Pasadena, CA 91105 (213) 796-2578

TITLE • AVAILABILITY • PRODUCTIONS

Shortcut to Cheyenne: manuscript*; Theatre Americana, CA; New Players Company, MD

Practical Aspects of Making a President: At Rise, 9838 Jersey Ave., Santa Fe Springs, CA 90670, 90¢; Theatre Guild of Webster Groves, MD

Treadmill to the Goodtime Star: At Rise, 90¢

Yankee Go Home: At Rise, 90¢

Three Days in the Life of Clar'bel Light: manuscript*; New England Westchester Group Theatre

Miss Light goes to War: manuscript*; Rochester Civic Theatre, MN: Actors Alley, Los Angeles, CA

Ms. Light and the Centerfold Man: manuscript*; Midwestern State University, TX; Actors Alley, Los Angeles, CA

Darwin High-Point: manuscript*

Picnic on the Meuse: manuscript*; KSFO, San Francisco, CA

Reluctant Mrs. Dracula: At Rise, 90¢

Legend of the Conway Line: manuscript*; Theatre Americana, CA; KSFO, San Francisco, CA

Seventeen Seconds: manuscript*; Barn Theatre, NJ; Texas Community Theatre, TX
  *$2.00, contact author

SYNOPSES

Picnic on the Meuse: Orville Disney left Oklahoma University to enlist in the Engineers. On November 11, 1918, he helped float a bridge across the Meuse in the face of German artillery and machine gun fire. Killed outright were seven from the Engineers and many from the marines. All were convinced the war would end at 11:00, as it did. The play ends with reading names from the casualty list as the Narrator summarizes Orville's post-war life; he returned to the farm, never married and committed suicide on August 1964. He was as much a casualty of the war as those killed outright. Copies of newspaper articles including Orville's obituary are attached for display in the lobby.

Full length. Setting: bare stage with black backdrop and scrim, some simple props. 10 males, 2–4 females.

Seventeen Seconds: Oliver Winston plans the perfect murder of his partner, Charles Jordan. The site is to be Jordan's hunting lodge. Oliver takes Jordan's wife, Sheila, to the lodge and tries to enlist her help, advancing various reasons she should help. She is undecided. Jordan turns up and commits suicide. Winston now finds that because of his plans for a perfect murder he is sure to be charged with Jordan's death and Sheila is left to be haunted by the question, if Jordan hadn't committed suicide, would she have helped murder him or not.

Full length. Setting: basement playroom of the lodge. 2 males, 2 females.

D

FELIX DOHERTY

Born in Halifax, Nova Scotia, Canada on April 27, 1908. A.B., and LL.B, from Boston College and Boston College Law School. Retired from editorial work in the aerospace industry. Wrote narration for **Immortal City,** a documentary on Rome and the Vatican art treasures. Recipient: C. Brooks Fry Award, Theatre Americana.

Address: 13639 Cornuta Avenue, Bellflower, CA 90706 (213) 866-5846

TITLE • AVAILABILITY • PRODUCTIONS

The Poet and the Prostitute (formerly **Song out of Sorrow**): manuscript*; Boston, MA; NYC

The King's Servant: manuscript*; Winooski, VT; Boston, MA

Paradise of Snakes (formerly **The Silver of San Tome**): manuscript*

God Save the King: manuscript*; staged reading, Los Angeles Actors Theatre, CA

Green Grows the Holly: manuscript*; Theater Americana, Altadena, CA

The Road from Camelot: manuscript*
    *contact author

SYNOPSES

The Poet and the Prostitute: A young prostitute saves the drug-addicted Victorian poet, Francis Thompson, from a vagrant's death on London's streets and shelters and encourages him. At the brink of suicide, his work attracts the attention of editor Wilfrid Meynell, to whom Thompson reveals his drug problem. Meynell urges a drug cure at his expense. A doctor warns that the frail Thompson may not survive the ordeal, but Thompson, convinced that his destiny as a man and poet are at stake, decides to take the chance.

Full length. Setting: one interior. 6 males, 1 female.

Green Grows the Holly: The play concerns the stormy courtship of Catherine of Aragon and the teenaged Henry Tudor (Henry VIII). Catherine is betrothed to Henry but her mother dies and her father delays payment of her dowry, so Henry VII requires his son to renounce his betrothal vow and arranges for another marriage. Relations between the two countries break down and the two countries are on the brink of war when Henry VII dies. Although Henry VIII's council opposes the match with Catherine, the young couple still love each other and Catherine convinces Henry that their personal desires are also compatible with the interests of England.

Full length. Setting: single set. 10 males, 6 females.

MARTIN BAUML DUBERMAN

Author of eight books including **Charles Francis Adams 1807-1886, James Russell Lowell, The Uncompleted Past, The Antislavery Vanguard, Black Mountain: An Exploration in Community,** etc. Currently Distinguished Prof. of History, Lehman, CUNY. Recipient: Bancroft Prize 1962 for **Charles Francis Adams;** The Vernon Rice Drama Desk Award, 1963–1964 for **In White America;** Finalist, National Book Award, 1966 for **James Russell Lowell;** Special Award from the National Academy of Arts and Letters, 1971 for "contributions to literature."

Address: 475 West 22nd St., New York, NY 10011

D

Martin Bauml Duberman (cont'd)

TITLE • AVAILABILITY • PRODUCTIONS

Elagabalus: Male Armor (collected plays), E.P. Dutton & Co., 201 Park Ave. South, New York, NY 10003, $8.95; The New Dramatists, NYC

Payments: Male Armor; The New Dramatists, NYC; The Back Alley Theater, Washington, DC

The Guttman Ordinary Scale (one act): **Male Armor;** The New Dramatists, NYC; John Drew Theater, NY

The Colonial Dudes (one act): **Male Armor;** also in **Best Short Plays of 1973,** Chilton Book Co., 201 King of Prussia Rd., Radnor, PA 19089, $8.95; Actors Studio, NYC; Dorset Summer Theater; John Drew Theater, NY

Metaphors (one act); **Male Armor;** also in **Collision Course,** Random House, Inc., 201 East 50th St., New York, NY 10022, $1.65; Cafe Au Go Go, NYC; New Dramatists, NYC;

In White America: Samuel French, 25 West 45th St., New York, NY 10036, $2.50; Sheridan Square Playhouse, NYC; two national tours; many foreign, amateur, and stock productions

The Recorder (one act): **Male Armor;** in one volume with **The Electric Map** under the title **The Memory Bank,** Dial Press, 1 Dag Hammarskjold Plaza, New York, NY 10017, $5.95; London; Off Broadway

The Electric Map (one act): **The Memory Bank:** Off Broadway

Visions of Kerouac: Little, Brown, 34 Beacon St., Boston, MA 02106, $4.95; The New Dramatists, NYC; Lion Theater Co., NYC

SYNOPSES

Payments: A young housewife persuades her husband to become a male prostitute in New York.
Setting: minimal. 9 males, 4 females.

Egalabalus: A wealthy young male from an aristocratic, political family attempts to live an androgynous life style.
Setting: a modern apartment in New York City (with some variants). 4 males, 4 females.

HELEN DUBERSTEIN

Born in New York City, June 3, 1926. Married to Victor Lipton; two daughters, Jacqueline and Irene. Playwright-in-residence at Circle Repertory Theatre Co., 1969–71; Goucher College, 1977; University of Hartford, 1977–78; Interlocken Arts Academy, 1979. Artistic Director, Theatre for New City, 1974–79. Has written poetry, latest is **Arrived Safely,** also **Changes; The Voyage Out; Succubus/Incubus; The Human Dimension.** Member, Dramatists Guild. Recipient: OADR Grant; National Foundation for the Arts; New York State Council on the Arts Grant; Iowa School of Short Fiction Award; Interlocken Award for Best Play.

Address: Westbeth, 463 West St., 904-D, New York, NY 10014

Agent: Helmut Meyer, 330 East 79th St., New York, NY 10021 (212) 288-2421

TITLE • AVAILABILITY • PRODUCTIONS

Street Scene: manuscript*; Chelsea Theatre Centre, NY; Heritage Theatre

D

Helen Duberstein (cont'd)

The Kingdom by the Sea (five one-act plays): manuscript*; Provincetown, MA; Circle in the Square, NYC

The Affair: manuscript*; Circle Repertory, NYC; Repertory Co. at Westbeth, NYC

Five Thousand Feet High: manuscript*; Westbeth Cabaret, NYC

A Visit from Grandma: manuscript*; The Dove Theatre Co., NYC

Love/Hate (one act plays): manuscript*; Omni Theatre Club, NYC

Your Unhappiness with Me Is of No Concern to Readers: manuscript*; Omni Theatre Club, NYC; ASTA

The Visit: manuscript*; The Assembly, as part of program; "Rape-In" with Westbeth Playwrights, NYC

Time Shadows: manuscript*; Circle Repertory Co., NYC; The Roundabout (taped by W.B.A.I), NYC

The Monkey of the Inkpot: manuscript*; The Actors Experimental Unit with Playwrights Cooperative, NYC

Copout!: manuscript*; New York Theatre Ensemble, NYC; University of Hartford, CT

The Play Within: manuscript*; New York Theatre Ensemble, NYC

When I Died My Hair in Venice: manuscript*; Circle Repertory Co., NYC

Foggia: manuscript*; Theatre-In-Zimmer, Hamburg˙

The Brain: manuscript*; The Open Space; Playwrights Group, Inc.,

The Puppeteers: manuscript*; as part of "Uptaught"

Under the Bridge There Is a Lonely Spot (with Gregory Peck): manuscript*; Plaza at Lincoln Center, NYC; Theatre for the New City, NYC

Four Corners: manuscript*; Quaigh Theatre, NYC; Circle Repertory Co. Workshop, NYC

We Never Thought a Wedding (folk opera): manuscript*; Theatre for the New City, NYC

The Broken Lease: manuscript*

Hotel Europe: New Works, John Jay Press, 444 West 56th St., New York, NY 10019

Axe of Creation: manuscript*; Four Corners Workshop
    *contact agent

SYNOPSES

Under the Bridge There Is a Lonely Spot (with Gregory Peck): Harriet's world is one of erotica, based on experiences and happenings in her youth which still hold a steel grip on her dreams and sexual turn-ons. Fearful of the excruciating pain she has experienced both as a child of parents who were unaware of her real existence, and as a pawn in early sexual experiences, used badly, raped in body, soul and mind, Harriet has come to terms with her half life. She has programmed herself into a country wife with a nice man and a nice child. She is living a nice life. Or is she? Her memories of her past come to haunt her, in person, with a visit of her mother who remembers the past as precious nostalgia. "The play succeeds beautifully in its intelligence (we are surely in the presence of an intellectual heavyweight and for that, thank god) . . . succeeds in its lyrical qualities and its abiding affection for a world peopled by flawed creatures . . . there is bite to these characters and a roundness . . . faced with the necessary complexities of being sensitively alive . . ." — Arthur Sainer, **Village Voice.**

Setting: old-fashioned farmhouse, both inside and outside (porch, kitchen, living room). 8 males, 4 females.

We Never Thought a Wedding: A folk opera which takes place in the forties. Concerns the relationship and inter-relationships of three couples. Val and Carlotta marry because they conceive of their friends, Leslie and Edith, as having an "ideal marriage" together with their child, Jonathon. As it turns out, Leslie and Edith invite Val and Carlotta to their wedding, as well as veritable crowds, two years later. Well! That is a wedding! The third couple, James and Lillian, are young, romantic and idealistic and they sing and dance their way in and out of all the singing and dancing!

Helen Duberstein (cont'd)

Setting: levels representing the loft of Edith and Leslie, and the apartment of Val and Carlotta: Broadway; a tinsely luncheonette. In the second act: the garishness of the wedding hall, and the ability to sweep it all away so that the last part of the act is actually played out on a bare stage. 3 males, 3 females plus a chorus of equal numbers of men and women.

Axe of Creation: Lisa Mayo of Spiderwoman Theater and Helen Duberstein formed a workshop to explore and produce a theater-piece based on dreams and hidden memories of women which would involve kinships amongst women, blood, surrogate and mythic. Several women of different ages, ethnic backgrounds, cultural heritage and sexual preferences met over a period of five months. All of them, they discovered, had experienced themselves outside of history, as it were, and had evolved a means of survival in a hostile environment which sought to make them disappear on many levels. In the first piece to evolve, **Axe of Creation,** each one tells her story of how she survives in a world that is not of her making.

Full length. Setting: a bordello. 7 or 8 females.

ROCHELLE HOLT DUBOIS

Born in Chicago, IL on March 17, 1946. B.A., University of Illinois; M.F.A., University of Iowa, Writers Workshop; Ph.D., Columbia Pacific University, CA. She has published **Pangs** (Lawton Press), **A Legend in His Time, From One Bird, The Train in the Rain** and **The Invisible Dog.** Recipient: Three grants, National Endowment for the Arts, Writer-in-residence; OADR Grant.

Address: 511 N. 42nd Avenue, Phoenix, AZ 85019

Agent: D.C. Erdmann, 516 Gallows Hill Road, Cranford, NJ (201) 232-7224

TITLE • AVAILABILITY • PRODUCTIONS

Walking into the Dawn: A Celebration: manuscript*; Magic Theatre, Omaha, NB (twice)

Golden Pyramids at Ohama: manuscript*; Goucher College, MD

Sharper Than a Serpent's Tooth: manuscript*; Tarpon Springs Recreation Center, Fl

Food: A Gastronomical Appetizer: Valhalia 4, Modern Drama, Ragnarok Press, Birmingham, Al

Birmingham, A Moving Play: manuscript*

House of Emotions (dance drama): manuscript*

Michael Field; Two Women Who Wrote as One Man: manuscript*

Life on Dixie Pike: manuscript*

You Tell Me Your Depression and I'll Tell You Mine: manuscript*

Love Letters: manuscript*

Panes: manuscript*
   *contact author or agent

SYNOPSIS

Walking into the Dawn: A Celebration: "This is a musical fantasy, an animated collage, a mobile for the stage. At times it seems to be a constantly whirling carousel. Scenes, sounds, players, their motions, the costumes, the moods and themes of the piece are constantly changing, evolving from one image into another. It celebrates woman, the essence of woman with reference to the ancient goddesses and all the women who have ever lived or will ever live. The motif is presented in a great variety of intricate theatrical bits; there are many short scenes, dances songs, changes and comic routines, all following one another swiftly." . . . Dr. Spencer, "Under the Sign Pisces," **Anais Nin Newsletter.**

D

THOMAS G. DUNN

Born in Albert Lea, MN on December 17, 1950.
B.A., University of Minnesota, summa cum
laude; M.A., University of Minnesota. Member of
Board of Contributors of Minneapolis Star. His
short stories and articles have been published in
numerous magazines. Past director of Play-
wrights Center. Tom is currently Executive
Director of the New Dramatists in New York.
Recipient: Summa Grant, 1971, University of
Minnesota; M.S.A.B. Project Award, 1976; Center
Stage Playwriting Contest, 1979.

Address: Apt. 124, 40 W. 72nd St., New York, NY
10023 (212) 362-6100

TITLE • AVAILABILITY • PRODUCTIONS

A Man Called Judas: manuscript*; KUOM Radio; University of Minneapolis

Tribute: manuscript*; Sacramento Play Festival, CA; high schools

Tales of Pacific N.W.: Bolger Publications, 3401 Como Ave., S.E., St. Paul, MN 55110, $3.00;
   Storytalers Tour; Wolf Trap Farm Park

King of Lodz: manuscript*; Playwright's Center, MN: Center Stage

Fishing Contest: manuscript*; Playwright's Center MN: Group Theater, SD

Jack and the Beanstalk: Bolger Publications, $4.00; Storytalers; Troupe Theatre

In Pursuit of the Sound of Hydrogen: manuscript*; Playwright's Center, MN; Midwest
   Playwright's Conference, WI

Daughters of Abraham: manuscript*; Playwright's Center, MN; Center Stage

Robbed: manuscript*; Playwright's Center, MN; Chimera

SYNOPSES

In Pursuit of the Sound of Hydrogen: A young scientist starts to evolve a new theory, dies and
becomes a cult figure.

Full length. Setting: minimal set. 3 males, 2 females.

Robbed: A young urban couple's life is changed forever by a series of burglaries the police are
helpless to control.

Full length. Setting: one set, minimal. 2 males, 1 female.

CHRISTOPHER DURANG

Born in Berkeley Heights, NJ on January 2, 1949.
B.A. in English from Harvard, 1971; M.F.A. in
Playwriting from the Yale School of Drama. He is
working on a screenplay for the Ladd Company
with Wendy Wasserstein. Recipient: CBS Play-
writing Grant; Rockefeller Grant; Guggenheim
Grant; Tony nomination. Best Book of a musical
(History of The American Film); Drama Desk
nomination for acting; Obie Award, 1980, for
Sister Mary Ignatius. . .

Agent: Helen Merrill, 337 West 22nd St., New
   York, NY 10011 (212) 924-6314

TITLE • AVAILABILITY • PRODUCTIONS

The Idiots Karamazov (with Albert Innaurato): Dramatists Play Service, 440 Park Ave. South, New York, NY 10016, $2.50; Yale Repertory Company, CT

The Nature & Purpose of the Universe: Dramatists Play Service, $2.50; Direct Theatre, NYC; Wonderhorse Theatre, NYC

Das Lusitania Songspiel (with Sigourney Weaver): manuscript*; Chelsea Theater Center, NYC; Vandam Theater, NYC

Titanic: manuscript*; Direct Theatre, NYC; Vandam Theater, NYC

A History of the American Film (music, Mel Marvin): Samuel French, 25 W. 45th St., New York, NY 10036, $2.50; O'Neill Center's National Playwrights Conference, CT; (Simultanteously) Hartford Stage Co., CT; Arena Stage, Wash. DC; Mark Taper Forum, CA; Broadway

Sister Mary Ignatius Explains It All for You: Dramatists Play Service, $2.50; Ensemble Studio Theatre, NYC

The Marriage of Bette & Boo: manuscript*; Williamstown Second Company, MA

The Vietnamization of New Jersey: Dramatists Play Service, $2.50; Yale Repertory Company, CT

Death Comes to Us All, Mary Agnes: Dramatists Play Service, $2.50; Yale School of Drama, CT

'Dentity Crisis: Dramatists Play Service, $2.50; Yale Repertory Company, CT

Beyond Therapy: manuscript*; Phoenix Theatre, NYC

The Actors Nightmare: manuscript*; Playwrights Horizons, NYC

Baby with the Bath Water: manuscript*

When Dinah Shore Ruled the Earth (with Wendy Wasserstein): manuscript*; Yale Cabaret, New Haven, CT
*contact agent

SYNOPSES

A History of the American Film: A comedy with music, chronicles the changes in America and American movies as it follows five archetypal characters. Loretta, the innocent heroine, is born in a silent D.W. Griffith film, falls in love with tough guy Jimmy in a 30's gangster movie, wanders into a screwball comedy, goes on for the ailing star in a Busby Berkeley musical, faces World War II, loses Jimmy in Casablanca, becomes an alcoholic, wins an Oscar for overcoming polio, finds 50's alienation in Hoboken, falls apart in the 60's and 70's (racism, exorcisms, earthquakes). The play ends with Jimmy and Loretta crawling out of the disaster movie rubble, planning the future.

Full length. 7 males, 6 females.

Sister Mary Ignatius Explains It All for You: Sister Mary Ignatius is giving her yearly lecture on how the world works, where heaven and hell are, who goes to purgatory, who goes to Limbo (unbaptized babies), what mortal sin is, what exactly went on in Sodom, what her family life was like (22 brothers and sisters; from her family, 5 became priests, 7 became nuns, 3 became brothers and the rest were institutionalized). She is assisted by Thomas, a 7-year-old child from Our Lady of Perpetual Sorrow School. Mid-way her lecture is interrupted by the arrival of 4 ex-students of Sister's, now in their 30's. They put on a Christmas pageant they used to perform in her class years ago and then settle down to chat with her. How their lives have strayed from her teachings distresses Sister greatly and she finds it necessary to shoot two of them.

One act. Setting: lecture hall. 3 males, 3 females.

D

SUSAN DWORKIN

Born in New York City on May 21, 1941. B.A.,
Wellesley College, Political Science. Co-author,
The MS. Guide to a Woman's Health, Doubleday-
Anchor Berkeley. Producing Director, Bergen-
stage, Inc., Teaneck, NJ. Contributing Editor,
MS. magazine. Articles have appeard in **Moment,
Hadassah** Magazine, **Cosmopolitan Interna-
tional.** Recipient: Grant, McDowell Colony.

Address: 46 Thames Blvd., Bergenfield, NJ 07621

Agent: Flora Roberts, 65 East 55th St., New York,
  NY 10022 (212) 355-4165

TITLE • AVAILABILITY • PRODUCTIONS

Roses (one act): manuscript*; Washington Theatre Club, Wash., DC

Mama's God of Love: manuscript*; Loft Theatre, NYC

The Farm Bill (one act): manuscript*; Triangle Theatre, NYC

Galilee (one act): manuscript*; Triangle Theatre, NYC

Picking Up Pieces: manuscript*; New Jewish Theatre Workshop, NYC

The Miami Dig: manuscript*; WPA Theatre, NYC; Bergenstage, NJ

The Public Good: manuscript*; Playwrights Horizons, NYC

Deli's Fable: manuscript*; Playwrights Horizons, NYC; Stage 46, NYC

The Forgotten Lover: manuscript*
  *contact agent

SYNOPSES

The Farm Bill: A woman with a menial government job attempts a personal revolt against the
USDA, brought on by her anxiety over her personal life and the connections she sees between her
problems and those of the American "land."

One act. Setting: an office. 2 males, 2 females.

The Miami Dig: A woman, by profession a ghost writer, visits her father-in-law and meets up with
his friends, an assortment of elderly people. She attempts in his apartment to unearth the history
of her own life, the heritage of her children and learns a new respect for what she previously
thought was dust, junk and garbage.

Two acts. Setting: an apartment. 4 males, 3 females.

Deli's Fable: An aging Jewish pediatrician has been hopelessly in love for many years with a
brilliant black designer who betrays him and returns to him repeatedly. She becomes ill with a
mysterious sickness. He calls in all his doctor friends to cure her and their desperate attempts to
do so create a great crisis in the love affair. The struggle of Solomon and Delia to find the source
of their strength to survive with each other is very much like the struggle of New Yorkers to live
with their fabulous, declining city.

Two acts. 4 males, 2 females.

CHARLES EASTMAN

Born in Los Angeles, educated Los Angeles City College. Television credits: **The Hamster of Happiness; NBC Experiment in Television.** Motion picture credits: original screenplay **Little Fauss and Big Halsy** for Paramount (published by Farrar, Straus & Giroux); original screenplay **The All-American Boy** for Warner Bros. (published by Farrar, Straus & Giroux) and directed by the author; original screenplay **The Hamster of Happiness (Second Hand Hearts)** for Lorimar Productions.

Address: 113 B 27th Street, Manhattan Beach, CA 90266 (213) 376-0411

TITLE • AVAILABILITY • PRODUCTIONS

La Peregrina: manuscript*; Theatre Event, Los Angeles, CA

Victorey: manuscript*; Theatre Event, Los Angeles, CA

Root of the Iceplant: manuscript*; Unitarian Church, Los Angeles, CA

The Hamster of Happiness: manuscript*; NBC Experiment in Television

The Unamerican Cowboy: manuscript*

Oli Oli Oxen Free: manuscript*

Busy Bee Good Food All Night Delicious (one act): manuscript*; Center Stage, Baltimore, MD

Borders: manuscript*; Center Stage, Baltimore, Md

Busy Bee Good Food All Night Delicious (full length) manuscript*
　　*contact author

SYNOPSES

La Peregrina: A dark comedy in two acts, a young couple traveling in Mexico in 1952 fall into the clutches of a "helping hand" and discover themselves and each other in their escape.

One Setting. 3 males, 3 females.

Oli Oli Oxen Free: An interior pastoral occurring in the mind of three young people involved in the eternal triangle.

Full length. One setting. 2 males, 1 female.

Busy Bee Good Food All Night Delicious and **Borders:** Two one-act plays with common theme and setting, an all-night bar and grill at the beach in Southern California. One play involves three customers in which no waitress appears and the other two waitresses and a busboy who have no customers.

One setting. 3 males, 3 females.

E

GUS EDWARDS

Born in Antigua, B.W.I. on March 8, 1939, Attended schools in St. Thomas, VI. Has trained at H.B. Studio, NYC. Twice participated at the National Playwrights Conference, O'Neill Theater Center in the New Drama for TV. Currently playwright-in-residence at the Negro Ensemble Co., NY and a member of the Plays In Process panel at T.C.G. Recipient: Rockefeller Playwrights Grant, 1979.

Address: 220 East 60th St., New York, NY 10022

Agent: Susan Schulman, 165 West End Ave., New York, NY 10023 (212) 877-2216/17

TITLE • AVAILABILITY • PRODUCTIONS

The Offering: Dramatists Play Service, 440 Park Ave. South, New York, NY 10016, $2.50; Negro Ensemble Co., NYC

Black Body Blues: manuscript*; O'Neill Theater Center's National Playwrights Conference, CT; Negro Ensemble Co., NYC

Old Phantoms: Dramatists Play Service, $2.50; Negro Ensemble Co., NYC

Aftermath: not available; O'Neill Theater Center's National Playwrights Conference, CT

These Fallen Angels: manuscript*; North Carolina School of Performing Arts, Greensboro, NC

Weep No More for Me: manuscript*; Negro Ensemble Co., NYC
    *contact agent

SYNOPSES

The Offering: A young black man visits his old mentor, who's now living in depressed circumstances in New York City, in order to give him some money. The visit turns out to be an unsettling affair involving adultery and even death.

Full length. Setting: one set, apartment interior. 2 males (black), 2 females (1 white, 1 black).

Old Phantoms: A southern landowner and father dies. After the funeral his three children (two sons and a daughter) are swamped with memories both good and bad about their domineering father and his attempts to shape and influence their lives.

Full length. Setting: one set, two levels, 5 males, 3 females, all black.

MARK R. EDWARDS

Born in Wichita, KS on June 6, 1945. B.A. in Creative Writing/Music from Wichita State U. M.A. in Theater, Kansas State U. Postgraduate work at U. of Kansas and Kansas State U. Worked as a writer for seven newspapers, two radio stations, the U. of Kansas and Larned State Hospital. As a free-lance writer he has contributed articles to small industrial magazines. Member: Theta Alpha Phi; Association of Kansas Theatre; MENC; Phi Mu Alpha Sinfonia. Recipient: Mikrokosmos Prose Award; Shubert Playwriting Fellowship; Second Prize, Wichita State U. Playwriting Contest.

Address: 220 W. 8th St., Larned, KS 67550 (316) 285-3766

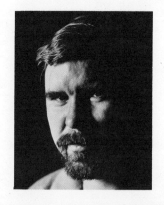

Mark R. Edwards (cont'd)

TITLE • AVAILABILITY • PRODUCTIONS

Larger Than Life: manuscript*; Kansas State U.

Saint Philemon and the Martyr Anictetus: manuscript*; Reader's Theatre, U. of KS

Wanted—Dead or Alive: Samuel French, 25 W. 45th St., New York, NY 10036, $1.25; Kansas State U.; Marymount College of Salina, KS

Hooray for Hollywood: self-published*; Kansas State U.; U. of Kansas

Children's Religious One-Acts: Contemporary Drama Services, Box 457, 1131 Warren Ave., Downers Grove, IL 60515, $9.50; Methodist Church, Larned, KS

Pawnee Fork: manuscript*; Larned Music Club, KS

Kate and the Colonel: Pig Iron Press, Inc., Youngstown, OH, $4.00; AKT Conference, KS; reading, Julian Theatre, CA

A Live Woman in the Mines: manuscript*; Pinecone Players, CO; Theatre Americana, Altadena, CA

Leonora: manuscript*
Televisionary: manuscript*
   *contact author

MARK EICHMAN

Born in Cedar Rapids, IO on October 2, 1949. Educated at California Lutheran College (B.A., 1971) and University of Arizona (M.A., 1976). He has also acted in Summer Stock and with Childrens Theatre Troupe in California and Arizona. Recipient: Western States Arts Foundation Playwriting Award, 1976.

Address: 375 Glenbrooke Road, Pontiac, MI 48054 (313) 683-2524

Agent: Audrey Wood, c/o International Creative Management, 40 West 57th St., New York, NY 10019 (212) 556-5600

TITLE • AVAILABILITY • PRODUCTIONS

Caged: not available; California Lutheran College

The Pawn: not available; University of Arizona

American Gothic: Dramatic Publishing Co., 163 Main St., Westport, CT 06880, $1.00; University of Arizona

As to the Meaning of Words: manuscript*; O'Neill Theater Center's National Playwrights Conference, CT, Hartman Repertory Co., Stamford, CT

Bugs and Other Animals: University of Arizona

Sharing: manuscript*
   *contact agent

SYNOPSES

American Gothic: On the basis of statistical information a magazine has selected America's most typical family, and sends a writer to their Iowa farmhouse to interview them. As the statistical family comes to life, the magazine writer discovers that any real personal interaction or meaning in their lives is impossible to grasp. The play is a grotesque portrait of the absurdity in assuming that America has a typical value system and way of life.

Setting: 1 interior. 3 males, 2 females.

E

Mark Eichman (cont'd)

As to the Meaning of Words: A full-length drama which examines the legal, moral, and ethical questions surrounding abortion. The "courtroom" becomes a setting for the play, and attention is focused on the difficulties faced by doctors and lawyers as they attempt to come to grips with the problem. As the action progresses, fact and emotion become inseparable, and those involved are drawn further away from the answers they seek.

Setting: unit setting. 9 males, 3 females.

Sharing: A light character portrait in which an old man's "tales of the past" form a link with his young grandson's dreams for the future, enabling them to communicate for the first time.

One act. Setting: one exterior. 1 male, 2 boys.

ROBERT H. EISELE

Born in Altadena, CA on June 9, 1948. B.A. (cum laude) and M.F.A. in Theatre Arts at U.C.L.A. He has had poetry published (**Poem Magazine**), and has written a novella and five film scripts, two of which are under option. Screenplay, **Partners,** soon to be released. He is an Equity actor and has choreographed stage combat. He is the regional editor of **West Coast Plays;** a member of S.A.G.; been in two films. He also holds a black belt in Chinese kenpo karate. He teaches acting and playwriting at Rio Hondo College in California. Recipient: Theatre Arts Corporation, National Playwriting Contest, 1979; American Conservatory Theatre Playwriting Fellowship, 1975–76; Oscar Hammerstein Playwriting Fellowship, Dramatist Guild Fund 1973–74; Donald Davis  Dramatic Writing Award, 1974; Regional Winner, American College Theatre Festival, Original Play, Pacific Southwest Circuit, 1974; Samuel Goldwyn Writing Award of Recognition, 1973.

Address: 1756 Glendon Ave., Los Angeles, CA 90024 (714) 846-3471 for messages or (213) 475-1698 (Home).

Agent: Ken Sherman & Associates, 9507 Santa Monica Blvd., Suite 212, Beverly Hills, CA 90210 (213) 273-8840

TITLE • AVAILABILITY • PRODUCTIONS

A Garden in Los Angeles: manuscript*; The Breughel Project, San Francisco, CA

Animals Are Passing from Our Lives: West Coast Plays, Vol. 3, P.O. Box 7206, Berkeley, CA 94707 $4.95; American Conservatory Theatre, CA; U.C.L.A.; American Playwrights Theatre

God's Got No Beard (one act): manuscript*; San Francisco Public Library, CA

The Cavalier (one act): manuscript*; Santa Monica College, CA

Coats: manuscript*; U.C.L.A.; American College Theatre Festival, Pacific South

Saint Salome: manuscript*

Mad Meg: manuscript*

The Missing String: manuscript*; U.C.L.A., CA

Jesus Treats (one act): manuscript*; U.C.L.A., CA

The Green Room: manuscript*; University of Colorado

A Dark Night of the Soul: manuscript*; St. Nicholas Theater Company, Chicago IL.

The Murder of Einstein: manuscript*; Alliance Theatre, Atlanta, GA; WETV, Atlanta, GA
*contact agent

E

Robert H. Eisele (cont'd)

SYNOPSES

Animals Are Passing from Our Lives: This is a vision of what we are becoming. A rural family works a dying land. A group of wanderers asks them for a safe resting ground away from the dangers of the road. But sanctuary turns into a trap for all. . . . This is a play about the dangers of losing contact, even for a moment, with the truth of our animal nature, our life force. Human beings cannot "degenerate" into animals, they can only lose sight of their instincts for love — and when they do, they lose themselves in the parade of animals, mute and speaking, that are passing from our live.

Full length (2 acts). Setting: front porch of a farmhouse and the yard, 3 males, 1 boy, 4 females.

A Dark Night of the Soul: It is the night before Jack's ordination day — only, he's suddenly lost all his religious belief. This is a tragic-comic look at how a family tries to force one of its members to follow the myth that's been created for him.

Full length. Setting: livingroom and backyard, sacristy of church. 6 males, 1 boy (no lines), 4 females.

The Greenroom: A group of actors prepare for a performance in a regional theatre. A bit player seems to have a strange power over his fellow actors, until one dares confront him with a deadly secret. The two are pitted against each other in a psychological battle that drives one of them to the brink of insanity.

Full length. Setting: the greenroom of a regional theater. 5 males, 3 females.

SAM A. EISENSTEIN

Born May 18, 1932, Bakersfield, CA. B.A., M.A., Ph.D. in Comparative Literature, U.C.L.A. Creative Writing professor at Los Angeles City College. Short stories in various magazines, including "Post Coitus Tristus," **Penthouse,** January 1970. Drama Reviewer for **L.A. Free Press, Coast Magazine, The Staff, Open City.** Book, **Boarding the Ship of Death,** Netherlands, Mouton and Co, 1974. Recipient: Fulbright grant to Japan, 1965; Office for Drama Research grant, 1971; Rockefeller grant, 1975.

Address: Los Angeles City College, Dept of
    English, Los Angeles, CA 90029 (213) 681-6819

TITLE • AVAILABILITY • PRODUCTIONS

A Masse for the Plagued: manuscript*; The Company Theatre, Los Angeles, in repertory, 1971

To Take Up Eternity Like a Mantle: Orion Magazine, vol. 17, March 1972*

The Portable Hoover: The Staff, March 10, 1972*

The Wall: The Staff, Sept. 17, Pacifica Station KPFK-FM, 1971

Trinidad: manuscript*

It Won't Be Long: Dramatika Magazine, spring 1974

Re: The Rosenbergs: Dramatika Magazine, winter 1974

Father and Son: manuscript*; KPFK; La Mama Hollywood, CA

The Lost Jill: manuscript*; Mark Taper Forum Lab; Pilgrimage Theater, Los Angeles, CA

The Adolf Hitler Show (with Ron Sossi): manuscript*; Odyssey Theatre, in repertory, CA

Thirty Years After: manuscript*; Reading, California Theatre Ensemble, Pasadena, CA
    *contact author

E

Sam A. Eisenstein (cont'd)
SYNOPSES

The Lost Jill: The lost Jill is Angela Brainard, who would be 26 on this anniversary of her birth if she were still alive, but who was kidnapped or lost on VE Day, 1945. The dates don't gibe. The family consists of Doris, a practical nurse, who spends the play in bed; Toby, the eldest son, 36, who is awaiting the birth of his child with Carol, 20, his wife; Peter, his brother, who is consumed with jealousy over Carol; two other sisters, Gina and Wendy, who are part-time hookers to support their families; Joseph, Gina's husband, an alchemist; and Jack Simmons, the newspaper man who arrives to bring order and "honesty" to the family, which does not want to know the "truth." There are dream games and many shifts of allegiance and an ambiguous ending in which the new child is given up for adoption to what may be the actual Lost Jill herself.

Full length. Setting: one-room apartment in Glendale, California. 4 males, 5 or 6 females.

Father and Son: Father, about 65, white, and son, about 40, obese and black, sit in their kitchen and abuse each other over the loss of their, respectively, wife and mother. The father jeers his son's lack of experience in the world. The son sarcastically demonstrates his father's impotence to change anything. The father lies enthusiastically about his wife's whoring and goddess status in Africa. When the father finally encourages his son to go forth, get out, the son loses faith and confidence and remains. They get ready for the coming of the mother. But it is just another day, and nothing happens at the end, except more waiting.

One act (fine curtain raiser for **The Lost Jill**). Setting: kitchen. 2 males.

A Masse for the Plagued: A troupe of actors takes shelter in a barn during the period of the Black Death in England. Their internal relationships are very complicated. They act out their parts, which they also accept in their "real" life. Townspeople come with their wares and their woes. The Plague also comes and the barn is sealed by the authorities. Solomon Eagle and his shadow, The Clown, appear, prophets of doom and resurrection, if the price is paid. Eagle is eternal, and seeks his death, but must pass on his mantle. Much madness erupts in the closed barn. The play includes music, songs, libretto.

Full length. Setting: barn. 12 males, 7 females.

MARK EISMAN

Born in Boston, MA on April 14, 1948. Educated at Duke University, Northwestern University (B.S. in Speech, 1970). TV writer (**The Great Space Coaster** series); writer-researcher for **Jeopardy!** Recipient: Emmy Award nomination, 1974; CAPS Playwriting Fellowship, 1979–80.

Address: 66 West 85th St., New York, NY 10024 (212) 873-0818

Agent: Susan Schulman, 165 West End Avenue, New York, NY 10023 (212) 877-2216

TITLE • AVAILABILITY • PRODUCTIONS

Fix!: manuscript*; O'Neill Theater Center's National Playwrights Conference, CT

Boardwalk (With 2 Houses): manuscript*; Players Repertory Theatre, Miami, FL

Sightlines: Kenyon Review, Winter 1980, Gambier, OH, $4.00; O'Neill Center's National Playwrights Conference, CT; Magic Theatre, San Francisco, CA

Payoffs: manuscript*; Cast Theatre, Los Angeles, CA

Orbits: manuscript*

Town Crier: manuscript*
  *contact author

Mark Eisman (cont'd)

SYNOPSES

Sightlines: If you knew you were going blind, which visual images would you "pack" to take with you? Ruth Thorner must make this painful journey into darkness. She is aided by Davis Pape, a man about to regain his vision after twelve years of sightlessness. Davis shares his insights into the worlds of vision and darkness, derived from his favorite book, Alice in Wonderland.

Full length: Setting: a waiting room. 1 male, 1 female.

Orbits: Frank Kazis, a professor of astronomy, can only imagine the initial encounter between his 19 year old bride and his 21 year old son. The two most important people in his life meet as the anesthesized scientist faces delicate surgery and ponders the most eagerly awaited astronomical event of the century.

Full length. 3 males, 2 females.

JAMES ELWARD

A.B. degree (Speech & Drama), Catholic University. Two years U.S. Army. Has written for TV (major hour shows as well as **The Secret Storm, The Doctors, The Guiding Light,** etc.). Under the pseudonym "R. James," wrote three mystery novels (**Storm's End, The House is Dark,** and **Tomorrow Is Mine,** Doubleday). Wrote libretto for the opera **The Man on the Bearskin Rug** (Boosey & Hawkes). Has acted every summer since 1955 at the Barnstormers Theater, Tamworth, New Hampshire. Has written lyrics for four musicals that have been produced there. Co-winner of Writer's Guild Award for Best Comedy Script. Member of the Actor's Studio Playwright's Unit.

Address: 14 Bank St., New York, NY 10014 (212) 255-4716

Agent: Joan Stewart, William Morris, 1350 Avenue of the Americas, New York, NY 10019 (212) 586-5100

TITLE • AVAILABILITY • PRODUCTIONS

Best Friends: Dramatists Play Service, Inc., 440 Park Ave. South, New York, NY 10016, $2.50; London; Vienna; numerous productions

Friday Night (collection of three one-act plays): Dramatists Play Service, $2.50; Pocket Theater, Off Broadway; colleges, community theaters, etc.

Hallelujah!: manuscript*; Lamb's Club; Central Presbyterian Arts Theater; The Barnstormers, Tamworth, NH

A Perfect Stranger: manuscript*

Subject to Change: manuscript**;

Finale: manuscript*
    *contact author
    **contact agent

E

JOEL ENSANA

Born in New Brunswick, NJ on February 25, 1935. B.A., San Francisco State College, Creative Writing; Graduate work in Drama. Resident Playwright, San Francisco One-Act Theater. Recipient: Shubert Fellowship; San Francisco State College, First Prize; Arts Council of Philadelphia Award; Norman Corwin Playwriting Contests; National Broadcasting Media Award, 1976.

Address: 102 Gold Mine Drive, San Francisco, CA 94131 (415) 647-4411

TITLE • AVAILABILITY • PRODUCTIONS

Please, No Flowers: The Best Short Plays of 1969, Chilton Press, Chilton Way, Radnor, PA 19089; Des Moines Drama Workshop, IA; American Conservatory Theatre, CA

The Date: Pyramid Magazine*; San Francisco State College, CA (stage & TV); Hungary

The Coronation: manuscript*; Mills College, CA; Berkeley One-Act, CA

Flotsam: manuscript*; San Francisco Playwrights Guild, CA

Mr. & Mrs. Lyle Conger: manuscript*; Black Repertory Theater

Party of One: Pyramid Magazine*

Ready for Teddy: manuscript*; KQED, CA; Quaigh Theater, NYC

Grand Exit: manuscript*; San Francisco One-Act Theater, CA

Castro St.: manuscript*; San Francisco Stock Company, CA

Halloween 2050 A.D.: manuscript*; Foolkiller's Theater, Kansas City, MO

Winchester House: manuscript*; Bare Stage Theater, Berkeley, CA

The Departure: manuscript*; KQED, CA

That Guggenheim Summer: manuscript*; Bare Stage Theater, Berkeley, CA

Dream Lover: manuscript*; Group Repertory Theater, Hollywood, CA
   *contact author

SYNOPSES

Please, No Flowers: A comic tragedy expressing the affirmation of life taking place in a funeral parlor.

One act (40 minutes). 3 males, 5 females.

Ready for Teddy: An erratic female meets Senator Kennedy on the Boston subway as he is escaping anti-busing mobs and she gets to express herself politically and otherwise.

One act (40 minutes). 1 male, 1 female.

That Guggenheim Summer: The last summer of American poet Hart Crane and his battle with his bisexuality while on a Guggenheim Grant in Mexico.

Full length. Setting: huge studio room in Mexico. 3 males, 3 females.

KEN EULO

Born in Newark, NJ on November 17, 1939. Educated at the University of Heidelberg. When not writing for the theater, Ken works on his poetry. Writing affiliations: Actors Studio Playwrighting Workshop, The O'Neill Playwrights, The Dramatists Guild, and the newly formed Italian Playwrights of America — The Forum. Recipient: Howard P. Foster Memorial Fund grant, 1972; Arken Industries and J & L Tanner Fellowship Award, 1973–74.

Address: 140 West 79th St., New York, NY 10024

Agent: Monica McCall, International Creative Management, 40 West 57th St., New York, NY 10019 (212) 556-5600

TITLE • AVAILABILITY • PRODUCTIONS

Final Exams: manuscript*; Courtyard Playhouse, NYC

Say Hello to Daddy: manuscript*; Pheasant Run Playhouse, Chicago, IL

Black Jesus: manuscript*; Lincoln Center, NYC

Puritan Night: manuscript*; Hartford Stage Company, CT; Lambs Club, NYC

Rise and Fall of Cris Cowlin: manuscript*

S.R.O.: manuscript*; O'Neill Theater Center's National Playwrights Conference, CT; Theatre Rapport, Los Angeles; Channel 31, New York

48 Spring Street (one act); Vol. I, **Off-Off Broadway Theatre Collection,** Galaxie Publishers, 426 W. 45 St., New York, NY 10036 (out of print)*; Theatre-in-the-Round; Ocean County College

The Elevator (one act): manuscript*; The Gate Theatre, NYC

Bang?: Janus: Media Publications, Inc., 314 Bayview Ave., Seaside Park, NJ 08752, $2.00; Plowright Playhouse; Boston College; University of Nebraska

Stationary Wave: manuscript*

The Frankenstein Affair: manuscript*; Courtyard Playhouse, NYC
  *contact author

SYNOPSES

Final Exams: Comedy-drama. Psychological murder mystery exploring the homosexual relationship of two young boys of twenty in college.

Full length. One set. 2 males.

The Frankenstein Affair: The story deals with the psychological happenings within Mary Shelley's mind. As it unfolds, the audience watches her live out her life while writing her famous novel, **Frankenstein.** Soon she gets caught up in her own story and begins to interact with the monster. She becomes possessed to finish her work. In rapid succession her life with Percy Shelley soon becomes overwhelmed with poverty, scandal, illness and death.

Full length. Setting: one set. 7 males, 2 females.

The Rise and Fall of Cris Cowlin: Comedy/drama that is an anti-war play. Six soldiers (misfits) are the army's new secret weapon. They are ordered to destroy a town in Vietnam in order to save it.

Full length. Setting: one unit set. 13 males, 2 females.

E

ALBERT EVANS

From the very beginning marched to the tune of a different drummer. Studied playwriting as an extension course at CCNY while writing paperback novels and freelance articles. Studied all aspects of drama at the Institute for Advanced Theatre Arts under the tutelage of some of the great European names while writing feelance advertising and fund-raising material. Original screenplay, with Marc Lipitz, **A Way of Life.** Has completed one novel, **The Almighty Eye** and working on **The Fractured Man.** Recipient: New York State Council on the Arts Grant; The Lab Theatre Grant: Work-in-progress Grant, Labor Theatre.

Address: 3800 Independence Ave., Bronx, NY 10463 (212) 884-5365

Agent: Elly Burke, Independent Artists, 200 W. 108th St., New York, NY 10025 (212) 222-8778

TITLE • AVAILABILITY • PRODUCTIONS

The Big Gate: manuscript*; Sheridan Square Playhouse, NYC; IASTA Playhouse, NYC

The Medal of Honor Winner: manuscript*; Peace Theater, Queens College, NY; Village Gate Cafe, NYC

Ghost Town: manuscript*; Peace Theatre, Riverdale, NY; Visual Arts Center, Greenwich Village, NYC

I Never Saw Another Butterfly: manuscript*; Performed as part of the religious service at Reformed Temple of Israel in Brooklyn, NY; Presented as part of fund raising drive of B'nai B'rith

Self Desctruct: manuscript*; Lab Theatre; Bronx Experimental Theatre, NY

Summer Camp: manuscript*; Riverdale Showcase NY; Lab Theatre and Bronx Experimental Theatre, NY

The Visitation: manuscript*; Riverdale Showcase; part of religious service at Broadway Methodist Temple and First Methodist Church of Mt. Vernon, NY; toured Community Centers

The Reconciliation: manuscript*; Playstreet Players

The American Iceberg: manuscript*; Several branches, NY Public Libraries; Riverdale Showcase, NY

Feedback: manuscript*; LAB Theatre; Labor Theatre
*contact author

SYNOPSES

The Reconciliation: The ancient battle of the sexists (sic) fought on new grounds. Super-male chauvinist Sam Winters is determined to make Nancy Coleman — his former secretary and his present boss at Wembly Sportswear, manufacturer of women's clothes — his mistress on his terms. Ms. Coleman is determined to marry him on *her* terms, with a new liberated-woman marriage contract.

Highly stylized, work uses rhyme, mime, shadow play, a new but inexpensive device termed "thought projection," as well as body movement close to dance. All of this has been carried out in workshop with comparative ease.

Full length. Setting: executive office. 4 males, 4 females.

The American Iceberg: In three separate but related one act plays the problems of aging in youth conscious America is examined from the viewpoints of an elderly woman in a nursing home, her children, her grandchildren and the people paid to take care of her. The play ends on an upbeat, life affirming note.

Three one acts. Setting: a living room and a nursing home visiting room. 3 males, 3 females.

Albert Evans (cont'd)

Feedback: The play poses the question of how many horrible deaths by contamination are acceptable from a power source that can feed the entire world. The greater the need for food due to a spreading world-wide draught, the more they turn up the power, the greater the number of deaths. Finally, which is worse: ancient death by starvation or modern death by Omega rays?

Full length. Setting: a small diner. 5 males, 4 females.

DON EVANS

B.S., Cheyney State; M.A., M.F.A., Temple University; Associate Professor of Black Studies at Trenton State College. He has written a variety of essays and articles in **Black World, Reporter, Essence** and **Players,** etc. Recipient: Outstanding Playwright of 1974, Arena Theatre.

Address: 32 Oak Lane, Trenton, NJ 08618 (609) 394-3705

Agent: Lucy Kroll, 390 West End Avenue, New York, NY 10024 (212) TR7-0627

TITLE • AVAILABILITY • PRODUCTIONS

Sugarmouth Sam Don't Dance No More: Best Short Plays of 1978, Chilton Press, Chilton Way, Radnor, PA 19089; H.B. Playhouse; ANTA Matinee Series, NYC

Matters of Choice: manuscript*; H.B. Playhouse; Players Co. of Trenton, NJ

It's Showdown Time: Dramatists Play Service, 440 Park Ave., So., New York, NY 10016, $2.50; New Federal Theatre; national tour

The Prodigals: Dramatists Play Service, $2.50

Mahalia: manuscript*; Henry Street Playhouse, NYC

Satchmo: manuscript*; McGlone-Bolden Assoc.
      *contact agent or author

SYNOPSIS

Matters of Choice: A middle-class black family returns home to find their house burglarized. Indignant that they are the victim, they set about a series of absurd moves to recover their losses. Uncertainty leads them to disrupt their household and accuse their friends.

Full length. Setting: single setting — two rooms in house. 4 black females, 3 black males, 1 white male.

E

TOM EYEN

Born in Cambridge, OH. Educated at Ohio State
State University, B.A. in English; American
Academy of Dramatic Arts. Taught drama for
Metropolitan Television Arts. Founder, Theatre
of the Eye, New York. Has directed and worked
as a publicity agent. Recipient: Rockefeller
Grant, 1967; Guggenheim Fellowship, 1970.

Address: 41 Fifth Ave., Penthouse B, New York,
NY 10003

TITLE • AVAILABILITY • PRODUCTIONS

Sarah B. Divine!: Sarah B. Divine! and Other Plays, c/o Drama Book Specialists, 150 West
52nd St., New York, NY 10019, $2.95, paperback; Spoleto, Italy; London

My Next Husband Will Be a Beauty: Sarah B. Divine! and Other Plays, New York

Why Hanna's Skirt Won't Stay Down: Sarah B. Divine! and Other Plays, New York; London

The Kama Sutra (An Organic Happening): Sarah B. Divine! and Other Plays, New York

Grand Tenement/November 22nd: Sarah B. Divine! and Other Plays, New York

Who Killed My Bald Sister Sophie?: Sarah B. Divine! and Other Plays, New York

**Aretha in the Ice Palace, or, The Fully Guaranteed Fuck-Me Doll: Sarah B. Divine! and Other
Plays,** New York; London

What Is Making Gilda So Gray?: Sarah B. Divine! and Other Plays, New York

The White Whore and the Bit Player: Sarah B. Divine! and Other Plays, New York; London

The Dirtiest Show in Town: manuscript*; London; New York

Women behind Bars: Samuel French, 25 W. 45th St., New York, NY 10036, $2.50; New York;
Washington

Frustrata, The Dirty Little Girl with the Paper Rose Stuck in Her Head Is Demented:
manuscript*; New York

Court: manuscript*; New York

Can You See a Prince?: manuscript*; New York

The Last Great Cocktail Party: manuscript*; New York

The Demented World of Tom Eyen: manuscript*; New York

Cinderella Revisited: manuscript*; New York

Miss Nefertiti Regrets: manuscript*; New York

Give My Regards to Off Off Broadway: manuscript*; New York

When Johnny Comes Dancing Home Again: manuscript*; New York

Alice Through a Glass Lightly: manuscript*; New York

Caution: A Love Story: manuscript*; New York

4 Noh Plays: manuscript*; New York

Lana Got Laid in Lebanon: manuscript*; New York

Gertrude Stein and Other Great Men: manuscript*; New York

The Neon Woman: manuscript*; Off-Broadway, NYC
        *contact author

LEE FALK

Born in St. Louis, MO. B.A., University of Illinois. He has produced over three-hundred plays and directed over one hundred. He managed the Boston Summer Theatre, Cambridge Summer Theatre, Marblehead Summer Theatre, and the Country Playhouse. He created and still writes the comic strips Mandrake the Magician and The Phantom.

Address: 7 West 81 St., New York, NY 10024

Agent: Robert Freedman, Brandt & Brandt, 1501 Broadway, New York, NY 10036 (212) 840-5760

TITLE • AVAILABILITY • PRODUCTIONS

Eris: Dramatists Play Service, 440 Park Ave. S., New York, NY 10016, $2.50; American Theatre showcase. Theatre La Bruyere, Paris; La Conservatore National D'Art, Paris

Home at Six: Dramatists Play Service, $2.50; numerous Amateur Groups in U.S. & Canada

Passionate Congressman: manuscript*; Cambridge, MA; Brattle Hall, MA

The Big Story: manuscript*; Cambridge, MA; Brattle Hall; Palo Alto, CA

Happy Dollar (musical, book): manuscript*; Houston, TX; Hollywood, CA

Mandrake the Magician (musical, book): manuscript*; Lenox Art Festival, MA
   *contact author

SYNOPSES

Eris: A man waits at night on a high bridge for late strollers . . . "sacrifices" to his god . . . his lost love who was a suicide on this bridge.

One act (1 hour). Setting: bench, railing of a bridge. 3 males, 1 walk-on.

Home at Six: John usually comes home at six. This day, when he returns at four, he finds his old mother, Mums, his nine-year-old son, Tim, his twelve-year-old daughter, Marge, his gem of a maid, Maude, his loyal wife, Kit, all transformed in appalling ways. Also his old blood buddy, best friend, Bob.

It amused me to write this play (dialogue and business) completely in words of one syllable.

Setting: traditional suburban livingroom. 2 males, 3 females, 2 children.

F

JULES FEIFFER

Born in New York City on January 26, 1929. Attended the Art Student League and Pratt Institute. Cartoonist for the **Village Voice** since 1956 and syndicated since 1959. Author of eleven collections of cartoons, two novels and films **Little Murders, Carnal Knowledge** and **Popeye.** Recipient: George Polk Memorial Award in journalism; Oscar, 1961, for **Munro**; Best Foreign Play, London Drama Critics and Obie Award, 1969 (both for **Little Murders**); Outer Critics Circle Award, 1970, for **The White House Murder Case.**

Agent: Robert Lantz, 114 East 55th Street, New York, NY 10022 (212) 751-2107

TITLE • AVAILABILITY • PRODUCTIONS

The Explainers: not available; Second City, Chicago, IL

Crawling Arnold: Dramatists Play Service, 440 Park Avenue South, New York, NY 10016, $1.25; Poets' Theater, Cambridge, MA

The World of Jules Feiffer: not available: Hunterdon Hills Playhouse, NJ

Feiffer's People: Dramatists Play Service, $2.50; Edinburgh; London

Passionella (part of **The Apple Tree**): Random House, out of print* Broadway

†**Little Murders:** Random House, 201 E. 50th St., New York, NY 10022; Off-Broadway; Broadway

The Unexpurgated Memoirs of Bernard Mergendeiler (in **Collision Course**): Random House, $1.65; Los Angeles, CA; NYC

God Bless: manuscript*; Yale Drama School, CT; Royal Shakespeare Company, London

The White House Murder Case: Grove Press, 196 W. Houston St., New York, NY 10014; Circle in the Square, NYC

Dick and Jane (in **O Calcutta**): Grove Press; Off-Broadway

Knock Knock: Samuel French, $2.50; Circle Repertory, NYC; Broadway

Hold Me!: Dramatists Play Service, $2.50; American Place Theatre, NYC

Grownups: manuscript*; American Repertory Theater, Cambridge, MA; optioned for Broadway
*contact agent
†Lincoln Center, Theatre on Film & Tape

ERNEST FERLITA

Born in Tampa, FL on December 1, 1927. B.S., Spring Hill College, AL; S.T.L., St. Louis University; D.F.A., Yale School of Drama. Books: **The Theatre of Pilgrimage** (Sheed & Ward); **Film Odyssey,** with John R. May (Paulist Press); **The Way of the River** (Paulist Press); **The Parables of Lina Wertmuller,** with John R. May (Paulist Press). Poems, **Seven Songs of Hiroshima** and **Quetzal** in **New Orleans Review.** Recipient: First Prize, Christian Theatre Artists Guild Playwriting Competition; Fulbright lectureship in American Drama, University of Parana, Brazil.

Address: Loyola University, New Orleans, LA 70118 (504) 865-3840

TITLE • AVAILABILITY • PRODUCTIONS

The Stones Cry Out: manuscript*

The Hills Send off Echoes: Baker's Plays, 100 Chauncy St., Boston, MA 02111, $1.25

New Fire: Baker's Plays, $2.00

The Ballad of John Ogilvie: manuscript*; Blackfriars Theatre, NYC

The Krewe of Dionysus: manuscript*; Santa Clara University, CA

The Mask of Hiroshima (music, Kevin Waters): manuscript*; Santa Clara University, CA

The Way of the Wolf: manuscript*; Lone Mountain College, CA

Ma-Fa (music, Robert Dwelley): manuscript*; Loyola University, LA

Black Medea: manuscript*; Spoleto Festival, USA, SC; New Federal Theatre, NYC

Purgatorio: manuscript*; Loyola University, LA

Dear Ignatius, Dear Isabel (music, Kevin Waters): manuscript*; Loyola College, Baltimore, MD

The Obelisk: manuscript*; Loyola University, New Orleans, LA
    *contact author

SYNOPSIS

Black Medea: The play is set in New Orleans in 1810, shortly after Toussaint's revolution in Haiti. Madeleine, a Haitian woman of royal African ancestry, has eloped to New Orleans with Jerome, Comte D'Argonne, a French settler's son, now dispossessed of his lands. Colonel Croydon wishes to marry his daughter to Jerome for the sake of his title. When Jerome acquiesces, Croydon insists that Madeleine leave New Orleans on the pretext that her involvement in the voodoo culture may stir up revolution among the slaves. Madeleine asks for a few days grace and then sends her two sons with the present of a bracelet. The clasp is poisoned and the bride dies. Madeleine kills her two sons to spite Jerome and flees. While the incidents parallel those of Euripides' play, **Black Medea** takes the form of a voodoo ceremony: her meetings with Croydon and Jerome take the form of acted flashback; the chorus is a group of voodoo worshippers led by Madeleine in her quest for vengeance.

Full length. Setting: four revolving triangular columns. 4 males, 5 females.

BARBARA FIELD

Born in Buffalo, NY and grew up in Atlantic City, NJ. B.A., University of Pennsylvania. M.A., University of Minnesota. Literary Manager, The Guthrie Theater since 1974. Member and co-founder, the Playwright's Lab. Has written the original libretto for a new opera, **Rosina**, premiered by the Minnesota Opera Company, 1980; Script for PBS, **From China to Us,** 1978. Two children. Recipient: Shubert Fellow in Playwriting, University of Minnesota 1970-71; Minnesota State Art Board Grant, 1973.

Address: 2719 Raleigh Avenue, Minneapolis, MN
    55416 (612) 926-9270

Agent: Lois Berman, 250 West 57th St., New
    York, NY 10019 (212) 581-0670/1

TITLE • AVAILABILITY • PRODUCTIONS

Materia Medica (Three comedies about disease, madness and death): manuscript*; Theatre of Involvement, Minneapolis; University of Minnesota; Walker Art Center, MN

The Late Show: manuscript*; Variety Hall Theatre, St. Paul, MN; University of Minnesota

F

Barbara Field (cont'd)

Playground: manuscript*; The Playwright's Lab, MN; Theatre of Involvement, MN

The Renaissance of Barnabe Barnes: manuscript*; University of Minnesota; University of Utah

She Sells Sea Shells: manuscript*; Theatre of Involvement, MN

Matrix: manuscript*; Theatre in the Round, Minneapolis, MN; Matrix Collective, Los Angeles, CA

A Christmas Carol (adaptation): manuscript*; The Guthrie Theater, MN; Actors Theatre of Louisville, KY

El Capitan: G. Shirmer, 4 East 49th St., New York, NY 10017; Minnesota Opera Co., MN; Houston Grand Opera, TX

The Magic Flute: manuscript*; Minnesota Opera Co., MN

Winds of Change: manuscript*; O'Neill Center's National Playwrights Conference, CT

Camille (adaptation): manuscript*; Guthrie Theatre, MN

Pen: manuscript*; O'Neill Center's National Playwrights Conference, CT

Sleight of Hand: not available; Playwright's Lab, MN; Harbour Front Theatre, Toronto, Canada

Coming of Age: manuscript*; Indiana Repertory Theater

Louvain/1915: manuscript*
    *contact agent

SYNOPSES

Matrix: Six women meet in a room of the palace. Three of them await the arrival of Don Giovanni. Two of them (from the Book of Esther) discuss their shared experiences with a lover-king. The sixth, an eighty-year-old eccentric crone named Alice Liddell, remembers the man who immortalized her in literature, Lewis Carroll. They may all be talking about the same man. They are all certainly coping with myths made by men about women.

Full-length comedy. Setting: a room, non-realistic. 6 females.

Coming of Age: Jake, an over-imaginative and under-motivated assistant professor of English, has come down to the seashore with his wife, Zoe, to write the scholarly paper which will earn him promotion to tenure. But both Jake and Zoe have brought "excess baggage" — in the shape of two bizarre gentlemen callers, who keep turning up to threaten, cajole, tease and taunt the couple into a recognition of home truths.

Full length. Setting: one set. 3 males, 1 female.

Louvain/1915: Set in Belgium during World War I, this play tells the story of two siblings, Annie and Theo, their parents and the disconcerting visitor who drops in to change the balance of the family.

Full length. Setting: one set. 5 males, 3 females.

JOHN FINCH

Born in Newburgh, NY on December 22, 1911. Educated at Wesleyan University, B.A., and Harvard University, M.A. Taught English and American Literature at Harvard and Dartmouth. Chairman, Department of Drama at Dartmouth, 1967-71, 1973-76. Served in U.S.N.R. in Pacific, land-based Solomon Islands and carrier-based on Yorktown, 1942-45. Director, Salzburg Seminar in American Studies, Salzburg, Austria, 1949-50. William R. Kenan Professor of Drama at Dartmouth 1968-1977. Retired in 1977 as William R. Kenan Professor of English and Drama Emeritus. Visiting Professor of Drama at Dartmouth, 1977-80.

Address: 1 Buell St., (P.O. Box 661), Hanover, NH 03755

TITLE • AVAILABILITY • PRODUCTIONS

The Wanhope Building: manuscript*; ANTA; Princess Theatre, NYC; Dartmouth, NH

The Winner: manuscript*; Hopkins Center, Dartmouth, NH

The Downstairs Dragon: manuscript*; Catholic University, Washington, DC; Yale University, CT
   *contact author

SYNOPSIS

The Downstairs Dragon: A comic fantasy for chilren and adults. Danny Jones, his father, mother, and dog, inherit the McCoy Museum, an old, dilapidated private museum, presided over by Mr. Cleats, the misanthropic curator, and Kitty, his niece, who is maintenance. The Joneses, evicted and broke, decide to live there. Despite the dust and cobwebs, it is a splendid place, except for the fact, discovered by Danny, Kitty, and the dog Rufus, that the cellar is inhabited by a dragon. Despite their efforts to slay it, sell it, explain it away, or turn it over to the government, the dragon persists. The resolution is the discovery that the only thing one can do with a downstairs dragon is to learn to live with it.

Full length. Setting: the main hall of the museum, dark, dusty, and cluttered. 12 males, 2 females, 1 dog (actor).

MIKE FIRTH

B.S., English, Iowa State University, 1965; M.F.A., Theater, Playwriting, Southern Methodist University. Editor of **Prolog**, for playwrights. Secondary teacher of English, Math, Physics, Drama. Computer programmer for National Theater File; Chairman, 1976, 1977. American Theatre Association Convention Playwrights Workshop. Recipient: Curtain Playwriting Award, 5th U.S. Army New Theatre Competition.

Address: 104 N. St. Mary, Dallas, TX 75214 (214) 827-7734

TITLE • AVAILABILITY • PRODUCTIONS

Some Live, Some Die: I.E. Clark, Box 246, Schulenberg, TX 78956, $1.00; Concordia Teachers College

The Keep: I.E. Clark, $1.50; Des Moines Comm. Theatre, IA; Ft. Hood Theatre, TX

Lady, No Lady: not available

Some Laugh, Some Cry: manuscript*

Apple A: manuscript*; Ft. Hood Theatre, TX
   *contact author

SYNOPSES

Some Live, Some Die: A few actors with a couple of chairs and a table and bits of costumes take a simple bit of philosophy and turn it into hard dogma. And anyone who suggests that the P.R. man might be Paul or that this play has any relation to the development of the Christian church, or waiting for Godot, will be pilloried.

One act. Setting: 4–6 folding chairs, table. 3 males, 1 female.

The Keep: The Keep is the greatest protection and the strongest prison. Five scenes show prisoners and guards in a future jail where the power of the mind does more to imprison or release than the walls.

Setting: a cell, represented by two benches. 2 actors minimum as tour d'force, 8 if no doubling, either sex.

F

BARBARA FISHER

Born in New York City on December 10, 1940.
B.A., Hunter College. Member, Authors Guild;
Dramatists Guild. Co-Director, Ten Penny Play-
ers since 1968. Co-Director, Waterways Project
since 1979. Co-Editor, **Waterways Project Maga-
zine.** Author/illustrator of fifteen children's
books for Ten Penny Players and NYC Board of
Education. Does performance readings of poet-
ry. Recipient: New York State Council on the
Arts; Rockefeller Brothers Fund; IBM Grant and
William C. Whitney Fund (for A Museum Project);
National Endowment for the Arts; J.M. Kaplan
Fund, CCLM (for **Waterways Project Magazine**).

Address: 799 Greenwich Street, New York, NY
10014

Agent: Philip Spitzer, 111-25 76th Avenue, Forest
Hills, NY 11375 (212) 263-7592

TITLE • AVAILABILITY • PRODUCTIONS

Noisy City Sam: manuscript*; New York City Parks

A Museum Project: manuscript*; Brooklyn Museum, NY

Mother Mandelbaum: Queen of the Fences: manuscript*

Jud: A Play for Two Voices: Ten Penny Players, NY

Jud & Honoria: manuscript*; Ten Penny Players, NY

Jud & the Oil Slick: manuscript*; Ten Penny Players, NY

Max St. Peter McBride: manuscript*
    *contact author

Please note that all the above are for children's audiences, to be performed by adults or puppets. The **Jud** series is fully illustrated; they are puppet plays. **Jud** is a penguin.

ROLF FJELDE

Born in New York City. Educated at Yale University, B.A. (Yale Drama School); Columbia University, M.A. Translator, Ibsen, **Peer Gynt; Four Major Plays,** Vols. I and II; **Complete Major Prose
Plays.** Original plays and Ibsen translations produced in England, Norway, Canada, and throughout the U.S. "Mr. Fjelde may well provide the
outstanding English-language Ibsen of this century." — Eric Bentley. Poetry and criticism in
various publications. TV, radio, and extensive
college and university lecture appearances in
Europe and America. Teaches dramatic literature at Pratt Institute and Juilliard. Recipient:
Yaddo fellowships in creative writing; American
Scandinavian Foundation fellowship; Ford Foundation fellowship in translation; Mellon Foundation grant in film studies.

Address: 261 Chatterton Pkwy., White Plains, NY
10606

Agent: Samuel French, 25 W. 45th St., New York,
NY 10036 (212) 582-4700

Rolf Fjelde (cont'd)

TITLE • AVAILABILITY • PRODUCTIONS

Switzerland (one act): manuscript*; O'Neill Theater Center's National Playwrights Conference, CT; Pratt Institute Playshop, NYC

The Rope Walk: manuscript*; O'Neill Theater Center's National Playwrights Conference, CT

Rafferty One by One: manuscript*; O'Neill Theater Center's National Playwrights Conference, CT; University of Missouri Theater
   *contact author

SYNOPSES

Switzerland: A seedy outsider obsessed with the tentacles of Swiss finance encounters a stolid horseplayer at the Automat. The initial zany comedy of their dialogue modulates into a poignant conclusion as the flaw they share — a presumption to knowledge beyond their capacities — first figuratively, then literally, poisons what they have in common.

One act. Setting: cafeteria table plus chairs. 2 males.

Rafferty One by One: Lorn Rafferty, on turning thirty, discovers that his eccentric life as a loner shows signs of psychological crisis: a minotaur has taken up residence in his closet. The maze Rafferty is in is then revealed in a vivid series of scenes with an Ivy League jogger, a gay fabric designer, a cigarette-ad cowboy, a militant feminist, a radio-controlled black psychiatrist, and a girl who would help him if her media ambitions would permit. One by one, the limitations, both of his own characer and the metropolitan environment, close in, until in frustration Rafferty enters a conspiracy with a whimsically mad bomber and is judged in an Alice-in-Wonderland trial. "Playwright Rolf Fjelde is obviously talented: many of his lines are witty, and his saga of a neurotic's struggle to liberate himself has strong satiric overtones." — **Show Business.**

Full length. Settings: six, to be realized in surreal, comedy-fantasy style. 4 males, 2 females, 1 boy aged 10.

LANNY FLAHERTY

Born in Pontotoc County, MS on July 27, 1942. After several years of construction work and informal travel and then service in the Military Police Corps of the Army in Germany, he received his B.F.A. from the University of Southern Mississippi and his M.F.A. from Southern Methodist University, Dallas, TX. He is a professional actor.

Address: 2130 Broadway, #1212, New York, NY 10023

Agent: Audrey Wood, I.C.M., 40 West 57th St., New York, NY 10019 (212) 556-5720

TITLE • AVAILABILITY • PRODUCTIONS

Showdown at the Adobe Motel: manuscript*; O'Neill Theater Center's National Playwrights Conference, CT; Hartman Theatre Co., Stamford, CT

A-Birthing at Nubbin Ridge: manuscript*

Whilom: manuscript*

Crisscrosscreeks: manuscript*

Cedars Mark the Campground: manuscript*
   *contact agent

Lanny Flaherty (cont'd)

SYNOPSES

Showdown at the Adobe Motel: Clyde Lee, an old man, is the last remaining resident of a dilapidated motel. A young woman, Mae June, attends to the old man's needs and listens to him tell of days when he and his buddy, Lank, worked in the early cowboy movies. Lank, who is now a revered television personage, visits his old buddy. They relive old times. Earnest competition between the two old men cemented their friendship in youth and now a memory forgotten precipitates their final showdown.

Full length. Setting: one set. 2 males, 1 female.

A Birthing at Nubbin Ridge: A southern family strewn asunder comes together after the close of the fighting of the War between the States. The men, war-torn and in pieces, struggle homeward to the women, who dispossessed and near starvation, endure and hold fast until their return. The play ends with the first planting in the coming spring.

Full length. Setting: either several realistic sets or one non-realistic set. 7 males, 6 females.

Whilom: A quartet of one acts all situated in the same southern locale, three in frontier days and one in the present. Can be played as separate plays or together as a full evening. Titles are: **Torrent, Contremps, Eider Down,** and **Consanguine.**

Setting: each play requires 2 sets, a turntable is recommended. Number of cast is variable, depending on doubling.

DON FLYNN

Born in St. Louis, MO on November 18, 1928. Graduate of University of Missouri. Working newspaperman from the **St. Joseph** (MO) **Gazette** to the **Kansas City Star, Chicago Daily News,** the late **New York Herald-Tribune,** now the **New York Daily News.**

Address: 303 Lantana Ave., Englewood, NJ 07631 (201) 568-9010

Agent: Harold Freedman, Brandt & Brandt, 1501 Broadway, New York, NY 10036 (212) 840-5760

TITLE • AVAILABILITY • PRODUCTIONS

Now It Makes Sense: manuscript*; Gateway Playhouse, Bellport, L.I., NY

The Black Sheep: not available; Off Off Broadway; The Actor's Place, NYC

The Petition (one act): manuscript*; O'Neill Theater Center's National Playwrights Conference, CT; Manhattan Theatre Club, NYC

A Money-Back Guarantee: manuscript*; Off Off Broadway: American Theatre Co.

The Man Who Raped Kansas: manuscript*; The Gilford Playhouse, Gilford, NH

Something That Matters: manuscript*; Off Off Broadway: American Theatre Co. NYC

The Pilgrims Landed Just down the Road: manuscript*; Quaigh Theater, NYC

A Meaningful Relationship: manuscript*; Shandol Theater, NYC

Around the Corner from the White House: manuscript*;

Pull the Covers over My Head: manuscript*; The Actor's Place, NYC
    *contact author or agent

F

SYNOPSES

A Meaningful Relationship: A play about that inevitable moment between a young couple who are living together when one says, "Isn't it about time we got married?". Cathleen thinks it's time she and Robbie got married. After all, her parents, Tom and Maureen, won't even come to visit if they're only living together.

Full length. Setting: an apartment. 3 males, 2 females.

Around the Corner from the White House: Reporter Mike O'Grady would gladly ignore the nut with the gun who took a wild shot at the Vice-Presidential candidate whose campaign he is covering — if the rest of the media would, too. But nobody dares ignore The Lady in Red, her lurid tale about her and the Veep might cost him and the President the election.

Full length. Setting: hotel room. 6 males, 4 females.

The Pilgrims Landed Just down the Road: Colin Blaine sneaks off from New York to Cape Cod to do his income tax and meet sexy neighbor, Sheila Schaeffer. When his college student daughter seeks him out for help because she is pregnant, everybody has more explaining to do than they can handle. Colin's wife, Sheila's husband and the daughter's boy friend also show up, much to the confusion of the motel owner.

Full length. Setting: a Cape Cod motel. 4 males, 3 females.

THOMAS M. FONTANA

Born in Buffalo, NY on September 12, 1951. B.A. in Theatre, State University College at Buffalo. He has written three screenplays and one TV movie. Playwright-in-residence, The Writers Theatre, NYC, 1975–; Williamstown Theatre Festival, 1978–80.

Address: 484 West 43rd St., #5N, New York, NY 10036 (212) 564-7885 or (212) 581-5295

Agent: Mary Harden, c/o Bret Adams, Ltd., 36 East 61st St., New York, NY 10021 (212) 752-7865

TITLE • AVAILABILITY • PRODUCTIONS

Old Fashioned: manuscript*; Chelsea Theater Center, NYC; Linwood Summer Theatre

Movin' Mountains: manuscript*; McCarter Theater Company, NJ; The Writers Theatre, NYC

The Overcoat (or **Clothes Make the Man**), (adaptation) manuscript*; Williamstown Theatre Festival, MA

The Underlings: manuscript*; Cincinnati Playhouse in the Park, OH; The Writers Theatre, NYC

An Awfully Big Adventure (an entertainment): manuscript*; The Writers Theatre, NYC

This Is on Me: Dorothy Parker (adaptation): manuscript*; Williamstown Theatre Festival, MA; Society Hill Playhouse, Philadelphia, PA

Johnny Appleseed (a Noh play): manuscript*; Studio Arena Theatre, NY
*contact agent

SYNOPSES

Old Fashioned: An innocent comedy set in the closing days of World War I in which two young privates try to overcome incredible odds to kiss the women they love before being shipped across the Atlantic.

Full length, includes period music. Setting: four sets. 10 males, 8 females.

Thomas M. Fontana (cont'd)

Movin' Mountains: Each member of an Italian-American family is forced to re-examine his or her beliefs when a tragedy strikes, culminating in the father taking an extreme action to prove his own faith.

Full length. Setting: unit set. 2 males, 2 females.

The Overcoat (or Clothes Make the Man): Adapted from the short story by Nikolai Gogol, a lonely clerk finds a reason for living when he decides to have a brand new overcoat made especially for himself.

Full length. Setting: unit set. Ensemble, much doubling, roughly 8 males, 4 females.

FRANK B. FORD

M.A., University of Connecticut, 1960. From 1962–64 he was a supervisor at the Turkish Air Force Language School, Izmir. Has published fiction and poetry in **Nugget; Fine Arts Magazine; The Delaware Literary Review.** The impetus of trying to write for the theatre comes from the pressure of having to script puppet shows for his family's traveling productions. Fellow, Virginia Center of the Creative Arts, Summer, 1980. Is Associate Professor of English at West Chester State College. Recipient: Grant from Office of Advanced Drama Research for play, **Waterman,** Guthrie 2.

Address: Dept. of English, West Chester State College, West Chester, PA 19380 (215) 436-2671

TITLE • AVAILABILITY • PRODUCTIONS

Waterman: Guthrie New Theater, Vol. 1, Grove Press, 196 W. Houston St., New York, NY 10014, $4.96; Guthrie 2, MN; New York Stageworks

Texas: manuscript*; New York Stageworks

Hamburger: manuscript*

Tetzel: manuscript*

Indignities: manuscript*; Earplay

Hoja!: manuscript*
  *contact author

SYNOPSES

Waterman: Each man tries only to grip his own life in the murderously surreal atmosphere of the Korean War. The outfit, The Third Shower Point, is behind the lines, thus ostensibly out of danger. Master Sergeant Waterman, a mercurially unhinging old trooper, confers with an alcoholic, Jesus Christ, his wife, and a Chinese major, to affirm his horrific belief that the unit is behind *enemy* lines. His vision prevails.

Setting: inside tent; company area. 8 males, 1 female.

Texas: In an atmosphere raw, hot, megalomaniacal, a mystical cowboy architect erects his own "Church of All" in the wilderness. Several cases of Lone Star beer slow and fuel the work, as does the intrusion of a Boston career girl. The architect tries to explain his work to the world but usually has to settle for the Marine, a sexy All American boy made cretinous by Vietnam. The architect invents a religion to fit his temple. A Texas millionaire must decide to support him and thus watch him burn out, or to stop him cold, make him act like other cowboys.

Full length. Setting: interior of Christmas Cafe; interior of ranch house; desert. 9 males, 1 female.

F

Hoja!: The wise old fool of Turkish folklore, an archetypal trickster, a quintessential survivor, up against the irrational and bloodthirsty Tamerlane, a gluttonous and vindictive mother-in-law, a sexually insatiable and completely mercenary wife.

Full length. Setting: classroom, Tamerlane's camp, interior of Hoja's house, courtyard, graveyard, 11 males, 4 females, optional dancers, musicians, dervishes.
Note: the play incorporates both shadow and hand puppetry.

JOE TAYLOR FORD

Born in Bowling Green, KY on December 23, 1940. B.A., M.B.A., The University of Chicago. Writer-in-Residence at Lyndon State College, VT. Recipient: John T. Kelley Memorial Playwriting Award, 1975.

Address: Butternut Farm, East Ryegate, VT 05042 (802) 592-3378

Agent: Susan Schulman, 165 West End Avenue, New York, NY 10023 (212) 877-2216

TITLE • AVAILABILITY • PRODUCTIONS

These Ruins Are Inhabited: manuscript*; Theatre East, Los Angeles, CA; American College Theatre Festival, University of New Hampshire

Hedda Gabler (adaptation): manuscript*; Studio Theatre, Bradford, Vt

The Last Minstrel Show: manuscript*; Locust Theatre, Philadelphia, PA; Charles Playhouse, Boston, MA

The Wives of Utah: manuscript*; Lyndon State College, VT

Marry Me: manuscript*

Club Cotton (musical): manuscript*

The Night James Boswell, Esquire, Wrote the Autobiography of Dr. Samuel Johnson:
manuscript*
*contact agent

SYNOPSES

These Ruins Are Inhabited: A comedy on a day in the life of senior citizens at the Greener Pastures Home For the Aged.
Full length. Setting: one interior set. 7 males, 6 females.

Marry Me: A comedy about a recently-divorced couple as they attempt to rebuild their lives apart after 15 years of marriage.
Full length. Setting: three interior sets. 4 males, 4 females.

The Wives of Utah: A play, in the form of **Under Milkwood,** about nineteenth century women who lived under Mormon polygamy.
Full length. Setting: one open set. 13 females.

F

RICHARD FOREMAN

Born in New York City on June 10, 1937. B.A.
from Brown U., RI and M.F.A. from Yale Drama
School. Founder-Director of the Ontological-
Hysteric Theater in NYC. Director of **Three Penny Opera** at the NY Shakespeare Festival at Lincoln Center; Director-screenwriter of feature
film, **Strong Medicine;** Book, **Plays and Mani-
festo's: Richard Foreman,** by N.Y.U. Press. His
opera, **Elephant Steps** was done in Lenox, MA
and NYC, recorded on Columbia Records. Recipient: Two CAPS grants; Rockefeller Playwright in
residence; Guggenheim Grant; NEA Librettist
Award; 3 Village Voice Obie Awards.

Address: 152 Wooster St., New York, NY 10012
(212) 260-3328

Agent: Performing Artservice, 463 West St., New
York, NY 10014 (212) 989-4953

TITLE • AVAILABILITY • PRODUCTIONS

Angelface; New York University Press,** 113–15 University Pl., New York, NY 10003; NYC

Ida-eyed: manuscript*; NYC

Total Recall: New York University Press**; NYC

Hotel China: New York University Press**; NYC

Dream Tantras: manuscript*; Lenox, MA

Evidence: manuscript*; NYC

Sophia = (Wisdom): Part 3; New York University Press**; NYC

Dr. Selavy's Magic Theater: manuscript*; NYC; Lenox, MA

Classical Therapy: New York University Press**; Paris, France

Particle Theory: manuscript*; NYC

Verticle Mobility: New York University Press**; NYC

Pain(t): New York University Press**; NYC

Hotel for Criminals: Belwin Mills Publishers, 25 Deshon Dr., Melville, NY 11746; Lenox, MA;
NYC

†**Pandering to the Masses;** in **Theater of Images,** Drama Book Specialists, 150 W. 52nd St.,
New York, NY 10019, $10.00; NYC

Rhoda in Potatoland; New York University Press**; NYC

Book of Splendor: Pt. 1: manuscript*; Paris, France

Book of Splendor: Pt. 2; Yale Theater Magazine,* New Haven, CT.; NYC

Blvd de Paris: manuscript*; NYC

The American Imagination; Belwin Mills Publishing; NYC

Place + Target: manuscript*; Rome, Italy

Penguin Touquet: manuscript*; New York Shakespeare Festival, NYC
    *contact author
    **All in one volume, Paper $10.00
    †Lincoln Center, Theater on Film & Tape

SYNOPSIS

The American Imagination: Music by Stanley Silverman. Act one treats of the adventures of the
famous French criminals, Fantomas, Irma Vep (the gang known as the Vampires) in their strug-

Richard Foreman (cont'd)

gles with the detective, Judex. The second act follows them as they come to America in search of Fantoma's daughter, the innocent Helene.

Full length. Setting: a Paris street and an American countryside by a lake. Scored for 6 musicians. 9 males, 5 females.

MARIA IRENE FORNES

Born in Havana, Cuba on May 14, 1930. Attended Havana public schools. Director and designer. Recipient: Whitney Fellowship, 1961; Centro Mexicano de Escritores, 1962; OADR Grant, 1965; Obie Award, 1965; Centas Foundation, 1967; Yale Fellowship, 1967; Tanglewood Fellowship, 1968; Rockefeller Grant, 1971; New York State Council on the Arts Grant, 1972; Guggenheim Grant, 1972.

Address: 1 Sheridan Square, New York, NY 10014 (212) 989-7216

Agent: Bertha Case, 345 West 58th St., New York, NY 10019 (212) 541-9451

TITLE • AVAILABILITY • PRODUCTIONS

The Widow: manuscript*

Tango Palace (There! You Died): Playwrights for Tomorrow, Vol. II (out of print); Actors Workshop, San Francisco, CA; Spoleto, Italy

The Successful Life of 3: Playwrights for Tomorrow, Vol. II; Firehouse Theatre, Minn., MN; Open Theatre, NYC

Promenade: Samuel French, 25 W. 45th St., New York, NY 10036 (call for terms); Judson Church, NYC; Kingston Mines, Chicago, IL

The Office: manuscript*; Broadway (previews)

A Vietnamese Wedding: with Promenade & Other Plays (out of print); Washington Square Church, NYC; Moore College, PA

The Annunciation: manuscript*; Judson Church, NYC

Dr. Kheal; in Promenade & Other Plays; Village Gate, NYC; London

The Red Burning Light; in Promenade & Other Plays; Open Theatre, NYC; Zurich

Molly's Dream; in Promenade & Other Plays; Tanglewood Workshop, MA; New York Theatre Strategy, NYC

The Curse of the Langston House: not available; Cincinnati Playhouse, OH

Aurora: manuscript*; New York Theatre Strategy, NYC

Eyes of the Harem: manuscript*; INTAR Theatre, NYC

Fefu and Her Friends: Wordplays: New American Drama*; American Place Theatre, NYC

Evelyn Brown (A Diary): manuscript*; Theatre For The New City, NYC
  *contact agent

F

PAUL FOSTER

Born in Penn's Grove, NJ. B.A., New York University Law School. President of the La Mama Theater, New York. Has just completed **The Boswell Journals,** a seven-play TV series and a filmscript, **Andrew Mellon.** Member: Societe des Auteurs et Compositeurs (Paris); The Authors League; The Dramatists Guild; PEN. Recipient: two Rockefeller Fellowships; two Irish University Drama Prizes; New York Drama Critics Award; two CAPS Fellowships; National Endowment for the Arts Fellowship; British Arts Council Award; Tony nomination; Guggenheim Fellowship; U.S. Dept. of State Lectureship.

Address: 236 East 5th St., New York, NY 10003

Agent: Charles Hunt, Fifi Oscard Agency, 19 West 44th St., New York, NY 10036 (212) 764-1100 and Samuel French, 25 West 45th St., New York, NY 10036 (212) 582-4700

TITLE • AVAILABILITY • PRODUCTIONS

Balls: Eight Plays from Off Off Broadway, Bobbs-Merrill, 4300 West 62nd St., Indianapolis, IN 46468, $4.95; Cherry Lane Theater, NYC

The Recluse: with **Balls;** Martinique Theater, NYC

The Hessian Corporal: with **Balls;** WNET

Hurrah for the Bridge: with **Balls;** La Mama E.T.C., NYC

The Madonna in the Orchard: Samuel French, 25 W. 45th St., New York, NY 10036, $4.75; La Mama E.T.C., NYC; O'Neill Theater Center, CT

Tom Paine: Samuel French, $2.50; La Mama E.T.C., NYC; London

The Stoned Angels: Out of print*; WNET

Satyricon; Samuel French, $4.75; La Mama E.T.C., NYC

†**Elizabeth 1;** Samuel French, $2.50; Broadway

Silver Queen Saloon; Samuel French, $2.50; La Mama E.T.C., NYC

!Heimskringla!; Samuel French, $5.00; WNET

Marcus Brutus; Samuel French, $6.25; Stage West, MA; Paris

Bogey's Back: manuscript*

The House on Lake Geneva: manuscript*
*contact agent
†Lincoln Center Theatre on Film & Tape

SYNOPSES

Tom Paine: The American revolutionary who named the United States of America, ends his life in a barn in lower Manhattan amid the war-poor. His life is enacted. "This brilliant play confirms Paul Foster's reputation as the most talented and significant of the Off-Off Broadway American Dramatists. Its use of new ideas and techniques dazzles with its audacity and skill and gives the play a highly individual and distinctive style." —**London Times.**
Full length. No set. 8 males, 4 females.

Elizabeth I: The life of the Virgin Queen who beheaded Mary Stuart and defeated the Armada. A company of touring actors enact the brilliant woman's daring life.
Full length. No set. 6 males, 4 females.

Marcus Brutus: The impending tragedy of the murder of Caesar is docketed for a modern hearing. "Flashes of comedy slash like knives into the play's fabric. He writes plays that try genuinely to

extend the range of the theater . . . as always with Foster, the proposition is dramatically right, its thrust is direct and its purpose very evident." —Clive Barnes, **New York Times.**
Full length. 9 males, 4 females.

RAY ERROL FOX

Born in Philadelphia, PA on July 13. Attended Boston University and had one year at Temple University Law School. He has written the lyrics for a number of film songs, including the award-winning **La Guerre Est Finie,** Fellini's **The Clowns.** He contributes dance and theater reviews and articles concerned with the Middle East, to various publications. He wrote the lyrics for the Performing Arts Repertory Theatre's **Young Ben Franklin** and the Broadway production of **The Sign in Sidney Brustein's Window.** His first book **Angela Ambrosia** was published by Alfred A. Knopf, Spring 1979, and will soon be a TV film.

Address: 88 Central Park West, New York, NY 10023

Agent: Susan Schulman, 165 West End Ave., New York, NY 10023 (212) 877-2216

TITLE • AVAILABILITY • PRODUCTIONS

The Confidence Man (musical: book and lyrics): manuscript*; Manhattan Theatre Club, NYC

Footloose & Fancy 3 (comedy): manuscript*

In the Presence of Mine Enemy: manuscript*

Occasion: manuscript*

To Sit on a Horse: manuscript*
*contact agent

TERRY CURTIS FOX

Born in Brooklyn, NY on May 22, 1948. B.A., University of Chicago, 1970. Formerly theater critic for **Village Voice;** formerly theater and film critic for the **Chicago Reader;** other publications include **Film Comment, Boston Real Paper, New York Magazine, Chicago Sun-Times, Tribune** and **Daily News.** Recipient: CAPS Playwriting Grant, 1979.

Agent: Elaine Markson, 44 Greenwich Avenue, New York, NY 10011 (212) 243-8480

TITLE • AVAILABILITY • PRODUCTIONS

Cops: Samuel French, 25 W. 45th St., New York, NY 10036, $2.50; Organic Theatre, Chicago, IL; Performance Group, NYC

Justice; Samuel French, $2.50; Playwrights Horizons, NYC; **Earplay**

F

Terry Curtis Fox (cont'd)

The Summer Garden: manuscript*; O'Neill Theater Center's National Playwrights Conference, CT

Mickey and Czerwicki Go to Heaven: manuscript*
  *contact agent

RICHARD FRANCE

Born in Boston, MA on May 5, 1938. Educated at the Yale School of Drama and Carnegie-Mellon University. Writes criticism, such as **The Theatre of Orson Welles** and his forthcoming edition of the Virgil Thomson/Gertrude Stein correspondence. Television producer, **Jewel Walker's Mime Circus,** PBS etc. Appeared in films. **Night of the Living Dead, The Crazies, Strong Medicine, The Sorrows of Dolores.** Writes for film, **War Is, The Week Bela Lugosi Died.** Recipient: Rockefeller Grant; Ford Grant; N.E.H. Research Fellow; N.E.A. Creative Writing Fellow (twice).

Address: 214 Porterfield Place, Freeport, NY 11520

Agent: Susan Schulman, 165 West End Ave., New York, NY 10023 (212) 877-2216

TITLE • AVAILABILITY • PRODUCTIONS

Station J: Irvington Press, 551 Fifth Ave., New York, NY 10017, $8.95; Body Politic, Chicago, IL; Gene Dynarsky Theater, Los Angeles, CA

The Image of Elmo Doyle: Dramatic Publishing Co., 86 E. Randolph St., Chicago, IL 60601, $1.10; Yale Drama School, CT; IASTA, NYC

Don't You Know It's Raining: manuscript*; Dallas Theater Center, TX

A Day in the Life: manuscript*; Salt City Playhouse, Syracuse, NY; Midwest Playwrights Festival, WI

The First Word and the Last; I. E. Clark, Box 246, Schulenberg, TX 78956, $1.00; Open Space Theatre, London; Mikery Theatre, Amsterdam

The Magic Shop: Performance Publishing, 978 N. McLean Blvd., Elgin, IL 60120, 90¢; Numerous productions

One Day in the Life of Ivan Denisovich; Performance Publishing, $1.75 (amateur version); Body Politic Theatre, numerous productions

Fathers and Sons; Performance Publishing, $1.95 (amateur version); Lawrence University, WI; Salt City Playhouse, Syracuse, NY

Envoys: manuscript* (also opera form); Yale School of Drama, CT; ATA Convention, Wash. DC

Feathertop; Performance Publishing, 90¢; Numerous Productions

Svengali (musical): manuscript*

Thyestes: manuscript*
  *contact agent

SYNOPSES

Svengali: The du Maurier novel **Trilby,** adapted as the book for a musical and relocated to the French Quarter of New Orleans before, during and after World War I.

Full length: Setting: several. 12 males, 10 females, a chorus.

Station J: An epic drama which follows the plight of the Japanese in this country during World War II. The play moves back and forth between scenes of the Shigeta family's evacuation from

Richard France (cont'd)

their San Francisco home and internment in a concentration camp and scenes (taken from actual speeches, court records and public testimony) which underscore the motives behind this national disgrace.

Full length. Setting: a unit set plus projection facilities. 8 males, 4 females.

A Day in the Life: "All heaven and earth/Shrouded white/Obliterate snow, unceasing snow." Using this haiku image as its point of departure, the play proposes that everyone deserves one day that is uniquely their own before the end overtakes them. Today belongs to Frederick Morton Unger. Set in the ever-encrouching whiteness of a "therapeutic" community, the play moves from reality to surrealism, from living characters to mannikins to shadows. Yesterday and today are accounted for, but whose day will it be tomorrow? The play ends with an all-embracing gesture to the audience indicating that this process of obliteration is not confined to the stage.

Full length. Setting: a dayroom with a nursing station, with a bedroom beyond. 6 males, 4 females and several mannikins.

J. e. FRANKLIN

Born in Houston, TX on August 10, 1937. B.A., University of Texas; Graduate hours, Union Theological Seminary, NY. Author, **Black Girl From Genesis to Revelations,** Signet Books. Skills include those of Artist-Therapist in intergenerational settings consisting of senior citizens and youths. Recipient: New York Drama Desk Award, 1971; Media Women Award, 1971; CAPS Award, 1972; Institute for the Arts and Humanities Dramatic Arts Award, Howard U., 1974; Better Boys Foundation Playwrighting Award, 1978; National Endowment on the Arts Creative Writing Fellowship, 1979; Rockefeller Grant, 1980

Address: 413 West 147th St., New York NY 10031

Agent: Victoria Lucas Associates, 888 Seventh Ave., Suite 400, New York, NY 10019 (212) 489-8008

TITLE • AVAILABILITY • PRODUCTIONS

Black Girl: Dramatists Play Service, 440 Park Ave., South, New York, NY 10016, $2.50; New Federal Theatre, NYC; Theater de Lys, NYC

The Prodigal Sister: Samuel French, 25 W. 45th St., New York, NY 10036, $2.50; New Federal Theatre, NYC; Theater de Lys, NYC

The Enemy: manuscript*; Herbert H. Lehman College, NY

Four Women: manuscript*; Herbert H. Lehman College, NY

MacPilate: manuscript*; Herbert H. Lehman College, NY

The Creation: manuscript*; Herbert H. Lehman College, NY

Another Morning Rising: manuscript*; Greenwood, SC

The In-Crowd: manuscript*; New Federal Theatre, NYC

Throw Thunder at This House: manuscript*; Theater for Artcentric Living, NYC; Skidmore College, Saratoga Springs, NY

Will the Real South Please Rise: manuscript*

Guess What's Coming to Dinner: manuscript*

The Hand-Me-Downs: manuscript*; Theater for Artcentric Living, NYC; LaMont-Zeno Theater, Chicago, IL

Cut Out The Lights And Call the Law: manuscript*; Negro Ensemble Company, NYC

F

J. e. Franklin (cont'd)

Fritz Was Here: manuscript*; Theater for Artcentric Living, NYC

Liars Die: manuscript*; Theater for Artcentric Living, NYC

The Broussard Bunch: manuscript*; Theater for Artcentric Living, NYC; Murphy House Theater, NY

Christchild: manuscript*; TV version at the O'Neill Theater Center's National Playwrights Conference, CT
*contact agent

SYNOPSES

Throw Thunder at This House: The first black undergraduate attending the University of Texas gets trapped by non-academic forces which degenerate into internecine warfare.
Full length. Setting: entertainment area of girl's dormitory. 4 males, 5 females.

Christchild: While trying to prove to his superstitious father that he was not born evil, an adolescent boy wrestles with the spiritual and biological questions surrounding his mysterious birth, his deformity and his suspect strength.
Full length. Setting: a livingroom. 3 males, 4 females.

The Hand-Me-Downs: A pre-adolescent girl and her older brother resolve problems of sibling rivalry and the shame they feel towards their father's illiteracy and old age.
Full length. Setting: a livingroom. 2 males, 2 females.

MARIO FRATTI

American, born in L'Aquilla on July 5, 1927. Educated at Ca'Foscari University, Venice, 1947–51, Ph.D. in languages and literature 1951. Served in the Italian Army, 1951–52: Lieutenant. Professor at Columbia University, 1967; Adelphi University, 1967–68; and Hunter College, 1967. Written one novel and one volume of poems, **Volti** (one hundred poems) published by Mariano-Bari, 1960. Recipient: RAI-Television Prize, 1959; Ruggeri Prize, 1960, 1967, 1969; Lentini Prize, 1964; Vallecorsi Prize, 1965; Unasp-Enars Prize, 1968; Arta-Terme Award, 1974; Richard Rodgers Production Award, 1980.

Address: 145 W. 55th St., New York, NY 10019
(212) 582-6697

Agent: Bruce Savan, A.P.A., 120 West 57th St., New York, NY 10019 (212) 582-1500

TITLE • AVAILABILITY • PRODUCTIONS

Five One-Act Plays in English (and French): EIST, Via del Tritone 132, Rome, Italy, $1.50

The Cage, The Suicide: Delta Publishing Co., 885 Second Ave., New York, NY 10017, $2.25; New York; Spoleto

The Wish: Religious Theatre, No. 6, Wichita State Univ., Wichita, Kansas 67208, $1.50; Denton, Texas; London

The Refusal: Poet Lore, Winter 1966, 36 Melrose St., Boston, Mass. 02166, $1.50; New York; London

Waiting: Poet Lore, Autumn 1968, $1.50; New York

The Third Daughter: First Stage, Vol. V, No. 3, Purdue University, Lafayette, Ind. 47907, $1.50; New York

Mario Fratti (cont'd)

The Coffin, Intermission Magazine, Hull House Assoc., 3179 No. Broadway, Chicago, Ill. 60657, $1.50; Rome; New York

The Refrigerators: Modern Intl. Drama, The Pennsylvania Univ., Univ. Park, PA. 16802, $2.00; New York; Milan, Italy

Betrayals: Drama & Theatre, Vol. 7, No. 3, Dept. of English and Speech, State University College, Fredonia, NY 14063, $1.50; Poland; India

The Academy, The Return: Best Short Plays of the World Theatre, Crown Publisher, 419 Park Ave. So., New York, NY 10016, $6.50; New York; Washington

The Bridge: Themes in the One-Act Play, R. D. Cox, McGraw Hill, 1221 Ave. of Americas, New York, NY 10020, $2.50; New York; Tokyo

Che Guevara: Enact, New Delhi, India*, Toronto; Tokyo

The Gift, The Friday Bench (also includes **The Wish,** and **The Coffin**): Edgemoor Publishers, 6110 B Edgemoor Drive, Houston, Texas 77036, $1.35; Rome; Milan; New York

Unique: Ann Arbor Review, Ann Arbor, Michigan. $1.50; Baltimore

The Doorbell: Ohio University Magazine, Athens, Ohio 45701, $1.50; New York; London

The Brothel: Mediterranean Review, Orient, NY 11957, $1.50; New York

Mafia: Proscenium Press, P.O. Box 361, Newark, Delaware 19711, $1.95; Florida

The White Cat & Races: Proscenium Press, $1.95; Rome; New York

Eleonora Duse: Breakthrough Press, Inc., 27 Washington Square, North, New York 10011, $1.50; Sarasota, Florida; New York

The Family: Breakthrough Press, $1.50; New York

The Chinese Friend: Breakthrough Press, $1.50; New York

The Seducers: Ora Zero Publisher, Via Monte Hermada 84, 33100, Udine, Italy, $1.50; Venice; New York

The Roman Guest: Ora Zero Publisher, $1.50; Pesaro, Italy

Chile 1973: Enact New Delhi, 4 Chamelion Road, Delhi 6, India, $1.50; New York; India

Patty Hearst: Enact New Delhi, $1.50; New York

The Only Good Indian: Drama & Theatre, Fredonia University, Dept. of English, Fredonia, NY 14063, $1.50; New York

The Anniversary: manuscript*

Dead Man's Bluff: manuscript*

Victim: Samuel French, 25 W. 45th St., New York, NY 10036, $2.50; Canada; Brazil

Kissinger: Enact, Pauls Press, B-258 Naraina Industrial Area, Phase I, New Delhi 110028, $2.00; California; India

Birthday (with **Third Daughter**): Samuel French, $2.50; Louisiana; Italy

Six Passionate Women: Enact, Pauls Press, $2.00; Actors' Studio; Italy

Nine (music, Maury Yeston): manuscript*; O'Neill Center's Composers, Librettists Conference, CT

Bosses: manuscript*
*contact author

SYNOPSES

The Anniversay: A thriller. Once a year, an older gentleman invites his "daughter" for dinner. It is not his daughter. Two murders. An unpredictable conclusion.
Full length. Setting: a livingroom. 2 males, 1 female.

Dead Man's Bluff: A thriller. A man is buried. He reappears. The corpse was identical. Who is he? A surprising plot. An unpredictable stunning conclusion.
Full length. Setting; a livingroom. 4 males, 2 females.

F

Mario Fratti (cont'd)

Six Passionate Women: A fast moving parody in the Billy Wilder tradition. Nino, a successful Italian filmmaker, has been stealing ideas all his life. William, his screenwriter, has been stealing Nino's women for years. Six "passionate" women plan a bizarre plot to outsmart and punish these two men. They succeed.

Full length. Setting: three beds. 2 males, 6 females.

GEORGE FREEK

Born in Champaign, IL on November 8, 1945. B.A. from U. of Illinois, M.A. in English from Southern Illinois U., working on Ph.D. in Modern American Literature. Has worked as a Graduate Teaching Assistant at S.I.U. Published numerous poems in many literary magazines (**Greenfield Review, Cincinnati Poetry Review,** etc.). Playwright-in-Residence, Southern Methodist University, 1980–81 and New American Theater, Rockford, IL. Recipient: Project Completion Grant, Illinois Arts Council; Fellowship, Midwest Playwrights Lab.

Address: 516 E. Menominie St., Belvidere, IL
    61008 (815) 547-7521

TITLE • AVAILABILITY • PRODUCTIONS

For Left-Handed Piano With Obbligato: manuscript*; Midwest Playwrights Lab, Madison, WI

Rhumba for 8 In 12 E-Z Lessons: manuscript*; Milwaukee Repertory Theater Co., WI

Transcendental Exercises: manuscript*; Academy Theatre, Atlanta, GA

Tarantella on a High Wire: manuscript*; Academy Theatre, Atlanta, GA

Danse Macabre #2: manuscript*; Milwaukee Repertory Theater Co., WI

The Cellar: manuscript*; The Changing Scene, Denver, CO

Filial Pieties: manuscript*; Southeastern Theatre Conference

Transformations: manuscript*; Lion Theatre Company, NYC

Figures from Giacometti: manuscript*; New American Theater, Rockford, IL
    *contact author

DAVID FREEMAN

A screenwriter and a playwright, David has also been a journalist and a publicist. He is also the author of **U.S. Grant in the City,** a collection of stories about New York.

Agent: Bridget Ashenberg, I.C.M., 40 W. 57th St.,
    New York, NY 10019 (212) 556-5600

David Freeman (cont'd)

TITLE • AVAILABILITY • PRODUCTIONS

Jesse and the Bandit Queen: Samuel French, 25 W. 45th St., New York, NY 10036, $2.50; O'Neill Theater Center's National Playwrights Conference, CT; New York Shakespeare Festival, NYC

Frank Buck Can't Make It: manuscript*; Island Repertory Theatre, Martha's Vineyard, MA; W.P.A. Theatre, NYC
*contact agent

SYNOPSIS

Jesse and the Bandit Queen: A two-character love story about the lives and times of the bandits Jesse James and Belle Starr. The play follows them through sixteen years of stormy romance, from obscurity to great notoriety, and finally to their deaths. In the course of the play, Belle and Jesse play themselves and all other figures in their lives. They find and tangle with one another, play one another, and finally become one another.

BRUCE JAY FRIEDMAN

Born in the Bronx on April 26, 1930. Bachelor of Journalism from the University of Missouri. U.S. Air Force 1951–53. He was editor of **Black Humor.** He is the author of four novels; **Stern, A Mother's Kisses, About Harry Towns, The Dick** and two collections of short stories **Far from the City of Class and Other Stories** and **Black Angels.** His latest book is **The Lonely Guys Book of Life.** Screenplay for **Stir Crazy.** Recipient: Obie Award for **Scuba Duba.**

Agent: Candida Donadio & Associates, 111 West 57th St., New York, NY 10019 (212) 757-5076

TITLE • AVAILABILITY • PRODUCTIONS

23 Pat O'Brien Movies: manuscript*; American Place Theater, NYC

Scuba Duba: Dramatists Play Service, 440 Park Ave. South, New York, NY 10016, $2.50; Off Broadway

A Mother's Kisses: manuscript*; New Haven, CT; Baltimore, MD

The Car Lover: Esquire, June 1968; NYC

Steambath: Samuel French, 25 W. 45th St., New York, NY 10036, $2.50; Off Broadway

First Offenders: manuscript*; Detroit, MI; Philadelphia, PA
*contact agent

F

CHARLES FRINK

Born in Norwich, Connecticut on March 13, 1928. Educated at Yale University — B.A., M.A., Ph.D. Has worked as tree surgeon, lifeguard, dish washer, carpenter, musician, teacher. Composer of dance scores **(The Minister's Black Veil)**, music for symphony orchestra **(Joe Hill, Nat Turner)**, music for chorus **(John Henry, Prayer of Columbus)**, and musical theater **(Donnegan's Crusade, Goddess in the Junkyard)**. All his writing, whether music, or drama, reflects his interest in history. Recipient: Composer's grant: National Endowment for the Arts. Commissions: Joseph Albano, Charles Weidman.

Address: 265 Gardner Ave., New London, CT 06320

TITLE • AVAILABILITY • PRODUCTIONS

A Day of Grace: manuscript*; O'Neill Theater Center's National Playwrights Conference, CT

Donnegan's Crusade: manuscript*; Mitchell College, New London, CT

Goddess in the Junkyard: manuscript*

An Echo of Bells: manuscript*

Dreams and Victims: manuscript*
    *contact author

SYNOPSES

Dreams and Victims: The first English settlements in Massachusetts: Plymouth Plantation, the "Godly Commonwealth" of the Puritans, and Merrymount, where refugees from England and Plymouth tried to create an earthly paradise combining Christian and pagan ideas. A clash of opposing visions of the New World.

Full length. Setting: several places in seventeenth-century Europe and Massachusetts; no literal scenery needed. 9 males, 7 females.

An Echo of Bells: A biographical play based on the life of William Billings, eighteenth-century Boston tanner and composer who wrote the marching song ("Chester") of the American Revolution.

Full length. Setting: street, wharves, churches of eighteenth-century Boston; no literal scenery. 6 males, 5 females, chorus.

Donneghan's Crusade: A musical play about a drunk who sobers up in order to wage a fight to save his cherished slum from urban renewal.

Full length. Setting: contemporary blighted area; no literal scenery. 11 males, 6 females, chorus.

MARTHA AYERS FUENTES

Born in Ashland, AL on December 21. B.A. from University of South Florida, Tampa. Member of the Society of Children's Book Writers with many published stories to her credit. T.V. credit, **The Rebel,** on **Faith For Today.** Member: Author's League of America; Dramatists Guild; American Theatre Association; Society of Children's Book Writers; Southeastern Writer's Association. Recipient: Lone Lister Creative Writing Award — Drama & Fiction; Sergel Drama Award for **Go Stare at the Moon.**

Address: 102 3rd Street, Belleair Beach, FL 33535

TITLE • AVAILABILITY • PRODUCTIONS

Two Characters in Search of an Agreement: Contemporary Drama, P.O. Box 68, Downers Grove Ill. 60515

Mama Don't Make Me Go to College, My Head Hurts: manuscript*; University of South Florida, FL

Go Stare at the Moon: manuscript*; University of Chicago, IL

What's the Matter With Uncle Leo?: manuscript*

Time of the Promise Green: manuscript*

Open the Door, Doctor. I Have Your Teeth. Where Have You Been?: manuscript*; Readings

The Barefoot Ballerina: manuscript*

Yesterday Where Shadows Go: manuscript*

Over the Glass Mountain: manuscript*

The Neighbors: manuscript*; Readings
  *contact author

SYNOPSES

Two Characters in Search of an Agreement: God and the devil, dressed as two traveling salesmen who have seen better days, meet in an all night diner to patch up their differences.

One act. Setting: an all-night diner. 6 males, 3 females, urchin children, 1 dinosaur.

Go Stare at the Moon: The aristocratic Latimer sisters, Suzann and Emmajean, are in conflict with the unscrupulous Cochran Clan who invade the ruins of their plantation after the Civil War. Emmajean is duped into a mock marriage to Earl Cochran, father of the Clan. She disintegrates mentally. Suzanne, in contrast, emerges strong, and regains ownership of the plantation.

Full length. Setting: the ruins of a Southern mansion showing the interiors of the rooms. 16 males, 5 females, 6 children.

What's the Matter With Uncle Leo?: When Leo Tagliarina, a devout Catholic, falls in love with his deceased wife's nurse, a beautiful Protestant married woman, he defies tradition, alienation from his family and ex-communication from his church, as he seeks to marry her.

Full length. Setting: two interiors. 3 males, 4 females.

F

CHARLES FULLER

Born in Philadelphia, PA. Recipient: CAPS Grant, 1975; Rockefeller Foundation Playwriting Grant, 1976; National Endowment for the Arts Playwriting Grant, 1977; Guggenheim Fellowship, 1977–78.

Agent: Esther Sherman, c/o William Morris Agency, 1350 Avenue of the Americas, New York, NY 10019 (212) 586-5100

TITLE • AVAILABILITY • PRODUCTIONS

The Rise: New Plays from the Black Theater, William Morrow, 105 Madison Ave., New York, NY 10016, $1.25; Harlem Cultural Center, NYC

The Village: A Party: manuscript*; McCarter Theatre, Princeton, NJ

The Perfect Party: manuscript*; Tamberlini's Gate, NYC

In My Many Names & Days: manuscript*; New Federal Theatre, NYC; Henry St. Settlement, NYC

The Candidate: manuscript*; Henry St. Settlement, NYC

In the Deepest Part of Sleep: manuscript*; Negro Ensemble Co., NYC; Denmark

First Love: manuscript*; Billie Holiday Theatre, NYC

The Lay Out Letter: manuscript*; Freedom Theatre, Philadelphia, PA

Charles Fuller Presents the Dynamic Jerry Bland & His Blandelles with the Fabulous Miss Marva Jane: manuscript*; Negro Ensemble Co., NYC

The Brownsville Raid: manuscript*; O'Neill Theater Center's National Playwrights Conference, CT; Negro Ensemble Co., NYC

Zooman and the Sign: Samuel French, 25 W. 45th St., New York, NY 10036, $2.50; Negro Ensemble Co., NYC

Sparrow in Flight: manuscript*; AMAS Repertory Theatre, NYC
*contact agent

SYNOPSES

The Brownsville Raid: A historical re-enactment of a military incident in 1906 in which one hundred-and-sixty seven soldiers were discharged from the U.S. Army for allegedly killing one of the townspeople of Brownsville, TX

Full length. Setting: a military barracks. 13 males, 1 female.

Zooman and the Sign: A drama which revolves around the killing of a twelve-year-old girl by a gang member and its result on the life of her family and the murderer.

GEORGE FURTH

Born in Chicago, IL on December 14, 1932. Educated at Northwestern University's School of Speech, B.S.; Columbia University for graduate work. In addition to writing has appeared as an actor on and Off Broadway, in many films and in almost every television program. Recipient: Tony Award; Drama Critics Award; Outer Circle Drama Critics Award; **Evening Standard** (London); Theater Club Award.

Attorney: Jerry N. Roth, 9455 Lloydcrest, Beverly Hills, CA 90210 (213) 274-5254

TITLE • AVAILABILITY • PRODUCTIONS

†**Company**: Music Theater International, 119 West 57th St., New York, NY 10019; Broadway

Twigs: Samuel French, 25 W. 45th St., New York, NY 10036, $2.50; Broadway

The Act: Feuer and Martin Productions, 158 East 63rd St., New York, NY 10021; Broadway

The Supporting Cast: Emanuel Azenberg Productions, 165 West 46th St., New York, NY 10036; Broadway

Merrily We Roll Along!: Harold Prince Productions, 1270 Avenue of the Americas, New York, NY 10020
  †Lincoln Center, Theatre on Film & Tape

FRANK GAGLIANO

Born in Brooklyn, New York on November 18, 1931. Educated at Queens College, New York; The University of Iowa, B.A.; Columbia University, M.F.A. Playwright-in-Residence, Royal Shakespeare Company, London, England, 1967–68/ Playwright-in-Residence, Florida State University, 1969–73/University of Texas at Austin: Lecturer in Playwriting and director of the E. P. Conkle Workshop for Playwrights, 1973–76. Benedum Professor of Playwriting (a newly-established chair in playwriting) at the University of West Virginia, Morgantown, West Virginia, 1976–. Recipient: Rockefeller Foundation Grants, 1965–67; O'Neill Foundation-Wesleyan University Fellowship, 1967; National Endowment for the Arts Fellowship in Playwriting, 1973; Guggenheim Fellowship in Playwriting, 1975.

Agent: Gilbert Parker, William Morris Agency, 1350 Avenue of the Americas, New York, NY 10019 (212) 586-5100

TITLE • AVAILABILITY • PRODUCTIONS

Night of the Dunce: Dramatists Play Service, Inc., 440 Park Ave. South, New York, NY 10016, $2.50; Barr-Wilder-Albee, Cherry Lane Theatre, NYC

Conerico Was Here to Stay: Samuel French, 25 W. 45th St., New York, NY 10036, $2.50; Barr-Wilder-Albee, Cherry Lane Theatre, NYC

Paradise Gardens East: with **Conerico Was Here to Stay;** Fortune Theatre, NYC

Father Uxbridge Wants to Marry: Dramatists Play Service, $2.50; O'Neill Theater Center's National Playwrights Conference; American Place Theatre, NYC

G

Frank Gagliano (cont'd)

The Hide-and-Seek Odyssey of Madeleine Gimple (children's play): Dramatists Play Service, $2.50; hundreds of children's theatres

The Prince of Peasantmania: manuscript*; O'Neill Theater Center's National Playwrights Conference, CT

Big Sur: Dramatists Play Service, $1.25; NBC "Experiment in Television"; Florida State University

In the Voodoo Parlor of Marie Leveau: manuscript*; The Phoenix Theatre, NYC; O'Neill Theater Center's National Playwrights Conference, CT

The Commedia World of Lafcadio B: manuscript*; The Phoenix Theatre, NYC; O'Neill Theater Center's National Playwrights Conference, CT

Congo Square (musical play; with Claibe Richardson): manuscript*; University of Rhode Island Theatre

The Resurrection of Jackie Cramer (musical theatre piece with Raymond Benson): manuscript*; University of Rhode Island Theatre, RI; The New Dramatists, NYC

The Total Immersion of Madeleine Favorini: manuscript*; University of Nevada, Las Vegas; New Dramatists, NYC
*contact agent

SYNOPSES

In the Voodoo Parlour of Marie Laveau: An unsung voodoo chamber opera, in which two separate, desperate people (a music critic and a once-famous soprano) go to the famous voodoo queen Marie Laveau for help during a New Orleans Mardi Gras at the turn of the century; and their past and present lives become entwined, and their futures are resolved in a grotesque climax of sex, voodoo ritual and murder. Told with spoken arias, duets and trios.

Full length. Setting: One interior set. 1 male, 2 females.

The Commedia World of Lafcadio B: An influenza epidemic is raging in the streets of New Orleans (circa 1917) and a charming con man devises farcical con games to con a whore, a ghost of a former voodoo queen, an absurd, rich bumpkin, Monsieur Influenza himself — and all this, to out-con the most horrifying con-monster of them all: Boredom!

One act farce. Setting: one interior. 2 males, 1 female.

The Total Immersion of Madeleine Favorini: Forty-two-year-old Madeleine Favorini journeys from despair to its opposite on a gynecological examining table that takes wing. Three actors portray 20 characters.

Full length one act. Setting: an examining table.

MARY GALLAGHER

Born in Van Nuys, CA on July 10, 1947. B.S., from Bowling Green State University, in English and Theater, 1969. Professional actress and director as well as a writer. Author of numerous short stories, published in **Cosmopolitan** and **Redbook**. Novel, **Spend It Foolishly,** Atheneum Press and Avon. Recipient: Office for Advanced Drama Research; Alaska State Council on the Arts; National Endowment for the Humanities through the University of Wisconsin at La Crosse; Heideman Award, Actors Theatre of Louisville.

Address: 268 West 73rd St., #3B, New York, NY 10023

Agent: Mary Harden, Bret Adams Ltd., 36 East 61st St., New York, NY 10021 (212) 752-7864

Mary Gallagher (cont'd)

TITLE • AVAILABILITY • PRODUCTIONS

Fly Away Home: manuscript*; American Conservatory Theatre, San Francisco, CA

Father Dreams: manuscript*; American Conservatory Theatre, San Francisco, CA; Loretto-Hilton Repertory Theatre, St. Louis, MO

Little Bird: manuscript*; Berkshire Theatre Festival, MA; 78th Street Theatre, NYC

Chocolate Cake: manuscript*; Actors Theatre of Louisville, KY

Love Minus: manuscript*

How to Say Goodbye: manuscript*
     *contact agent

SYNOPSES

Father Dreams: Through a stream of memories, dreams and fantasies, a young man struggles to understand his father's mental illness and its effect on his family and himself.

Full length. Setting: one abstract simple setting. 2 males, 2 females.

Little Bird: A conflict between two young sisters threatens to sever their close relationship. By learning to accept their own and each other's frailties and those of the men they love, they heal this breach and move beyond it.

Full length. Setting: one realistic but simple setting. 2 males, 2 females.

Chocolate Cake: Two very different women with the same secret have an encounter which opens the eyes of the younger one and may change her life.

One act. Setting: one simple set. 2 females.

HERB GARDNER ‡

Born in Brooklyn, NY in 1934. Attended Carnegie Institute of Technology and Antioch College. Member of Dramatists Guild and ALA. Screenplays: **A Thousand Clowns** and **Who is Harry Kellerman and Why Is He Saying Those Terrible Things About Me?** Novel, **A Piece of the Action.** Cartoonist, The Nebbish. Recipient: Screen Writers Guild Award; Emmy Award, **Annie, The Woman in the Life of a Man.**

Agent: Sam Cohn, International Creative Management, 40 West 57th St., New York, NY 10019 (212) 556-5600

TITLE • AVAILABILITY • PRODUCTIONS

A Thousand Clowns: Samuel French, 25 W. 45th St., New York, NY 10036, $2.50; Broadway

The Goodbye People: Samuel French, $2.50; Broadway

Thieves: Samuel French, $2.50; Broadway

One Night Stand (music, Jule Styne): manuscript*; Broadway (previews)

Life And/Or Death: manuscript*; Circle Repertory, NYC
     *contact agent

G

LOUIS GARFINKEL

Born in Seattle, Washington, on February 11, 1928. Educated at University of California, Berkeley; University of Washington School of Drama; University of Southern California, B.A. '48. Louis has produced and directed motion pictures as well as written them. His films include: **The Young Guns, Face of Fire, A Minute to Pray a Second to Die, The Doberman Gang, Little Cigars,** and **The Deer Hunter,** winner of five Academy Awards including Best Picture of 1978. His TV credits include over seven-hundred scripts for ABC-TV's **Day in Court** and **Morning Court.** Member: Dramatists Guild; Writers Guild of America West; Academy of Motion Picture Arts and Sciences; Los Angeles P.E.N.

Address: 14127 Margate St., Van Nuys, CA 91401 (213) 788-2776

Agent: Robert Stein, Kohner-Levy Agency, 9169 Sunset Blvd., Los Angeles, CA 90069 (213) 550-1060

TITLE • AVAILABILITY • PRODUCTIONS

Molly (based on Gertrude Berg's **The Goldbergs**): manuscript*; The Alvin Theater, NYC

I Shall Return: manuscript*; Norfolk, VA; Shubert, Boston, MA
  *contact agent

BARBARA GARSON

Born in Brooklyn, 1941. B.A. in Classical History from the Univ. of Calif. at Berkeley. During the Vietnam war, Barbara worked in a Coffee House for G.I.'s near Fort Lewis army base. Her play **Macbird** was originally written for an anti-war teach-in. In addition to plays she writes for magazines, including **Harpers, New York Times, Village Voice, Ms.** Her book **All the Livelong Day, The Meaning and Demeaning of Routine Work,** is a collection of stories about people doing every day jobs, published by Doubleday and Penguin. She has written numerous skits and puppet shows for political occasions including material for FTA, the Jane Fonda-Donald Sutherland anti-war show that toured army bases around the world. Recipient: A.B.C. grant, writing for **Cameras,** administered by Yale

University, 1967; Louis M. Rabinowitz Foundation Grant, 1973; New York State Council on the Arts, special grant for production for Younger Audiences, 1975; National Endowment for the Arts Fellowship; Guggenheim Fellowship; Obie Award.

Address: 463 West Street, Apt 1108A, New York, NY 10014

Agent: Elaine Markson, 44 Greenwhich Ave., New York, NY 10011 (212) 243-8480

TITLE • AVAILABILITY • PRODUCTIONS

Macbird: Grove Press, 53 E. 11th St., New York, NY 10003, $1.75; Village Gate, New York; Over two-hundred productions

Barbara Garson (cont'd)

Going Co-Op (written with Fred Gardner): manuscript*; Theatre for the New City, NYC; Central Arts Theatre, NYC

The Dinosaur Door: manuscript*; Theatre for the New City, NYC
    *contact author or agent

SYNOPSES

The Dinosaur Door: On a class trip to the Natural History Museum, Daisy Bannanowitz, her little brother Mark, and Jordan, the bad kid in the class, are lured into a hidden section of the museum, behind the Dinosaur Door. There they manage to foil Phenomenon, a former museum janitor who is using the forgotten fossils, stored in old cartons, to create a single streamlined species which will replace all existing animals. He is doing this because he simply can not stand the messy multiplicity of evolution. Phenomenon's side kick, a reconstructed neanderthal, who despite his species differences has remarkably human feelings, eventually helps the children and museum animals to overcome the villain. Then wounded, he crawls back into extinction.

In the end, the children must decide whether to stay in what is now a paradise, where they can eat all the soda and Yodels and Yankee Doodles they want, stop at the water faucet, touch the displays, go to bed when they choose, free of all adult regulation and irrationality. But they choose to rush back out just in time into the familiar world with their nervously controlling teacher, Mrs. Newron and Daisy's loving but guiltily bumbling mother.

Full length, with songs. Setting: in the museum. The setting in the Natural History museum can very easily be re-worked to use the specific details of any local museum. In fact, the author is anxios to help with necessary re-writes when possible. 3 little girls, 4 little boys, 5 males, 4 females, assorted children and prehistoric animals.

Going Co-Op: A situation comedy about an apartment house in Manhattan going co-op. The tenants who can't afford to buy begin to organize (and get to know each other.) They are aided comically by a radical collective including the guitar-playing son of a postal worker who lives in the building. It ends with the victory of the tenants but the poignant and prophetic break-up of the collective. Set in the late '60s.

Full length, with songs. Setting: apartment house. 11 males, 9 females.

JACK GELBER

Born in Chicago, IL on April 12, 1932. B.S., University of Illinois in journalism. Has directed such plays as **The Kitchen, Indians, The Chickencoop Chinaman** and **The Kid.** Novel, **The Ice.** Wrote the screenplay for **The Connection.** Was Associate Professor in Graduate Theater at Columbia University and now heads the Playwriting Program at Brooklyn College. Recipient: Obie Award, 1959; New York Drama Critics Award, 1959; Vernon Rice Award, 1959; Guggenheim Grant, 1963 and 1966; Rockefeller Playwright-in-residence Grant, 1972; Obie, Best Director; National Endowment for the Arts Fellow, 1974; CBS Fellow, 1974

Address: 215 Marlborough Road, Brooklyn, NY
    11226

TITLE • AVAILABILITY • PRODUCTIONS

The Connection: Grove Press, 196 W. Houston St., New York, NY 10014; Living Theatre, NYC

The Apple: Grove Press; Living Theatre, NYC

Square in the Eye: Grove Press; Theatre de Lys, NYC

The Cuban Thing: manuscript*; Broadway

G

Jack Gelber (cont'd)

Sleep: Hill & Wang, 19 Union Square, New York, NY 10003, $2.95; American Place Theatre, NYC

Barbary Shore (adaptation): manuscript*; New York Shakespeare Festival, NYC

Rehearsal: manuscript*; American Place Theatre, NYC

Starters: manuscript*; O'Neill Theater Center's National Playwrights Conference, CT
   *contact author

CLARK GESNER

Born in Augusta, ME in 1938. Raised in New England and Plainfield, NJ. A.B. in English, Princeton University, 1960. Army Special Services, 1961–63. Staff writer and composer for **Captain Kangaroo** (C.B.S.-TV) 1963–66. Much writing and composing in New York for the past twelve years, for theater, records, and TV, especially **Sesame Street** and **The Electric Company.** Wrote book, **Stuff, etc.,** by John Gordon (pseud.) Lippincott. Filmmaker, writer, director, etc.

Address: 87 Remsen St., Brooklyn, NY 11201
   (212) 875-5835

Agent: Leo Bookman, William Morris Agency, 1350 Avenue of the Americas, New York, NY 10019 (212) 586-5100

TITLE • AVAILABILITY • PRODUCTIONS

You're a Good Man, Charlie Brown (musical): Tams Witmark, 757 Third Ave., New York, NY 10017; Numerous productions

The Utter Glory of Morrissey Hall (musical): Samuel French, 25 W. 45th St., New York, NY 10036, $2.50; Pacific Conservatory of the Performing Arts, Santa Maria, CA; Broadway

The Ransom of Red Chief (children's musical): manuscript*
   *contact author

WILLIAM GIBSON

Born in New York. Attended City College of New York. Besides his plays, he has written **The Cobweb** (novel), **Winter Crook** (poems), **The Seesaw Log** (chronicle), **A Mass for the Dead** (chronicle and poems), **A Season in Heaven** (chronicle), **Shakespeare's Game** (critical analysis), Atheneum.

Address: Stockbridge, MA 01262

Agent: Flora Roberts, 65 East 55th St., New York NY 10022 (212) 355-4165

TITLE • AVAILABILITY • PRODUCTIONS

Dinny & the Witches: Dramatists Play Service, Inc., 440 Park Ave. South, New York, NY 10016, $2.50; Off Broadway

William Gibson (cont'd)

A Cry of Players: Dramatists Play Service, $2.50; Lincoln Center

Two for the Seesaw: Samuel French, 25 W. 45th St., New York, NY 10036, $2.50; Broadway

The Miracle Worker: Samuel French Inc., $2.50; Atheneum Publishers, 597 Fifth Ave., New York, NY 10017; Broadway

Golden Boy (musical): Atheneum Publishers, 597 Fifth Ave., New York, NY 10017; Broadway

American Primitive: Dramatists Play Service, $2.50; Washington, D.C.

The Body & the Wheel: Dramatists Play Service, $2.50; University of New Hampshire

The Butterfingers Angel, Mary and Joseph, Herod the Nut, and the Slaughter of 12 Hit Carols in a Pear Tree: Dramatists Play Service, $2.50; Syracuse Stage, NYC

Golda: Samuel French, $2.50; Broadway

Goodly Creatures: manuscript*; Round House Theatre, Wash. D.C.; Shakespeare & Co., Lenox, MA
*contact agent

SYNOPSES

The Butterfingers Angel, Mary and Joseph, Herod the Nut, and the Slaughter of 12 Hit Carols in a Pear Tree: A comedy with some dark moments, based on the Nativity story, a retelling in modern terms and language; written for church presentation at Christmas, but has been done professionally at other seasons.

Setting: bare stage, three platforms. 6 males, 4 females, 4 children.

HENRY GILFOND

Books published: **Black Hand at Sarajevo; The Reichstag Fire; Heroines of America; Plays for Reading; Favorite Short Stories; Voodoo; Journey Without End.** Has ghosted sports books and biographies of John Kennedy and Robert Kennedy. Written radio and TV scripts for **Cavalcade of America, American Inventory, New World A'Coming.** Edited: **New World Monthly; Dance Observer.**

Address: P.O. Box 357, Hampton Bays, NY 11946
(516) 283-3904

Agent: Bertha Case, 345 West 58th St., New York, NY 10019 (212) 541-9451

TITLE • AVAILABILITY • PRODUCTIONS

The Wick and the Tallow: recorded by Folkways

Region of the Cross: workshop productions at Circle-in-the-Square

Edge of the Knife: manuscript*;

Moses: manuscript*

Trade a Day: manuscript*

Moon over Deep Bay: manuscript*
*contact agent

G

Henry Gilfond (cont'd)
SYNOPSES

The Wick and the Tallow: A house in which the husband, three daughters and a son-in-law struggle against a matriarchy and against each other. Throughout the play there is a promise of murder. It is a mood play of which Norris Houghton wrote "reminiscent of ways of Yeats and Lorca, a comparison I mean as a compliment, in its combination of passion and a kind of poetic symbolism."

Full-length verse. Setting: livingroom/kitchen. 1 male, 4 females.

Trade a Day: Intrigue in a lush brothel. A sailing man tries to lure one of the women into a life at sea. The illegitimate son of the madam threatens to destroy the brothel. Callous politics, chicanery and comic action, with a man-hating whore taking center stage, as another whore creates a Missa Solemnis on the brothel piano.

Full-length verse. Setting: main room of brothel, with escalator, if possible. 5 males, 5 females.

JACK GILHOOLEY

Born in Philadelphia, PA on June 26, 1940. Syracuse U. (B.A. Drama), Villanova U (M.A. Theatre), U of Pennsylvania (M.A. American Civilization). Currently Director of Theatre at Jersey City State College, where he teaches Playwriting and Introduction to Theatre. Member: New Dramatists; Actor's Equity; Screen Actors' Guild. Guest writer, Directors Unit, Actor's Studio. Recipient: Shubert Playwriting Fellowship; Fenimore Playwriting Award; Jane L. Gilmore Playwright Award; MacDowell and Millay Colony Fellowship; National Endowment for the Arts Grant.

Address: 639 West End Ave., Apt. 12-C, New York, NY 10025 (212) 595-3997

Agent: Mary Harden, c/o Bret Adams Ltd., 36 East 61st St., New York, NY 10021 (212) 752-7864

TITLE • AVAILABILITY • PRODUCTIONS

The Last Act (one act): manuscript*; Thirteenth Street Playhouse, NYC; Theatre for the New City, NYC

Entrepreneurs of Avenue B (one act): manuscript*; Thirteenth Street Playhouse, NYC; Vassar College

Homefront Blues: manuscript*; Manhattan Theatre Club, NYC

The Last Christian: manuscript*; New Dramatists, NYC; The Open Space in Soho, NYC

The Comeback: manuscript*; Theatre for the New City, NYC; Upstairs at the Downstairs, NYC

Avenue B: manuscript*

The Time Trial: manuscript*; New York Shakespeare Festival, NYC; Syracuse U., NY

The Competitors: manuscript*; La Mama E.T.C. Co., NYC

Mummer's End: manuscript*; Folger Theatre, Wash., D.C.; Asolo Theater, FL

The Elusive Angel: manuscript*; O'Neill Theater Center's National Playwrights Conference, CT; Phoenix Theatre, NYC

Afternoon in Vegas: manuscript*; Theatre by the Sea, NY; American Conservatory Theatre, CA

The Brixton Recovery: manuscript*; Indiana Repertory Theatre, IN; PAF, NY

The Ravelles' Comeback: manuscript*

Descendants: manuscript*; Indiana Repertory Theatre, IN

Jack Gilhooley (cont'd)

Mummers: manuscript*

Shirley Basin: manuscript*

Dancin' to Calliope: manuscript*; Earplay

SYNOPSES

The Time Trial: Seven auto-racing freaks in their twenties, restless and resentful from an inability to alter their dead-end existence in a small town, look forward to the return of the local hero (a world champion driver). But his racing death, under highly suspect circumstances, changes their lives and separates them forever.

Full length. Setting: grandstand and automobile graveyard. 4 males, 3 females.

Afternoons in Vegas: This play concerns four women in Rocco Moranzo's Pussycat Lounge off "The Strip." Bunny, the roller-derby queen, represents a sort of vicarious glamor for the other three until Randy, a rich golfer arrives to jeopardize their comradeship.

Full length. Setting: a lounge. 1 male, 4 females.

Descendants: Three generations of the Gavin family are reunited by the dying mother. The desperate attempts to bury the past animosities that have scattered the sons and daughters ultimately serve to reopen old wounds and initate the granddaughter.

Full length. Setting: a livingroom. 3 males, 3 females.

FRANK D. GILROY

Born in New York City on October 13, 1925. B.A., Dartmouth College, also attended Yale School of Drama. Has written novels; **Private, From Noon till Three.** For TV, he wrote for **Playhouse 90, Omnibus, Kraft Theatre,** etc. Films; **The Fastest Gun Alive, Desperate Characters, From Noon till Three, Once in Paris.** President of the Dramatists Guild, 1969–71. Recipient: Obie Award, 1962; Pulitzer Prize, 1964; New York Drama Critics Circle Award, 1965; Berlin Film Festival, 1971.

Address: c/o Dramatists Guild, 234 West 44th St., New York NY 10036

TITLE • AVAILABILITY • PRODUCTIONS

The Middle World: not available; Dartmouth College, NH

Who'll Save the Plowboy?: Samuel French, 25 W. 45th St., New York, NY 10036, $2.50; Phoenix Theatre, NYC

The Subject Was Roses: Samuel French, $2.50; Broadway

Far Rockaway: Samuel French, $2.50; Channel 13, NYC

That Summer—That Fall: Samuel French, $2.50; Broadway

The Only Game in Town: Samuel French, $2.50; Broadway

Present Tense includes **Come Next Tuesday, Twas Brilling, So Please Be Kind:** Samuel French, $2.50; Sheridan Square Playhouse, NYC

Last Licks: manuscript*; Broadway

The Next Contestant: Samuel French, $1.25; Ensemble Studio Theatre, NYC

Dreams of Glory: Samuel French, $1.50; Ensemble Studio Theatre, NYC
    *contact author

G

MAXWELL GLANVILLE

Trained many of the black actors on the present professional scene. Has had some experience as producer, director, stage manager, instructor, coach, master of ceremonies, play editor, and in playwriting, poetry reading and writing. Recently completed two screenplays. Also an autobiographical account of his life on the American theatrical scene in the form of a novel, **The Bitch.** Former newspaper columnist for the **Amsterdam,** New York, **News; Age; Chicago Defender,** New York edition; and local organs. Recipient: YMCA Award for Service to Community in Theatre, 1965; Bed-Stuy Civic Club and American Community Theatre Award for "unselfish, devoted and inspirational work in the field of theatre and arts for the community;"

Special Audelco Award for Sustained and Superior Contributions to Black Theatre, 1979; Pioneer in Black Theatre; WLIB Community Civic award; scholarship to New School for Social Research in 1942–43 (acting and study of drama); offered Rosenwald Scholarship in 1943 but had to refuse because of greetings from Uncle Sam. Currently staff writer and showbiz columnist for **Big Red.**

Address: 775 Concourse Village East, Bronx, NY 10451 (212) 992-1441

TITLE • AVAILABILITY • PRODUCTIONS

Subway Sadie (playlet; co-author with Charles Griffen): manuscript*; Greenwich Mews Theatre, NYC

For Any Evil: manuscript*

The Bonus (one-act comedy): manuscript*; American Community Theatre; Clark Center YWCA

Cindy (one-act fairy tale): manuscript*; American Community Theatre; Adam Clayton Powell Jr. Theatre

Long Stretch—Short Haul: manuscript*; American Community Theatre; Brownsville, Brooklyn

Dance to a Nosepicker's Drum (co-author with Rudolph Gray, Jr.): manuscript*; Clark Center YWCA; Concourse Village, Bronx

The Injectors (playlet): manuscript*

Twit for Twat (co-author with Gertrude Grenidge; musical comedy based on Shakespeare's **Measure for Measure):** manuscript*; reading at New Florida Theatre, NYC
*contact author

SYNOPSES

The Bonus: What happens when a newly-married young couple decide to go on a vacation and they are visited by the mother-in-law? Hubby's bonus spurs him to want to go but wifey feels obligated to entertain Mom who is not at all what we expect.

One-act comedy. Setting: livingroom. 1 male, 2 females.

Long Stretch-Short Haul: Three actors are out of work and looking like crazy while doing odd jobs. They hold meetings regularly to check their situation. Love interest is there because a secretary loves one who is indifferent while another loves her to whom she is indifferent.

Full length comedy. Setting: Street area and living room. 6 males, 3 females.

Cindy: The Cinderella story told in black lifestyle. One-act comedy-fairy tale based on a fairy tale.

Setting: livingroom with two exits. 2 males, 4 females.

JOANNA McCLELLAND GLASS

Ms. Glass is a native of Canada. Her novel, **Reflections on a Mountain Summer,** was published by Alfred Knopf in the U.S. and by Macmillan in London. It was "read" in ten segments on B.B.C. in 1976. A short story, **At the King Edward Hotel,** was published in England by Macmillan in 1977, in a collection titled **Winter's Tales 22.** This collection has appeared in the U.S., published by St. Martin's Press. Recipient: National Endowment for the Arts Grant, 1979.

Agent: Lucy Kroll Agency, 390 West End Ave., New York, NY 10024 (212) 877-0627

TITLE • AVAILABILITY • PRODUCTIONS

Santacqua: not available; H. B. Playwrights Unit, NYC

Canadian Gothic-American Modern (companion one acts); Dramatists Play Service, 440 Park Avenue South, New York, NY 10016, $2.50; Manhattan Theatre Club, NYC; Berkeley, CA

Artichoke: Dramatists Play Service, $2.50; Long Wharf Theatre, New Haven, CT; Alley Theatre, Houston, TX

The Last Chalice: not available; Manitoba Theatre Centre

To Grandmother's House We Go: Samuel French, 25 W. 45th St., New York, NY 10036, $2.50; Alley Theatre, Houston, TX; Broadway
*contact agent

SYNOPSES

Canadian Gothic: A story of class clash, miscegenation, pride and loss set in a small Canadian city.

Setting: three chairs. 4 characters: Mother, Father, Daughter, and a Cree Indian

American Modern: A wife, middle-class, middle-aged, has become a scavenger who makes daily forays into Long Island gutters. She relates to her husband the events of her first visit to a psychiatrist.

1 male, 1 female.

(These two plays are companion pieces, running an hour each, and are intended to be performed together.)

Artichoke: Walter Morley commits adultery with a water witch, who then leaves her addled child on Margaret Morley's doorstep. Margaret raises the child but banishes Walter to the smokehouse. Eventually, the Morleys entertain a summer visitor, Gibson McFarland, an international authority on Alexander Pope. Margaret has a summer affair with Gibson, causing Walter to move in with Jake and Archie, two old farmers who act as a chorus. A serious comedy about pride, compromise, and acceptance of self.

Setting: a vast prairie farm. 5 males, 1 female, 1 girl.

To Grandmother's House We Go; Grandie, 81, lives with her old, retired brother, Jared; her widowed daughter, Harriet; and her elderly maid/companion, Clementine. On Thanksgiving weekend Harriet's three children, all in states of marital disarray, arrive with requests for support and refuge. A serious comedy about changing values and standards, the disintegration of family. The theme is stated by Harriet: "Is there a life after children?"

Full length. Setting: an antique-cluttered Victorian living room. 2 males, 6 females.

G

SETH GLASSMAN

Born in New York City on July 10, 1947. Educated at City University of New York, B.A., Phi Beta Kappa, magna cum laude; New York Univ., M.A. Drama. Directing credits include: three seasons as Artistic Director of the Woodstock Stage Company; **Summertree,** Off-Broadway; **2 × 5,** a musical cabaret, Off-Broadway. Presently Artistic Director of the Stage Company; Director-in-Residence at The Vocal Arts Foundation where he conducts workshops for actors, directors, and club and opera performers.

Agent: Audrey Wood, ICM, 40 West 57th St., New York, NY 10019, (212) 556-5722

TITLE • AVAILABILITY • PRODUCTIONS

Billy (musical): manuscript*; Billy Rose Theater, Broadway

Zooo!: manuscript*

The Wooing of Mad Margaret: manuscript*
   *contact agent

RUTH GOETZ

Born in Philadelphia, PA on January 11, 1912. Wrote many plays with her husband, Augustus, also the films, **The Heiress, Carrie, Rhapsody, Trapeze** and **Stagestruck.** Treasurer of the Dramatists Guild. Recipient: Academy Award for **The Heiress.**

Address: c/o The Dramatists Guild, 234 West 44th St., New York, NY 10036 (212) 398-9366

TITLE • AVAILABILITY • PRODUCTIONS

Franklin Street; not available; National Theatre, Wash., DC

One Man Show; manuscript*; Broadway

The Heiress (adaptation); Dramatists Play Service, 440 Park Ave. South, New York, NY 10016, $2.50; Broadway

The Immoralist (adaptation); Dramatists Play Service, $2.50; Broadway

The Hidden River (adaptation); Dramatists Play Service, $2.50; Playhouse Theatre, NYC

Sweet Love Remembered; manuscript*; New Haven, CT

Madly in Love (adaptation); not available; Summer Theater

Play on Love (adaptation with Bart Howard); not available; London
   *contact author

LLOYD GOLD

Born in Atlanta, GA, raised in the small north Georgia town of Dalton. Attended Tulane University and received B.A. degree from Emory University in 1972. Received M.F.A. degree from Brandeis University in 1974.Plays produced at Emory and Brandeis. He attended the Edward Albee Foundation at Montauk, Long Island. Screenplay for Aurora Productions, **Don't Tell Me Your Name.** Recipient: Shubert Playwriting Fellowship; Fellowship from the National Endowment for the Arts.

Address: 160 Bleecker St., New York, NY 10012

Agent: Flora Roberts, 65 East 55th St., New York, NY 10022 (212) 355-4165

TITLE • AVAILABILITY • PRODUCTIONS

Renaissance: manuscript*

The Turnip: not available; Emory University

A Grave Undertaking: Dramatists Play Service, 400 Park Avenue South, New York, NY 10016, $2.50; O'Neill Theater Center's National Playwrights Conference, CT; Seattle Repertory Theatre, WA

Davis J.: manuscript*; Birmingham Festival Theatre, AL

When the Stars Begin to Fall: manuscript*;

Bright Wings: manuscript*

Selective Service: manuscript*; Actors Theatre of Louisville, KY
*contact agent

SYNOPSES

A Grave Undertaking: A Grave Undertaking is the story of an undertaker who hates death, his blue baby daughter, and the priest she loves. It is set in the Garden District of New Orleans during the Mardi Gras of 1956. In the course of the play's action the undertaker, Herman Starr, tries to save his daughter from certain death; the daughter, Monica, risks that death for a glimpse of the world outside her house; and the priest, Dominic Savio Paquette, is forced to confront both death and life as never before.

"Mr. Gold has written a richly textured play full of a certain density, surprising in the strength of its emotions, rewarding in the range and scope of its imagination. Undoubtedly Mr. Gold is a playwright to be reckoned with." —Clive Barnes

Setting: single set of southern charm and Gothic decay. 7 males, 2 females.

Bright Wings: Blaise Callahan's wife is a saint. A real one. He goes to Rome from New Orleans to witness his late wife's canonization. Her goodness and mercy have followed him all the days of his life — and he is perfectly miserable. In Rome, Blaise discovers a world filled with devils and angels, usually indiscernible from each other. And, in the end, he discovers a man — himself.

Full length. Setting: flexible and fluid. 5 males, 1 female.

G

ROSE LEIMAN GOLDEMBERG

Born in Staten Island, NY on May 17, 1928. B.A.,
Brooklyn College (magna cum laude), M.A., Ohio
State University, also studied at American
Theatre Wing and Columbia University. Has
taught Playwriting, Acting and Directing at the
University level. Author of three books; **Here's
Egg on Your Face** (Hewitt House), **Antique
Jewelry: A Practical and Passionate Guide**
(Crown), **The Complete Book of Natural
Cosmetics** (Simon and Schuster). CBS-TV
special, **Land of Hope; The Burning Bed** (CBS);
B.B.C. radio adaptation of **Letters Home;** ABC-
TV Movie of the Week, **Mother and Daughter: The
Loving War** and CBS-TV miniseries, **Women**
among others. Recipient: Two faculty research
grants for Playwriting, Fairleigh Dickinson
University; two New Jersey State Council on
Arts Grants; First Prize, Sullivan County Dramatic Workshop; Earplay Purchase Award; Armstrong Award; First Honorable Mention, Concord Bicentennial Contest.

Address: 548 Martense Avenue, Teaneck, NJ 07666

Agent: Susan Breitner, (201) 779-4268 or (212) 753-6880

TITLE • AVAILABILITY • PRODUCTIONS

Apples in Eden: manuscript*

Absolutely Everything: manuscript*

A Little Travelling Music: manuscript*

Rites of Passage: manuscript*; New Dramatists, NYC; Astor Place Theater, NYC

Gandhiji: manuscript*; O'Neill Theater Center's National Playwrights Conference, CT; Fairleigh
   Dickinson University, NJ

The Merry War: manuscript*; New Dramatists, NYC; Fairleigh Dickinson University, NJ

Marching As to War: Dramatists Play Service, Inc., 440 Park Ave. South, New York, NY 10016,
   $1.25; East Village Theater, NYC

The Rabinowitz Gambit: manuscript*; Cleveland Playhouse, OH; New Theater Workshop, NYC

The Crossroad: IJL, 315 Park Avenue South, New York, NY 10022; Carillon Hotel, FL

Fences: Plays for Living, Family Service Association of America, 44 East 23rd St., New York,
   NY 10019, $2.00; Various productions

This Big House: Plays for Living, $2.00; Various productions

The Underground Bird: Plays for Living, $2.00; Various productions

Letters Home: Samuel French, 25 W. 45th St., New York, NY 10036, $2.50; American Place
   Theatre, NYC; Theater at New End, London

Personals: not available; American Place Theatre, NYC
   *contact agent

SYNOPSES

Rites of Passage: Charley Gordon's wife is dying — but to him she's terribly alive: four Louisas
who swirl around him in his solitude accusing him of some terrible unfaith. He also must deal
with his young daughter who can't accept her mother's fate, and with his own need, on many
levels, for a lonely, vulnerable schoolteacher who comes to visit. His exorcism of the Louisas and
his coming to grips with the core of his guilt is the crux of the play.

Full length. Setting: an apartment in upper New York state. 1 male, 6 females, 1 girl of 11.

The Rabinowitz Gambit: A Jewish father presides over the "engagement" (pawn-to-King-four) of
his brilliant chess bum son and a suicidal irresistable blonde "shiksa" — in a seedy hotel room in

G

New York on New Year's Eve. In the course of it all, they discover some secrets of life — and game playing — and love.

Setting: hotel room in New York. 4 males, 1 female.

Letters Home: Based on Aurelia Plath's editing of the letters of her brilliant poet daughter, Sylvia, **Letters Home** tells the powerful story of a mother who fought to keep her daughter from suicide.

Full length. Setting: open stage, freely furnished, where two women live. 2 females.

JOLENE GOLDENTHAL

Born in Boston, MA, A.B., Smith College; attended Yale School of Drama; M.A., Trinity College; University of Hartford, video and TV. Has written art criticism for **The Hartford Courant** and feature articles for **Antiques World, National Antiques Review, Trinity Reporter.** Lecturer, Hartford College for Women: The Playwright and the Play. Founder/Artistic Director, The Hartford Playwrights, Inc. Recipient: First Prize, Cedar Rapids Community Theatre; First Prize RAPT Playwriting Competition.

Address: 132 Jefferson St., Hartford, CT 06103
(203) 677-1484/249-5203

TITLE • AVAILABILITY • PRODUCTIONS

Mequasset by the Sea: manuscript*; ATA, NYC; Chelsea Theater/New Works Project, NYC

Remembering Mrs. Crowley: manuscript*; Hartford Stage Company, CT; Expressionist Theatre II, NYC

Island: manuscript*; Hartford Stage Company, CT; Shelter West, NYC

The Station: manuscript*; Cedar Rapids Community Theatre, IA

A Stranger in a Strange Land: manuscript*; Galaxy, Norfolk, VA; Foundation de l'Ecole Internationale, Switzerland

Five P.M.: manuscript*; Sausalito Drama Festival, CA

Birthday: manuscript*

The Carriage: manuscript*; CPTV; Old State House, CT

The Yellow Leaf: manuscript*; WMGM

Charade: manuscript*; Center Players

I Thought I Saw a Snowman: manuscript*

A Quiet Walk: manuscript*
    *contact author

G

A. E. O. GOLDMAN

Born on June 21, 1947. B.A., Amherst College,
M.A., Harvard University. Articles in the following: **New York Times** (Travel-1976; Op Ed 1979);
Readers Digest, foreign language editions (15
separate articles); **International Herald Tribune.**
Unpublished novel, **Picture of the People.** Recipient: CAPS semifinalist, 1974–75, for **Dabones
of Babylon.**

Address: 30 E. Hartsdale Avenue, Apt. 3L, Hartsdale, NY 10530

Agent: Barbara Rhodes, 140 West End Avenue,
New York, NY 10023 (212) 580-1300

TITLE • AVAILABILITY • PRODUCTIONS

Trapshod: manuscript*; Actors Voyage East, NYC

She's Bad Today: manuscript*; O'Neill Theater Center's National Playwrights Conference, CT

Dabones of Babylon: manuscript**

Secrets of a Shrinking Universe: manuscript**

Goethe with Shades: manuscript*
    *contact agent
    **contact author

SYNOPSES

Dabones of Babylon: Ash Siedman, always the pompous elitist and amused manipulator of lives
is forced by illness to become physically and emotionally dependent on Tony daBone —
unschooled, abrasive and utterly innocent, who comes crashing into his newly confined live.

Full length. Setting: a hospital room. 5 males, 4 females.

Secrets of a Shrinking Universe: The cosmic vs. the mundane. Dr. David Gordon, cosmologist is
losing control of his pulsing world. His students are revolting, his faculty retrenching, his wife
receding (into madness). It is 1969 and America is fresh upon the moon and an expanse is
shriveling in around him.

Full length. Setting: a large cluttered office in a university. 4 males, 1 female.

Goethe with Shades: John Henry Wolfson, academic, is being pursued, out in California (remak-
ing Faust or rather **I Love Lucifer** for the screen: occult! disaster! *and* sex) he is bedeviled by a
mysterious stranger from back east. It is a comedy between two coasts, two life styles, two men,
two sides of a single woman and of course, the damned dialectic.

Full length. Setting: studio/office, other areas only suggested. 3 males, 1 female.

JAMES GOLDMAN ‡

Born in Chicago, IL on June 30, 1927. Ph.B., and M.A. from University of Chicago. Post-graduate work at Columbia. Screenwriter: **The Lion in Winter; They Might Be Giants; Nicholas and Alexandra.** Novels: **Waldorf; The Man From Greek and Roman; Myself as Witness.** Recipient: Academy Award, 1968; American Screenwriters Award and British Screenwriters Award, 1967; Drama Critics Award.

Agent: Sam Cohn, International Creative Management, 40 West 57th St., New York, NY 10019 (212) 556-5600

TITLE • AVAILABILITY • PRODUCTIONS

Blood, Sweat and Stanley Poole (with William Goldman): Dramatists Play Service, 440 Park Ave. South, New York, NY 10016, $2.50; Broadway

Family Affair (book): manuscript*; Broadway

They Might Be Giants: manuscript*; Theatre Royal, Stratford, England

The Lion in Winter: Samuel French, 25 W. 45th St., New York, NY 10036, $2.50; Broadway

Follies: Music Theatre International, 119 West 57th St., New York, NY 10019; Broadway
*contact agent

LEE GOLDSMITH

Born in NYC on January 4, 1923. Educated at George Washington High School, N.Y.C.; 3½ years in Army, WW II (Pacific Service). First writing: special material lyrics for Evelyn Knight, Kaye Ballard, Hermione Gingold. Has also worked as comic book script writer and court reporter.

Address: 3124 Florida Ave., Miami, FL 33133 (305) 442-4726

Agent: Leo Bookman, c/o William Morris Agency, 1350 Avenue of the Americas, New York, NY 10019 (212) 586-5100

TITLE • AVAILABILITY • PRODUCTIONS

Sextet: manuscript*; Off-Broadway

Sheba: manuscript*; 1st Chicago Center, IL

Golddiggers of 1633: manuscript*; Players Repertory Theater, MIami, FL; Golden Apple Dinner Theater, Sarasota, FL

Shine: (lyrics) manuscript*
*contact author

SYNOPSES

Sextet: Interplay of relationships among two heterosexual couples and one homosexual couple during course of dinner party.

4 males, 2 females.

Sheba: Musical version of Inge's **Come Back Little Sheba.**

2 males, 2 females, 4 male chorus singer/dancers.

G

Lee Goldsmith (cont'd)

Golddiggers of 1633: Irreverent musical version of Moliere's **School for Wives.**

6 males, 2 females.

PATRICIA GOLDSTONE

Born in Los Angeles, CA on June 16, 1951. B.A. from Vassar College (magna cum laude); Anglo-Irish Literature Diploma; M. Lit., Trinity College, Dublin (first degree honors). Journalism, in the field of sociology/entertainment. Published in **New West, MacClean's, Washington Post, L.A. Times, American Film, Sight and Sound** and several European publications. Has written several screenplays and one novel. Recipient: Maguire Fellowship for study in Western Europe for two years.

Address: 114 S. Flores St., Los Angeles, CA
90048 (213) 653-0423

Agent: Susan Breitner, (201) 779-4268 or
(212) 753-6880

TITLE • AVAILABILITY • PRODUCTIONS

Anne in the Camps: manuscript*; Vassar College, NY

The Sisters of Mercy: manuscript*; Vassar College, NY

The Circus Animals' Desertion: manuscript*; Trinity Players Theatre; Wexford Opera Festival

The Sunday Shoe: manuscript*; Trinity Players Theatre; Radio Telefis Eireann Radio Players

The Disturbing Death of Ernie Melia: manuscript*
    *contact author

SYNOPSES

The Circus Animals' Desertion: Fantasy/drama on the life and times of W. B. Yeats.

Full-length and one-act version available. Setting: minimal set. 4 males, 3 females.

The Disturbing Death of Ernie Melia: Mystery/drama on the fate of one Irish laborer at the hands of police in London at the height of the 1974 IRA bomb campaign.

Long one act. Setting: minimal set. 9 males, 3 females, male parts can be doubled or tripled up.

Anne in the Camps: Fantasy/drama tracing Anne Frank's path after "The Diary" ends. Set within a deserted train station in modern Europe as, after death, she meets her father once again.

Long one act. Setting: Minimal set. 2 males, 2 females.

GLORIA GONZALEZ

Born in New York City. Studied playwriting with Harold Callen at The New School; Rick Sevy, Theatre Arts Workshop; studied directing/ playwriting with Lee Strasberg; studied acting with Anthony Mannino. Worked as an investigative newspaper reporter for ten years on various dailies. TV credits: **Gaucho,** After School Special ABC-TV; **The Day the Women Got Even,** Movie of the Week; and has developed comedy pilots for Columbia Pictures, MGM and Warner Brothers. Author of juvenile novels, **The Glad Man** and **Gaucho,** published by Alfred A. Knopf. Regular contributor to the **Dramatists Guild Quarterly.** Member: The Dramatists Guild; Author's League of America; Writer's Guild of America, East; Women in Film, Inc. Recipient: Jacksonville College Playwriting Contest.

Address: 5907 Boulevard East, West New York, NJ 07093

Agent: Selma Luttinger, Brandt and Brandt, 1501 Broadway, New York, NY 10036 (212) 840-5760

TITLE • AVAILABILITY • PRODUCTIONS

Curtains: : Dramatists Play Service, 400 Park Ave. South, New York, NY 10016, $1.25; **Best Short Plays, 1976,** Chilton Books, Radnor, PA 19089; Jacksonville University; Hudson Guild, NYC

Let's Hear It For Miss America!: manuscript*; Country Dinner Playhouse, FL

Double Play: under option

A Sanctuary in the City: manuscript*; Theatre Americana, Altadena, CA

The Puppet Trip: manuscript*

A Day in the Port Authority: manuscript*; Theatre at Noon, NYC

Woola-Boola (musical): manuscript*

Black Thoughts on a Bright Monday: manuscript*

Revolutionaries Don't Sit in the Orchestra: manuscript*

A Former Gotham Girl: manuscript*; Corner Theatre, Baltimore, MD; New Playwrights Theatre, Washington, D.C.

Cafe Con Leche: manuscript*

Lights: manuscript*; Theatre Webster Groves, St. Louis, MO

Moving On!: Samuel French, 25 W. 45th St., New York, NY 10036, $2.50; Theatre at Noon, NYC

Love Is a Tuna Casserole: manuscript*; New York Theatre Ensemble, NYC
   *contact agent

SYNOPSES

The Puppet Trip: A celestial classroom. The "students" are Marilyn Monroe, Chief Sitting Bull, Clarence Darrow, Booker T. Washington, Lizzie Borden and Babe Ruth. Their assignment: to decide whether or not to resume an earthly existence — with, in some cases, a change in sex . . . race . . . nationality.

Full length. Setting: bare classroom except for desks. 5 males, 2 females.

Light!/Curtains!: Two zany "valentines" to show biz.

5 males, 3 females.

G

ROBERT GORDON

B.A. and M.A. from UCLA in Speech; M.A. in Creative Writing from San Francisco State University. Teaching playwriting at San Francisco State University. Has completed two novels, **The Quest for Steven Yelm** and **Leaks**. Stories and plays published in such quarterlies as **Paris Review, Transatlantic Review, The Literary Review, Texas Quarterly**. Recipient: Goldwyn Literary Award for a collection of stories; Playwright-in-residence with the American Conservatory Theatre, 1972–73; Tangley Foundation Grant in Writing; Dramatists Guild travel grant; T.C.G. Travel Grant.

Address: 50 Davis Lane, Penngrove, CA 94951

Agent: Robert Lantz, Lantz Office, 114 East 55th St., New York, NY 10022 (212) 751-2107

TITLE • AVAILABILITY • PRODUCTIONS

Person to Person: manuscript*; O'Neill Theater Center's National Playwrights Conference, CT; San Francisco Actor's Ensemble, CA

The Tunes of Chicken Little: Playwrights for Tomorrow, Vol. 13, University of Minnesota Press, $4.95 (paperback); American Conservatory Theatre, San Francisco, CA

The Light and the Dark of It: manuscript*

Once and for All: manuscript*; O'Neill Theater Center's National Playwrights Conference, CT; Goodman Theatre, Chicago, IL

Young Caesar (puppet opera): manuscript*; Cabrillo Music Festival; Cal Tech, Los Angeles, CA

Going Over: manuscript*; American Shakespeare Theatre, Stratford, CT

And: West Coast Plays, #2 Box 7206, Berkeley, CA 94707, $4.95; American Conservatory Theatre, San Francisco, CA; Bare Stage, San Francisco, CA
*contact author or agent

SYNOPSES

Person to Person: A serio-comic treatment of modern evasion and its consequences. This play presents a poignant tale of one super-aggressive but intelligent speech teacher (Gale) and her confrontation with a potential love, a young hippie-ish detective put on her trail by her husband who wishes to become her ex-. Gale is a lonely, hence hostile, dart-throwing neurotic who is beset with anger and guilt at her own deficiencies, yet is saved by a blissful sense of humor that tells her the truth about herself. "Playwright Gordon sensitively probes the depths of his characters' anguish but is also intelligent enough to realize that a maudlin display would only belabor his points." —**Berkeley Gazette**.

Full length. Setting: the livingroom of Gale's apartment, which is altered in Act II to reveal part of another apartment. 2 males, 2 females.

The Tunes of Chicken Little: A chicken in a cage at a county fair plays the piano when a light goes on. His encaged situation and his eventual death signify fact and symbol for the people who come in contact with Chicken Little. The play cuts across both traditional time and space. Time-wise, the play shifts — with a single line or entrance of a character — forward or back in time and the people often speak to each other across time and space. The subjects of freedom versus imprisonment, and identity are explored throughout. Some of the characters: a judge who prefers studying mushrooms to the law; Nat, who owns and fears Chicken Little; Rutherford, considered "retarded" by society but open to much experience denied others; Carol, young and pretty, who only wants to be happy and thinks it should be easy; a lesbian couple, trying to work through to a more satisfying relationship; Rhoda, who keeps the facts straight; and her husband, who wants to be comfortable.

Full length. Setting: consists of lightweight modules plus a cage large enough to hold a man-chicken. A coatrack at either end of the stage holds the various props. 9 males, 8 females.

Robert Gordon (cont'd)

Once and For All: The themes of death and personal evasion in a contemporary American family are explored in this dark comedy. In the first scene, **Once**, there are two young brothers, one a dead war veteran who is suspicious of language, the other alive and a great verbalist. The live one feels guilty over the death of his brother. In the second scene, **And,** their mother delivers a lengthy monologue to her husband as he lies dead on the couch. In the third scene, **for All,** which takes place in a cemetery, all four have a chance to work through some of their fears and confusions. ". . . resounds with something of the same slow anguish and despair that marks . . . Joseph Heller's **Something Happened.** Both present pictures of distress and ambivalence which afflict America these days." —**Denver Post.**

One act (runs about 1 hour, 10 minutes). Setting: non-naturalistic, and should economically suggest the livingroom in scene two and the cemetery in scene three. Scene one requires a mannikin and an artificial tree. 3 males, 1 female.

RUTH GORDON

Born in Wollaston, MA on October 30, 1896. Married Gregory Kelly (dec.), Married Garson Kanin, 1942. First acted in **Peter Pan** at Empire Theatre, NYC, 1915. Has made many films and appeared extensively on television. With husband Garson Kanin, has co-authored films **Adam's Rib, A Double Life, The Marrying Kind** and **Pat and Mike.** Wrote the plays **Years Ago** (became the film **Actress**); **Over Twenty-One; The Leading Lady; A Very Rich Woman.** Author of **Myself Among Others.** Autobriography, **My Side,** 1976 (Harper & Row), **An Open Book,** 1980 (Doubleday). Recipient: Academy Award (Oscar) for **Rosemary's Baby** (1972); Emmy Award, **Taxi,** (1979).

Address: 200 West 57th St., Suite 1203, New York, NY 10019 (212) 556-7850

Agent: Milton Goldman, International Creative Management, 40 West 57th St., New York, NY 10019 (212) 556-5703

TITLE • AVAILABILITY • PRODUCTIONS

Years Ago: Dramatists Play Service, 440 Park Ave. South, New York, NY 10016, $2.75; Mansfield Theatre, NYC

The Leading Lady: manuscript*; Dramatists Play Service, $10 deposit, $2 reading fee; National Theatre, NYC

Over Twenty-One: manuscript*; Dramatists Play Service, $10 deposit, $2 reading fee; Music Box, NYC

A Very Rich Woman (adapted): Samuel French, 25 W. 45th St., New York, NY 10036; $2.50; Belasco Theatre, NYC

Ho! Ho! Ho!: manuscript*; Stockbridge, MA.
  *contact agent

G

CHARLES GORDONE

Born in Cleveland, OH on October 12, 1925. B.A., Los Angeles State College. Served in the U.S. Air Force. Actor and Director. Member: Actor's Studio; Ensemble Studio. Recipient: National Institute of Arts and Letters; Drama Desk Award; Critic's Circle Award; Obie Award (acting); Pulitzer Prize.

Address: 17 West 100 Street, New York, NY 10025

Agent: Rosenstone/Wender, 3 East 48th St., New York, NY 10017 (212) 832-8330

TITLE • AVAILABILITY • PRODUCTIONS

A Little More Light Around The Place (adaptation): manuscript*; Sheridan Square Playhouse, NYC

No Place to Be Somebody: Samuel French, 25 W. 45th St., New York, NY 10036, $2.50; Sheridan Square Playhouse, NYC; Playwrights Unit, NYC

Gordone Is a Muthah: Best Short Plays of 1973, Chilton Press, Chilton Way, Radnor, PA 19089; Carnegie Recital Hall, NYC

Baba Chops: manuscript*; Wilshire Ebell, Los Angeles, CA

The Last Chord: manuscript*; Billie Holiday Theatre, NYC

Anabiosis: manuscript*; City Players, St. Louis, MO
    *contact agent

PHILIP KAN GOTANDA

Born in Stockton, CA on December 17, 1949. B.A. in Asian Studies from U. of California at Santa Barbara; J.D. from Hastings College of Law; studied ceramics in Japan. Co-founder of Asian American Musicians Organization. As a singer/songwriter of original Asian American music, he has performed extensively throughout the western coast of the US and Canada. Recipient: Artist-in-residence at Okada House at Stanford University; Rockefeller Grant, 1980-81.

Address: 229 Willard N., #7, San Francisco, CA 94118 (415) 387-0577

TITLE • AVAILABILITY • PRODUCTIONS

The Avocado Kid or Zen in the Art of Guacamole: manuscript*; East West Players, LA, CA; Asian American Theater Co., San Francisco, CA

Song for a Nisei Fisherman: manuscript*; Asian American Theater Co. San Francisco, CA; Stanford University, CA

Bullet Headed Birds: manuscript*; Asian American Theater Co., San Francisco, CA; Stanford University, CA

Zero: manuscript*
    *contact author

SYNOPSES

Song for a Nisei Fisherman: It is a play with music that chronicles the life of a Nisei (second

Philip Kan Gotanda (cont'd)

generation Japanese American) man from the time of his childhood in Hawaii until his death through a melange of story, music and memory. The play utilizes the complete cycle of fishing — catching, cleaning, cooking, eating, catching — as a cyclical metaphor for his life.

One act, one and a half hours. Setting: simple stage and most props should be mimed. 1 central character and 6 males and 4 females.

The Avocado Kid or Zen in the Art of Guacamole: An Asian-American musical based on the Japanese fairy tale **Momotaro, the Peachboy.** A boy pops out of an avocado and sets out on an odyssey. Along the way, he meets Jinya Wolf (a woman raised by wolves), Bigfoot (a vegetarian soft-shoeing sasquatch) and a Dodo bird who dresses in "duck drag." He ultimately duals with Jagaimo, the Bandit and the Fabulous Bandelles, a new-wave meat-eating band. Music cuts across a wide variety of musical styles.

Full length. 6 males, 4 females, 5 parts can be either sex.

JOSEPH GATH GOTTFRIED

Born in Tel Aviv, Israel on March 24, 1935. Studied playwriting with Gene Frankel, The New School and New York University. Member of the Dramatists Guild. Has written an illustrated children's story, **Pepito,** and four short films: **The Wrong Side of the Park** (produced in 1974 by NATAS), **Mermaid, Heart of Stone,** and **Technicolor Spectacles.**

Address: 25 Tudor Pl., New York, NY 10017 (212) 682-4815

TITLE • AVAILABILITY • PRODUCTIONS

Tidings: manuscript*; Playbox, NYC

Play House: manuscript*; Mercer Street Art Center, NYC

Dr. Denton's Secret: manuscript*; Lolly's Theatre Club, NYC

Thespians: manuscript*

Dune Road: manuscript*; American Theatre of Actors

Summer Reunion: manuscript*

Choices: manuscript*

Bungalow: manuscript*

Murdermask: manuscript*
   *contact author

SYNOPSES

Playhouse: Joel and Steve have been lovers for two years when Mary Jane, whom Joel married to become an American citizen, shows up, pregnant. Fun-loving, fag-hag Mary Jane manages to win over the apprehensive Steve, but when he tries to talk his lover into keeping the child, Joel refuses to "play house." Mary Jane, who's determined to find a home and father for her baby, threatens her husband to have him deported unless he lets her stay and keep the child. Joel, who's equally determined not to destroy his relationship with Steve, throws her out. Lost at first, survivor Mary Jane looks up another gay couple and manages to get invited over.

Full length. Setting: small New York apartment. 2 males, 1 female.

G

BARBARA GRAHAM

Born in Pittsburgh, PA on November 22, 1947. Attended New York University and San Francisco State University. She is a former actress and director. Currently Artistic Director of Tale Spinners, a multi-generational theatre troupe which performs plays relating to aging and the aged. Staff theatre reviewer for the **San Francisco Bay Guardian** since 1978. Playwright-in-residence, Berkeley Stage Company, 1978-79.

Address: 873 Alvarado St., San Francisco, CA 94114

Agent: Bridget Aschenberg, I.C.M., 40 West 57th St., New York, NY 10019 (212) 556-5720

TITLE • AVAILABILITY • PRODUCTIONS

Jacob's Ladder: West Coast Plays, P.O. Box 7206, Berkeley, CA 94707, $5.00; Berkeley Stage Company, CA; WPA Theatre, NY

The Care and Feeding of Poultry: manuscript*; Eureka Theatre, San Francisco, CA

Elderly Gentleman Seeks: manuscript*; People's Theatre Coalition, San Francisco, CA; Eureka Theatre, San Francisco, CA
*contact agent

SYNOPSES

Jacob's Ladder: Leona, an up-and-coming painter of thirty-three, lives alone with her nine-year-old son, Jacob, in a storefront flat in San Francisco. Will, Jacob's father and Leona's husband returns after an absence of nineteen months to assert his paternal claim to the boy. Having established a new life in Mexico City following the breakdown of his marriage to Leona, Will is anxious to share his life with Jacob. The issue is one of scarcity: two parents, one child; both parents want to raise the chld. The dynamics are further complicated by the presence of Peter, Leona's 27-year-old lover.

Full length. Setting: Leona's flat, consisting of living quarters plus studio space. 3 males, 2 females.

The Care and Feeding of Poultry: A comedy in which Emily and Michael Cantor — adults in their thirties — have moved back to their parents' cramped apartment in New Jersey. Each for his or her own reasons has found it difficult to cope with the world. Corrine and Jack, their parents, plan a birthday celebration for Emily — even though it isn't really her birthday — in order to give her a boost. Annie, Jack's mother and the children's grandmother attempts to help Emily in her own way by incantation, swinging a chicken over Emily's head and presenting her with a one-way ticket out of New Jersey. In this play, flying chickens and magic and denial of reality collide with reality, forcing the characters to accept what actually is rather than isolated worlds of their own invention.

Full length. Setting: a livingroom, a park, a blood bank. 3 males, 5 females.

Elderly Gentleman Seeks: Benjamin Bloom, a 75 year old widower, wishes to maintain his independence and continue living in his own home, despite difficulties. His middle-aged daughter, Sylvie, has decided that it is impractical and unsafe for her father to continue to live alone and she begins to take steps to secure another living arrangement for him (some sort of institution). Willie, his granddaughter, comes up with an alternative solution to her grandfather's housing problem and convinces him to put an ad in the paper for roommates. Two elderly women, Rowena and Lillie, show up and talk Benjamin into letting them move in. Sylvie realizes that no amount of professional supervision can protect her father and herself from old age and death. 6 songs, lyrics and music by Richard Koldewyn.

One act, about one hour. Setting: split stage, Benjamin's kitchen and the Housing Authority. 2 males, 4 females, a pianist.

PERCY GRANGER

Born in Ithaca, NY on August 8, 1945. Attended Oklahoma public schools, Harvard University with a B.A. in English Literature, cum laude. He has written for film, television, radio (over fifty scripts for **Radio Mystery Theater** and **Sears, now Mutual, Radio Theater**) and stage. Literary manager for the Ensemble Studio Theatre, 1977–78.

Address: 650 West End Ave., New York, NY 10025

Agent: Rick Leed, Hesseltine-Baker, 119 West 57th St., New York, NY 10019 (212) 489-0966

TITLE • AVAILABILITY • PRODUCTIONS

Eminent Domain: manuscript*; O'Neill Theater Center's National Playwrights Conference, CT; McCarter Theatre Co., NJ

Studs Edsel: manuscript*; Folger Theatre Group, Wash., DC; Ensemble Studio Theatre, NYC

The Enchanted Cottage (musical adaptation): manuscript*; St. Nicholas Theater Co., IL

Leavin' Cheyenne/Working Her Way Down: manuscript*; St. Clements, NYC

Vivien: manuscript*; Ensemble Studio Theatre, NYC; Newhouse Theater, Lincoln Center, NYC

Solitude Forty: manuscript*; WPA, NYC; U of Oklahoma
    *contact agent

HARRY GRANICK

Self-educated. Published poetry, short stories, articles; recorded songs and narratives set to music. Wrote radio dramas and documentaries in its best period; television scripts until blacklisted. One of ten selected for Theatre Guild's Playwrights Workshop under Kenneth Rowe; member of New Dramatists during first twelve years. Books: **Run, Run!**, Simon and Shuster, a full-length novel for ten-year-olds. **Underneath New York**, Rinehart & Co., non-fiction description. **Warsaw Ghetto**, a tone poem, performed by the Dean Dixon Orchestra, Martin Wolfson narrator, at Carnegie Hall. Drama critic for **Masses and Mainstream** and for **New Theater Magazine**, England. Recipient: Peabody Award, Radio Documentary; Theater Conference Grant; Sergal Play Contest, Third Prize for **Witches' Sabbath;** Five Arts Contest, First Prize, for **Witches' Sabbath.**

Address: 100 LaSalle Street, New York, NY 10027 (212) 749-1730

Agent: Bertha Klausner, International Literary Agency, 71 Park Ave., New York, NY 10016 (212) 685-2642

TITLE • AVAILABILITY • PRODUCTIONS

The Guilty: manuscript*; Margo Jones Theater, TX; college and summer stock productions; many overseas productions

Witches' Sabbath: manuscript*; Syracuse U.; Off-Broadway

Promenade: manuscript*

The Hooper Law: manuscript*; Margo Jones Theater, TX

G

Harry Granick (cont'd)

The Hells of Dante: manuscript*

The President and the Psychiatrist: manuscript*

The Jew of Venice: manuscript*

Pigeons (comedy): manuscript*

The Long Smoldering (A Holocaust Play): manuscript*

The Bright and Golden Land: manuscript*; PAF Playhouse, LI; Shelter West, NYC

Two for One: manuscript*
  *contact agent

SYNOPSES

Witches' Sabbath: France, Fourteenth Century, a time of wars. An impoverished knight, held two years by his English captors, returns to his barony without horse and armour, embittered by his wife's failure to ransom him. Now he is intolerably wounded to learn of his wife's infidelity. Rejecting the regional Inquisitor's offer of help to restore him to power, he institutes his own inquisition to compel compliance with his demands. There follows his retainers' mass rape of a serf on her wedding night, their murder of her husband and a witches' Sabbath uprising at this outrage; the Baron is himself charged with heresy as is his Lady.

Highly theatrical, universal in theme, with an affective love story. Unit set. With doubling, 21 males, 6 females.

The Long Smoldering: Unique in the massive literature of the Holocaust, the play grapples, not with the event itself, but with the two thousand years of racist persecution that prepared the way for what Hitler hoped would be the Final Solution. Despite weight of material, action is continuous from morn to morn, no flashbacks.

Full length. Setting: one set. 2 males, 2 females.

The Bright and Golden Land: A family memoir of immigrant life, funny, touching, upbeat, for those who remember and those who never knew.

Full length. Setting: one unit set. 4 males, 2 females.

AMLIN GRAY

Born in New York City on April 19, 1946. Graduated from Fox Lane High School, Bedford, NY. Trained as an actor at the American Musical and Dramatic Academy and the Royal Academy of Dramatic Art. Playwright-in-residence at the Milwaukee Repertory Theatre, 1977-. Recipient: National Endowment for the Arts Creative Writing Fellowship, 1979-80.

Address: c/o Milwaukee Repertory Theater, 929 N. Water St., Milwaukee, WI 53202 (414) 964-3945

Agent: Lois Berman, 250 West 57th St., New York, NY 10019 (212) 581-0670

TITLE • AVAILABILITY • PRODUCTIONS

Founding Father: manuscript*; O'Neill Theater Center's National Playwrights Conference, CT; Cubiculo Theater, NYC

Pirates, or Rackham in Love: manuscript*; O'Neill Theater Center's National Playwrights Conference, CT;

Namesake: manuscript*; Milwaukee Repertory Theater, WI

Bo: manuscript*; Milwaukee Repertory Theater, WI; Intiman Theatre, Seattle, WA

Amlin Gray (con't)

†How I Got That Story: manuscript*; Milwaukee Repertory Theater, WI; Theater Three, TX

The Fantod: manuscript*; Theatre X, Milwaukee, WI; Actors Theatre of St. Paul, MN

Sixties: manuscript*; Milwaukee Repertory Theater, WI

Outlanders: manuscript*; Actors Theatre of St. Paul, MN; Milwaukee Repertory Theater, WI
    *contact author or agent
    †Lincoln Center Theatre on Film & Tape

SYNOPSES

How I Got That Story: A reporter struggles to come to grips with an Asian revolution. The play is written for two actors: one plays the reporter, the other plays the revolution. "An explosion of young talent . . . By turns painfully funny and just plain painful, **How I Got That Story** recaptures both the black comedy and the bottomless tragedy of Vietnam and it does so with the simple magic of pure theater." Frank Rich, **New York Times**
Full length. Setting: unit set. 2 males.

Bo: In a sometimes ironic, sometimes impassioned tirade against a sociologist who has employed and exploited her, a woman hobo of the 30s reveals her life as a "sister of the road." "An enthralling monologue. . . . a narrative gem." — Jay Joslyn, **Milwaukee Sentinel**
Curtain raiser (20 minutes). Set in whatever theater it is being performed in. 1 female.

The Fantod: "The play wittily parodies and gently probes Victorian sensibilities and literature. The story deals with the arrival at a placid British estate of a mysterious, mesmerizing nobleman schooled in the exotic philosophies and opiates of the East. His alarmingly bright gaze fixes on the hypersensitive daughter of the household. The play is a clash between ego and innocence, unbridled hedonism and mannered repression, all carefully controlled to combine the flamboyant menace of the Broadway Dracula with the verbose conventions of Victorian society." — American Theatre Critics Association, citing the play as one of nine outstanding new plays produced in the regional theater in 1978–79.
Full length. Setting: one set. 3 males, 3 females, 1 pianist (optional).

WILLIAM M. GREEN

B.F.A., University of Texas, Austin, TX. His published novels included, **Spencer's Bag, Avery's Fortune, The Salisbury Manuscript, See How They Run** and **The Man Who Called Himself Devlin.** At various times, he has performed as an actor, nightclub entertainer, and producer-director of TV program trailers.

Address: 303 West 66th St., New York, NY 10023

Agent: Jo Stewart, I.C.M., 40 West 57th St., New York, NY (212) 556-5600

TITLE • AVAILABILITY • PRODUCTIONS

The Rock of Kosciusko Street: manuscript**; U. of Texas

The Odyssey of Howard Singleton: manuscript**;

That Merry Gang: manuscript**;

Nell a musical comedy (book with Dennis Turner): manuscript*; Manhattan Theatre Club, NYC
    *contact author
    **Contact the Graham agency, 317 W. 45th St., New York, NY 10036

G

William M. Green (cont'd)
SYNOPSIS

Nell: Set in one of the bawdiest periods in England's history, here is the story, very loosely based on certain actual events, of how a lecherous king and one of his more inventive mistresses, foiled one of the most heinous of all political plots . . . and had a good time in the bargain. Basically it's a lusty bedroom farce in musical comedy form. A full-length musical with a baroque rock score and lyrics.

Full-length musical. 5 males, 4 females.

ROMA GRETH

Born in Philadelphia, PA. Freelance writer for fifteen years doing a lot of advertising, short stories, religious writing and articles. Recipient: The Scene Award; Washington Area Feminist Theatre Bicentennial Award; Playwright's contest, Oxnard, CA; University of Miami Playwriting Award.

Address: 148 Clymer St., Reading, PA 19602

Agent: Charles Hunt, Fifi Oscard, 19 West 44th St., New York, NY 10036 (212) 764-1100

TITLE • AVAILABILITY • PRODUCTIONS

A Second Summer: not available

On Summer Days: not available

Narcissus: The Smith, 5 Beekman St., New York, NY 10038, $3.00; Plaza Players, Oxnard, CA

Worms: The Scene, #1, 5 Beekman St., New York, NY 10038, $2.50; Omni Theatre club, NYC; Brookdale Community College, NJ

The American War Women: manuscript*; WPA, NYC; Washington Area Feminist Theatre

Cassiopea: manuscript*; Lincoln Center Showcase, NYC; George Washington U., DC

Curtain Call: manuscript*; WPA, NYC; Expressionist Theatre, NY

The Greatest Day of the Century: manuscript*; Aspen Playwrights Conference, CO; American Place Theatre, NYC

Halfway: manuscript*; WPA, NYC; Women's Prison, Claymont, CA

The Heaven Mother: manuscript*; Academy Theatre, GA; NY Shakespeare Festival, NYC

November People: manuscript*; Actors Place, NYC; Off Off Broadway showcase

The Pottstown Carnival: manuscript*; Atlantic City Playhouse, NJ; Off Off Broadway showcase

Quality of Mercy: manuscript*; Playwrights Horizons, NYC; Syracuse Stage, NY

The Believers: manuscript*

Windfall Apples: manuscript*; O'Neill Theater Center's National Playwrights Conference, Ct; IRT, NYC

Four Lanes to Jersey: manuscript*; reading, St. Clements, NYC
*contact author

SYNOPSES

The Greatest Day of the Century; On the day World War II ends, the excitement and confusion cause four characters in a small Pennsylvania city to face themselves and their problems. It is a

Roma Greth (cont'd)

day when a friendship between two young women ends, virginity is spent and a father faces his son's homosexuality.

Full length. Setting: one exterior set. 2 males, 2 females.

Narcissus: A modern telling of the legend of Echo and Narcissus. Cuban refugees in a slum area of Miami. Some Spanish necessary.

Full length. Setting: one exterior set. 4 males, 7 females.

Four Lanes to Jersey: Comedy with music about two pipeline welders drifting from Texas to the East Coast.

Full length. Setting: one unit set. 2 males, 2 females.
  *contact author

SUSAN GRIFFIN

Born in California on January 26, 1943. B.A. and M.A., San Francisco State University. Books Published: **Dear Sky** (poetry) 1971; **Let Them Be Said** (poetry) 1973; **Letter** (poetry) 1974; **The Sink** (short stories) 1974; **Le Viol** (essay, Fr. translation) 1971; **The Poletis of Rape** (essay) 1971. In the fall of 1976, Harper & Row published a collection of her poetry. She has taught creative writing for several years privately and with the University of California & San Francisco State. She has also taught drama and studied acting. **Woman & Nature** was published in 1978 by Harper & Row; **Pornography and Silence: Culture's Revenge Against Nature,** Harper & Row, 1981. Recipient: Ina Coolbirth Prize for Poetry, 1963; NEA Grant for poets working with radio, 1974; Emmy for **Voices,** 1975. Three undergraduate Scholarships; UC, Berkeley.

Address: 1008 Euclid Ave., Berkeley, CA 94708 (415) 527-4570

Agent: Ellen Neuwald, 905 West End Ave., New York, N.Y. (212) 663-1582

TITLE • AVAILABILITY • PRODUCTIONS

Cat and the Cock: not available; Freedom Theatre

The Everlasting Reich: manuscript*; S.F. Repertory Theatre, CA

Voices: Samuel French, 25 W. 45th St., New York, N.Y. 10036, $2.50; Lunch Box Theatre; KPFA (Pacifica Radio, Berkeley); KQED (Public Television, S.F.)

The Little Deaths: manuscript*
  *contact agent

SYNOPSIS

Voices: Voices is the story of the lives of five women, told by each woman as she is facing a different kind of crisis in her life. Grace's children have left home, and she is wondering what she will do. Maya, a student of sociology, an intellectual, divorced and raising two children, is aware that she has little time to examine her own life. Kate, an actress who has shaped her own life, faces old age and death. Erin, who lives in a self-imposed isolation, contemplates suicide. Rosalinde, the youngest, sees life as a series of experiments in living.

Setting: no setting required. Character breakdown: 5 females, aged 65–70; 43–48; 37–32; 28–23; 22–17.

G

TOM GRIFFIN

Born in Providence, RI on February 14, 1946. B.A.
from the U. of Rhode Island, 1969. Professional
actor with the Trinity Square Repertory Co. in
Providence. Has had fiction published in **Transatlantic Review** and **Playboy.** Recipient: Nomination by Los Angeles Drama Critics Circle for Distinguished Achievement in Playwriting, 1979.
Playboy Editorial Award in Best New Contributor
Category, 1973.

Agent: Gilbert Parker, William Morris Agency,
1350 Avenue of the Americas, New York, NY
10019 (212) 586-5100

TITLE • AVAILABILITY • PRODUCTIONS

Will the Gentlemen in Cabin Six Please Rise to the Occasion: manuscript**; Joanne Meredith
Rep. Co., LA, CA; New Playwrights Project, U. of RI

Workers: manuscript**; St. Clement's Theatre, NYC; U. of Rhode Island

The Taking Away of Little Willie: manuscript*; Mark Taper Forum, LA, CA; Theatre Three,
Dallas, TX

Einstein and the Polar Bear: manuscript*; O'Neill Theater Center's National Playwrights Conference, CT; Hartford Stage Company, CT; optioned for Broadway

　*contact author
　**contact agent

SYNOPSES

The Taking Away of Little Willie: An extraordinary man with a retarded adult son is confronted by
family and community pressures to have the son institutionalized. Set in a seaside resort town in
New England, the play is both a comedy and a serious look at one day in the life of two highly
disparate families.

Full length. Setting: one set. 4 males, 3 females.

Einstein and the Polar Bear: A once famous novelist, now reclusively isolated from the literary
mainstream, meets a woman who touches his life in ways neither of them could ever have an-
ticipated.

Full length. Setting: one set. 4 males, 2 females.

WILLIAM GRIFFIN

Born in Boston, MA. A.B. in Philosophy and Eng-
lish from Boston College. M.A. in Dramatic
Literature from Catholic University. He was an
editor at MacMillan Publishing where he was
responsible for Brooks Atkinson's **Broadway,**
Flamini's **Scarlett, Rhett, and a Cast of
Thousands: The Filming of "Gone With the
Wind,"** Sennett's **Your Show of Shows** and
Howard's **"GWTW: The Screenplay."** He is now
the head of Southern Writers, a literary agency.

Address: 5120 Prytanica St., New Orleans, LA
70115 (504) 899-5889

TITLE • AVAILABILITY • PRODUCTIONS

Seat of War: manuscript*; Boston College, MA

The Omega Point: manuscript*; Circle-in-the-Square Playwrights Workshop, NYC; Edward
Albee Workshop, NYC

William Griffin (cont'd)

A Fourth for the Eighth: manuscript*; Evergreen Theater, Hollywood, CA

Campion: manuscript*; O'Neill Theater Center's National Playwrights Conference, CT

The Contemporary Flesh: manuscript*

The Classical Spirit: manuscript
   *contact author

SYNOPSIS

Campion: In 1580 a priest landed incognito on the English coastline. In 1581 he was captured hiding in a country house. For his actions between these two dates, he was accused of heresy and treason, tried and convicted, sentenced to death and executed. In this harsh, non-romantic treatment of an historical incident involving the queen of England (Elizabeth I) and a Jesuit priest (Edmund Campion), the playwright comes to grips with what should be the central issues in all historical/political/religious plays: how and why can the "prisoner" hold out against all natural, and sometimes supernatural, odds?

Full length. Setting: a dungeon in the Tower of London. 8 males, 2 females.

ANTONI GRONOWICZ

Born in Poland. Ph.D., Lwow University, Poland. Author of fourteen novels and bio-novels; **Bolek; Chopin; Tchaikovsky; Bela Schick; Modjeska; Rachmaninoff; Paderewski; Hitler's Wife; Pattern; Four from the Old Town; The Piasts; Gallant General; An Orange Full of Dreams; The Hookmen.** Recipient: National Play Competition, Provincetown Academy of Arts, 1970; International Competition, Geneva, Switzerland, 1979; Ford Foundation Grant.

Address: 132 East 82nd St., New York, NY 10028
   (212) 288-6479

Agent: Morton L. Janklow Associates, Inc., 598
   Madison Avenue, New York, NY 10022
   (212) 421-1700

TITLE • AVAILABILITY • PRODUCTIONS

Recepta: manuscript*; Lwow Theater, Poland

Painted School: manuscript*; Discovery Theater, Chicago, IL

Lost Money: manuscript*; Toronto Playwrights Center, Canada

Rocos: manuscript*; Göteburg Theater, Sweden

The United Animals: manuscript*; Play Festival, Geneva, Switzerland

Shores of Pleasure—Shores of Pain: manuscript*; Provincetown Theater

Chisler's Paradise: manuscript*

Forward Together: manuscript*; Cambridge Theater, England

Greta: manuscript*; Syrena Theater, Warsaw, Poland

Colors of Conscience: manuscript*
   *contact agent or author

G

THEODORE FARO GROSS

Born in Arlington, VA on July 1, 1949. Raised
and educated in US, Israel and Europe.
Graduated Brandeis in 1969. Reporter and editor-
in-chief of **Boston After Dark** and the **Boston
Phoenix**. Has written for film, radio, national
press and beginners in English. Poet. Resident
Playwright of the New Works Project in New
York.

Address: 100 Riverside Drive, New York, NY
10024

Attorney: Robert Youdelman, 424 Madison Ave.,
New York, NY 10017 (212) 755-1568

TITLE • AVAILABILITY • PRODUCTIONS

Charles & Tribulations: manuscript*

House of Cards: manuscript*; O'Neill Theater Center's National Playwrights Conference, CT

Fire at Luna Park: manuscript*; O'Neill Theater Center's National Playwrights Conference, CT

Who's Who in America?: manuscript*; Jamestown Community College, NY

  *contact attorney

JOHN GUARE

Born in NYC on February 5, 1938. Graduated
Georgetown U., A.B.; Yale School of Drama,
M.F.A. Dramatists Guild Council member.
Taught playwriting at NYU. Associate Professor
of Playwriting, Yale School of Drama, 1978–80.
Wrote film **Taking Off,** with Milos Forman; also
Atlantic City, directed by Louis Malle. Recipient:
Obie Award; Most Promising Playwright, 1976,
Variety Poll of New York Drama Critics, **Cop Out;**
New York Critics Circle Prize, 1971, Obie Award,
Best Play–Outer Critics Circle Prize and Los
Angeles Drama Critics Circle Prize for **House of
Blue Leaves;** Tony Award for Best Musical, 1972;
Tony Award for Best Libretto, New York Drama
Critics Prize for Best Musical for **Two Gentlemen
From Verona**; Rockefeller Grant, 1968 and 1977;

ABC-TV; Yale Grant, 1966; Audrey Wood Wesleyan Grant, 1967; Cannes Film Festival Jury Prize,
Taking Off; Hull-Warringer Award, 1979; Jefferson Award, 1978; **Soho Weekly,** Best Play of 1979.

Agent: R. Andrew Boose, c/o Barovick Konecky, 1 Dag Hammarskjold Plaza, New York, NY 10017
(212) 940-8343

TITLE • AVAILABILITY • PRODUCTIONS

A Day for Surprises: Dramatist Play Service, 440 Park Ave. S., New York, NY 10016 $1.25, Caffe
Cino, NYC

Kissing Sweet: with **A Day for Surprises;** WNET

Something I'll Tell You Tuesday: Dramatist Play Service, $1.25; Caffe Cino, NYC

Loveliest Afternoon of the Year: with **Something I'll Tell You Tuesday;** Caffe Cino, NYC

To Wally Pantoni, I Leave a Credenza: manuscript*; Barr-Wilder-AlbeeWorkshop, NYC; WNBC,
Experiment in Television

Muzeeka: Dramatists Play Service, $1.25; O'Neill Theater Center's National Playwrights Confer-
ence, CT; Mark Taper Forum, Los Angeles, CA

Cop-Out: Samuel French, 25 West 45th St., New York, NY 10036, $2.50; O'Neill Theater Center's National Playwrights Conference, CT; Broadway

Home Fires: with **Cop-Out;** Broadway

†**House of Blue Leaves:** Samuel French, $2.50; O'Neill Theater Center's National Playwrights Conference, CT; Off Broadway

Two Gentlemen From Verona: Tams–Witmark, 757 Third Ave., New York, NY 10017; New York Shakespeare Festival, NYC; Broadway

Rich and Famous: Dramatists Play Service, $2.50; Academy Festival Theater, Lake Forest, IL; Williamstown Theater, MA

Marco Polo Sings a Solo: Dramatists Play Service, $2.50; New York Shakespeare Festival, NYC

Landscape of the Body: Dramatists Play Service, $2.50; Academy Festival Theater, Lake Forest, IL; New York Shakespeare Festival, NYC

Bosoms and Neglect: Dramatists Play Service, $2.50; Goodman Theater, Chicago, IL; Broadway

In Fireworks Lie Secret Codes: manuscript*; Actor's Theater of Louisville, KY; Actors Studio, NYC

Lydie Breeze: manuscript*; Workshop, NYC

*contact agent
†Lincoln Center, Theatre on Film & Tape

SYNOPSIS

Bosoms and Neglect: A forty-year-old man and the women in his life; from the woman he knows least (a pick-up on the day he's running away with his best friend's wife); to the woman he's known longest, his eighty-three-year-old mother.

Full length. Setting: three sets. 1 male, 2 females.

A. R. GURNEY, JR.

Born in Buffalo NY, on November 1, 1930. Attended St. Paul's School, Concord, NH; Williams College, B.A., 1952; Yale School of Drama, M.F.A., 1958. Teaches literature at M.I.T., Cambridge, MA. Novels: **The Gospel According to Joe; Entertaining Strangers.** Recipient: Vernon Rice Drama Desk Award, 1970–71. Rockefeller Award for Playwriting, 1977–78.

Address: 20 Sylvan Ave., West Newton, MA 02165 (617) 244-3164

Agent: Gilbert Parker, William Morris Agency 1350 Avenue of the Americas, New York, NY 10019 (212) 586-5100

TITLE • AVAILABILITY • PRODUCTIONS

Three People (one act): **Best Short Plays 1955-56,** Beacon Press, 25 Beacon St., Boston, MA 02108 (out of print)*

Love in Buffalo (musical): manuscript*; Yale School of Drama, CT

Who Is Sally? (one act): manuscript*; Schlitz Television Playhouse

Tom Sawyer (musical) (co-author): manuscript*; Kansas City Starlight Theatre, KS

Turn of the Century (one act): **Best Short Plays 1957-58,** Beacon Press (out of print)*

G

A. R. Gurney, Jr. (cont'd)

Around the World in 80 Days (musical): Dramatic Publishing Co., 86 East Randolph St., Chicago, IL 60601; $2.00

The Thursday Club (one act): manuscript*; WHDH-TV

The Life of the Party (one act): manuscript*; WGBH-TV

The Bridal Dinner: First Stage magazine, Purdue University 1964; manuscript*; M.I.T. Community Players, MA

The Politician (TV series in four parts): manuscript*; WGBH-TV, MA

The Comeback (one act): Dramatists Play Service, Inc., 440 Park Ave. S., New York, NY 10016, $1.00; Club 47, Inc., of Cambridge, MA

The Rape of Bunny Stuntz: Samuel French, 25 West 45th St., New York, NY 10036, $1.25; Playwrights Unit, NYC

Another Aida (one act): manuscript*; Theatre Company of Boston, MA

The David Show: Samuel French, $1.25; Boston University Playwrights Workshop at Tanglewood, MA; Players Theatre, NYC

The Golden Fleece (one act): Samuel French, $1.25; Playwrights Unit, NYC; Mark Taper Forum, Los Angeles, CA

Tonight in Living Color (Two one-act plays; **The David Show,** revised, and **The Golden Fleece**): Actors Playhouse, NYC

The Problem (one act): Samuel French, $1.25; New Theatre Co-operative, Atma Coffeehouse, Boston, MA

The Open Meeting (one act): Samuel French, $1.25; New Theatre Co-operative, Atma Coffeehouse, MA

The Love Course (one act): Samuel French, $1.25; Theatre Company of Boston, MA

Scenes from American Life: Samuel French, $2.50; Boston University Playwrights Workshop at Tanglewood; Studio Arena Theatre, Buffalo, NY

The Old One-Two (one act): Samuel French, $1.25; Spingold Theatre, Brandeis University, MA

Children: Samuel French, London; Dramatists Play Service, $2.50; The Mermaid Theatre, London; Manhattan Theatre Club, New York, NY

Who Killed Richard Cory?: Dramatists Play Service, $2.50; Circle Repertory Company, NYC

The Middle Ages: Dramatists Play Service, $2.50; Mark Taper Lab, Los Angeles, CA; Hartman Theatre, Stamford, CT

The Wayside Motor Inn: Dramatists Play Service, $2.50; Manhattan Theatre Club, NYC; Thetford Players, Thetford, VT

The Golden Age: manuscript*; Aspen Playwrights Festival, Aspen, CO; Greenwich Theatre London

*contact agent

SYNOPSES

Scenes from American Life: A collage of scenes of middle-class life in America from 1930 into the future.

Two acts. Single set; piano. 4 males, 4 females.

Children: The erosion of traditional values in a Wasp family.

Two acts. Setting: a terrace on an island off the Massachusetts coast. 1 male, 3 females.

Who Killed Richard Cory?: Variations on the E. A. Robinson poem.

Two acts. Setting: single, multi-purpose set. Variable cast.

JACK RAPHAEL GUSS

Born in the USSR on May 11, 1919. B.A., University of California; post-graduate work, University of Zurich, Geneva, the Sorbonne. Story Editor: **Channing, Slattery's People, The Young Lawyers, The Bold Ones, Medical Center, Switch, Eischeid.** Currently Story Editor of **Trapper John.** Producer of **Quincy.** TV credits: **World Premiere, Medical Center, Ben Casey, The Bold Ones, Slattery's People, Cannon, Switch, Night Gallery.** Films: **The Lady in Cement, 20th Century.** Recipient: Writers Guild Nomination **(Channing).**

Address: 10500 Mars Lane, Los Angeles, CA 90024

Agent: Sam Adams, Adams, Ray and Rosenberg, 9220 Sunset Blvd., Los Angeles, CA 90069 (212) 278-3000

TITLE • AVAILABILITY • PRODUCTIONS

The Umbrella: manuscript**; Locust Street Theatre, PA; Comedy Theatre, London

Black on White (musical): manuscript*

Fathers: manuscript*; Actors Studio Workshop, NYC

The Red Pigeon: manuscript*; The Theatre, L.A., CA

    *contact agent
  **in collaboration.

OLIVER HAILEY

Oliver Hailey, a native Texan, received his BFA from the University of Texas and his MFA from the Yale School of Drama. In addition to productions throughout the United States, his plays have been performed in England, Germany, Belgium, Austria, Scotland, Australia, Canada, and Israel. The 1975 television season saw two of Mr. Hailey's plays presented on PBS: **For the Use of the Hall,** Hollywood Television Theatre series, and **Who's Happy Now?,** Mark Taper Forum's Theatre in America series. He has served as program consultant to Norman Lear for the television series **Mary Hartman, Mary Hartman.** For two seasons he was story editor for **McMillan & Wife.** He wrote the TV play for **Sidney Shorr,** (NBC, Movie-of-the-Week). He has taught play-

writing at the UCLA Extension Bureau. He is married to novelist Elizabeth Forsythe Hailey, author of **A Woman of Independent Means.** They have two daughters, fifteen and eleven. Recipient; Vernon Rice Drama Desk Award, 1963, for **Hey You, Light Man!.** Citation of Merit from the Los Angeles Drama Critics for the Melrose Theatre production of **Father's Day, 1973.**

Address: 11747 Canton Pl., Studio City, CA 91604

Agent: Shirley Bernstein, Paramus Artists Assoc., 1414 Avenue of the Americas, New York, NY 10019 (212) PL 8-5055

H

Oliver Hailey (cont'd)

TITLE • AVAILABILITY • PRODUCTIONS

Hey You, Light Man!: Dramatists Play Service, 440 Park Ave. South, New York, NY 10016, $2.50 Yale University, CT; Off Broadway

First One Asleep, Whistle: manuscript*; Broadway

Who's Happy Now?: Dramatists Play Service, $2.50; O'Neill Theater Center's National Playwrights Conference, CT; Mark Taper Forum, L.A., CA

Father's Day: Dramatists Play Service, $2.50; Mark Taper Forum, L.A., CA; Elitch Gardens, Denver, CO

Continental Divide: Dramatists Play Service, $2.50; Washington Theatre Club, Wash., DC; Berkeley Repertory Theatre, CA

For the Use of the Hall: Dramatists Play Service, $2.50; Trinity Square Repertory Co., Providence, RI; Hollywood Television Theatre

And Where She Stops Nobody Knows: manuscript*; Mark Taper Forum, L.A., CA; Cricket Theatre, MN

Animal: Dramatists Play Service, $1.25; Off Off Broadway; Edinburgh Festival, Scotland

Picture: with **Animal;** Off Off Broadway; Mark Taper Forum, L.A., CA

Crisscross: with **Animal;** Evergreen Theatre, L.A., CA

Red Rover, Red Rover: Dramatists Play Service, $2.50; Cricket Theatre, MN; Melrose Theatre, L.A., CA

Tryptich: manuscript*; UCLA Resident Theater Co., L.A., CA

I Won't Dance: manuscript*; Studio Arena Theatre, Buffalo, NY; Broadway

I Can't Find It Anywhere: manuscript*; Actors Theatre of Louisville, KY

   *contact agent

SYNOPSES

Father's Day: Left with their alimony, their children and neighboring apartments on New York's posh upper East Side, three divorcees share their loneliness, their thoughts on sex and marriage, and their bitter memories of lost trust and closeness. When their ex-husbands arrive for a Father's Day reunion they are all, at first, as civilized and sophisticated as the situation demands—but then the veneer begins to crack, and beneath the fusillade of funny lines their aching emptiness, and hurt show through. In the end they face the truth about themselves and the rejection which they must accept, as the humor of the play gives way to a moment of touching, revealing, yet quietly shattering resignation.

Full length. Setting: terrace of an East Side New York apartment. 3 males, 3 females.

Who's Happy Now?: The setting is a West Texas small town bar, and the action covers three periods in the main character's life, at six, sixteen and twenty. He and his resilient, but resigned, mother frequent the bar so that the boy may at least get to know his father—who comes there every night with his girlfriend, a waitress named Faye Precious. As the years pass a sort of whimsical accommodation is achieved between these very different people, and the boy grows up divided between avenging his mother for the father's disloyalty and getting back at him for his own hurts, while still trying to win the paternal love and approval he so desperately wants. The son's talent for song writing eventually gives him the means to get away—but when he asks his mother to join him, she refuses. Once before she had tried to leave, but couldn't, and she has learned that it is better to shed her pride and keep even a share in the man she loves than to stand on this and have nothing.

Full length. Setting: West Texas small town bar. 3 males, 2 females.

For the Use of the Hall: A Long Island summer house on a freezing winter weekend is the setting for an examination of success and failure by American standards. In this "somewhat" autobiographical play, a failed playwright, a nun, an art speculator and an author of children's books confront the iron will of Charlotte, the play's protagonist and heroine, who demands first place from life—and thereby succeeds in reducing the size of all the lives she touches.

Full length. Setting: large, commodious central room of a summer cottage on Long Island. 2 males, 4 females.

WILLIAM HAIRSTON

He has written **The World of Carlos,** a novel, published by G.P. Putnam's Sons. He wrote several films and many television shows for the U.S. Information Agency (Washington, D.C.); Directed for the stage in New York City; Created and edited a newspaper for the D.C. Government, **D.C. Pipeline.** He is a former professional actor; stage, movie and TV; Has worked in theatre management for New York Shakespeare Festival and Arena Stage. He is listed in **Who's Who in America.** Studied writing and television play writing at N.Y.U. and Columbia University. Film/TV treatment of Hans Habes **Walk in Darkness.** Conceived and coordinated **Rhythm 'N' Blues** with music by Spencer Williams. Recipient: National Endowment for the Arts—Literary Study Grant. The Ford Foundation—Theatre Administration Grant.

Address: 9909 Conestoga Way, Potomac, MD 20854 (301) 299-2418

Agent: Isle Lahn, Paul Kohner, Michael Levy Agency, 9169 Sunset Blvd., Hollywood, CA 90069 (212) 550-1060

TITLE • AVAILABILITY • PRODUCTIONS

Black Antigone: manuscript*; North Carolina District and State Drama Festival

Curtain Call, Mr. Aldridge, Sir!! (adapted from a radio play by Ossie Davis): manuscript*; Off Broadway

Swan Song of the 11th Dawn: manuscript*; Workshop, "Reading", NYC

Walk in Darkness (adaptation): manuscript*; Greenwich Mews Theatre, NYC

Ira Frederick Aldridge: manuscript*;

Passion Flowers (adaptation): manuscript*;

   *contact agent

MARTIN HALPERN

Born in NYC on October 3, 1929. B.A., M.A., University of Rochester; Ph.D., Harvard, 1959. Poems widely published in journals and in two volumes, **Two Sides of an Island and Other Poems,** U. of North Carolina Press, 1963 and **Selected Poems,** Golden Quill Press, 1976. Presently Professor of Playwriting and Dramatic Literature, Brandeis University. Recipient: Fullbright Scholarship, 1956–57; Howard Foundation Fellowship, 1962–63; Special Award in Poetic Drama, California Olympiad of the Arts, 1968; Bronze Windmill Award, Corporation for Public Broadcasting and Radio Nederland, 1971; Harold C. Crain Award, San Jose State University Theatre, 1978.

Address: 14 Waban Street, Natick, MA 01760 (617) 655-4796

Agent: Bret Adams, 36 East 61st St., New York, NY 10021 (212) 752-7864

H

Martin Halpern (cont'd)
TITLE • AVAILABILITY • PRODUCTIONS

Mrs. Middleman's Descent: First Stage, Fall, 1966, Purdue University, Lafayette, IN 47907; Poets' Theatre, Cambridge, MA; University of California, Berkeley, CA

Reservations: First Stage, Winter, 1966; Judson Theatre, NYC; Image Theatre, Cambridge, MA

Tameem: Breakthrough Press, 27 Washington Square North, New York, NY 10011*; Laurie Theater, Brandeis U, MA; California Olympiad of the Arts.

The Messiah: manuscript*; Spingold Theater, Brandeis, MA

The Lower Drawer: manuscript*; Berkshire Theatre Festival, MA

The Damned Thing: manuscript*; Corp. for Public Broadcasting & WHA.

The Siege of Syracuse: manuscript*; Laurie Theater, Brandeis, MA

Visitations: manuscript*; Berkshire Theatre Festival, MA

What the Babe Said: Pioneer Drama Service, P.O. Box 22555, Denver, CO, $1.50; Arena Stage, Washington, DC; Circle Repertory Company, NYC

Total Recall: Best Short Plays of 1978, Chilton Press, Chilton Way, Radnor, PA 19089; Arena Stage, Washington, DC; Circle Repertory Company, NYC

Trespassers (originally **The Tenants**): manuscript**; Brandeis University, MA

No Moves Back: manuscript**; San Jose State Theatre, CA

Opus One-Eleven: manuscript*

Day Six: manuscript**

Heart of the Lotus: manuscript*; Brandeis University, MA

> *contact author
> **contact agent

SYNOPSES

Day Six: A misanthropic recluse, who has total recall of the Bible and earns his living ghost-writing sermons for various clergy, is visited by a lonely divorcee in quest of spiritual communion. What begins as an ironic clash of opposites concludes, after much mutual self-revelation, in a true communion and reawakening of love in both protagonists.

Full length. Setting: studio apartment in New York. 1 male, 1 female.

Heart of the Lotus: The clash between a benign but fanatical contemporary religious cult (fictitious) and an unorthodox "deprogrammer" over the mind of a brilliant student; part suspense story, part philosophical study of issues like religious freedom, mind control and the effect on contemporary society of the absence of strong transcendent beliefs and values.

Full length. Setting: motel room, two other small playing areas. 3 males, 3 females.

No Moves Back: Two retired musicians (American Jewish), longtime friends and chess adversaries, confront the coming of old age through an afternoon of comic and serious soul-searching with each other and with various passersby in a city park where they meet for what could be their last chess match.

Full length. Setting: an abstractly rendered city-park scene. 5 males, 3 females.

KELLY HAMILTON

Composer, lyricist, and playwright. Born in San Francisco, California. Educated at College of Notre Dame, N.Y.U., and U.C.L.A.; member of Lehman Engel's BMI Musical Theatre Workshop. For several years, Kelly successfully ran his own repertory theatre in the San Francisco Bay Area, during which time he wrote, produced, designed and directed more than half a dozen of his early musicals—earning critical plaudits, but, more importantly, building a sound foundation of experience in all phases of the musical theatre. Recipient: Joseph Jefferson Award, Best Production, **Dance on a Country Grave;** David B. Marshall Award in Musical Theatre, for **Saga.**

Address: 23 West 73rd St., #911, New York, NY 10023 (212) 580-9764

Agent: Gilbert Parker, William Morris Agency, 1350 Avenue of the Americas, New York, NY 10019 (212) 586-5100

Music Publisher: Tommy Valando, 1270 Ave. of the Americas, No. 2110, New York, NY 10020

TITLE • AVAILABILITY • PRODUCTIONS

Surprise! (musical): manuscript*; Comedia II, Hollywood, CA; Diablo Valley College, San Francisco, CA

Dance on a Country Grave (musical): manuscript*; Brigham Young University, UT; Arlington Park Theatre, Chicago, IL; Hudson Guild Theatre, NYC

Saga (musical): manuscript*; Wonderhorse Theatre, NYC

Trixie True, Teen Detective (musical): Samuel French, 25 West 45th St., New York, NY 10036, $2.50; Theatre de Lys, NYC

    *contact agent

SYNOPSES

Dance on a Country Grave: Dark, romantic musical based on Thomas Hardy's **Return of the Native.** Thirteen piece orchestration by Eddie Sauter. Set in nineteenth century on the brooding English moors, the central story is of beautiful Eustacia Vye's romantic involvement with young Clym Yeobright, whom she uses in her desperate attempt to escape her bleak surroundings. Subplots, lyrical songs, and rustic folk humor are woven throughout to balance Hardy's stark, main theme of man's inability to defy his fate. "Kelly Hamilton, remember that name, is a composer and lyricist of very special gifts. The music has a haunting lyricism, while his lyrics include genuine poetry, psychological revelation, and literacy to an astonishing degree."—Dettmer, **Chicago Today.** "Ambitious and inspired."—**Variety.**

Setting: requires a single, many-leveled abstraction suggesting the heaths and moors of Southern England. 4 males, 4 females, plus chorus of approximate 8–10 mixed character parts.

Saga: Highly stylized, free-flowing, all-music-lyric-and-dance musical, with an especially rhythmic, folk-oriented score. Three central characters are caught up in a mystic tapestry of American folk-legends; the shifting relationships (within themselves, and with others), motives and emotions of these three characters become an allegory for the restless spirit that spawns, shapes—and, perhaps, divides—a new country.

Setting: a single abstraction, may require intricate lighting and projections. 1 male, 2 females, plus very strong supporting cast-chorus (much doubling of roles) of approximately 10–20.

Surprise!: Stylish musical comedy based on Moliere's **Tartuffe,** with a touch of Commedia dell' Arte flavor. Tartuffe, a conniving hypocrite, weasels his way into the home and affections of Orgon, a Paris merchant. While posturing as a holy man, Tartuffe is busy seducing Orgon's wife and raising general havoc with the family and servants.

Setting: 1 unit set, suggesting a 17th-century Paris salon and the surrounding boulevards. 5 males, 4 females, plus comic chorus of approximately 6–8.

H

WALLACE HAMILTON

Native New Yorker. Harvard, B.A. Wrote **Christopher and Gay: A Partisan's View of the Greenwich Village Homosexual Scene** (Saturday Review Press). Novels: **Coming Out** (New American Library); **David at Olivet** and **Kevin** (both St. Martin's Press).

Address: 334 East 11th St., New York, NY 10003
(212) 674-8269

Agent: Lucianne Goldberg, 255 West 84th St., New York, NY 10024 (212) 787-2717

TITLE • AVAILABILITY • PRODUCTIONS

The Burning of the Lepers: manuscript*; Arena Stage, Washington, DC; Off Broadway

The Midnight Cry: manuscript*; Off Off Broadway

Anthony in the Desert: manuscript*; Harford College, MD

Time Now: manuscript*; Corner Theatre, Baltimore, MD

Bunny Boy: manuscript*; Center Stage, Baltimore, MD; Corner Theatre, Baltimore, MD

Matinee: manuscript*; Corner Theatre, Baltimore, MD; Off Off Broadway

Tegaroon: manuscript*; Corner Theatre, Baltimore, MD; Berkshire Theatre Festival, Stockbridge, MA

Rite for Bedtime: manuscript*; Off Off Broadway

Bonus March: manuscript*; Center Stage, Baltimore, MD

A Touch of Orpheus: manuscript*; Corner Theatre, Baltimore, MD; Off Off Broadway

Wanting: manuscript*; Corner Theatre, Baltimore, MD

A Month of Fridays: manuscript*; Off Off Broadway

The Transplants: manuscript*; Off Off Broadway

Friend of the Family: manuscript*; Off Broadway

The Queen's Will: manuscript*; Off Off Broadway

Invitation to a Bear-Baiting: manuscript*

The Rain Barrel: manuscript*

    *contact agent

SYNOPSIS

Invitation to a Bear-Baiting: Wesley Stuart, a gay man in his early fifties who is assistant manager of an antique gallery, finds that his alcoholism is standing in the way of his appointment as gallery manager. His lover, Ned, in his early twenties, aspires to be a professional guitarist and singer, but fails disastrously at his first public performance. Out of these two failures a bond of determined survival is forged.

Full length. Setting: one interior. 5 males.

GEORGE HAMMER

Educated at The City College of New York, B.S., M.S.; Columbia University, Ed.D.. Playwright, actor, designer, professor in the City University of New York, and psychotherapist in private practice. Member, The Dramatists Guild. Recipient: Best Play Award, Barn Theatre, Montville, NJ.

Address: 20 Fifth Ave., New York, NY 10011
(212) 982-3977

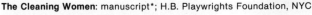

TITLE • AVAILABILITY • PRODUCTIONS

The Cleaning Women: manuscript*; H.B. Playwrights Foundation, NYC

Comes Tomorrow: manuscript*; H.B. Playwrights Foundation, NYC

When Princes Could Be Waiters: manuscript*; H.B. Playwrights Foundation, NYC

The Golden Land: manuscript*; H.B. Playwrights Foundation, NYC

Seventy-Three Hundred Hamburgers Later: manuscript*; New York Theatre Ensemble, NYC

Changes: A Love Story: manuscript*; Barn Theatre, Montville, NJ; Quaigh Theatre, NYC

   *contact author

SYNOPSES

Comes Tomorrow: The Alenskys are Russian Jewish immigrants living on the Lower East Side of New York during the Depression of the 1930's. Ruth and Joshua, the children of the family, each in his own way seeks to free himself from the domination of their mother. In the end, Pincus, a widower from the old country, wins Ruth's love and carries her off on his bicycle.

Full-length comic-drama. Setting: a kitchen. 3 males, 2 females.

The Golden Land: David Kahn, an immigrant who built a business during the 1930's Depression, is beset by problems. His business is in debt and the gangster from whom he has borrowed money is trying to take over his company; the union is organizing his shop and his daughter is in love with the union organizer; and his brother may get arrested as a con-artist. A surprise birthday present solves his problems.

Full-length comic drama. Setting: a livingroom. 5 males, 1 female.

Seventy-Three Hundred Hamburgers Later: A couple, married for twenty years, leads a life of sameness and boredom. Their real means of communicating is by participating in each other's fantasies, based on 1930's movies and other memories. Deals with alienation and language.

One-act comic-drama. Setting: a room. 1 male, 1 female.

VALERIE HARRIS

Born in Philadelphia, PA on October 7, 1952. B.A., Cheyney State College, PA; M.A., Performing Arts/Theater, American U., Washington, D.C. Has published essays in many publications including **Glamour, Artworker's News, Black Art** and **Fireweed: Women and Performance.** Guest editor/interviewer for **Heresies #8: Third World Women in the U.S.** Also works in independent film as a story consultant and script writer, works to be produced by Camera News, Inc. Member the Dramatists Guild and New Dramatists. Recipient: Outstanding Achievement in Playwriting Award, 1978, Case Western Reserve U.

Address: c/o Camera News, Inc., 160 Fifth Ave., Suite 911, New York, NY 10010

H

Valerie Harris (cont'd)

TITLE • AVAILABILITY • PRODUCTIONS

Boxes: manuscript*

Nights Alone: manuscript*; Washington, DC; Cleveland, OH

The Redesther Play: manuscript*

Ice Game: manuscript*; Washington, DC; New York, NY

*contact author

SYNOPSES

Nights Alone: An old, white humpbacked woman shares her bungalow with a young black derelict. They spend their nights alone together re-enacting scenes from her past in an attempt to understand her present reality. "A fascinating and gripping play . . . an event that is a credit to the theater and to a splendid new playwright". **The Cleveland Press**

One act. Setting: abstract interior. 1 youngish black male, 1 older white female.

Ice Game: Six costumed performers hired to entertain at a masquerade ball are forced to "take five" on a frozen lake when the "premier performer"—the Pierrot—refuses to go on. The others first engage in various manipulations to keep him from leaving the troupe, but finally in resignation they entice him into a deadly game that ultimately releases him from his "life-time contract."

One act. Setting: a frozen lake surrounded by trees. 4 males, 2 females.

JOSEPH HART

Born in Brooklyn, NY on May 1, 1945. Educated at Fordham University, B.A.; New York University, Theater — M.A. Works as actor, director, teacher as well as playwright. Founder-Director, New York University Drama Society; Founder-Director, Melting Pot Theatre, Off Off Broadway; Director, Rutgers Theatre Workshop; Director, Popsickle Players Children's Theatre and Shoestring Players Children's Theatre. Actor in New York Shakespeare Festival, TV, summer stock, Rutgers Prof. Repertory. Teaches acting, directing, ensemble technique, children's theatre, and creative dramatics. Poetry and fiction also published. Playwright in Residence, Cubiculo Theatre; Resident Playwright, Rutgers Theatre Arts Department. Resident Playwright, Aspen Playwrights Conference. Member, Ensemble Studio Theatre. Recipient: Fellowship in Theatre at N.Y.U., 1967–69; offered Shubert Fellowship to Pittsburgh Playhouse, 1970.

Address: 155 N. 6th Ave., Highland Park, NJ 08904 (201) 572-3969

TITLE • AVAILABILITY • PRODUCTIONS

Absinthe: manuscript*; New York University, Mainstage, NYC

Sonata for Mott Street: Drama & Theatre, edited by Henry Salerno, Dept. of English, SUNY at Fredonia, NY 14063, $1.00; Cubiculo Theatre, NYC

Brooklyn Bridge Is Falling Down: manuscript*; Cubiculo Theatre, NYC

Ghost Dance: Drama & Theatre; Stage Magic Play Service, I.E. Clark, Box 246, Schulenberg, TX 78956, $1.50; Rutgers University Mainstage, NJ; University of Alaska

The Memoirs of Charlie Pops: manuscript*; Cubiculo Theatre, NYC; Soho Repertory, NYC

Wiglaf, A Myth for Actors (ensemble piece): **Actor Training 3, Institute for Acting Research** with Drama Book Specialists (publishers); **Prairie Schooner Quarterly,** 318 Andrews Hall, University of Nebraska, Lincoln, NB 68503; Rutgers University Experimental Theatre, NJ; Cubiculo Theatre, NYC

Joseph Hart (cont'd)

The Dark Moon and the Full: Best Short Plays, 1977, Chilton Pub. Co., Radnor, PA 19089

Window and Wall: manuscript*; Cubiculo Theatre, NYC; Irish Rebel Theatre

Lot's Wife: manuscript*; Aspen Playwrights Conference, CO; Rutgers University, NJ

Election Night: manuscript*; Theatre West, L.A., CA

Triple Play: manuscript*; American Renaissance Theatre, NYC

   *contact author

SYNOPSES

The Memoirs of Charlie Pops: The last day in the life of a neighborhood folk hero in New York City's "Little Italy." Charlie, now sixty years old, a widower stricken with cancer of which he is supposed to know nothing, must decide between surrendering to a slow painful death or committing an act of vengeance which will bring about a swift and deadly reprisal. In killing his archenemy, John Black, Charlie takes charge of his fate, frees his young nephew, Robert, from the web of the mob's feudal world, and achieves for himself a humor and a dignity he was unable to find in any of his memories. The play is set against the background of the San Gennaro street festival. Its humor, color, and exuberance lend emphasis to the story of "Charlie Pops." "Hart's **Pops** snaps and crackles with life."—Bruce Chadwick, **New York Daily News.**

Full length. Setting: two interiors—kitchen and barren luncheonette. 6 males, 3 females.

Lot's Wife: A big, adventurous retelling of the story of Abraham's family, particularly the memorable and mysterious woman to whom the Bible gives only one sentence. It is a two-part play—**The Husband** and **The Wife**—which holds some of our most traditional notions under the light and heat of a modern consciousness. A woman searches for beauty and meaning in a world where men and Gods contend for raw power.

Full length. Setting: unit set. 13 males, 7 females.

Window and Wall: Two related plays set in a small house in Irish Catholic Brooklyn. Each tells the story of an old person and a young person caught at a moment when life must change and the inevitability of death or adulthood must be accepted. The first play speaks from the feminine point of view, the second from the masculine. The emphasis is on comedy as Aggie Reilly celebrates her seventy-eighth Good Friday with a bottle of Irish whiskey, and a father and son stage their own version of the Dempsey-Sharkey prize fight. In each play youth and age help each other to accomplish one of life's necessary changes.

Setting: two interiors. 3 males, 4 females.

LEZLEY HAVARD

Born in London, England on August 9, 1944. She went into the theater at fifteen. She has worked as an actress, stage manager and director. She started writing in 1975. Recipient: Clifford E. Lee Playwriting Award; Canada Council for the Arts Grant, (twice), Best Play, Women-Write-For-Theatre; Best Play, Multi-Cultural Play Festival.

Address: 410 South Keystone, Burbank, CA
   91506 or Alliance Theatre, 15 16th St.,
   Atlanta, GA 30309

Agent: Earl Graham Agency, 317 West 45th St.,
   New York, NY 10036 (212) 489-8288

TITLE • AVAILABILITY • PRODUCTIONS

Hide and Seek: Dramatists Play Service, 440 Park Avenue South, New York, NY 10016, $2.50
   Lennoxville Festival Theatre, Quebec; Broadway

Victims: Playwrights Co-op, Playwrights Canada, 8 York St., Toronto, Ont. M5T 1R2 Canada
   Windsor Players, Windsor, Canada; Alliance Theatre, Atlanta, GA

Lezley Havard (cont'd)

In the Name of the Father: manuscript*; Alliance Theatre, Atlanta, GA

The Actors: manuscript*

   *contact agent

SYNOPSES

Hide and Seek: A supernatural thriller. A couple, after fifteen years of marriage, are expecting their first child. In an effort to escape the city they move into an old farmhouse in the country. The wife is delighted by the visits of a small child who plays on their swing. When she tries to establish the child's identity, she discovers that the child has been missing for five years.

Full length. Setting: one unit set. 4 males, 4 females, 1 young girl

In the Name of the Father: A play that explores father and son relationships. An indictment of patriarchial society, its repressive attitudes and myths, its concepts of what a father should or should not be.

Full length. Setting: one set. 3 males.

The Actors: A sad and amusing night of crisis in the lives of two out of work actors, living in depressing, economically disasterous conditions.

Full length. Setting: one set. 2 males.

SAM HAVENS

Born in Beaumont, TX on November 15, 1936. B.A. and M.A. from Lamar U., Beaumont, TX. Has worked as an announcer and director for KFDM-TV, acted in summer stock, taught in public school and instructed and directed at Alley Theatre Merry-Go-Round School. Since 1970, Chairman of the Drama Dept. at U. of St. Thomas, Houston. Recipient: Ford Foundation Grant; Texas Committee for the Humanities and Public Policy and NEH commission to write a play for **Plays For Living**; participated in Commonwealth Stage Festival of New Plays.

Address: 3415 Audubon, Houston, TX 77006
   (713) 523-0306

Agent: Earl Graham, 317 W. 45th St., New York,
   NY 10036 (212) 489-8288

TITLE • AVAILABILITY • PRODUCTIONS

Bubba: I.E. Clark, Inc., Saint John's Road, Schulenberg, TX 78956, $2.25; Lamar U., TX;
   Barter Theatre, VA

Canzada and the Boys: manuscript*; Dallas Theater Center, TX; Theatre Port-Royal, Montreal

Blanko: manuscript*

Couple of the Year: manuscript*; Theatre in the Works, Commonwealth Stage, MA; Dallas
   Theater Center, TX

Bumper to Bumper: Plays for Living, Family Service Center, 3635 W. Dallas, Houston, TX;
   Plays for Living, Houston, TX

   *contact agent

Sam Havens (cont'd)

SYNOPSES

Canzada and the Boys: The story of a retired teacher who has taken three lonely young men under her wing. The group finds happiness and comfort together but their world is shattered by the arrival of Canzada's son.
Full length. Setting: a den. 4 males, 1 female.

Couple of the Year: The story of Lionel, a successful architect who, on this particular Easter Sunday, reaches a crisis point in his life. He decides to stop the world and take a look at his life and especially his marriage with wife, Jill.
Full length. Setting: a second-grade classroom in a church school. 2 males, 2 females.

Bubba: The story of a young wife, nicknamed Bubba, who discovers she is more brother to her husband than wife. She decides to rebel and assert her own identity — which includes restoring her real name, Sarah Jane.
Full length. Setting: NYC apartment. 2 males, 2 females.

ALLAN HAVIS

Born in New York City on September 26, 1951. Attended Walt Whitman High School, City College of New York, B.A., Hunter College, M.A., and Yale Drama School, M.F.A. Harper & Row published his novel for young readers, **Albert the Astronomer.** Recipient: John Golden Fellowship in 1974 & 1975; Marc A. Klein Playwriting Award from Case Western Reserve University, OH.

Address: 226 East 85th St., New York, NY 10028

Agent: Helen Merrill, 337 W. 22nd St., New York, NY 10011 (212) 924-6314

TITLE • AVAILABILITY • PRODUCTIONS

The Boarder & Mrs. Rifkin: manuscript*; Hunter Playwrights, NYC

Oedipus Again: manuscript*; Case Western Reserve U., OH

Watchmaker: manuscript*; Kuku Ryku Theatre Lab, NYC

Heinz: manuscript*; Yale Drama School, CT

Interludes: manuscript*; Ensemble Co. Summer Cabaret, CT; Yale Drama School, CT

Family Rites: manuscript*; Yale Drama School, CT

Approaching Chimera: manuscript*

Year of the Mink: manuscript*

   *contact author

SYNOPSES

Interludes: A dark comedy about a quartet of young people living in New York's Greenwich Village. Written in a short, jaggered style, the story flirts with incest, murder and self-mutilation. Beverly and Josh have an unusual marriage.
One act. Setting: one set, the livingroom of a basement apartment. 2 males, 2 females.

Family Rites: An experimental drama about a family reunion. Scott and Debra, now grown up, return to their family and partake in many familiar customs which have become disquieting.
One act. Setting: one set, sections of a suburban home. 3 males, 2 females.

H

DAVID KERRY HEEFNER

Born on July 18, 1945 in Des Moines IA. Educated at Drake University and graduated from Goodman School of Drama of Art Institute of Chicago with majors in directing and acting. Worked extensively as actor and director in Broadway, Off-Broadway, regional, stock, etc. Has written comedy and special material for T.V., club and review performers. Listed in **Burns Mantle Best Plays,** one of ten best from Off Off Broadway for adaptation and direction of **Finnegans Wake.** Assoc. Director of Hudson Guild Theatre 1975–1978; currently producing director. Recipient: N.Y. State Council on the Arts for Residency at Hudson Guild Theatre, as Literary Manager for 1976–77.

Address: Hudson Guild Theatre, 441 W. 26 St.,
  New York, NY 10001 (212) 760-9836

TITLE • AVAILABILITY • PRODUCTIONS

Today We Saw a Turtle: manuscript*; Thresholds, NYC; New York Free Theatre, NYC

Finnegans Wake (from Joyce): manuscript*; Thresholds, NYC; Manhattan Theatre Club
  (Reading), NYC

A Season in Hell (The essence of Rimbaud): manuscript*; Thresholds, NYC; WNYC-TV

Reunion among Ruins: manuscript*; New York Theatre Ensemble, NYC

The Life of God: An Autobiography: manuscript*

**American Hystery 1. Further Wonders of the Divil in Massachusetts 2. The Death of Martha
  Washington, Jr.**: manuscript*; Hudson Guild Theatre, NYC
  *contact author

SYNOPSIS

American Hystery: Two plays dealing with actual historical incidents involving hysteria. Both plays are farces using the same five actors. **Further Wonders of the Divil in Massachusetts** deals with the efforts of Cotton and Increase Mather, the witch-hunting father and son team, to squelch a case of possession which popped up just a year after the infamous Salem trials. **The Death of Martha Washington, Jr.** reveals what George Washington's stepdaughter saw through a crack in his study door, causing her to perish in a fit.

Setting: one interior setting for each play. 3 females, 2 males.

HAROLD HEIFETZ

Graduate of the University of Illinois 1941 and a graduate student at the University of Chicago and the California Institute of Technology, he served in the Navy for over three years. He has written two novels: **Jeremiah Thunder** (Doubleday) and **Hard Charger** (Bantam), non-fiction, **Zen and Hasidism,** (Quest Books). He is the Chairman of ANTA, West Playwright Unit in Los Angeles, CA.

Address: 12142 Emelita St., North Hollywood,
  CA 91607 (213) 980-3837

Agent: Bertha Case, 345 West 58th St., New
  York, NY 10019 (212) 541-9451

Harold Heifetz (cont'd)

TITLE • AVAILABILITY • PRODUCTIONS

Mama and Her Soldiers: manuscript*; Curtain Call Theatre, Hollywood, CA

Harry Kelly: manuscript*; East/West Players, Hollywood, CA

Billy God: manuscript*; ANTA, West, Hollywood, CA

Hungry Mother Mountain: manuscript*; ANTA, West, Hollywood, CA
*contact agent

SYNOPSES

Harry Kelly: Barbed wire fence down center of stage. Inside is a Japanese girl, farming a small plot. It is a Japanese War Relocation Camp during WW II. Outside the barbed wire fence is a Mohave Indian. They fall in love through the barbed wire.

One setting. There is a "Greek" chorus of Japanese members of the camp, and a white Colonel of the army. 1 female, 2 males and chorus.

Billy God: A play, two acts, about the black numbers racket, and a Jew who becomes part of it, and at the end is crucified.

7 blacks, 1 white.

JACK HEIFNER

Born in Corsicana, TX on March 31, 1946. B.F.A. in Theater Arts from Southern Methodist University. Worked as an actor with The American Shakespeare Festival as well as summer stock and Off Broadway. Also technical and design jobs. Founding member of The Lion Theatre Company. Member: Dramatists Guild; ASCAP; Actor's Equity; Screenwriters Guild. Co-producer, **Das Lusitania Songspiel. Vanities** is the longest running play in Off Broadway history. Recipient: CAPS Grant, 1977; National Endowment for the Arts Grant, 1978; ASCAP Award, 1978.

Address: 77 West 85th St., 5A, New York, NY 10024

Agent: Mary Harden, c/o Bret Adams Ltd., 36 East 61st St., New York, NY 10021 (212) 752-7864

TITLE • AVAILABILITY • PRODUCTIONS

Casserole: manuscript*; Playwrights Horizons, NYC

Vanities: Samuel French, 25 W. 45th St., New York, NY 10036, $2.50; Co-production–Playwrights Horizons and Lion Theatre Company, NYC; P.A.F. Playhouse, NY

Patio/Porch: Dramatists Play Service, 440 Park Ave South, New York NY 10016, $2.50; Broadway; Dallas, TX

Tornado: manuscript*

Music-Hall Sidelights (adaptation): manuscript*; Lion Theatre Company, NYC

Star Treatment: manuscript*; Lion Theatre Company, NYC

America Was: manuscript*
*contact agent

H

LILLIAN HELLMAN

Born in New Orleans, LA on June 20, 1907. Attended New York University; Columbia University and Tufts, M.A. She has written book reviews, magazine articles, screenplays (**Dead End, The Little Foxes, The Chase**). Editor of **The Letters of Anton Chekhov** and Hammett's **The Big Knockover.** Author of **An Unfinished Woman, Pentimento, Scoundrel Time.** Member: American Academy of Arts & Sciences; National Academy of Arts and Letters. Recipient: New York Drama Critics Circle Award; Brandeis University Creative Arts Award; National Institute of Arts & Letters Gold Medal.

Address: 630 Park Ave., New York, NY 10021

Agent: Don Congdon, c/o Harold Matson Company, 22 East 40th St., New York, NY 10017 (212) 679-4490

TITLE • AVAILABILITY • PRODUCTIONS

The Children's Hour: Dramatists Play Service, 440 Park Ave South, New York, NY 10016, $2.50; Broadway

Days to Come: Collected Plays, Little Brown; Broadway

Little Foxes: Dramatists Play Service, $2.50; Broadway

Watch on the Rhine: Dramatists Play Service, manuscript, $10 deposit, $2 reading fee; Broadway

The Searching Wind: Dramatists Play Service, manuscript; Broadway

Another Part of the Forest: Dramatists Play Service, $2.50; Broadway

Montserrat (adaptation): not available; Broadway

Autumn Garden:: Dramatists Play Service, $2.50; Broadway

Regina*: Broadway

The Lark (adaptation): Dramatists Play Service, $2.50; Broadway

Candide: Collected Plays; Broadway

Toys in the Attic: Dramatists Play Service, $2.50; Broadway

My Mother, My Father and Me (adaptation): Dramatists Play Service, manuscript; Broadway
  *contact agent

NANCY HENDERSON

Born in Wilmington, NC. Educated at Mary Baldwin College, B.A.; University of North Carolina, M.A., Dramatic Art. She has written four books for juveniles published by Julian Messner, including two books of children's plays, and **Celebrate America: A Baker's Dozen of Plays,** and **Walk Together: Five Plays on Human Rights.** One of these plays, **Look Behind The Mask,** was produced by children on TV in Chapel Hill, North Carolina. She is also author of the correspondence course in playwriting now in use at UNC (recently revised with Mary Patterson) and has taught creative writing there and in many workshops. Recipient: First Prize in two national competitions for **Lo, The Angel,** University of Wisconsin and Dramatists Alliance and for **Hot Pink Blues** which won the annual contest of the Black River Playhouse, Chester, NJ and was produced there.

Address: 13 Bank St., New York, NY 10014 (212) 929-7770

Agent: Roberta Pryor, I.C.M., 40 West 57th St., New York, NY 10019 (212) 556-5730

TITLE • AVAILABILITY • PRODUCTIONS

Lo, The Angel: manuscript*; Univ. of North Carolina; Dramatist Alliance

Speed, Bonnie Boat (published under author's maiden name, Nancy Wallace): Walter Baker, 100 Summer St., Boston, Mass. 02111; Univ. of North Carolina

Medusa of Forty-Seventh Street: Samuel French, 25 W. 45th St., New York, NY 10036, $1.25; Old Reliable Theatre Tavern (Off Off Broadway), The Playbox NYC

Monochrome: manuscript*, Old Reliable Theatre Tavern, NYC

Hot Pink Blues: manuscript*; Black River Playhouse, Chester, NJ

Feel Free (with co-author, Charlotte Kraft): manuscript*; Gene Frankel Theatre Foundation, NYC; (OOB); New Players, Baltimore, MD

Walk Together: Five Plays on Human Rights (for children): Julian Messner, Inc., 1230 Avenue of the Americas, New York, NY 10020, $6.64; Ralph Bunche and other NYC schools; WRDU-TV,

Celebrate America: Julian Messner, $7.79

96 A: manuscript; Eccentric Circles Theatre, NYC
*contact agent

SYNOPSES

Hot Pink Blues: Verna Claiborne, her husband Aspen, and her cousin Jessamine, have fled New York because Aspen has embezzled their money in his brokerage firm. They escape to a luxurious tropical beach hotel where the unreal atmosphere highlights the hollowness of their lives and the suffering beneath comic facades. Verna longs for love and freedom, meets a man who might be a potential lover/rescuer; he turns out to be a private eye. Impending death from a hurricane startles Verna into awareness, but leaves the others unmoved.

Full length. Setting: modern hotel interior. 3 females, 4 males.

96A: A gentle, fearful wife, is sent on trips by her bored husband. But travel has opened up her life, shown her wants of her own, capacity for change, hidden strengths. She finds a lover in Greece. She learns that she can save or destroy her husband, whose career is in jeopardy. In deciding the course of her life, she becomes a challenging and interesting woman.

Full length. Setting platforms, minimal furniture and props suggesting a series of places in London, Greece and Rome. 3 males, 5 females, several bit parts.

Nancy Henderson (cont'd)

Feel Free: A psychological comedy that studies the human foibles of the human potential movement, with compassion for the characters involved. Thatcher, a middle-aged medievalist who furtively enjoys sex but cannot love, meets Celeste, a thirty-eight-year-old virgin who is determined to achieve awareness, at a weekend personal growth workshop. The play is about their conflicts and pursuit of the elusive love goal, along with six other people striving for personal growth.

Two acts. Setting: lounge in a country inn. 4 females, 4 males.

BETH HENLEY

Born in Jackson, Mississippi, May 8, 1952. B.F.A. in Theatre, Southern Methodist U., one year in acting in M.F.A. program, U of Illinois. Written TV pilot for **Morgan's Daughters,** Paramount. Recipient: Co-winner Great American Playwriting Contest, Actor's Theatre of Louisville, 1978; Pulitzer Prize.

Address: 839 N. Hayworth Ave., Los Angeles, CA 90046

Agent: Gilbert Parker, William Morris Agency, 1350 Ave. of the Americas, N.Y., NY 10019 (212) 586-5100

TITLE • AVAILABILITY • PRODUCTIONS

Crimes of the Heart: manuscript*; Actor's Theatre of Louisville; Actor's Theatre of California

The Miss Firecracker Contest: manuscript*; The Victory Theatre, CA; New Stage Theatre, Jackson, MS

Am I Blue?: manuscript*
  *contact agent

SYNOPSES

Crimes of the Heart: Three indomitable southern sisters are fighting to deal with their hopes and troubles. Babe, twenty-four, is out of jail on bail. She has just shot her husband, Senator Zachery Botrelle, because, "she didn't like his looks." Meg, twenty-seven, has flown in from Los Angeles, where her career as a singer has collapsed and she has been reduced to working as a clerk in a dog food company. Lenny, the oldest, has just turned thirty and feels she will never find love because she has been afflicted with a "deformed ovary" and can never bear children.

Full length. Setting: a large kitchen. 2 males, 4 females.

The Miss Firecracker Contest: Carnelle, twenty-four, is striving to win the Miss Firecracker Contest — a beauty contest held every Fourth of July in her hometown, Brookhaven, MS. Carnelle's two cousins, Elain and Delmount, both return home in time to see her through the contest. Elain, a fading beauty, has left her rich husband in Natchez. Delmount, twenty-eight, recently released from a lunatic asylum is intent on selling the house and "every stick of furniture in it." Popeye Jackson, twenty-three, appears on the scene to make Carnelle's costume for the contest — she can hear voices through her eyes.

Full length. Setting: a livingroom; the carnival grounds. 2 males, 4 females.

RICHARD HENRICKSON

Born in Portland, OR on November 27, 1948.
Bachelor of Science and Master of Music
Degrees, The Juilliard School; professional
violinist, recording producer, composer/arranger
in New York City. Richard has worked as composer and lyricist with several playwrights on
various musical plays. Recipient: First American
Finalist and Performing Grand Prize winner,
Grand Prix de Paris International de la Chanson
for **Lovely Dancer (lonely dancer),** 1976; Medaille
d'Or, Prix d'Academie Internationale de la Chanson, **How Do You Want to Love Me.**

Address: 243 West End Avenue, New York, NY
10023

Agent: Beautiful Music Unlimited, Ltd., 545 Fifth
Avenue, New York, NY 10017 (212) 582-8800

TITLE • AVAILABILITY • PRODUCTIONS

Cleopatra (with Bruce Feld): Elan Associates, Ltd., c/o Eli Ask, 218 West 22nd St., New York,
NY 10011

The Great American Success: manuscript*

Ozone Hour (with Ian Horvath and Dennis Nahat): manuscript*; Hanna Theatre, Cleveland, OH
*contact agent

SYNOPSES

The Great American Success: A Queens, New York, rock 'n' roll quartet is hired by their former
violinist, Richard Henrickson, to be a "bad rock group" in his Broadway production of **The Great
American Success,** a musical play. The quartet are comedians in their own right and steal the
show, which bombs on opening night. Never aware that they were hired by their "buddy" Richard
because they were supposed to be terrible musicians, they return to their anonymous existence,
rehearsing in a telephone-less abandoned bowling alley in Queens, never to learn that record
companies want to offer them contracts. The play is a play within a play, a mirror image of itself,
and, except for background music, employs music and lyrics in only real-life situations.

Two acts, 2½ hours, 25 musical segments, 18 with lyrics. Settings: abandoned bowling alley; an
office; a restaurant, with the first being repeated at the end and the actual broken-down and
setting-up stage being employed between the second and third. 18 males, 9 females.

Ozone Hour: A rock ballet musical play that traces the history of rock from the 50s to the 80s. The
setting is the late 60s Golden Age of Rock with flashbacks into the light hearted 50s and visions
into the disillusioned future. The main character is a white-suited, red-vested, mustached
Mephistopheles-style drug pusher, pimp, and devil who witnesses apathetically the progress and
ultimate demise of rock. A brutal ending wherein a glitter rock star is murdered on a chrome
"cross" by three male and two female punk rockers comments on the simultaneous seriousness
and tongue-in-cheek humor of rock theater.

Full length. Setting: one set with various platforms for rock musicians and dancers. Fog machine,
flash-pot explosions, scrims, heavily lighted. 15 males, 15 females. Two versions, 35 minutes and
2 hours.

H

VENABLE HERNDON

Born in Philadelphia, PA on October 19, 1927. Princeton, B.A. 1950, Harvard, M.A. 1951 (French and Russian Literature). Founder (with three others) of literary quarterly, **Chelsea Review,** for eighteen issues. Film **Alice's Restaurant** (with Arthur Penn), United Artists screenplay published by Doubleday. Commissioned to do the following film scripts: **Location; Until the Monkey Comes; Uncle Sam's Wild West Show; Jimmy Shine** (after Schisgal play). Biography, **James Dean: A Short Life,** Doubleday, New American Library, Futura (England), Hayakawa Shobo (Japan). Recipient: Stanley Drama Award, 1967.

Address: 238 West 22nd St., New York, NY 10011
(212) 741-0578

TITLE • AVAILABILITY • PRODUCTIONS

Until the Monkey Comes: Volume 2, **New American Plays,** Mermaid Dramabook, Hill & Wang, Farrar, Straus, & Giroux, 19 Union Sq., New York, NY 10003, $1.95; Martinique, New York: Hull House, Chicago; Berlin

Independence Night: manuscript*; Loft Theatre, New York

Bag of Flies: manuscript*; Cubiculo, New York

Sugar Mill (composer Ken Guilmartin): manuscript*

Tom Thumb (after Fielding's **Tragedy of Tragedies;** with composer Bob Dennis): manuscript*
*contact author

SYNOPSES

Sugar Mill: Every spring the island of Bueno's biggest sugar mill does a pageant celebration in Honor of Jesus Guerra — Guerra's revolution. J. G.-G., a peasant becomes a baseball star, bats ball that hits dictator Moralista in head, is arrested, escapes island in weather ballon, lands on cigar factory roof in Tampa, returns to conquer Bueno; drive out Moralista. While re-enactment of revolution proceeds, J.G.-G's former lieutenants, including nightclub-brothel Madam, now misfits in the new society, learn that Jesus is coming to close brothel. They plot to kill him. At the last minute he saves them and himself. Tone is lyrical, ironic. A musical.

Full length (two acts). Setting: a sugar mill. 5 females, 5 males (doubling and tripling in other roles).

Independence Night: Susanna, nineteen, returns from boarding school to spend summer with parents, drifts into sexual encounter with father, struggles to work through emotional effects of this with father, and mother. Other people are grandmother, a guest, a lifeguard. Straight drama.

Full length (two acts). Setting: summer house at beach. 4 males, 2 females.

Until the Monkey Comes: During winter vacation, group of college friends assembles in an absent parent's penthouse to party and battle about lives sophisticated too early by material privilege and psychic hardship. Comedy with undertones of violence. "Enter Venable Herndon, playwright, and last night at the Martinique, his **Until the Monkey Comes. . . .** It is a very unpleasant drama which quite fascinated your agent from first to last, even in its weaker aspects, and it is going to make a dent." —Jerry Tallmer, **New York Post.**

Full length (two acts). Setting: Manhattan penthouse with terrace over East River. 4 males, 2 females.

MARS HILL

Born in Pine Bluff, AR on November 18, 1927. Raised in Chicago. Received B.A. degree in Architecture, University of Illinois; M.A. degree in Black Studies, SUNY at Albany. His work has been mainly developing a theater in the Capitol District of Albany. Movies: **Odds Against Tomorrow**, 1960; TV: **Occupation**, 1972, **Eclipse**, 1974, Channel 10, Albany. Teaches workshop in Black Drama at Arbor Hill Community Center. Taught first Black Theater course at SUNY at Albany, 1970. Attended Festac 77 in Laos, Nigeria. Panelist for CAPS, 1981. Recipient: Black Business Men's Achievement Award; Community Achievement Award from Neighborhood House, 1972; Third World Theater Survival Award, New Heritage Repertory Theater, Inc., 1979; CAPS Award, 1980.

Address: 5 Homestead Ave., Albany, NY 12203 (518) 482-6683 (home) (518) 457-5651 (office)

Agent: Richard Fulton, 850 Seventh Ave., New York, NY 10019 (212) 582-4099

TITLE • AVAILABILITY • PRODUCTIONS

Two Ten: manuscript*; Trinity Institute, Albany, NY

The Man in the Family: manuscript*; Siena College, Albany, NY

Occupation: manuscript*; Arbor Hill Community Center, Albany, NY

The Buzzards: manuscript*

Peck: manuscript*

To Have and to Have Not: manuscript*

The Street Walkers: manuscript*; Trinity Institute; State University of New York at Albany, NY; Siena College; House of Kuumba, New York

The Cage: manuscript*

A Very Special Occasion: manuscript*

Huzzy: manuscript*; First Church; Afro-American Studio

Celebration: manuscript*; Trinity Institute; NBT

House and Field: manuscript*; Trinity Institute; Uhuru Sasa School, Brooklyn, NY

First in Way: manuscript*; Trinity Institute; Arbor Hill Community Center

Monkey Motions: manuscript*

Malice in Wonderland: manuscript*

Eclipse: manuscript*

Cavorting with the Whartons: manuscript*; Empire State Plaza, Albany NY
*contact agent

SYNOPSES

Malice in Wonderland: About a closely-knit family who has moved into a changing neighborhood. The family is part of that upward mobility blacks were going through during the middle sixties. The highlight of the play is when Malesia, a wayward sister, purges the members of the family during the absence of the mother, who has visited a dominating influence of absolute rule and color consciousness on three generations.

Setting: livingroom, with screened porch, of the Hays family, located in a good section of the suburb of a large midwestern city. 7 males, 5 females.

Huzzy: Two old women, award-winning gossipers, coincidentally run into each other on a bus traveling south from Chicago. The principal gossiper begins telling a story of a Huzzy who had

Mars Hill (cont'd)

stolen her favorite daughter's husband. While she is telling the story, a sexy young girl gets on the bus and sits beside a near-middle-age man who is sleeping. As the trip wears on the man and the girl become friendly, which adds fuel to the already hot story gossiper number one has going about that Huzzy. The friendship of the man and the girl develops to the extent that the gossipers start to compare the girl to the Huzzy they are talking about. They lose all control when the girl and the man become involved in a kissing scene. The gossipers lose all interest in the Huzzy they were talking about and concentrate on the one in front of their very eyes. The play is a barrel of laughs.

Setting: middle section of a bus. 1 male, 3 females.

Cavorting with the Whartons: The play deals with the efforts of a middle-aged black mother to go to college. All of her eight children are on their own except her youngest daughter, who has just received a fully paid scholarship to Howard University. Her best friend, So So, who has two degrees, devises a way for her cultural and social club, The Whartons, to sponsor her. Hilarious antics are encountered when the mother's family and the club is approached, since the club normally gives scholarships to young students just out of high school.

VERNON HINKLE

Born in Amsterdam, NY on June 23, 1935. B.A. from Ithaca College, NY and M.F.A. from Yale Drama School, 1961. Bradford College, M.A., Head of Drama Dept. until 1971. Eclectic writing career including magazine articles, speeches for corporate executives, etc. Novels: **Music to Murder By** (Tower Pub.); five other novels under pseudonym, H.V. Elkin.

Address: 470 West 24th St., New York, NY 10011
(212) 242-3872

TITLE • AVAILABILITY • PRODUCTIONS

Characters in a Play: manuscript*; La Mama, NYC

The Circus Once: manuscript*; reading, HB Studio, NYC

Musicians of Bremen (children's musical): manuscript*; Level II, Philadelphia, PA; Phoenix Prod., Washington & Baltimore

Showcase (formerly **The Concept**): manuscript*; O'Neill Theater Center's National Playwrights Conference, CT

Suicides in Limbo: manuscript*; reading, HB Studio, NYC

Reflections: manuscript*

Edna: manuscript*; Kansas Wesleyan U.

If I'm Dead, Start without Me: manuscript*
*contact author

SYNOPSES

Showcase: Three actors and a professor assemble in a workshop situation to stage the professor's thesis about dreams and reality. The professor sits at an electronic console providing lights and sound effects he considers appropriate, as, in comic scenes four years apart, the young actor plays a character in search of his adolescent dream (a dream girl); an ingenue and a character woman play the women in his life (four each). The professor's objective commentaries on the action become irritating to the subjective actor, leading to a conflict between them. As a

Vernon Hinkle (cont'd)

result, the actor, the character he plays and, vicariously, the professor, discover reality is a better kind of dream.

Full length. Setting: a bedroom and a console area. 2 males, 2 females.

Edna: Dr. Robert Worth, image conscious and grant greedy, finds himself in a delivery room with an unwed mother, Babs, who refuses to have her baby because of all the pain and suffering in the world. Then Robert's inability to change her mind is suddenly being broadcast on TV. Fearing this will endanger his receiving a Foundation grant, he promises to protect the baby for the rest of its life, and Edna is born. Turning it to his advantage, Robert uses Edna to prove his theory that life without tension produces eternal youth. Edna lives her early years in a cloistered environment where she is programmed for later forays. She remains relatively immune to life's problems despite the efforts of Gerard who, in several roles, tries to expose her to them. However, the tensions Gerard intends for Edna are absorbed by Robert. This, plus Robert's inability to satisfy some "need" Edna cannot articulate, causes his insanity and death. Then, over Bab's objections, Gerard is able to lead the now sixty-year-old but still childlike Edna out into the real world where there is pain but also love.

Full length. Setting: a circular environment with changing set pieces. 2 males, 2 females.

If I'm Dead, Start without Me: A doctor, an artist and a novelist return to the lakeside house they shared ten years ago as college roommates. Two of their number are missing, a ukulele player having drowned in the lake before graduation and a teacher who died recently. A woman who had been the object of a love triangle among them joins them and, fulfilling the teacher's deathbed wish, the foursome hold a seance to summon the departed roommates to the reunion. In the darkness, the novelist is strangled to death by a ukulele string. Enter the detective-landlord, and a complex plot begins to unravel, with many surprises and nothing turning out to be what it seemed.

Full length. Setting: hunting lodge-type living room. 4 males, 1 female.

J. KLINE HOBBS

Born in Battle Creek, MI on May 9, 1938. B.A., Michigan State University; M.A., Columbia University; M.L.S., Western Michigan University. Director and actor — radio, Off Broadway and regional theatre. Teacher, summer theatre workshop and adult education. Producer/Director videotape poetry reading series, **Riverlight Poetry Fair** and Regional Playwrights Conference, Kalamazoo College, 1978. Artistic Director, Riverlight and Co., 1981–. Editor, **Business of the Theatre,** Gale Publishing Information Guide Series. Poems: periodicals, little magazines and **New York Times.** Anthologies: **Modern American Lyrics: The Best of Contemporary Poetry,** 1963; **Forty Salutes of Michigan Poets,** 1975; **Under Covers with the Troubadour Poetry Guild,** 1976. Resident artist at Olivet college. Resident artist and lecturer at Kalamazoo College. Books: **Diary of the Ultimate One Night Stand . . .** and **Arrivals and Departures.** Recipient: Michigan Council for the Arts; CETA Grant; Kalamazoo Foundation for Regional Theatre.

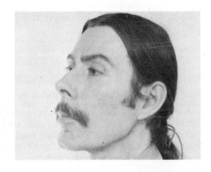

Address: 657 East Michigan Ave., Battle Creek, MI 49017 (616) 962-2453

TITLE • AVAILABILITY • PRODUCTIONS

The Hypocritical Satellites: manuscript*; Michigan State University Experimental Theatre

Notes on a Hypothetical Second Coming: Selections in **Under Cover with the Troubadour Poetry Guild,** Stovepipe Press, c/o Ben Tibbs, 5700 Vintage Lane, Kalamazoo, MI 49007, $1.50; Olivet College Writers Workshop; Michigan Arts Festival

H

J. Kline Hobbs (cont'd)

Of Pickles and Purple Peacocks: manuscript*

120 Northeast of Chicago: manuscript*

Pedants Delusions: manuscript*; Columbia University, NYC

This Was Planned To Be a Choral Drama: manuscript*; Kalamazoo College, MI
　　*contact author

SYNOPSES

120 Miles Northeast of Chicago: Tully is on weekend vacation with his best friend, L.D., and Sudy, the girl L.D. is sleeping with. Suspecting that Cal, the tenant of the neighboring cottage is "queer," Tully and L.D. harass him. When they leave, Sudy apologizes, but Cal rejects her. Then Lef, Cal's ex-lover, shows up and Tully nearly ends up "singing soprano" for the rest of his life for his continued remarks about Cal. During a beach pearty in the evening, Sudy ingratiates herself with Cal and Lef forgives Tully. Sudy and Tully tell how L.D., the guy everybody loves, is incapable of returning love and can only manipulate people to bolster his idea of himself. Frustrated by this relationship, Sudy seduces Cal, and Tully goes off into the dunes with Lef. In the morning all four have an awakening sense of themselves and their lives. Cal takes Sudy to a bus and plans to see her the next weekend. When Tully recognizes the futility of his attachment for L.D., he goes with Lef. Unaware that Sudy's and Tully's illusions about themselves and their love for him have ended, L.D. goes to bed.

Full length. Setting: front porches and yard between two shabby cottages. 4 males, 1 female.

This Was Planned To Be A Choral Drama: The audience comes into a vandalized and debris strewn theater. When they are settled, a man and two women enter with brooms and pails. While they clean, they tell about disasters which made a spectacular production "Return of the King of Kings," impossible. In its place they review their own lives. As each recalls important childhood, adolescent and adult experiences before they met, they assume roles of each others mothers, fathers, sisters, girl friends and boy friends. After adultery, divorce, impotence and affairs as they develop careers, they have all reoriented their lives and vowed "to have as much respect for each other and each others' vocations as monks and nuns do." They explain that what they say "may mean something to only one or two now and maybe a few more later on." Having completed cleaning the theater, they leave.

One act (60 minutes). Setting: debris strewn stage. 1 male, 2 females.

CHARLES HORINE

Born in Delphos, OH on May 8, 1912. B.A., Ohio Wesleyan University. Has written for films and, under the pseudonym Chuck Horner, for television. Television credits include **The Arthur Godfrey Show; Garry Moore; Jack Paar; NBC-TV's Today Show; CBS-TV News.** Recipient: Emmy Award for CBS-TV Special **Razzmatazz.**

Address: 137 Riverside Dr., New York, NY 10024
　　(212) 873-0778

TITLE • AVAILABILITY • PRODUCTIONS

Me and Thee: Dramatists Play Service, 440 Park Avenue South, New York, NY 10016, $2.50;
　　Broadway

Hurrah for the Fun: manuscript*

Physician: manuscript*

Charles Horine (cont'd)

The Office Party: manuscript*

Wilson in Love: manuscript*; Tryout, The Marshall University Players, Huntington, WV

City Mouse . . . Country Mouse: manuscript*

The Trial of John D. Lee: manuscript*
  *contact author

SYNOPSES

Hurrah for the Fun: An **Ah Wilderness** of the Thirties, its title is ironic, since there was little to shout "hurrah" for in those depression days, as the Morton family finds out during a Thanksgiving reunion at the ancestral farm. But there are laughs, some tears and lots of nostalgia as the various unemployed and financially ruined Mortons come home to roost. John, the son of David and Anna Morton, the farm's sturdy tenants, brings his girlfriend, Julie, home from college to meet "the folks" in one short weekend, grows up in more ways than one.

Full length. Setting: farmhouse living room. 5 males, 4 females.

City Mouse . . . Country Mouse: A young New York City career girl has her own version of **The Captain's Paradise** as she manages to live with two different men, one during the week, the other on weekends in the country. Or does she manage it? . . . This is obviously a comedy and in finding out how she tries to bring it off, there are lots of laughs.

Full length. Setting: city apartment, front of a small cabin. 5 males, 3 females.

Wilson in Love: This is a two-character play based on the correspondence between Woodrow Wilson and his first wife, from their first meeting till their marriage. Dr. Arthur Link, the outstanding Wilson scholar, call this play, "Wonderful . . . a truly great story."

Full length. Setting: Just the suggestion of two living rooms on a divided stage. 1 male, 1 female.

ISRAEL HOROVITZ

Born in Wakefield, MA, 1939. He wrote his first play at 17. He was a student at the Royal Academy of Dramatic Art (1961–63) and returned to London as Playwright-in-Residence — Royal Shakespeare Company, in 1965. Films: **The Strawberry Statement, Believe in Me,** has written novels (**Cappella, Nobody Loves Me**) and poetry (**Spider Poems and Other Writings**) as well as various articles in numerous publications. Instructor of playwriting at The City College of New York, where he earned an M.A. in English Literature in 1977. Joined the faculty of Brandeis University as Fanny Hurst Visiting Professor of Theatre Arts, 1974, and returned in 1975 and has been asked to remain as playwright-in-residence, ad finem. Nationally-ranked masters-

runner. Married to Gillian Adams, second ranking female marathoner (**Runner** magazine ranking). Founder, Artistic Director, The Playwrights Lab and of the Gloucester Stage Company. Recipient: Obie Award (1968, 1969); Rockefeller Fellowship; Show Business Grand Award; Vernon Rice Drama Desk Award; Emmy Award, 1979; CAPS grant; National Endowment for the Arts award; Award in Literature of the American Academy of Arts and Letters; French Critics Prize; nominated for the Pulitzer Prize, 1968, 1969; Prix du Jury, Cannes Film Festival, 1972; **Los Angeles Weekly** Best Play Award, 1981.

Agent: Robert Lantz, 114 East 55th St., New York, NY 10022 (212) 751-2107

TITLE • AVAILABILITY • PRODUCTIONS

The Comeback: manuscript*; Emerson Theatre, Boston, MA

H

Israel Horovitz (cont'd)

The Death of Bernard the Believer: manuscript*;

This Play Is About Me: manuscript*; South Orange, NJ

The Hanging of Emanuel: manuscript*; South Orange, NJ

The Killer Dove: manuscript*; New Jersey

Hop: manuscript*; Cafe Cabaret, S. Orange, NJ

Skip: manuscript*; Cafe Cabaret, S. Orange, NJ

Jump: manuscript*; Cafe Cabaret, S. Orange, NJ

It's Called the Sugar Plum: Dramatists Play Service, 440 Park Ave. South, New York, NY 10016, $1.25; O'Neill Theater Center's National Playwrights Conference, CT; Astor Place Theatre, NYC

The Indian Wants the Bronx: Dramatists Play Service, $1.25; O'Neill Theater Center's National Playwrights Conference, CT; Astor Place Theatre, NYC

Brownstone: manuscript*;

Rats: Dramatists Play Service, $1.25; Cafe Au Go-Go, NYC: Actors Playhouse, NYC

Morning (Chiaroscuro): Morning, Noon and Night, Samuel French, 25 West 45th St., New York, NY 10036, $2.50; O'Neill Theater Center's National Playwrights Conference, CT; Spoleto, Italy

Leader: Dramatists Play Service, $1.25; Off Broadway

The Honest-to-God Schnozzola: manuscript*; Gramercy Arts, NYC

Acrobats: Dramatists Play Service, $2.50; Theatre de Lys, NYC

Line: with **Acrobats;** La Mama, NYC

Dr. Hero: Dramatists Play Service, $2.50; Actors Co., Long Island, NY

Clair-Obscur: manuscript*; Paris

Alfred the Great: Avon Books, 224 West 57th St., New York, NY 10019; O'Neill Theater Center's National Playwrights Conference, CT; Actor's Studio, NYC

Our Father's Failing: with **Alfred the Great;** O'Neill Theater Center's National Playwrights Conference, CT; Pittsburgh Playhouse, PA

Alfred Dies: with **Alfred the Great;** Pittsburgh Playhouse, PA

Spared: Dramatists Play Service, $2.50; Brandeis University, MA; Manhattan Theatre Club, NYC

Turnstile: manuscript*; Dartmouth, NH

Trees: with **Leader;** NET-TV

Shooting Gallery: Dramatists Play Service, $1.25; Manhattan Theatre Club, NYC

Play for Germs: with **Shooting Gallery;** NET-TV

Uncle Snake: Dramatists Play Service, $2.50; Bicentennial Play, Central Park, NYC

The Primary English Class: Dramatists Play Service, $2.50; O'Neill Theater Center's National Playwrights Conference, CT; Brandeis University, MA

The Reason We Eat: manuscript*; Hartman Repertory Company, Stamford, CT

Stage Directions: with **Spared;** Actors Studio, NYC

Hopscotch: Dramatists Play Service, $2.50; American Cultural Center, Paris

The 75th: with **Hopscotch**

Sunday Runners in the Rain: manuscript*; Actors Playhouse, NYC; New York Shakespeare Festival, NYC

The Widow's Blind Date: manuscript*; Actors Studio, Playwright's Lab, NYC

The Good Parts: manuscript*; Actors Studio, NYC

Man with Bags (adaptation): Samuel French, $3.95; Baltimore, MD

A Christmas Carol (adaptation): Dramatists Play Service, $2.50; Center Stage, Baltimore, MD

Israel Horovitz (cont'd)

The Former One-on-One Basketball Champion: manuscript*; Gloucester Stage Company, Gloucester, MA; Actor's Studio, NYC

Mackerel; Talon Books, 201/1019 East Cordova, Vancouver, British Columbia, V6A 1M8, Canada; Hartford Stage Company, Hartford, CT; Open Circle Theatre, Toronto

Park Your Car in the Harvard Yard: manuscript*;

The Pig Bit: manuscript*

The Great Labor Day Classic: manuscript*

*contact agent

TINA HOWE

Born in New York City. B.A. from Sarah Lawrence College, post-graduate study at Columbia Teachers College and the Sorbonne. Has done varied work including high school English teacher, salesperson, typist, lecturer, newspaper reporter, translator, editor and research assistant.

Address: 333 West End Avenue, New York, NY 10023

Agent: Flora Roberts, 65 East 55th St., New York, NY 10022 (212) 355-4165

TITLE • AVAILABILITY • PRODUCTIONS

The Nest: manuscript*; Act IV Theater, Provincetown, MA; Mercury Theater, NYC

Birth and After Birth: The New Women's Theatre, Vintage Books, 201 E. 50th St., New York, NY 10022, $5.95

Museum: Samuel French, 25 W. 45th St., New York, NY 10036, $2.50; Los Angeles Actors Theater, CA; New York Shakespeare Festival, NYC

The Art of Dining: Samuel French, $2.50; New York Shakespeare Festival, NYC; Kennedy Center, Washington, D.C.

SYNOPSES

Museum: Seventeen men and twenty-two women attend the final day of a group show of modern artists held in a major American museum.

Full length. Cast size is flexible due to doubling and tripling possibilities.

The Art of Dining: People reveal their anguish and joy over food as they dine at three separate tables of a tiny new restaurant in New Jersey run by a harassed young husband and wife who make mayhem and wonderful dishes in the adjoining kitchen.

Full length. Setting: one set. 2 males, 5 females.

H

LEE HUNKINS

Born in NYC on January 1, 1930. Graduated from George Washington High School in Manhattan. Attended New York University. Has been affiliated with the Writers Workshop at the New York Shakespeare Festival. Her TV play, **Hollow Image,** was a two-hour special on ABC in 1979. Recipient: ABC Theatre Award in the New Drama for Television Project at the O'Neill Theater Center's National Playwrights Conference.

Agent: Flora Roberts, 65 E. 55th St., New York, NY 10022 (212) 355-4165

TITLE • AVAILABILITY • PRODUCTIONS

The Square Peg: not available; American Community Theatre, NYC

The Cage: not available; American Community Theatre, NYC

Another Side of Tomorrow: not available; American Community Theatre, NYC

Fading Hours: not available; American Community Theatre, NYC

26501: manuscript*; American Community Theatre, NYC; Old Reliable Theatre, NYC

Revival: manuscript*; Old Reliable Theatre, NYC: Afro American Total Theatre, NYC

The Dolls: manuscript*; Old Reliable Theatre, NYC; Afro American Total Theatre, NYC

Maggie: not available; Negro Ensemble Summer Festival, NYC

    *contact agent

SYNOPSES

26501: The play concerns the predicament of a guide for the newly departed, who tires of his role and in punishment is sent back to earth.

One act: Setting: bare stage with a desk and a chair. 2 males.

Revival: This play concerns the problem of friendship and animosity among four homeless men.

One act. Setting: a clearing near the railroad tracks. 4 males.

The Dolls: A palpable play concerning three life size puppets who come to life.

One act. Setting: A stage and a dressing room. 4 males, 2 females.

F. V. HUNT

Born in Cleveland, OH. Attended New York University Graduate Drama Department. Communications Specialist by occupation, produced radio and TV shows. Member, Dramatists Guild, Authors League of America, P.E.N. Founder, American Women Playwrights Association 1973; produced seven plays by women playwrights at Columbia University Theatre Workshop and three staged readings at the McBurney YMCA. Co-produced **The World Through Women's Eyes;** Consultant, 1978–80, for CAPS. Recipient: Brotherhood Award, 1965, for producing, writing, and moderating **Open City,**, a weekly half-hour talk program on WINS Radio; five fellowships to Edward MacDowell Colony; fellowship to New York University Graduate Drama School and Gene Frankel Theatre Studio; P.E.N. Grant.

Address: 505 LaGuardia Pl., New York, NY 10012

Attorney: Steven Roth, Sidamon-Eristoff, Morrison, Warren, Ecker & Schwartz, 551 Fifth Avenue, New York, NY 10017 (212) 661-2820

TITLE • AVAILABILITY • PRODUCTIONS

The Park (continuing series of seven plays, including: **Tennis Anyone; Shish Kebab; Dough; Waiting for Clarence; Bottoms Up; Expresso & Brioche; Androgyne**): manuscript*; Troupe Theatre, NYC; Dramarena Theater, NYC

Sand: manuscript*; Theatre for the New City, NYC; New York Theatre Ensemble, NYC

Two from Ulysses: manuscript*; Columbia University, NYC; Theatre Workshop

Cashmere Love: manuscript*; Northeastern University, Boston, MA; Cubiculo Theatre, NYC

Off White: under option, Rick Hobard, Hobard Productions; New York Shakespeare Festival, staged reading, NYC

Woman with a Gun: manuscript*; Open Space Theater, NYC, reading

Arizona: manuscript*

Phil: manuscript*

*contact author or Steve Roth

SYNOPSES

Phil: A young woman painter, living in Soho, struggles for emotional and sexual identity through two relationships—a former female roommate and a young man writer living in the loft above hers. A modern drama.

Full length. Setting: painter's studio. 1 male, 2 females.

Arizona: A black comedy. A husband and wife retiring to Arizona await the arrival of their actor son. As they wait, the recently-dismissed maid returns with her boyfriend to pick up a reference. Her boyfriend is aggressive and macho. Knowledgeable about art he proceeds to lecture the couple on their art collection while his girlfriend (the maid) gathers objet d'art into her bag. In a struggle over the couple's jewelry, the boyfriend is killed and put into a bedroom. When the son arrives, dressed as Dracula for his new role, the father and son get into a nasty argument and the son is killed by the father. The parents now have two bodies on their hands and two tickets to Arizona. Surprise ending.

Full length. Setting: an apartment. 3 males, 2 females.

H

FREDERIC HUNTER

Formerly a reporter for **The Christian Science Monitor** and a foreign service officer of the U.S. Information Service, Fred now writes full time for films, television and the theater.

Address: 4998 La Ramada Dr., Santa Barbara, CA 93111 (805) 964-1627

Agent: Esther Sherman, Wiliam Morris Agency 1350 Avenue of the Americas, New York, NY 10019 (212) 586-5100

TITLE • AVAILABILITY • PRODUCTIONS

A Marriage of Convenience: manuscript*; University of California at Los Angeles

The Hemingway Play: manuscript*; O'Neill Theater Center's National Playwrights Conference, CT; Harvard University Summer Repertory, MA

The Disposable Woman: manuscript*; Dallas Theater Center, TX

Panzram's Revenge: manuscript*

Subway (3 one acts): manuscript*; Fifth Street Studio Theater, Los Angeles, CA

Dramatic Instincts: manuscript*
   *contact author

PAUL HUNTER

Born in Los Angeles. Educated at Principia Upper School and Principia College (B.A.). Has worked as a television writer, freelance journalist, advertising copywriter, graphics designer and theatrical press agent. Recipient: Los Angeles Drama Critics Circle Award in 1972 for **An Interview with F. Scott Fitzgerald;** Drama-Logue Critics' Award for **Love & Marriage & Then What?**

Address: 510 South Burnside Ave., Los Angeles, CA 90036 (213) 935-4974

Agent: Ben Conway & Associates, 999 N. Doheny Drive, Los Angeles, CA 90069 (213) 274-8133

TITLE • AVAILABILITY • PRODUCTIONS

An Interview with F. Scott Fitzgerald: Best Short Plays of 1972, Chilton Book Co., 201 King of Prussia Rd., Radnor, PA 19089, $7.95; Evergreen Stage, Los Angeles; Playbox Theatre, NY

Hostile Terrain: manuscript*; Circle Theatre, Los Angeles, CA; Zephyr Theatre, Los Angeles, CA

Scott and Zelda: manuscript*; Oxford Playhouse, Los Angeles; Theatre de Lys matinee series, NYC

How Do You Live with Love?: manuscript*; Garden Theatre Festival, Los Angeles; White Barn Theatre, Westport, CT

When in Rome: manuscript*; Theatre West, Los Angeles, CA

Love & Marriage & Then What?: manuscript*; Cast Theatre, L.A., CA

Zelda Alone: manuscript*

   *contact agent

SYNOPSES

Zelda Alone: A one-woman play about the last day in the life of Zelda Fitzgerald. Setting is her room in a mental institution, and she moves in and out of memory as she tries to come to terms with the contradictions in her life.

Full length.

When In Rome: American Christy Corner attempts to break off her affair with a charming, impulsive Italian, heir to a thriving motel chain, by fleeing to a small pensione in Rome. She has to share a bathroom with the guest next door who turns out to be an attractive American businessman. Guess what happens? You're wrong!

Full length. Setting: two small rooms in a Roman pensione and the bathroom which connects them. 3 males, 3 females.

KATHY HURLEY

Born in Plainfield, NJ on April 1, 1947. B.A., Arizona State University four-year academic scholarship, summa cum laude; M.A., Illinois State University and the University of Colorado (graduate fellowships). Member of Dramatists Guild, Authors League of America, Actors Equity Association and A.F.T.R.A. Recipient: The Stagebrush Theatre Playwriting Award; Heckshire Grant for Children's Theatre; National Endowment for the Arts Playwriting Residency Grant for the New York Metropolitan Short Play Festival.

Address: Manhattan Plaza, 484 West 43rd St., #22P, New York, NY 10036

Agent: Gloria Safier, 667 Madison Avenue, New York, NY 10021 (212) 838-4868

TITLE • AVAILABILITY • PRODUCTIONS

For an Eggshell: manuscript*; Stagebrush Theatre; Stonesoup Theatre

The Alchemist's Book: Samuel French, 25 West 45th St., New York, NY 10036, $2.00; Henry Street Settlement, NYC

Byron or Beauty Like the Night: manuscript*; Octagon/Bert Wheeler Theatre; Actors' Alliance

The Black Princess (children's musical): manuscript*; Double Image Theatre, NYC; Lincoln Center Library of the Performing Arts, NYC

At the Bus Stop: manuscript*; Double Image Theatre, NYC; One Act Play Festival, NYC

The Forgotten Treasure (children's musical): manuscript*; Double Image Theatre, NYC; New York City Programs in the Park Series

The Fading of Miss Dru: manuscript*; Actors Alliance; New York Metropolitan Short Play Festival

From Our Point of View: manuscript*; Long Island Theatre Guild; Double Image Theatre, NYC

Yes, But What Do You Do for a Living?: manuscript*; Actors Alliance; New York Metropolitan Short Play Festival

*contact agent

H/I

DAVID HENRY HWANG

Born in Los Angeles, CA on August 11, 1957. Attended Harvard School in North Hollywood, CA; A.B. in English from Stanford University, (Phi Beta Kappa). Co-founded Stanford Asian American Theatre Project and directed original student production of **FOB** at Stanford University's Okada House. Also directed premiere of Philip Gotanda's **A Song for a Nisei Fisherman**. Led Asian American studies classes and writing workshops. Published poet, jazz pop musician.

Agent: Helen Merrill, 337 W. 22nd St., New York, NY 10011 (212) 924-6314

TITLE • AVAILABILITY • PRODUCTIONS

FOB: manuscript*; O'Neill Theater Center's National Playwrights Conference, CT; New York Shakespeare Festival, NYC

Family Devotions: manuscript*; New York Shakespeare Festival, NYC

The Dance and the Railroad: manuscript*; New Federal Theatre, NYC; New York Shakespeare Festival, NYC

The House of Sleeping Beauties: manuscript*

Love that Waits: manuscript; Lennox Art Center, Stockbridge, MA

   *contact agent

SYNOPSES

FOB: Steve is a newcomer from Hong Kong; Grace immigrated to America as a young girl. They also identify with Gwan Gung and Fa Mu Lan, Chinese warrior spirits. Dale, an American born Chonk, enters and together they experience Asian immigration and American assimilation in new terms.

Full length. Setting: the back room of a Chinese restaurant in Torrance, CA. 2 yellow males, 1 yellow female.

The House of Sleeping Beauties: A Japanese author enters a house where old men come to fantasize their youth, as they sleep beside the bodies of young, drugged women.

One act. Setting: one set. 1 yellow male, 1 yellow female.

McCREA IMBRIE

Born in Atlantic City, NJ on May 15, 1918. McCrea writes for films in addition to the theatre. Recipient: Audrey Wood Award, 1972.

Address: 21 Pine Drive; Roosevelt, NJ 08555 (609) 448-4492

Agent: William Morris Agency, 151 El Camino, Beverly Hills, CA 90212 (213) 274-7451

TITLE • AVAILABILITY • PRODUCTIONS

Down Under (with R. Kidder): manuscript*

Marvin (with N. Selden): manuscript*

A Responsible Spider: manuscript*

Someone's Comin' Hungry (with N. Selden): manuscript*; Pocket Theatre, NYC

A Girl Like Norman Mailer (with N. Selden): manuscript*

McCrea Imbrie (cont'd)

Still Life (with Timothy Imbrie): manuscript*; Classic Stage Theatre; Ham & Clove Stage Co., NYC

Car (with N. Selden): manuscript*; Berlin Festival; Actors Studio Workshop, NYC

Raincheck (with N. Selden): manuscript*; Berlin Festival; West Germany

Mister Shandy (with N. Selden): manuscript*; Roundabout Theatre, NYC: Actors Studio Workshop, NYC

The Feeling Shop (with N. Selden): manuscript*; Actors Studio Workshop, NYC

Clearing (with N. Selden): manuscript*; Actors Studio Workshop, NYC; Huntington Theatre Workshop, NY

Gino (with N. Selden): manuscript*

The Policeman's Wife (with N. Selden): manuscript*

Leaves for a Sunday Afternoon (with N. Selden): manuscript*

*contact agent

SYNOPSES

Still Life: A man and his wife are preparing for a party they are giving. None of their guests come but a stranger arrives. They are wary and afraid of the stranger. They abuse him and make him their prisoner. The stranger finally convinces the couple he means them no harm. They release him. The man and his wife try to seduce and possess the stranger. He rejects them. The couple kill the stranger.

Full length. Setting: almost bare stage. 2 males, 1 female.

Clearing: A business man decides to commit himself to a mental hospital because he can no longer endure the loss of self, arising from the break-up of his business. His wife of twenty-five years takes his decision as a rejection of herself and their marriage. She struggles to have him start a new life with her. The play begins when they are about to leave for the mental institution. A hitchhiker forces himself upon them and tries to change their lives.

Full length. Setting: bare stage with or without a representational car. 2 males, 1 female.

Someone's Comin' Hungry: Paul Odom, a young black war veteran, finds the activism of his white and very pregnant wife, Connie, a source of contention in their marriage. The birth of their son stirs deep changes in each of them and they encounter each other with an honesty neither was willing to risk before. Paul's father, who lives with them, and Connie's mother, as well as a young black girl upstairs, join the confrontation.

Full length. Setting: living room showing bedroom area and kitchen of an East Village apartment. 2 males, 3 females.

ROBERT E. INGHAM

Born in Bedford County, VA on January 27, 1934. Attended the U. of Virginia and the Yale School of Drama (M.F.A. in Playwriting). Taught acting and directing at Grinnell College in Iowa and the U. of Montana. He has worked at the Milwaukee Repertory Theatre and many other places. Recipient: John Golden Scholar; John Golden Fellow; RCA-NBC Fellow; American Theatre Critics Association, Best Play done outside New York, 1979-80, **Custer.**

Address: 3555 Asbury Ave., Dallas, TX 75205

Agent: Helen Harvey, 410 W. 24th St., New York, NY 10011 (212) 675-7445

I

Robert E. Ingham (cont'd)

TITLE • AVAILABILITY • PRODUCTIONS

Simple Life; Three New Yale Playwrights, Crown Press, 1 Park Ave., New York, NY 10016; Yale Drama School, CT

No Better: manuscript*; Grinnell College

Custer: manuscript*; O'Neill Theater Center's National Playwrights Conference, CT; Milwaukee Repertory Theatre, WI

*contact author

ALBERT INNAURATO

Born in Philadelphia, PA in 1948. Graduated Yale School of Drama, 1974. M.F.A. in Playwriting. He has suffered through many odd jobs in New York while continuing the writing of his plays. Recipient: Guggenheim Grant, 1975–76; Rockefeller Grant.

Agent: Helen Merrill, 337 West 22nd Street, New York, NY 10011 (212) 924-6314

TITLE • AVAILABILITY • PRODUCTIONS

The Idiots Karamazov (with Christopher Durang): Dramatists Play Service, 440 Park Ave. South New York, NY 10016, $2.50; Yale Repertory Company, CT; Houston, TX; etc.

Urlicht: Bizarre Behavior, Avon Books, 224 West 57th St., New York, NY 10019, $3.50; Theatre of Living Arts, Philadelphia, PA; Playwrights Horizons, NYC

Transfiguration of Benno Blimpie: Dramatists Play Service, $1.25. Also **Bizarre Behavior;** O'Neill Theater Center's National Playwrights Conference, CT; Direct Theatre, NYC; etc.

Earthworms: West Coast Plays, 1979, P.O. Box 7206, Berkeley, CA 94707, $4.95. Also **Bizarre Behavior;** O'Neill Theater Center's National Playwrights Conference, CT; Playwrights Horizons, NYC

Gemini: Dramatists Play Service, $2.50. Also **Bizarre Behavior;** Playwrights Horizons, NYC; PAF Playhouse, NYC

Ulysses in Traction: Dramatists Play Service, $2.50. Also **Bizarre Behavior;** Circle Repertory Company, NYC

Passione: Dramatists Play Service, $2.50; Playwrights Horizons, NYC; Broadway

Wisdom Amok: Bizarre Behavior; Berkeley Stage Company, CA

ANTHONY INNEO

Simultaneously educated in the streets of Newark, NJ while attending its schools, followed by two years at Fairleigh Dickinson University, also attended the American Musical and Dramatic Academy. Emphasis has always been placed on his acting career but he has been a member of the Italian Playwrights Forum since its inception. Numerous readings of his plays have been done throughout the city.

Address: 352 West 46th St., #6C, New York, NY 10036 (212) 977-4311

TITLE • AVAILABILITY • PRODUCTIONS

From Now On: manuscript*; Italian Playwrights Forum, NYC

I Have This Friend: manuscript*

Temporarily in Order, or Use It While You Can: manuscript*

Pele and Hiiaka: manuscript*; Italian Playwrights Forum, NYC

Just Between Us: manuscript*

    *contact author

SYNOPSES

From Now On: The internal and external destruction of an international rock group called Trinity Plus. Original rock music covers ten years.

Full length. Setting: multi-leveled. 11 males, 4 females, doubling included, no orchestra.

Just Between Us: The story of a famous architect and his nephew/writer who have a meeting of the minds. The topic: incest.

Full length. Setting: diningroom and kitchen. 2 males which can be adjusted to 2 females.

Pele and Hiiaka: A musical story of the undivided love between two sisters; the eldest of seven whose name is Pele and the youngest who is affectionately called Haiiaka-i-ka-poli-o-pele, which means Hiiaka, the darling of Pele. It is the historical event of the Hawaiian goddesses. Original music.

Full length.

CORINNE JACKER

Northwestern University, B.A. and M.A. TV credits include **Actors Choice; The Last G.I.'s; Adams Chronicles; Visions.** Recipient: Obie Award, 1975; New York Emmy Citation, 1970; Emmy Citation, 1975; Cine Golden Eagle, 1971; Rockefeller Grant, 1979–80.

Address: 110 West 86th St., New York, NY 10024

Agent: Lois Berman, 250 West 57th St., New York, NY 10019 (212) 581-0670

J

Corinne Jacker (cont'd)

TITLE • AVAILABILITY • PRODUCTIONS

Harry Outside: Dramatists Play Service, 440 Park Avenue South, New York, NY 10016, $2.50;
O'Neill Theater Center's National Playwrights Conference, CT; Circle Repertory Company,
NYC

Bits and Pieces: Dramatists Play Service, $2.50; Manhattan Theatre Club, NYC; E.P.Conkle
Workshop, Dallas, TX

Breakfast, Lunch and Dinner: with **Bits and Pieces;** Actors Studio, NYC; E.P.Conkle Workshop,
Dallas, TX

Travellers: manuscript*; O'Neill Theater Center's National Playwrights Conference, CT;
Cincinnati Playhouse-in-the-Park, OH

Making It: manuscript*; Circle Repertory Company, NYC

Night Thoughts: Dramatists Play Service, $2.50; St. Clements, NYC: Circle Repertory Company,
NYC

Terminal: with **Night Thoughts;** Circle Repertory Company, NYC

My Life: Dramatists Play Service, $2.50; Circle Repertory Company, NYC

The Other People's Tables: manuscript*; Billy Munk Theatre, NYC

Chinese Restaurant Syndrome: Best Short Plays of 1979, Chilton Press, Chilton Way, Radnor,
PA 19089, $10.50; Billy Munk Theatre, NYC

Later: Dramatists Play Service, $2.50; Phoenix Theatre, NYC

After the Season: manuscript*; American Festival Theatre, Lake Forest, IL; pre-Broadway

Domestic Issues: manuscript*; Yale Repertory, CT

*contact agent

SYNOPSIS

Harry Outside: A famous and successful architect, Harry Harrison (after confinement for a mental
breakdown), can no longer accept the restrictions and second-rate standards of modern society.
He cannot even bear to stay indoors and has instead set up his studio in the woods. As he labors
on a new and absorbing project his life is intertwined with others, family and friends, who in
various ways, love and admire him.

Full length. Setting: a clearing in the woods. 3 males, 4 females.

R. EUGENE JACKSON

Born in Helena, AR on February 25, 1941. B.A.,
Memphis State University; M.A., Kent State
University; Ph.D., Southern Illinois University.
Presently Associate Professor of Drama and
Chairman of the Department of Dramatic Arts at
the University of South Alabama, teaching
theatre history, playwriting, children's theater.
Recipient: won second place in playwriting con-
tests in Atlanta, Kansas City, Carbondale, IL;
Pioneer Drama Service, Best Play, 1979.

Address: 1901 Oakleaf Court, Mobile, AL 36609
(205) 661-1426, Home — (205) 460-6305, Office

TITLE • AVAILABILITY • PRODUCTIONS

Ferdinand and the Dirty Knight: Pioneer Drama Service, 2172 S. Colorado Blvd., Denver, CO
80222, $1.50; Kent State U., OH; San Francisco State College, CA

A Thousand & One Spells to Cast: manuscript*; Kent State U., OH

R. Eugene Jackson (cont'd)

Little Red Riding Wolf: I.E. Clark, P.O. Box 246, Schulenburg, TX 78956, $1.50; Pixie Players, Mobile, AL

Who Can Fix the Dragon's Wagon?: I.E. Clark, $2.50; Wisconsin State U., Eau Claire, WI

Felicia & the Magic Pinks: manuscript*; Pixie Players, Mobile, AL

Triple Play: Dramatic Publishing Co., 86 E. Randolph St., Chicago, IL 60601, $1.00

The Mother Goose Follies: manuscript*; Southern Illinois U.

Snowballs & Grapevines: manuscript*; U. of South Alabama

The Castle of Otranto: manuscript*

No Way: manuscript*;

Cinder-Ella (musical): manuscript*; U. of South Alabama; Children's Musical Theatre, Mobile, AL

The Creepy Castle Hassle: Performance Publishing Co., 978 N. McLean Blvd., Elgin, IL 60120, $2.50; Little Theatre Company, Mobile, AL

The Crazy Paper Caper: Performance Publishing Co., $2.50; Mobile Recreation Dept.

Beauty & The Beast (musical): manuscript*; U. of South Alabama

Jamestown Diary (musical): manuscript*; Children's Musical Theatre, Mobile, AL

A Mother Goose Celebration (musical): manuscript*; Children's Musical Theatre, Mobile, AL

From Sea to Shining Sea (musical): manuscript*; Children's Musical Theatre, Mobile, AL

The Wonderful Wizard of Oz: I.E. Clark, $2.00; Pixie Players, Mobile, AL

The Sleeping Beauty (musical): Pioneer Drama Service, $2.00; Children's Musical Theatre, Mobile, AL

The Swiss Family Robinson (musical): manuscript*; Children's Musical Theatre, Mobile, AL

The Adventures of Peter Cottontail (musical): manuscript*; Children's Musical Theatre, Mobile, AL

Brer Rabbit's Big Secret (musical): Pioneer Drama Service, $2.00; Children's Musical Theatre, Mobile, AL

Arthur, King of England (musical): manuscript*; Children's Musical Theatre, Mobile, AL

Hangin' Loose: manuscript*

The Wolf Man Strikes Again: manuscript*

Pinocchio (musical): manuscript*; Children's Musical Theatre, Mobile, AL

The Jumping Off Place (musical): manuscript*; Children's Musical Theatre, Mobile, AL

Superkid: I.E. Clark, $2.50

Under the Gaslight (musical melodrama): manuscript*; U. of South Alabama

Snowhite and the Space Dwarfs (musical): Pioneer Drama Service, $2.50; Children's Musical Theatre, Mobile, AL

Super Snooper (musical): manuscript*; Children's Musical Theatre; Mobile, AL

A Golden Fleecing: Pioneer Drama Service, $2.50; University of South Alabama

Rag Dolls: I.E. Clark, $2.00

Rumpelstiltskin Is My Name: I.E. Clark, $2.00

Is That a Fact? (musical): manuscript*; Children's Musical Theatre, Mobile, AL

Unidentified Flying Reject: manuscript*

Bumper Snickers (co-author): I.E. Clark, $2.00

   *contact author

J

JIM JACOBS

Born in Chicago, IL on October 7, 1942. Attended Chicago City College. Worked as advertising copywriter, rock'n' roll musician, professional actor, both in regional theatre and on Broadway. Nominated for Joseph Jefferson Award's Best Actor of the Year, Chicago 1969–70 Season, for title role in **Jimmy Shine**. Member of ASCAP, Actors Equity Association, Screen Actor's Guild, The Dramatists Guild. Co-author/lyricist/composer of **Grease**. **Grease** nominated for seven Tony Awards including Best Book for a Musical; also nominated for Grammy Award for Best Original Cast Album. On Dec. 8, 1979, it became the longest running show on Broadway (9 years), finally closing after 3,388 performances.

Agent: Bridget Aschenberg, c/o ICM, 40 West 57th St., New York, NY 10019 (212) 556-5720

TITLE • AVAILABILITY • PRODUCTIONS

Grease (co-author with Warren Casey): Samuel French, 25 West 45th St., New York, NY 10036, $2.00; Broadway; numerous other productions worldwide

Island of Lost Coeds: in progress.

SYNOPSIS

Grease: The new '50s rock 'n' roll musical. **Grease** parodies the teen-age life style of the late 1950s, yet the show is ageless. Anyone who went to high school, remembers Elvis, faked an ID card to buy beer, or cruised the drive-in circuit in an old custom car, will enjoy the super-cool, fun-packed songs, dances and neat-o dialogue of **Grease.**

Full length. Setting: one basic set of high school corridor covered with '50s memorabilia; and various flats suggestive of different locales in the neighborhood. 8-9 males (one-small role can be doubled), 8 females.

MICHAEL JACOBS

Born in New Brunswick, NJ on June 28, 1955. Studied Theater at Ithaca College, NY and The Neighborhood Playhouse School of Theater, NYC. He has written TV pilots and short stories. He is a member of the Dramatists Guild.

Agent: Rosenstone/Wender, 3 East 48th St., New York, NY 10017 (212) 832-8330

TITLE • AVAILABILITY • PRODUCTIONS

Daddy's Boys: manuscript*

Cheaters: Samuel French, 25 West 45th St., New York, NY 10036; Boston; Broadway

Getting Along Famously: manuscript*

   *contact agent

SYNOPSIS

Cheaters: Two young people, living together, are confused about the value of marriage. They would seek help from their parents, but they are unaware that their parents are unaware that they are having affairs with the parents of their children's lovers. The children decide an introductory

Michael Jacobs (cont'd)

dinner between the families might be apropos to discuss whether loyalty to one other in life is worthwhile anymore. But once introductions are made, it's everyone for himself.

Full length. Setting: one set, livingroom that changes, (farce change). 3 males, 3 females.

ARTHUR JASSPE, Ph.D.

Born in New York City. Ph.D., New York University, M.A., Columbia University (T.C.) Professor of English, Winston-Salem State University, North Carolina, 1968–1969. Wrote **Exact Change Only,** novel; scholarly book, **Critical Theory and Playwriting Practice of Contemporary American Playwrights: 1920–1940,** Ann Arbor, Michigan, University microfilms, Inc., 1959; articles: **A Proposal for Enhancing the Playwright's Condition, The Dramatists Guild** Quarterly; **Achievement in Dramatic Art, News-letter No. 19;** American Society for Theatre Research, Princeton, New Jersey; **We Need Benny These Days, Dramatist Bulletin,** The Dramatists Guild. Music compositions: **I Wandered Lonely As a Cloud** (song); **April** (Mixed Chorus); **Introduction and Rondo for French Horn and Orchestra, String Quartet Cameo No. 2,** (Orchestra); **Minute Overture** (Orchestra); **Cameo,** (Orchestra); **Alma Mater** (A Symphonic Overture). Has also directed College varsity productions, as well as Army Special Service shows during his term of military service. Recipient: Founders Day Certificate, New York University; War Service Scholarship, New York State.

Address: 80 First Ave., New York, NY 10009 (212) 674-3706

Agent: Herbert J. Kimmel, Esq., Flatiron Building, 175 Fifth Ave., New York, NY 10010 (212) 477-1386

TITLE • AVAILABILITY • PRODUCTIONS

Seven Days Hath December: manuscript*; Readings, Greenhouse Theatre, NYC

Amertyl: manuscript*; Readings, Greenhouse Theatre, NYC

The Tarleton Story: manuscript*

The Oldest Drugstore in New York: manuscript*; Readings, Greenhouse Theatre, NYC

The Ratings Sweep: manuscript*; Readings, Greenhouse Theatre, NYC

Harrison of the Mounted: manuscript*; Readings, Greenhouse Theatre, NYC

Gene and Jeanne: manuscript*; Readings, Greenhouse Theatre, NYC

SYNOPSES

The Oldest Drug Store in New York: A continuing series of one-act plays concerning the adventures in and around a drug store. Various males and females as required for each and every play.

Setting: a drug store (including a fountain).

The Ratings Sweep: A continuous series of one-act plays in and around a television station.

Major characters are 6 males. Various other parts. Setting: back stage of a New York television station.

Gene and Jeanne: Boy meets girl—girl meets boy in an unusual manner.

Setting: a very nice street or plaza; summertime. 1 male, female.

J

JOHN JILER

Born in New York City on April 4, 1946. B.A., University of Hartford, CT in English. John has acted and written for experimental theaters throughout Europe and North America before returning here several years ago to seek a professional career. Since then he has appeared often on the New York stage and written his first body of new work since 1971. Recipient: Chicago Drama Critics League, Best Supporting Actor.

Address: 93 Nassau St., #.915, New York, NY
   10038

TITLE • AVAILABILITY • PRODUCTIONS

The Library: manuscript*; University of Hartford, CT

African Star: manuscript*; O'Neill Theater Center's National Playwrights Conference, CT

Where There's a Will: not available; Circle H Ranch, Glen Gardner, NJ

Ball: manuscript*

Guava Lagoon: manuscript*

Early Bird: manuscript*

   *contact author

SYNOPSES

Guava Lagoon: A tale about a mental institution in the thickest part of the Jamaican rain forest, run by natives for wealthy white neurotic Americans.

Setting: Guava Lagoon. 5 males, 4 females.

Early Bird: The paths of a vulgar/poetic newsvendor and a young black ballerina cross briefly and sadly in New York.

One act. Setting: a street corner newstand. 3 males, 1 female.

C. ROBERT JONES

Born in Rock Hill, SC. B.A., University of South Carolina; M.A., University of Georgia; M.F.A., Catholic University of America. Resident Director, Little Theatre, Savannah, GA. Chairman, Founder, Department of Theatre Arts, Gardner-Webb College. Currently Playwright-in-Residence and Associate Professor of Theatre Arts, Mars Hill College. Guest director (opera), Stetson University, Parkway Playhouse. Author, **Lanky Tales,** short stories for children. Composer, **Rhapsodie Espagnole** (piano). Has written book, music, lyrics for all his musicals listed here. Recipient: Fulbright Grant; David B. Marshall Award, Musical Theatre.

Address: P.O. Box 531, Mars Hill, NC 28754
   (704) 689-4437

TITLE • AVAILABILITY • PRODUCTIONS

The Crown (musical): Baker's Plays, 100 Chauncy St., Boston, MA 02111, $2.50; Little Theatre of Savannah, GA; numerous others

The Spelling Bee (musical): Baker's Plays, $1.60; Gardner-Webb College; numerous others

C. Robert Jones (cont'd)

Something Beautiful: Baker's Plays, $1.25; Numerous productions

Marked for Murder: Baker's Plays, $1.25; Numerous productions

Love is Better Than the Next Best Thing: Baker's Plays, $2.25; Numerous productions

Mandy Lou (musical): Dramatic Publishing Co., 4150 N. Milwaukee Ave., Chicago, IL 60641, $2.25; Southern Appalachian Repertory Theatre; Charleston Summer Theatre, SC

Rivals (musical): manuscript*; Owen Theatre, Mars Hill College, NC

A Belonging Place** (with music): manuscript*; Southern Appalachian Repertory Theatre

Wednesday's Children**: manuscript*; Southern Appalachian Repertory Theatre

Heart of the Tiger**: manuscript*; Licklog Players, NC

A Time for Singing: manuscript*; Gardner-Webb College

> *contact author
> **Etchings in Firelight,** collective title for trilogy

SYNOPSES

Mandy Lou: A musical comedy that is also a gentle spoof of the **Gone With The Wind** south and old-fashioned melodramas. Mandy Lou, a seventeen-year-old debutante, returns from finishing school to find her father in jail, wrongly accused of forgery, and crafty overseer Rufus Tattnall, trying to wrest away her home, Bellemaison Plantation. To top it all, there is a mix-up in Mandy Lou's cotillion partners, an unknown baby left on the doorstep, and some surprising news about a shipwreck twenty years before. Family show with fourteen songs. The play holds the attendance record for the theater that premiered it.

Full length. Setting: one unit set. 8 males, 9 females.

Rivals: Musical comedy adaptation of Sheridan's comedy updated to 1889. Mrs. Malaprop has spirited her nieces, Lydia Languish and Juliette Melville, away from London to stave off the attentions of young suitors, Absolute and Faulkland. The plot closely follows the original, ending happily with even Mrs. Malaprop getting her man. Twenty-three songs. Original cast album available.

Full length. Setting: one unit set. 6 males, 5 females, extras.

Etchings in Firelight; A trilogy covering two generations of the Ammons family in North Carolina between 1895 and 1932. Each play stands on its own. **Heart of the Tiger** tells the story of Abel Ammons and his first wife, Kate, whose marriage is disapproved by a domineering father. A power-play ensues between father and daughter with unexpected results. 6 males, 4 females.
A Belonging Place, a play with music, begins during World War I at Kate's death in the flu epidemic. Hilda Marx, a German opera singer and one of 2,000 German nationals interned in the town, becomes nurse to ten-year-old Marcie Ammons. A love story between Abel and Hilda is complicated by the fact that Abel's son, Ben, is a soldier in France and Hilda's fiance is one of the other interned Germans. 6 males, 4 females, 3 children.
Wednesday's Children, set between 1929 and 1932, is the story of Abel's two children, Marcie and Ben, and the complications brought into their lives by their neighbor, Laura Lee Ledbetter, and a handsome young school principal, Clay Delaney, who is loved by both girls. Laura Lee's rejection by Clay sets up a chain of events which changes the lives of everyone in a wrenching and devastating way. 7 males, 6 females, 3 children.

The three plays are full length and use the same unit set.

J

SILAS JONES

Born in Paris, KY on January 17, 1940. Studied
Literature and Creative Writing at Washington
State, Los Angeles City College and Writers
Guild of America's Open Door Program. Director
of Writers Workshops at Performing Arts Society of Los Angeles, 1974, and Paradox Playhouse,
Los Angeles, 1978. Certified to teach Drama and
Creative Writing in Los Angeles. Has published
short stories, **The Price of Dirt, Children of All** (a
sci-fi children's book featuring black super-
heroes); wrote TV documentary, **TV's Black Image Syndrome** and **Protest and Beyond** (NBC);
created **Denise Douglass, DDS,** sitcom optioned
to Twentieth-Century Fox. Member, WGA, West,
Dramatists Guild of America. Recipient: Gwen-
dolyn Brooks Literary Award, 1972, Best Short
Story; ARTACT Playwriting Award.

Address: 7818 South Hobart Blvd., Los Angeles, CA 90047 (213) 971-8443

TITLE • AVAILABILITY • PRODUCTIONS

Waiting for Mongo: manuscript*; Negro Ensemble Company, NYC

The Afrindi Aspect: manuscript*; Negro Ensemble Company, NYC

The Eighth Planet: manuscript*

Off: manuscript*

Vagaries: manuscript*

   *contact author

SYNOPSIS

Waiting for Mongo: A nightmare comedy. Virgil, a schizophrenic black teenager, is literally
camping out in a church cellar, waiting for the Black Brigade's leader, Mongo, to save him from a
lynch mob who thinks he has molested a white girl. In a dream sequence, Virgil and Mongo
singlehandedly destroy the Sheriff and his deputies, but when Virgil wakes, the real mob is breaking down the church doors. Is Virgil afraid? Of course not. He simply removes his combat boot
and, using it as a phone, calls Mongo . . . . "Jones has created his own play and style. The play is
the star."—Martin Gottfried, **New York Post.** "Jones is a genuine talent." — **Village Voice.** "Jones
has the precious gift of irony." — **Emory Lewis.**

Setting: a dilapidated southern black church, basement and church proper, 6 males, 3 females.

ERNEST A. JOSELOVITZ

Born in Danbury, CT on June 18, 1942. B.A. from
U.C.L.A. and M.F.A. from University of Min-
nesota. Member, Playwrights Unit, American
Conservatory Theatre, San Francisco. Play-
wright-in-residence, New Playwrights' Theatre,
Wash., DC, 1978-81; Playwriting instructor, New
Playwrights' Theatre School and George Mason
U. Recipient: Shubert Playwriting Fellowship;
John Golden Travelling Fellowship; Starr Play-
writing Prize; O.A.D.R. Travel/Consultation
Grant; Theatre Communications Group Travel
Grant; N.E.A. Theater Residency Grants, 1978-9;
Rockefeller Foundation, Arts DC, Script Devel-
opment Grant, 1979; DC Commission on the Arts
and Humanities, 1979, 1981; N.E.A. Writer's
Grant, 1980.

Ernest A. Joselovitz (cont'd)

Address: 1401 N St., N.W., Wash., DC 20005 (202) 667-3623

Agent: Robert Freedman, Brandt & Brandt, 1501 Broadway, New York, NY 10036 (212) 840-5760

TITLE • AVAILABILITY • PRODUCTIONS

Parable: not available; Greyfriars' Society Theatre, Pasadena, CA

The Inheritance: Playwrights For Tomorrow, Vol. 13, University of Minnesota Press, 2037 University Ave., S.E., Minn., MN 55414, $4.95; University of Minnesota

Hagar's Children: Dramatists Play Service, 440 Park Ave. South, New York, NY 10019, $2.50; New Playwrights' Theatre, Wash., DC; New York Shakespeare Festival, NYC

Sammi: Dramatists Play Service, $1.25; Jewish Repertory Theatre, NYC

Righting: Dramatists Play Service, $1.25

The Bubble: manuscript*; One Act Theatre Company, San Francisco, CA

Splendid Rebels: manuscript*; New Playwrights' Theatre, Wash., DC; Corner Theatre, Baltimore, MD

Triptych: manuscript*; Jewish Repertory Theatre, NYC; Greater Washington Jewish Community Center, Wash., DC

Holding On: manuscript*; New Playwrights' Theatre, Wash., DC

Inaugural: manuscript*; Bloomington Playwrights' Project, IN

Rehearsal for Murder: manuscript*

Break Up: manuscript*

Jesse's Land: manuscript*

   *contact agent

SYNOPSES

Jesse's Land: A story of love and pride that spans three generations of a Jewish-American family. Seventy-year-old Connecticut farmer Jesse Kletchik estranged from everyone else, is meeting his only grandson, David, for the first time. At stake is the future of his land. Within the framework of that final crisis of his life, its source is enacted: the marriage of his son to city-bred Willa Neuwald, whose drive and ambition are Jesse's match. Her determination to gain some part of his land as a future for herself and coming child meet his equal pride and insecurity making that giving impossible. And from the explosive rivalry grows a deep affection, the roots of that love the same as their incompatible needs.

Full length. Setting: the Kletchik farmhouse — the kitchen and then the living–dining room. 3 males, 2 females.

Hagar's Children: Drama with music. Bridgehaven Farm, a home for emotionally disturbed teenagers. It's the day before Christmas, a day of boisterous celebration, of memories and explosive tensions for the abused and discarded youngsters who are struggling for the first time to combat their deep sense of worthlessness and emotional chaos. One of them kills the farm's mascot, and still has the knife. Which one? The House, their world and last hope, is threatened. They themselves must overcome it. "abrasively astonishing . . . so intense and harrowing—that it jumps into a perfect somersault of theatre . . . " — Clive Barnes, **NY Times**

Setting: single-unit set, two levels, the Bridgehaven Farm House — bedrooms, living room, dining room, forestage. 6 males, 3 females.

Splendid Rebels: 1917: Emma Goldman, radical feminist, whose objection to entry into World War I becomes a defense of the rights for conscientious objectors, and a fateful conflict with the forces of an emerging national police led by the young and ambitious J. Edgar Hoover. Emma Goldman, with her lifelong companion, the doctrinaire anarchist Sasha Berkman, her lover and "King of the Hoboes," Dr. Ben Reitman, and her counsel in defense, Clarence Darrow, confront the forced conformity of wartime and postwar hysteria of the "red scare," For the nation, it marks the end of an era. For Emma Goldman, it forces a choice between political and personal commitment.

Full length. Setting: single unit set to include Emma Goldman's New York City apartment, a courtroom, various other locations. 13 males (many of which can double), 3 females.

J

ROBERT FARRAS JOSEPH

Born in Philadelphia, PA on November 30, 1935.
Educated at the University of Pennsylvania, B.A.
Graduate work at U.C.L.A. and Trinity University,
San Antonio, Texas. Author of the novels **The
Diva** (1975) and **Kate's Way** (1977), published by
G.P. Putnam's Sons. Has written for **CBS Play-
house** and for **Filmation,** both television. Recipi-
ent: Charles MacArthur Award (Honorable Men-
tion) for the play **Kool-Aid's Girls, 1974.**

Address: 2407 Bayshore Avenue, Ventura, CA
93001

Agent: Film Artists Management Enterprises,
Inc., 8278 Sunset Blvd., Los Angeles, CA 90046
(213) 656-7590

TITLE • AVAILABILITY • PRODUCTIONS

A Perfect Place for Appeal to Reason (one act): manuscript*; Trinity University Theater, San
Antonio, TX; Evergreen Stage Company, Los Angeles, CA

Have a Heart (one act): manuscript*; Evergreen Stage Company, CA

The Surrogate Groom (one act): manuscript*; Evergreen Stage Company, CA

A Lull in the Fighting (Vacation from War): manuscript*; CBS Playhouse

Presence of Mine Enemies: manuscript*; Theater of Arts, Los Angeles, CA

Kool-Aid's Girl: manuscript*; Evergreen Stage Company; Theater Exchange, Los Angeles, CA

Holly-Haven: manuscript*
*contact author

SYNOPSES

Kool-Aid's Girl: A touching and exciting love-hate story of Russ, a disillusioned paraplegic trying
to kick the drug habit and the memory of a marriage gone sour, and his nurse, Caroline, a determined pollyanna exconvict on parole who is still pining for the jailbird lover who "done her
wrong." Flashes of humor and tenderness light up this eminently actable play about two yearning
people, each "caged" in his own emotional prison, who finally break out of their self-imposed patterns of isolation to admit their overpowering need for each other in the nick of time. The dialogue
scintillates with wry wit, and the poignantly intimate scenes of self-revelation are a director's
delight.

Two acts. Setting: a picturesque houseboat in a small marina in Sausalito. 1 male, 1 female.

Holly-Haven: Three elderly silent screen stars solve problems and anxieties by acting out
memories of their old films while their young custodian struggles to save the mansion in which
they are housed from imminent destruction. A comedy-drama with elements of fantasy counter-
balanced with naturalism.

Full length, three acts. Setting: the decaying ballroom of an old Hollywood mansion. 4 males, 3
females.

Presence of Mine Enemies: While going about his harrowing duties in an infantry battalion aid
station in Vietnam, an army doctor reminisces about his civilian life and finds curious parallels
with his present situation.

Full length, two acts. Drama. Setting: an aid station. 7 males, 2 females.

JOSEPH JULIAN

Born in St. Marys, PA. Brought up in Baltimore, Maryland, where he attended Forest Park High School and Johns Hopkins University. A man of all media, Julian has written for the **Theatre Guild-U.S. Steel T.V. Hour** and has acted in hundreds of other television programs, such as **The Untouchables, Perry Mason, Alfred Hitchcock, Somerset** and **The Edge of Night.** He has been featured in numerous Broadway plays, including **The Rope Dancers** and **A Case of Libel.** In the glory days of radio he performed in over ten thousand dramatic broadcasts, which provided source material for his book. **This Was Radio — A Personal Memoir,** published by The Viking Press, with an introduction by Harold Clurman.

Address: 333 Central Park West, New York, NY 10025 (212) 222-1657 or 582-8800

TITLE • AVAILABILITY • PRODUCTIONS

Double Feature: manuscript*; Provincetown Playhouse, MA

Presento: manuscript*; Theatre Guild-U.S. Steel Hour (T.V. version)

The Gimmick: manuscript*; The Theatre Guild Westport Playhouse, CT; Elitch's Gardens, Denver, CO

See What I Mean: manuscript*; New Stages

A Man Around the House: manuscript*; Bucks County Playhouse, PA; O'Neill Theater Center's National Playwrights Conference, CT

Only More So: manuscript*

Ups and Downs and Evens: manuscript*; O'Neill Theater Center's National Playwrights Conference, CT

An Act of Kindness: manuscript*; O'Neill Theater Center's National Playwrights Conference, CT; American Renaissance Theatre, NYC
*contact author

SYNOPSES

The Gimmick (A Comedy of Lies): A clever young copywriter who hates the "lies" of advertising, prevails on his wife to support them while he writes an "honest" play. Money runs out, wife gets fed up. Inspiration! He places ad in newspaper that states simply: "SEND ME A DOLLAR." Seventy-five thousand people do. Wife accuses him of deceiving all those who have responded. He rationalizes ad as honest because he promised nothing. Finally he is relieved of money by a philosophical gunman pretending to be a U.S. Revenue agent, and recognizes his own self-deception through the slick robber's rationalization of his profession: i.e., important social function of the thief — without them economy would collapse — people would no longer put money in banks, etc.

Full length. Setting: one interior set. 7 males, several male bits, 3 females.

A Man Around the House: Attractive widow tries to give young teen-age son moral direction in spite of her own anxieties, confusion and hunger for love. She gives boy conventional answers to his questions about sex, like, "Wait until you get married to a nice girl." She has an affair with an affable policeman who takes an interest in the boy. She accepts him as a representative of authority and moral right. Boy discovers them in bed and accuses his mother of hypocrisy in advice to him. She eventually sees fallibility of policeman (who is married), and realizes one must never abdicate one's conscience to another person. She must work out her own answers.

Full length. Setting: one interior set. 5 males, 3 females, and walk-ons.

Only More So: A wildly comic satire on our preoccupation with material things. It turns our values

J/K

Joseph Julian (cont'd)

upside down in order to get a better look at them. The story dramatizes the life of the world's greatest advertising man as he dictates his autobiography. The highlight of his career is the launching of the enormously popular TV game show, **Nationalist Chinese Roulette,** where a contestant loads a revolver with both bullets and blanks, points it at his head and pulls the trigger. The fewer blanks in the gun the greater the prize. Losers are given a decent burial so the viewers won't have that let-down feeling. There is corruption and game fixing which recalls the great TV quiz scandals of the fifties.

Full length. Setting: multi scenes. 3 male leads, 1 female, 10 bits plus extras. Requires fluid production — a director's challenge.

DIANE KAGAN

Born in Maplewood, NJ. Educated at Florida State University, B.A., Drama and Dance. Studied with Martha Graham and Stella Adler. Member of The New Dramatists. First book (fiction) published by Random House, Fall 1975: **Who Won Second Place at Omaha?** An actress as well, she made her Broadway debut in Enid Bagnold's **The Chinese Prime Minister;** also appeared in **Any Wednesday,** standby for Claire Bloom in **A Doll's House,** Rochelle Owens' **Emma Instigated Me, Macbeth** and **Little Black Sheep** at Lincoln Center, for Chelsea Theater in **The Family.** Co-starred in **Huey Long** (NBC-TV). Featured in Tennessee Williams' play **Vieux Carré.**

Address: 158 East 82nd St., New York, NY 10028

Agent: Audrey Wood, 40 West 57th St., New York, NY 10019 (212) 556-5600

TITLE • AVAILABILITY • PRODUCTIONS

Phoebus††: manuscript**; La Mama E.T.C., NYC

High Time and on the Rocks††: manuscript**; WPA Theatre, NYC

Luminosity without Radiance††: manuscript**; Manhattan Theatre Club, NYC

The Final Voyage of Aphrodite: manuscript*

Who Won Second Place at Omaha? (play version): manuscript*

The Corridor: manuscript*; The New Dramatists, NYC; Open Circle Theatre, Baltimore, MD

Marvelous Brown: manuscript*; The New Dramatists, NYC; White Barn Theatre, CT

> *contact agent
> **contact author
> ††in collaboration.

SYNOPSES

The Corridor: Two people who fail to live in the moment, who murder the present — make a journey through time, evasive, uneven. In their desperate hope for the future, and their iron grip on the past, the present slips away — until it forces its way upon them and catches them unaware.

Full length, three acts. Setting: one set. 3 characters (1 male, 1 female, 1 girl).

The Final Voyage of Aphrodite: Aphrodite, in conflict with her image, calls in an objective person to view her life and help her to understand the circumstances of her birth.

Full length. Setting: one set. 3 males, 5 females.

BERNARD M. KAHN

B.A. and M.A. from the University of Michigan (English and Speech). Four-year member of the varsity swimming team. Three-year All American swimmer. Winner of the 100-meter backstroke at the 1953 Maccabbiah Games in Israel. Wrote over one hundred TV shows for the various networks.

Address: 9889 Santa Monica Blvd., Beverly Hills, CA 90212 (213) 553-0221

Agent: Shirley Bernstein, 1414 Avenue of the Americas, New York, NY 10019 (212) PL 8-5055

TITLE • AVAILABILITY • PRODUCTIONS

The Best of Everybody: manuscript*; Studebaker Theatre, Chicago, IL

Our Very Own Hole in the Ground: manuscript*; La Mama Theatre, E.T.C., NYC

The Matinee: manuscript*; The Theatre of Los Angeles, CA

Caught: manuscript*; under option

> *contact author

GUS KAIKKONEN

Born in Detroit, MI on May 7, 1951. Attended Georgetown University. Also an actor. Recipient: CAPS, 1977; American Theatre Critics Association, 1979 (for one of the ten best plays to open outside New York); Playwriting Grant (twice) from Michigan State Arts Council.

Address: 124 MacDougal St., New York, NY 10012

Agent: Dale Davis and Company, 1650 Broadway, New York, NY 10019 (212) 581-5766

TITLE • AVAILABILITY • PRODUCTIONS

Time Steps: manuscript*; Playwrights Horizons, NYC; BoarsHead Theatre, MI

Fool of Hearts: manuscript*; BoarsHead Theatre, MI; Cohoes Music Hall, Cohoes, NY

The Chinese Viewing Pavilion: manuscript*

What Are Friends For?: manuscript*; Actor's Theatre of Louisville, KY

> *contact agent

SYNOPSES

Time Steps: The unplanned reunion of a particularly disparate midwestern family at the retired parents' summer home.

Full length. Setting: unit set, the living room, porch and lawn of the home. 5 males, 5 females, 1 child.

Fool of Hearts: Arthur is in love for the first time. The object of his affections is Julia, his roommate's neglected fiancee, a girl who has loved and lost once too often. She arrives to take him to Thanksgiving dinner and Arthur convinces her to stay, if only for a few hours.

Full length. Setting: one set, the livingroom and hallway of Arthur's apartment. 1 male, 1 female.

K

Gus Kaikkonen (cont'd)

The Chinese Viewing Pavilion: Four friends from college imagine they will be friends forever. The play takes a look at the friendship in two year intervals.

Full length. Setting: one set, a Chinese viewing pavilion on a farm near the Delaware River. 5 males, 3 females.

LEE KALCHEIM

Born in Philadelphia, PA on June 27, 1938. Educated at Trinity College. B.A.; Yale University Drama School. Lee writes for television and films in addition to the theater. His T.V. credits include **Alfred Hitchcock, N.Y.P.D., Odd Couple, ABC Movie of Week (Class of '63), All in The Family** (Emmy Award). Also TV movies for CBS and NBC, as well as **Henry Winkler Meets William Shakespeare** and **The Secret of Charles Dickens.** Recipient: Rockefeller grant; 1965 Emmy Award; Christopher and Writers Guild Award.

Address: 38 West 9th St., New York, NY 10011

Agent: Audrey Wood, I.C.M., 40 West 57th St., New York, NY 10019 (212) 556-5722

TITLE • AVAILABILITY • PRODUCTIONS

A Party for Divorce: manuscript*; Albee-Barr-Wilder Workshop, NYC; Provincetown Playhouse, NYC

Match Play: New Theatre in America; Dell Publishing Co., 1 Dag Hammarskjold Plaza, New York, NY 10017, $1.95; Provincetown Playhouse, NYC

. . . And The Boy Who Came To Leave: Vol. 2, **Playwrights for Tomorrow,** Univ. of Minn. Press, 2037 University Ave. S.E., Minneapolis, Minn. 55455, $1.95; Off Broadway; Theater in The Round; Astor Place Theater, NYC

An Audible Sigh: manuscript*; O'Neill Theater Center's National Playwrights Conference, CT

The Surprise Party: manuscript*; New Dramatists, NYC

Who Wants to Be the Lone Ranger: manuscript*; Trinity College; Mark Taper Forum, CA

The Prague Spring: manuscript*; O'Neill Theater Center's National Playwrights Conference, CT; Cleveland Playhouse, OH; University of Rhode Island

Win with Wheeler: manuscript*; O'Neill Theater Center's National Playwrights Conference, CT

Friends: manuscript*

*contact agent

SYNOPSIS

An Audible Sigh: An eccentric, well-known writer, Gale McGee . . . an iconoclast . . . marries a young girl and moves from his absurd life in California into her middle-class environment in a Connecticut home . . . "temporarily." He tries to work, but his natural environment is one of conflict, and soon he is at odds with his new mother-in-law, Florence, and his new wife, Lucy. Through the conflict, Lucy "finds" her mother but never quite gets to Gale: a writer—an observer to the end — removed from even his own feelings.

GARSON KANIN

Born in Rochester, NY on November 24, 1912. Graduated from American Academy of Dramatic Arts, 1933. Acted for and was assistant to George Abbott 1935-37; was under contract to Samuel Goldwyn 1937 and RKO 1938-40. Served in U.S. Army E.T.O. 1941-45 attaining rank of Captain. Married actress Ruth Gordon, 1942, with whom he has co-authored many notable films. Author of many short stories, books of fiction and non-fiction, articles and screenplays. Has also written, produced, directed and acted for the stage. Member: Writers Guild; Authors Guild; Authors League; Directors Guild; Dramatists Guild; SDG; DGA; ASCAP; AFTRA; SSD&C; AMPAS; Actors Fund; The Players; The Friars; The Lambs, The Coffee House; New York Athletic Club. Recipient: **For The True Glory,** Academy Award; Citation, N.Y. Film Critics' Circle & Best Film of the Year from The National Board of Review; Sidney Howard Memorial Award for **Born Yesterday;** Donaldson Awards (1946); AADA Alumni Award of Achievement (1958).

Address: 200 West 57th St., Suite 1203, New York, NY 10019 (212) 586-7850 or (212) 586-7851

Agent: Nat Lefkowitz, c/o Wm. Morris Agency, 1350 Ave. of the Americas, New York, NY 10019 (212) 586-5100

TITLE • AVAILABILITY • PRODUCTIONS

Born Yesterday: Dramatists Play Service, 440 Park Ave. South, New York, NY 10016, $2.25; Lyceum Theatre, NYC

The Smile of the World: Dramatists Play Service, 60¢ (unbound); Lyceum Theatre, NYC

The Rat Race: Dramatists Play Service, $10.00 deposit, $2.00, Reading Fee; Ethel Barrymore Theatre, NYC

The Live Wire: Dramatists Play Service, $10.00 deposit, $2.00, Reading Fee; The Playhouse, NYC

The Good Soup (adapted)*: Plymouth Theatre, NYC

Do Re Mi:* St. James Theatre; London

A Gift of Time (adapted): Samuel French, 25 W. 45th St., New York, NY 10036, $2.50; Ethel Barrymore Theatre, NYC

Come on Strong: Dramatists Play Service, $2.50; Morosco Theatre, NYC

Fledermas (with Howard Dietz): Metropolitan Opera, NYC

Remembering Mr. Maugham (adapted): manuscript*; Theresa Kaufman Concert Hall, NYC, The Players, NYC

Dreyfus in Rehearsal (adapted): manuscript*; Ethel Barrymore Theatre, NYC
   *contact agent

K

JACK A. KAPLAN

Born in Brooklyn, NY on October 29, 1947. Educated at Brooklyn College (B.A.); Indiana University; Pace University; New School for Social Research. Also writes short stories, composes songs, draws cartoons. Has done some acting and stage managing, also critic for **Show Business.** Member, Dramatists Guild. Recipient: Ottillie Grebanier Award for Playwriting (from Brooklyn College, 1969).

Address: 1909 East 17th St., Brooklyn, NY 11229
(212) 339-2978

TITLE • AVAILABILITY • PRODUCTIONS

Queen Karen: Laser Magazine, Brooklyn College, 1970*

Alligator Man: Dramatists Play Service, 440 Park Avenue South, New York, NY 10016, $1.25; Cubiculo Theatre, NYC; 78th Street Theatre Lab, NYC

Nothing but Punks: manuscript*

Chipmunk Heaven: manuscript*; St. Clement's Church, NYC

Second Heaven: manuscript*

An Old Family Recipe: manuscript*

Mr. Coincidence: manuscript*

A Joker in Paradise: manuscript*

The Man from Porlock: manuscript*; Playwright's Center, San Francisco, CA

    *contact author

SYNOPSES

An Old Family Recipe: Who is the best cook in Rabbit Egg? Beth Pierce, married to the flag-waving chief lieutenant of the volunteer fire department, or Sandy Herne, wife of an ambitious young intern fresh out of medical school and Manhattan? It's old vs. young, conservative vs. liberal and especially Traditional American vs. Continental Gourmet cooking in a rivalry that splits the town until Chester Gilby, erstwhile newspaper editor, holds a pie-baking contest to settle the dispute with surprising results.

Full length. Setting: stylized interiors and exteriors. 5 males, 6 women.

The Man from Porlock: One of the archvillains of literary history — the man who prevented Samuel Taylor Coleridge from completing **Kubla Khan** — gets a chance to defend himself.

One act. Setting: interior. 2 males.

Alligator Man: Telesphonte Broussard is the proudest member of Cajun country's famous alligator-poaching family, and the most successful — having killed more gators and sold more hides than anyone else. Only when he kills the girlfriend of Gruesome Gator, he makes his first mistake. Gruesome is bent on revenge. He buys a belt from Broussard made from his girlfriend's hide, and by "kidnapping" the gator man's spinsterish sister-in-law, lures him into the far reaches of the cypress swamp. There, amidst a raging hurricane, the alligator and the man have their fight to the finish. The townsfolk don't know what has happened, except that Broussard's sister-in-law seems suddenly "liberated" and there is a new gator-hide peddler in town: specializing in "albino" gator hides! In this play the humans are played by whites and the alligators by blacks, introducing tacitly the theme of racism in a play ostensibly about ecology, the macho mentality, and appearance vs. reality. The cast also includes a comic federal agent (a la Raymond Chandler), two gossipy old women, Broussard's sexy wife and Gruesome's equally sexy girlfriend.

One act comedy. Setting: swamp, town square, livingroom. 3 males, 5 females. With music.

JEROME KASS

Born in Chicago, IL on April 21, 1937, raised in New York City. B.A. and M.A. from N.Y.U., doctoral work at Brandeis University. Taught in the English Departments of Brandeis, Queens College. For the past several years, he has written mostly for TV and films: **Young Marrieds at Play** (for **Hollywood Television Theatre**); **A Brand New Life (ABC Movie of the Week); Queen of the Stardust Ballroom (CBS Special); My Old Man** (CBS). Recipient: Winner of Writer's Guild Award, Best Original Teleplay 1975, for **Queen of the Stardust Ballroom;** Emmy nominee, 1975; Tony nominee, 1978.

Address: 2023 Greenfield Avenue, Los Angeles, CA 90025

Agent: Bill Robinson, Robinson & Assoc., 132 South Rodeo Dr., Beverly Hills, CA 90210 (213) 275-6114

TITLE • AVAILABILITY • PRODUCTIONS

Princess Rebecca Birnbaum; Make Like a Dog; Suburban Tragedy; Young Marrieds at Play (all one acts): **Four Short Plays by Jerome Kass,** Dramatists Play Service, 440 Park Ave. South, New York, NY 10016, $2.50; produced under the omnibus title **Monopoly,** by The Establishment Theatre Co. at Stage 73; various other productions.

Miracle of the Magazine Man: manuscript*; O'Neill Theater Center's National Playwrights Conference, CT

Saturday Night: Dramatists Play Service, $2.50; Sheridan Square Playhouse, NYC; Actors Forum, Los Angeles, CA

A Collection of Short Plays: manuscript*; Triangle Theatre; various productions worldwide

The Resurrection of Bernard Mandlebaum: manuscript*

Liberation: manuscript*

The Eulogy of Jacob Herman Garfinkle: manuscript*

*contact agent

SYNOPSES

Saturday Night: Two lonely women, leading dull and uneventful lives, spend Saturday nights together spinning poetic and erotic fantasies. They are often so carried away that they can no longer distinguish reality from fantasy. On the Saturday night of the play, one of the women, Rochelle Harris, is forced to confront the tragic reality of her life when certain very real events interrupt her night of fantasy. "Jerome Kass's **Saturday Night** is a beautiful, beautiful play . . . I haven't seen anything so intelligently and well written, so filled with compassion and so theatrically balanced in some time . . . It is serious and funny and painfully sensitive . . . it is quite nearly mesmerizing."—Martin Gottfried.

Full length. Setting: a Bronx living room. Time: the early '60s. 4 males, 2 females.

The Eulogy of Jacob Herman Garfinkle: Jacob's wife has died and Jacob has locked himself in his apartment, waiting to join her in death. His two old friends, Oscar, the intellectual and spiritualist, and Izzie, the sensualist, force their way into the apartment and use every means possible to bring Jacob back to life. In the end, the three old men decide to move in together and spend the rest of their lives as roommates.

One act. Setting: a Bronx livingroom. 3 males.

K

MICHAEL KASSIN

Born in Chicago, IL on September 10, 1947. B.A., summa cum laude, University of Minnesota; M.A., University of Minnesota. Professional acting credits include The Guthrie Theater; The Richard Allen Center; Mixed Blood Theatre. Recipient: Guthrie Theater Award; Playwrights' Lab Grant; Commissions from Cricket Theatre and the Actors Theatre of Louisville.

Address: 776 Bronx River Road, Bronxville, NY 10708

Agent: Bret Adams Ltd., 36 East 61st St., New York, NY 10021 (212) 752-7864

TITLE • AVAILABILITY • PRODUCTIONS

A Parable of Abram: not available

Federation of United Colored Kinsmen: not available

Night School: not available

No Mourning After Dark: manuscript*; Center Stage, MN; Front & Center Players, San Diego, CA

Brother Champ: manuscript*; Mixed Blood Theatre, MN; Shirtsleeve Theatre, NYC

Today a Little Extra: manuscript*; Center Stage, MN; Actors Theatre of Louisville, KY

Sophie and Willa: manuscript*; Playwrights Lab, MN; Center Stage, Baltimore, MD

Sorry: manuscript*

   *contact agent

SYNOPSES

Today a Little Extra: A tragi-comedy about an old kosher butcher and the young unkosher hotshot who buys him out. It is a changing of the guard, a story of traditions passed in pain, laughter and love.
Full length. Setting: 2 sets — butcher shop, old woman's apartment. 2 males, 1 female.

Brother Champ: Based on the true story of a South Carolina convict-turned-boxer, Brother Champ is a play-within-a-play in which a young man finds himself by learning to stand apart from his past.
Full length. Setting: a social club. 7 males.

Sophie and Willa: A comedy about two women, one old and Jewish, the other thirtyish and Black, who, as roommates, teach each other to accept love by accepting themselves.
Full length. Setting: a sparsely furnished livingroom. 1 male, 2 females.

C. H. KEENEY

Born in Jasper, OR on September 13, 1899. Educated at the University of Oregon. Served as student instructor of make-up for five years. Writer of short stories, drama and music. Most recent publication, **Make-Up Made Easy,** Pioneer Drama Service. Member: Dramatists Guild; ASCAP; Authors Club of Hollywood. Listed in: **International Author's and Writers Who's Who; International Who's Who of Intellectuals; ASCAP Biographical Dictionary; Personalities of the West & Midwest; Biographical Directory of Playwrights.** Fellow of The International Biographical Association. Recipient: Midwestern Writers Conference Prize; Kansas League Festival.

Address: 6517 South Newlin Avenue, Whittier,
CA 90601

TITLE • AVAILABILITY • PRODUCTIONS

Old Skin Flint: On Stage Tonight, Baker Plays, 100 Chauncey St., Boston, MA 02111, $2.50;
Numerous productions

Once an Actor: in **On Stage Tonight;** Numerous productions

Major Milliron Reports: in **On Stage Tonight;** Numerous productions

Pity the Poor Fish: in **On Stage Tonight;** Numerous productions

Willie's Weekness: manuscript*; Local high schools

The Builder: manuscript*; High schools and little theatres

Flight Three Five Nine: manuscript*; High schools and little theatres

For the Love of Mike: manuscript*; Throughout US & Canada

Begone, Begonia: Heuer Publishing, Cedar Rapids, IA; Numerous productions

Not to the Swift or True Love Conquers All: manuscript*

How to Work Your Way Through College on a Credit Card: manuscript*

The Lawful Mr. Bean: manuscript*

The Widow's Might or What Happened to Henry: Pioneer Drama Service, 2172 South Colorado
Blvd., P.O. 22555, Denver, CO 80222, $1.00

Meddler, U.S.A.: manuscript*

*contact author

SYNOPSES

Flight Three Five Nine: Living room of modest home on the West Coast during Second World War, housing a mother and her two grown daughters. The elder daughter's husband has been killed in the war and this is the night that the husband of the younger daughter is being flown home on leave. As the three women prepare to leave for the airport to greet him, there is some sort of mistaken mixup between the local radio station and the tower at the airport, and the talk between it and the incoming plane is broadcast. The plane gets into severe trouble mechanically and, while battling heavy fog, the dramatic reports of this and reaction of the women build the show to a terrific climax — but all turns out right in the end.

One act. One set. 3 females and off-stage voices of 3 or 4 males.

The Lawful Mr. Bean: The story of Roy Bean, from the time he came to Vinegaroon until his death in Langtry. All the best stories about him are brought to life including his love for Lily Langtry that is accented by dream sequences. It is a play with music rather than a strict musical.

Full length. Setting: one main set. Large cast of 39 can be doubled or tripled down to 15 males, 6 females and 1 boy.

K

SHANNON KEITH KELLEY

Born in Cape Girardeau, MO on February 12, 1948. B.S. in Secondary Education, Southeast Missouri State U., M.F.A. in Theatre, Ohio University. **About in the Dark,** a poetry chapbook; represented in **Anthology of Magazine Verse** and **Yearbook of American Poetry for 1980;** poetry in **Kansas Quarterly, Chouteau Review, Poet & Critic, Star-Dancer** and **The Cape Rock.** Recipient: Commission from Actors Theatre of Louisville, 1980, **Dennis and Rex.**

Address: 111-50 76th Road, 5K, Forest Hills, NY 11375

Agent: Helen Merrill, 337 West 22nd St., New York, NY 10011 (212) 924-6314

TITLE • AVAILABILITY • PRODUCTIONS

Blind Home Coming Near: manuscript*; Ohio U., Playwrights Workshop

Headsets (formerly, **E d Cel's Psycho-Deli Hours Went That-A-Way):** manuscript*; Ohio U., Mainstage Experimental

Big Apple Messenger: manuscript*; Mark Taper Forum Lab, CA

Time Was: manuscript*; South Coast Repertory Co., CA

Dennis and Rex: manuscript*

   *contact agent

SYNOPSES

Big Apple Messenger: This comedy-drama explores the relationships of the men who operate a branch office of a messenger service in Manhattan's garment district. During one workday, the incremental progression of individual lives unfolds against a backdrop of work. At the end of the day, each man has learned more about himself; certain characters are changed irrevocably by their new insights, others only tangentially affected. Each is sustained by the shared grind of work.

Full length. Setting: an office. 14 males — 9 Caucasian, 3 Black, 2 Puerto Rican.

Time Was: Oran Darby, a fifty-year-old drifter, seeks out the one woman he has ever loved — and has not seen for eighteen years: Madge, at forty a very successful business woman who has built her life and nurtured her daughter on the fictitious tragic loss of her husband. The drama addresses the issues of love and responsibility, the necessity of sustaining illusions and what happens when those illusions become one's reality.

Full length. Setting: one set. 3 males, 2 females.

Headsets: This comedy concerns the efforts of Ed Cel, a late-night telephone operator (and former rock disc jockey/college dropout), to come to grips with his past by facing the people he encounters over the phone and in person. Other characters in the play are: Tanya, a sixty-year-old operator who dreams of sky diving; MelonShine, a black wino and "regular" phone customer; Half-Arm, a Viet Nam vet with an arm gone and a drug habit; 482 JM, a psychology major who works the switchboard at the Tidy Night Inn.

Full length, 12 scenes. Setting: telephone office switchboard, two telephone booths, a hotel console, a basement room. 3 males, 2 females.

TIM KELLY

Born in Saugus, MA on October 2, 1937. B.A., M.A., Emerson College, MA. Screenwriter. Recipient: New England Theatre Conference Award; Pioneer Drama Service Award; Sarasota Centennial Arts Festival Poetic Award; Religious Drama Award, California Festival of the Arts; Sergel Drama Prize; Bicentennial Playwriting Award, U. of Utah; International Thespian Society Award; ABC Fellow, Yale U.; National Endowment for the Arts; Santa Fe Theatre Corp, Best Children's Play; Texas Community Theatre Stagecenter Award; Promising Playwright Award, Colonial Players, MD; Forest A. Roberts Playwriting Award; Virginia Weisbroad Playwriting Award; David Nederlander Playwriting Award; Sweepstakes Playwright Award.

Address: 8730 Lookout Mountain Avenue, Hollywood, CA 90046 (213) 656-9453

Agent: New York-William Talbot, Samuel French, Inc., 25 West 45th St., New York, NY 10036 (212) 582-4700
   West Coast-Bob Lewis, Goldfarb-Lewis, 8733 Sunset Blvd., Los Angeles, CA 90069 (213) 659-5955

TITLE • AVAILABILITY • PRODUCTIONS

Toga! Toga! Toga!: Pioneer Drama Service, 2172 S. Colorado Blvd., Denver, CO 80222, $2.50; Numerous productions

Krazy Kamp: Pioneer Drama, $2.50; Numerous productions

Airline: Pioneer Drama, $2.50; Numerous productions

Sherlock Holmes: Pioneer Drama, $2.50; Numerous productions

Pecos Bill and Slue-Foot Sue Meet the Dirty Dan Gang: Pioneer Drama, $2.50; Numerous productions

The Brothers O'Toole: Pioneer Drama, $2.00; Numerous productions

Lizzie Borden of Fall River: Pioneer Drama, $2.50; Numerous productions

Cry of the Banshee: Pioneer Drama, $2.50; Numerous productions

The Time Machine: Pioneer Drama, $2.00; Numerous productions

Lady Dracula: Pioneer Drama, $2.50; Numerous productions

Not Far from the Gioconda Tree: Pioneer Drama, $1.25; Numerous productions

Marsha: Pioneer Drama, $1.25; Numerous productions

Reunion on Gallows Hill: Pioneer Drama, $1.50; Numerous productions

Happily Never After: Pioneer Drama, $1.25; Numerous productions

Mark Twain in the Garden of Eden: Pioneer Drama, $1.25; Numerous productions

Memorial: Pioneer Drama, $1.25; Numerous productions

It's a Bird! It's a Plane! It's Chickenman!: Pioneer Drama, $1.25; Numerous productions

A Marriage Proposal — Western Style: Pioneer Drama, $1.25; Numerous productions

The Keeping Place: Pioneer Drama, $1.25; Numerous productions

The Natives Are Restless: Pioneer Drama, $1.50; Numerous productions

The Eskimos Have Landed: Pioneer Drama, $1.25; Numerous productions

The Shame of Tombstone: Pioneer Drama, $2.00; Numerous productions

Hawkshaw the Detective: Pioneer Drama, $2.50; Numerous productions

Alias Smedley Pewtree: Pioneer Drama, $1.50; Numerous productions

Seven Wives for Dracula: Pioneer Drama, $1.50; Numerous productions

K

Tim Kelly (cont'd)

Young Dracula: Pioneer Drama, $2.50; Numerous productions

Bride of Frankenstein: Pioneer Drama, $2.50; Numerous productions

Frankenstein Slept Here: Pioneer Drama, $1.50; Numerous productions

It's Bigfoot: Pioneer Drama, $1.50; Numerous productions

The Incredible Bulk at Bikini Beach: Pioneer Drama, $1.50; Numerous productions

The Invisible Man: Pioneer Drama, $1.50; Numerous productions

Sherlock Meets the Phantom: Pioneer Drama, $1.50; Numerous productions

Monster Soup: Pioneer Drama, $1.50; Numerous productions

The Wonderful Wizard of Oz: Pioneer Drama, $2.50; Numerous productions

Alice's Adventures in Wonderland: Pioneer Drama, $2.50; Numerous productions

Captain Nemo and His Magical Marvelous Submarine Machine: Pioneer Drama, $2.00; Numerous productions

King of the Golden River: Pioneer Drama, $2.00; Numerous productions

Wedding Belles and Lumberjacks: Pioneer Drama, $2.50; Numerous productions

The Mouse and the Raven: Pioneer Drama, $1.25; Numerous productions

Lost in Space and the Mortgage Due: Eldridge Publishing Co., Franklin, OH 45005, $2.00 Numerous productions

Unidentified Flying High School: Arthur Meriwether, Inc., 1529 Brook Drive, Downers Grove, IL 60515, $2.00; Numerous productions

M*A*S*H (full length): Dramatic Publishing Co., 4150 N. Milwaukee Ave., Chicago, IL 60641, $2.00; Numerous productions

M*A*S*H (one act): Dramatic Pub. Co., $1.00; Numerous productions

A-Haunting We Will Go: Dramatic Pub. Co., $2.00; Numerous productions

Virtue Victorious: Dramatic Pub. Co., $2.00; Numerous productions

No Opera in the Op'ry House Tonite: Dramatic Pub. Co., $2.00; Numerous productions

The Timid Dragon: Dramatic Pub. Co., $1.00; Numerous productions

Victoria at Eighteen: Dramatic Pub. Co., $1.00; Numerous productions

The Tale That Wagged the Dog: Dramatic Pub. Co., $1.00; Numerous productions

Silent Snow, Secret Snow: Dramatic Pub. Co., $1.00; Numerous productions

Up the Rent: Dramatic Pub. Co., $1.00; Numerous productions

The Marvelous Playbill: Dramatic Pub. Co., $1.00; Numerous productions

Ladies of the Tower: Dramatic Pub. Co., $1.00; Numerous productions

Bluebeard Had a Wife: Dramatic Pub. Co., $1.00; Numerous productions

West of the Pecos: Dramatic Pub. Co., $1.50; Numerous productions

The Uninvited: Dramatists Play Service, 440 Park Ave. South, New York, NY 10016, $2.25; Numerous productions

The Remarkable Susan: Dramatists Play Service, $1.25; Numerous productions

Second Best Bed: Dramatists Play Service, $1.25; Numerous productions

The Cave: Dramatists Play Service, $1.25; Numerous productions

Two Fools Who Gained a Measure of Wisdom: Dramatists Play Service, $1.25; Numerous productions

Everything's Jim Dandy: I.E. Clark, Saint John's Road, Schulenburg, TX 78956, $2.25; Numerous productions

The Frankensteins Are Back in Town: I.E. Clark, $2.25; Numerous productions

Dracula, "The Vampire Play": I.E. Clark, $2.25; Numerous productions

Sweeney Todd, "Demon Barber of The Barbary Coast": I.E. Clark, $2.25; Numerous productions

The Fall of the House of Usher: I.E. Clark, $2.25; Numerous productions

Lantern in the Wind: I.E. Clark, $1.25; Numerous productions

Jocko, or The Monkey's Husband: I.E. Clark, $1.25; Numerous productions

Murder in the Magnolias: Baker's Plays, 100 Chauncy St., Boston, MA 02111, $2.25; Numerous productions

The Soapy Murder Case: Baker's Plays, $2.25; Numerous productions

Captain Fantastic: Baker's Plays, $2.25; Numerous productions

Dirty Work in High Places: Baker's Plays, $2.25; Numerous productions

The Deceitful Marriage: Baker's Plays, $1.25; Numerous productions

How to Get Rid of a Housemother: Baker's Plays, $1.25; Numerous productions

While Shakespeare Slept: Baker's Plays, $1.25; Numerous productions

The Last of Sherlock Holmes: Baker's Plays, $1.25; Numerous productions

If Sherlock Holmes Were a Woman: Baker's Plays, $1.25; Numerous productions

Always Marry a Bachelor: Baker's Plays, $1.25; Numerous productions

Tap Dancing in Molasses: Baker's Plays, $1.25, Numerous productions

Creeps by Night: Baker's Plays, $1.25; Numerous productions

Widow's Walk: Baker's Plays, $2.25; Numerous productions

The Butler Did It: Baker's Plays, $2.25; Numerous productions

Crazy, Mixed-Up Island of Dr. Moreau: Baker's Plays, $1.25; Numerous productions

Enter Pharoah Nussbaum: Baker's Plays, $2.25; Numerous productions

Loco-Motion, Commotion, Dr. Gorilla and Me: Baker's Plays, $2.25; Numerous productions

The Great All-American Musical Disaster: Baker's Plays, $2.25; Numerous productions

The Green Archer: Baker's Plays, $2.25; Numerous productions

Merry Murders at Montmarie: Performance Publishing, 978 N. McLean Blvd., Elgin, IL 60120, $2.25; Numerous productions

The Canterville Ghost: Performance Pub. $2.25; Numerous productions

The Case of the Curious Moonstone: Performance Pub. $2.25; Numerous productions

Charley's Charmers: Performance Pub. $2.25; Numerous productions

Sherlock Holmes' First Case: Performance Pub. $2.25; Numerous productions

The Convertible Teacher: Performance Pub. $2.25; Numerous productions

Whatever This Is — We're All In It Together: Performance Pub. $2.25; Numerous productions

The Yankee Doodle: Performance Pub. $2.50; Numerous productions

Nashville Jamboree: Performance Pub. $2.50; Numerous productions

Lemonade Joe Rides Again: Performance Pub. $2.25; Numerous productions

W.C.Fieldworthy — Foiled Again: Performance Pub. $1.10; Numerous productions

Barrel of Monkeys: Performance Pub. $1.10; Numerous productions

The Witch Who Wouldn't Hang: Performance Pub. $1.10; Numerous productions

Country Gothic: Performance Pub. $1.10; Numerous productions

Navajo House: Performance Pub. $1.10; Numerous productions

Frankenstein: Samuel French, 25 West 45th St., New York, NY 10036, $2.50; Numerous productions

The Burning Man: Samuel French, $2.50; Numerous productions

Egad, The Woman in White: Samuel French, $2.50; Numerous productions

The Hound of the Baskervilles: Samuel French, $2.50; Numerous productions

The Silk Shirt: Samuel French, $1.25; Numerous productions

K

Tim Kelly (cont'd)

The Gift and The Giving: Samuel French, $1.25; Numerous productions

Raggedy Dick and Puss: manuscript*; Aspen Playwrights Conference, CO; Seattle Repertory Theatre, WA

Beau Johnny: manuscript*; Pioneer Memorial Theatre, Salt Lake City, UT

Jack The Ripper: I.E. Clark, $2.50; Hillberry Theatre, Detroit, MI

Yankee Clipper: manuscript*; Back Alley Theatre, Los Angeles, CA

Under Jekyll's Hyde: Pioneer Drama Service, $1.50

Terror By Gaslight: Dramatists Play Service, $2.50

Airline: Pioneer Drama Service, $2.25

The Adventure of the Clouded Crystal: manuscript*

Sherlock Holmes and the Adventure of the Speckled Band: I.E. Clark, $2.50

Ten Weeks with the Circus: Pioneer Drama Service, $2.50

Dark Deeds at Swan's Place: Samuel French, $3.00

The Lalapalooza Bird: I.E. Clark, $1.25

*contact agent

SYNOPSES

The Adventure of the Clouded Crystal: Sir Arthur Conan Doyle, creator of Sherlock Holmes, and Harry Houdini, world's greatest magician and escape artist, are dear friends, although the issue of "spiritualism" often causes them to argue. Doyle arranges a seance with a famed medium in the hope Houdini will become a "believer." Houdini, however, plans to expose the medium as a fraud. What he doesn't count on is the cleverness of the woman. The dramatic and often funny sparks fly as the two lock themselves in combat.

Long one act. Setting: sparsely-furnished room. 2 males, 2 females.

Jack The Ripper: In the London home of Dr. Thaddeus Sargeant, news that a deranged killer called Jack the Ripper is roaming the nearby alleys causes terror. The housekeeper is morbidly fascinated and when a stranger comes to the house bearing an uncanny resemblance to newspaper descriptions of the madman, she's convinced the entire family is in mortal danger. The household contains two felons, both of whom are looked upon as experiments in rehabilitation by the doctor's daughter. Visitors include a police inspector who investigates the murder of a previous maid and Lady Flora Chilton who is determined to rid Whitechapel of its social ills. Suspicion falls on each character as the London fog swirls and more killings indicate the killer, as well as the police, are drawing closer to the house. The play offers a solution to the famous case, as well as an explanation as to why Jack was never found.

Full length. Setting: a Victorian parlor. 4 males, 4 females.

Raggedy Dick and Puss: (Please note this is not a children's play). It is about Richard Burton (Raggedy Dick), the greatest English traveler and explorer of the 19th Century, master of thirty-eight languages, atheist, iconoclast, eroticist and suspected pronographer. Isabel (Puss), his wife, was a devoted Roman Catholic with prudish tastes. After Burton's death she spent seventeen days and nights alone in his study reading all his unpublished works, deciding what would survive and what would be consigned to the flame. She destroyed what Burton considered his greatest effort, the one work that best reflected himself — **The Scented Garden.** This work is an attempt to explain what led up to that incredible holocaust. It is a play, not precise history.

Full length. Setting: Richard Burton's study. 1 male, 1 female.

SHEPPARD KERMAN

Born in Brooklyn, NY on August 26, 1928. B.S.S. in English, C.C.N.Y. Member, New Dramatists Committee, 1952–56; Dramatists Guild; Equity; AFTRA; SAG. President of "In-Perspective Communications, Inc.," multi-media productions. Broadway and film actor. Narrator of TV commercials. Creator of scenic projections for **Seesaw; Mary Martin/Ethel Merman Special; Beatlemania; Sunset** and **Platinum.** TV credits include **Danger, Matinee Theater, Studio One, Camera 3.** Author of poetic work **The Candy Man.** Lyricist to Marvin Hamlisch, Lee Pockriss, John Strauss. Creator of over one-hundred multi-media works for industry including musicals, motivational pieces and speeches. Producer and director. Recipient: Showbusiness awards, Best Actor 1950 and 1951 as Everyman and Marc Antony in Dryden's **All for Love;** Obie Award for **Mr. Simian;** Los Angeles Drama Critics Circle Award, for visual design concept (**Beatlemania**).

Address: 41B Dunes Lane, Port Washington, NY 11050 (516) 883-2813

Agent: Bret Adams, 36 East 61st St., New York, NY 10019 (212) 752-7864

TITLE • AVAILABILITY • PRODUCTIONS

The Dark and the Day: manuscript*; New Dramatists, NYC

Bilby's Doll: manuscript*; New Dramatists, NYC

Cut of the Axe: Lincoln Center Collection; Broadway;

Players on a Beach: manuscript*; Masters' Institute Theater

Nine Rebels: manuscript*

Mr. Simian: manuscript*; Theater Collection of New York Public Library, Lincoln Center Collection; Astor Place Playhouse, NYC

The Husband-in-Law: manuscript*

The Tune of the Time: manuscript and tape of show*; Civic Theater, Atlanta, GA

Distant Relations: manuscript*
    *contact author

SYNOPSES

Mr. Simian: A plague in Lisbon forces an exodus. The play involves five passengers, including a trained chimpanzee, en route to South America and safety on board a vessel. The desire of the "simian" to become a man, thus escaping the bonds of his cage, is the main thrust of the play. In comic and theatrical fashion, and through a series of confrontations with the extreme views of the passengers and crew, "Mr. Simian" succeeds in his metamorphosis. In symbolic fashion, he becomes the master of his own fate.

Full length, three acts. Setting: deck and hold of a ship. 5 males, 1 female.

Nine Rebels: Written in the form of **La Ronde,** the play studies, with humor, satire and drama, the attempt at nine forms of rebellion (from criminal to religious activities) and their limitations. Theatrically philosophical in nature, it offers wide scope to actor, director and scenic designer.

Full length, two acts. Setting: a municipal courtroom, a chic livingroom, a newspaper office, patio of estate, headquarters in revolutionary country, doctor's office, priest's study, bedroom of low-income dwelling. Ideal for use of scenic projections and set pieces. 14 males, 8 females.

Players on a Beach: A highly stylized comic-poetic summary of aspiration, particularly in the theater. A play is being rehearsed on a beach. A novice is chosen for the leading role. He is exposed to the amusing machinations of director, producer, leading lady, critics and other members of

K

Sheppard Kerman (cont'd)

the "company." His hopes are dashed when the play is suddenly converted to a musical (our hero can't sing). The play has been called "a classic of its genre."

One act (1 hour, 10 minutes). Setting: a beach. 9 males, 6 females, extras.

E. K. KERR

Born in Indianapolis, IN on April 20, 1937. A.B. from Indiana University. Studied acting at the Neighborhood Playhouse. Has appeared on Broadway, Off Broadway, stock, repertory and soap operas.

Address: 537 Grand Avenue, #E3, Leonia, NJ 07605

Agent: Gilbert Parker, William Morris Agency, 1350 Ave. of the Americas, New York, NY 10019 (212) 586-5100

TITLE • AVAILABILITY • PRODUCTIONS

Juno's Swans: manuscript*; Ensemble Studio Theatre, NYC: PAF Playhouse, LI

The God Play: manuscript*

   *contact agent

SYNOPSES

Juno's Swans: A comedy about sisters: one lives in New York City and became an actress. The older sister stayed back home in the midwest and married a man who is a successful banker. The play begins as the older sister pays a very unexpected visit to her actress sister. There is a climactic scene with Dimitrios Tsigounis, a tyrannical Greek director and the two sisters who finally come to a mutual understanding. One reviewer entitled his review "Move over Neil Simon." Another reviewer said, "Neil Simon, move over."

Full length. Setting: one set.

The God Play: A comedy about the creation, up to the present time. God, middle-aged, gruff, and his two collaborators, B2 and Ernie, try to hold it all together. It keeps threatening to fall apart. There is a happy ending.

Full length. 3 characters.

JEAN KERR

Born in Scranton, PA on July 10, 1923. Educated at Marywood College, Scranton, PA and Catholic University, Washington, DC. Author of **Please Don't Eat the Daisies, The Snake Has All the Lines, Penny Candy, How I Got to be Perfect.**

Address: 1 Beach Avenue, Larchmont, NY 10538

Agent: Irving P. Lazar, 1 East 66th St., New York, NY 10021 (212) 355-1177

Jean Kerr (cont'd)

TITLE • AVAILABILITY • PRODUCTIONS

Song of Bernadette (with Walter Kerr): Dramatic Publishing Co., 4150 N. Milwaukee Avenue, Chicago, IL 60641, $2.00; Numerous productions

Our Hearts Were Young and Gay (adaptation): Dramatic Publishing Co., $2.00; Numerous productions

Jenny Kissed Me: Dramatists Play Service, 440 Park Avenue South, New York, NY 10016, $2.50; Broadway

Touch and Go (with Walter Kerr): Brandt & Brandt, 1501 Broadway, New York, NY 10036; Broadway

John Murray Anderson's Almanac (sketches): not available; Broadway

King of Hearts (with Eleanor Brooke): Dramatists Play Service, $2.50; Broadway

Goldilocks (with Walter Kerr): Samuel French, 25 West 45th St., New York, NY 10036, $2.50; Broadway

Mary Mary: Dramatists Play Service, $2.50; Broadway

Poor Richard: Samuel French, $2.50; Broadway

Finishing Touches: Dramatists Play Service, $2.50; Broadway

Lunch Hour: Samuel French, $2.50; Broadway

LARRY KETRON

Born in Kingsport, TN on July 27, 1947. Educated, University of Tennessee; East Tennessee University. Two years U.S. Army, one year Viet Nam. Writes for theatre, television. Member, The Dramatists Guild.

Address: 21 West 76th St., New York, NY 10023

Agent: Gilbert Parker, c/o William Morris Agency, 1350 Avenue of the Americas, New York, NY 10019 (212) 586-5100

TITLE • AVAILABILITY • PRODUCTIONS

Cowboy Pictures: manuscript*; Playwrights Horizons, NYC

Augusta: manuscript*; Playwrights Horizons, NYC: Theatre de Lys, NYC; Off Broadway

Stormbound: manuscript*; Playwrights Horizons, NYC

Patrick Henry Lake Liquors: Dramatists Play Service, 440 Park Avenue South, New York, NY 10016, $2.50; Manhattan Theatre Club, NYC; PAF Playhouse, NY

Quail Southwest: Dramatists Play Service, $2.50; Manhattan Theatre Club, NYC; Carnegie-Mellon, Summer Theatre, Pittsburgh, PA

Rib Cage: Dramatists Play Service, $2.50; Stage West, MA; Manhattan Theatre Club, NYC

The Frequency: manuscript*; American Conservatory Theatre, CA; WPA Theatre, NYC

Character Lines: Dramatists Play Service, $2.50;WPA Theatre, NYC: St. Nicholas Theatre, Chicago, IL

  *contact agent

K

FAIZUL B. KHAN

Born in Guyana, South America on September
20, 1944. As an actor, he has played Off Off
Broadway, Off Broadway and on Broadway. He
has also appeared in films, television and in
regional theater. He is a skilled union carpenter.
Recipient: National Endowment Creative Writing
Grant, 1979–80.

Address: 3451 Giles Place, Bronx, NY 10463
(212) 549-6985

TITLE • AVAILABILITY • PRODUCTIONS

The Shanty: manuscript*; Theatre at St. Clement's, NYC

Don't Go Gentle into the Night: manuscript*

*contact author

SYNOPSES

The Shanty: The play revolves around a hard-working, skilled carpenter (West Indian), who refuses
to participate in the politics of the union or the contractors and attempts to succeed because of
his skill and not his politics. It involves eight other carpenters of multi-racial and diverse political
backgrounds, caught in this struggle between the union and the contractor. It deals with the corruption and brutality among these construction workers, good men forced to take paths they
might have avoided—in order to survive.

Full length. Setting: a carpenter's shanty in a Brooklyn ghetto. 10 males.

Don't Go Gentle into the Night: Luis Garcia witnesses a murder by criminals controlling the activities in the area. He can't go to the police for fear of being killed. Because he was set up, the
police find incriminating evidence against him and he gets caught in a struggle for survival for
himself and his family. Being poor, he cannot pack up and relocate and he cannot depend on the
police for protection. He is squeezed by both sides with no place to hide. The constant struggle of
the poor trying to survive in the bottom of the heap.

Full length. Setting: Hell's Kitchen area in Manhattan. 5 males, 1 female.

JEFFREY KINDLEY

Born in Portland, OR on June 2, 1945. Educated
at Columbia College, B.A.; Columbia University,
M.A., Ph.D. Teaching experience: Department of
English and Comparative Literature, Columbia
University, 1970–1976. Other written works
(poetry): **The Under-Wood,** 1966. Member, The
New Dramatists. Recipient: E.P. Conkle Play-
wrights Workshop Grant, University of Texas,
Austin, TX, 1975.

Address: 27 West 96th St., #2C, New York, NY
10025 (212) 662-0528

Agent: Gilbert Parker, William Morris Agency,
1350 Avenue of the Americas, New York, NY
10019 (212) 586-5100

TITLE • AVAILABILITY • PRODUCTIONS

Among Adults: manuscript*; Manhattan Theatre Club (under title **By Mutual Consent**), NYC;
Galaxy Theater Company, NYC

The Counterpart Cure: manuscript*; The New Dramatists, NYC

Jeffrey Kindley (cont'd)

Saint Hugo of Central Park: manuscript*; E.P. Conkle Playwrights Workshop, University of Texas, Austin, TX; BBC Radio

Is There Life After High School? (music & lyrics, Craig Carnelia): manuscript*; Hartford Stage Company, CT

   *contact agent

SYNOPSES

The Counterpart Cure: Farce about a doctor who specializes in fulfilling his patients' fantasies by altering their identities. Characters change personality, appearance, even sex, under the doctor's direction, and the actors trade parts from act to act.

3 acts. Setting: a doctor's office, showing waitingroom, office, and examining room. 4 males, 4 females.

Saint Hugo of Central Park: Comic biography of a modern-day saint. A teenager from Brooklyn devotes himself to the ascetic life and becomes a media hero overnight when he's discovered to have unusual curative powers.

2 acts, with music by Craig Carnelia. Setting: minimal. 8 males, 7 females.

JOHN W. KIRK

Born in 1932. M.A., Ohio State University; Ph.D., Florida. Member: Phi Beta Kappa. One of the founders of the University Resident Theatre Association. His interests have included acting, directing, and dramatic theory. Has written a text **A Philosophy of Play Direction,** and a critical study of Kenneth Burke, **Dramatism and The Theatre.** Has been Chairman of the Theatre Department at Illinois State University and is currently a full professor devoting his time to teaching and playwriting. Recipient: Illinois Arts Council, Completion Grant; Midwest Playwrights Lab.

Address: R.R. No. 1, Box 306, Hudson, IL
   61748 (309) 452-4000

TITLE • AVAILABILITY • PRODUCTIONS

Judas: manuscript*; Illinois State University; A.C.T.F., Milwaukee, WI

The Third Richard: manuscript*; Illinois State University; Midwest Playwrights Lab, WI

Tom & Mary, Mary & Tom: manuscript*; Illinois State U.

Balls: A Jock Comedy: manuscript*; Illinois State University

Martin Luther: Apostle of Defiance: manuscript*; Body Politic Theatre, Chicago, IL; National tour.

   *contact author

SYNOPSES

Judas: The events immediately prior to and during the week of Christ's crucifixion are viewed in historical context. Judas, the business manager and strategist of the band of disciples is confronted with an eccentric wish on the part of the "Rabbi," a charismatic, if uneducated Gallilean, to fulfill the Old Testament prophecies by sacrificing himself at the Passover festivities in Jerusalem. Judas struggles to dissuade the Nazarine from such a desperate and foolish plan. Jesus stuns Judas by telling him he must engineer the event by betraying the master to the authorities. Judas, sworn to secrecy, tries to prevent the catastrophe, but finally is caught up in a swirl of events that lead to Judas' destruction and the Nazarine's martyrdom.

K

John W. Kirk (cont'd)

Full length. Setting: 1st act, interior; 2nd act, multiple, space staging. 6 males, 1 female. 10 minor males.

The Third Richard: Richard III, maligned and misrepresented by history and literature, returns to pursue the truth, expose his detractors and recover his good name which has been denied him by four hundred years of "Tudor lies." One by one, the important figures of his past return and battle Richard. In the course of the action Will Shakespeare, Thomas More and other figures from the past are brought back to answer to Richard. In the end Richard discovers that the truth is a two-edged sword. Once the door is opened, the truth threatens to overwhelm him before he reaches a new understanding of himself and his past.

Full length. Setting: open staging. 7 males, 3 females.

Tom and Mary, Mary and Tom: Tom and Mary, a young, troubled married couple, are visited by Nicky and Rollo, toughs from the surrounding ghetto neighborhood. The ensuing confrontation escalates until the close of the act finds Tom in helpless frustration as he listens to the sound of Mary and Nicky making love in the other room. The second act finds Tom and Mary dipping deep into the "mythos" to find the resources to reject this primitive animal assault. They finally find the means to punish their tormentors and to create a new and stronger basis for their relationship.

Full length. Setting: one interior. 3 males, 1 female.

JAMES KIRKWOOD

Born in Los Angeles, CA in 1930. He has been on radio, done nightclub satire with Lee Goodman, acted for four years on TV's **Valiant Lady,** and performed in many plays. He is the author of: **There Must Be a Pony!** (novel, Little, Brown & Co., 1960; currently Avon Books paperback); **Good Times/Bad Times** (novel, Simon & Schuster, 1968; currently Fawcett Paperback); **American Grotesque** (non-fiction account of Clay Shaw-Jim Garrison conspiracy trial in New Orleans, Simon & Schuster, 1970); **P.S. Your Cat is Dead!** (novel, Stein & Day, 1972; currently Warner's Paperback); **Some Kind of Hero** (novel, T.Y. Crowell & Co., 1975); **Hit Me with a Rainbow** (Delacorte, 1980). Screenplay: **Some Kind of Hero,** Paramount. Member, Actors Equity, S.A.G., A.F.T.R.A., P.E.N., Dramatists Guild. Re-

cipient: New York Drama Critics Award for **A Chorus Line** (co-author of book), 1975; Tony Award, 1976, Best Musical Book; Pulitzer Prize, 1976, for Best Drama.

Address: 58 Oyster Shores Rd., East Hampton, NY 11937

Agent: Esther Sherman, William Morris Agency, 1350 Ave. of the Americas, New York, NY 10019 (212) 586-5100

TITLE • AVAILABILITY • PRODUCTIONS

There Must Be A Pony!: manuscript*; six summer theatres (Westport, Ogonquit, etc.)

U.T.B.U. (Unhealthy To Be Unpleasant): Samuel French, Inc., 25 West 45th St., New York, NY 10036, $2.50; Helen Hayes Theatre, NYC

P.S. Your Cat Is Dead!: Samuel French, $2.50; Studio Arena Theatre, Buffalo, NY; Golden Theatre, NYC

†**A Chorus Line:** Knopf, 201 E. 50th St., New York, NY 10022; Shubert Theatre, NYC

Surprise: manuscript*; John Drew Theatre, NY

*contact agent or author
†Lincoln Center, Theatre on Film & Tape

James Kirkwood (cont'd)

SYNOPSES

P.S. Your Cat Is Dead!: Jimmy Zoole, a 38-year-old actor, who has recently been robbed twice, the second robbery relieving him of the only copy of his first novel, is merely at the beginning of his run of bad luck. By New Year's Eve, the run escalates to a full gallop. He is fired from a play, his cat is on the critical list, and he catches his girl friend, Kate, packing to leave him. After she's gone, Jimmy, on the brink of a breakdown, discovers a burglar, Vito, hiding under his bed about to rip him off for the third time. Jimmy Zoole sets out to avenge himself and all of us for the perverse breaks in life. He knocks the burglar out, ties him to the kitchen sink and keeps him prisoner over New Year's. What happens when he does this is the upbeat story — by turns hilarious, shocking and moving — as these two disparate characters develop a most unusual friendship, interrupted by the return of Kate with her new boyfriend and later on by a trio of merrymakers who turn out to have more on their minds than just making merry. A darkly hued comedy, it deals with surviving and opening oneself up to friendship and new experiences.

Setting: a loft apartment in Greenwich Village on New Year's Eve. 5 males, 2 females.

U.T.B.U.: U.T.B.U. (Unhealthy to Be Unpleasant) is a whacky organization dedicated to righting the world's ills by summary extermination of all the nasty people in it. The leader is a blind man, and his present target is an erstwhile actor whose 94-year-old mother won't give him the money to produce the play in which he wants to make a come back, and whose demise he therefore intends to hasten with an assortment of Gothic tortures. The **UTBU** leader has an arsenal of two devices: a devastating cane that's hard on shins, and some detonations which he is inspired to use on stage mothers and other assorted villains, and which have caused him to be headlined as the mad bomber. At the climax, the head-on confrontation of the **UTBU** leader and the actor is capital comedy. We regret to advise the next of kin of both that neither survives the unhealthy encounter.

Farce. 4 males, 6 females.

WARREN KLIEWER

Born in Mountain Lake, MN on September 20, 1931. B.A., English, University of Minnesota; M.A., English, University of Kansas; M.F.A., Playwriting, University of Minnesota. Publications: Poems, stories and articles in periodicals. Three volumes of poetry, most recently **Liturgies, Games, Farewells, 1974.** Editor and publisher of seven volumes of **Religious Theatre,** 1964–1971, in which were published fourteen new plays by eleven new playwrights in addition to numerous articles. Recent directing assignments: Artistic Director for the National Humanities Series and the Carolina Readers' Theatre. Director for the American Heritage Festival. Artistic Director for multi-media productions, the Communications Community, New Rochelle, NY. He is also a professional actor, and taught for thirteen years. Member, New Dramatists; Dramatists Guild; S.S.D.C.; A.E.A. and S.A.G.

Address: 281 Lincoln Ave., Secaucus, NJ 07094 (201) 863-6436

TITLE • AVAILABILITY • PRODUCTIONS

Ever So Humble: manuscript*; Lincoln Center Library Theatre, NYC; St. Boniface Cultural Center; tours to colleges and museums

A Lean and Hungry Priest (music by Dan Newmark): **Playwrights for Tomorrow,** Vol. 12, edited by Arthur H. Ballet, University of Minnesota Press, Minneapolis, MN, $4.95; Scorpio Rising Theatre, CA

How Can You Tell the Good Guys from the Bad Guys?: Samuel French, 25 West 45th St., New York, NY 10036, $2.50

K

Warren Kliewer (cont'd)

Half Horse, Half Cockeyed Alligator: manuscript*; Fulton Opera House, American Heritage Festival

Seventy Times Seven: Religious Theatre, No. 4: manuscript*; Eagles Mere, PA

The Daughters of Lot: Kansas Quarterly, 1970. Contact the Editors, English Dept., Kansas State University, Manhattan, KS

A Trial Can Be Fun, If You're the Judge: Fortress Press, 2900 Queen Line, Philadelphia, PA 19129, $2.00; Firehouse Theatre, Minneapolis, MN

A Bird in the Bush (opera libretto with music by Herbert Bielawa): University of Southern California

The Booth Brothers: manuscript*; New Dramatists, NYC

The Berserkers: manuscript*; New Dramatists, NYC

Round the Cherry Tree: manuscript*; Many productions

The Museum of Olde Tyme Life: manuscript*

The Two Marys: manuscript*; New Dramatists, NYC

Madame Cleo Here, at Your Service: manuscript*; Washington Theatre Club; Princeton U., NJ

Hypocrites, Frauds and Cheats: manuscript*; Tour — Jersey City, NJ; Providence, RI

A Small Winter Crisis: manuscript*; New Dramatists, NYC

   *contact author

SYNOPSIS

The Museum of Olde Tyme Life: A man returns to his hometown on his sixtieth birthday, expecting to rediscover nostalgic memories of his youth but finding instead that the whole town is being turned into a museum commemorating the Black Hills Gold Rush. He then discovers that this is a deception, for the real purpose of the museum is to conceal a senseless crime committed thirty-eight years ago against the old man who had founded the community.

Full length. Setting: interior of an old barn. 1 male, 2 female.

NORMAN KLINE

Born in Lynn, MA on April 7, 1935. Former Artistic Director, HB Playwrights Foundation, New York City. Currently Managing Director, The Emelin Theatre for the Performing Arts, Mamaroneck, New York. Teacher of comedy writing, HB Studio. Studied with Zero Mostel and Herbert Berghof. Graduated from the American Academy of Dramatic Arts. Contributed material for **New Faces, 1968** and **Spread Eagle Revues,** Wash., D.C. Recipient: Virginia Merrit Helfer Award for Playwriting, Colonial Playhouse, Annapolis, Maryland; Commissioned by the Corporation for Public Broadcasting to write radio plays for **Earplay;** New York State Council on the Arts Playwrights Award for young audiences.

Address: 103 Willow Ave., Larchmont, NY 10538
   (914) 698-3045

TITLE • AVAILABILITY • PRODUCTIONS

Faces: manuscript*; HB Playwrights Foundation, NYC; Cincinnati Playhouse-in-the-Park, OH

The American Hamburger League: manuscript*; New Theatre, NYC

K

Commitments and Other Alternatives: manuscript*; Milwaukee Repertory Theatre, WI; Theatre Sans Souci, Copenhagen

*contact author

SYNOPSIS

Faces: "Kline's work invites a comparison with Feiffer and Thurber. A kaleidoscope of short scenes anatomizing life among the sodality of white, middle-class American suburbia. Not exactly a revue, or a vaudeville, or a cartoon strip, it has the qualities of all three." — **Toronto Star.**

Setting: contemporary. 3 males, 3 females.

JOANNE KOCH

Born in Chicago, IL on March 28. B.A., Cornell University, Phi Beta Kappa, Woodrow Wilson Fellowship. M.A., English and Comparative Literature, Columbia University. Syndicated columnist, Newspaper Enterprise Association, 1970–75. Articles in **Psychology Today, Chicago Tribune, Parade, McCalls.** Co-author with Lewis Z. Koch of **The Marriage Savers** (1976) and **Marriage & Family** (1981, Houghton Mifflin). Columnist, **Washingtonian** magazine. Recipient: Family Service Association, Media Award; American Psychoanalytic Association, Media Award; Barnes Shakespeare Prize, Cornell University; Forbes-Heerman Playwriting Contest.

Address: 343 Dodge Ave., Evanston, IL 60202
(312) 864-5660

Agent: Audrey Wood, c/o ICM, 40 West 57th St., New York, NY 10019 (212) 556-5722

TITLE • AVAILABILITY • PRODUCTIONS

Teeth: manuscript**; Victory Gardens Theater, Chicago, IL; Midwest Playwrights Laboratory, Madison, WI

Haymarket: Footnote to a Bombing: manuscript*; Midwest Playwrights Laboratory, Madison, WI; Chicago Women's Theatre Group, IL

Coming Out: manuscript*; Chicago Women's Theatre Group, IL

The Mentor: manuscript*

Socks: manuscript*

Car Pool: manuscript*

   *contact author
   **contact agent

SYNOPSES

Teeth: The battle of the sexes is put in a new perspective when a female journalist tries to help women combat unwanted advances. With the help of her amateur inventor brother and her lawyer love, she discovers a new method for keeping male intruders at bay. But the device must be tested. The heroine finds the perfect man for the job, but it takes a surprising denouement to make all those concerned realize that some vulnerabilities just can't be protected.

Full length. Setting: a contemporary apartment. 5 males, 4 females.

Haymarket: On May 4, 1886, a bomb was thrown during a worker's protest meeting in Chicago. Seven policemen died. Four men were executed for the bombing, though no conclusive evidence was found. One cheated the hangman by blowing himself up in prison. Years later the widow of

Joanne Koch (cont'd)

one of the executed men commits her sane son to an insane asylum. This last event remains only a footnote to the bombing, yet it is organically related to the tragic episode known as Haymarket. This play explores that connection.

Full length. Setting: minimal set requirements. 6 males, 5 females.

Coming Out: A young woman prepares to introduce her parents to the parents of her fiance. She learns that Mom and Dad, who run a health food store and always seemed very conventional, are swingers. The engagement party proceeds, as the fiance takes this news rather badly. Outside a blizzard rages, bringing into the house an old man who has pretended to collapse in the snow: he got tired of being a recluse. He turns out to be the perfect person to deal with this dilemma, helping the priggish young fiance when he realizes that his own parents seem to know these future in-laws all too well. The young couple manages to make a graceful exit from the loving but misguided older generation.

Full length. Setting: one set. 4 males, 3 females.

ARTHUR KOPIT

Born in New York City on May 10, 1937. B.A., Harvard University. Recipient: Shaw Travelling Fellowship, Harvard, 1959; Guggenheim Fellowship, 1967; Rockefeller Grant, 1968; National Institute of Arts and Letters, 1971; National Endowment for the Arts, 1974; Vernon Rice Award and Outer Circle Award, 1964; Fellow, Center for the Humanities, Wesleyan University; Playwright-in-Residence, Wesleyan; CBS Fellow, Yale.

Address: 5 Glen Hill Road, Wilton, CT 06897

Agent: Audrey Wood, International Creative Management, 40 West 57th St. New York, NY 10019 (212) 556-5722

TITLE • AVAILABILITY • PRODUCTIONS

The Questioning of Nick: The Days the Whores Came Out to Play Tennis: Samuel French, 25 West 45th St., New York, NY 10036, $3.45; Harvard University, MA

Gemini: not available; Harvard University, MA

Don Juan in Texas (with Wally Lawrence): not available; Harvard University, MA

On the Runway of Life You Never Know What's Coming Off Next: not available; Harvard University, MA

Across the River and Into the Jungle: not available; Harvard University, MA

Sing to Me Through Open Windows: with **The Questioning of Nick;** Harvard University, MA

Oh Dad, Poor Dad, Mamma's Hung You in the Closet and I'm Feelin' So Sad: Samuel French, $2.50; Harvard University, MA; London

Asylum: not available; Theatre de Lys, NYC

Chamber Music: with **The Questioning of Nick;** Society Hill Playhouse, Philadelphia, PA

The Day the Whores Came Out To Play Tennis: with **The Questioning of Nick;** Players Theatre, NYC

The Hero: with **The Questioning of Nick;** New York Theatre Ensemble, NYC

Indians: Samuel French, $4.95; London, England; Arena Stage, Washington, DC

The Conquest of Everest: with **The Questioning of Nick;** New York Theatre Ensemble, NYC; WNHC, New Haven, CT

K

Arthur Kopit (cont'd)

Secrets of the Rich: not available; O'Neill Theater Center's National Playwrights Conference, CT

†Wings: Samuel French, $2.50; Yale Repertory Theatre, New Haven, CT; Broadway

Good Help is Hard to Find: manuscript*; Ensemble Studio Theatre, NYC

*contact agent
†Lincoln Center, Theatre on Film and Tape

ROBERT KORNFELD

Harvard A.B.; attended numerous other institutions including Columbia, N.Y.U., Circle in Square workshops in acting, directing, playwriting with, respectively, Bill Ball, Frank Corsaro, Edward Albee. First job was writing drama series for station XEQ, Mexico City, starring Arturo de Cordova. In addition to writing has been a salon photographer, had fourteen one-man shows, been included in approximately one hundred museum shows at Metropolitan Museum of Art, Boston Museum of Fine Arts, etc. etc., in U.S. and Europe. Poems published in Europe: in France in **Cahiers d'Art et d'Amitie,** in Italy in **Il Tempo** and **Botteghe Oscure.** French monologues recited in Paris nightclubs. Edited book on folklore, reporter for **San Francisco Examiner.** Author, **Great Southern Mansions** (Walker & Co.). Recipient: Two first prizes, Little Theatre National Contests; Broadway Drama Guild National Playwright's Competition, 1979.

Address: 5286 Sycamore Ave., Riverdale, NY 10471

Agent: Curtis Brown, Ltd., 575 Madison Ave., New York, NY 10022 (212) 755-4200

TITLE • AVAILABILITY • PRODUCTIONS

An Hour With Poe: Out of Space, Out of Time: manuscript*; Lincoln Center, NYC; Gould Memorial Theatre, NY

Passage in Purgatory: manuscript*; Albee Workshop, NYC; Circle-in-the-Square, NYC

Kicking the Castle Down: manuscript*; Gramercy Arts Theatre, NYC

Glory Hallelujah!: manuscript*; 18th Street Playhouse, NYC

Clementina: manuscript*; Riverdale Contemporary Theatre, NY

Tell the Stars: manuscript*; Spoleto Festival of the Two Worlds; O'Neill Theater Center, Post Season

Reunion (co-author): manuscript*; Cubiculo Theatre, NYC

Playing Ludwig: manuscript*

The Art of Love: manuscript*

To Be a Woman: manuscript*

The Bridge (co-author): manuscript*

The Passion of Frankenstein: manuscript*; New York Stage Works, NYC

Shark in the Sky: manuscript*

Mrs. Bullfrog: manuscript*

*contact agent

K

CHARLOTTE KRAFT

Born in Palmerton, PA. A.A., Colby Jr. College;
B.A., University of Michigan. Studied playwriting
at Circle in the Square, New School, Gene
Frankel and Ben Zavin Workshops. Freelance
writer and author of books, magazine articles,
audio-visual scripts and workshop materials on
social problems, health and cultural change.
Book, **Beat the System: A Way to Create More
Human Environments** (with Robert Allen). Recipient: Black River Theatre Contest; Religious
Drama Prize (Valpairaiso University and Coventry Cathedral, England).

Address: 103 Reade St., New York, NY 10013
(212) 964-0513 or Box 775, Groton, MA 01450

TITLE • AVAILABILITY • PRODUCTIONS

Kuber's Secret: manuscript*; Black River Theatre, NJ; Morristown Unitarian Fellowship, NJ

Jump!: manuscript*; Theatre Experience, NJ; KBS Actor's Cafe, E. Orange, NJ

Geneva Crossroads: manuscript*

Feel Free (with Nancy Henderson): manuscript*; Gene Frankel Theater, NYC; New Players
Theatre, MD

Trappings: manuscript*; Wit's End Theatre Experience, NJ; Script Development Workshop,
NYC

Sky-Jack: manuscript*; Black River Theatre, NJ; Morristown Unitarian Fellowship, NJ

A Life in the Day of . . . : manuscript*; Black River Theatre, NJ; Morristown Unitarian Fellowship, NJ

Spaceman's Hallowe'en: manuscript*

Thirtieth of February: manuscript*

Snow White and the Seven Solutions (with Richard Ryder): manuscript*; Artists for Survival,
Street Festival, NYC

Red Riding Hood and the Big Bad Nuclear Power Wolf: manuscript*

  *contact author

SYNOPSES

Thirtieth of February: Great-Uncle Kuber, a brilliant, aging scientist who is concerned about the
loss of humanity in the technological advances of the world, has invited his relatives to his farm,
supposedly for a vacation. They find, however, that instead of relaxing they are expected to take
part in a demanding schedule of value-generating experiments. Renata, one of the young aunts,
falls in love with Kuber's assistant, Bernard and tries to challenge Kuber's authority through him.
Her rebellious spirit and Kuber's superior knowledge come in conflict with shattering results for
all of them.

Full length. Setting: farm kitchen, recreation room. 3 males, 2 females.

Trappings: Cora, a determined woman of forty-two, is recently divorced and trying to extricate
herself from the psychological traps of her fifteen-year-old marriage. Her precocious thirteen-
year-old is entering the unpredictable territory of puberty. Steve, a narcissistic, virile young man,
has just dropped out of college and into their household. The tumultuous three-way relationship
that develops helps Cora to grow emotionally and spiritually.

Full length. Setting: office, kitchen. 6 males, 5 females.

GAIL KRIEGEL

Born in New York City on October 17, 1942. B.A., Fairleigh Dickinson University; M.F.A., City University of New York. Instructor at Brooklyn College, NY. Recipient: National Playwriting Award for Children; CAPS Grant; Fellowship at City University.

Address: 431 Washington Ave., Brooklyn, NY 11238 (212) 857-6359

Attorney: Barry Mallin, Esq., 170 Broadway, New York, NY 10038 (212) 840-1541

TITLE • AVAILABILITY • PRODUCTIONS

Rainbow Junction: manuscript*; Brooklyn Academy of Music, NY; Town Hall, NYC

The Prince of Macy's: manuscript*; Harlequin Theatre, NYC; Hollywood Stage, CA

Holy Places: manuscript*; St. Nicholas Theatre, Chicago, IL; American Place Theatre, NYC

O. 2V: manuscript*

   *contact attorney

SYNOPSES

Holy Places: Rona, a runner, is unable to face the loss of her father and creates a myth around his death which she uses to free herself from the suffocating relationships she has with her mother and her long-time boyfriend.

Full length. Setting: one interior, one exterior. 2 males, 2 females.

O. 2V: The encounter of a white woman teacher, embittered by the loss of her husband in the Vietnam War, with eight black veteran students, all survivors of the Vietnam War.

Full length. Setting: a college classroom. 9 males, 1 female.

HELEN KROMER

Born Columbus, OH. Educated Ohio State U.; B.A., American Academy Dramatic Art, New York; Columbia U. Graduate School (English drama). Career in freelance contractual writing along with periods of teaching, feature writing, public relations work, various philanthropic agencies. Has written plays, books, radio and TV scripts, documentary films, filmstrips, musical revues, historical symphonic dramas. Recipient: 1963-71 yearly: Popular Panel Awards, American Society of Composers, Authors and Publishers. 1967, Honorary Doctor of Humanities Degree, Christian Theological Seminary, Indianapolis, IN; 1960—Danforth Grant; Golden Reel Award at American Film Festival, 1956; George Washington Honor Medal; Freedoms Foundation Award 1957; Blue Ribbon Awards, A.F.F., 1956, '59, '64.

Address: 173 West 78th St., New York, NY 10024 (212) 874-4463

Agent: McIntosh & Otis, 475 Fifth Ave., New York, NY 10017 (212) 689-1051

K/L

Helen Kromer (cont'd)
TITLE • AVAILABILITY • PRODUCTIONS

Like It Is (a musical revue, music, Fred Silver): Baker's Plays, Inc., 100 Chauncy St., Boston, MA 02111, book & lyrics $2.25; Repertory Theater, Indianapolis, IN

Sure As You're Born (musical revue, music, Gene Benton): Baker's Plays Inc., $2.25; Repertory Theater

Hannah: A Parable in Music (music, Fred Silver): Baker's Plays, Inc., $2.25; Veterans Memorial, OSU Players and Columbus Players Club, OH

Verdict of One: Baker's Plays, Inc., $2.00; Oberlin U. by Cleveland Play House, OH

For Heaven's Sake! (a musical revue, music, Fred Silver): Baker's Plays, Inc., $2.25; North American Ecumenical Youth Assembly, Ann Arbor, MI

Under One Roof (one-act play): in anthology, **We, Too, Belong,** Dell Publishing Co., Inc., 1 Dag Hammarskjold Plaza, 10017, $.95

Take Any Street (one-act play): Friendship Press*, 475 Riverside Drive, New York, NY 10025

*contact author

SYNOPSES

Hannah: A Parable in Music: Hannah Huckleby, a middle-aged widow, moves into a community and joins the local church choir but she sings off key and the choir members decide she must be dismissed. Three delegates sent one after another become involved instead with the Huckleby household as Hannah's helplessness in the face of overwhelming problems touches them. In the process they are changed and they change the household. Hannah goes on being her bumbling "angel unaware" self, except astonishingly, she has learned to sing on key.

Full length. Setting: livingroom showing bedroom area, kitchen and front yard of middle-class semi-rural home. 6 males, 5 females, 1 girl, 1 boy.

Verdict of One: Based on the physicist's premise that "all the progress of mankind to date results from the making of careful measurements," the play suggests that conversely, retrogression can also be measured. Through a series of flashbacks, a crime of rape-murder committed on a crippled girl by an emotionally disturbed teenager is investigated not in terms of commission but of omission. Edward Roe Cox, promising young physicist, is indicted for complicity in the crime though he was two miles away when it was committed. The prosecution, following the intricacies of societal involvement, brings Cox to the point of confession, measuring events by scientific criteria.

Full length. Setting: a courtroom. 11 males, 5 females, and 3 roles either men or women.

STAN LACHOW

Born in Brooklyn, NY in 1931. B.A.U.W.W. at Roger Williams College. An actor and director for the stage. Conducted playwriting workshops at Rockland Community College in NY.

Address: Cherry Lane, Tallman, NY 10982
(914) 357-7694 or (212) 586-6300

TITLE • AVAILABILITY • PRODUCTIONS

It's to Laugh: manuscript*; Cubiculo Theatre, NYC; Courtyard Playhouse, NYC

I'm Not Jewish and I Don't Know Why I'm Screaming: manuscript*; Cubiculo Theatre, NYC; Oribus Theatre

Wrinkles: manuscript*

Harry and Thelma in the Woods: manuscript*

Subways, Hallways and Rooftops (3 one acts): manuscript*; Courtyard Theatre, NYC; Troupe Theatre

  *contact author

SYNOPSES

Wrinkles: Marge Klinger, a forty-three-year-old attractive Queens housewife, is getting wrinkles. She feels there must be more to life than she has thus far experienced, and feels trapped in her kitchen. During the course of a day she is confronted by: George, her husband, who believes, "That ever since Roosevelt died it's never been the same"; Lenny, their mutual friend, dentist, and Marge's lover for the past ten years, who no longer wants an old friend for a mistress; Shirley, his suburbanite wife who comes to visit Marge; Hildegarde, Marge's daughter, who has found a peace Marge does not wish to share; Papa, a crazy old boarder . . . Marge is sure he's a Nazi . . . and finally, Jeremiah, a young gas meter reader who has memorized **The Encyclopedia Brittanica,** and who shows Marge a way out of her kitchen.

Full length. Setting: kitchen and dinette area of an attached home in Queens. 4 males, 3 females.

Harry and Thelma in the Woods: Harry Konigsberg is attempting to end a twenty-year marriage to Thelma. He is a middle-aged writer of animal training books who wants to be another Hemingway. Thelma sings off key but is sure it can be cured.

Full length. Setting: the woods. 1 male, 1 female.

MYRNA LAMB

Born in Newark, NJ on August 3. Attended Newark schools; New School for Social Research; Rutgers University. Studies with Actors Mobile Theatre; Circle in the Square Workshop; School of Visual Arts. Extensive background in lecturing and readings. Completed screenplays, **Blood Alley, Balloon;** treatments for **King of the Blitz, Point Pleasant America.** Recipient: Biennale de Paris production grant, 1971; Rockefeller Fellowship residency grant for New York Shakespeare Festival, 1972; Guggenheim Fellowship, 1973; National Endowment for the Arts Music Program grant, 1974, 1975; New York Shakespeare Festival grant (Playwrights on Payroll), 1977.

Address: 400 West 43rd St., #43 T, New York, NY 10036 (212) 244-3168

TITLE • AVAILABILITY • PRODUCTIONS

Monologia: The Mod Donna and Scyklon Z, Samuel French, 25 West 45th St., New York, NY 10036, $2.25; Interart Theatre, NYC; Village Gate, NYC

Pas de Deux: with **Monologia;** Oberlin College, OH; Boston radio

The Butcher Shop: with **Monologia;** Oberlin College, OH

In the Shadow of the Crematoria: with **Monologia;** Martinique Theatre, NYC; Village Gate, NYC

L

Myrna Lamb (cont'd)

The Serving-Girl and the Lady: with **Monologia;** Martinique Theatre, NYC; Village Gate, NYC

But What Have You Done for Me Lately: with **Monologia;** Washington Square Church, NYC; Village Gate, NYC

Two-Party System: manuscript*; Interart Theatre, NYC

I Lost a Pair of Gloves Yesterday: manuscript*; Manhattan Theatre Club, NYC; One Act Theatre Co., Berkeley, CA

The Mod Donna: Samuel French, $2.25; New York Shakespeare Festival, NYC; Biennale de Paris

Apple Pie: manuscript*; New York Shakespeare Festival, NYC; Centre for Theatre Research, Buffalo, NY

Jillila: manuscript*

Crab Quadrille: manuscript*; Interart Theatre, NYC

The Sacrifice: manuscript*; AMDA Theatre, NYC

Olympic Park: manuscript*; New York Shakespeare Festival, NYC (reading)

Ballad of Brooklyn: manuscript*; Brooklyn Academy, NY

The Comeback Act: manuscript*; Interart Theatre, NYC

Mother Ann: manuscript*

*contact author

SYNOPSES

The Comeback Act: After a twenty-five-year hiatus, the two principals of a sister act meet in a "backstage" area. In their vaudeville team context, they play out their old routines in a last rehearsal of the "Comeback Act." In rhymes, song, doggerel, dance and patter, they work with an old M.C. to the passionate and poignant climax of their new act.

Full length. Setting: backstage. 3 females or 2 females and 1 male.

Olympic Park: World War II in Newark as experienced by four teenage girls in a working class neighborhood that loses its young men. Bonds of love, humor and clarity with Marie and Yolanda enable young Violet to survive domestic brutality and a terrible loss of innocence. The play is meant to be filmatic and has a taped score available.

Full length. Setting: simple lighted areas with a backdrop of an amusement park representation. 1 young male, 4 young females, 1 older male, 2 older females.

Crab Quadrille: A comedy-farce with strong hints of environmental pollution set in a New Jersey shore beach house. "Crabby" complaining novelist Joanna, faces mid-life crisis, career reverses and the disintegration of a long-term love affair with Sam, the husband of her best friend, Irene. Into this tottering domestic arrangement steps Steve, a strange young man who wishes to set up a "Crabcakes Franchise" empire on the bleached bones of their menage. Is he a true profiteer or a false prophet? Joanna writes the ending.

Full length. Setting: one non-literal beach house representing two identical apartments in a two family house. 2 males, 3 females.

L

DIANE CHARLOTTE LAMPERT

Bronx-born lyricist Diane Charlotte Lampert has run a full musical cycle: from country, pop, soul and rock to folk opera and jazz; from theatre and TV to nightclubs and over 20 motion pictures. She received an Academy Award nomination for best song, with composer Peter Schickele, for the Universal Pictures science fiction film **Silent Running** (now a cult film), and is the only lyricist the late jazz great Cannonball Adderley ever worked with. Ms. Lampert has written more than fifty hit songs, several top ten and number one in every form of popular music. Recipient: First Prize, Italian Song Festival; two gold records, Australia; "Break It to Me Gently," No. 1 hit with Brenda Lee; "Your Name Is Beautiful," No. 1 country hit with Carl Smith; "Ain't Nothin'," Top Ten with Billy "Crash" Craddock; "The Olive Tree," Top Ten in London with The Seekers.

Address: 45 East 66th St., New York, NY 10021

Agent: Earl Graham, Graham Agency, 317 West 45th St., New York, NY 10036 (212) 489-8288

TITLE • AVAILABILITY • PRODUCTIONS

King of Schnorrers (Bernard Hermann, composer, book, Shimon Wincelberg): manuscript*; Goodspeed Opera House, CT

Big Man — The Legend of John Henry (Cannonball and Nat Adderley, composers, book, Paul Avila Mayer and George W. George): manuscript*; (and Fantasy Records); Newport Jazz Festival, RI; Musical Hall, Detroit, MI

Nell Gwyn, The Protestant Whore (Peter Schickele, composer, book, Wm. M. Green and Dennis Turner): manuscript*; Lyric Theater of New York; Manhattan Theatre Club, NYC

Smaze!! (composer, Peter Schickele): manuscript*; New Earth Exposition, Los Angeles, San Francisco and Boston; Orange County Community College, Middletown, NY

*contact author

JAMES LAPINE

Born in Mansfield, OH on January 10, 1949. B.A. from Franklin and Marshall College and M.F.A. from California Institute of the Arts. Worked as a Graphic Designer and Photographer prior to his involvement in the theater. His interest began when he was working as the Resident Graphic Designer for the Yale Repertory Theatre. Recipient: Obie Award for **Photograph**, 1978; Millay Colony, Albee Foundation; George Oppenheimer/Newsday Award, 1980

Address: 49 Ann St., New York, NY 10038

Agent: George Lane, William Morris Agency, 1350 Avenue of the Americas, New York, NY 10036 (212) 586-5100

L

James Lapine (cont'd)

TITLE • AVAILABILITY • PRODUCTIONS

Photograph (adaptation): manuscript*; Open Space Theatre, NYC

Twelve Dreams: manuscript*; Lenox Arts Center, MA

Table Settings: Samuel French, 25 West 45th St., New York, NY 10036, $2.50; Playwrights Horizons, NYC; Chelsea Theater Center, NYC

   *contact agent

CRISPIN LARANGEIRA

Born in New York City on September 24, 1940. Attended Universities of London, Paris, Suisex and Madrid. M.F.A. in Dramatic Arts, U. of Connecticut. Teaching at high schools, psychiatric hospitals, colleges. Creator/coordinator, Latino Drama Unit at NY Shakespeare Festival. Literary Advisor, Henry Street, New Federal Theater. Consultant, WNET. Headwriter, PBS KCET-TV. Screen writer, CBS/Center Theater. Founder, Arts Ensemble. Recipient: Guggenheim Fellowship; Shubert Grant; National Endowment for the Arts Grant; P.E.N. Grant; CAPS Grant; New York State Council on the Arts.

Address: Mitch Douglas, I.C.M., 40 West 57th St., New York, NY 10019 (212) 556-5738

TITLE • AVAILABILITY • PRODUCTIONS

Daydreams: manuscript*; Ensemble Studio Theatre, NYC

People of the Empire: manuscript*; New York Shakespeare Festival, NYC

Crack: A Moral Fable in at Least Two Pieces: manuscript*; New York Shakespeare Festival, NYC

Cosmo and Company: manuscript*; New York Shakespeare Festival, NYC; Arthur Kill Correctional Facility

Whispers: manuscript*; Long Wharf Theatre, CT; O'Neill Theater Center's National Playwrights Conference, CT

Kolyma: manuscript*; New Dramatists, NYC

Friends: manuscript*; O'Neill Theater Center's National Playwrights Conference, CT; New Federal Theatre, NYC

Good Times Are Here Again: manuscript*; New York Shakespeare Festival, NYC

Comes A Time: manuscript*; Ensemble Studio Theatre, NYC

Three: manuscript*

See/Saw: manuscript*

Chamber #8: not available at this time

Fancies: manuscript*; Hudson Guild Theatre, NYC

At Last a Meeting of Minds Takes Place: manuscript*

   *contact agent

SYNOPSES

People of the Empire: Set in Trinidad, Colorado, in 1903, at the time of the great UMW coal miners strike. The strike remains a backdrop to the lives of people of the town swept up within it. Darvis had been a leader of men in a previous strike but its failure and many deaths has broken him. His

Crispin Larangeira (cont'd)

brother, Caemon, is full of fire but is corrupted by Flanagan, an agent of the mine owners. Marita, mistress to Darvis and Jacob, a Jew from Russia, embodies the destructive forces unleashed by the emerging society which pays no mind to the human being in its frenetic drive to industrial organization.

Full length. Setting: fluid staging. 6 males, 4 females.

Whispers: Jana Latvis, in prison and exile since 1941, secretly writes of her past in the hopes that someday the truth of what she has seen will be known and do some good. Neftaly Savaty, a Jew just let out of the camps, somewhat in a state of shock, and trying to walk across Siberia to his home in Minsk, comes to her cabin in the middle of the night, frozen, starving and frightened. Their common bonds of suffering at first bring them together but then turn to guilt and hatred because of what each did to survive. It will take all their strength to reach a point where each will still recognize the humanity of the other and go his and her own way.

Full length. Setting: a cabin. 1 male, 1 female.

See/Saw: A man and a woman, actors, meet during preparation and rehearsal of a play. He falls so madly in love with her, he decides to leave the set when she, due to an on-going relationship, cannot return his love. She is hurt in a serious fire. He comes to her. He stays with her. They fall into a strange distant love from which finally, she again breaks loose. His life and his career slide downhill. She comes to him.

Full length. Setting: multi sets. 1 male, 1 female.

CARL LARSEN

Born on August 28, 1934, Orange County, CA. Education: El Camino College (two years). Actor's Studio-Playwright's Unit (one year). Published two novels, eight collections of poetry, 1973: New York State Poets-in-the-Schools Program. Recipient: 1953, DeCamp Playwriting Award.

Address: 84 Susquehanna Ave., Lock Haven, PA 17745

Agent: The Foley Agency, 34 East 38th St., New York, NY 10016 (212) 686-6930

TITLE • AVAILABILITY • PRODUCTIONS

The Clocks: Pioneer Drama Service, 2172 S. Colorado Blvd., Denver, CO 80222, $1.25; Broadway Show League; Fulton Theatre Company; Milwaukee Repertory Theater, WI

Several Objects Passing Charlie Greeley: manuscript*; Milwaukee Repertory Theater, WI; PBS-TV

Bury My Knee At Wounded Groin: manuscript*; Hollywood Little Theater, CA

The Plot to Assassinate the Chase Manhattan Bank: Pioneer Drama Service, $1.25; Theatre East, NYC

Centipede: Pigiron*, P.O. Box 237, Youngstown, OH 44501, $1.00

You Guys Kill Me: manuscript*

   *contact agent

SYNOPSES

The Clocks: Four clocks, with six words, alter the Nature of Time.

One act. Setting: empty stage, 4 stools. Cast of 4, either male or female.

L

Carl Larsen (cont'd)

Several Objects Passing Charlie Greeley: Charley Greeley, from his coffin, views the past life of a loser with his mistress and his mother.

One act. Setting: the Rock of Ages Memorial Funeral Chapel. 1 male, 2 females.

Bury My Knee at Wounded Groin: The survivors of the Siege at Fort Forlorn prepare for the final onslaught.

One act. Setting: the ladies room at a frontier fort. 3 males.

JACK LARSON

Born in Los Angeles, CA. Educated in Los Angeles and Pasadena City College. Writing in verse forms that interested composers, he began collaborations with Virgil Thomson (opera, **Lord Byron), (Song Cycle),** Ned Rorem, Gerhard Samuel (monodrama, **The Relativity of Icarus,** now a ballet by the Joffrey Company), and wrote text and scenario for a new ballet for the Joffrey, **Orpheus Times Light[2],** also **A Place for Peace** with Virgil Thompson. New adaptation of monodrama **Lelio** (Berlioz) premiered at Hollywood Bowl by Los Angeles Philharmonic; new concert adaptation of **Egmont** (Goethe-Beethoven), Los Angeles Music Pavilion and Carnegie Hall. Recipient: Rockefeller Foundation Grant; Ford Foundation grant; Koussevitzky Grant; commissions from the Metropolitan Opera, Mark Taper Forum,

Los Angeles Philharmonic (for concert adaptation of dramatic works **Lelio** and **Egmont),** San Francisco Chamber Symphony (for two monodramas for chamber orchestra and voice).

Address: 449 Skyeway Rd., Los Angeles, CA 90049

Agent: Robert Lantz, 114 East 55th St., New York, NY 10022 (212) 751-2107

TITLE • AVAILABILITY • PRODUCTIONS

The Candied House (rhymed verse): manuscript*; Leo S. Bing Theater, Los Angeles County Museum of Art

Cherry, Larry, Sandy, Doris, Jean, Paul (rhymed verse): manuscript*; The Loft, NYC; Edinburgh Festival, London

Chuck (one act, verse): **Collision Course,** Random House, Inc., 201 East 50th St., New York, NY 10022, $4.95; Mark Taper Forum, Los Angeles, CA; Off Broadway

June-Moon (one act, verse): **New Theatre for Now,** Delta Books, 1 Dag Hammarskjold Plaza, New York, NY 10017, $2.25; Mark Taper Forum, Los Angeles, CA; various university productions

The Carob Trees (American Noh play): manuscript*

Fun Zone: manuscript*; Edinburgh Festival

Byron (adapted from opera libretto): manuscript*; Mark Taper Lab, Los Angeles, CA

Son-Like (monodrama, adaptation of Stravinsky's **The Soldiers Tale):** Peer-Southern Publishers, 1740 Broadway, New York, NY 10019

Love Songs for Two Monsters (song-play, music by Paul Chihara): manuscript*

*contact agent

Jack Larson (cont'd)

SYNOPSES

Cherry, Larry, Sandy, Doris, Jean, Paul: Girl has boys, girl loses boys, girl gets boys. Girl (Cherry) has gay boys (Larry, Sandy) on their first trip to Europe. Girl loses boys to girls (Doris and Jean). Girl gets boys back with aid of soldier (Paul). "Altogether delightful . . . Written in bubbling but unobtrusive verse couplets." — B. A. Young, **London Financial Times.**

Full length. Setting: room in London boarding house. 3 males, 5 females.

The Candied House: A mystery play based on Grimm's **Hansel and Gretel** where the characters do not live happily ever after, but as happily as possible.

Full length, in rhymed verse. Setting: a room; a wood; inside the Candied House. 3 males, 3 females.

LOUIS LaRUSSO II

Born in Hoboken, NJ, October 13, 1935 and stayed there until the Army called in 55–56. Later worked as a longshoreman while attending the A.A.D.A. After ten years of filling the well, the plays became honest enough to write. Recently has written several film scripts. Recipient: Tony nomination, 1976; Drama Desk nomination, 1976.

Address: 111 Willow Terrace, Hoboken, NJ 07030

Agent: Audrey Wood, c/o International Creative Management, 40 West 57th St., New York, NY 10019 (212) 556-5722

TITLE • AVAILABILITY • PRODUCTIONS

Hello, Thank You, and Goodbye: manuscript*; Lolly's Cabaret Theatre, NYC

The Poets: manuscript*; Churchyard Playhouse, NYC

Rocco and Raymond: manuscript*

Swordsmen in Love: manuscript*

Sigiliano: manuscript*

The Honeymoon: manuscript*; Eastside Playhouse, NYC

Thanksgotten: manuscript*; Churchyard Playhouse, NYC

Lamppost Reunion: Samuel French, 25 West 45th St., New York, NY 10036, $2.50; The Little Theatre, NYC

The Golden Ducks of Summer: manuscript*; under option

Momma's Little Angels: Dramatists Play Service, 440 Park Ave. South, New York, NY 10016, $2.50; Off Broadway

Wheelbarrow Closers: Samuel French, $2.50; Broadway

Vesper's Eve: manuscript*

The Zonk City Blues: manuscript*

Sea Mother's Son: manuscript*

Acorns in Moondust: manuscript*

Marlon Brando Sat Right Here: manuscript*; Boltax, NYC

Sunset: manuscript*; Buffalo Arena, NY

L

Louis LaRusso II (cont'd)

Toyland: manuscript*; Actors Repertory, NYC

Lifetime Revue: manuscript*

Knockout: Samuel French, $2.50; Broadway

Lackawanna Rogues: manuscript*

River Street is Haunted: manuscript*

The Tales of Robin Hood: manuscript*

    *contact agent

ARTHUR LAURENTS

Born in Brooklyn, NY on July 14, 1918. Attended Cornell U., NY. Author of novels: **The Way We Were; The Turning Point.** Films: **Rope; The Snake Pit; Anastasia; Bonjour Tristesse; The Way We Were; The Turning Point** and others. Has written radio plays and directed. Member, Dramatists Guild Council. Recipient: Tony Award; Screen Writers Guild Award; Drama Desk Award; Golden Globe Award; Sidney Howard Memorial Award; Variety Award and others.

Address: Quogue, NY 11959

Agent: Shirley Bernstein, Paramuse Artists Associates, 1414 Avenue of the Americas, New York, NY 10019 (212) 758-5055

TITLE • AVAILABILITY • PRODUCTIONS

Home of the Brave: Dramatists Play Service, 440 Park Ave. South, New York, NY 10016, $2.50; NYC

Heartsong: manuscript*; New Haven, CT; Boston, MA

The Bird Cage: Dramatists Play Service, manuscript; Broadway

The Time of the Cuckoo: Samuel French, 25 W. 45th St., New York, NY 10036, $2.50; Broadway

A Clearing in the Woods: Dramatists Play Service, $2.50; Broadway

Invitation to a March: Dramatists Play Service, $2.50; Broadway

The Enclave: Dramatists Play Service, $2.50; Wash. D.C.; Off Broadway

Scream: manuscript*; Houston, TX

West Side Story: Music Theatre International, 119 West 57th St., New York, NY 10019; Broadway

Gypsy: Tams-Witmark, 757 Third Avenue, New York, NY 10017; Broadway

Anyone Can Whistle: Music Theatre International; Broadway

Do I Hear A Waltz?: Rodgers & Hammerstein, 598 Madison Avenue, New York, NY 10021; Broadway

Hallelujah, Baby!: Music Theatre International; Broadway

The Madwoman of Central Park West: manuscript*; Off Broadway

    *contact agent

SHIRLEY MEZVINSKY LAURO

Born in Des Moines, IA. B.A. from Northwestern U. School of Speech and M.A. from U. of Wisconsin. Author of novel, **The Edge.** Professional actress, freelance editor, full-time college instructor of drama. Resident playwright at Ensemble Studio Theatre. Executive Committee member, Studio Ensemble Studio Theatre; Steering Group, Dramatists Guild Women's Committee, 1981. Recipient: Great American Play Contest, 1979; Double winner — Samuel French Short Play Award, 1979; Edna St. Vincent Millay Colony Fellow, 1977; CAPS Alternate, 1977; Off Off Broadway Playwright's Residency Award, 1980.

Address: 275 Central Park West, New York, NY 10024

Agent: Gilbert Parker, William Morris Agency, 1350 Avenue of the Americas, New York, NY 10019 (212) 586-5100

TITLE • AVAILABILITY • PRODUCTIONS

The Contest: manuscript*; Alley Theatre, TX; Ensemble Studio Theatre, NYC

I Don't Know Where You're Coming From At All!: Samuel French, 25 West 45th St., New York, NY 10036, $2.50; Ensemble Studio Theatre, NYC; Double Image Theatre, NYC

Open Admissions: Samuel French, $2.50; In **Off Off Broadway Festival Plays;** Ensemble Studio Theatre, NYC; Double Image Theatre, NYC

Nothing Immediate: Samuel French (with **Open Admissions);** Double Image Theatre, NYC; Actor's Theatre of Louisville, KY

The Coal Diamond: Dramatists Play Service, 440 Park Ave. South, New York, NY 10016, $2.25; Ensemble Studio Theatre, NYC; Actor's Theatre of Louisville, KY

Margaret and Kit: manuscript*

*contact agent

SYNOPSES

The Coal Diamond: A comedy based on the shifting relationships of four office women working in an insurance company in a Southeastern Missouri town in 1955. It is lunchtime and the women are playing bridge, but the stakes are higher than the card game. At issue is the pecking order in the office and the power structure.

One act. Setting: one interior set, corner of an office. 4 females.

The Contest: A bittersweet play set in a small, midwestern town in 1943. The story revolves around the relationships in a lower-middle class family of Jewish origins. Lily, the wife and mother, is a contest "junkie," hoping to win big so that she can change her family's life. Joe, her husband, is a gentle man resigned to his station as a factory worker. Caught in the emotional cross-fire between her mother's ambitions and her father's dreams, Beverly Sue, the daughter struggles for her own identity. The play centers on a Mounds Candy Bar contest that the mother has entered against the father's vehement wishes.

Full length. Setting: one interior set. 3 males, 6 females.

Nothing Immediate: A suspense story centering on two women thrown together in a rundown motel in a small Iowa town. Sandra, a young Jewish woman from New York, arrives to be near her father who lies gravely ill in a near-by hospital. Edna, the motel-keeper, is a right-wing religious fanatic of pioneer American stock whose business is failing and whose only relative has been a Viet Nam casualty. As Edna registers Sandra, an uncanny tension between the two women mounts as Edna begins to reveal a deep hostility toward Sandra and the world she represents.

One act. Setting: one interior (Lobby). 3 females.

L

EDDIE LAWRENCE

Born in Brooklyn, NY. Attended Brooklyn College, B.A.; Atelier Leger, Paris; Academie de la Grande Chaumiere, Paris. Mr. Lawrence is best known for his irreverent and outrageous character creation, "The Old Philosopher." His major acting credits on the legitimate stage include acclaimed roles in **Bells Are Ringing, The Threepenny Opera** and **Sherry.** He has done many TV talk shows. Among the people that he has written for are Victor Borge, Louis Nye, Carl Reiner, Jack E. Leonard, Sid Caesar, and Leo Durocher. He can be seen on the movie screen in **Act of Love** and in **The Night They Raided Minsky's.** He wrote the French film **The Ladies and the Men,** consisting of four Maupassant short stories and a series of twenty-five comedy shorts for Paramount Pictures as well as being a

contributor to **Esquire** and **Mad** magazines. Mr. Lawrence is also an accomplished painter, having studied under Fernand Leger. Mr. Lawrence paints under the name Lawrence Eisler and has taught acting, with emphasis on comedy. Recipient: Mystery Writers of America Award.

Address: 435 East 57th St., New York, NY 10022 (212) 688-7774

TITLE • AVAILABILITY • PRODUCTIONS

Louie and the Elephant: manuscript*; Off Broadway

The Beautiful Mariposa: manuscript*; Provincetown Playhouse (American Theatre Festival)

The Adventure of Eddie Greshaw: manuscript*; Provincetown Playhouse (American Theatre Festival)

Jonas (adapted from French): manuscript*

The Natives Were Restless: manuscript*

An Evening of Courteline: manuscript*; American Theatre, Paris

The Colonel is an Emigre: manuscript*

Kelly (book and lyrics; music by Moose Charlap): manuscript*; Broadway

A Nose for a Nose: manuscript*

Pistols in the Park: manuscript*

The Expressionist (book and lyrics; music by Moose Charlap): manuscript*

Animals (3 one-acts): manuscript*; Princess Theater, NYC
　　*contact author

SYNOPSES

The Expressionist: A musical inspired by the life of Paul Gauguin, who, at forty-five, gave up what most men aim for in life and plunged into the unknown world of painting. The time between his two trips to the islands and his futile attempt to become successful in Paris. It is as comic as it is tragic.

Two acts. Setting: simple; should be dominated by Gauguin's paintings. A large cast where everyone doubles.

A Nose for a Nose: a farce. A woman "in search of herself" joins a band of self-styled vigilantes who mete out punishment to evil-doers everywhere. Almost everyone is hoist by his own petard.

Two acts. Setting: all very simple except for the imaginative use of a swimming pool. 13 males (less if doubling is employed), 4 females.

The Natives Were Restless: A comedy. A restless band of ex-GIs, mostly painters, in Paris after World War II. La Vie Boheme isn't what it seems to be.

Two acts. Setting: The Dome Cafe in the Montparnasse. Cast: a large one; every actor has his moment.

JEROME LAWRENCE

Born in Cleveland, OH. Graduated Ohio State U., Phi Beta Kappa. Doctor of Fine Arts, Villanova U., Doctor of Humane Letters, Ohio State U., and Doctor of Literature, Fairleigh Dickinson U. Only playwright on Drama Panel, U.S. State Dept. Culture Exchange. Founding father of: Armed Forces Radio Service; American Playwrights Theatre and Margo Jones Award. Author of biography, **Actor: The Life and Times of Paul Muni.** Master Playwright at N.Y.U., visiting professor: Baylor; Ohio State; Salzburg Seminar in American Studies. Board Member: American Conservatory Theatre; National Repertory Theatre; Dramatists Guild; Authors League. Director at Dallas Theatre Center, Dublin Theatre Festival, Barter Theatre, many others.

Lawrence and Lee's plays have been translated and performed in thirty-one languages. Recipient: Multiple awards including two Peabody Awards in Broadcasting; Donaldson Award; Two Tony Awards; Outer Circle Critics Award; American Theatre Association Lifetime Achievement Award; ASCAP; **Variety** Critics Poll; British Drama Critics Winner and many others.

Address: 21056 Las Flores Mesa Drive, Malibu, CA 90265

Agent: Harold Freedman, Brandt & Brandt, 1501 Broadway, New York, NY 10036 (212) 840-5760

TITLE • AVAILABILITY • PRODUCTIONS

Laugh, God!: Contemporary Play Publications*; Ohio State University, OH

Live Spelled Backwards: Dramatists Play Service, 440 Park Ave. South, New York, NY 10016, $1.25; Beverly Hills, CA; Columbus, OH

The following plays were all written with Robert E. Lee

Inherit The Wind: Dramatists Play Service, $2.50; Dallas, TX; Broadway

Auntie Mame: Dramatists Play Service, $2.50; Wilmington, DE; Broadway

The Gang's All Here: Samuel French, 25 W. 45th St., New York, NY 10036, $2.50; Philadelphia, PA; Broadway

Only In America: Samuel French, $2.50; Philadelphia, PA; Broadway

A Call on Kuprin: Samuel French, $2.50; Philadelphia, PA; Broadway

Sparks Fly Upward (formerly **The Diamond Orchid**): Dramatists Play Service, $2.50; New Haven, CT; Broadway

Mame (Score, Jerry Herman): Tams-Witmark, Inc., 757 Third Ave., New York, NY 10017; Philadelphia, PA; Broadway

The Night Thoreau Spent in Jail: Samuel French, $2.50; American Playwrights Theatre throughout the country

Dear World (score, Jerry Herman): Tams-Witmark; Boston, MA; Broadway

The Crocodile Smile: Dramatists Play Service, $2.50; The Player's Ring, Los Angeles, CA; Playhouse-in-the-Park, Philadelphia, PA

The Incomparable Max: Dramatists Play Service, $2.50; Barter Theatre, VA; Broadway

Jabberwock: Samuel French, $2.50; Ohio State University, OH; American Playwrights Theatre

First Monday In October: Samuel French, $2.50; Cleveland Play House, OH; Kennedy Center, Washington, DC; Broadway

Look, Ma, I'm Dancin'! (score, Hugh Martin): manuscript*; score: Chappell Music, 810 7th Avenue, New York, NY 10019; Boston, MA; Broadway

Shangri-La (score, Harry Warren, Lawrence and Lee): manuscript*; score: Edwin H. Morris Music, 810 7th Avenue, New York, NY 10019; New Haven, CT; Broadway

Top of the Mark: manuscript*

L

Jerome Lawrence (cont'd)

Paris, France: manuscript*

Eclipse: manuscript*

Some Say in Ice: manuscript

Dilly (score, Vernon Duke, Lawrence & Lee): manuscript*

Houseboat in Kashmir: manuscript*

Short and Sweet: manuscript*

The City Has Lost Its Angels: manuscript*

Annie Laurie (musiplay): Harms, Inc. c/o Warner Bros., Inc., 75 Rockefeller Plaza, New York, NY 10019, $1.50; Los Angeles, CA; Chicago, IL

Roaring Camp (music, Dvorak; lyrics, Lawrence & Lee): Harms, $1.50; Los Angeles, CA Chicago, IL

The Familiar Stranger (musiplay): Harms, $1.50; Los Angeles, CA; Chicago, IL

   *contact agent

SYNOPSES

The Night Thoreau Spent in Jail: The most produced play of our time: the long journey of the soul of Henry David Thoreau from being a hermit to rejoining the human race — during his one night in jail. "The play of the century" . . . .**Scholastic Magazine.**

Full length. 11 males, 5 females.

Sparks Fly Upward: A scathing portrait of the flammable Evita Peron.

Full length. 16 males, 6 females.

Inherit The Wind: A modern theater classic about man's right to think. "Literature of the theatre." . . . Brooks Atkinson.

LANCE LEE

Born in New York City on August 25, 1942. Attended Boston University; B.A., Brandeis University; M.F.A., Yale School of Drama. He has taught at the Universities of Southern California and California (Los Angeles campus). His poetry, stories and reviews have appeared in, among others, **Chicago Review, Poem, Literary Review, Riverside Review, Cottonwood Review,** etc. **Two of A Kind,** with David Levy, purchased by NBC-TV. Has played a prominent role in local environmental issues. Recipient: Arts of the Theatre Fellowship, 1966; Rockefeller Grant (through the Office for Advanced Drama Research), 1971; National Endowment for the Arts, 1976-77.

Address: 1127 Galloway St., Pacific Palisades, CA 90272

Agent: Alleen Hussung, Samuel French, 25 West 45th St., New York, NY 10036 (212) 582-4700

TITLE • AVAILABILITY • PRODUCTIONS

Rasputin: manuscript*; Yale School of Drama, CT; O'Neill Theater Center's National Playwrights Conference, CT

Fox, Hound & Huntress: Volume 10, **Playwrights for Tomorrow,** U. of Minnesota Press, $3.45; Odyssey Theatre, CA

Lance Lee (cont'd)

Gambit: manuscript*; O'Neill Theater Center's National Playwrights Conference, CT; Victory Gardens Theatre, Chicago, IL

Time's Up: Samuel French, 25 West 45th St., New York, NY 10036, $2.50; Goodman Theatre, Chicago, IL; Theatre Upstairs, Los Angeles, CA

Life Scenes: manuscript*

*contact agent

SYNOPSES

Rasputin: A full-length play on the hypnotic and powerful Russian monk who helped bring the Romanovs down. But an unconventional treatment, focusing on the inherent flaws in character exploited by Rasputin in his remorseless drive for power. His rise is a definition of failure, his success the cornerstone of his fall. With intimate, confrontational scenes, the play ellipses seventeen years of history into one seemingly unbroken drive. It is very specifically not a pageant or a costume drama.

Full length. Setting: modular and abstract, changing scene to scene only in minor detail. 9 males, 4 females.

Gambit: John Hollinrake, a world-famous author/revolutionary humanist, has withdrawn to the northern California coast with his young wife. But an interviewer from a prestigious review pursues him; the local Women's Literary Committe shatters his privacy; and his long-suffering and exasperated wife torments him with an affair, all conspiring to make him face the failure in himself that drove him here. The action is realistic, within the format of a chamber play.

Long one act. Setting: a room of a house overlooking a garden. 6 males, 5 females.

Time's Up: Time's Up is a psychological "whydunit" about two people who can't bear their dreams coming true. They turn to a crisis center and, unknown to each other, confront the audience in a verbal symphony where their differences and strangeness melt before our eyes. The happiness they seek through an understanding and overcoming of their problems fall short of freeing them from the "mind-forg'd manacles" we all bear and which seem, in an ending of warmth and compassion, to be part of what it means to be human.

Long one act. Setting: almost a bare, unchanging box set divided in two by an invisible wall that gives us two partly glimpsed offices in a crisis center. 1 male, 1 female, and the audience (as the passive therapists).

LESLIE LEE

Born in Bryn Mawr, PA, now lives in New York City. B.A., University of Pennsylvania; M.A., Villanova University. Currently Assistant Professor in Theater at the College at Old Westbury, SUNY. He has published fiction, **The Day After Tomorrow,** a novella; film scripts, **The First Breeze of Summer,** for **Theatre in America** series; **Almos' A Man,** adaptation, for he American Short Story series; **The Split Cherry Tree,** ABC-TV, and **Go Tell It On The Mountain,** adaptation for PBS, among others. Recipient: Rockefeller Foundation Playwriting Fellow, 1966-68; Shubert Foundation Playwriting Grant, 1971-72; Obie Award; Best Play Tony Nomination; Outer Circle Critics Award, 1976; Mississippi ETV Award; Special Mention, Black Filmmakers.

Address: 708 Washington St., #2B, New York, NY 10014

Agent: Ellen Neuwald, 905 West End Avenue, New York, NY 10025 (212) 633-1582

L

Leslie Lee (cont'd)

TITLE • AVAILABILITY • PRODUCTIONS

Elegy to a Down Queen: manuscript*; La Mama E.T.C., NYC

Cops & Robbers: manuscript*; La Mama E.T.C., NYC

Elegy to a Down Queen (musical version): manuscript*; La Mama E.T.C., NYC

The Night of the No-Moon: manuscript*; New Dramatists, NYC

The War Party: manuscript*; New Dramatists, NYC

Between Now and Then: manuscript*; New Dramatist, NYC: Hal Prince Theater, Philadelphia, PA

As I Lay Dying, a Victim of Spring: manuscript*; Walnut St. Theater, Philadelphia, PA

The Book of Lambert: manuscript*; St. Clements Theatre, NYC

†**The First Breeze of Summer**: Samuel French, 25 West 45th St., New York, NY 10036, $2.50; Negro Ensemble Co., NYC; Broadway

Killing Time (A play with music): manuscript*; Village Gate, NYC

Life, Love and Other Minor Matters (a musical revue): manuscript*; Village Gate, NYC

Willie: manuscript*; O'Neill Theater Center's National Playwrights Conference, CT

    *contact agent
    †Lincoln Center, Theatre on Film & Tape

ROBERT E. LEE

Born in Elyria, OH. Attended Ohio Wesleyan University; Lit. D., Northwestern University; H.H.D., Ohio State University; Honorary M.A., Pasadena Playhouse, College of Theatre Arts. Co-founder of Armed Forces Radio Service; American Playwrights Theatre; Margo Jones Award. Professor of Playwriting at UCLA. Lecturer on theater, world-wide. Major Lawrence & Lee Collections at Lincoln Center, NY; Ohio State University; Harvard. Their plays have been translated and performed in thirty-one languages. Recipient: Peabody Awards in Broadcasting, (twice); Donaldson Award; Tony Awards, (twice); Outer Circle Critics Award; American Theatre Association Lifetime Achievement; ASCAP; **Variety** Critics Poll; British Drama Critics Winner and many others.

Address: 15725 Royal Oak Road, Encino, CA 91436

Agent: Harold Freedman, Brandt & Brandt, 1501 Broadway, New York, NY 10036 (212) 840-5760

TITLE • AVAILABILITY • PRODUCTIONS

Sounding Brass: Samuel French, 25 West 45th St., New York, NY 10036, $2.50; Reformed Church, Bronxville, NY

Ten Days That Shook the World: manuscript*; Freud Theatre, UCLA

The following plays were all written with Jerome Lawrence

Inherit the Wind: Dramatists Play Service, 440 Park Avenue South, New York, NY 10016, $2.50; Dallas, TX; Broadway

Auntie Mame: Dramatists Play Service, $2.50; Wilmington, DE; Broadway

The Gang's All Here: Samuel French, $2.50; Philadelphia, PA; Broadway

Robert E. Lee (cont'd)

Only in America: Samuel French, $2.50; Philadelphia, PA; Broadway

A Call on Kuprin: Samuel French, $2.50; Philadelphia, PA; Broadway

Sparks Fly Upward (formerly **Diamond Orchid**): Dramatists Play Service, $2.50; New Haven, CT; Broadway

Mame (score, Jerry Herman): Tams-Witmark, Inc., 757 Third Ave., New York, NY 10017; Philadelphia, PA: Broadway

The Night Thoreau Spent in Jail: Samuel French, $2.50; American Playwrights Theatre throughout the country

Dear World (score, Jerry Herman): Tams-Witmark; Boston, MA; Broadway

The Crocodile Smile: Dramatists Play Service, $2.50; The Player's Ring, Los Angeles, CA; Playhouse-in-the-Park, Philadelphia, PA

The Incomparable Max: Dramatists Play Service, $2.50; Barter Theatre, VA; Broadway

Jabberwock: Samuel French, $2.50; Ohio State University, OH; American Playwrights Theatre

First Monday in October: Samuel French, $2.50; Cleveland Play House, OH; Kennedy Center, Washington, DC; Broadway

Look, Ma, I'm Dancin'! (score, Hugh Martin): manuscript*; score: Chappell Music, 810 7th Avenue, New York, NY 10019; Boston, MA; Broadway

Shangri-La (score, Harry Warren, Lawrence and Lee): manuscript*; score: Edwin H. Morris Music, 810 7th Avenue, New York, NY 10019; New Haven, CT; Broadway

Top of the Mark: manuscript*

Paris, France: manuscript*

Eclipse: manuscript*

Some Say in Ice: manuscript

Dilly (score, Vernon Duke, Lawrence & Lee): manuscript*

Houseboat in Kashmir: manuscript*

Short and Sweet: manuscript*

The City Has Lost Its Angels: manuscript*

Annie Laurie (musiplay): Harms, Inc. c/o Warner Bros., Inc., 75 Rockefeller Plaza, New York, NY 10019, $1.50; Los Angeles, CA; Chicago, IL

Roaring Camp (music, Dvorak; lyrics, Lawrence & Lee): Harms, $1.50; Los Angeles, CA; Chicago, IL

The Familiar Stranger (musiplay): Harms, $1.50; Los Angeles, CA; Chicago, IL

   *contact agent

SYNOPSES

First Monday in October: The play deals with the behind the scenes frictions on the United States Supreme Court—particularly when an attractive but arch-conservative woman is appointed—and the resulting fireworks with the High Court's reigning liberal. Issues: porno movies and scheming multi-nationals. How mighty judicial matters can be resolved with humor and humanity.

Full length. Setting: unit set plus thrust. 12 males, 1 female.

Sounding Brass: St. Paul sans sainthood: this was written for the chancel. What if Paul had actually revisited the warring church in Corinth, instead of lambasting the new Christians with letters from the mainland? The flawed Saul of Tarsus battles for the loyalty of his most important church and nearly loses. Very free-form.

Full length. Setting: flexible. 8 males, 3 females, chorus optional.

Jabberwock: Based on Improbabilities lived and imagined by James Thurber in the fictional city of Columbus, Ohio. This is the greening of Jamie in the days when Woodrow Wilson was keeping us out of war.

Full length. Setting: unit set, the Thurber house. 14 males, 13 females.

L

RICHARD LEES

Born in Ann Arbor, MI on October 21, 1948. Educated at Stanford, the U. of Michigan and the Yale School of Drama. Besides his plays, he is the author of one novel and one screenplay. Recipient: Avery Hopwood Award; William Morris Fellowship; John Golden Fellowship; CBS Foundation Prize; Rockefeller Grant in Playwriting; NEA Artist-in-residence grant.

Address: 18333 Hatteras, #18, Los Angeles, CA 91356

Agent: Helen Merrill, 337 West 22nd St., New York, NY 10011 (212) 924-6314

TITLE • AVAILABILITY • PRODUCTIONS

Arrival: manuscript*; U. of Michigan, MI

Shoppin': manuscript*; U. of Michigan, MI

Scenes in Isolation: manuscript*; Canterbury House Theatre

Seth: manuscript*; Yale Studio Theatre, CT

Alma's Rules: manuscript*; Yale Repertory Sunday Series, CT

Out of Sync: Yale/Theatre, Spring 1975, Box 854, Meriden, CT 06450

At the End of Long Island: manuscript*; O'Neill Theater Center's National Playwrights Conference, CT; Mark Taper Forum Lab, LA, CA

Right of Way: manuscript*; Guthrie Theatre, MN; South Coast Repertory, CA

Ophelia Kline: manuscript*; Playwrights Horizons, NYC

A Punk in the Country: manuscript*

   *contact agent

MARK LEIB

Born in Tampa, FL on March 21, 1954. B.A., Harvard College, 1975; Bristol University, England, Postgraduate Certificate in Drama, 1976; M.F.A., Yale Drama School, 1980. Recipient: CBS Foundation Prize in Playwriting, 1978.

Address: 23 Avon Street, Cambridge, MA 02138

Agent: Helen Merrill, 337 West 22nd St., New York, NY 10011 (212) 924-6314

TITLE • AVAILABILITY • PRODUCTIONS

Muddle: not available; Van Dyck Theatre, Bristol, England

Against the Law (formerly **The Law**): manuscript*; Edinburgh Festival, Scotland; Yale Cabaret, New Haven, CT

Mark Leib (cont'd)

Laplotte: An Escape in the French Style: not available; Yale Cabaret, New Haven, CT

Terry by Terry: manuscript*; O'Neill Theater Center's National Playwrights Conference, CT; American Repertory Theatre, Cambridge, MA

Figaro (adaptation): manuscript*

  *contact agent

CHARLES LEIPART

Born in Chicago, IL on April 28, 1944. B.S., Northwestern University, School of Speech, 1966, Honors in Stage Directing. Apprenticed to Howard Bay, Goodspeed Opera House; Technical apprentice, Trinity Square Repertory, 1966-67. Professional actor on stage, in films and TV. Graduate seminar, stage directing with Harold Clurman, Hunter College, 1979. Member, John Ford Noonan's Playwrights' Workshop, 1977-79.

Address: 115 West 71st St., #5A, New York, NY 10023

Agent: Susan Schulman, 165 West End Avenue, New York, NY 10023 (212) 877-2216

TITLE • AVAILABILITY • PRODUCTIONS

Deja Vu: manuscript*; New York Cast Company, NYC

The Harvest Moon Ball: manuscript*

Stiletto or The Crime of Fashion: manuscript*

The King of Poland: manuscript*; New York Cast Company, NYC

Romance: manuscript*

Mr. Opportunity & The Undefeated Rhumba Champ: manuscript*; APA, American Theatre of Actors, NYC

My Early Years: manuscript*

Mr. & Mrs. 'A': manuscript*

Trio for Heartstrings: manuscript*

  *contact agent

SYNOPSES

Romance: A contemporary, two character love story.
Full length. Setting: stylized, open setting suggesting a studio apartment. 1 male, 1 female.

Mr. & Mrs. 'A': A house in the woods, an unexpected visitor.
Full length. Setting: living-dining interior. 1 male, 2 females.

Trio for Heartstrings: Three variations on the theme of romantic longing for three players.
Full length. Setting: one flexible unit set. 1 male, 2 females.

L

HARDING LEMAY

Born in North Bangor, NY. Educated, after high
school, at the Neighborhood Playhouse School
of the Theatre. Has written for television since
1968, including drama **They** for WNET, and headwriter 1971–79, daytime serial, **Another World.**
Creator and head writer of serial, **Lovers and
Friends.** Author of **Inside, Looking Out,** published 1971 by Harpers Magazine Press and nominated for National Book Award the following
year as best American biography. Non-fiction, **8
years in Another World,** Atheneum, 1981. Recipient: Emmy Award for best writing, Daytime
Serial, for **Another World,** 1975.

Address: 146 East 19th St., New York, NY 10003

Agent: Marie Stroud, Stroud Management,
    18 East 48th St., New York, NY 10017
    (212) 688-0226

TITLE • AVAILABILITY • PRODUCTIONS

Look at Any Man: manuscript*; New Dramatists, NYC; Neighborhood Playhouse, NYC

From a Dark Land: manuscript*; New Dramatists, NYC

The Little Birds Fly: manuscript*; New Dramatists, NYC

Return Upriver: manuscript*; New Dramatists, NYC

The Death of Eagles: manuscript*; New Dramatists, NYC; Univ. of Michigan

The Joslyn Circle: manuscript*; New Dramatists, NYC: Dublin Theatre Festival

The Off Season: manuscript*; New Dramatists, NYC

How He Became a Writer: manuscript*; New Dramatists, NYC

    *contact agent

SYNOPSES

The Little Birds Fly: Six grown children return home for their father's funeral to a farmhouse near
the Canadian border in New England. During several days, they survey the wreckage they left
behind them when they escaped, the boys by running away, the girls by getting married. The
Mother, in her late fifties, is insane, the father committed suicide, and the two central figures, a
skeptical sophisticated New Yorker and the eldest daughter who married a rich Bostonian Jew,
come to terms with their anguished past and move together back into more productive lives.
Three other children, including an eighteen-year-old girl, have stayed on the farm; three brothers
are laborers.

Drama, three acts. Setting: the kitchen of a run-down farmhouse in winter. The time is the present.
6 males, 4 females.

The Joslyn Circle: An intellectual comedy about a family of noted American writers and a young
midwesterner who marries one of them, twenty years his elder, and who tries to enlist their support in his political activities. The theme is of the destructive narcissism of the creative person as
displayed in domestic relationships. Characters: three women in their fifties, a famous novelist,
her anthropologist, activist sister, and their noted poet cousin; three men: the novelist's Jewish
intellectual husband, the thirty-year-old third husband of the anthropologist, and a homosexual
bachelor brother of the poet. The surface of the play is brittle comedy; beneath the surface is a
tangle of complex, contradictory relationships haunted by childhood, a dead brother, and famous
ancestors.

Three acts. Set in the present in a drawing room outside of Boston. 3 males, 3 females.

How He Became a Writer: A New York publisher and her chauffeur/companion are taken in by a
widowed farm woman and her grandson when their car is turned off the route to Montreal

Harding LeMay (cont'd)

because of flooding. A contest over the immediate future of the grandson, about to graduate from high school, ensues with unpredictable results for all concerned.

Full length. Setting: kitchen of the farmhouse, 1930s. 3 males, 4 females.

STEPHEN LEVI

Born in Springfield, IL on January 12, 1941. Educated at Los Angeles City College. Studied acting with Stella Adler, Herbert Berghof, Uta Hagen and Lee Strasberg. Has performed with the American Shakespeare Festival, Barter Theatre and the New York Shakespeare Festival. Has written screenplays and directed many productions throughout the country. Married with one daughter. Member of the New Dramatists.

Address: 519 Second Avenue, #3W, New York, NY 10016 (212) 889-2604

TITLE • AVAILABILITY • PRODUCTIONS

Daphne in Cottage D: Dramatist Play Service, 440 Park Ave. South, New York, NY 10016, $2.25; Boston; Broadway

Angel on My Shoulder: Samuel French, 25 W. 45th St., New York, NY 10036, $2.50; Pineville Dinner Theatre, NC; Shady Lane Playhouse, IL

Getting Mama Married: Samuel French, $2.50; New Dramatists, NYC; Shady Lane Playhouse, IL

Je T'Aime, Jessica: manuscript*; HB Playwrights Foundation, NYC; Holland

Cherry Soda Water/The Gulf of Crimson: manuscript*; New Dramatists, NYC; Playwrights Foundation, NYC

Memorial to the Honored Dead: manuscript*; New Dramatists, NYC; Playwrights Lab, MN

The Undiscovered Country: manuscript*; Los Angeles City college; Pasadena City College, CA

Missing Persons: manuscript*; New Dramatists, NYC

The Offering: manuscript*

The Dance on Saturday Night: manuscript*

Prudence in Transit: manuscript*

An Opposite Attraction: manuscript*

Goodbye Cruel World: manuscript*; New Dramatists, NYC

The Fairy Godmother: manuscript*

*contact author

L

IRA LEVIN

Born in New York City on August 27, 1929. B.A.
from New York University. Served in the United
States Army where he wrote training films.
Author of **A Kill Before Dying, Rosemary's Baby,
This Perfect Day, The Stepford Wives, Boys from
Brazil.** Member of the Dramatists Guild; Author's
Guild; ASCAP. Recipient: Edgar Allan Poe
Award.

Agent: Rosenstone/Wender, 3 East 48th St.,
New York, NY 10017 (212) 832-8330

TITLE • AVAILABILITY • PRODUCTIONS

No Time for Sergeants: Dramatists Play Service, 440 Park Ave. South, New York, NY 10016,
$2.50; Broadway

Interlock: manuscript, Dramatists Play Service, reading fee $2.00; deposit, $10.00; Broadway

Critics Choice: Dramatists Play Service, $2.50; Broadway

General Seeger: Dramatists Play Service, $2.50; Broadway

Drat! The Cat! (music, Milton Schafer): Inquire, Samuel French, 25 West 45th St., New York,
NY 10036; Broadway

Dr. Cook's Garden: Dramatists Play Service, $2.50; Broadway

Veronica's Room: Samuel French, $2.50; Broadway

Deathtrap: Dramatists Play Service, $2.50; Broadway

Break A Leg: Samuel French, $2.50; Broadway

JONATHAN LEVY

Born in New York. B.A. from Harvard; attended
University of Rome, Italy; M.A. and Ph.D. from
Columbia. Has taught at Juilliard School of
Music and University of California at Berkeley.
Playwright in residence at Manhattan Theatre
Club; president and co-founder of Playwrights
for Children's Theatre and a member of the
Albee-Barr Playwrights Unit and the New
Theatre Playwrights Unit. He was Fannie Hurst
Visiting Professor of Theatre Arts at Brandeis
University, 1979; Chairman, Dept. of Theatre
Arts, SUNY, Stony Brook, 1980; Co-Chairman,
Theatre for Youth Panel, National Endowment
for the Arts, 1979; Policy Panel, National Endow-
ment for the Arts, 1980. He has also written
opera libretto (**Boswell's Journal**) and **Wild Rose,**
fiction, verse, and criticism for the **Village
Voice, Harper's Bookletter, Cricket,** and **Bottighe Oscure.** Recipient: CAPS grant; Lincoln Center
Institute, Senior Fellow; Charlotte Chorpenning Award, 1979.

Address: 1165 Fifth Ave., New York, NY 10029

Agent: Susan Schulman, 165 West End Avenue, New York, NY (212) 877-2216

L

TITLE • AVAILABILITY • PRODUCTIONS

The Pornographer's Daughter: manuscript*; Manhattan Theatre Club, NYC

Theatre Games: manuscript*; Theatre Calgary, Canada

Marco Polo: A Fantasy for Children: manuscript*; O'Neill Theater Center's National Playwrights Conference, CT; Manhattan Theatre Club, NYC

Master Class: manuscript*; Manhattan Theatre Club, NYC

Monkey Play: manuscript*; Clark Center for the Performing Arts, NYC

Charlie the Chicken: manuscript*; American Shakespeare Festival

The Marvellous Adventures of Tyl: Contemporary Children's Theater, edited by B.J. Lifton, Avon Books, 250 West 55th St., New York, NY 10019, $5.95; Triangle Theatre, NYC

The Shrinking Bride: manuscript*; Mercury Theater

The Master of the Blue Mineral Mines: manuscript*; Barr-Albee Playwrights Unit, NYC

The Little Green Bird (adapted from the Italian of Carlo Gozzi): manuscript*; The Young Hampton Players, Southampton, NY

Jack N's Awful Demands: manuscript*; The Playbox Theatre, NYC

Ziskin's Revels: manuscript*; The New Theatre Workshop, NYC

An Exploratory Operation: manuscript*; The New Jewish Theatre Workshop, NYC

The Play of Innocence and Change: New Plays for Children, P.O. Box 273, Rowayton, CT 06853, $2.50; The Children's Theatre of the 92nd Street YMHA, NYC

Turandot (adapted from the Italian of Carlo Gozzi): **The Genius of the Italian Theatre,** edited by Eric Bentley, New American Library Inc., 1301 Avenue of the Americas, New York, NY 10019 (out of print)*

Sabbatai Zevi: manuscript*; The Theatre Company of Boston, MA

Old Blues: manuscript**; Impossible Ragtime Theatre, NYC

Arts and Letters: manuscript**; New York Stage Works, NYC

*contact agent
**contact agent

SYNOPSES

Charlie the Chicken: A domestic comedy about Charlie, a performing chicken, and his master, Ferenc Horvath, a seedy Hungarian vaudevillian. Charlie has a brilliant, questing mind and a thirst for knowledge and experience. Horvath, who needs him as a docile stooge, offers him stuffed toys, tap dancing and unlimited bottled beer. An admirer pays them an unexpected visit backstage and Charlie's longings erupt, with bad consequences.

One act. Setting: a run-down theatre, front and back stage. 2 males, 1 female, and a pianist of either sex.

Master Class: An ancient Russian diva, reduced to giving elementary classes, takes a young voice student through Schubert's **Death and the Maiden.** In the harrowing process, she gives the student a glimpse of what a serious life in art is about, and intimations of mortality.

One act. Setting: a college music classroom. 2 females and a pianist of either sex.

The Marvellous Adventures of Tyl: A play for children loosely based on the Tyl Eulenspiegel legend. In a series of transformations, the play takes the hero from birth to mock death, by way of a series of wild, instructive adventures.

Full length. Setting: minimal and flexible. 4 males, 3 females.

L

DAVID LIFSON

Born in New York City on December 29, 1908. Received B.S. Degree at Washington Square College, M.A. and Ph.D. at New York University. Professor of English and Humanities, Monmouth College, NJ; Director of Theatre at Pratt Institute, Brooklyn, 1958–1963; Stage Manager on Broadway; Assistant Director on radio; Producer-Director professional summer stock theaters. Published author of **Yiddish Theatre in America, Epic & Folk Plays of the Yiddish Theatre** and a novel **Headless Victory** (A.S. Barnes & Co. 1978). Contributor to **Encylopaedia Britannica.** Drama critic for various publications. Drama editor, Jewish Telegraph agency. Recipient: Fulbright-Hays Scholar for Research in Theatre, 1970–1971; Otto Kahn Fellowship at Metropolitan Opera; writing and production grants from Monmouth College; New York University Award for Scholarship.

Address: 40 East 10th St., New York, NY 10003 (212) 473-5323

Agent: Bertha Klausner, Writers International Agency, 71 Park Ave., New York, NY 10016 (212) 685-2642

TITLE • AVAILABILITY • PRODUCTIONS

Familiar Pattern: manuscript*; Provincetown Playhouse, NYC

Greet Tomorrow: manuscript*

Buffoons: manuscript*

News Item: manuscript*

At the Gate: manuscript*

The Troubador: manuscript*

Gift of the Magi: manuscript*; Maryland State College, MD

Children at the White House: manuscript*; Pratt Institute, NYC

Gimpy: manuscript*; N.Y.U.

Mummers and Men: manuscript*; Provincetown Playhouse, NYC

Recruits: Fairleigh-Dickinson Press, Rutherford, NJ, $14.50

Farvorfen Vinkel: manuscript*

Hirsch Lekert: manuscript*

Yankel Boyla: manuscript*

Hurrah for Us: manuscript*

Oh, Careless Love!: manuscript*

How to Rob a Bank: manuscript*; PAF Playhouse, Long Island, NY

Le Poseur: manuscript*; Italian Ministry of Culture, NY

Ivory Tower: manuscript*

Eye of the Storm: manuscript*

Masquerade: manuscript*

The Flatbush Football Golem: manuscript*

Emeritus: manuscript*

    *contact agent

David Lifson (cont'd)

SYNOPSES

The Flatbush Football Golem: (lyrics by Lifson & Kalmanoff, music, Martin Kalmanoff) A Hassidic Yeshiva in Brooklyn is endowed a football team. After being defeated, one of its devout Kabbala students creates a Golem who leads the team to victory. The play has a conflict of orthodoxy vs. feminism as well as the football theme.

Emeritus: A play about an aging director/actor in an eastern European country (Socialist) whose inadequate pension obliges him to coach young actresses. He plots with one actress to obtain money from a young, visiting Fulbright-Hays Fellow.

PAUL STEPHEN LIM

Born in Manila, Philippines on January 5, 1944. B.A., and M.A., from Kansas University. Lecturer, English Department, University of Kansas. Writer of short stories, poetry, essays and book reviews. Member of Dramatists Guild; Authors League of America; The Society of Midland Authors; American Association of University Professors; Phi Beta Kappa Society. Recipient: American College Theatre Festival; Palanca Memorial Awards, 1976, 1977, 1978; Shubert Playwriting Fellowship, 1976; Kansas Arts Commission Grant, 1979.

Address: 934 Pamela Lane, Lawrence, KS 66044
(913) 842-6287

TITLE • AVAILABILITY • PRODUCTIONS

Conpersonas: Samuel French, 25 West 45th St., New York, NY 10036, $2.50; American College Theatre Festival, Washington, DC; University of Kansas

Homerica: manuscript*; University of Kansas

Points of Departure: manuscript*; East West Players, Los Angeles, CA; Asian American Theatre Workshop, San Francisco, CA

Woeman: manuscript*; University of Kansas; Shelter West, NYC

Chambers: manuscript*; Midwest Playwrights Laboratory, Madison, WI

Flesh, Flash and Frank Harris: manuscript*; Lawrence Community Theatre, KS

Hatchet Club: manuscript*

Zooks! (musical): manuscript*

*contact author

SYNOPSES

Flesh, Flash and Frank Harris: An embittered old Frank Harris reminisces in his apartment in Nice and, through a series of flashbacks, recreates the many ups and downs in his life — his friendship with the likes of Oscar Wilde and George Bernard Shaw, his successes and failures with women, his battle with censors upon the publication of **My Life and Loves** — and ultimately comes to grips with the many ghosts from his past, including his younger and middle-aged self.

Full length. Setting: platforms suggesting a variety of places. 8 males, 4 females doubling and tripling in 36 speaking parts.

Woeman: A newspaper photographer is in the process of being committed to a mental institution and his mother calls a meeting at his apartment to dispose of his worldly goods. The play captures in various flashbacks the nature of the man's relationships with the five most important

L

Paul Stephen Lim (cont'd)

women in his life. Thematically, the play examines the nature of marriage in the "Me Decade" and also the more extreme consequences of divorce on children.

Full length. Setting: a studio apartment. 1 male, 5 females.

Homerica: Each of the three acts can be performed independently of the others but, if presented together, the play traces sexual mores in America — past, very Victorian and repressed; present, wild and abandoned; future, scientific. The play is a statement on the possible consequences of the sexual revolution on the nuclear family, especially on children.

Full length. Setting: bookstore, singles' bar, travel agency. 8 males, 5 females doubling and tripling in 31 parts.

ROMULUS LINNEY

Born in Philadelphia, PA on September 21, 1930. B.A. Oberlin College; M.F.A., Yale School of Drama. Author of three novels, **Heathen Valley, Slowly, By Thy Hand Unfurled** and **Jesus Tales.** TV: CBS, **American Parade;** PBS, **Feeling Good.** Adjunct Professor of Playwriting and Fiction, Brooklyn College; School of the Arts, Columbia University; Connecticut College and others. Recipient: National Endowment for the Arts Grants; Commissions for plays from: Appalachian Regional Commission; Kennedy Center; Virginia Museum Theatre; Phoenix Theatre; Actor's Theatre of Louisville; Guggenheim Fellowship; Obie Award.

Address: 235 West 76th St., New York, NY 10023
(212) 362-9183

Agent: Gilbert Parker, William Morris Agency, 1350 Avenue of the Americas, New York, NY 10019
(212) 586-5100

TITLE • AVAILABILITY • PRODUCTIONS

The Sorrows of Frederick: Dramatists Play Service, 440 Park Ave. South, New York, NY 10016, $2.50; Mark Taper Forum, Los Angeles, CA; Birmingham Repertory Theatre

Democracy: Dramatists Play Service, $2.50; H.B. Playwrights Foundation, NYC; Virginia Museum Theatre

The Love Suicide at Schofield Barracks: Dramatists Play Service, $2.50; H.B. Playwrights Foundation, NYC; ANTA Theatre, NYC

Holy Ghosts: Dramatists Play Service, $3.95; East Carolina University; Garrick Theatre, NYC

Old Man Joseph and His Family: Dramatists Play Service, $2.50; Chelsea Theatre Center, NYC

Appalachia Sounding: manuscript*; Carolina Readers Theatre Tour

The Death of King Phillip: manuscript*; New England Chamber Opera; H.B. Playwrights Foundation, NYC

Southern Comfort: not available; H.B. Playwrights Foundation, NYC; Lincoln Center Library, NYC

Childe Byron: manuscript*; Virginia Museum Theatre; Actor's Theatre of Louisville, KY

Tennessee: Best Short Plays', 1980, Chilton Press, Chilton Way, Radnor, PA 19089, $10.95; Ensemble Studio Theatre, NYC

Goodbye, Howard: manuscript*; Earplay

Choir Practice: manuscript*; Newhouse Theatre, Lincoln Center, NYC

El Hermano: manuscript*; Ensemble Studio Theatre, NYC

Romulus Linney (cont'd)

The Captivity of Pixie Shedman: manuscript*; Phoenix Theatre, NYC

　*contact agent

SYNOPSES

The Sorrows of Frederick: A stage life of Frederick the Great of Prussia, moving from a battlefield in his old age, to his youth, maturity and old age again.

Full length. Setting: unit set. 12 or more males, 1 female.

Childe Byron: The lifespan of Lord Byron, as hallucinated before her death by his daughter, Ada, Countess of Lovelace.

Setting: one set. 4 males, 4 females.

Tennessee: An old mountain woman's return from Tennessee to the farm in North Carolina where she was born and her discovery that Tennessee was not where she thought it was.

Setting: unit set. 3 males, 3 females.

DANIEL LIPMAN

Daniel received a B.F.A. from Boston University's School of Fine Arts and an M.A. from the University of Michigan. He was Playwright-in-Residence at the University of Michigan's Professional Theatre Program, 1971–72. Has written for TV, two episodes, **Family** (with Ron Cowen). Screenplay, **Firefly** (with Ron Cowen). Recipient: Avery Hopwood Award for Drama for **Last Respects,** 1972.

Address: 620 Via de la Paz, Pacific Palisades, CA 90272

Agent: Audrey Wood, International Creative Management, 40 West 57th St., New York, NY 10019 (212) 556-5722

TITLE • AVAILABILITY • PRODUCTIONS

Last Respects: manuscript*; Professional Theatre, University of Michigan; University of California at Berkeley

Casanova and His Mother (one act): manuscript*; O'Neill Theater Center's National Playwrights Conference, CT; St. Clements, NYC

Orion's Hound: manuscript*

Gene & Jean (with Ron Cowen): not available; Stockbridge, MA

　*contact agent

SYNOPSIS

Orion's Hound: A comedy about Skip Hulldecker, an ex-astronaut, who became an "instant" hero by being the fourth man to walk on the moon. Now, ten years later, Skip is forgotten (he still feels like a failure because his father wanted him to be first on the moon) and he has to deal with his world, his family, and himself coming apart at the seams: a mere payment for the American obsession with success.

Full length. Setting: the main bungalow of a ramshackle motel in New Mexico. 7 males, 2 females.

L

JOSEPH LIZARDI

Born in Caguas, Puerto Rico on February 12, 1941. Educated at the City University; AAS Bronx Community College; B.A. Baruch College. Joseph writes for television and films in addition to the theatre. **The Dope War** (screenplay) and **Spanish Harlem** (screenplay) have both been optioned for production by Woody King Associates.

Address: 5 Ontario Avenue, Plainview, NY 11803
(516) 822-7385

Agent: Bertha Klausner, 71 Park Avenue, New York, NY 10016 (212) 685-2642

TITLE • AVAILABILITY • PRODUCTIONS

Summerville: manuscript*; West Side Community Theater, NYC

The Contract: manuscript*; Carnegie Hall Repertory Theater, NYC

The Agreement: manuscript*; Carnegie Hall Repertory Theater, NYC

The Commitment: manuscript*; Henry St. Playhouse, NYC; New Federal Theater, NYC

The Block Party: manuscript*; Henry St. Playhouse, NYC

El Macho: manuscript**; Puerto Rican Traveling Theater, NYC

The Powderroom: manuscript**; Arena Players, Long Island Repertory Theater

Blue Collars: manuscript*; Arena Players, Long Island Repertory Theater

The Family Room: manuscript*

The Runaway: manuscript*

Three on the Run: manuscript*

Save the Children: manuscript*

Couples: manuscript**

December in New York: manuscript**

    *contact author
    **contact agent

SYNOPSES

December in New York: A young couple faces the biggest crisis of their young but shaky marriage with the sudden arrival of her mother and his father for the Christmas holidays. It is a humorous look at a serious contemporary problem.
Full length. Setting: livingroom of a Manhattan apartment. 3 males, 2 females.

The Family Room: A wealthy and ultra-conservative Long Island family plunge into a sudden panic when their daughter arrives home from college with what they consider an extremely un-suitable fiance.
Full length. Setting: family room of a Long Island mansion. 3 males, 3 females.

Couples: A comedy about four different couples. A husband suddenly returning to the wife he abandoned three months before. A married man's sudden confrontation with the biggest crisis of the affair he has been having with a married woman. A married couple suddenly coming to grips with their shaky marriage while waiting out a blizzard in a cheap motel. And an elderly couple's sudden awareness that there is love and sex after sixty-five.
Full length. Setting: a motel room; a living room. 3 males, 3 females.

ROY LONDON

Born in New York City; B.A. Antioch College (Drama-Mathematics). Consultant and writer for the Museum of the City of New York and Museum of the Diaspora in Tel Aviv. Writer of several films for TV, most recent **California Gold Rush** and **Auction!,** a mystery pilot. **People of North Carolina,** poetry for film and published. Actor: Broadway, Off and Off Off Broadway, film and TV, Royal Shakespeare Company, repertory. Director: Manhattan Theatre Club, Ensemble Studio Theatre, Circle Repertory. Teacher: Acting (Manhattan Theatre Club). Playwright in Residence, Circle Repertory Company. Recipient: National Endowment for the Arts grant in playwriting (1974–75). Commission from **Earplay**; New York State CAPS grant, 1977.

Address: 449½ N. Sycamore, Los Angeles, CA 90036

Agent: Bret Adams, Ltd., 36 East 61st St, New York, NY 10021 (212) 752-7864

TITLE • AVAILABILITY • PRODUCTIONS

The Amazing Activity of Charlie Contrary and the Ninety-Eighth Street Gang: Dramatists Play Service, Inc., 440 Park Ave. South, New York, NY 10016, $2.50; Circle Repertory Company, NYC

In Connecticut: manuscript*; GeVa, Rochester, NY; Circle Repertory Company, NYC

Mrs. Murray's Farm: Dramatists Play Service, $2.50; Circle Repertory Company, NYC

Emily Tis Thee I Love: manuscript*

Here Wait: manuscript*; Cast Theatre, Los Angeles, CA

  *contact author

SYNOPSES

In Connecticut: A family breaking apart and refinding each other on moving day; a young moving man who studies philosophy and an older couple who lose the house to which they intended to retire; a series of lies found out; a comedy of crossed intentions resolving itself in everyone moving to a place they had not expected to go. Contemporary.

Setting: living room of a restored Early American Connecticut home, 1976. 3 males, 4 females.

Mrs. Murray's Farm: The Battle for Manhattan (1776) . . . what might have happened. Farce.

Setting: kitchen and dining room of Mrs. Murray's farm, eighteenth century New York. 4 males, 4 females.

The Amazing Activity of Charlie Contrare and the Ninety-Eighth Street Gang: A sixteen-year-old-boy breaks up into himself as he envisions life at thirty, sixty, and ninety. His mother breaks down.

Setting: kitchen of a New York apartment and an open playing area that is mutable. 5 males, 4 females.

L

LARRY LOONIN

Born in Brooklyn, NY on January 5, 1941. B.A.,
Brooklyn College, Philosophy, 1962. He has
directed over one hundred plays, fifty of them for
Off Broadway. He has also acted in plays and
movies. Theater critic for 4 different
newspapers.

Address: 800 East 17th St., Brooklyn, NY 11230
(212) 434-6558 or (212) 586-6300

TITLE • AVAILABILITY • PRODUCTIONS

Run to the Sea: manuscript*; Cafe Cino, NYC

Our First Gobi Fossils: manuscript*; Cafe A-Go-Go, NYC

Happenings: manuscript*; Martinique Theatre, NYC

What You Will: manuscript*; Charles St. Theatre, MA

Bourgeois Blues: manuscript*; Poly Arts Theatre, MA

Exhausting the Possibilities: manuscript*; Theater for the New City, NYC

Factory Ping Pong (with Peggy Ings): manuscript*; Charlestown Working Theater, MA

Business of Relations (with Peggy Ings): manuscript*; Charlestown Working Theater, MA

Incidents (with Yvonne Rainer): manuscript*; Cafe Cino, NYC

The Cenci Myth: manuscript*; Emerson College, MA

    *contact author

ERIC MEREDITH LORD

Born Chicago, IL on March 10, 1923. Studied
playwriting with the late Lajos Egri. Member
A.E.A., S.A.G., A.F.T.R.A., and the National
Playwright Company, Hollywood. Professional
actor since the days of radio soap operas in the
early forties. Appears in summer stock and such
television shows as **Mission Impossible** and
Hogan's Heroes. A one-time stockbroker; he
recently played the role of one in a McDonald's
Hamburger commercial. He lives alone in
Newport Beach, Calif. where he is working on a
screenplay. Recipient: Winner of First Prize in
the second annual John Gassner Memorial
Playwriting Awards (New England Theatre Conf.)

Address: 1560 Placentia Ave., F16, Newport
Beach, CA 92660 (714) 548-8783

Agent: Lee Goren, Talent Enterprises, 1607 El Centro, Hollywood, CA 90028 (213) 462-0913

TITLE • AVAILABILITY • PRODUCTIONS

The Wayward Angel: Exposition Press, 50 Jericho Tpk., New York, NY 11753, $4.00; Ojai
Community Center, CA

Eric Meredith Lord (cont'd)

Rigamarole: manuscript*; Santa Ana City Hall Annex, CA

The Regent & the Prune: manuscript*

One Down: manuscript*

Lions Four, Christian's Nothing: manuscript*

Wisdom of the Elders: manuscript*

Courage and Rose: manuscript*

Many Happy Returns: manuscript*

    *contact author

SYNOPSIS

Many Happy Returns: An honest executive is tricked into recovering from a nervous breakdown in the beachfront home of a nurse who was once his lover. Three weird weekend guests, all outpatients of a nearby mental institution, bring chaos, wisdom and love as gifts as they see through the corporate trickery going on in our hero's absence. They conspire to help him because they know he is still loved by the nurse who has befriended them. The villain is caught and terrified by the inmates. The hero returns with the proof of his innocence and the lovers are happily re-united, ready to brace themselves for another weekend in their "satellite Cuckoo's Nest."

A comedy in three acts. One interior set. 4 males, 2 females.

ROBERT LORD

Born in Rotorua, New Zealand in 1945. B.A. in Political Science and English Literature. Tried countless jobs: insurance clerk, journalist, oil rigger, cosmetic salesman, teaching, writing short stories. He worked in New Zealand theater: writing, stage management, directing, publicity, and acting. Attended the first two Australian Playwrights Conferences. He likes the United States so much that he is now a permanent resident. He has recently written **Pictures,** which has just been filmed in New Zealand. Recipient: Katherine Mansfield Young Writers Award; four grants from the Queen Elizabeth II Arts Council of New Zealand.

Address: 250 West 85th Street, #14J, New York, NY 10024

Agent: Gilbert Parker, c/o William Morris, 1350 Avenue of the Americas, New York, NY 10019 (212) 586-5100

TITLE • AVAILABILITY • PRODUCTIONS

It Isn't Cricket: Act Magazine, P.O. Box 9441, Wellington, New Zealand*; Downstage Theatre, Wellington, New Zealand, Australian National Playwrights Conference

Balance of Payments: manuscript*; Unity Theatre; Wellington Downstage Theatre

Friendship Centre: manuscript*; Pegasus Players, Christchurch, New Zealand

Meeting Place: Act Magazine*; Downstage Theatre; Phoenix Theatre, NYC

Nativity: manuscript*; Theatre Co-op, Auckland, New Zealand

Heroes & Butterflies: manuscript*; Mercury Theatre, Auckland; Downstage Theatre, New Zealand

Well Hung: manuscript*; Downstage Theatre; Nimrod Theatre, Sydney; Trinity Square Repertory Company, Providence, RI

L

Robert Lord (cont'd)

Dead and Never Called Me Mother: manuscript*; O'Neill Theater Center's National Playwrights Conference, CT

Glitter and Spit: manuscript*

I'll Scream If I Want To: manuscript*; Provincetown, MA

High as a Kite: manuscript*; Downstage Theatre, Wellington, New Zealand

Cop Shop: manuscript*; Toronto Arts Productions, Canada

A Family Portrait: manuscript*

   *contact agent

SYNOPSIS

Well Hung: A farce set in a police station of a small country town. The two officers who maintain the station find their lives disordered by the arrival of a senior detective to solve a murder case. During the investigation a great deal is revealed about the occupants of the station but very little about the case at hand. One policeman is something of a stud and has been having an affair with the other's wife. An elderly woman who is either an abortionist or a used car dealer confuses the situation, as does the local idiot who may or may not have done the murder. The situation becomes very confused and numerous people get shut in numerous cupboards and such. Seduction, accusation, infidelity feature prominently. At the end all is revealed (except who did the murder) with disastrous results and a murder and a suicide follow, changing the tone of the play somewhat abruptly. A neat if not happy ending is provided by the visiting detective.

Full length. Setting: single set, the main office of the station. 5 males, 2 females.

TOBI LOUIS

Educated at University of Wisconsin, New York University, A.B., M.A.; American Academy of Dramatic Art; Martha Graham School; Katherine Dunham School of Dance; Herbert Berghof; Lee Strasberg; Sharon Thie; Aaron Frankel. She has written a book of poems, **Realizations,** and is currently working on **Private Thoughts of Public Women** (non-fiction). She has been an Editorial Consultant for play and television productions. Her TV and film credits include: **Cry of a Summer Night, Portrait of a Woman, Roadside Cafe,** and **Love in 4 Flats** as well as many commercials for television. She is a member of the Dramatists Guild, Actors Equity, AFTRA, Writers Guild East and CBS-TV Writer's Workshop. CAPS Panel on Playwriting, 1978, Columbia Films Professional Writers' Workshop, 1979. Recipient of the John Golden Fellowship for Playwriting; Private grant for works in progress.

Address: 269 West 72nd St., New York, NY 10023

Personal Manager: Joseph Burstin, 16 Garfield St., Blauvelt, NY 10913 (914) 359-2087

TITLE • AVAILABILITY • PRODUCTIONS

Thicker Than Water: manuscript*; New Dramatists, NYC

Fly from the Wrath: manuscript*; New Dramatists, NYC; The Actors Company, NYC

When Love Is Done: manuscript*

Autumn's Laughter: manuscript*

Time Is a Thief: manuscript*; O'Neill Theater Center's National Playwrights Conference, CT; New Dramatists, NYC

Cry of a Summer Night: manuscript*; Actor's Playhouse, NYC; CBS-TV Writer's Workshop

Tobi Louis (cont'd)

Sounds of Laughter: manuscript*; Actor's Playhouse, NYC

Fantasy: manuscript*; O'Neill Theater Center's National Playwrights Conference, CT; The Play Box, NYC

The Witty and the Dumb: manuscript*; The Small Place, NYC

Tears Are for a Very Young Man: manuscript*

Sin and Sorcery: manuscript*

The Insides of Orchid Price: manuscript*; Hunter College Playhouse, NYC

Solitude, Frenzy and the Revolution: manuscript*; N.Y. Cultural Center, NYC; Manhattan Theatre Club, NYC

Take a Chance: manuscript*

Persons, Places 'n Rings: manuscript*

Sing To Me of Far Away Places: manuscript*

   *contact author or agent

SYNOPSES

Solitude, Frenzy and the Revolution: An unusual tale of justice which opens with a macabre encounter at a bus stop. A play with satiric overtones that uses language in a rhythmic, new way.

Full length. Setting: open set. 4 males, 1 female.

The Insides of Orchid Price: Orchid Price, a doctor's son, wealthy and well-educated, is lost — alienated from his self — and desperately trying to find his way through to tomorrow. He cannot understand his father; he cannot enjoy or handle sex; he is afraid to trust his own judgment and feelings. He does not understand his own rebellion, but must rebel. His black alter ego, Goliath Goforth, the son of poor but hard-working parents, is in opposite straits. He is full of self-knowledge, acceptance, and a positive attitude toward life and his place in it. Through his guidance and concern (in the guise of a philanthropic roommate), Orchid is helped along the road to maturity and self-knowledge. " . . . It is an excellent play and an auspicious first choice for the Hunter College Playwrights season" — **Ariel**

Full length. Setting: open set. 6 males, 2 females.

Take a Chance: A musical comedy that walks the thin line between reality and fantasy. It explores the problems of love and communication in the lifestyle of the singles set and their place in an ever-increasing technological society.

Full length. Setting: open set. 6 males, 2 females.

CHARLES LUDLAM

Born in Floral Park, NY on April 12, 1943. Received drama scholarship to Hofstra University. B.A. in Dramatic Literature, 1965. Writer, director and actor. Founder of The Ridiculous Theatrical Company. Appeared in Mark Rappaport's film, **The Imposters** and is now working on his film, **The Sorrows of Dolores.** Has conducted many Teaching Workshops. Recipient: Obie Award to Charles Ludlam and The Ridiculous Theatrical Company; Second Prize for **Bluebeard** at International Avant Garde Theater Festival; Obie Award for performances in **Corn** and **Camille;** Special Obie Award for **Professor Bedlam's Educational Punch & Judy Show;** Obie Award for design, **Der Ring Gott Farblonjet;** Guggenheim Fellowship; Commission from the NY State Council on the Arts; Rockefeller Bros. Grant. Theater panelist, N.Y. State Council on the Arts, two years.

Address: 55 Morton St., New York, NY 10014

L/M

Charles Ludlam (cont'd)
TITLE • AVAILABILITY • PRODUCTIONS

Big Hotel: manuscript*; Gate Theater, NYC

Conquest of the Universe/When Queens Collide: manuscript*; Gate Theater, NYC

Turds In Hell (with Bill Vehr): **Drama Review,** 51 West 4th St., New York, NY 10012; Gate Theater, NYC; The Masque Theater, NYC

The Grand Tarot: manuscript*; Millenium Film Workshop, NYC

Bluebeard: Best Plays of Off Broadway, 1970, Bobbs Merrill, 4 W. 58th St., New York, NY 10019; La Mama E.T.C., NYC; The Trocadero at Christopher's End, NYC

Eunuchs of the Forbidden City: Scripts, New York Shakespeare Festival, 425 Lafayette St., New York, NY 10003; Berlin and World Tour; Theater For The New City, NYC

Corn: manuscript*; Thirteenth St. Theater, NYC

Camille (adaptation): manuscript*; Thirteenth St. Theater, NYC

Hot Ice: Drama Review, T-62; Evergreen Theater, NYC

Stage Blood: manuscript*; Evergreen Theater, NYC

Professor Bedlam's Educational Punch & Judy Show: manuscript*; Evergreen Theater, NYC

Caprice: manuscript*; The Performing Garage, NYC; Provincetown Playhouse, NYC

Jack & The Beanstalk: manuscript*; Brooklyn Academy, NY; Albany, NY

The Adventures of Karagoz: manuscript*; Festival Mondial de Theatre, Nancy, France

Der Ring Gott Farblonjet: manuscript*; Truck and Warehouse Theater, NYC

The Enchanted Pig: manuscript*; Ridiculous Theatrical Co., NYC

The Ventriloquist's Wife: manuscript*; Cabaret, NYC

A Christmas Carol (adaptation): manuscript*; Ridiculous Theatrical Co., NYC

Utopia Incorporated: manuscript*

Reverse Psychology: manuscript*; Ridiculous Theatrical Co., NYC

Love's Tangled Web: manuscript*; Ridiculous Theatrical Co., NYC

   *contact Ridiculous Theatrical Co., 1 Sheridan Square, New York, NY 10014

SYNOPSIS

Hot Ice: The saga of an underground war between the Cryogenic Society (an organization which believes in freezing the dead in the hope of later resuscitation) and the Euthanasia Police (who are devoted to the ideal of the "good death") and is cast in the mold of the gangster epic. This play proved to be something of an expose when it was first performed. On closing night, the man who invented the cryogenic concept voluntarily came up on the stage after the play. Since the play used actors planted in the audience as a device, the audience thought he was part of the play.

Full length. Setting: Euthanasia Police Headquarters, Office of the Cryogenic Foundation. 7 males, 7 females, 1 narrator.

JEROME McDONOUGH

Born in Sequin, TX, November 26, 1946. Educated at West Texas State University, B.S. and M.A. Graduate intensification, Creative and Theatre Writing. Teacher of Theatre, English, Creative Writing. Director, performer. Teacher, Creative Writing, Amarillo College. Published in **Dramatists Guild Quarterly, Writer's Digest, Prolog.** Recipient: Winner, Texas Educational Theatre Association Playwriting Contest, 1975. International Thespian Society, List of most produced short plays, 1980.

Address: 6106 Dartmouth, Amarillo, TX 79109
  (806) 353-5871

Agent: Jay Garon, 415 Central Park West,
  New York, NY 10025 (212) 866-3654

TITLE • AVAILABILITY • PRODUCTIONS

The Betrothed: Samuel French, 25 W. 45th St., New York, NY 10036, $1.25; Colleges, high
  schools, United States and Canada

Filiation: I.E. Clark, Inc., Box 246, Schulenburg, TX 78956, $1.25; High schools, college labs

Fables: I.E. Clark, Inc., $1.25; West Texas State Univ., colleges, high schools

The Old Oak Encounter: I.E. Clark, $1.50; College labs

Transceiver: Samuel French, $1.25; High schools

A Short Stretch at the Galluses: Eldridge Publishing Co., Franklin, OH 45005, $1.00;
  High schools, community theaters

Asylum: I.E. Clark, Inc., $1.25; Poet's Repertory Theater, Texas Christian U., high schools and
  college labs

Dirge: Baker's Plays, Inc., 100 Chauncey St., Boston, MA 02111, 85¢; High schools

The Noble's Reward: Eldridge Publishing Co., $1.00; High schools

A Stretch at the Galluses (full-length musical western farce): manuscript*; Amarillo Little
  Theatre, Perryton Players

Requiem: I.E. Clark, $1.25; High schools and colleges

Stages: I.E. Clark, $1.25; High schools and colleges

Eden: I.E. Clark, $1.75; High schools and colleges

O, Little Town: I.E. Clark, $1.25; High schools and junior highs

It's Sad, So Sad When an Elf Goes Bad: I.E. Clark, $1.25; High schools, junior highs,
  community theaters

The Nearest Star: I.E. Clark, $1.25

  *contact author

SYNOPSES

Asylum: A highly theatrical play in several connected scenes dealing with the premise that anyone should be allowed to live the way he sees fit without being constantly in danger of being "healed" by some opposing faction. An ensemble play, **Asylum** is the essence of simple theatre with the emphasis placed on innovative performance and direction. Approximately 40 minutes.

Open space. A wheelchair. An ensemble numbering twelve or more performers.

Requiem: The brief moments between the wars begin **Requiem** but then the draft notices are posted again and the tragic cycle recommences. But a Mother has had enough of the death of her children. She refuses to surrender her son and daughter. "The war machine cranks up and they want my oil again," she soliloquizes. Her battle with the Sergeant and her ultimate sacrifice are the soul of the play.

One act. Setting: bare stage. Mixed ensemble of 12 or more.

M

Jerome McDonough (cont'd)

Stages: A play about plays, specifically about a play that is not working. As the power struggle between the author and the director and his staff rages, the actors begin to wonder who, if anyone, is in charge. When all but three actors are fired, the question becomes even more pointed. When it is over, is it over?

One act. Setting: platform unit set. Mixed ensemble of 10 or more.

EUGENE McKINNEY

Born in Fort Worth, TX on October 2, 1922. M.A. and B.A. from Baylor University. For thirty years a teacher of playwriting. Since 1963, Playwright-in-residence, Trinity U. Since 1959, Professor of Playwriting at the Dallas Theater Center. Author of many TV shows produced on all three networks. Recipient: Play series established by Dallas Theater Center in his honor (Eugene McKinney New Play Reading Series). Winner of Brussel World Fair Film Festival for best short-run fiction film, (producer).

Address: 423 Fantasia, San Antonio, TX 78216
(512) 344-9582

TITLE • AVAILABILITY • PRODUCTIONS

The Answer Is Two: not available; Baylor Theater; U. of Corpus Christi

A Different Drummer: Samuel French, 25 W. 45th St., New York, NY 10036, $2.50; Baylor Theater; Omnibus (TV)

Of Time and the River: not available; Baylor Theater; Dallas Theater Center

The Ivory Tower, Two Flights Down: Baylor Press, Waco, TX 76703; Baylor Theater

The Cross-Eyed Bear: not available; Dallas Theater Center, TX

The People in the Glass Paperweight: Samuel French, $1.25; Directions, ABC-TV

When You're by Yourself, You're Alone: Samuel French, $1.25; Directions, ABC-TV; Alpha-Omega Players

The Family Game: manuscript*

*contact author

JOHN McLIAM

Born in Hayter, Alberta, Canada on January 24, 1918. B.A. in English from St. Mary's College, Moraga, CA; Graduate studies in English, U. of CA in Berkeley. As an actor, Mr. McLiam has been in six Broadway shows and in many major motion pictures. On television, he has appeared on most major series and many network specials.

Address: 5003 Alhama Dr., Woodland Hills, CA 91363 (213) 347-0384

John McLiam (cont'd)

TITLE • AVAILABILITY • PRODUCTIONS

Sin of Pat Muldoon: Dramatists Play Service, Inc., 440 Park Ave. South, New York, NY 10016, $2.50; Broadway

Whizney Land: manuscript*; Theatre West, Los Angeles, CA

The Cock May Crow: manuscript*; Theatre West, CA

As on a Darkling Plain: manuscript*; Theatre West, CA

    *contact author

SYNOPSES

Whizney Land: A social, satirical, farce comedy on the dehumanization of carnival entertainers.
Setting: one set. 6 males, 5 females.

The Cock May Crow: A musical trial-drama based on the life of Robert Burns. Structured as a moral-political inquisition, Burns' songs and poems and life style are an organic part of evidence submitted by defense and prosecution.
Setting: one multi-set. 5 males, 5 females. Authentic folk music in public domain, 1-6 musicians.

As On A Darkling Plain: The plight of a trusting, honest man in a hypocritical, acquisitive society.
Setting: one set. 5 males, 5 females.

TERRENCE McNALLY

Born in St. Petersburg, FL on November 3, 1939. Educated at Columbia University, B.A., 1960. Recipient: Stanley Award; Guggenheim Fellowships (twice); Obie Award, **Bad Habits;** Achievement in Playwriting Citation, American Academy of Arts and Letters and The National Institute of Arts and Letters for **The Ritz;** Hull-Warriner Award.

Address: 218 West 10th St., New York, NY 10014

Agent: Rosenstone/Wender, 3 East 48th St, New York, NY 10017 (212) 832-8330

TITLE • AVAILABILITY • PRODUCTIONS

The Roller Coaster: not available; Columbia Review, 1960

And Things That Go Bump In The Night: Dramatists Play Service, 440 Park Avenue South, New York, NY 10016, $2.50; Guthrie Theatre, MN; Broadway

The Lady of the Camellias: not available; Winter Garden, NYC

Next: Dramatists Play Service, $2.50; Off Broadway

Tour: with **Next;** Cafe au Go-Go, NYC

Botticelli: with **Next;** WNET, NYC

Sweet Eros: Dramatists Play Service, $2.50; Gramercy Arts, NYC

Cuba Si!: Dramatists Play Service, $2.50; Theatre de Lys, NYC

Witness: with **Sweet Eros;** Gramercy Arts, NYC

Noon: Samuel French, 25 West 45th St., New York, NY 10036, $2.50; Broadway

Terrence McNally (cont'd)

Last Gasps: with **Cuba Si!;** WNET, NYC

Bringing It All Back Home: with **Cuba Si!;** New Haven, CT

Bad Habits: Dramatists Play Service, $2.50; Astor Place Theatre, NYC; Broadway

Where Has Tommy Flowers Gone?: Dramatists Play Service, $2.50; Yale Repertory, CT;
Off Broadway

Let It Bleed: not available; Off Off Broadway

The Ritz (formerly **The Tubs):** Samuel French, $2.50; Yale Repertory, CT; Broadway

Whiskey: Dramatists Play Service, $2.50; St. Clements Theatre, NYC

SYNOPSES

Where Has Tommy Flowers Gone?: The picaresque adventures of a self-styled "street" person
and some of the people he meets.

Full length. Setting: unit set. 3 males, 3 females, 1 dog.

Bad Habits: A comedy about human perfectibility. Two inter-related plays — one acts.

6 males, 2 females.

The Ritz: A farce about sexual identity set in a male bath house.

Full length. Setting: one unit set. 12 males, 2 females.

JANET McREYNOLDS

Born in Bluffton, AR on July 19, 1933. Ph.D. in
English, minor in Theater at the University of
Minnesota. Author of novel, **I Have a Great
Desire** (Houghton Mifflin, 1961). Screenplay,
Commencement, Sunshadow Films, 1979. Reci-
pient: NEA Grant for Creative Writing, 1978.

Address: 2990 18th St., Boulder, CO 80302
(303) 443-8566

TITLE • AVAILABILITY • PRODUCTIONS

Hey, Rube: manuscript*; Mark Taper Forum Lab, Los Angeles, CA; Interart Theatre, NYC

The Man Who Knew John Dillinger: manuscript*; the Changing Scene, Denver, CO

"Fight Like Hell 'Til You Get To Heaven: Cottonwood Press, P.O. Drawer 112, Crawford, NB
69339, $3.00

Motherright: manuscript*

*contact author

SYNOPSES

Hey, Rube: This play was suggested by a crime which occurred in the '60s. A young girl was tor-
tured over a period of months and finally murdered by a woman with whom she was boarded and
the woman's two daughters. The play starts with a courtroom scene and the story is told in
flashbacks. The focal point of the play is the close identity the woman feels with her victim. She
keeps insisting, "I am the one who was murdered." A carnival atmosphere adds a bizarre element.

Full length. Setting: four playing areas. 4 males, 10 females.

Janet McReynolds (cont'd)

The Man Who Knew John Dillinger: Jimmy MacIntosh is a man in his seventies, a victim of amnesia. He believes that he is the last surviving member of the Dillinger gang and has been looking for "Johnny" the past forty years. He falls into the clutches of a practical nurse, Rosie Freeman, who first befriends him then betrays him to the police in a replay of "the woman in red." Rosie's patient, Esther and two children from upstairs contribute their own poignant stories to the theme of lost identities.

Full length. Setting: two playing areas. 1 male, 2 female, 2 children.

Fight Like Hell 'Til You Get To Heaven: The story of Mother Jones, the militant labor agitator. The play uses the occasion of Mother Jones's 100th birthday party to recapitulate her tumultuous career. It is panoramic in scope, using incidents from major labor conflicts from the 1880's through the 1920's.

Full length. Setting: minimal set; scrim for slide projections. 14 males, 8 females, 8 children.

EDWARD H. MABLEY

Born in Binghamton, NY. Author of **Dramatic Construction,** a technical analyses of twenty-four famous plays (Chilton Press); **The Motor Balloon "America",** (Stephen Green Press); also wrote forty-five radio and television plays for CBS and NBC. Recipient: Two National Theatre Conference Fellowships.

Address: 15 West 72nd St., #19-P, New York, NY 10023 (212) 787-1047

Agent: Brandt & Brandt, Dramatic Dept., 1501 Broadway, New York, NY 10036 (212) 840-5760

TITLE • AVAILABILITY • PRODUCTIONS

Temper the Wind (with Leonard Mins); not available; Syracuse University, NY; Broadway

Glad Tidings: manuscript, Samuel French, 25 W. 45th St., New York, NY 10036; American Theatre, St. Louis, MO; Broadway

Red Sky at Morning (with Joanna Roos): manuscript*; Olney Theatre, MD

June Dawn (with Dorothy Evans); Samuel French, $2.50; Many productions

Spring Journey (with Joanna Roos): Samuel French, $2.50; Many productions

Discrimination for Everybody: Samuel French, $1.25; Various productions

The Mermaid in Lock No. 7 (Elie Siegmeister, composer): Henmar Press, C.F. Peters, 373 Park Ave. South, New York, NY 10016; Point State Park, PA; Flemish Chamber Opera, Belgium

The Plough and the Stars (Elie Siegmeister, composer): Carl Fisher, Inc., 56 Cooper Square, New York, NY 10003; Baton Rouge, LA; Bordeaux, France

Bon Voyage (Vera Brodsky Lawrence, composer): manuscript*; York Players, NYC

Night of the Moonspell (Elie Siegmeister, composer): Carl Fisher, Inc.; Shreveport, LA

She Still Stoops to Conquer: manuscript*

The Feathered Serpent: manuscript*

Piggy Bank Rag (music by Joplin, Lamb, Woods, Matthews): manuscript*

Doubleplay: manuscript*

    *contact author

SYNOPSES

Bon Voyage: Musical adaptation of **Le Voyage de Monsieur Perrichon.** Two piano score from melodies by Offenbach.

Full length. Setting: unit set, four locations. 4 males, 2 females, 5 or more extras.

M

Edward H. Mabley (cont'd)

The Feathered Serpent: Murder mystery set amid the ruins of an ancient Mayan city in a Central American jungle.

Full length. Setting: one exterior set. 6 males, 4 females.

Doubleplay: About the rehearsal of a play—the problems and personalities of the actors can be quite unlike those of the characters they are portraying.

Full length. Setting: bare stage. 7 males, 4 females.

E. MACER-STORY

Born in Minneapolis, MN on January 20, 1945. B.S., Speech/Theater, Northwestern University, 1965. M.F.A., Columbia University, Playwriting, 1968. Professional psychic with private practice and author of numerous articles on U.F.O. research and the para-normal. **Congratulations: The UFO Reality,** Crescent Press, 1978; **Angels of Time: Astrological Magick,** Raven Press, 1981. Poems in various magazines and chapbooks. Recipient: Shubert Fellowship, Columbia, 1968.

Address: Old Chelsea Station, Box 662, New York, NY 10113 (212) 929-5032, office

TITLE • AVAILABILITY • PRODUCTIONS

The Little Old Hermit of the Northwest Woods: manuscript and tape*; Hamilton-Kirkland College

Handsel and Gretal Meet the Ghost of J. Edgar Hoover: manuscript and tape*; Fanuiel Hall, outdoors, Boston, MA

Fetching the Tree: manuscript and tape*; Polyarts, Boston, MA; Horticultural Hall, MA

Lady Video & The Ecosensor: manuscript and tape*; Boston Commonwealth Armory, MA; Funk Fest

New Day: manuscript and tape*; City of Boston, New Years Celebration, MA

Visiting Momma: manuscript*; Theosophical Society, Boston, MA

The Autobiography of Morgan Lefay: manuscript and tape*; Americana Hotel, NYC

Radish: manuscript and tape*; 18th Street Theater, NYC

Red Riding Hood's Revenge: manuscript and tape*; Inferno Disco, NYC

The Blues Deduction: manuscript*; Playwrights Platform, Boston, MA

Desiderata: manuscript*; Theater for the New City, NYC

Aphrodite/The Witch Play: manuscript*; Theater for the New City, NYC

The Observation Chamber: manuscript*; 18th Street Theater, NYC

*contact author

FRANKLYN MacGREGOR

Born in Atlanta, GA. Educated at Yale University and Oxford University (England). Novels written: **The Madagascar Corundum; The Bhatar Transfer; The Inestimable Education of Horace Oakley Anderson III** (play adaptation). Presently engaged in international business and cultural affairs.

Address: c/o E. Black, 40 Central Park South,
   Apt. 11-D, New York, NY 10019
   (212) 832-0534

TITLE • AVAILABILITY • PRODUCTIONS

The Big Alabama Wonder: manuscript*; DuPont Hour on NBC-TV; Town and Gown Theatre, Birmingham, AL

The Governor: manuscript*

The Friends of My Heart: manuscript*

The Inimitable Education of Horace Oakley Anderson III: manuscript*

The Monument: manuscript*; Courtyard Theatre, NYC

The Possessor: manuscript*

   *contact author

SYNOPSES

The Monument: The action takes place at Benedict and Peggy Arnold's home at West Point on September 25, 1780. It is the day of Arnold's defection and escape, and the capture of the British agent, Major Andre, who had known Peggy Arnold well in Philadelphia. By coincidence, General Washington and his staff arrive that morning for breakfast. Arnold asks Peggy to delay Washington, using every means at her command, so he can escape. She agrees. Washington arrives, unaware of Arnold's defection and flight, only to find out later in the day, when his relationship with Peggy becomes confused and emotional.

Full length. Setting: living room of Arnold's home. 9 men, 2 women.

The Possessor: Based on the last three years of the life of Eugene O'Neill. Everyone in the play has real life antecedents, although different names are used. It is about a writer, Garrity, who has reached a stage in life where he is unable to write or function as a man and muses back over his life via flashbacks and other means, to try to discover the reasons for his malaise — principally his relationships with his children, his wives, his parents and brother.

Full length. One set: living room/study of Garrity's home in Connecticut on the sea. 7 males, 7 females.

M

C. K. MACK

Born in New York City on November 20, 1941. Mount Holyoke College, B.A. Studied with Uta Hagen at the HB Studio and graduate work at Columbia University. Guest lecturer, Wagner College; visiting playwright, Hampshire College, MA. Novel, **The Chameleon Variant** with David Ehrenfeld (Dial Press, 1980). Film strips and TV pilot for Joshua Tree Productions. Recipient: 1976 Stanley Drama Award.

Address: 115 Central Park West, New York, NY 10023

TITLE • AVAILABILITY • PRODUCTIONS

Family House: not available; New Dramatists, NYC

Esther: manuscript*; New Dramatists, NYC; White Barn Theatre, Westport, CT

A Safe Place: manuscript*; New Dramatists, NYC: Women's Project, American Place Theatre, NYC

Survial Games: manuscript*; New Dramatists, NYC; Berkshire Theatre Festival, MA

   *contact author

SYNOPSES

Esther: A play about the legendary Jewish queen of Persia and the power game she learns to play in an alien political arena as she grapples with finding her true identity. Through cinematically designed scenes we watch her evolution.

Full length. Setting: no set. In the round. 5 males, 1 female.

A Safe Place: A psychological mystery play, dealing with a professor of anthropology who is studying tribal society in the Amazon, while back in New England, his daughters are falling under the influence of an evangelical cult leader.

Full length. Setting: one set, impressionistic, suggesting three environments and their merging. 2 males, 8 females.

Survival Games: A comedy about a changing relationship of a couple in a changing world in four scenes from the early sixties to the late nineties.

Full length. Setting: no set. 1 male, 1 female.

WENDY MacLAUGHLIN

Born March 23, 1931 in Kansas City, MO. Attended Bennett Junior College. Studied at the Neighborhood Playhouse, NYC and with Martha Graham, also the University of Missouri. For two years, she was a host on public television where she interviewed theater personalities and reviewed plays. She is married and has four children. Recipient: Hidden Talent Contest Winner, U. of Missouri; American College Theater Festival, Regional Winner, also National Alternate Winner; Semi-finalist and Finalist, Actors Theater of Lousiville.

Address: 5400 Sunset Drive, Kansas City, MO 64112 (816) 444-8267

TITLE • AVAILABILITY • PRODUCTIONS

Watch Out Little Boy or You'll Fall In: manuscript*; University of Missouri

Chapel: manuscript*; Theater Workshop, Cable TV, Kansas City, MO

Crown of Thorn: manuscript*; University of Missouri; University of Iowa

Watermelon Boats: three-quarter-inch cassette*; Actors Theater of Louisville, KY; KCPT, Kansas City, MO

Secret: manuscript*; Missouri Association of Playwrights

Catch a Crab: manuscript*; Commissioned by Actors Theater of Louisville, KY

*contact author

SYNOPSES

Crown of Thorn: This play examines the life of the priest/scientist, Pierre Teilhard deChardin, who has been called the most visionary thinker of the twentieth century. Convinced that all life evolved from the same speck of dust and continuous evolution was leading toward the unity of mankind, he found himself in direct conflict with Catholic doctrine of the time. He was forbidden to publish and given the choice of remaining silent or leaving the church. His final decision is not easily understood but springs from the soul search of a total human being . . . a man who lived life fully . . . wrestling with temptations, relationships, ego and ultimately his own faith. The drama is cosmic in scope incorporating music, dance, poetry and visuals.

Full length. Setting: open and free. Uses a slide projector to open each scene. 4 males, 2 females, chorus optional size.

Watermelon Boats: Kitty and Kate are two friends who meet three times at a lake and float boats made from watermelons. They discuss sex, their hopes, dreams, fears and secrets . . . finally arriving at a big truth of life and friendship.

A 10-minute play or a 22-minute TV drama. Setting: two ladders and empty stage. 2 females who age from 10 to 20.

Secret: The story concerns a woman dissident writer who has been imprisoned in a Soviet insane asylum for eight years because of her religious and political views. The action takes place in the hours before she is to be exiled for writing about the atrocities she suffered while incarcerated. Three generations of Russian women share the apartment: Lisa, the nine-year-old child willing to risk danger for her mother and the cause. Marina, the older mother-in-law, seeking safety and obscurity above all else. Anna, the writer, who discovers through a relationship with an attractive Soviet folk singer, the truth about herself and her motives. In the end, it is the innocent child who suffers for the weakness of her elders in not fighting for the truth and freedom before we are killed spiritually and physically.

Full length. Setting: an apartment in Russia today. 3 males, 3 females.

M

ROSS MacLEAN

Born in Detroit, MI on May 18, 1954. First Los Angeles playwright to be produced by La Mama Hollywood. Worked there as writer, actor, director and stage hand. Writer/director for drama therapy program with mentally and emotionally handicapped adults. Organized midnight theater program at La Mama and has worked in many capacities at small theaters in L.A. Playwright-in-Residence at Deja Vu Coffeehouse, first L.A. underground theater.

Address: c/o 1705 N. Kenmore Ave., Hollywood, CA 90027 (213) 653-3202; (213) 660-9862

TITLE • AVAILABILITY • PRODUCTIONS

Hero of the Jungle: manuscript*; La Mama Hollywood, CA

Story: manuscript*; La Mama Hollywood, CA

December Wedge: Dramatics Magazine, Vol. 50, #2, 3368 Central Parkway, Cincinnati, OH 45225, $2.00; Deja Vu Coffeehouse, L.A., CA

Nelson '76: manuscript*; Los Angeles Garden Theater Festival

Four Play: manuscript*; A.C.T. Workshop, San Francisco, CA

Multiple Fractures: manuscript*; Deja Vu Coffeehouse, L.A., CA

Food: Dramatics Magazine, Vol. 51, #3, $2.00; Deja Vu Coffeehouse, L.A., CA; New York Theatre Ensemble, NYC

An Experiment in Lust: manuscript*; Deja Vu Coffeehouse, L.A., CA; The Fourth E, NY

Sluts: manuscript*; Deja Vu Coffeehouse, L.A., CA

   *contact author

SYNOPSES

Sluts: Hedonism flirts with authority to an unhealthy degree. A group of gay men, finding themselves hard pressed by the outside society, make efforts to prove they are normal human beings, deserving of a place in the world. Unfortunately, they succeed. Moving from the caste of outcasts to renegades, they are absorbed into the mainstream at the expense of their uniqueness, their moral liberty and their own individuality.

Full length. Setting: a public street. 6 males, 2 females.

Food: Joe and his wife, Carol, are dinner guests at the home of Carol's brother Mack, and his wife Bonnie. Joe is unemployed. Mack had invited them over initially as a kindness to help his sister out, but this is the third week the two have been showing up for free meals and Carol's husband shows no signs of supporting himself. Mack is suffering financially from this sponging and the quality of the meals has turned wretchedly poor. The play is a sharp argument on dependence, responsibility and the decline in the quality of living.

One act. Setting: a dinner table. 2 males, 2 females.

M

DAVID MAMET

B.A. English Literature, Goddard College, VT, 1969. Special Lecturer, Drama, Marlboro College, VT. Artist-in-Residence, Drama, Goddard College. Instructor, Acting, Pontiac, IL. Special Lecturer, Drama, U. of Chicago, IL. Director, St. Nicholas Theater Company, Chicago, IL. Playwright-in-Residence and Associate Artistic Director, The Goodman Theatre, 1978–. Council Member, The Dramatists Guild, 1979–. Recipient: Joseph Jefferson Award, 1973–74; Children's Theatre Grant, NY State Council on the Arts, 1976; New York Critics Circle Award, 1977; **Village Voice** Obie, Best New Plays, 1976; John Gassner Award, 1979.

Agent: Rosenstone/Wender, 3 East 48th St., New York, NY 10017 (212) 832-8330

TITLE • AVAILABILITY • PRODUCTIONS

The Duck Variations: Samuel French, 25 West 45th St., New York, NY 10036, $2.50; Body Politic Theater, Chicago, IL; St. Clement's, NYC

Sexual Perversity in Chicago: with **The Duck Variations;** Organic Theater Company, Chicago, IL; St. Clement's, NYC

Squirrels: manuscript*; St. Nicholas Theater Company, Chicago, IL

The Poet and the Rent: Samuel French, $2.00; St. Nicholas Theater Company, Chicago, IL

Reunion: Grove Press, 196 West Houston St., New York, NY 10014, $2.95; St. Nicholas Theater Company, Chicago, IL

Dark Pony: with **Reunion;** Yale Repertory, CT

American Buffalo: Samuel French, $2.50; Goodman Theatre, Chicago, IL; St. Nicholas Theater Company, Chicago, IL

A Life in the Theatre: Samuel French, $2.50; Goodman Theatre, Chicago, IL; Off Broadway

†**The Water Engine:** Grove Press, $3.95; St. Nicholas Theater, Chicago, IL; New York Shakespeare Festival, NYC

Mr. Happiness: with **The Water Engine;** Broadway

†**The Woods:** Samuel French, $2.50; St. Nicholas Theater, Chicago, IL; New York Shakespeare Festival, NYC

Revenge of the Space Pandas: Dramatic Publishing Co., 4150 N. Milwaukee Ave., Chicago, IL 60641, $2.00; St. Clements, NYC; Circle Repertory Co., NYC

Sanctity of Marriage: not available; Circle Repertory, NYC

Lone Canoe: manuscript*; Goodman Theatre, Chicago, IL

Lake Boat: manuscript*; Harold Clurman Theater, NYC

The Sermon (one act): manuscript*; Ensemble Studio Theatre, NYC
    *contact agent
    †Lincoln Center Theatre on Film & Tape

SYNOPSES

Sexual Perversity in Chicago: Nine weeks in the life and loves of Bernard Litko and his protege, Danny Shapiro; Deborah Soloman, Dan's new inamorata; and Jane Weber, Deborah's roommate. "The human organism perceives the passage of time because of its limited understanding of the essential immortality of the germ plasm. We are restricted in our understanding because we produce bisexually and the individual organism is not complete unto itself. This is why we refer to sexual experimentation as 'making time.' "

31 short scenes; 1 hour, 20 minutes. Minimal set. 2 young men, 2 young women.

American Buffalo: Donny Dubrow runs a junkshop in Chicago. His junkshop is a cover for his

M

David Mamet (cont'd)

operations as a small-time fence. Donny and Bob plan the robbery of a valuable coin collection. Their plans and their relationship are altered by the play's third character, Teacher, a petty thief and gambler. "Mine eyes have seen the glory of the coming of the Lord. He is peeling down the alley in a Black and Yellow Ford."

Full length. Setting: junkshop, 3 males: 1 young, two older.

JOE MANCHESTER

Born in New London, CT on March 17, 1932. Educated at Carnegie Tech (playwriting major) and New York Law School. He has written TV and screenplays in addition to plays. Frequent lecturer in high schools and colleges on the subject of theater. Produced the Broadway play, **The Deadly Game** by Friedrich Duerrenmatt, which was chosen as one of the ten best plays of 1959–60 by Louis Kronenberger.

Address: P.O. Box 242, Waterford, CT 06385

Agent: Barry Lee Cohen, 450 Park Avenue, New York, NY 10022 (212) 758-4540

TITLE • AVAILABILITY • PRODUCTIONS

Run, Thief, Run!: Dramatists Play Service, 440 Park Avenue South, New York, NY 10016, $1.00; Numerous productions

Balloon Shot: Dramatists Play Service, $1.25; Numerous productions

The Secret Life of Walter Mitty (musical): Samuel French, 25 West 45th St., New York, NY 10036, $2.50; Off Broadway; Equity Library Theatre, NYC

Exept for Susie Finkel: Samuel French, $2.50; Cleveland Play House, OH; Playhouse-on-the-Mall

SYNOPSES

The Secret Life of Walter Mitty: Upon reaching his fortieth birthday, Walter Mitty, the James Thurber character whose name has become a household word, reflects on his rather drab, ordinary life. Defeated in his quest for wealth and glory by family responsibilities, a mortgage, a routine job and his own propensity for dreaming rather than doing, Walter creates elaborate fantasies in which he, of course, is always the hero.

Full length. 11 males, 13 females and as many more extras as desired

Except for Susie Finkel: Jonas Fox, swinging bachelor, is enjoying a real life that's better than most people's fantasy life when, one day Shoshana Gluber enters. Shoshana Gluber?!?! Shy, awkward, introverted and plain—hardly a candidate for the centerfold of Playboy—this stranger has come from the Bronx to his apartment in Manhattan to marry Jonas!

Full length. Setting: interior. 3 males, 2 females.

WILLARD MANUS

Born in New York City on September 28, 1930. B.A., Adelphi College. He has published four novels under psuedonyms, two under his own name, **The Fixers** and **Mott the Hoople** and his newest, **The Boys of 'Nam.** Written for **The Nation, Holiday, Venture** etc. Was foreign correspondent for **Financial Post** (Canada) and many other papers. Presently writing for TV, **The Secrets of Midland Heights,** Lorimar Productions.

Address: 248 Lasky Drive, Beverly Hills, CA 90212 (213) 556-1975

Agent: Ms. Mary Alice Kier, STE Representation, Inc., 211 S. Beverly Drive, Beverly Hills, CA 90212 (213) 550-3982

TITLE • AVAILABILITY • PRODUCTIONS

Junk Food: manuscript*; Open Stage Theatre, London; Many state theaters in Germany and Austria

The Bleachers: manuscript*; Magic Lion Theatre, Berkeley, CA; New York Shakespeare Festival, NYC

Man in the Sun: manuscript*

Pork Chops (adaptation): manuscript*

The Yard: manuscript*

The Deepest Hunger (adaptation): manuscript*; Commissioned, Actors Theatre of Louisville, KY

SYNOPSES

The Bleachers: A study of the human community that once frequented the bleacher seats of the old Polo Grounds in New York City. The play follows these rabid baseball fans through a ballgame between the New York Giants and the Brooklyn Dodgers in the mid '50s. As the bleacherites scream and cheer and curse and joke their way through the game, we come to learn who they are and what their dreams and hopes and agonies are made of. The play in the end is a comic requiem for a way of life destroyed by the wrecker's ball.

Long one act. Setting: the bleachers seats. 9 males, 2 females.

The Yard: The Yard is a cross-section of the poor man's social and athletic club known as a city school yard. Here, every Sunday morning, come the neighborhood folk — white, black, latin — to play ball, sun themselves, gossip, dance, drink beer and to continue some of the battles and conflicts that make modern urban life the jangling, funny, violent, heady adventure that it is.

Full length. Setting: corner of a big city school yard. 8 males, 2 females.

The Deepest Hunger: This is the study of a young brother and sister who have been sent to live on a poor dirt farm in Oklahoma as foster children, even though their natural parents are still alive. But the time is 1941, the mother works in a war plant, the father is in prison and so the children must struggle alone to find a place for themselves in a strange and often hostile world they never made.

Long one act. Setting: backyard of the dirt farm. 1 man, 1 boy, 2 women, 2 girls.

M

ROBERT WESLEY MARTIN

Born in Salem, NH on June 8, 1927. B.A., Boston
University. Studied at Reed College; Indiana
University; New School for Social Reseach;
Mildred I. Reed Writer's Colony. Taught school
for ten years including Master's Degree Program
for Science Teachers at Wesleyan University.
Free lance writer and editor. Has had approx-
imately two-hundred articles published in
Science and Math Weekly. Associate member of
the Dramatists Guild; the Authors League of
America. Elected member of National Associa-
tion of Science Writers, Inc.

Address: 148 10th Ave., 4C, New York, NY 10011
(212) 243-6941

TITLE • AVAILABILITY • PRODUCTIONS

Mildred: manuscript*; Image Theatre; The Dove Company

Peter Sent Me: manuscript*; University of the Streets; Cubiculo Theatre, NYC

Cornelius, the Last: manuscript*

There Was a Door: manuscript*; Image Theatre; Hudson Guild Theatre, NYC (reading)

Pelican Revisited: manuscript*; Omni Theatre Club; Augustine Films

Apricot Cranberry Mince-Meat Peach Pie: manuscript*; Hudson Guild Theatre, NYC (reading)

Spermatocidalmania: manuscript*

The Four Fs: manuscript*

The Locket: manuscript*

Bolo: manuscript*

Jack's World: manuscript*

Man Who Tried to Hate: manuscript*

Shadows: manuscript*

Slow Express: manuscript*

Nothing is Forever: manuscript*

To Grow a Rose: manuscript*

Twisting Slowly in the Wind: manuscript*

   *contact author

SYNOPSES

Spermatocidalmania: After ten years of marriage and five children, feminist, liberated Rachel
decides that her oboist/teacher/hen-pecked husband, Lance, should get a vasectomy. When
Lance balks, Rachel delivers her ultimatum: "Get it, or else . . . " Lance becomes impotent;
Rachel, feeling guilty, undergoes Primal Scream Therapy with an unorthodox female psychiatrist
who tries to seduce Lance. Rachel "finds herself" through therapy and Lance "finds success"
with his oboe composition; but can they and will they understand each other?

Full Length. Setting: One multiple set showing livingroom; partial views of admitting office; doctor's office. 8 males, 3 females.

Cornelius, the Last: Cornelius, a thirty-two-year-old biochemist, returns from Italy after creating a
human fetus from chemicals found on earth. His mother, deeply steeped in Eastern Orthodoxy,
can't understand her son's rejection of God and of the religiosity she has taught him. On Easter
Eve, when Christ is to enter the home to purify it, Cornelius becomes torn by conflicts with his
family, friends, God, and himself. He wants to play God because he created life. Will Christ arise
and enter the house to praise Cornelius, or rid the house of evil?

Full length. Setting: one — showing livingroom and partial view of bedroom. 7 males, 4 females.

Robert Wesley Martin (cont'd)

Nothing Is Forever: A recovering alcoholic struggles with friends, family and his conscience as he tries to perceive the world as it is today, not what it was yesterday or will be tomorrow. He has a choice to make — a world without booze or back to the uncertain yesterdays. His acceptance of himself as he is gives him strength to cope.

Full length. Setting: symbolic. 6 males, 2 females.

SHARON STOCKARD MARTIN

Born in Nashville, TN on June 18, 1948. Educated at Howard University, Bennington College, B.A.; Southern University, M.A.; Yale School of Drama, M.F.A. Was a member of Ed Bullins' Writers' Workshop, Free Southern Theater Writers' Workshop, and Frank Silvera Playwright's Workshop, Theater and arts critic. Script Reader for Yale Repertory Theatre and N.E.A. Free lance writer. Recipient: Shubert Fellow, Yale School of Drama, 1974–75 and C.B.S. Foundation Prize in Playwriting, 1976; Kennedy Center, Black Playwright Award, 1979; Mary Roberts Rinehart Grant, 1980.

Address: 4533 Chantilly Drive, New Orleans, LA 70126 (504) 242-4020

TITLE • AVAILABILITY • PRODUCTIONS

Proper and Fine: Fanny Lou Hamer's Entourage: The Search, Scholastic Black Literature Series*; Free Southern Theatre

Edifying Further Elaborations on the Mentality of a Chore: manuscript*; Free Southern Theatre

The Ole Ball Game: A Song without Words or Music: manuscript*

The Undoing of the 3-Legged Man: manuscript*

Entertaining Innumerable Reflections on the Subject at Hand: manuscript*; Dashki Project Theatre, New Orleans, LA

To My Eldest and Only Brother: manuscript*

Canned Soul: manuscript*; Yale Cabaret, CT; Free Southern Theatre

Deep Heat: manuscript*; Yale University, CT; Davenport College

Baby Death, SOS and Other Anxiety Pieces for the Contemporary American Stage: manuscript**; Yale Cabaret, CT; Free Southern Theatre

The Moving Violation: Sea Urchins Press, **Anthology of Contemporary Black American Plays,** P.O. Box 9805, Oakland, CA 94613; Dashiki Project Theatre, LA

Bird Seed: manuscript*; Free Southern Theatre

Hair Products: manuscript*

*contact author

SYNOPSES

The Moving Violation: Jackson, stopped by policemen and subjected to complete humiliation, returns to his wife Dawson and her bizarre brothers, a compulsive eater, a street hustler, a pseudo-intellectual and a man in love. A strange ordinance, delivered through the mail, restricts them to the house. The six, driven by their own obsessions, struggle to understand the unorthodox logic that imprisons them, cope with their increasingly threatening environment and regain their freedom.

Full length. Setting: house interior and street outside. 8 males, 2 females.

M

Sharon Stockard Martin (cont'd)

Hair Products: Doris, Pepsi, Clarissa, Inez and eight-year-old Sholandra are difficult customers in an understaffed urban black beauty parlor. Oliver, the proprietor hires Bobbie to help. The seven clash over opposing standards of black beauty, but more fundamentally, the issue of deteriorating black male-female relations.

Full length. Setting: interior of a deteriorating beauty parlor. 4 males, 6 females.

JAMES PAUL MARVIN

Born in Lansing, MI on May 23, 1953. Attended Alma College, MI. Graduated with honors from the U. of Illinois in Champaign-Urbana, B.F.A. Also M.F.A. from Trinity U., San Antonio, TX. Currently an actor, teacher and playwright at the Dallas Theater Center. Recipient: Ruby Loyd Apsey Playwriting Contest at the U. of Alabama.

Address: 3515 Travis, #210, Dallas, TX 75204
 (214) 521-0368

TITLE • AVAILABILITY • PRODUCTIONS

Silver Whispers: manuscript*; Trinity University, TX

Point of Departure: manuscript*; TEACH, San Antonio, TX

Dr. Jekyll and Mr. Hyde: manuscript*; University of Alabama; Dallas Theater Center, TX

 *contact author

SYNOPSES

Silver Whispers: A poetic drama which uses four characters to show the development of two love affairs. The play uses realistic scenes as well as poetic monologues to trace the feelings of these four young people as we see them fall in love.

One act. 2 males, 2 females.

Point of Departure: Susan (a young high school student) is on her way to New York for an abortion. During her stay in the bus station, she comes in contact with a number of different characters. The basic conflict rests in each character as they search for the reasons that have brought them to this crossroad in their lives.

Full length. Setting: small bus station. 4 males, 5 females.

Dr. Jekyll and Mr. Hyde: Adaptation. "Marvin's adaptation retains much of the flavor of Stevenson, but abstracts various elements of the story and juxtaposes them in fresh ways. Moreover, the Jekyll-Hyde character himself is portrayed by two actors . . . the result is engrossing as an experiment in ritualistic and representational techniques seldom seen . . ." **Birmingham News.** Relying on interpretative movement, sounds of human voices and the inner feelings of the characters, the classic story is told in the form of a nightmare.

Full length. 5 males, 3 females.

MARK MEDOFF

Born in Mt. Carmel, IL on March 18, 1940. Grew up in Miami Beach, FL. Married, wife, Stephanie; children, Debra, Rachel and Jessica. B.A., University of Miami, 1962; M.A., Stanford University, 1966. Professor of English and Drama, Dramatist in Residence, and Chairman of the Drama Department, New Mexico State University, Las Cruces, NM. Experienced actor and director; dedicated horticulturist, racquetball and tennis player. Recipient: Obie Award for Distinguished Playwriting; Drama Desk Award; Outer Critics Circle; John Gassner Playwriting Award; Jefferson Award for Best Principal Actor, 1973–74 Chicago Season; Guggenheim Fellowship in Playwriting, 1974–75; Westhafer Award, 1973–1974; New Mexico State University (its highest award to a member of the faculty); Tony Award, 1980; Governor's Award for Excellence in the Arts; Drama Desk Award; Outer Critics Circle Award, 1979–80.

Address: c/o Drama Department, Box 3072, New Mexico State University, Las Cruces, NM 88003
(505) 646-4517

Agent: Gilbert Parker, William Morris Agency, 1350 Avenue of the Americas, New York, NY 10019
(212) 586-5100

TITLE • AVAILABILITY • PRODUCTIONS

The Odyssey of Jeremy Jack (a children's play; with Carlene Johnson): Dramatists Play Service, 440 Park Ave. South, New York, NY 10016, $2.50; Numerous productions

Four Short Plays including: **The Froegle Dictum, Doing a Good One for the Red Man, The War on Tatem, The Ultimate Grammar of Life:** Dramatists Play Service, $2.50; Numerous productions

When You Comin' Back, Red Ryder?: Dramatists Play Service, $2.50; Off Broadway

The Kramer: Dramatists Play Service, $2.50; also in **Playwrights for Tomorrow,** Vol. 13, University of Minn. Press, 2307 University Ave. SE, Minneapolis, MN 55414, $4.95 (paperback); ACT, San Francisco; Mark Taper Forum, Los Angeles, CA

†**The Wager:** Dramatists Play Service, $2.50; Off Broadway

The Halloween Bandit: manuscript*; PAF Playhouse, NY; Jewish Repertory Theatre, NYC

Firekeeper: manuscript*; Dallas Theater Center, TX

The Conversion of Aaron Weiss: manuscript*; University of Rhode Island/New Repertory Project, RI; Guthrie 2, MN

†**Children of a Lesser God:** Dramatists Play Service, $2.50; Mark Taper Forum, Los Angeles, CA; Broadway

　　*contact agent
　　†Lincoln Center, Theatre on Film & Tape

M

LEONARD MELFI

Born in Binghamton, NY on February 21, 1935.
Attended St. Bonaventure U, American Academy
of Dramatic Arts and studied with Uta Hagen/
Herbert Berghof. Author of **Notes of a New York
Playwright** in each issue of **Dramatists Guild
Quarterly;** two novels, **The End of Marriage
Forever!** and **Bright Angel Bright;** film for Sophia
Loren, **Lady Liberty; Earplay, The Flower Girl;**
poetry in **Exodus** and **Provincetown Review;**
Channel 13, TV plays, **Puck, Puck, Puck!** and
What a Life!; artist of abstract paintings, show-
ing, May, 1978 at The Stanhope, NYC. Recipient:
Two Rockefeller Grants for Playwriting; Guggen-
heim Fellowship for Playwriting; Kennedy Cen-
ter Commission; New York State Council on the
Arts Commission; State University of New York
Commission.

Address: 45 West 87th St., #5-A, New York, NY 10024 (212) 873-9445 — home, (212) 582-4240 —
service

Agent: Helen Harvey, 410 West 24th St., New York, NY 10011 (212) 675-7445

TITLE • AVAILABILITY • PRODUCTIONS

There's No Sugar in Scotch: manuscript*; Staged reading, NYC

The Frost Fire: manuscript*; Staged reading, NYC

The Late Drummer Boy: manuscript*; Staged reading, NYC

Watch the Cars and Lights: manuscript*; Circle-in-the-Square, NYC

Friends and Monsters: manuscript*; Theatre Genesis, NYC

Lazy Baby Susan: manuscript*; La Mama E.T.C., NYC

Sunglasses: manuscript*; Theatre Genesis, NYC

Birdbath: Encounters, Samuel French, 25 W. 45th St., New York, NY 10036, $4.95;
La Mama, E.T.C., NYC; Theatre Genesis, NYC

Lunchtime: In **Encounters;** La Mama E.T.C., NYC

Halloween: In **Encounters;** Playwrights Unit, NYC

Ferryboat: In **Encounters;** Theatre Genesis, NYC

The Shirt: In **Encounters;** O'Neill Theater Center's National Playwrights Conference, CT

Times Square: In **Encounters;** La Mama E.T.C., NYC; Germany

Out-of-Town Traffic: manuscript*; Theatre Geneis, NYC

Midnight Mass: manuscript*; Bronx Community College, NY

The Elevator Escapade: manuscript*; Theatre Genesis, NYC

Pussies and Rookies: manuscript*; La Mama E.T.C., NYC

Uptight All Right: manuscript*; Bronx Community College, NY

Stimulation: manuscript*; La Mama E.T.C., NYC

Night (from **Morning, Noon and Night):** Samuel French, $2.50; Broadway

Jack and Jill (from **Oh! Calcutta!):** Grove Press, 196 W. Houston St., New York, NY 10014,
$1.95; Broadway; World tour

Niagara Falls: New Theatre For Now, Dell Publishing, 750 Third Ave., New York, NY 10012,
$2.25; Cafe La Mama, NYC; Mark Taper Forum, L.A., CA

Having Fun in the Bathroom: manuscript*; La Mama E.T.C., NYC

Port Authority: manuscript*; Bronx Community College, NY

Dear Carmine DeSapio: manuscript*; La Mama E.T.C., NYC

Disfiguration: manuscript*; Mark Taper Forum, L.A., CA

Stars and Stripes: Collision Course, Vintage Books, 201 East 50th St., New York, NY 10022, $1.65; Cafe Au Go Go, NYC

The Raven Rock: manuscript*; Cafe La Mama, NYC

The Breech Baby: manuscript*; The Loft Workshop, NYC

The Jones Man: manuscript*; Act IV, Provincetown, MA; Actors Experimental Unit, NY

Wet and Dry: manuscript*; Act IV, Provincetown, MA; The Loft Workshop, NYC

Alive!: manuscript*; The Loft Workshop, NYC

Cinque (Horse Opera): Samuel French, $2.50; Royal Court, London; La Mama, E.T.C., NYC

Horse Opera: manuscript*; La Mama E.T.C., NYC

A Springtime Man: manuscript*; La Mama E.T.C., NYC

Beautiful!: manuscript*; Theater for the New City, NYC

Ah! Wine!: manuscript*; New York Theatre Ensemble, NYC

Sweet Suite: manuscript*; Theatre for the New City, NYC

The Flower Girl: manuscript*; Troupe Theater, NYC

Porno Stars at Home: Samuel French, $2.50; Courtyard Playhouse, NYC

Fantasies at the Frick: Samuel French, $2.50; The Open Space In SoHo, NYC

Horn of Plenty: manuscript*; New York Public Library, NYC

Taxi Tales: Later Encounters, Samuel French, $4.95; Broadway; IRT Theatre, NYC

Rusty and Rico and Lena and Louie: Later Encounters; Broadway; IRT Theatre, NYC

Erotic Behavior Upstate: manuscript*

Butterfaces: manuscript*; Theatre for the New City, NYC

The Baby Kids: manuscript*

The Son of Redhead: manuscript*; Newhouse Theatre, Lincoln Center, NYC

 *contact agent

SYNOPSES

Erotic Behavior Upstate: A very contemporary American comedy involving a free, unmarried "older woman" and her romantic relationships with young fraternal twin brothers and another young man who has just escaped from a mental institution in his pajamas, now forming a "quaint quadrille."

Full length. Setting: one set. 3 males, 1 female.

Butterfaces: A play-within-a-play murder mystery pertaining to a group of actors and actresses, a playwright, a director and a little boy, all participating in an Off Off Broadway production, during the present time.

Full length. Setting: one set. 4 males, 5 females.

The Baby Kids; A modern play dealing with a group of ex-teenaged alcoholics (and also pill addicts), all living together in a "communal type" New York City brownstone, under the spirit and guidance of a much older woman who has just suffered a stroke.

Full length. Setting: one set. 7 males, 4 females.

M

STEVE METCALFE

Born in New Haven, CT on July 4, 1953. B.A., Westminster College, New Wilmington, PA. M.A. work at Boston University in Acting. Actor in Off Broadway shows. Commissioned to write play for Manhattan Theatre Club. Recipient: Double Image Theatre Play Contest.

Address: 169 West 78th St., #4, New York, NY
   10024 (212) 595-7814

Agent: Esther Sherman, William Morris Agency,
   1350 Avenue of the Americas, New York, NY
   10019 (212) 586-5100

TITLE • AVAILABILITY • PRODUCTIONS

Vikings: Samuel French, 25 West 45th St., New York, NY 10036, $2.50; Manhattan Theatre
   Club, NYC; Royal Poinciana Theatre, Palm Beach, FL

White Linen: manuscript*

Island Cafe: manuscript*; Drama Committee, NYC

Jacknife: manuscript*; Quaigh Theatre, NYC: Double Image Theatre, NYC

Baseball Play: manuscript*; Double Image Theatre, NYC; Quaigh Theatre, NYC

   *contact agent

SYNOPSES

Vikings: Three generations of a family face the approaching death of the grandfather.

Full length. Setting: 3 areas; a kitchen, a bedroom, family room. 3 males, 1 female.

White Linen: A play based on the exploits of western outlaws Bill Longley and John Wesley Hardin, with 12 original songs.

Full length. Setting: minimal. 8 males, 1 female.

Jacknife: A confrontation between a lonely truck driver/Viet Nam vet and a college student.

One act. Setting: a college dorm room. 2 males.

ARTHUR MILLER

Born in New York City on October 17, 1915. A.B., University of Michigan. Did work in the Federal Theater Project and CBS and NBC workshops. Author of the film, **The Misfits.** His books include **Situation Normal; Focus; I Don't Need You Anymore.** Recipient: Hopwood Award; Theatre Guild National Award; New York Drama Critics Award (twice); Pulitzer Prize, **Death of a Salesman;** Tony Award, **The Crucible;** Gold Medal from National Institute of Arts; O'Henry Award; Brandeis University Creative Arts Award.

Agent: Kay Brown, International Creative Management, 40 West 57th St., New York, NY
   10019 (212) 556-5600

TITLE • AVAILABILITY • PRODUCTIONS

They Too Arise: *; Ann Arbor, MI

Honors at Dawn: *; Ann Arbor, MI

The Man Who Had All the Luck: *; Broadway

That They May Win: Best Plays of 1944, Dodd Mead, out of print; New York

All My Sons: Dramatists Play Service, 440 Park Avenue South, New York, NY 10016, $2.50; Broadway

Death of a Salesman: Dramatists Play Service, $2.50; Broadway

An Enemy of the People (adaptation): Dramatists Play Service, $2.50; Lincoln Center, NYC

The Crucible: Dramatists Play Service, $2.50; Broadway

A View From the Bridge: Dramatists Play Service, $2.50; Broadway

†A Memory of Two Mondays: Dramatists Play Service, $2.50; Broadway

After the Fall: Dramatists Play Service, $2.50; Lincoln Center, NYC

Incident at Vichy: Dramatists Play Service, $2.50; Lincoln Center, NYC

The Price: Dramatists Play Service, $2.50; Broadway

The Creation of the World and Other Business: Dramatists Play Service, $2.50; Broadway

The Archbishop's Ceiling: manuscript*; Kennedy Center, Washington, DC

The American Clock: manuscript*; Spoleto Fetival, NC; Off Broadway

*contact agent
†Lincoln Center Theatre on Film & Tape

JASON MILLER

Graduated University of Scranton. Studied at Catholic University. Has worked as actor in films and on stage. Stage credits: Champlain and Cincinnati Shakespeare Festival; New York Shakespeare Festival, where he created the role of Rogozhin in Robert Montgomery's play, **Subject to Fits.** Most prominent film appearance was as Father Karras in **The Exorcist.** Television: played F. Scott Fitzgerald in ABC Theatre Dramatic Special entitled **F. Scott Fitzgerald in Hollywood.** Recipient: Antoinette Perry (Tony) Award, 1973, Best Play; Drama Critics Circle Award, 1972, Best Play; Drama Desk Award, 1972, Most Promising Playwright; Outer Circle Award, 1972, Best Play; Pulitzer Prize, 1973; Variety Poll, 1972.

Agent: Earl Graham, Graham Agency, 317 West 45th St., New York, NY 10036 (212) 489-8288

TITLE • AVAILABILITY • PRODUCTIONS

It's a Sin to Tell a Lie: Dramatists Play Service, 440 Park Avenue South, New York, NY 10016, $2.50; various productions

Circus Lady: with **It's a Sin to Tell a Lie**

Lou Gehrig Did Not Die of Cancer: with **It's a Sin to Tell a Lie**

That Championship Season: Dramatists Play Service, $2.50; Off Broadway; Broadway

Nobody Hears a Broken Drum: Samuel French, 25 West 45th St., New York, NY 10036, $2.50; Off Broadway

M

Jason Miller (cont'd)

SYNOPSIS

Nobody Hears a Broken Drum: During the Civil War, when capitalists exploited their labor, especially in the coal mines of Pennsylvania, there was one colony of irascible Irish who joined with union organizers, and then went on a tear when a mine collapsed and killed half a dozen compatriots. The leader called a strike, and the owner accepted the terms—provided the leader would give himself up as the killer of a company man during one of the riots. This encounter was the basis of the formation of the notorious Molly McGuires, and from here to the end, it is a headlong lunge through history, as men fight for bread and clothing, and authority fights for law and order. In the end, the leader readies hmself for the gallows with another tankard and another song.

SUSAN MILLER

Born in Philadelphia, PA on April 6, 1944. Educated at Pennsylvania State University, B.A.; Bucknell University, M.A. Instructor of English at Penn State 1969–1973. Lecturer of Playwriting Seminar at U.C.L.A. 1975–76. Co-author of screenplay **One for the Money/Two for the Show** and **A Whale for the Killing.** Commission for Barbara Schultz's PBS series, **Visions.** Recipient: Rockefeller Grant in Playwriting, 1975; National Endowment for the Arts, 1976; Obie for **Nasty Rumors and Final Remarks,** 1979.

Address: 847 North Kilkea Dr., Los Angeles, CA 90046

Agent: Flora Roberts, 65 East 55th St., Suite 702, New York, NY 10022 (212) 355-4165; London, Michael Imison, Dr. Jan Van Loewen Ltd., 81-83 Shaftesbury Ave., London W IV PBX, England

TITLE • AVAILABILITY • PRODUCTIONS

No One is Exactly 23: manuscript*; Published in **Pyramid Magazine,** Issue 1, 1968, 32 Waverly St., Belmont, MA 02178; Pennsylvania State University; Dickinson College

Daddy/A Commotion of Zebras: manuscript*; Alice Theatre, NY

Silverstein & Co.: manuscript**; New York Shakespeare Festival (reading), NYC

Confessions of a Female Disorder: Gay Plays, Avon Books, 250 W. 55th St., New York, NY 10019, $3.50; O'Neill Theater Center's National Playwright Conference, CT; Mark Taper Forum, New Theatre for Now, Los Angeles, CA

Denim Lecture: manuscript**; Mark Taper Forum, Lab Theatre, Los Angeles, CA; Pennsylvania State University

Flux: manuscript**; New Phoenix Repertory Co., (sideshow), NYC; American Rep. Co., London

Cross Country: West Coast Plays, Vol. 1, P.O. Box 7206, Berkeley, CA 94707, $4.95; Mark Taper Forum, Los Angeles, CA; American Film Institute (as work in progress)

Nasty Rumors and Final Remarks: manuscript*; New York Shakespeare Festival, NYC

    *contact author
    **contact agent

SYNOPSES

Confessions of a Female Disorder: The non-linear journey of a woman who is wrestling with her sexuality, her work, a new awareness of other women, and her relationship with her husband. Moving laterally in time, her quest is often interrupted by someone or some event that she is not ready to deal with: i.e., during a college scene, her husband shows up in her dorm room. Ronnie, the central character, sometimes speaks to the audience as if she were footnoting. During her

Susan Miller (cont'd)

college years, Ronnie has an intimate and confusing relationship with another young woman, Coop. In their adult life, they consummate this sexually, although it opens a new set of choices.

Full length. Setting is flexible, may be done simply, using abstracts. If realistic, then some indication of a dormitory room shower stall, psychiatrist's office in the first act. In the second act, just a kitchen. 6 males, 7 females.

Silverstein & Co.: On one part of the stage are the Silversteins: Dr. Ernie Silverstein who performs abortions in league with his renegade son Nelson; Ethel Silverstein, his wife who chairs committees; Pam, their sixteen-year-old daughter who is having some sort of real or embellished nervous breakdown; Sandra . . . a friend of the family who is both Nelson's lover—and Pam's sexual guide. On another part of the stage are the Rabbis and members of Nelson Silverstein's congregation. Nelson, who was more or less banished from his home, now calls himself a rabbi/spiritual leader. The interaction between one part of the stage and the other is filled with ritual, myth, and union between brother and sister. When Pam begins acting strangely, her father calls Nelson to come home. He does. Only to upset once again the balance of Ethel's home.

Full length. Setting: livingroom, bedroom area. Synagogue area . . . which requires only a podium and benches or stools. 5 males, 4 females, 5-7 people who are the "Chanters" in Synagogue.

T. C. MILLER

Born in Long Beach, CA in 1944. B.A., UC Berkeley; M.A., Northwestern; M.F.A., Ohio U. Has also published criticism. Now teaches and directs in the Theatre Arts Department at California State University, Fresno. Clever (if slow) backcourt man on department's intra-mural basketball team. Recipient: Shubert Fellowship, 1969; shared first prize in the Citizens' Theatre (Glasgow) New Play Competition, 1972; Fringe First Award, Edinburgh Festival, 1978.

Address: Theatre Arts, CSUF, Fresno, CA 93740

TITLE • AVAILABILITY • PRODUCTIONS

Symposium: UCLA Alumni Magazine*; UCLA, Brooklyn College, Ohio University, CSUF

Tape: not available

Moral Facts: not available; Brooklyn College, NY

Donald Duck: not available; Magic Theater, CA

The F. S. Perls Memorial Dream Theater: not available; CSUF, Clark Center, NYC

The Boccaccio Rhythm Theater: manuscript*; CSUF, Good Company Players

The Miss Hamford Beauty Pageant and Battle of the Bands: Dramatic Pub. Co., 86 E. Randolph St., Chicago, IL 60601, $2.00; American Conservatory Theatre; CSUF Good Company Players

The Emperor of Late Night Radio: manuscript*; New York Shakespeare Festival, NYC; Players Repertory Theatre

Paranoia in the Polo Lounge: manuscript*; CSUF, ACTF Region 1 Festival

The Incompetents: manuscript*; Oregon Shakespeare Festival

An Evening with the Avenger: manuscript*; CSUF; Edinburgh Fringe Festival

    *contact author

T. C. Miller (cont'd)

SYNOPSIS

The Incompetents: A Jewish girl from West Los Angeles joins a neo-Hindu cult. Her parents go to court seeking a conservatorship. The hearing examines the girl's experience from the viewpoint of the law, of psychologists and of mystics. The problem is that, when one is adapted to a corrupt culture (as most of us are) any religious act may seem bizarre.

Full length. Setting: a dining room, a courtroom. 8 males, 4 females.

DAVID SCOTT MILTON

Born Pittsburgh, PA. Worked at a variety of jobs including actor, photographer, and private detective. Feature film, **Born to Win,** starring George Segal, was 1971 New York Film Festival selection. Novels are **The Quarterback, Paradise Road** and **Kabbalah. Heavyweights** (Putnam) due 1981. Adapted David Hare play, **Knuckle,** for **Hollywood Television Theater.** Received Mark Twain Journal Award for **Paradise Road.**

Agent: Marty Shapiro, Shapiro-Lichtman,
2 Century Plaza, Suite 1320, 2049 Century Park East, Los Angeles, CA 90067
(213) 557-2244

TITLE • AVAILABILITY • PRODUCTIONS

The Interrogation Room: manuscript*; Theater Genesis, NYC

Halloween Mask: manuscript*; Theater Genesis, NYC

The Uncle: manuscript*; Theater Genesis, NYC

The Metaphysical Cop: manuscript*; Off-Center Theater, NYC

Moscow Purge Trial, 1938: manuscript*; Theater Genesis, NYC

Scraping Bottom: manuscript*; New York Theater Ensemble, NYC; Clark Center Players, NYC

The Barefoot Antelope: manuscript*; American Place Theatre, Writers Development Program, NYC

Duet for Solo Voice (one-act and two-act versions): manuscript*; American Place Theatre, Off Broadway

Bread: manuscript*; American Place Theatre, NYC

Duet: Samuel French, 25 West 45th St., New York, NY 10036, $1.25; Coconut Grove Theater, FL; Golden Theater, Broadway

Skin: manuscript*

  *contact agent

SYNOPSES

Moscow Purge Trial, 1938: A documentary play taken from the actual manuscript of the last, great Russian purge trial. In its present form it runs five hours and has a cast of thirty. The play has an Alice-in-Wonderland absurdity, chilling, gallows humor—all the more terror-filled because in its essentials it's true. Presents the Stalinist version of Maxim Gorky's death, Hitler-Trotsky conspiracy, murder, sabotage and treason. History turned on its ear. Lies as truth. Much, much more.

Courtroom setting. 27 males, 3 females.

Bread: Sinister goings-on in a Pittsburgh bakery. Stanley, the owner of the bakery, is being undermined by his ex-prostitute, bookkeeper mistress, her pimp lover, and his own son. Rollicking humor, ominous machinations, terror, farce, surrealism. Begins with loving realistic

David Scott Milton (cont'd)

detail—bakers kneading and baking bread, the cranking of machinery, the flow of the ovens; ends up in a wild nightmare.

Full length. Setting: complete bakery, including ovens, office area. 5 males, 1 female.

Skin: A young man and woman who may or may not be sadistic, psychopathic killers, invade a home owned by a man who may or may not be a doctor, real estate agent, oriental mystic, freeway sex fiend. A metaphysical comedy. Requires some nudity or skillful faking of same.

Setting: a California beach house. 2 males, 1 female.

BARBARA MOLETTE

B.A., Florida A. & M. University; M.F.A., Florida State University. Writer, consultant and lecturer — costume and makeup design, playwriting, and Afro-American theatre aesthetics. Co-authored filmstrip with Carlton Molette, **Stage Makeup for Black Actors,** distributed by Paramount Theatrical Supplies, Alcone Co., NY. Recipient: Graduate Fellowship — Florida State University, 1968–69. Included in the current edition of **Who's Who of American Women.**

Address: 8102 Braesview, Houston, TX 77071
(713) 777-2269

CARLTON MOLETTE

B.A., Morehouse College; M.A., University of Iowa; Ph.D., Florida State University in Theatre Administration. Playwright, director, designer, actor, technician, publicist, producer for over one-hundred productions in professional, educational and community theatre. Writer, lecturer and consultant-playwriting, Afro-American theatre aesthetics and theatre design and technology. Co-authored filmstrip with Barbara Molette, **Stage Makeup for Black Actors,** distributed by Paramount Theatrical Supplies, Alcone Co., N.Y. Recipient: Ford Foundation Scholarship, 1955–59; Carnegie Foundation Doctoral Fellowship, 1966–68; Atlanta University Center Faculty Research Grant, 1970. Present position: Dean, School of Communications, Texas Southern University.

Address: 8102 Braesview, Houston, TX 77071 (713) 777-2269

TITLE • AVAILABILITY • PRODUCTIONS

Dr. B. S. Black** (musical): manuscript*; Spelman College, Federal City College, Texas Southern University

Noah's Ark**: manuscript*; Spelman College

Booji**: manuscript*; Spelman College

M

Carlton Molette (cont'd)

Rosalee Pritchett**: Dramatists Play Service, 440 Park Avenue South, New York, NY 10016, $1.25; Negro Ensemble Company, NYC: Free Southern Theatre; Spelman College

Dr. B. S. Black (non-musical): manuscript*; Howard University; Spelman College; Southwestern State College

　　*contact author
　**co-authored with Barbara Molette.

SYNOPSES

Dr. B. S. Black: Musical based very loosely on Molière's **Dr. in Spite of Himself.** Black con artist is recipient of wife's revenge. He is beaten by two rural gentlemen into confessing he is a doctor of black medicine and sets out to cure Magnolia, the daughter of Chauncy White, III. Sidetracked at the White estate by Tilly Mae and the "sweet utensils of her trade," B. S. eventually solves the dilemma by uniting Leroy and Magnolia and sets his sights on politics.

Full length. Setting: southern urban street scene; bungalow front yard and street corner in front of liquor store. Rural plantation, interior and exterior. 4 females and 5 males. Chorus optional. Minimum musical instruments—keyboard, bass and drums.

Noah's Ark: Noah, college professor; wife, Gladys; son, Daniel, live in the year before 1984. War rages in Africa and Daniel, a college student, is slated for induction in the army. Noah, an ardent pacifist, conducts his own private, non-violent war with the powers that be.

Setting: interior, family room/den of middle class, black urban home in the south. 4 females and 3 males.

Booji: the play chronicles a black attorney's attempts to make "the system" work for black people, and the difficulties he encounters from blacks and whites alike. During the course of the play, we discover Walter's many-faceted relationships with, among others, his wife, his law partner, a former army buddy turned radical, an evanescent socialite, and a traitor.

ROBERT MONTGOMERY

Born in Cincinnati, OH in 1946. M.A. from Dartmouth College, 1968, M.F.A. in Playwriting, Yale School of Drama, 1971. Taught at Fordham U in 1979. Has written songs, taught playwriting at the National Theater Institute, Waterford, CT and acted. He married in 1968 and has a daughter. Recipient: Guggenheim Fellowship, 1972; NEA Grant, 1975; Drama Critics Most Promising Playwright Award, 1971.

Agent: Ellen Neuwald, 905 West End Ave., #94, New York, NY 10025 (212) 663-1582

TITLE • AVAILABILITY • PRODUCTIONS

Lotta: manuscript*; New York Shakespeare Festival, NYC

Subject to Fits: Samuel French, 25 West 45th St., New York, NY 10036, $2.50; Yale, New Haven, CT; New York Shakespeare Festival, NYC

Electra: manuscript*; St. Clement's Church, NYC; tours

Green Pond (music by Mel Marvin): manuscript**; Toured South Carolina; Chelsea Theater Center, NYC

　　*contact author
　**contact agent

EDWARD J. MOORE

Born June 2, 1935 in Chicago, IL. Playwright; Actor. Education: Goodman Theatre, Chicago, IL; H.B. Studios and Uta Hagen. Founder, The New York Playwrights' Workshop (Greenwich Village). Member, Screen Actors Guild; American Federation of TV and Radio Artists; Actors Equity Association; Drama Guild. Broadway Debut; **After the Rain,** Golden Theatre. Off Broadway Debut: **The White House Murder Case** by Jules Feiffer. Played Harry Bales Off Broadway in his own play **The Sea Horse.** Recipient: Vernon Rice Drama Desk Award, Outstanding New Playwright 1974, **The Sea Horse.** Otis Guernsey's **Ten Best Plays of 1973–74.**

Address: 11 Carmine St., New York, NY 10014

Agent: Earl Graham, 317 West 45th St., New York, NY 10036 (212) 489-8288

TITLE • AVAILABILITY • PRODUCTIONS

The Sea Horse: Samuel French, 25 West 45th St., New York, NY 10036, $2.50; various domestic and international productions

The Bicycle Man: manuscript*

   *contact agent

SYNOPSIS

The Sea Horse: Gertrude Blum has donned an armor-like exterior that shields her from herself and from all men, whom she violently distrusts. She has hidden herself within a body gone to fat and become self-sufficient and afraid to allow herself a deep relationship with another human being. Harry Bales, a boisterous, romantic, compassionate merchant seaman between trips, has finally determined to make a home and establish his own business, and he has found himself in love and eager to marry — Gertrude. His wooing of this formidable and suspicious woman makes a lusty, amusing touching and dramatic play of great power and affirmation. This play ultimately speaks to the spirit and celebrates the strength of human devotion and constancy.

Full length. Setting: a run-down west coast waterfront bar. 1 male, 1 female.

HONOR MOORE

Born in New York City on October 28, 1945. B.A., Radcliffe College, cum laude, 1967; Yale School of Drama, 1967–69. Poetry published in **New West, American Review, Chrysalis** and other magazines and in anthologies, **We Become New, Tangled Vines.** Editor, **The New Women's Theatre: Ten Plays by Contemporary American Women.** Journalism and reviews published in **Ms** and **Yale/Theatre.** Represented in the anthology, **The Writer on Her Work: Women Writers Reflect on Their Art and Situation.** Has given poetry readings and poetry and playwriting workshops. Listed in **A Directory of American Poets and Fiction Writers.** Recipient: CAPS, 1976; Van Ameringen Foundation, 1979-80.

Address: 100 Hudson St., New York, NY 10013 (212) 431-4594

Agent: Audrey Wood, I.C.M., 40 West 57th St., New York, NY 10019 (212) 556-5722

M

Honor Moore (cont'd)
TITLE • AVAILABILITY • PRODUCTIONS

Mourning Pictures: New Women's Theatre, Vintage, c/o Random House, 201 E. 50th St., New York, NY, $5.95; Lenox Arts Center, MA; Broadway

Years: manuscript*; Women's Project, American Place Theatre, NYC

The Terry Project (with Victoria Rue): manuscript#

> *contact agent
> #contact V. Rue, 463 W. 19th St., New York, NY 10011

SYNOPSES

Years: The chronicle of a friendship between two young women, best friends in high school — one an aspiring conductor, the other an aspiring poet — who commit themselves, meeting four or five times during the decade of their twenties, both to a new kind of committed female friendship and to their work: the story told in scenes, letters, flashbacks, journal entries.

Full length. Setting: unit set with pieces to indicate change of place and time. 2 females.

The Terry Project: Adaptation of the writings (journals, prose, poetry) of a young woman who has been diagnosed as schizophrenic. The piece renders her life and world using her writings which the authors have arranged as a play. Unlike other stories of mental illness in that it is written from the "ill" person's point of view and does not primarily concern the therapeutic experience. Utilizes abstract sound and some music but is *not* a musical.

Full length. Setting: unit set with visually rich pieces, curtains, etc. to suggest place both in this world and in Terry's other world. 4 males (one juvenile), 9 females, chorus of 6-8 men and women.

Mourning Pictures: An episodic play with songs that traces the relationship between a 27-year-old daughter and her 50-year-old mother when the mother is dying of cancer. Other characters are the father, a younger sister, her boyfriend, and several doctors who can be played by one actor. A singer sings songs which form a counterpoint to the action. " . . . it is a stunning first play about the exploration of what a daughter and a mother say to each other and to themselves when the mother is dying . . . it gives us a deep sounding of one woman's development as a daughter, a woman and a writer." — Susan Braudy, **Ms. Magazine.** "Miss Moore is a very good writer, and there is scarcely a word too many in her text. She has pruned it and left room within it for silences that put me in mind of passages in Eliot's **Four Quartets.**" — Brendan Gill, **The New Yorker.**

Full length. Setting: a unit set utilizing a small number of properties to suggest several different places. Music available by arrangement with the author and the composer, Noa Ain **(Mourning Pictures** may also be performed without music.). 3 males (ages 50–55, 20, 35–50), 3 females (ages 50, 27, 18), 1 singer (a woman).

JUDITH MORLEY

Born in New York City on April 29, 1923. Degree in Drama, U. of Miami; Graduate work in theater at Columbia and Adelphi. Early work in Miami; University of Miami; Radio Station WKAT & **Miami Daily News.** Later, in N.Y., she was a script writer and interviewer for NBC and the **Voice of America.** During a hiatus, she entered politics and became a Democratic State Committee-woman. She studied acting with Stella Adler, et al and playwriting with George Tabori and Mario Fratti. She is a member of the Dramatists Guild, Equity, AFTRA & SAG. Is currently working with a New York group in creating performance pieces in the context of myth, ritual and altered states of awareness. Founder of the WOW Theatre Workshop of the Women's Interart Center. Recipient: Drama Scholarship, U. of Miami; A. M. Drummond Award; five plays chosen as SWAP plays for the Southwest Theatre Conference:

Address: 250 Scudders Lane, Roslyn Harbor, NY 11576 (516) 676-3118 or (212) JU6-6300

TITLE • AVAILABILITY • PRODUCTIONS

The Fledgling: not available; U. of Miami, FL

Ham and Borscht: not available; U. of Miami, FL

Jo-Ella: manuscript*; SWAP play, Oklahoma State U., Courtyard Theater, N.Y.

No Vacancy: manuscript*; SWAP

Travel Lightly: manuscript*

Short Hop to Ohio: manuscript*; SWAP

A Nice Boy for Joanie: N.Y.S. Community Theater Journal, Vol. IV, 1, State U. at Albany, 135 Western Ave., Albany, NY 12203

The Haircut: manuscript*; Numerous productions

Mother's Day: manuscript*; WOW Theatre Workshop NY

Thank You, Thank You, Doctor: manuscript*

Nirvana Manor: manuscript*; Eccentric Circles, NYC

　　*contact author

SYNOPSES

Nirvana Manor: Musical comedy about the suburban dream/nightmare, 1951–76, or the rise and fall of suburbia.

Full length. Large cast, all ages. Setting: flexible.

Mother's Day: The play's pivotal character is an attractive woman of fifty who has given up the glory and the awards: to live in symbiotic relationship with her aged mother . . . Her equilibrium is shattered when a series of incidents reveal her inability to deal with long-standing, hidden, sexual conflicts, or to deviate from the "script" which she and those around her seem almost compelled to act out.

The Haircut: A high school student who dares to question the authority of both man and God is terrorized by a teacher who cannot handle the threat of the boy's individuality. Young people dealing with real problems.

Full length. Setting: school corridor, and split-level suburban home. 6 males, 5 females.

M

ALDYTH MORRIS

B.A., Utah State University; post-graduate work, University of Hawaii. Was managing editor of the University of Hawaii Press for 15 years. Was assistant editor to C. A. Moore for four books **(The Japanese Mind, the Chinese Mind, The Indian Mind,** and **The Status of the Individual East and West)** and for the Journal **Philosophy East and West** from 1953 to 1965. Author of articles on various subjects. Recipient: Award of Merit from Dramatists Alliance for one-act play **The Wall;** production award for best new play showing man in ethical crisis for **Secret Concubine;** honorable mention in national contest Puppeteers of America; Christopher Award, 1978.

Address: 1028 Fifteenth Ave., Honolulu, HI 98616

TITLE • AVAILABILITY • PRODUCTIONS

Fourth Son (Carefree Tree): Samuel French, 25 West 45th St., New York, NY 10036 + ; Phoenix Theatre, NYC; Hawaii Chinese Civic Association, Honolulu, HI

Secret Concubine: Samuel French + ; Princeton Players, Princeton University, NJ; Carnegie Theatre, NYC

Damien Letter: manuscript*; Honolulu Community Theatre; Monomoy Theatre, Cape Cod

Tusitala: Robert Louis Stevenson in the Pacific: manuscript*; State Lyceum Circuit, Hawaii

The Dog That Was: manuscript*

Sword and Sumarai: manuscript*; Honolulu Community Theatre, Drama Department; Brigham Young University, Provo, UT

Neither Kith nor Kin: manuscript*; concert reading, New York

The Dragon of the Six Resemblances (Fingernail of My Beloved) (children's play): manuscript*; Laboratory Theatre, University of Hawaii

Damien: manuscript*; U. of Hawaii; P.A.F., NY

Captain Cook: manuscript*; U. of Hawaii; U. of Detroit, MI

Stevenson: manuscript*; Hawaii Performing Arts; Hawaii Public Theater

*Contact Jeffrey Steingarten, 29 W. 17th St., New York, NY 10011
+ Available in manuscript from Samuel French, $15.00 security deposit, $2.00 reading fee, 75¢ postage and handling.

SYNOPSIS

Damien: A one-man play that deals with the heroic Belgian priest who voluntarily went to live among the lepers of Molokai, "the one clean man among a flock of almost a thousand lepers," lived with them for sixteen years and himself died of the disease. His heroism stirred the entire world and undoubtedly hastened the finding of a way to control the disease.

EDMUND MORRIS

B.A. LLB (law degree). Films: **Walk on the Wild Side, Project X, Savage Guns.** Over two-hundred teleplays. Wrote for **Philco Playhouse, Suspense, Medical Center**... (too many to mention). Taught Playwriting, stage direction, acting at Piscator's Workshop, New York; University of Denver.

Address: 1122 18th St., Santa Monica, CA 90403
(213) 394-4785

TITLE • AVAILABILITY • PRODUCTIONS

The Wooden Dish: Dramatists Play Service, 440 Park Avenue South, New York, NY 10016, $2.50; Phoenix Theatre, London; Booth Theatre, NYC

End of Innocence: manuscript*

Parlor Game: manuscript*

    *contact author

SYNOPSES

End of Innocence: Rome, Nine A.D. The Emperor Augustus, discovering the adultery of his granddaughter Julia, exiles her as he did her mother for the same crime. He must find a scapegoat and divert the populace's attention. His victim is the poet Ovid who he believes has ridiculed his attempts to purge Rome of pornography and vice. Ovid must choose exile and death or betray a trust and his own conscience.

Full length. Unit set (four different set pieces). 10 males, 5 females.

Parlor Game: A play based upon the careers of the notorious Everleigh sisters who ran the most fashionable and famous brothel in Chicago at the turn of the century. The sisters, very proper ladies themselves, are determined to defeat the efforts of a reform Mayor to close them down and to frustrate the efforts of a group of competitive madams and their pimps, "the Friendly Friends," from causing them more grief. One night a client dies in one of the houses and his nude body is taken to the Everleigh Club and the police summoned. The sisters discover the treachery and the body is taken elsewhere. The night is spent trying to get rid of the body and to resolve a personal conflict in the lives of the sisters.

Full length. One set. 6 males, 8 females.

FRANK MOFFETT MOSIER

Born Ringgold County, IA on May 15, 1929. B.A., William Jewell College, 1951; M.F.A. in Playwriting, State University of Iowa, 1956. Past Member of New Dramatists Committee and Actors' Studio Playwrights Unit. 1960–75, head of English department and Assistant Principal, Quintano's High School for Young Professionals, New York City; 1969–75, associated with Actor's Place at St. Luke's (Managing Director, 1972–75), an Off Off Broadway Theatre. Member, organizing executive Committee, OOBA (The Off Off Broadway Alliance), and former member, Board of Directors. Free lance writer on horticultural subjects. Co-director, Fresno Ballet Co. where his ballet, **The Death of a Poet** was done. Recipient: Ford Foundation fellowship (playwright-observer on Saul Levitt's **Andersonville Trial**, 1959-60.

Address: 3637 North Wishon Ave., Fresno, CA 93704

M

Frank Moffett Mosier (cont'd)

TITLE • AVAILABILITY • PRODUCTIONS

Christine Fonnegra: manuscript*; State University of Iowa

The Winter Soldier (MFA thesis): manuscript*

Come Up and See My Casserole and **The Birth of Venus** (both one act): manuscript*; Lincoln Center Library of the Performing Arts, NYC; Actor's Place at St. Luke's, NYC

The Eagle & the Rock and **Iscariot** and **The Degenerate** (all one act): manuscript*; New Dramatists, NYC; Actor's Place, NYC; various college and community theatres

The Reunion, Two Sisters and **First Book of Kings** (all one act): manuscript*; Actor's Place at St. Luke's, NYC

King for a Day: manuscript*

The Duchess of Santiago: manuscript*; Actor's Studio (selected portions), NYC

Op: manuscript*; Actor's Studio, NYC: Actor's Place at St. Luke's, NYC

The Satyr Play: manuscript*

Der Lumpentanzer: manuscript*

  *contact author

SYNOPSES

The Duchess of Santiago: Ann-Elizabeth, eighteen, daughter of liberal Wasps, discovers the Santiago family living in peaceful squalor, and sets about to upgrade their lifestyle and aspirations, using her generous allowance as capital. She does everything right—from her viewpoint—and it all turns out horribly for the six Santiagos. She degenerates into a **nobless-oblige** patroness, the family disintegrates and Angel—the teen-age Santiago son—vainly tries to warn her away from his family and finally kills her. In personal terms, a parable of the evils of the welfare state.

Full length. Setting: a walk-up apartment in East Harlem. 3 males, 5 females (including 2 kids).

The Satyr Play: Silenus, a real satyr, has been genetically engineered as a park curiosity in a future society where apartheid separates the chaotic masses of the old inner cities from the emotionally insulated middle class, dwelling in park-surrounded suburbs. Silenus plots with city revolutionaries to destroy the society of which his grotesquerie is a symbol. In his forest-glen (exterior) home, on "D-Day," he masks his purpose by hosting a bacchanalian revel. He destroys the suburbs with hidden neutron bombs, and is killed by the revellers. A young urbanite revolutionary and a non-conformist suburban schoolgirl escape together to help rebuild a society.

Full length. 6 males (one a dwarf), 2 females.

Der Lumpentanzer: Four women, "suitemates" at a small religion oriented midwestern college in the early 1950s, are reunited thirty years later as two are being honored at the school's Achievement Day. The three "ugly ducklings" have done well professionally in science, literature and music. Their talented, beautiful leader in college days is trapped playing wifey to a mediocre businessman. Can they raise her consciousness and should they?

Full length. Setting: one unit set. 8 females, 4 at 20 and same characters at 50.

PAUL MROCZKA

Born in March, 1954. B.A., Franklin and Marshall College; M.F.A., Dramatic Writing, Brandeis University. He has been an instructor at Brandeis; an Editor of **Vortex;** and New Plays Editor for the **New England Entertainment Digest;** Currently, Advisor to Lowell Festival, 1981, New Play Competition, Lowell, MA and instructor of playwriting for New Hampshire Gifted Child Program. Recipient: Bultman Award for Playwriting, Loyola University of the South, 1979; Shubert Fellow in Playwriting, Brandeis, 1978.

Address: 908 Johns Drive, Scranton, PA 18505
 (717) 342-3673

TITLE • AVAILABILITY • PRODUCTIONS

Killers: manuscript*; Other Room Theatre, PA

The Circle: manuscript*; Green Room Theatre, PA: Other Room Theatre, PA

The Sandwich: manuscript*; Other Room Theatre, PA

The Big Sell: manuscript*; Berkeley Stage Co., CA; Nat Horne Theatre, NYC

Twaddles: manuscript*; Brandeis University, MA

The Last Laugh: manuscript*; Brandeis University, MA

A Flat Monotone: manuscript*; Brandeis University, MA

A New Man: manuscript*; Brandeis University, MA

Battle Cry: manuscript*; Merrick Theatre, Brandeis; WCVB-TV, Boston, MA

Timepieces: manuscript*; Brandeis University, MA

Cowboys! (with John R. Briggs): manuscript*

Beaches: manuscript*

 *contact author

SYNOPSES

Cowboys!: A musical farce. A humorous look at the old west, its characters and the way it has been portrayed through the motion picture. The play takes place in the Wyoming Territory with the arrival of a traveling medicine show wagon and a troop of players.

Full length. 5 males, 3 females.

Beaches: Two women, lost in their own worlds of joy and pain, have been meeting on a beach for the past month. Their needs and secrets, locked away for years, are finally exposed.

Full length. Setting: the beach. 1 male, 2 females.

The Big Sell: Jack "Big Apple" O'Connor controls his prison cell with maniacal precision and brutality. Today his fellow inmates attempt to stop him from making a hit on another prisoner. A struggle to break the controlling power that one man has over many.

One act. Setting: a prison cell. 6 males.

N

LYNDA MYLES

Born in New York City. Attended Michigan State
University; B.A. from Columbia University, NY.
Studied acting with Uta Hagen and Herbert
Berghof and has acted on Broadway, Off Broad-
way as well as on T.V. and in regional theater.
Has written non-fiction for **New York Magazine,**
done a play for **Earplay** and her play, **Wives,** was
optioned by Titus Productions, ABC-TV.

Address: 203 West 81st St., #6A, New York, NY
10024 (212) 873-3737

Agent: Alan Morris, Sandra Landau, c/o Sy
Fischer Co., 1 East 57th St., New York, NY
10022 (212) 486-0426

TITLE • AVAILABILITY • PRODUCTIONS

Wives: manuscript*; O'Neill Theater Center's National Playwrights Conference, CT

SYNOPSIS

Wives: A comedy in which the action goes backwards in time for ten years telling the story of
three women — their divorces and their marriages.

Full length. Setting: a livingroom. 3 males, 3 females.

N. RICHARD NASH

Born in Philadelphia, PA on June 8, 1913. B.S.,
University of Pennsylvania. Screenplays:
Welcome Stranger (with Arthur Sheekman); **Nora
Prentiss** and **Porgy and Bess.** Has written widely
for TV (Philco Theater, etc.) Novels: **East Wind,
Rain; Aphrodite's Cave.** Recipient: Maxwell
Anderson Verse Drama Award, 1940; Interna-
tional Drama Award; Prague Award; Karl Gosse
Award; Archer Award.

Address: 850 Seventh Ave., Suite 406,
New York, NY 10019 (212) 582-0285

Agent: Joan Scott, Writers & Artists Agency,
450 N. Roxbury Drive, Beverly Hills, CA
90210 (213) 550-8030

TITLE • AVAILABILITY • PRODUCTIONS

Parting at Imsdorf: contact agent*; Broadway

Second Best Bed: Samuel French, 25 West 45th St., New York, NY 10036, manuscript;
Broadway

The Young and Fair: Dramatists Play Service, 440 Park Avenue South, New York, NY 10016,
$2.50; Broadway

Rouge Atomique: Dramatists Play Service, $1.00

See the Jaguar: Dramatists Play Service, manuscript, $10 deposit, $2 reading fee; Broadway

The Rainmaker: Samuel French, $2.50; Broadway

Girls of Summer: Samuel French, manuscript

Handful of Fire: Samuel French, $2.50; Broadway

Wildcat: Tams-Witmark, Inc., 757 Third Ave., New York, NY 10017; Broadway

N. Richard Nash (cont'd)

110 In the Shade: Tams-Witmark; Broadway

The Happy Time: Dramatic Publishing Co., 4150 N. Milwaukee Ave., Chicago, IL 60641 $2.25; Broadway

Echoes: Samuel French, $2.50; Broadway

Sarava: Mitch Leigh, 200 West 59th St., New York, NY 10019; Broadway

*contact agent

ELYSE NASS

Born in New York City on February 14, 1947. B.A. in Psychology-Women's Studies, summa cum laude, Richmond College, City University of New York, 1973; Worked as a writer in the CETA Artists Project, NYC. Was feature writer for **New York Womensweek,** also contributed articles to **Dramatists Guild Quarterly, Art Workers News.** Playwright-in-residence, Quaigh Theatre, 1978–79. Playreader for Lincoln Center, 1967–69; Chelsea Theater Center, 1967; and Quaigh Theater, 1978–79. Fellow, Virginia Center for the Creative Arts, Sweet Briar, Summer 1977. Member, Professional Playwrights Unit of Puerto Rican Traveling Theater and P.E.N. Listed with **Poets and Writers, International Authors and Writer's Who's Who, Dictionary of International Biography.**

Address: 60-10 47th Ave., Woodside, NY 11377

Agent: Selma Luttinger, Brandt & Brandt, 1501 Broadway, New York, NY 10036

TITLE • AVAILABILITY • PRODUCTIONS

Detours: manuscript*

The Real Wife-Beater: manuscript*

Inbetween: manuscript*

Second Chance: Best Short Plays of 1980, Chilton Book Co., 201 King of Prussia Rd., Radnor, PA 19089, $12.95; Quaigh Theatre, NYC

City Life: manuscript*

Backwards: manuscript*; Reading, Society of Stage Directors & Choreographers Workshop, NYC

W.H.E.N.: manuscript*

Love from the Madhouse: DeKalb Literary Arts Journal, Winter 1975, DeKalb College, 555 N. Indian Creek Dr., Clarkston, GA 30021, $1.25; Reading, Women Arts Committee, Provincetown, MA

A Is for Alpha: manuscript*

The Marriage Museum: manuscript*; New American Playwrights Series, Brooklyn College, NY; West Side Discussion Group Theatre, NYC

Washington Squares: manuscript*; Gotham Art Theater, NYC

Reunion '68: manuscript*; Gotham Art Theater, NYC

Memory Shop: manuscript*; Playwrights Workshop Club, NYC

Zebras in Blue Nightgowns: manuscript*; Theater for the New City, NYC

Mango: manuscript*; West Broadway Workshop, NYC; Lincoln Center Library, NYC

Down: not available

N

Elyse Nass (cont'd)

Avenue of Dream: Dramatists Play Service, 440 Park Avenue South, New York, NY 10016, $1.25; Playwrights Workshop Club, NYC: WBAI-FM, NYC

Cry Louder Than a Black Cat: not available

Transience and Clay: not available

Willows for Her Harp: not available

　*contact author or agent

SYNOPSES

The Marriage Museum: The play deals with a marriage of convenience between a jet-set couple who lead double lives and their involvement with a young couple.

Full length. Setting: elegant livingroom. 2 males, 2 females.

Avenue of Dream: An examination of a mother-daughter relationship set in a slum environment.

One act. Setting: small, shabby livingroom. 2 females.

Second Chance: A comedy-drama about an elderly widow who decides to take up acting as a hobby and her prudish neighbor's effort to dissuade her.

One act. Setting: a nicely furnished livingroom. 2 females.

JOHN NASSIVERA

Born in New York on July 28, 1950. B.A., Boston University in English & Romance Languages; Ph.D., McGill University in Comparative Literature. Taught at McGill and Columbia Universities before joining New Dramatists, 1979–80. Has written reviews, translations and poetry. Producing Director for the Dorset Theatre Festival, VT and Director for the Dorset Colony House for Writers.

Address: 528 Riverside Drive, 3E, New York, NY 10027 (212) 663-1729 or (802) 867-2223

Attorney: Brit Geiger, Rubin, Baum, Levin, Constant & Friedman, 645 Fifth Avenue New York, NY 10022 (212) 759-2700

TITLE • AVAILABILITY • PRODUCTIONS

The Penultimate Problem of Sherlock Holmes: Samuel French, 25 West 45th St., New York, NY 10036, $2.50; Dorset Theatre Festival, VT; Hudson Guild Theatre, NYC

Sweeney Todd or the String of Pearls (adaptation, with Michael Wright): manuscript*; Dorset Theatre Festival, VT

Phallacies: manuscript*; Dorset Theatre Festival, VT; New Playwrights' Theatre, Washington, DC

Four of a Kind: manuscript*; Williams College, MA

　*contact author or attorney

SYNOPSES

Phallacies: A play based (loosely) on the Freud/Jung split of 1913, with a poor patient named Zeno caught in the middle.

Full length. Setting: unit set. 5 males, 4 females.

John Nassivera (cont'd)

Four of a Kind: A play about four women at Barnard College; the first act is set in 1910 and the second act takes place in the present.

Full length. Setting: 1 interior set. 4 females.

The Penultimate Problem of Sherlock Holmes: A "Holmes" play that isn't; in the guise of a Holmesian mystery, the play is an examination of Doyle's relationship to his famous detective and his involvement in the Spiritualist movement.

Full length. Setting: 1 interior set. 6 males, 3 females, 2 off-stage voices.

JANET L. NEIPRIS

Born in Boston, MA on March 11, 1936. B.A., Tufts University; M.A., Simmons College; M.F.A., Brandeis University (Playwriting). She is on the faculty of N.Y.U. and writes primarily for the stage in addition to television and radio. Television credits include: **How Does Your Garden Grow** and **The Baxters** (WCVB-TV, Boston); **Woman '76** (WBZ-TV, Boston); **Impact** (WJZ-TV, Baltimore). Recipient: Sam S. Shubert Playwriting Fellowship; National Endowment for the Arts Fellowship, 1979–80.

Address: 59 Whitney St., Westport, CT 06880

Agent: Helen Merrill, 337 West 22nd St., New York, NY 10011 (212) 924-6314

TITLE • AVAILABILITY • PRODUCTIONS

Statues: manuscript*; Brandeis University, MA; Cubiculo Theater, NYC

Exhibition: manuscript*; Brandeis University, MA; Cubiculo Theatre, NYC

The Bridge at Belharbour: manuscript*; Brandeis University, MA: Cubiculo Theatre, NYC

Jeremy and the Thinking Machine: manuscript*; Cape Ann Playhouse, Rockport, MA; Thirteenth Street Theatre, NYC

Separations: manuscript*; Reading—Manhattan Theatre Club, NY; Arena Stage, Wash., DC

Flying Horses: not available; University of Montana

The Desert: manuscript*; Milwaukee Repertory Theatre, WI; American Premier Stage, Boston, MA

*contact agent

SYNOPSES

Statues: Jennie Ames, a twenty-nine-year-old teacher from Pepperell, Mass. comes to a statuary factory in a torn-down area of Charlestown to get a statue of Christopher Columbus for a local play. She encounters Roberto Da Fralizzi, forty-five, the statue maker, who is confronted with the shifting values of his neighborhood and the church which no longer buys statues, but only love beads and guitars. Jennie finds not the statue but an openness in Roberto which encourages the same in her, culminating in a frenetic game of statues which promises a beginning, a connection, a coming to life for both.

Set: interior of a religious statuary factory. 1 male, 1 female.

Exhibition: Katy Valentine and Alex Ainbinder meet in a museum in New York City on Christmas Eve where Katy obsessively sketches a painting done by a former lover. Alex, a depressive and obsessive personality, who says "The day I find out I don't have cancer—that's a good day" all but stands on his head to get Katy's attention. He succeeds in destroying her faith in the artist and she succeeds in destroying the painting, but they still don't go off together, much as they

N

Janet L. Neipris (cont'd)

long for some kind of connection. The truth is elusive in this play and Katy, who claims to be a former Rockette says "I don't know if this true. I make up lots of things." But one truth is clear, Katy and Alex cannot make this relationship happen—Christmas Eve, alone and all. A play about missed connections.

Set: interior of a museum, New York City. 1 male, 1 female.

The Bridge at Belharbour: A plumber, Tom Fahey, father of seven children and owner of a newly built above-ground swimming pool, comes to unplug the sink in a summer home inhabited by Valerie Marino. Valerie, whose husband has mysteriously disappeared, stalks her prey ferociously, seductively piercing his defenses, probing beyond the boundaries of human decency. The play plunges through the hell of the American dream and leaves its victim, the whistling plumber, depleted, and Valerie, all smiles but with a questionable victory.

Set: kitchen of a summer home in Marblehead, MA, overlooking the ocean. 1 male, 1 female.

STANLEY NELSON

Born in Brooklyn, NY on June 9, 1933. Educated at University of Vermont, B.A., 1957. Stanley writes poetry and fiction in addition to plays. His poetry has appeared in more than fifty periodicals and he has poetry published: **Idlewild, The Brooklyn Book of the Dead, The Travels of Ben Sira, Chirico Eyes** and **101 Fragments of a Prayer.** Short stories, **The Unknowable Light of the Alien.** He is the editor of **The Scene** (an annual anthology of Off Off Broadway plays) and of **The Scene** Award Series, (full-length plays).

Address: 372 Pacific St., Brooklyn, NY 11217
(212) 624-2344

TITLE • AVAILABILITY • PRODUCTIONS

Emanons: Red Cedar Review*: Bastiano's Cellar Studio; Brookdale Community College Theatre; various New York productions

Shuffle-Off: manuscript*; Bastiano's Cellar Studio; Cubiculo Theatre, NYC

Mr. Optometrist: manuscript*; Bastiano's Cellar Studio; New York Theater Ensemble, NYC

The Harrison Progressive School: The Scene/1, The Scene, 5 Beekman St., New York, NY 10038; Bastiano's Cellar Studio; Theatre East; various other productions

Mrs. Peacock: One scene published in **Scene/2, The Scene;** manuscript*; The Old Reliable Theatre, NYC; Omni Theatre; London; various New York productions

The Plan: manuscript*; New York Theater Ensemble, NYC

Ruth and the Rabbi: manuscript*; Omni Theatre; Bastiano's Cellar Studio

Tsk, Mary Tsk: manuscript*; Stagelights I; Stagelights II

El Exejente: manuscript*; Playhouse Theatre; Bastiano's Theatre

The Butler Carries the Sun Away: manuscript*; Playhouse Theatre; Stagelights II

Rite of Spring: one segment in **The Scene/3,** manuscript*; WPA Theatre, NYC

The Master Psychoanalyst: manuscript*; The Old Reliable Theatre, NYC; Theatre 77; Oklahoma college tour of sixteen U.S. colleges

The Poetry Reading: manuscript*; Cubiculo Theatre, NYC: Bastiano's Theatre

No One Writes Drawing Room Comedies Anymore: manuscript*; Joseph Jefferson Theatre, NYC; Theatre East

Poe: From His Life and Mind: manuscript*; Theatre 77; The Night House Theatre; tour of thirty U.S. colleges

Schlurp: manuscript*; New York Theater Ensemble, NYC

Stanley Nelson (cont'd)

Once I Put an Ad in the Void: manuscript*

*contact author

SYNOPSES

The Master Psychoanalyst: During the early early days of psychoanalysis, one of Freud's most brilliant students, Victor Tausk, committed suicide under mysterious circumstances. Subsequent researches have implicated Freud himself in the events leading up to this suicide. **The Master Psychoanalyst** is a fictionalized account that investigates the basis of this accusation—and explains the intense, often bizarre relationships that evolved with the inner circle of Freud's early followers.

Full length. Setting: a psychoanalyst's office; a room in a sanatorium. 2 males, 4 females.

Mrs. Peacock: Mrs. Peacock, a resident of Old Folks Home, is engaged in a personal power-struggle with Miss Saltino, a thirtyish, sadistic nurse. Mrs. Peacock is struggling against the system to preserve her individuality and identity. She has remained aloof from the other residents, but this isolation is broken by the appearance of Mr. Ditchik, a spry senior citizen who likes to do Yiddish song and dance routines, and Mr. Saffron, a lusty grandfather who escapes from Old Folks Home. In this play, it is the "old fogies"—represented by Mrs. Peacock, Mr. Ditchik, and Mr. Saffron—who are the rebels, and the "young fogies"—Miss Saltino, Mrs. Peacock's daughter, Mrs. Saffron's son—who represent the Establishment.

Full length. Setting: Mrs. Peacock's room; a nurse's station. 3 males, 3 females.

Poe: From His Life and Mind: Edgar Allan Poe, one of the authentic geniuses of American literature, died in a Baltimore hospital after being left on the street by political thugs. This event is used to launch a surreal investigation of Poe's disturbed mind during the last years of his life, when he was beset by poverty, neglect of his talents, and most especially, the death of Virginia Poe ("Annabel Lee"). Characters from Poe's life are interwoven with the characters Poe created in his poems and stories.

Full length. Setting: the Poe Cottage in Fordham. 6 males, 6 females.

JAMES NICHOLSON

Born in St. Louis, MO on February 16, 1946. B.A., Washington University, 1968; M.F.A., Florida State University, 1974. Fellow, Midwest Playwrights Laboratory, 1980. Recipient: Missouri Arts Council Playwriting Award, 1978, for **Stardust;** First Prize, National Theatre Foundation's Award, 1979, for **Proud Flesh.**

Address: 8423 Midland Blvd., St. Louis, MO, 63114 (314) 429-2331

TITLE • AVAILABILITY • PRODUCTIONS

Down by the Gravois (Under the Anheuser-Busch): manuscript*; Milwaukee Repertory Theater Company, WI; Actors Theatre of Saint Paul, MN

Crop Rotation: manuscript*; Plays in Progress, Players Repertory Theatre, Miami, FL

Stardust: manuscript*

Proud Flesh: manuscript*

Beyond Here are Monsters: manuscript*; Midwest Playwrights Laboratory, WI

*contact author

SYNOPSES

Down by the Gravois (Under the Anheuser-Busch): A portrait of a middle-class American Irish-Catholic family. The two youngest children, twenty-eight-year-old Jimmie (who never quite manages to leave home) and twenty-two-year-old Sharon (who always comes back), anxiously

N

James Nicholson (cont'd)

seize any excuse to avoid coping with the stagnancy of their lives while the entire family does its best to cope with the unpredictable behavior of the patriarch of the clan, the senescent Dan O'Grady. The major metaphor of the play is beer and it flows freely—especially when the entire family gathers to celebrate Dan's birthday.

Full length. Setting: the living room of a middle-class urban home, with a stairway leading upstairs and exit access to kitchen and bathroom. 8 males, 7 females.

Stardust: The Stardust Burlesque—a local institution on what was once the hottest strip in town—has been killed by a local zoning quirk; the restaurant next door has become a church and it is illegal to operate a bawdy house within ninety yards of a church. An attempt at a nostalgic closing night fails miserably as the denizens of the Stardust are subjected to a series of urban indignities culminating in a bungled holdup.

One act. Setting: the interior of a burlesque house. 8 males, 3 females.

Beyond Here Are Monsters: Deep in the Amazonian jungle lurks a tribe of Indians; the Kreen-Ankra, who have never been seen by civilized man and have never met another person they have not killed. A small group of intrepid (and eccentric) English explorers and their native Indian servant have camped in the Kreen-Ankra's only remaining garden in an attempt to starve them out of hiding before they are exterminated by the onslaught of civilization.

Full length. Setting: a camp in the midst of the jungle. 4 males, 1 female.

JEAN NUCHTERN

Born in New York City on November 20, 1939. Attended Professional Children's School. B.A., Hofstra College. Poet-journalist. As a dance journalist, she has been published in **The Village Voice; The Soho Weekly News; Dance Magazine; Dance Scope; Ballet News** and others. Recipient: **Writer's Digest,** Short Story Award.

Address: 411 West End Avenue, New York, NY 10024

TITLE • AVAILABILITY • PRODUCTIONS

The Hold-Up: manuscript*; Stagelights Theatre, NYC

Round Trip: manuscript*; Plowright Playhouse, PA; American Theatre Co., NYC

The Elizabeth Stuart Company: manuscript*; The Open Space, NYC

Carrie: manuscript*; Reading, Open Space, NYC; Reading, Womanbooks, NYC

White Asparagus: manuscript*; Reading, Manhattan Plaza, NYC; staged reading, Women in the Arts, NYC

Magic Time: manuscript*; Reading, Theatre Off Park, NYC

   *contact author

SYNOPSES

Round Trip: A two-character play in which one person speaks. Ethel Rosen visits her catatonic husband in a psychiatric home in upstate New York to see if there's a chance of him changing his condition. Realizing there is no hope, she tells her silent husband she's remarrying.

One act. Setting: a visiting room. 1 male, 1 female.

Jean Nuchtern (cont'd)

The Elizabeth Stuart Company: A play about the machinations in a modern dance company. It also deals with a young woman's rise from chorus member to soloist.

Full length. Setting: three simple settings. 2 males, 2 females.

Magic Time: What happens when a radical theater presents a lascivious production of **Marat/Sade** and is closed down by the local rednecks?

Full length. Setting: a kitchen and a doorway to a house. 4 males, 3 females.

JOHN OLIVE

Born in Fukuoka, Japan on December 12, 1949. B.A. and M.A. in Theatre Arts, U. of Minnesota. Has written radio plays: **Pentecost** for **Earplay; The Long Corridor** for BBC; and **Satori in Dayton's;** opera, **The Silver Fox,** done at the Minnesota Opera Workshop and Opera Omaha. Also a professional actor. Founding member of the Playwrights' Lab. Recently appointed Playwright-in-Residence at the Actors Theatre of St. Paul. Recipient: Minnesota State Arts Board Grant, 1978.

Address: 2212 Glenwood Ave. N., Minneapolis, MN 55405 (612) 377-5273

Agent: Susan Schulman, 165 West End Ave., New York, NY 10023 (212) 877-2216/7.

TITLE • AVAILABILITY • PRODUCTIONS

Thin Lady Fat Man: manuscript*; Theatre-in-the-Round, Minneapolis, MN

Minnesota Moon: manuscript*; Playwrights' Lab, MN; Circle Repertory Co., NYC

Texas Dry: manuscript*; O'Neill Theater Center's National Playwrights Conference, CT

Standing on My Knees: manuscript*; Playwrights' Lab, Minneapolis, MN; North Light Repertory Co., Chicago, IL

Gift of the Magi (adaptation, music by Libby Larsen): manuscript**; Story-Talers, Minneapolis, MN; Actors Theatre of St. Paul

Clara's Play: manuscript*; Boars Head Theater, Lansing, MI
    *contact agent
    **contact author

SYNOPSES

Minnesota Moon: Two high school buddies, Alan and Larry, are sitting in the moonlit yard of an abandoned farmhouse in southern Minnesota, drinking beer, laughing, sharing stories and saying good-bye: Alan leaves the next day for college. It's 1968 and Vietnam looms in their futures. "Haunting"—**New Yorker** . . . "Evanescent"—**New York Times.**

One hour. Setting: one set. 2 young males.

Standing on My Knees: A portrait of a poet's struggle with schizophrenia. The play follows her from her release from the hospital, through her relationships with an old friend, a new lover and a psychiatrist and ends with a relapse. It's a play about loneliness and about the relationship of creativity and mental illness.

Full length. Setting: one set. 1 male, 3 females.

The Gift of the Magi: A holiday musical, loosely adapted from the short story by O. Henry. A young, very poor couple, Jim and Della, live on New York's Lower East Side at the turn of the cen-

O

John Olive (cont'd)

tury. They long to buy each other Christmas presents. Jim sells his watch to buy Della gold combs for her beautiful hair and Della sells her hair to buy a chain for Jim's watch. Music by Libby Larsen, piano score only.

Full length, 1 hour and 15 minutes. Setting: one set. 1 male, 1 female, two or three other performers who play a variety of characters. A touring version which uses only three performers and is designed for young audiences also exists.

RICHARD ARTHUR OLSON

Born in Chicago, IL on January 28, 1943, Aquarius. B.A., Princeton, 1965; MFA, Yale Drama School, 1969. Influenced by Jung and Zen. Practices yoga. Has maintained daily journal since high school. Married, Carol Bankerd, 1971; Daughter, Auguste, 1977. Has directed at Harvard, Vassar, Yale, Theatre Company of Boston, Tabor Opera House, Aspen Theater Workshop and Theater of the Open Eye.

Address: 122 West 80th St., New York, NY
10024 (212) 595-3718

TITLE • AVAILABILITY • PRODUCTIONS

The Bookcase: manuscript*; Chatham Road Players, IL

The Writer: manuscript*; Exit Coffeehouse, New Haven, CT

Seven Loving Women: manuscript*; Aspen Theatre Workshop, Aspen, CO

Drive-In: manuscript*; Yale Experimental Theatre, CT

The Sphinx: manuscript*; Yale Experimental Theatre, CT

We Four: manuscript*; Yale Experimental Theatre, CT

Marathon: manuscript*

The Dinner Party (new title, **By the Way**): manuscript*

As Above, So Below: manuscript*; G. Jung Foundation, NY, reading

Untitled: Lines for Three Performers: manuscript*; Private readings

Improvisation for Actor, Dancer and Musician: *; Theater of the Open Eye, NYC

   *contact author

SYNOPSES

Rather than providing synopses of any particular plays, Mr. Olson would like to give a summary of his work as a whole. His first play, **The Bookcase**, somehow prophesized his situation today: in that play, a playwright creates a play through the improvisations of the characters in his own life, including actors, a director, a composer and a critic. This consciousness of illusion and reality in the theater continued with several of his plays, eventually dispensing with plot and characters completely; so that by the late 1970s, in **The Dinner Party, As Above, So Below** and **Untitled,** the reader sees only successive sections of lines, with no indication as to who is saying what line, what they are doing, or where they are. What he had in mind was a group of performers who would be using these lines as vehicles for their own self-expression, discarding the social roles they left behind in the outside world and seeking a group transcendent experience in the process. In 1980, at the Theater of the Open Eye, he participated in the sort of improvisation about which he had been writing, interacting with a dancer and a musician. He is now working on a scripted monologue.

KEVIN O'MORRISON

Born in St. Louis, MO, he was tutored privately for university equivalent. He has written for TV: **The House of Paper, A Sign for Autumn** (NBC); **And Not a Word More,** (CBS) and written films, all in the documentary field. His acting credits include **The Watergate Coverup Trial** (PBS). Drama Consultant, under aegis of Office for Advanced Drama Research, 1966; Artist-in-Residence, Trinity University, TX, 1974; Visiting Professor, University of Missouri, 1976; Adjudicator for New Plays Program, American College Theatre Festival, 1979–80; Playwright-in-Residence to more than thirty colleges and universities. Recipient: CAPS Playwriting Fellowship, 1975; N.E.A. Playwriting Fellowship, 1979–80; National Repertory Theatre, New Play Contest, 1981.

Address: 20 East 9th St., New York, NY 10003

Agent: Janet Roberts, William Morris Agency, 1350 Avenue of the Americas, New York, NY 10019 (212) 586-5100

TITLE • AVAILABILITY • PRODUCTIONS

Three Days Before Yesterday: Playwrights For Tomorrow, Vol. 4, University of Minn. Press (under title **The Long War);** University of Minnesota; Triangle Theatre, NYC

Requiem: manuscript*; University of Montana

The Morgan Yard: Samuel French, 25 West 45th St., New York, NY 10036, $2.50; O'Neill Theater Center's National Playwrights Conference, CT; Cleveland Play House, OH

†**Ladyhouse Blues: :** Samuel French, $2.50; O'Neill Theater Center's National Playwrights Conference, CT; Phoenix Theatre, NYC, Dallas Theatre Center, TX

Dark Ages: manuscript*; Impossible Ragtime Theatre, NYC

A Party for Lovers: manuscript*

Report to the Stockholders: manuscript*

*contact agent
†Lincoln Center, Theatre on Film & Tape

SYNOPSES

Ladyhouse Blues: In South St. Louis, people used to say, "When you're standin' there hurtin' so bad you could die, an' you know you won't—that's the blues." And in August, 1919—in the midst of war-born inflation, while her eldest daughter is being wasted by tuberculosis—Liz Madden, a widow at forty-one, tries with what laughter, tears, and raillery she can muster, to hold her three younger daughters around . . . at least until Bud, her only son, "can get back from the Navy."

Full length. Setting: kitchen of floor-through "flat" in South St. Louis. 5 females.

A Party for Lovers: Even as bulldozers and jackhammers threaten his fashionable restaurant-home in New York's East 50's, eighty-three-year-old Vito Vitale holds a betrothal party for the daughter of his old age and her fiance, and tries to resist the mounting force of his family's attempts to persuade him to uproot himself — "for his own good."

Full length. Setting: two "practical" French windows, to suggest upstairs bedroom and terrace of NYC brownstone. 4 males, 4 females.

Report to the Stockholders: Chairman of the Board gives an accounting of his stewardship, cradle to the grave: 1915 to "now."

Full length, with 32 original songs, music by Larry Grossman. Setting: 2 or 3 cubes; cyclorama or drapes.

O

SALLY ORDWAY

Educated at Hollins College, B.A., M.A. in Theatre from Hunter College, NY. Member of the Westbeth Playwrights' Feminist Collective. Recipient: Fellowships at Yaddo, MacDowell Colony and Edward Albee Foundation; ABC-TV Fellowship in Writing for the Camera, Yale, 1967-68; National Endowment for the Arts Grant; CAPS Grant, 1978.

Address: 344 West 38th St., #10B, New York, NY 10018 (212) 695-7743

TITLE • AVAILABILITY • PRODUCTIONS

There's a Wall between Us, Darling: manuscript*; also **Yale/Theatre,** Summer 1968, Box 854, Meriden, CT 06450; Theatre Genesis, NYC; The Actor's Place

Free! Free! Free!: manuscript*; Theatre Genesis, NYC; Hunter College, NYC

A Desolate Place near a Deep Hole: manuscript*; Caffe Cino, NYC; Loeb Drama Center, NYC

A Passage through Bohemia: manuscript*; O'Neill Theater Center's National Playwrights Conference, CT; Theatre for the New City, NYC

Movie, Movie on the Wall: Scripts Magazine #2*; O'Neill Theater Center's National Playwrights Conference, CT; Mark Taper Forum, CA

We Agree: manuscript*; New York Theatre Ensemble, NYC

Allison: manuscript*; Music Barn Theatre; Peace Festival at Westbeth, NYC

Australia Play: manuscript*; New York Theatre Ensemble, NYC

Playthings: manuscript*; Theatre for the New City, NYC

The Chinese Caper: manuscript*; Theatre for the New City, NYC

Sex Warfare: manuscript*; Westbeth Playwrights' Feminist Collective, NYC

Crabs: Scripts Magazine, #2*; Company Theatre of Los Angeles, CA; Almost Free Theatre, London

Family, Family: The Scene, 1974*; Town Hall, NYC; Southampton College

San Fernando Valley: Scripts Magazine #2*; New York Theatre Ensemble, NYC; Academy Theatre, GA

War Party: manuscript*; St. Clement's Theatre, NYC

Memorial Day: manuscript*; St. Clement's Theatre, NYC

The Hostess: manuscript*; Westbeth Playwrights' Feminist Collective, NYC; Royal Court Theatre, NYC

S.W.A.K.: manuscript*; Phoenix Theatre, NYC; Playwrights Horizons, NYC

Film Festival: manuscript*; Playwrights Horizons, NYC

No More Chattanooga Choo Choo: manuscript* .

   *contact author

SYNOPSES

Family, Family: The short history of Margaret's growth and self-fulfillment within her own nuclear family. Men play the women and women play the men in this play.

One act. Setting: minimal. 2 males, 2 females.

S.W.A.K.: This cinematically structured play comically probes the struggles of three single New

Sally Ordway (cont'd)

York women to cope with unloving lovers, intense therapy, the mother relationship and the rediscovery of their new strengths. Among the three, the central character is Carrie, a woman in her thirties. We see through her eyes as she tries to work out her own life. The play is about what women are becoming today.

Full length. Setting: minimal. 2 males, 4 females.

OWA

Born in New York City on July 28, 1944. Writer-in-Residence at the Frank Silvera Writers' Workshop, 1979. Recipient: Rockefeller Grant; Critics Choice, Samuel French/Double Image Short Play Festival, 1976.

Address: 507 East 93rd St., New York, NY 11212

Agent: Weldon Irvine, P.O. Box 38, St. Albans, NY 11412 (212) 724-2800

TITLE • AVAILABILITY • PRODUCTIONS

The Soledad Tetrad

Part I. A Short Piece for a Naked Tale: manuscript*; La Mama E.T.C., NYC

Part II. Transitions for a Mime Poem: Center Stage, An Anthology of Afro-American Playwrights, Sea Urchin Press, Box 9805, Oakland, CA 94613; La Mama E.T.C., NYC; Bijou, NYC

Part III. That All Depends on How the Drop Falls: manuscript*; Negro Ensemble Co., NYC; New York Theatre Ensemble, NYC

Part IV. the bloodrite: manuscript*; Frank Silvera Writers' Workshop, NYC; O'Neill Theater Center's National Playwrights Conference, CT

Funnylingus: manuscript*; Frank Silvera Writers' Workshop, NYC

cyklops I: manuscript*; Fordham University, NYC

In Between the Coming and the Goings

Rejections: manuscript*

Egwuwu: manuscript*; Frank Silvera Writers' Workshop, NYC; Martinique Theatre, NYC

heaven must be a very complicated place: manuscript*

Concert Grande: manuscript*

Rascallion: manuscript*

The Garden of Eden: manuscript*

 *contact agent

SYNOPSES

the bloodrite: Morality drama. A business man meets an ex-offender on a New York pier which leads to conversation and a deadly confrontation.

Full length. Setting: a waterfront pier. 3 males, 1 female.

O

Owa (cont'd)

Transitions for a Mime Poem: A man-woman introspective in verse and dramatic dialogue with mime and music.

One act. Setting: no set. 1 male, 1 female.

heaven must be a complicated place: A study in the struggle of an urban family to meet the challenge of the post World War II Amerika.

Full length. Setting: a kitchen. 3 males, 2 females.

DANIEL W. OWENS

Born in Malden, MA. B.A. in English from University of Massachusetts. Ed.M. from Harvard University School of Education. Part-time lecturer, University of Massachusetts, in Black Theatre and Playwriting. Teacher at Boston English High School. Resident playwright, New African Company of Boston. Director of Playwrights Workshop, National Center of Afro-American Artists. He is now the Co-ordinator of the Workshop Program at the Frederick Douglass Creative Arts Center. Has published poetry in **Journal of Black Poetry** and **Negro Voices Today: An Anthology by Young Negro Poets.**

Address: 873 St. Nicholas Ave., New York, NY 10032

TITLE • AVAILABILITY • PRODUCTIONS

Nigger, Nigger Who's the Bad Nigger: manuscript*; New African Company, Boston, MA; National Center of Afro-American Artists

The Box: manuscript*; New African Company; University of Illinois at Urbana

Clean: manuscript*; New African Company

Joined: manuscript*; People's Theater of Cambridge, MA

Imitatin' Us, Imitatin' Us, Imitatin' Death: manuscript*; New African Company

Refusal: manuscript*; National Center of Afro-American Artists

Where Are They??: manuscript*; Black Drama Students at Yale, CT

Bus Play and Slipt: manuscript*; Dan Owens Company

Misunderstanding: manuscript*; National Center of Afro-American Artists

What Reason Could I Give: manuscript*; O'Neill Theater Center's National Playwrights Conference, CT

Emily Tillington: manuscript*; Emerson College, MA

Acife and Pendabis: manuscript*; Afro-American Studio Theater, NY

One Shadow Behind: manuscript*; People's Theater of Cambridge, MA

Bargainin' Thing: manuscript*; O'Neill Theater Center's National Playwrights Conference, CT

The Noirhommes: manuscript*

Tho More You Get, The More You Want (musical): manuscript*; Frederick Douglass Creative Arts Center, NYC

Lagrima Del Diablo: manuscript*; Negro Ensemble Company, NYC

The Michigan: manuscript*; Negro Ensemble Company, NYC

> *contact author

ROCHELLE OWENS

Born April 2, 1936. Her plays have been produced throughout the world. In addition to
writing for the Theater, she has published eight
books of poetry and three collections of plays,
the newest of which is **Spontaneous Combustion.** She has given many readings in this country and Europe. Founding member of the New
York Theatre Strategy and a sponsor of the
Women's InterArt Center. Was Playwright-in-
Residence at the American Place Theatre. A
Rochelle Owens collection has been established at the Boston University Mugar Library and
the University of California, Davis, CA. Recipient: Several Obies; Drama Desk Award;
Honors from New York Drama Critics Circle;
Guggenheim Grant; Yale School of Drama
Fellowship; CAPS Grant; Rockefeller Grant; Na-
tional Endowment for the Arts Grant.

Address: 606 West 116th St., New York NY 10027

Agent: Donald C. Farber, 600 Madison Ave., New York, NY 10022 (212) 758-8000

TITLE • AVAILABILITY • PRODUCTIONS

Futz: Samuel French, 25 West 45th St., New York, NY 10036, $5.95; Theatre de Lys, NYC;
Actor's Playhouse

Beclch: manuscript, Samuel French; Theatre of Living Arts, PA: Gate Theatre, NYC

Homo: manuscript, Samuel French; La Mama tour of Sweden; La Mama Theatre, NYC

Istanboul: manuscript, Samuel French; Judson Poets Theater, NYC: Actor's Playhouse, NYC

The Karl Marx Play: Samuel French, $5.95; American Place Theatre, NYC: European Tour

Kontraption: with **The Karl Marx Play;** New York Theatre Strategy, NYC

He Wants Shih: with **The Karl Marx Play;** New York Theatre Strategy, NYC

O.K. Certaldo: with **The Karl Marx Play;** Reading

Farmers Almanac: with **The Karl Marx Play;** Actors Studio, NYC

Coconut Folk-Singer: with **The Karl Marx Play;** WBAI; Germany

The String Game: manuscript, Samuel French

Emma Instigated Me: manuscript*; American Place Theatre, NYC

Game of Billiards: manuscript*

The Widow and the Colonel: Dramatists Play Service, 440 Park Avenue South, New York, NY,
10016, $1.25; Voice of America

Who Do You Want, Piere Vidal?: manuscript*; French cafe theater

Mountain Rites: Best Short Plays, Chilton Press, Chilton Way, Radnor, PA 19089;
Erie Buffalo Workshop, NY

Chucky's Hunch: manuscript*; Theatre for the New City, NYC

*contact author

SYNOPSIS

Istanboul: Three times Obie award-winning play. Set in fifteenth-century Constantinople. Getting
riches, religion and love in the turbulent and doomed queen of cities. Exciting women roles won
two awards for actresses in the fabulously rich part of St. Mary of Egypt. "Bristling with
humor."—CBS-TV. "A rare and daring dramatic imagination."—**New York Times.**

Full length. 4 males, 5 females.

O

OYAMO
A/K/A
CHARLES F. GORDON

Born in Elyria, OH. Educated at Miami University, Oxford, Ohio (American Studies); Brooklyn College (Lighting and Stage Design); New York University, Washington Square College (Journalism); B.A., College of New Rochelle; M.F.A., Yale School of Drama. Drama critic: **Black Theatre Magazine**. Technical Director: New Lafayette Theatre Company. Writer-in-Residence, African-American Cultural Center, Buffalo, New York. Film script, commissioned by Sidney Poitier and Harry Belafonte. Recipient: Rockefeller Foundation's Playwright-in-Residence; New York State Council on the Arts Grant (CAPS), 1973, 1975; Special Guest, VOK-TV, Nairobi, Kenya, 1973; Guggenheim Fellowship, 1973-74.

Address: P.O. Box 251, Morningside Station, New York, NY 10026

Agent: Helen Marie Jones, P.O. Box 251, Morningside Station, New York, NY 10026
  (212) 926-5164 or (212) 868-3330

TITLE • AVAILABILITY • PRODUCTIONS

The Advantage of Dope: manuscript (film and theatre)*

The Breakout: manuscript*; ; O'Neill Theater Center's National Playwrights Conference, CT; Manhattan Theatre Club, NYC

Crazy Niggers: manuscript*; The Street Theater, Inc., Eastern Drama Workshop

His First Step: New Lafayette Theater Presents, ed. by Ed Bullins, Anchor Press, Doubleday & Co., Inc., 245 Park Ave., New York, NY 10017, $3.95; New York Shakespeare Festival, NYC

The Juice Problem: manuscript*; O'Neill Theater Center's National Playwrights Conference, CT

Nine As One: manuscript*

The Barbarians: manuscript*; Frank Silvera's Writers' Workshop, NYC

Screamers: manuscript*

A Star is Born Again: manuscript*; African-American Theatre Center, Buffalo, NY

Hillbilly Liberation: Write agent*, $5.00

The Resurrection of Lady Lester: manuscript*; Yale Repertory, CT

  *contact agent

SYNOPSES

The Barbarians: Revolutionary-ritual on the real barbarians of this society, and their ultimate submission to the actual source of power.

Two acts. 9 males (4 black, 5 white), 3 females (1 black, 2 white).

Crazy Niggers: A play showing who are, and the absurdity of, the real crazy niggers and other folk.

Three acts. 13 males (10 black, 3 white), 8 females (7 black, 1 white).

The Juice Problem: An erotic love chartoon, the characters, all black, doing whatever is necessary to survive and "get over."

Three acts. 4 males, 5 females.

WILLIAM PACKARD

Graduated Stanford University with honors in Philosophy. Playwright-in-Residence, Institute of Advanced Studies. He has three collections of poetry, **To Peel an Apple, Peaceable Kingdom,** and **First Selected Poems.** He has translated and adapted from the French, Japanese, Chinese, Italian, Burmese, Korean and Babylonian. Founder and editor of the **New York Quarterly.** Professor at the Washington Square Writing Center; teaches at Hofstra University, Wagner, the New School and Cooper Union. His novel, **Saturday Night at San Marcos,** will be published soon. He also teaches playwriting at the H.B. Studio. Recipient: Robert Frost Award to Breadloaf; Outer Circle Critics Award.

Address: 232 West 14th St., New York, NY 10011

Agent: Bertha Case, 345 West 58th St., New York, NY 10019 (212) 541-9451

TITLE • AVAILABILITY • PRODUCTIONS

In the First Place: Experiment Press*; The White Barn, Westport, CT; ANTA Matinee Series, NYC

Once and for All: Experiment Press*; IASTA, NYC

On the Other Hand: Experiment Press*

From Now On: Experiment Press*; HB Studio, NYC
(The above plays are all early verse plays.)

Sandra and the Janitor: Best Short Plays of 1971, Chilton Book Co., 201 King of Prussia Rd., Radnor, PA 19089, $7.50; HB Studio, numerous stock and regional productions

The Funeral: Four Plays: Bird Girl Press, P.O. Box 521, Old Chelsea Station, New York, NY 10011, $3.95

The Marriage: in **Four Plays;** Gene Frankel Theatre, NYC

War Play: in **Four Plays;** Gene Frankel Theatre, NYC

My Name Is Bobby: manuscript*

The Killer Thing: Bird Girl Press, $10.00

> *contact agent

SYNOPSES

The Funeral: Family is gathered for funeral of father, but is actually psychic funeral of daughter, who is systematically destroyed in course of play.

Long one act. Setting: funeral home. 3 males, 2 females.

War Play: Soldier in eastern war, young girl from native town, ghastly effect of war is gradually disgorged.

Long one act. Setting: a field. 1 male, 1 female.

The Killer Thing: A thirteen-year-old girl runs away from home, encounters a hermit in the woods; later an anonymous man comes on to the same hermit, admits he raped and killed the thirteen-year-old girl, in addition to about twenty-seven other persons he has killed and buried out in the woods.

Full-length. 2 males, 1 female.

P

WILLIAM E. PARCHMAN

Born in Louisville, KY on July 30, 1936, and educated at Murray State University in Kentucky and the American Theatre Wing in New York City. Bill has written for TV's **Captain Kangaroo.** Director: New Nassau Repertory Company, Nassau County, Long Island, NY. Recipient: Playwriting fellowships from Florida State University and Wesleyan University, Conn. Winner of Stanley Award, New York City Writers Conference, Wagner College, for **The Prize in the Crackerjack Box.**

Address: 65 Fourth Ave., Mineola, NY 11501
(516) 747-2168

TITLE • AVAILABILITY • PRODUCTIONS

The Prize in the Crackerjack Box: manuscript*; O'Neill Theater Center's National Playwrights Conference, CT; New Dramatists, NYC

The Party: manuscript*; O'Neill Theater Center's National Playwrights Conference, CT

Mocking Bird: manuscript*; O'Neill Theater Center's National Playwrights Conference, CT

Needmore: manuscript*; New Dramatists, NYC

Needmore's Mother: manuscript*; Asolo Theatre, FL

The King of the Hill Is Down: manuscript*; New Dramatists, NYC

    *contact author

SYNOPSES

The Prize in the Crackerjack Box: A very modern comedy about an idealistic, innocent young man named Sy Fiffer, conditioned by his environment, movies, television, novels, etc., to expect "the best of all worlds." In the play we can see his unfortunate experiences with his ex-wife, his new love, the military establishment, psychiatry, a teeny bopper. The American society and morality are closely examined with song and satire.

Full length. Comedy. Time: the present. Can be performed with one or two set pieces and varied lighting. 17 males, 9 females. It is possible to double-cast some roles.

The King of the Hill Is Down: An assassination attempt is made on a Presidential candidate who has returned to his rural home town. The Law sets out to discover who shot him. Unfortunately, both the sheriff and his deputy are suspects, as well as the victim's old girlfriend who is now the local TV "Weather Woman." The hospital waiting room set up by the police as a command post is invaded by a gun-toting young couple who appear to be intent on finishing the assassination. The mystery is solved in the end and the guilty party gets his punishment — and we all know a little more about the motives of assassins and the American heritage that encourages them.

Three acts. Setting: small-town hospital waiting room. Time: several years from now. 4 males, 3 females.

STEPHEN DAVIS PARKS

Born in Foristell, MO on November 20, 1949. B.S., Colorado State University; M.A. in Creative Writing, San Francisco State University. He began his theater career as an actor and attended the Neighborhood Playhouse School, NYC. He has had poetry published in numerous journals. Has worked as a carpenter.

Address: 2307 Bryant St., San Francisco, CA 94110

Agent: Lois Berman, 250 West 57th St., New York, NY 10019 (212) 581-0670

TITLE • AVAILABILITY • PRODUCTIONS

The Idol Makers: manuscript*; O'Neill Theater Center's National Playwrights Conference, CT; Mark Taper Forum, Los Angeles, CA

Skidding Into Slow Time: manuscript*; O'Neill Theater Center's National Playwrights Conference, CT; Cast Theatre, Los Angeles, CA

*contact agent

PETER PARNELL

Born in New York City on August 21, 1953. Attended public schools on Long Island; B.A. from Dartmouth College, 1974, magna cum laude. Recipient: Reynolds Travelling Fellowship in Playwriting, 1975-76.

Agent: Flora Roberts, 65 East 55th St., New York, NY 10022 (212) 355-4165

TITLE • AVAILABILITY • PRODUCTIONS

Scooter Thomas Makes It to the Top of the World: not available at this time; O'Neill Theater Center's National Playwrights Conference, CT

Sorrows of Stephen: Samuel French, 25 West 45th St., New York, NY 10036, $2.50; New York Shakespeare Festival, NYC

P

ROBERT PATRICK

Born in Kilgore, TX on September 7, 1937. Attended Eastern New Mexico U. Was there at the
beginning of the Off Off Broadway movement at
the Caffe Cino and La Mama. He is dedicated to
the idea that the Theater is a personally responsible art form on a level with painting, poetry,
novels, etc. An essentially new idea born with
Off Off Broadway because Off Off Broadway was
the first wide-spread, long-term, theater movement free of critical, political, academic, financial, religious, military and legal restrictions.
Has written for many magazines, TV, films and
poetry journals. Recipient: CAPS Grant; Rockefeller Grant; Citizens Theatre, Glasgow, Best
World Playwriting Award; **Show Business,** Best
Play Award

Address: c/o La Mama, 74A East 4th St., New York, NY 10003

TITLE • AVAILABILITY • PRODUCTIONS

The Haunted Host: Robert Patrick's Cheep Theatricks: Samuel French, 25 West 45th St.,
New York, NY 10036, $4.45; Caffe Cino, NYC

I Came to New York to Write: in **Cheep Theatricks;** Old Reliable, NYC

Joyce Dynel: in **Cheep Theatricks;** Old Reliable, NYC

Arnold Bliss Show: in **Cheep Theatricks;** Old Reliable, NYC

Help, I Am: in **Cheep Theatricks;** Old Reliable, NYC

Lights, Camera, Action: in **Cheep Theatricks;** Caffe Cino, NYC

One Person: in **Cheep Theatricks;** Old Reliable, NYC

Preggin and Liss: in **Cheep Theatricks;** Old Reliable, NYC

The Richest Girl in the World Finds Happiness: in **Cheep Theatricks;** La Mama E.T.C., NYC

Cornered: in **Cheep Theatricks;** Gallery Theatre, NYC

Still-Love: in **Cheep Theatricks;** Playbox, NYC

The Golden Circle: Samuel French, $1.75; Spring Street Co., NYC

Mirage: in **One Man, One Woman,** Samuel French, $4.45; La Mama E.T.C., NYC

Bank Street Breakfast: in **One Man, One Woman;** I.A.T.I., NYC

Love Lace: in **One Man, One Woman;** Los Angeles, CA

Cheesecake: in **One Man, One Woman;** Caffe Cino, NYC

Something Else: in **One Man, One Woman;** New York Theatre Ensemble, NYC

Cleaning House: in **One Man, One Woman;** W.P.A., NYC

Play-by-Play: Samuel French, $2.50; La Mama, E.T.C., CA

Kennedy's Children: Samuel French, $2.50; Playwrights Horizons, NYC

Love: A Game of Any Length: At Rise, Vol. 12, #4, 9838 Jersey Ave., Santa Fe Springs, CA
90670, $3.00; Our Lady of the Lake College, San Antonio, TX

Simultaneous Transmissions: The Scene, #2, The Smith, 5 Beekman St., New York, NY 10038,
$3.50; Kranny's Nook, Brooklyn

T-Shirts: Gay Plays, Avon Books, 224 W. 57th St., New York, NY 10019, $3.95; Out-And-About,
Minn., MN

My Cup Ranneth Over: Dramatists Play Service, 440 Park Avenue South, New York, NY 10016,
$1.25; Everyman Co., Brooklyn, NY

Mercy Drop: Calamus Press, 121 Second Ave., New York, NY 10003; W.P.A., NYC

Ludwig & Wagner: with **Mercy Drop** etc., Calamus Press; La Mama, NYC

Hymen and Carbuncle: with **Mercy Drop** etc., Calamus Press; Dove Co., NYC

Robert Patrick (cont'd)

Diaghilev & Nijinsky: Mercy Drop & Other Plays, Calamus Press

Un Bel Di: Performance (o.p.)*; Arts Elast, NYC

See Other Side: Yale/Theatre* (o.p.); Old Reliable, NYC

Indecent Exposure: manuscript*; Caffe Cino, NYC

Halloween Hermit: manuscript*; Caffe Cino, NYC

Lily of the Valley of the Dolls: manuscript*; Caffe Cino, NYC

Let Me Tell It to You (Dr. Paroo): Dramatics Magazine—3/78, 3368 Central Pkwy., Cincinnati, OH 45225, $2.00

A Bad Place To Get Your Head: manuscript*; Dove Co., NYC

The Overseers: manuscript*; Old Reliable, NYC

The Path of the Greater Narwhal: manuscript*; Boston Conservatory, MA

The Conservation Menace: manuscript*; La Mama E.T.C., NYC

Hippie as a Lark: manuscript*; Stagelights II, NYC

The Golden Animal: manuscript*; Old Reliable, NYC

Angel, Honey, Baby, Darling, Dear: manuscript*; Old Reliable, NYC

Angels in Agony: manuscript*; Old Reliable, NYC

Fog: G.P.U. News, P.O. Box 92203, Milwaukee, WI 53202, 75¢; Old Reliable, NYC

Mutual Benefit Life: Dramatists Play Service, $2.25; Production Co., NYC

Report to the Mayor: manuscript*; Everyman Co., Brooklyn, NY

The Sleeping Bag: manuscript*; Playwrights Workshop, NYC

Absolute Power over Movie Stars: manuscript*; Old Reliable, NYC

Female Flower: manuscript*

The Family Bar: with **Mercy Drop** etc., Calamus Press; Deja Vu, L.A., CA

Youth Rebellion: manuscript*; Old Reliable, NYC

Silver Skies: manuscript*; Old Reliable, NYC

The Warhol Machine: manuscript*; Playbox Studio, NYC

Judas: West Coast Plays #5, P.O. Box 7206, Berkeley, CA 94707, $4.95; Santa Maria, CA

Starwalk: Dramatika (o.p.)*

Tarquin Truthbeauty: manuscript*; Old Reliable, NYC

How I Came to Be Here Tonite: manuscript*; La Mama E.T.C., L.A., CA

OOOOOOOOPS: manuscript*; Old Reliable, NYC

Salvation Army: manuscript*; Old Reliable, NYC

Hoop-La: manuscript*

I Am Trying to Tell You Something: manuscript; The Space, NYC

The Chattering Illiterates: manuscript*

 *contact author

SYNOPSES

Judas: Young Judas, training for an executive position with the conquering Romans, drifts from both Rome and his religion to follow the cult of Jesus. Pilate tries to save Jesus to prove to Judas the power of Rome—with disastrous results.

Full length. Setting: one unit set, modern dress. 7 males, 1 female.

My Cup Ranneth Over: Paula and Yucca have been roommates from college to New York. Everyone always thought haughty Paula would be the success, but slovenly Yucca's eccentric music suddenly takes off and Paula must deal with her own shock and jealousy.

One act. Setting: modern livingroom. 2 females.

P

Robert Patrick (cont'd)

Mutual Benefit Life: Four young New Yorkers have come to Los Angeles: nineteen-year-old Carol wants to be a star; Scott, Laura and Greg have their own reasons. Scott's amnesia gives Laura her chance to deceive Scott, her husband Greg, and Carol, and to try for romance and stardom for herself.

Full length. Setting: a Los Angeles living-dining area. 2 males, 2 females.

SYBILLE PEARSON

Born in Czechoslovakia on January 25, 1937. Attended New York City College. Acted under the name of Sybil White. Taught Remedial English at City College. She is married and the mother of two sons.

Address: 215 West 88th St., New York, NY
10024 (212) 874-2315

Agent: Audrey Wood, c/o I.C.M., 40 West 57th
St., New York, NY 10019 (212) 556-5722

TITLE • AVAILABILITY • PRODUCTIONS

A Little Going Away Party: manuscript*; The Womens Project, American Place Theatre, NY; Virginia Polytechnical & State University

Sally and Marsha: manuscript*; O'Neill Theater Center's National Playwrights Conference, CT; Yale Repertory, CT

*contact agent

SYNOPSES

Sally and Marsha: A story of two housewives, Sally and Marsha, who meet and become friends. It looks at their needs and their affection for each other.

Full length. Setting: a livingroom-and-kitchen combination. 2 females.

A Little Going Away Party: A story about a moving day, a separation and a death; lived through by Mrs. Wells and her daughter, Claire, and Alex, the moving man.

Long one act. Setting: a basement of an old country house. 1 male, 2 females.

CHINA CLARK PENDARVIS

Staff writer, ABC, **The Bill Cosby Show.** Writing teacher for Cell Block Theatre, Columbia University. Director and founder of **Neo Black Women in Poetry.** Has recorded album of poetry, **China Clark and Neo Black Women in Poetry,** 1976. Teacher at the Network for Learning. Recipient: CAPS, 1975; Hannah del Vecchio, 1974; Woolrich Foundation, 1973.

Address: 145 E. Eighteenth St., 3B, Brooklyn, NY 11226 (212) 856-6826

TITLE • AVAILABILITY • PRODUCTIONS

Profection in Black: New York Shakespeare Festival, 425 Lafayette St., New York, NY 10003, $2.00; Negro Ensemble Company, NYC

In Sorrow's Room: Era, Box 1829, G.P.O. New York, NY 10011, $2.50; African Total Theatre, NYC

Neffie: Era, $2.50; Urban Arts Theatre, NYC

The Chinese Screen: manuscript*; La Mama, ETC, NYC

Sugar Brown—Divine & May: manuscript*

   *contact author

SYNOPSES

In Sorrow's Room: Deals with the independence of a young beautiful black woman. Sorrow has left her domineering mother to find herself. She is pursued constantly by men who seem interested only in her body and not her art or ideas.

4 females, 3 males.

Neffie: A tale of undying love. Music—dance—fantasy.

5 females, 7 males.

JAMES D. PENDLETON

Born in Fort Bragg, NC on December 12, 1930. B.S. from Davidson College and M.A. from U. of NC. Writer for Mutual Radio Network, **Red, White, & Blue in Black** and **Blacks in America,** records for Everette/Edwards Co. Married to singer Catharine Cox Pendleton and has three daughters. He is an associate professor of English at Virginia Commonwealth U. His TV play, **Rite of Passage,** was done in the New Drama for TV at the O'Neill Theater Center's National Playwrights Conference. Recipient: Rochester Civic Theater Playwriting Award; North Carolina School of the Arts Playwriting Award; Converse College Drama Award; James Helms Playscript Award; TRAV-TV Television Writing Award.

Address: Route 1, Box 319, Midlothian, VA 23113, (804) 794-5375, 257-1670

Agent: Lois Berman, 250 W. 57th St., New York, NY 10019 (212) 581-0670

P

James D. Pendleton (cont'd)

TITLE • AVAILABILITY • PRODUCTIONS

A Last Supper: manuscript*; Winston-Salem, NC; Chapel Hills, NC

The Defender: manuscript*; Richmond, VA

The Obscene Verse of Magdalene Randallman: manuscript*; Clarion, PA

The Trial of Judas: manuscript* (in German); Chr. Kaiser Verlag, Munich, Germany; Richmond, VA

The Brief and Violent Reign of Absalom: Religious Theatre, Wichita, State University, manuscript*; Scottsbluff, NB

Nightsong: manuscript*; Spartanburg, SC; Richmond, VA

The Oaks of Mamre: Bakers Play, 100 Chauncy St., Boston, MA 02111, $1.00; Richmond, VA; Chicago, IL

Rite of Passage: manuscript*; **Earplay**

*contact agent

SYNOPSES

A Last Supper: Philip, about forty, plans to ask Laura, same age, to go away with him to Europe. Laura is fully prepared to leave her sterile marriage and spend the rest of her life with Philip but, during the evening, a strange crippled man comes out of the shadows in the back of the restaurant, claims to know them both, and so shatters the mood that Philip tells Laura that he is going to live in Rome alone, leaving her desolate.

One act. Setting: a fashionable restaurant, 1929. 3 males, 1 female.

Nightsong: Eric, a scientist, has worked hard to develop a substance to destroy the harmful insect in the world. He has also discovered that his poison kills helpful insects and that the harmful insects have developed strains too strong for his science. In his work, he has neglected Erna, his wife, who merely wants to live comfortably and be loved. As Eric confronts his failures, he also wants more and more to live and be loved, but he discovers that his neglect has so hardened Erna that she cannot give him the love he wants. He is left contemplating the super-strong insects he has helped produce.

One act. Setting: a home laboratory. 1 male, 1 female.

Rite of Passage: Thomas Jefferson, in his first term as president, faces a number of political crises including the charge that he has fathered three children by the slave woman, Sally Hemings. Jefferson is forced to re-evaluate his own life's work and to face, in a new way, the kinship between the black and white races and its relation to the American nation that he helped to found.

Full length. Setting: In and around Monticello, 1801-3. 6 males, 3 females.

LEONARD L. PERLMUTTER

B.A., University of Rochester; M.A. and M.F.A., University of Miami (Playwriting). Biographical sketch in **Who's Who in the South and Southwest; Dictionary of International Biography.** He is a professional industrial engineer, currently registered in the District of Columbia. Recipient: 1970 Sam Shubert Playwriting Fellowship; Florida Theatre Conference Award; **The Doomsday Conspiracy,** (New Earth Books), grant from the New York State Council on the Arts.

Address: 5610 N.W. 49th Terrace, Ft. Lauderdale, FL 33319 (305) 731-7204

Agent: Ann Elmo, 60 East 42nd St., New York, NY 10017 (212) 686-9282

P

TITLE • AVAILABILITY • PRODUCTIONS

Ma, Pa and Me: manuscript*; University of Miami, FL

Decision: manuscript*; Hollywood Playhouse, Hollywood, FL

Easy Money: manuscript*; Fort Lauderdale Civic Theatre, FL

The Conquests of Helen: manuscript*; Tamarac Workshop for the Performing Arts, Tamarac, FL

The Inheritance: manuscript*; Tamarac Workshop for the Performing Arts, Florida

The Dawn Man: manuscript*

Skin Deep: manuscript*

Second Chance: manuscript*

The Doomsday Conspiracy: manuscript*

*contact author

SYNOPSES

Skin Deep: A plastic surgeon believes that beauty is more than skin deep but a woman novelist who interviews him does not. She has her ugly nose transformed into a beautiful one. The change destroys a lesbian relationship between the novelist and her secretary, thereby proving the surgeon's point. The surgeon discovers a beauty cream which can make women younger and he can become rich as a result. His wife, who previously wanted to divorce him, now changes her mind. In the end she leaves him because he has decided to build a non-profit poor peoples' hospital. The surgeon then begins dating the novelist.

Set. Doctor's office. 1 male, 5 females.

Second Chance: The entire action takes place aboard an airplane. The stewardess is in love with the pilot but his parents are opposed to the marriage because the girl is a Polish coal miner's daughter, while they are college professors and their son went to Harvard. A supernatural visitor tells the passengers the plane has gone down and they are all dead, but they will be given a chance to save themselves. Their salvation lies in having the parents withdraw their opposition to the marriage. The mother agrees but the father does not. The lovers are united and in each other's arms as the plane crashes a second time.

Set: Cutaway section of an airplane. 8 males, 2 females.

The Doomsday Conspiracy: The U.S. Government is going to be overthrown by the most powerful forces in the country. Politics and intrigue! Adventures on tropical islands; jealousy and lust for power, greed. Not only will you laugh but you will long for the outcome. Can two bickering reporters save democracy?

Full length. Setting: bar of a posh Caribbean resort hotel. 5 males, 2 females.

AVRA PETRIDES

Born and raised in Manhattan. Ms. Petrides is an actress as well as playwright. She was seen as Honey in Albee's **Who's Afraid of Virginia Woolf?** when it was first presented on Broadway and has appeared on, Off and Off Off Broadway, also on tour here and abroad in contemporary works, classics and her own plays. She is a member of the New Dramatists and the Actors' Studio.

Address: 1414 Third Ave., New York, NY 10028
(212) 737-0664

Agent: Charles Hunt, c/o Fifi Oscard, 19 West 44th St., New York, NY 10036 (212) 764-1100

Avra Petrides (cont'd)

TITLE • AVAILABILITY • PRODUCTIONS

Phoebus: manuscript*; La Mama E.T.C., NYC

Luminosity: manuscript*; Manhattan Theatre Club, NYC

On the Rocks: manuscript*; The WPA, NYC; WBAI-FM

High Time: manuscript*; The WPA, NYC

In the Dark: manuscript*; New Dramatists, NYC

Soft Shoulders: manuscript*; New Dramatists, NYC

The Bloom is off the Rose: manuscript*

The Dirty Old Man: manuscript*

Evdoxia Smith on the Moon: manuscript*

*contact author

SYNOPSES

In the Dark: Two burglars accidently rob a one-hundred-and-three-year-old woman of her life.

One act. Setting: the barest suggestion of a livingroom. 2 males, 1 female.

Soft Shoulders: A Siamese twin's twin has mysteriously left her side. She goes in search of her.

One act. Setting: bare stage with a white line down its center, suggesting a road. 1 male, 2 females.

Evdoxia Smith on the Moon: Evdoxia Smith, the great Heterogeneous Ballerina loses her ability to "elevate."

Full length. Setting: bare stage. 3 males, 3 females play 20 roles.

HOWARD PFLANZER

Born in New York City on October 18, 1944. B.A. in Languages and Literature, City College of New York, M.F.A. in Playwriting and Dramatic Literature, Yale School of Drama. Television Writers Workshop, Columbia Pictures. Advanced Certificate, Piano and Music Theory. Has written articles on the Theatre and published fiction **(New Voices)**. New York premiere, Brecht's **The Wedding** and **The Beggar or the Dead Dog.** Produced and directed for WBAI-FM, 1975. TV film, **The Return Process,** WNHC-TV, writer/director. Recipient: John Golden Fellow, Yale School of Drama, 1967–68; Playwrights Unit-Puerto Rican Traveling Theatre.

Address: 590 West End Avenue, #9C,
New York, NY 10024 (212) 787-1037

TITLE • AVAILABILITY • PRODUCTIONS

On the Bridge: manuscript*; Theatre Im Zentrum, Austria; Playbox Studio, NYC

It's Your Turn Now: manuscript*; Theatre Im Zentrum, Austria

Inventory: manuscript*

Set Up For Glory: manuscript*

Boris, Beware: manuscript*

The Man Who Loved Music: manuscript*

The Model Ghetto: manuscript*

The Guest of Honor: manuscript*; WBAI-FM; KPFA-FM

You're Having Company: manuscript*; WBAI-FM

Black and Whitey: manuscript*; WBAI-FM

Closet Drama: New Voices*

The Cop: manuscript*; Playwrights Horizons, NYC

Exotic Arms: manuscript*

Matt the Killer: manuscript*; Playwrights Horizons, NYC

The Teachers Room: manuscript*; Playwrights Horizons, NYC

The Rabbi: manuscript*

Mass Media: manuscript*

The Final Act (formerly **Tricks of the Trade):** manuscript*; Symphony Space, NYC

> *contact author

SYNOPSES

The Final Act: a comedy about a magician and his wife; their parting, separate journeys and apocalyptic reunion.

Full length. Setting: three playing areas which serve as indoor and outdoor locations. 3 males, 3 females.

The Rabbi: A Rabbi is caught in a conflict between his every day life and the mysterious and terrifying realms of the Kabbalah.

Full length. Setting: space with several playing areas. 4 males, 3 females.

The Teachers Room: A sinister comedy about the murder of a teacher and the surprising result of a strange and disruptive investigation on the other teachers. Everyone is interrogated by two detectives who are in every way beyond the law.

Full length. Setting: space with several playing areas. 7 males, 2 females.

LOUIS PHILLIPS

Born in Lowell, MA on June 15, 1942. B.A., Stetson University, FL; M.A., Radio, TV and Motion Pictures, University of North Carolina; M.A., English and Comparative Literature, City University of New York. Author of a comic novella, **Theodore Jonathan Wainwright Is Going to Bomb the Pentagon** and numerous books for children, including **The Brothers' Wrong and Wrong Again** (McGraw Hill), **The Man Who Stole the Atlantic Ocean** (Prentice-Hall). His poetry has appeared in many magazines and anthologies, including **New American Poetry.** Recipient: State University of New York Research Fellowship, 1972; State University of New York Playwriting Contest, 1973, 1975; Winner of First **Earplay** Contest.

Address: 447 East 14th St., #12D, New York, NY 10009 (212) 260-2088

Agent: Charles Hunt, Fifi Oscard Agency, 19 West 44th St., New York, NY 10036 (212) 764-1100

TITLE • AVAILABILITY • PRODUCTIONS

Pilgrimage: manuscript*; Actors Voyage East, NYC; Cricket Theater, MN

P

Louis Phillips (cont'd)

The Last of the Marx Brothers' Writers: West Coast Plays, #2, P.O. Box 7206, Berkeley, CA 74707, $4.95; Old Globe Theater, CA; Solari Theater Ensemble, CA

The Banquet: manuscript*

Alchemy Da Vinci: manuscript*; Harpur College, NY

God Have Mercy on the June-Bug: manuscript*; In the Works, U. of MA

A Convention of Tuba Players Convenes in Fat City: manuscript*; Colonnades Theatre Lab, NYC

Who Here Has Seen the Color of the Wind: manuscript*; Colonnades Theatre Lab, NYC; School of Visual Arts, NYC

The Envoi Messages: Modern International Drama, 10/75, Harpur College, Binghamton, NY 13901; Indiana Repertory Theater

Arbuckle's Rape: manuscript*; Westbeth Exchange for the Arts, NYC; National Radio Theater

the Immortals: manuscript*; Players Repertory Theater, FL

The Goalie: manuscript*; Colonnades Theatre Lab, NYC

Warbeck: manuscript*; **Journal of Irish Literature,** Proscenium Press, P.O. Box 361, Newark, DE 19711; Colonnades Theatre Lab, NYC

Life Guard: manuscript*; WPA Theater, NYC

The Ballroom in St. Patrick's Cathedral: manuscript*; Colonnades Theatre Lab, NYC

The Great American Quiz Show Scandal: manuscript*; University of California, San Diego, CA

Radio Station WGOD Is on the Air: Prologue Press, 447 E. 14th St., New York, NY 10009, $3.00

Dead Stars: manuscript*

Precision Machines: manuscript*; Foolkiller Theater, Kansas City, KS

   *contact agent

SYNOPSES

The Ballroom in St. Patrick's Cathedral: Described by Emory Lewis as "a drama of originality and glowing beauty," the play centers on a family of Greek-Americans in a small Massachusetts town during the closing days of World War II. "It is a naturalistic play, whose setting and details of character and dialogue could not be more specific and lifelike."

Full length. Setting: simple, yet functional set, containing several areas. 11 males, 6 females.

The Last of the Marx Brothers' Writers: Jimmy Bryce, an ex-vaudevillian and comedy writer lives in a run-down hotel in Los Angeles. As he waits for a young comic writer to arrive for comedy lessons, Bryce remembers his past life. His memory conjures up his ex-wife Alice and an original "Marx-brothers-like" character called Flammo or Julius Dumont. The play is studded with wild verbal and slapstick comic turns and tries to explore the world of terror and surrealism that lies on the other side of comedy. "It's **Duck Soup** with meat and potatoes." — **Los Angeles Free Press.**

Setting: Broken-down hotel room. 4 males, 1 female, 2 off-stage voices.

The Envoi Messages: A fourteen-year-old girl delivers telegrams for Western Union during the Depression. "If you have any feeling for true drama, **The Envoi Messages** will excite and entice you — to hunger for more of the same." — **The Daily Reporter,** Indiana.

Setting: "The set is simple and functional, yet provides for the myriad special effects needed to take the messenger to darkest Africa, the Wild West, and outer space." (From a review of Envoi.) 8 males, 4 females (with much doubling and tripling of roles).

PEGGY PHILLIPS

Born in New York City. Educated at Columbia University. Has been a publicist for theatre, films and allied arts, as well as a story editor for television and films. Her TV writing credits include most of the major network shows including a year as head writer of the NBC-TV series, **Days of Our Lives.** Other TV credits include **Lassie, My Three Sons, National Velvet, Playhouse 90, Studio One, Matinee Theatre,** and two years in England as writer and story editor for the **Robin Hood** series and others. She was General Press Representative for the first two years of Center Theatre Group in the Mark Taper Forum and Ahmanson Theatres of Los Angeles' Music Center.

Address: 15155 Albright St., Pacific Palisades, CA 90272 (213) 454-1281

TITLE • AVAILABILITY • PRODUCTIONS

The Brink of Glory: manuscript*; Brander Matthews Theatre, Columbia University

To Charlie, With Love: manuscript*; Brander Matthews Theatre, Columbia University

Brass Ring: manuscript*; Lippitt Theatre, RI

The Summer Soldier: manuscript*; Reading-Group Theatre

Listen Professor: Samuel French (out of print); Forest Theatre, NY

Paper Moon: manuscript*; Old Towne Theatre, Smithtown, LI, NY

It Never Was You: manuscript*; Theatre West, Los Angeles

A Golden Sorrow: manuscript*

*contact author

SYNOPSIS

A Golden Sorrow: A romantic historical adventure based on a little-known incident in the immediate post-Napoleonic era in Europe . . . a confrontation between Franz, Duke de Reichstadt and Napoleon's bastard son, Alexandre Walewski. Although nearly the same age, both young men are vastly different in background and character, yet both are loved by the same woman. The result of their confrontation very nearly disturbs the balance of Europe. The play is based on history, but like every story it has its own reality. In the light of personal interpretation of the characters and of their reactions, the author has chosen to believe that what might have happened did happen.

Full length. Multiple scenes but handled in one setting through the use of simple elevations. 10 main characters; 5 others.

P

JOHN PIELMEIER

Born in Altoona, PA on February 23, 1949. B.A. from Catholic University of America, M.F.A. from Pennsylvania State University. As an actor, he has worked extensively in regional theater. He is a member of New Dramatists and The Playwrights Lab of the Actors Studio. Recipient: Shubert Fellowship in Playwriting; Co-winner, 1980 Festival of New American Plays at Actors Theatre of Louisville for **Agnes of God**; Special Mention, Playbill Award.

Agent: Andy Gellis, c/o J. Michael Bloom, Ltd.
400 Madison Avenue, New York, NY 10017
(212) 832-6900

TITLE • AVAILABILITY • PRODUCTIONS

Soledad Brothers (adaptation): not available; Penn State University, PA

A Chosen Room: manuscript* + ; Guthrie Two, MN; New Dramatists, NYC

Song of Myself: manuscript*

Sleight-of-Hand: manuscript*; Reading, J.F.K. Center, Wash., D.C.; optioned

Agnes of God: manuscript*; O'Neill Theater Center's National Playwrights Conference, CT; Actors Theatre of Louisville, KY

Jass: manuscript*; New Dramatists, NYC

A Ghost Story: manuscript* + ; Commission, Actors Theatre of Louisville, KY

　　*contact agent
　　+ when performed together, they use title of **Haunted Lives**

DRURY PIFER

Born in Germiston, South Africa, Commercial aviator. Drama reviewer, San Francisco, 1975–76. **New West** magazine columnist, 1975–76. Novel, **Circle of Women,** Doubleday. Recipient: National Endowment for the Arts Creative Writing Fellowship, 1980.

Address: 1101 Blackshire Road, Wilmington, DE
19805 (302) 656-7320

TITLE • AVAILABILITY • PRODUCTIONS

The Fish: manuscript*; Magic Theater, San Francisco, CA; Pacifica Radio

Suspended: manuscript*; Pacifica Radio; U. Delaware Radio

Head: manuscript*; Pacifica Radio

Waiting for His Majesty: manuscript*; Berkeley Stage Co., Berkeley, CA

Baby: manuscript*; Berkeley Stage Co., Berkeley, CA

Feuerbach's Wife: manuscript*; Berkeley Stage Co., Berkeley, CA

Objay Dart for Judith: manuscript*; Berkeley Stage Co., Berkeley, CA

Smack!: Proscenium Press, P.O. Box 361, Newark, DE 19711, $2.59; Berkeley Stage Co., Berkeley, CA

Winterspace: manuscript*; Berkeley Stage Co., Berkeley, CA

Pagano: manuscript*; Delaware Theatre Co.

An Evening in Our Century: manuscript*; Berkeley Stage Co., Berkeley, CA

Angel in the House: not available at this time; Delaware Theatre Co.

*contact author

SYNOPSES

An Evening in Our Century: Amnesty International has cast a steady light on the practice of torture and Amnesty information as used in this play to explore the psychology of men who will do anything for information. Alex, the old pro, wants to "humanize" the process and invites a young lawyer, Snimen, to help him reorganize things. Snimen resists, but Alex knows Snimen better than the lawyer knows himself. A frightening play that probes the power of the individual to resist.

Full length. Setting: interior of a government office. 4 males, 1 female.

Smack!: Claire, a young woman divorced from Jack, a California thinker and poet, finds that her junk shop income won't cover even minimum expenses, not to mention the orthodontist for her son. Jack is broke, but his dad, Frank, a tightwad and retired actor, has money. Claire cooks up a deal with Joe Adorable, a pusher, to make everyone rich fast. Unfortunately, she has overlooked both the moral issue and Molly, Frank's lady, an ex-stripper who knows all about good and evil. The untangling of this dark comedy is witty and fast paced.

Full length. Setting: a tatty livingroom and a jail cell. 3 males, 3 females.

Feuerbach's Wife: A young Russian official, in scratchy Soviet-issue underwear tries to interrogate an old commissar who has finally run afoul of the Revolution. History in the grand manner unfolds, but the young interrogator finds her fascination and respect undermined by the old man's manner and her terrible long johns. Soon it is no longer clear who is on trial. An absurd comedy in the Chekhovian manner which questions everything from Marx and his dialectic to Pavlov and his dog.

One act. Setting: a basement. 1 male, 1 female.

ROBERT PINE

Born in New York City on February 21, 1928. Bachelor of Civil Engineering, New York University, 1949; M.A., Economic Geography, Columbia University, 1958; M.S., City Planning, Pratt Institute, 1968. Studied Playwriting, Columbia University. Freelance writer and editor. Published book, **Sag Harbor — Past, Present and Future.** Recipient: New York State Council on the Arts grant.

Address: 60 East 9th St., New York, NY 10003
(212) 254-9493

Agent: Susan Schulman, 165 West End Avenue, New York, NY 10023 (212) 877-2216

TITLE • AVAILABILITY • PRODUCTIONS

Delta: manuscript*

Points of Departure: manuscript*

The Little Shop: manuscript*; Reading, Ensemble Studio Theatre, NYC

P

Robert Pine (cont'd)

The Therapist: manuscript*

Strategic Sacrifice: manuscript*

Levine: manuscript*

Landscape with Waitress: Samuel French, 25 West 45th St., New York, NY 10036, $2.50; New York Stage Works, NYC; Ensemble Studio Theatre, NYC

Nine Hundred Million Chinese: manuscript*; Reading, Soho Artists Theatre, NYC

Refugees: manuscript*

Glenn Miller Died for Our Sins: manuscript*; Reading, Ensemble Studio Theatre, NYC

*contact author

SYNOPSES

Landsape with Waitress: A man enters a restaurant alone, orders his dinner, then begins to fantasize about a romantic relationship with the waitress — revealing much about himself in the process.

One act. Setting: a portion of a restaurant with tables. 1 male, 1 female.

Glenn Miller Died for Our Sins: A young boy growing up during World War II — His family, religious and love problems force him to come to grips with who he is.

Full length. Setting: one multiple set with three areas. 6 males, 2 females.

JOSEPH T. PINTAURO

Born in Ozone Park, NY on November 22, 1930. B.B.A. from Manhattan College; M.A. from Fordham in American Literature; B.A. in Philosophy, St. Jeromes College, Ontario; Four years of Theology at Niagara U. Ten books of poetry published by Harper & Row, also a quartet of books under the title of **Rainbow Box.** Novel, **Cold Hands,** by Simon & Schuster. Summit will publish his next novel, **Light At the Beach.** Worked as a copywriter for eight years for Young & Rubicam.

Address: Box 531, Sag Harbor, NY 11963
(516) 725-4141

Agent: Audrey Wood, c/o I.C.M., 40 West 57th St. New York, NY 10019 (212) 556-5600

TITLE • AVAILABILITY • PRODUCTIONS

A, My Name Is Alice: manuscript*; Circle-in-the-Square Workshop, NYC

The Interview: manuscript*; Caffe Cino, NYC; The Cubiculo, NYC

Holy Communion: manuscript*; The Cubiculo, NYC: The Loft, NYC

Cousin's Castle: manuscript*

Cacciatore III: Uncle Zepp: Cacciatore, Dramatists Play Service, 440 Park Avenue South, New York, NY 10016, $2.50; Actors Repertory Company, NY; University of Rhode Island

Cacciatore I: Charlie and Vito: Cacciatore, Dramatist Play Service; Actors Repertory Company, NY; Hudson Guild Theatre, NYC

Cacciatore II: Flywheel and Anna: Cacciatore, Dramatist Play Service; Actors Repertory Company, NY; Hudson Guild Theatre, NYC

The Snow Orchid: manuscript*; O'Neill Theater Center's National Playwrights Conference, CT; Circle Repertory Company, Plays in Progress, NYC

P

Joseph T. Pintauro (cont'd)

Mary McDougal and the Monk: manuscript*

Parakeet Street: manuscript*

   *contact agent

SYNOPSES

Flywheel and Anna: Flywheel, a bus driver, sells his and his wife's apartment and with the money that he secretly squirreled away over their thirty years of hard times, buys a tiny cottage on Shelter Island as a retirement present for Anna. When he presents her with the key on their first week of "supposed" vacation, the grief of those years almost crushes her as she recalls her lifetime of doing without. When she then discovers that their apartment is sold, her anger is uncontainable and her words, as she lashes out at Flywheel, reveal the deep pain, the regret, as well as the love that was in their relationship.

One act. Setting: one room of a summer cottage. 1 male, 1 female.

Charlie and Vito: Charlie, on the eve of his wedding, goes to younger brother's room for advice on what to do about his morning trousers which are much too large. A discussion develops around their dead brother Eddie, who certainly would have been best man if he hadn't been killed six months earlier in a construction accident. The tremendous differences in the two living brothers sharpens and ensnares them into an argument over long endured grievances. But both loved Eddie, and the dead brothers' power radiates into their argument and provides new understanding.

One act. Setting: Vito's bedroom. 2 males.

The Snow Orchid: An electronics engineer, Rocco Lazarra, returns from one year of therapy which he underwent after trying to take his life. His wife is an agoraphobic Sicilian, his oldest son is a homosexual and his youngest, a dope smoking drop out from high school. He brings with him orchids he has started to raise. The family resents this invasion and Rocco's attempts to change them with his new found wisdom. They lash out in revenge against the man and his orchids, and the orchids respond in kind.

Full length. Several levels. 3 males, 1 female.

RAYMOND PLATT

Born in West Chester, PA. B.A., Temple University. Checkered career includes stints as liquor store manager, English teacher, labor disputes arbitrator, advertising copy chief, and wine taster. Has just completed, and is actively pursuing publication of the only known novel (**House Rules**) which contains an original one-act play.

Address: 142 West End Ave., New York, NY 10023

TITLE • AVAILABILITY • PRODUCTIONS

The Blue Period of Merv and Louise Sandstrom: manuscript*

The Dilly: Performance Publishing Co., 978 North McLean Blvd., Elgin, IL 60120, $1.10; Stagelights Theatre

The Name Plate: manuscript*; Theatre Rapport, Los Angeles, CA

Helen's Hand: Performance Publishing Co., $1.10; New York Theatre Ensemble, NYC

The Entertainment: manuscript*; Stagelights Two

P

Raymond Platt (cont'd)

Now That the Children Are Grown: Performance Publishing Co., $2.25; amateur and school productions

The Zodiac Flap: Performance Publishing Co., $2.25; amateur and school productions

The Snowbound King: manuscript*; New York Theatre Ensemble, NYC

Memory Is a Spongecake: manuscript*; Hippodrome Cafe, Off Off Broadway

Morrison/Peterson: manuscript*

Souffle of Turbot: manuscript*; Stagelights Theatre

Watching Over Wally: manuscript*

The Testing Bit: manuscript*; New York Theatre Ensemble, NYC
   *contact author

SYNOPSIS

Watching Over Wally: Wally is the adored, though sensationally oversexed, brother of three innocent spinsters. Conflict, and merriment, ensue when, in deep debt to a gourmet loan shark, Wally is forced to lodge three charming prostitutes in his sisters' apartment. A policeman-pimp who is fanatical about ice cream, and the environmentalist mother of one of the prostitutes, add to the complications. "A dirty play for clean people," W.O.W. manages to explore sexuality with hilarity and without a single off-color word!

Full-length farce. Setting: livingroom. 3 males, 7 females.

ABE POLSKY

Born in Philadelphia, PA on August 13, 1935. Graduated from U.C.L.A., majoring in Theatre Arts. He is experienced in writing plays, screenplays and teleplays. Wrote and co-produced feature film, **The Baby,** original screenplay, **The Firebrand.**

Agent: Lois Berman, 250 W. 57th St., New York, NY 10019 (212) 581-0670/Sam Adams, 9200 Sunset Blvd., Los Angeles, CA 90069 (213) 278-3000

TITLE • AVAILABILITY • PRODUCTIONS

Devour the Snow: Dramatists Play Service, Inc., 440 Park Ave. S., New York, NY 10016, $2.50; Hudson Guild Theatre, NY; Broadway

SYNOPSIS

Devour the Snow: A riveting courtroom drama from the harrowing saga of the ill-fated Donner Party, some of whose members perished (only to be cannibalized by others) while snowbound in the Sierra Nevada mountains. Lewis Keseberg, a German emigrant and survivor of the tragic expedition, has brought a suit for slander against several other survivors, who have accused him of being a grave robber and murderer. As the trial testimony proceeds, the awful facts of the expedition's demise are revealed. Keseberg does not deny the horror of what occurred, or the madness which made him a party to it, but he cannot live with the accusation that all involved will be burdened until the end of their lives with the terrible, numbing anguish of what they went through.

Full length. Setting: single interior/exterior. 8 males, 3 females.

VICTOR POWER

Born in Dublin, Ireland, on October 16, 1930. Educated St. John's College, Waterford, Ireland; University of Iowa, M.A. (Journalism); M.F.A., University of Iowa (Writers Workshop); Ph.D. course completed (in Drama). Taught at the University of Iowa Drama Department, King Abdulaziz University, Saudi Arabia, and Loyola University, Chicago. Employed as broadcaster and producer by Radio Eireann, WSUI Educational Radio, Iowa City and WMT-TV (CBS for Eastern Iowa). Fiction and scholarly articles appeared in **North American Review, Drama & Theater, Educational Theatre Journal, The New Statesman, Eire-Ireland,** Novella, **The Rugged Rascal Ran,** in **Ohio Journal,** Winter 1974 (Ohio State University). Novella, **Lackendara,** in **Ohio Journal,** March, 1976. Novel, **Circle of Knives** (1976), presently in process of negotiation European publication. Recipient: Shubert Playwriting Fellowship, University of Iowa, 1968; Norman Felton doctoral Playwriting Fellowship, 1969, Oireachtas prizes for Gaelic plays, 1959, 1961; "All Ireland" prize for best new play in 1964, 1965; First Prize in the U.S. and Canada for **The Mudnest** in **Story, The Yearbook of Discovery,** 1969; **The Escape** awarded the Illinois Arts Council-WTTW Channel 11 Drama Contest prize in 1974; Illinois Arts Council Creative Writing Fellowship for fiction; Illinois Arts Council Literary Award; NEA Playwright-in-Residence Grant; Translation Center Award, Columbia University, **Apple on the Treetop.**

Address: 1817 Buckingham Dr. N.W., Cedar Rapids, Iowa, 52405 (319) 396-0626

Agent: Bobbe Siegel, 41 West 83rd St., New York, NY 10024 (212) 877-4985

TITLE • AVAILABILITY • PRODUCTIONS

Young Men in a Hurry: manuscript*; Taidhbhdhearc Theater, Galway (in Gaelic); Broadcast, Radio Eireann Players

The Mudnest: Story, The Yearbook of Discovery, Four Winds Press*; WSUI; University of Iowa Radio Players

The Escape: Drama & Theater, State College of New York at Fredonia, NY 14063, $1.50; University of Iowa; Happy Medium Theater, Chicago, IL

Who Needs Enemies?: manuscript*; University of Iowa

Johnnie Will: manuscript*; Equity Showcase, Victory Gardens Theater, Chicago, IL; Body Politic Theater, Chicago, IL

Blood Brothers: manuscript*; WFMT, Chicago Radio Players

Mr. Dunne & Mr. Dooley (one-man show); manuscript*; Chicago, IL

Mother Jones: manuscript*; Body Politic Theater, Chicago, IL

Don't Tell My Mother I'm Living in Sin: manuscript*

*contact author

SYNOPSES

The Escape: The play is set in Ireland in 1968, on a southern seashore. A young priest, Peter McCann, is contemplating doing away with himself. As he stands on the water's edge, the various stages of his priestly life, various parishes he has been in and characters he has met, flash before his eyes. A hilarious episode in England ends in a showdown between McCann and his anglicized pastor, occasioned by the visit of Queen Elizabeth to the parish. His friend, The Dean, a father-figure, represents his conscience-type alter ego. There is humor and comedy in this play which on another layer deals with serious issues. There are two texts — the published multi-media version as staged by the University of Iowa, and the professional version as performed in the Happy Medium Theater, Chicago, in which the role of the Dean is strengthened. This play received national attention in the **National Catholic Reporter,** and was hailed by Protestant and Jewish groups who saw a relevance in the theme to their own religious dilemmas.

8 males (two of whom double for other parts), 1 female.

P

Victor Power (cont'd)

Johnnie Will: Concerns the family problems which arise in a modern Irish rural household when the Northern Ireland political situation impinges on the tranquility of an Irish backwater. The play concerns change . . . the old ways versus the new, the application of modern scientific farming to old-fashioned ways of doing things. Martin Tierney, the head of the house, is appalled by the threat of hoof and mouth disease to his prize herd of cattle, and wishes to use the skills of a quack doctor rather than those of his future son-in-law, a veterinarian. His two daughters are in conflict, his son cannot abide him, and arrives with a divorcee from Belfast, and there is what Gary Houston, book editor of the **Chicago Sun Times,** describes as "some excellent characterization and some exquisite conflict." There is wit, drama and suspense with a strong story line.

4 males, 4 females.

The Mudnest: Based on a news story of a middle-aged Irish bachelor, one of the sixty-thousand unmarried farmers west of the River Shannon, who answers an advertisement from a middle-aged female teacher who, now that her mother has passed away, is jolted into the reality of her aloneness. The play opens as she arrives at the farmhouse in County Waterford, and the play is a comic, often pathetic, unfolding of their courtship. The forces arrayed against their alliance are not only within them, but also externally, from the bachelor uncle but also from an embittered "other" woman who had her eye also on the prize.

4 major characters: 2 male, 2 female. 4 minor characters: 2 male, 2 female.

TONI PRESS

Born in New York City on August 22, 1949. B.A., University of California, Los Angeles; M.A., University of Connecticut. Playwright-in-Residence with The Cherubs Guild Corporation at The Wonderhorse Theatre. Recipient: Shubert Foundation for workshop production, 1975; Wisconsin Arts Board Grant, 1978; Midwest Professional Playwrights Lab.

Address: 34 Montgomery Place, 1B, Brooklyn, NY 11215 (212) 857-8369

TITLE • AVAILABILITY • PRODUCTIONS

Children of the Land: manuscript*; Madison Civic Repertory, WI

John: manuscript*; Playwright's Lab, Minn., MN; New York Stageworks, NYC

We're Here to Help: manuscript*; Madison, WI

The Feast: manuscript*; Playwright's Lab, Minn., MN

Mash Note to an Old Codger: New Plays by Women, Shameless Hussy Press, Box 3092, Berkeley, CA 94703, $3.95; The Company Theatre, Los Angeles, CA

Vera, with Kate: manuscript*; Wonderhorse Theatre, NYC

Tremont: manuscript*

Carolyn: manuscript*

Patty and Josh: manuscript*

*contact author

JAMES PRIDEAUX

Born in South Bend, IN on August 29, 1935. Educated Ball State University, Muncie, IN and University of Michigan. Regular contributor to **Playboy Magazine.** Writer of CBS's **Secret Storm** for two years. TV credits include **Mrs. Lincoln's Husband** on NBC's **Sandburg's Lincoln; Lemonade; The Last of Mrs. Lincoln** on Hollywood **Television Theatre** and **Return Engagement,** Hallmark Hall of Fame. Recipient: New York Drama Desk Award as "Most Promising Playwright 1972-73."

Address: 840 North Larrabee St., West Hollywood, CA 90069

Agent: William Morris Agency, 151 El Camino, Beverly Hills, CA 90212 (213) 274-7451

TITLE • AVAILABILITY • PRODUCTIONS

The Bench: manuscript*; Sniffen Court Comedy Club

Ain't It Awful about Marie Antoinette?: manuscript*; Sniffen Court Comedy Club

Postcards: Dramatists Play Service, 440 Park Avenue South, New York, NY 10016, $1.25; Broadway; Off Broadway

Lemonade: Dramatists Play Service, $2.50; Hollywood Television Theatre; Off Broadway, Albee-Barr-Wilder Playwrights Unit

The Autograph Hound with **Lemonade;** Off Broadway, Albee-Barr-Wilder Playwrights Unit

The Last of Mrs. Lincoln: Dramatists Play Service, $2.50; Broadway; Hollywood Television Theatre

Stuffings: Dramatists Play Service, $2.50; Lincoln Center Library Theatre, NYC

An American Sunset with **Stuffings**

Under Macdougal: manuscript*; Playwrights Horizons, NYC; Ball State University Theater

The Orphans; Dramatists Play Service, $2.50; The Youngstown Playhouse; Theatre 40, Los Angeles, CA; Missouri Repertory Theatre

The Housekeeper: manuscript*; optioned for Broadway

Mixed Couples: manuscript*; Broadway

Jane Heights: manuscript*; Coronet Theatre, Los Angeles, CA

   *contact agent

P/R

JOHN PYROS

B.A. Brooklyn College; Ph.D. New York University. He taught at college level for six years. He is a Producer/director of Dramatika Produce. He has published theater & film criticism for **Quarterly Journal of Speech; American Theatre Journal; Cineaste; Moving Out; Take One; Exchange; Small Press Revue; Negro American Literary Forum;** etc. Publisher/editor; **Dramatika Magazine;** critic-at-large, WWQT, Clearwater, FL; Author, **Mike Gold: Dean of American Proletarian Writers,** 1980; **William Wantling — Poet,** 1981; Editor, **Hippie Literature,** Stony Hills Press, 1981. Recipient: CCLM Award winner, Grant; American Film Institute for an oral history of Stan Vanderbeek, Southern Fellowships Foundation Grant, 1967; Brecht-Monroe Foundation Playwights Award, Wagner College.

Address: 429 Hope St., Tarpon Springs, FL 33589

TITLE • AVAILABILITY • PRODUCTIONS

The Bacchae Rock: manuscript*; New York University

M. L. Bloom: manuscript*; Troy State College, AL

Dear Whitey: manuscript*; Southern University, LA

A Play of Sadness: manuscript*; Berry College, GA

P.S. I Love You: manuscript*

Batman Bops the Book Bandits: manuscript*; Lincoln University, PA

Actors Exercise: L'Esprit, Cumberland College, NJ, Vol. 2, No. 1, $1.00; Cumberland College, NJ

To Solve a Problem: L'Esprit, Vol. 3, No. 2; Cumberland College, NJ

Smith, Bessie, Death of the: manuscript*; Off-Bowery Theatre, NYC

The Freek Advise: Intrepid, Buffalo, NY, Vol. 21, No. 22, $2.00

Last Moments of John D. Rockefeller: manuscript*; Rutgers College, NJ

Last Moments of W.A. Mozart: manuscript*; Center Stage, PA

Sheenie and Shine: manuscript*; Painted State, PA

Winston Tastes Good: manuscript*; Gegenschein Placenter, NY

Janis: manuscript*; Artists Alliance, Tampa, FL

A How To Manual: manuscript*; Loft Gallery, Clearwater, FL

   *contact author

DAVID RABE

Born in Dubuque, IA on March 10, 1940. Attended Loras College and Villanova University for M.A. in Theatre. Recipient: Obie Award; **Variety** Award; Drama Desk Award; Elizabeth Hull-Kate Warriner Drama Guild Award (twice); John Gassner Outer Critics Circle Award; New York Drama Critics Award for **Streamers;** Tony Award for **Sticks and Bones.**

Agent: Ellen Neuwald, Inc., 905 West End Ave., New York, NY 10025 (212) 663-1586

David Rabe (cont'd)

TITLE • AVAILABILITY • PRODUCTIONS

Basic Training of Pavlo Hummel: Samuel French, 25 West 45th St., New York, NY 10036, $2.50; New York Shakespeare Festival, NYC

†Sticks and Bones: Samuel French, $2.50; New York Shakespeare Festival NYC; Broadway

The Orphan: Samuel French, $2.50; Broadway

In the Boom Boom Room: Samuel French, $2.50; Vivian Beaumont, NYC

Streamers: Samuel French, 2.50; Long Wharf Theatre, CT; Mitzi Newhouse, NYC

　　†Lincoln Center, Theatre on Film & Tape

FREDERICK A. RABORG, JR.

Born in Richmond, VA on April 10, 1934; married (Eileen Mary), 6 children; educated at California State College, Bakersfield, B.A., English Literature; graduate studies in literary criticism and children's literature; taught journalism and creative writing, Bakersfield College (1970-75); currently book reviewer for **The Bakersfield California** and free lance writer; former columnist and critic for **The Bakersfield News-Bulletin** and editor of literary quarterly **Pantry** (1964-65); short stories and articles have appeared in such magazines as **The Horn Book, Swank, Chic, Short Story International, Cavalier, Nugget, Rogue, Catholic Home, Editor and Publisher** and others; one poetry volume, **Why Should the Devil Have All the Good Tunes?;** author of seventeen paperback novels under various names; served as national judge for Kern County Drama Festival; served as battalion sergeant major, 8th F.A. Bn. U.S. Army, Korea and Hawaii, won American Spirit Honor Medal. Recipient: First Prize, Class International Intercollegiate Creative Writing Contest, 1969-70; International Thespian Society Competition Award; various awards from The New York Poetry Forum.

Address: P.O. Box 2385, Bakersfield, CA 93303 (805) 323-4064

Agent: Ann Elmo, 60 East 42nd St., New York, NY 10017 (212) 686-9282

TITLE • AVAILABILITY • PRODUCTIONS

Glass: manuscript*

The Other Side of the Island: manuscript*; Bakersfield Community Theatre Guild, CA; Kern County Drama Festival

Making It!: manuscript*; Bakersfield Community Theatre Guild, CA

Ramon and the Artist: manuscript*; **Dramatics Magazine** May/June 1976; North High School, Bakersfield, CA

One Evening in Thalia: manuscript*; Bakersfield Playwrights and Actors Conservatory Theater Organization, CA

Brutesong: manuscript*; Bakersfield Community Theatre Guild, CA

Simas, in Chains!: manuscript*; Bakersfield Playwright and Actors Conservatory Theater, CA

Tribal Rites: manuscript +; Bakersfield Playwrights and Actors Conservatory Theater, CA

Daisy at the Dance: manuscript*

　　*contact agent
　　+ contact Lawrence Harbison, Samuel French 25 W. 45th St., New York, NY 10036

R

Frederick A. Raborg, Jr. (cont'd)

SYNOPSES

Simas, in Chains!: Suitable in form to incorporate original modern dance and original music. Dialogue in verse.

This play is based on documentation of the Simas Kudirka defection off the coast of Martha's Vineyard; it may be performed on bare stage, with fully rigged set (single) or as reader's theatre; provides an excellent light show with the use of appropriate templates.

Full length. 4 females, 6 males.

Tribal Rites: Designed for either fully-rigged or bare stage. An explicit, adult drama — a chthonic ritual suggestive of a comic cycle — rooted in myth, occurring in Frank's Franks, a decrepit restaurant in Skyway, an amusement park by the sea. The chief female is the goddess, Rhea; Andre is an Oscar Wilde-type wag, the keeper of the gate; elements of Beckett come to mind. It is a contemporary Greek drama of sacrifice and rebirth.

Full length. 3 females, 14 males.

PETER RAMSEY

Born in St. Paul, MN on August 25, 1921. Educated at Harvard University; University of Minnesota; The American Theatre Wing. Over fifteen years experience in theatre, including acting and stage managing. Two years a volunteer in the Peace Corps, Santiago, Chile, in a special project of community development using the performing arts. Published twenty-five magazine articles, primarily in the juvenile field for **Golden Magazine.** Four month residence at the Huntington Hartford Foundation, California.

Address: 459 West 43rd St., New York, NY 10036
(212) 541-8364

Management: William Herndon, 117 Christopher St., New York, NY 10014 (212) 675-0093

TITLE • AVAILABILITY • PRODUCTIONS

Three Acts of Charity: manuscript*; Merry-Go-Round Theatre, Sturbridge, MA; Richmond Repertory Theatre, England

Earnest Is the West: manuscript*

Paris Then: manuscript*

See What the Lions in the Back Cage Will Have: manuscript*; Chile, South America

Natasha's Theme from the Idiot: manuscript*

Mention My Name in St. Paul: manuscript*

   *contact author or agent

SYNOPSES

Three Acts of Charity: A tale of murder, lust and greed set against the gentility of the Hudson River Manor House in the year 1868. With each clap of thunder the plot thickens as a naive girl fights for survival amid the machinations of two sisters, a handsome gypsy, a flighty maid and an ever-present detective.

Full length, comedy. Setting: an ornate parlor. 4 females, 3 males.

Earnest Is the West: A paraphrase of Oscar Wilde's **The Importance of Being Earnest;** set in Dodge City and the glorious old West.

Peter Ramsey (cont'd)

Full length. Two sets: the Last Chance Saloon and the porch of the ranch house. 5 males, 4 females.

Mention My Name in St. Paul: A story of three young men coming of age just before the second World War and the effects of the war on them, their relationships and the people involved with them and the destruction of the one who does not go into the war. Told through laughter as well as tears.

Full length. Setting: a unit set or projections. 5 males, 7 females.

BOB RANDALL

Born in New York City on August 20, 1937. Educated at New York University, B.A. In addition to plays, Bob has written several television pilots, contributed to TV specials, one of which was his adaptation of **6 Rms Riv Vu.** His first novel, **The Fan,** was published by Random House and a Literary Guild Selection; **The Next,** Warner Books, 1981, **The Unlisted,** due 1981, Simon & Shuster. Recipient: Drama Desk Award, 1973; twice nominated for an Emmy; Edgar Allen Poe Award, 1978.

Address: 169 East 78th St., New York, NY 10021

Agent: Bret Adams, 36 East 61st St., New York, NY 10021 (212) 752-7864

TITLE • AVAILABILITY • PRODUCTIONS

6 Rms Riv Vu: Samuel French, 25 West 45th St., New York, NY 10036, $2.50; Broadway; television

The Magic Show: manuscript*; Broadway

    *contact agent

DENNIS J. REARDON

Born in Worcester, MA on September 17, 1944, moved around a lot; B.A. University of Kansas ('66); taught English at Indiana University ('66–'67); U.S. Army ('68–'69); married Georgia Wooldridge ('71). Recipient: Hopkins Award to the outstanding scholar in English literature, University of Kansas, 1965 and again in 1966; Shubert Playwriting Fellowship, University of Michigan, 1970; First Prize, Avery Hopwood Drama competition, 1971, for **Siamese Connections.**

Address: 106 MacDougal St., Apt. 9, New York, NY 10012

Agent: Ellen Newwald, 905 West End Ave., New York, NY 10025 (212) 663-1582

TITLE • AVAILABILITY • PRODUCTIONS

The Happiness Cage: Samuel French, 25 West 45th St., New York, NY 10036, $2.50; Anspacher

R

Dennis J. Reardon (cont'd)

Theater, New York Shakespeare Festival, NYC; Newman Theater, New York Shakespeare Festival, NYC

Siamese Connections: manuscript*; Professional Theater Program, University of Michigan, Ann Arbor, MI; Actors Studio, NYC

The Leaf People: manuscript*; Booth Theater, Broadway

*contact agent

SYNOPSES

The Happiness Cage: Patients in a Veterans' Hospital are induced to participate in a program of experimental brain implantations designed to achieve conformable neurological "happiness." One resists, preferring the limitations of his own identity to the technologically achievable bliss. "In his three produced plays Reardon has grappled with the ghost of O'Neill (perhaps unknowingly) while establishing himself as one of America's most promising playwrights." **Contemporary Dramatists,** London. "Dennis Reardon is a playwright of immense talent." — Rex Reed, **New York Daily News.** "A playwright of proven quality." — Clive Barnes, **New York Times.**

Full length. Setting: inside a Veterans' Administration hospital. 10 males, 3 females.

Siamese Connections: A somber, brooding exploration of an American farm family. The characters are all trapped like pinned butterflies on a dream gone bad. The protagonist, a young man sickened by the spiritual vacuity of his existence but bound by archetypal ties of blood and love to his defeated family, wages an intense war of emotional survival. The battle carries beyond the rational into a sad nightmare terrain where the Dead come back with more Life than they possessed while still breathing.

Full length. Setting: an American farm — part of a front yard and a non-representational suggestion of the porch and bedroom of a farmhouse. 4 males, 3 females.

The Leaf People: An adventure story with music depicting the first contact by white men with a hostile tribe of Amazonian Indians. The play endeavors to reveal our fundamentally shared humanity — both bad and good — while it celebrates the beauty of cultural diversity.

Full length. Setting: a Brazilian rain forest. From 11 males, 6 females up to 17 males, 8 females, depending on available resources. (The Broadway version also employed five on-stage musicians, but recorded music will work.)

JEAN REAVEY

Born in New York City. Attended Barnard College, American University, B.A. in Communications. Also novelist and poet. Widow of George Reavey, poet, translator and critic. Her works were first produced in the early sixties. Was Playwright-in-Residence at New Phoenix and member of the Open Theatre. Member: P.E.N. and The Dramatists Guild. Wrote opera, **Who Stole the American Crown Jewels?**

Address: 221 East 85th St., New York, NY 10028
(212) 744-8607

TITLE • AVAILABILITY • PRODUCTIONS

Poised for Violence: manuscript*; WBAI

Bunny Hop: manuscript*; La Mama E.T.C., NYC

Mercy Me: manuscript*; Theatre I.T.D., Zagreb, Yugoslavia; Sarajevo Festival, Yugoslavia

Window: manuscript*; La Mama E.T.C., NYC

Telephone Pole: manuscript*; Playwrights Unit, NYC: Cubiculo, NYC

American Kaleidescope (co-authored): Dramatic Publishing Co., 4150 N. Milwaukee Ave., Chicago, IL 60641, $2.00; Stage 73, NYC; Camera 3, CBS-TV

Ten Ton Toys: manuscript*; Washington Square Methodist Church, NYC

Adora: Letter Edged in Black Press, manuscript*; New York Theatre Ensemble, NYC, Nameless Theatre

The Incredible Julia: manuscript*; Dubrovnik Festival, Yugoslavia; The Quaigh Theatre, NYC

The Blanderbets: manuscript*

Cracks in the Grand Old Manse: manuscript*

Jigsaw (musical): manuscript*; Quaigh Theatre, NYC

Sounds of a Triangle: Klingo's Glove, Madame de Mosque-Kee-Toe, Adora: manuscript*; Nameless Theatre

Two Avenues of Reproach: manuscript*

Home-Grown Dilemma: manuscript*

Eldorado Dream: manuscript*

*contact author

SYNOPSES

Two Avenues of Reproach: A costumed farce wherein two ladies of the 1880s on a wharf in Salem turn to horrifying their spouses by relating the "joys of killing." It is up to a Captain and his Mate to turn these concerns to a ship bearing one-hundred-thirty-seven young women sold into slavery by their fathers. The fate of the ship is thus linked inextricably with the turn in morality when killing is no longer such a joy.

Full length. Setting: a wharf. 4 males, 2 females.

Home-Grown Dilemma: A family sit-com told in a surrealistic manner wherein the mother is so beset she splits apart, which sends the father headlong for help from a police detective, while the five year old son, who is responsible for his parents' dilemma, pursues his course of being impossible, intelligent and intellectual.

Full length. Setting: the family room. 3 males, 3 females.

Eldorado Dream: The story of Jesus Christ and that of artistic creativity meet in a golden space — the Eldorado Dream — as told through multi-media and the conflicts between an art dealer and his stable of artists.

Full length. Setting: an art dealer's home. 4 males, 1 female.

SYLVIA REGAN

Born in New York City on April 15, 1908. Educated at Hillhouse High School, New Haven, Conn., and American Academy of Dramatic Arts, New York, Broadway actress from 1927 through 1931. Theater promotion for Theatre Union, 1932–1936, Mercury Theater, 1936–1939. First play produced in 1940, **Morning Star,** Longacre Theatre, New York. Recipient: With late husband, Abraham Ellstein, Ford Foundation Grant for Grand Opera, **The Golem,** produced by New York City Opera Company, 1963.

Address: 55 East 9th St., New York, NY 10003
(212) 473-0125

Agent: Barbara Rhodes, 140 West End Ave., New York, NY 10023 (212) 580-1300

R

Sylvia Regan (cont'd)

TITLE • AVAILABILITY • PRODUCTIONS

Morning Star: manuscript; Dramatists Play Service, 440 Park Ave. South, New York, NY 10016; Longacre Theater, NY, Embassy Theatre, Swiss Cottage, London

Great to be Alive (musical comedy): manuscript;** Winter Garden Theater, NY

The Fifth Season: Samuel French, 25 West 45th St., New York, NY 10036, $2.50; Cort Theater, NY; Cambridge Theater, London

The Golem (grand opera): manuscript and libretto**; New York City Opera Co., NYC

Zelda: Dramatists Play Service, $2.50; Barrymore Theater, NYC

The Twelfth Hour: manuscript*

The Wind-Up Toys: manuscript*

    *contact agent
    **contact author

SYNOPSES

The Twelfth Hour: The time is April, 1945. The last twelve hours in the life of Benito Mussolini (now sixty-two) and his long time paramour, Clara Petacci (now thirty-two). Guerillas, representing the National Committee for the Liberation of Italy have caught them in their attempt to escape, and hole them up secretly in the attic bedroom of a farmhouse, ostensibly for safe-keeping until the Duce can be brought back to Milan, and tried as a war criminal. The secret is not kept. The next day they are taken away, their fate a matter of history. Since nothing is known of the twelve hours the two actually spent in such a room, the action of the play is based partly on historical fact (in the Duce's remembrance of time past), and the dramatist's fictional conjecture based on their qualities of character.

Full length. Setting: Italian farmhouse attic bedroom, which remains set during occasional simple side settings for flashbacks. 3 females, 18 males (can be doubled, several male walk-ons.)

The Wind-Up Toys: The time is present day Moscow. A young gentile Russian couple, have, with happy anticipation, just moved into a flat in a new housing development, after sharing a communal flat with five others. They are quickly forced to make difficult choices, when their good friends, a young Jewish couple, apply to go to Israel. The man is arrested, tried and convicted on trumped-up charges. In their attempt to help the innocent friend, the tentacles of the State reach out to them with disastrous results.

Full length. Setting: an apartment. 8 males, 8 females. (can be doubled)

RICHARD REICH

Born: Vienna, Austria. Completed college in Austria, then emigrated to the United States. Began writing plays in English, some of which were translated into German and produced on television in Austria, Germany and Switzerland.

Address: 875 West End Ave., New York, NY 10025 (212) 222-8405

TITLE • AVAILABILITY • PRODUCTIONS

The Tin Cup: not available; Margo Jones Theatre, Dallas, TX

Richard Reich (cont'd)

The Dark Corridor: manuscript*; New Lindsey Theatre Club, London, England; White Barn Club Theatre, Westport, CT

House without Windows: Dramatists Play Service, 440 Park Avenue South, New York, NY 10016, $2.50; Theatre Royal, Windsor, England

Night Shade: manuscript*; Straight Wharf Theatre, Nantucket, MA

Nordland: manuscript*; Akademie Theatre, Vienna, Austria

Orchestra: manuscript*; Theater in der Josefstadt, Vienna, Austria

Departemento de Soltero: manuscript*; Theatre of Modern Art, Buenos Aires, Argentina

Girls Are the Funniest: manuscript*; Pheasant Run Playhouse, St. Charles, IL

Semilla: manuscript*; Joaquin De Vedia Theatre, Buenos Aires, Argentina

Pets: manuscript*; Provincetown Playhouse, New York

Naked Underneath: manuscript*

Mirrored Man: manuscript*

The Red Dress: manuscript*

*contact author

SYNOPSES

Naked Underneath: The wife is a successful cookbook author, the husband an unsuccessful serious writer. Frustrated by his wife's success, he decides to write a sex-bestseller — with the help of a call girl.

Set: one. 4 males, 2 females.

Mirrored Man: A man who, with his wife, is about to be driven from his home, ready to flee, to surrender, to give up, finds his conscience in the empty frame of a broken mirror and realizes that he must not run away, that he has to stay: "A man is supposed to be a mirror, a mirror in which others recognize themselves. Throughout all those thousands of years, if everyone of those who ran away had stayed, had stood his ground, this would be a better place to live in now — don't you think?" . . .

1 set: 8 males, 2 females.

SY REITER

Born on November 29, 1921. B.A., Brooklyn College, 1943; M.A. and Ph.D.,, New York University. Author, **World Theater,** Horizon Press, 1973 and Dell paperback, 1974. Teaches Writing for Musical Theater, Playwriting and Dramatic Literature at Brooklyn College, C.U.N.Y.

Address: 215 West 78th St., New York, NY 10024 (212) 874-1177

TITLE • AVAILABILITY • PRODUCTIONS

Cask of Amontillado (one act opera): Aldo Provenzano, 429 Burning Tree Road, Cherry Hill, NJ 08034; Eastman School of Music, NY

Adam and Eve (one act opera): manuscript*; Joseph Jefferson Theater, NYC

R

Sy Reiter (cont'd)

Alice Through the Looking Glass (musical): Dramatic Publishing Co., 4150 N. Milwaukee Ave., Chicago, IL 60641, $1.75; Numerous productions

The Well (total theater piece based on Noh drama):manuscript*; Joseph Jefferson Theater, NYC

Gift of the Magi (musical): Dramatic Publishing Co., $1.00; Numerous productions

Three Shepherds and a Lamb (Christmas opera): manuscript*; Union Presbyterian Church of Brooklyn, NY

Joan and the Devil (musical): manuscript*; 13th Street Theater, NYC

Ivanhoe: manuscript*; Reading, Actors Studio, NYC

*contact author

SYNOPSES

Joan and the Devil: Satan comes to a small town early in the century, on a Fourth of July, looking for a woman who can give him a real contest. He meets such a person in the young Joan.

Full length musical. Setting: one set. 6 males, 7 females. Piano — vocal score.

Ivanhoe: Although based on Scott's novel, the themes and relationships are contemporary to us; Rebecca and the Templar are the main characters.

Full length. Setting: no set required. 10 males, 2 females.

RONALD RIBMAN

Born in New York. Educated at Brooklyn College, University of Pittsburgh. Recipient: Fellow, Rockefeller Foundation 1966, 1968, 1975; Straw Hat Award, 1973, **The Poison Tree;** Fellow, Guggenheim Foundation 1970; Fellow, National Foundation for the Arts, 1973; Obie Award, Best Play, **The Journey of the Fifth Horse** 1966; Emmy Nomination, Best Play, **The Final War of Olly Winter;** Drama Critics Award and Dramatists Guild Award, 1976–77, for **Cold Storage.**

Address: R.R. 1, Sabbath Day Hill, South Salem, NY 10590

Agent: Flora Roberts, Inc., 65 East 55th St., New York, NY 10022 (212) 355-4165

TITLE • AVAILABILITY • PRODUCTIONS

Harry, Noon and Night: Samuel French, 25 West 45th St., New York, NY 10036, $2.50; American Place Theater, NYC

Journey of the Fifth Horse: Samuel French, $2.50; American Place Theater, NYC

Ceremony of Innocence: Dramatists Play Service, 440 Park Avenue South, New York, NY 10016, $2.50; American Place Theater, NYC

Passing Through to Exotic Places: contains **The Son Who Hunted Tigers in Jakarta, Sunstroke, The Burial of Esposito;** Dramatists Play Service, $2.50; Sheridan Square Playhouse, NYC

Fingernails Blue As Flowers: Dell Pub. Co., 1 Dag Hammarskjold Plaza, New York, NY 10016; American Place Theater, NYC

A Break in the Skin: manuscript*; Yale Repertory Theater, CT

The Poison Tree: Samuel French, $2.50; Ambassador Theater, NYC

Cold Storage: Samuel French, $2.50; American Place Theater, NYC; Broadway

*contact agent

HOWARD RICHARDSON

Born in Spartanburg, SC on December 2, 1917. Mars Hill Junior College, 1936; A.B., M.A., University of North Carolina; University of Paris; Ph.D., University of Iowa. Lecturer; staff writer, **Warren Wade,** NBC-TV series, 1947; author series plays produced by Albert McCleery, NBC-TV, 1948–50; story editor, later assistant producer, American Inventory, NBC-TV, 1955–56; instructor of playwriting, Abbe Theatre School, NYC, 1947–48 and Clark Center Performing Arts, New York City, 1960–62; visiting associate professor, University of Oregon, 1963–64; Visiting lecturer, San Fernando Valley State College, 1964–65; Chairman, Dept. of Speech, College of Virgin Islands, 1966; Artist-in-Residence, North Carolina State University and East Tennessee State University. Tour leader, Gateway Holidays, 1966–. Member Dramatists Guild; Writers Guild of America; Actors Equity Assoc.; American Theatre Assoc.; American College Theatre Festival; Speech Association of America. Recipient: Maxwell Anderson Award, 1942.

Address: 207 Columbus Avenue, New York, NY 10023 (212) 874-2616

Agent: Abbott Van Nostrand, Samuel French, Inc., 25 West 45th St., New York, NY 10036 (212) 582-4700

TITLE • AVAILABILITY • PRODUCTIONS

Dark of the Moon (with William Berney): Samuel French, 25 West 45th St., New York, NY 10036, $2.65; Broadway; London

Design for a Stained Glass Window (with William Berney): Baker's Plays, 100 Chauncy St., Boston, MA, $2.25; Mansfield Theatre, NYC: Calvery Theatre, NYC

Mountain Fire (with William Berney): manuscript*; Colosseum Theatre, London; Hayloft Theatre, Allentown, PA

Cat in a Cage (with Frances Goforth): manuscript*; Theatre in the Dale, New Milford, CT; Theatre Noctombule, Paris

Widow's Walk (with Frances Goforth): manuscript*; Barter Theatre, VA

Protective Custody (with William Berney): manuscript*; Walnut Theatre, Philadelphia, PA

Ark of Safety (with Frances Goforth): Samuel French, $2.50; Appalachian Theatre, Mars Hill, NC: Gilbrith Theatre, U. of E. TN

Evening Star (with Frances Goforth): Samuel French, $2.50; Civic Auditorium, Kingsport, TN; Arts Club, Washington, DC

A Thread of Scarlet: Samuel French, $2.50; Juneau-Douglass Little Theatre, AK; Encompass Theatre, NYC

The Laundry: Samuel French, $2.50; Gate Theatre, NYC

*contact agent

SYNOPSES

Protective Custody: This melodrama treats the subject of brain-washing and shows how it is possible by force to convert a person of reactionary beliefs into a dedicated communist. On one level this is a play of exciting intrigue and characterization, but in addition it probes into the basic differences that divide the ideologies of the world today. Dolly Barnes, a successful New York newspaper columnist, on an assignment in central Europe, is kidnapped and detained in a Communist prison. Marc Bradley, a British diplomat who defected to the east, has been sent to convert Dolly to the Communist philosophy. As Mark slowly begins to gain possession of her personality, the play reveals the various methods ranging from physical and mental torture to modern psychiatric techniques by which a prisoner may be converted against his will.

Full length. Setting: two playing areas — a cell in the prison and an interrogation chamber. 4 males, 3 females.

R

Howard Richardson (cont'd)

Mountain Fire: The authors returned to the same form and style of their **Dark of the Moon** in this fantasy of the southern Smoky Mountains. The story is a re-telling of the Bible legend of Sodom and Gomorrah, told as a fable of two rival hillbilly towns. It blends mountain folk tunes with primitive religious fervor and country music. It tells the story of Lot and his young bride, Becky, and her love of the traveling salesman, Joe. It is a parable of two conflicting cultures. Told through a blend of music, poetry, dance.

Full length. Setting: minimum amount of scenery necessary to suggest outdoors in the Smoky Mountains. 13 males, 6 females.

Evening Star: Written particularly for senior adult theater with roles for actors in their sixties or older. The action takes place on board a reconverted Mississippi paddle wheel showboat, now a home for retired actors. The boat is in jeopardy of going bankrupt and in a last ditch effort to save it, the actors organize a benefit performance with results that are both sad and comic. A comedy drama, a geriatric **Love Boat,** it reveals the loves, old jealousies and past ambitions of the passengers. It is realistic in its tender and sympathetic treatment of the problems of aging and has become a popular favorite of retirement centers throughout the country.

Full length. Setting: several playing areas — the lobby, dining salon, captain's bridge and outer deck of the ship. 5 males, 7 females.

ROBERT RICHE

Graduate, Yale University, B.A. Married, two children. Television credits include NBC Movie of the Week, **Run for Your Wife,** ABC series pilot **Studio 84** and comedy serialization **Cereal.** Recipient: Connecticut Foundation for the Arts grant, 1975; National Endowment for the Arts grant, 1974; Office for Advanced Drama Research production grant, 1972; Breadloaf Writers Conference, fellowship in creative writing; Stanley Drama Award, 1979.

Address: 45 New St., Ridgefield, CT 06877

Agent: Robert Freedman, Harold Freedman,
   Brandt & Brandt, Dramatic Dept. Inc.,
   1501 Broadway, New York, NY 10036
   (212) 840-5760

TITLE • AVAILABILITY • PRODUCTIONS

The Stag at Eve: manuscript*

Message from the Grassroots: Samuel French, 25 West 45th St., New York, NY 10036, $2.50; Bristol Old Vic, England, numerous amateur productions

The Great 200th Anniversary H-Bomb Crisis: manuscript*; Magic Theatre of Berkeley, CA

Why is That Dumb Son of a Bitch Down the Street Happier Than I Am?. manuscript*; New Playwrights' Theatre of Washington, DC

Thanksgiving at Aunt Betty's: manuscript*; Washington Theatre Club, Washington, DC

We Hold These Truths: manuscript*; Theatre Off Park, NYC

Daddy Beautiful, Hot Pants and Little Blue Jewel: manuscript*

Last Dance before the Music: manuscript*; Walden Theatre, NYC

   *contact agent

SYNOPSES

Why Is That Dumb Son of a Bitch Down the Street Happier Than I Am?: Harold Conroy, forty-seven, former Navy boxing champion, ex-radical, architect, sculptor, ex-drunk, male chauvinist, wise guy, father and husband, has refused to work for the past two years. He vaguely dreams of a

R

commission to create a sculpture for the new annex to the State University library; complications arise when he is actually awarded the job. Conroy's contrary nature runs hilariously counter to his wife's determination to turn their artistically talented son into a tennis jock, and against his neighbor's running offer to commission him to design a string of Mexican Taco Shacks for suburban Connecticut. The neighbor's wife, an amateur belly dancer, offers comfort and advice for which she is rewarded with something of a rude surprise. How does a misfit comic buffoon like Conroy measure up against a sober world that can see him only as a nuisance? A funny serious play.

Full length. Setting: one interior. 6 males. 4 females.

Last Dance Before the Music: The Playwright is called onstage from the audience to be in attendance at the premiere performance of his "autobiographical play," a carefully structured work which the Director informs him will be done as improvisation — for the sake of "greater depth." In a macabre turn, the Playwright is asked to play himself during the performance, and opposite a former love of his life, a beautiful girl, whom he had written into the play, but whom he has not seen in twenty years. The increasingly frightening conflict between the Director (whom it becomes apparent is Death) and the Playwright is essentialy over the Playwright's affirmative interpretation of his life versus the Director's insistence that the interpretation is a lie. The issues under consideration revolve around the morals and values of modern man. The question of who wins in life and who loses are probed deeply, and with humor, and the play offers some startling answers.

Full length. Setting: bare stage, with props. 5 males, 2 females.

JEAN RILEY

Born in Appleton, WI on July 11, 1916. B.A., Pasadena Playhouse College of Theatre Arts. Author of original play for television, **The Pink Burro;** creator of **Me and Benjy;** managing editor, interracial newspaper in Los Angeles; also columnist for **The Northrop News.** Has edited the following biographies: **Where's the Rest of Me?** (Ronald Reagan); **I Blow My Own Horn** (Jesse Lasky); and **I Love Her, That's Why!**(George Burns). Has worked as an actress at The Players Guild; Hartman Theatre; The Columbus (Ohio) Summer Theatre.

Address: 855 Wellesley Ave., Los Angeles, CA
    90049 (213) 826-0185

Consultant: Bernard Sindell, Sindell Agency,
    11706 Montana Ave., Los Angeles, CA 90049
    (213) 820-2069

TITLE • AVAILABILITY • PRODUCTIONS

Backdoor of Heaven (musical) co-author: manuscript*; Pasadena Playhouse, CA

The Pink Burro: manuscript*; Palm Springs Playhouse, CA

On Stage Inn: manuscript*; Pioneer Playhouse, Danville, KY

The Dirty Dove: manuscript*; TV rights to Universal

Reedee: manuscript*

    *contact author

SYNOPSES

The Pink Burro: A three-act comedy about two retired vaudevillians, Lillian and Frank Anders. Never having reached the top themselves, they settle down to operate a small hamburger-and-coffee shop on the outskirts of Palm Springs. All of Lillian's hopes and plans and every cent made in the pink-painted eatery are directed toward making a star of their daughter who, however, has

R

Jean Riley (cont'd)

made other plans. As the faded star, Lillian, sings, dances, talks, and plans for her family with abandon. As a woman desperately desirous of making her dreams come true for her darling daughter, she is not averse to being brassy and cheap and hoydenish but her desperation surfaces during this conflict-filled weekend of the colorful Desert Circus.

Set: interior of small, flamboyant roadside restaurant. 6 males, 5 females.

Reedee: Reedee is pushing seventy and looks every minute of it. She lives alone in a crummy mobile home with her overweight dachshund. Her sister, Jan, is in her fifties and also will win no beauty contests. Jan works in the steno pool of a major studio. Cleverly conniving, Jan tackles the hottest young impresario in town and gets his enthusiastic interest in her proposed screenplay — after all, motion pictures about sport figures are cleaning up and Jan has a potential blockbuster: the story of her sister who was The World's Champion Lady Wrestler 50 years ago! They have to work fast because this is the week-end that will make them rich and famous! The girls have a ball. They reminisce, laugh, cry, get drunk, fight and come out of the fray triumphant.

Full length. Setting: interior/exterior of a small seedy mobile home. 2 females, 2 dogs.

JONATHAN RINGKAMP
(Brother Jonathan, O.S.F.)

Born in Brooklyn, NY on March 6, 1929. M.F.A. from Pratt Institute, NY. Also studied at Accademmia di Belli Arti, Venice, Italy. He has written films, **Rapallo and Sons, The Killing Hour,** and is now writing a novel and completing the third play in a trilogy called **The Goddams.** TV play for **Visions,** 1975. Recipient: Fulbright Scholarship; runner-up, CAPS and Sergel Prize.

Address: 133 Remsen St., Brooklyn, NY 11201
(212) 834-4755

Agent: Flora Roberts, 65 East 55th St.,
New York, NY 10022 (212) 355-4165

TITLE • AVAILABILITY • PRODUCTIONS

†**Everyman and Roach** (with Geraldine Fitzgerald): manuscript*; Street theatre, La Mama, NYC

Mister Esteban (with Geraldine Fitzgerald): manuscript*; Street theatre, Lincoln Center (outside), NYC

Elena: manuscript*; Street theatre, Brooklyn Academy of Music, NY

If God Wouldn't Eat with A German: manuscript*

The Dog Ran Away: manuscript*; Ensemble Studio Theatre, NYC; Milwaukee Repertory Theatre, WI

You Didn't Have to Tell Me: manuscript*; Ensemble Studio Theatre, NYC

Jack Swift American Myth: manuscript*; Street theatre

Play Dead: manuscript*; Reading, Ensemble Studio Theatre, NYC; Actors Studio, NYC

Veteran: manuscript*; Reading, Ensemble Studio Theatre, NYC: Everyman Theatre, NYC

The Arbor: manuscript*; Manhattan Theatre Club, NYC

Change of Mind: manuscript*; Ensemble Studio Theatre, NYC

Ground Lies Fallow: manuscript*; Reading, Actors Studio, NYC

Shakespeare on Shakespeare: manuscript*; Strasberg Institute, NYC

Bella Figura: manuscript*; Ensemble Studio Theatre, NYC

The Wall at Higgs Memorial Beach**: manuscript*

Gregorius the Great: manuscript*

> *contact author or agent
> **in progress
> †Lincoln Center Theatre on Film & Tape

LOUIS RIVERS

Born in Savannah, GA on September 18, 1922; educated at Savannah State College, B.A.; studied speech and drama with Walter Kerr at Catholic University, Washington, DC; received M.A. in dramatic arts from New York University; studied playwriting with Elmer Rice; studied playwriting with John Gassner at Yale University; received Ph.D. from Fordham University; presently a professor at New York City Community College. Recipient: John Hay Fellowship for Creative Writing; NEA Fellowship, New York University; Experienced Teacher Fellowship, Hunter College; EPDA Fellowship, Kingsboro Community College.

Address: 333 Lafayette Ave. Brooklyn, NY 11238
(212) 857-1567

TITLE • AVAILABILITY • PRODUCTIONS

Black English: manuscript*

Black Pictures: manuscript*

Bouquet for Lorraine: manuscript*

A Case of Peppermint Gum: manuscript*

Crabs in a Bucket: manuscript*

Ghosts: manuscript*

Madam Odum: manuscript*; New Heritage Theater, NYC; Memphis, TN

Mr. Randolph Brown: manuscript*

Nights Passage into Purple Passion: manuscript*

A Papa for Jimmy Jr.: manuscript*

The Scabs: manuscript*

Seeking: manuscript*

Spiritual Rock Incident at Christmas Time: manuscript*

This Piece of Land: manuscript*; American Theater Company, NYC; Memphis, TN

The Witnesses: manuscript*

Soldiers of Freedom: manuscript*; American Theater Company, NYC

More Bread and the Circus: manuscript*

> *contact author

SYNOPSES

Madam Odum: A domestic comedy in two acts, one interior. The inter-actions take place on the campus of a small southern black college in the late 1960's. It is concerned with the resistance of

R

Louis Rivers (cont'd)

one female college professor, Madam Odum, self-styled musical prima donna, who is being forced to retire.

5 black females, 4 black males.

This Piece of Land: One-act domestic, exterior. The play takes place on a small farm in South Carolina during the hot summer of 1934. Emphasis is on the beautiful thought of the play, not plot, which is very simple. The heroine who is terminally ill is determined to help her husband hold onto their piece of land much longer than the present circumstances would allow.

2 black females (1 minor role), 5 black males, 1 white male.

Spiritual Rock Incident: A musical in two acts. It is the retelling of the Biblical story of the divine conception in modern black idioms with rock, gospel, blues and traditional music. The empty stage and auditorium are the setting, and the play is presentational. The musical instruments are two pianos and a drum.

5 black men (2 baritones; a pianist, an organist; a drummer who is a baritone; a tenor), 8 black women (3 who sing and dance; 1 mezzo soprano; 3 dramatic sopranos, 1 contralto.)

SUSAN RIVERS

Born in San Francisco, CA on November 2, 1954. B.A. in Dramatic Art, University of California. Teacher and performer. Member of Eureka Theatre Playwrights Forum. Recipient: NEA Playwright-in-Residence Grant, Julian Theatre, San Francisco, CA.

Address: 577 Castro St., #302, San Francisco, CA 94114 (415) 626-2807

TITLE • AVAILABILITY • PRODUCTIONS

Maude Gonne Says No to the Poet: West Coast Plays, P.O. Box 7206, Berkeley, CA 94707, $4.95; Bay Area Playwrights Festival, San Francisco, CA; Mark Taper Forum, L.A., CA

Bloodletting: manuscript*; Eureka Theatre, San Francisco, CA; American Conservatory Theatre, San Francisco, CA

The Lion and the Portugese: manuscript*; Reading, Seattle Repertory Co., WA

Penelope's House: manuscript*; Julian Theatre, San Francisco, CA

Song of a Nomad Flute: manuscript*; Eureka Theatre, San Francisco, CA

Still Life: manuscript*

Palm Sunday: manuscript*; Eureka Theatre, San Francisco, CA

   *F.K.Van Patten, c/o Eureka Theatre, 2299 Market St., San Francisco, CA 94107

SYNOPSES

Maude Gonne Says No to the Poet: In this fictional treatment of the relationship between Maud Gonne, Irish revolutionary and actress, and the poet W.B. Yeats, Maud and her daughter Izzie, prepare to testify at the trial of Maud's estranged husband, John MacBride — on trial for his life because of his part in the Easter Revolution of 1917. Maud must face up to the disastrous consequences of her manipulation of MacBride, and yearns for the counsel and solace of her old lover, Yeats. Confronted with evidence of her dwindling powers, she refuses to attend the trial. Later, Yeats appears with the news of MacBride's execution. He repeats a proposal of marriage made

Susan Rivers (cont'd)

thirty years earlier. How and why Maud tells him "no" frames the dilemma of human relationships explored in the play; the desire for vulnerability subjugated by the need for control.

One act. Setting: Maud's flat. 1 male, 2 females.

Song of a Nomad Flute: Based on the legend of Lady Wen Chi, a Chinese noblewoman abducted by marauding nomads in 200 A.D. Wen Chi's resistance to change and insistence on isolation precipitates a violent struggle between herself and the nomad chieftain T'ai Han. He pits himself against her death wish and conspires with the harsh elements of the steppes to strip her layers of acquired personality and reveal, at the core, the durable consciousness of life Wen Chi always possessed. Stylistically, the play draws upon elements of Oriental theatre; it requires a great deal of movement, stresses the visual and is highly theatrical.

Full length. Setting: a large, flexible space. 8 males, 8 females, 1 child.

Still Life: A young teacher is brought face-to-face with the fragility of her aspirations in the contemporary world. With her lover breaking away in pursuit of his career and her colleagues battling to save the school from closing, Elsie finds herself turning for answers to an unlikely source: Maisie, the schizophrenic mother of her best friend. Maisie not only turns Elsie's values on end but throws the household into chaos as she careens towards a breakdown, forcing each character into an abrupt moment of self-recognition and leaving Elsie, alone by the end, with a stronger more resilient vision.

Full length. Setting: a San Francisco flat. 2 males, 3 females.

LANIE ROBERTSON

Born in Knoxville, IA on May 4, 1941. Attended fourteen schools in twelve states before graduating high school. Attended U. of Kansas, studied at U. of London, Ph. D. in British Literature, Temple University. **The Insanity of Mary Girard** in **Best Short Plays,** 1978.

Address: 484 West 43rd St., #9C, New York, NY
     10036

Agent: Rick Leed, Hesseltine-Baker Ltd.,
     119 West 57th St., New York, NY 10019
     (212) 489-0966

TITLE • AVAILABILITY • PRODUCTIONS

The Runneth Over Cup: manuscript*

El Tigre de Payare: not available

Dark Night of the Theatre: not available

The Murder of Mrs. Magoo: manuscript*; YM-YWHA, Philadelphia, PA

The Decision: not available

In Separate Chambers: manuscript*; Theater Center, Philadelphia, PA

Washington Revolting: manuscript*

The Park Bench Play: manuscript*

Siamese: manuscript*; Painted Bride Arts Center

He/She: Pizza Pie: manuscript*; East West Art Gallery, NYC

Commentaries on "The Tibetian Book of the Dead": manuscript*

The Curing of Eddie Stoker: manuscript*; YM-YWHA, Philadelphia, PA

R

Lanie Robertson (cont'd)

The Carlisle Commission: manuscript*; Philadelphia, PA; Boston, MA

Back County Crimes: Samuel French, 25 West 45th St., New York, NY 10036, $2.50; Williamstown Theatre Festival, MA; Playwights Horizons, NYC

The Insanity of Mary Girard: Samuel French, $2.50; Theater Center, Philadelphia, PA; Edinburgh Festival, Scotland

Geographies of Northern Provinces: manuscript*; Theater Center, Philadelphia, PA

Closing the Halls Where Once Fatima Stood: manuscript*; The Repertory Company, Philadelphia, PA

What Does a Blind Leopard See?: manuscript*; Theater Center, Philadelphia, PA

The Mickey Mouse Murder Case: manuscript*

Bringing Mother Down: manuscript*; Actors Theatre of America, NYC

The Trials of Mrs. Surratt: manuscript*

    *contact agent

SYNOPSES

Back County Crimes: Similar in structure to **Spoon River Anthology** and **Our Town,** it's life and violent death in a small town tied together by a running commentary by the county's sole physician of many years. These are a series of vignettes which present comic or tragic back woods tales of murder, adultery and various other crimes which altogether celebrate the complexity and beauty of life.

Full length. Setting: platform set. 34 characters (may be done with 4 males, 6 females..

The Insanity of Mary Girard: In 1790, Mary Girard, pregnant with another man's child, is incarcerated by her husband in the asylum for "lunaticks." Throughout the play the "furies" who are other inmates dance about Mary and become persons in her life. At the end she decides to become insane as a way of rejecting the world which has placed her unjustly in this place.

One act. Setting: bare set. 3 males, 4 females.

The Mickey Mouse Murder Case: Minnie, Bugs, Porky, Claracow and Bull gather to celebrate Mickey's fiftieth birthday at a seedy bar in Miami Beach. After Mickey arrives and reveals he is determined to "make a comeback" as a movie star, two "murders" take place. Who is trying to kill off Mickey and why? The play is a black comedy.

One act. Setting: a bar room. 4 males, 2 females.

BETSY JULIA ROBINSON

Born in New York City on February 7, 1951. Graduated from Briarcliff High School, NY. B.A. from Bennington College, studied at the National Theatre Institute. Also an actress. Has written comedy material for actors, cable TV, and comedy revues; articles for technical magazines and **Wisdom's Child** and fortunes for Goldberg's Funny Fortune Cookies. She is a member of the Dramatists Guild.

Address: 57 West 70th Street, New York, NY 10023 (212) 799-4223

TITLE • AVAILABILITY • PRODUCTIONS

The Shanglers: New Plays By Women, Shameless Hussy Press, Box 3092, Berkeley, CA 94703, $3.95; Company Theatre, L.A.

Betsy Julia Robinson (cont'd)

Gladys Mazurky: manuscript*; Ensemble Studio Theatre Workshop, NY

Kin: manuscript*

Inventory: manuscript*

The Last Available Burial Ground on Manhattan Island: At Rise, 9838 Jersey Ave., Santa Fe Springs, CA 90670, $3.00; Ensemble Studio Theatre, NY

Out to Lunch: manuscript*; Ensemble Studio Theatre, NY

    *contact author

SYNOPSES

Gladys Mazurky: A story of a girl and her identity crisis. Gladys, shy and naive with a mild stutter, moves to New York City because a former college buddy has invited her to share the rent on her apartment. She arrives to an empty apartment. Her absent roommate welcomes and forever communicates with her through quickly scrawled notes. Gladys lands a job as a girl friday for a new literary magazine which turns out to be a job as a label typist for a porno magazine distributor. Things and relationships grow from bad to worse, her stutter increases, til at the brink of total collapse, she discovers the art of lying and realizes that she can keep herself for herself. A comedy.

Short two acts. Setting: one set with minimal pieces denoting many different localities. 2 males, 2 females.

Kin: About the importance of and need for kinship, no matter how destructive the relationships. The first Christmas for Lorna and her children, Chrystal and Maxwell, after the suicide of the husband/father. The extended family arrives. Toilet, thermostat, electricity and people break down until all is chaos. Finally a calm settles only to be destroyed by Chrystal's announcement that she is leaving home and family forever. A rather black comedy.

Full length, 3 acts. Setting: livingroom. 3 males, 4 females.

Inventory: Alison has dropped out of college and returned home where she is now working, taking inventory in her best friend's father's toy store. Through constant interruptions, misunderstandings and arguments, she finally manages to sort everything out. A comedy.

Full length, 2 acts. Setting: Stockroom of a toy store. 3 males, 4 females.

S. GARRETT ROBINSON

Born in Columbus, OH on January 18, 1939. Education: B.S. in Microbiology and Physiological Chemistry, Ohio State University; M.L.S. in Library and Information Science and Technology, Rutgers; past Instructor, Black Theatre and the Creative Writing Workshop for The Department of Black Studies, Jersey City State College, Jersey City, NJ. Playwriting participant, Theatre for the Forgotten (Prisoners Work Release Program). Presently, Science Librarian, Hunter College School of Health Sciences (CUNY). Garrett writes primarily for Black Theatre (adults and children). However, he has had a reading of several unproduced works about Appalachian urban whites. He has also written and published several songs. Recipient: The Schuster Faculty Fellowship Award for An Afro-Hispanic Bilingual Theatre Project in East Harlem.

Address: 313 East 10th St., New York, NY 10009

Agent: Lily A. Robinson, Robinson Enterprises, 313 East 10th St., New York, NY 10009 (212) 260-0762

R

S. Garrett Robinson (cont'd)

TITLE • AVAILABILITY • PRODUCTIONS

Hamhocks (a tragi-comedy musical): manuscript*; New Heritage Repertory Theatre of Harlem (NHRT), NYC

The Whiteshop (a cultural spoof): manuscript*; NHRT, Theatre for the Forgotten, Rikers Island, NYC

The Land of Lem: manuscript*; Afro-American Repertory Theatre (AART), Afro Culture Center of Harlem, NYC

The Magic Drum (an Anansi African folktale adapted for children): Wazum Publications, Box 600, New York, NY 10009; AART at Harlem Hospital and Intermediate School 201 of Harlem, NYC

Ajuba and the Magic Gourd: manuscript*; readings

Cophetua (an African love story): manuscript*; readings

*contact author

SYNOPSIS

Land of Lem: Is a dramatic form that fuses African and Euro/Greek dramatic concepts. Characters in the play are caught up in the forces of spiritualism and materialism. Tympano-phonetic structures and rhythms are used to define the characters' reflection of the forces as they are channeled through the personality of a human entity. A classical form of black English based on the Baptist Evangelistic (King James Biblical influence) speech patterns is used as a rhythm vehicle. The ideologies of the black country of the 60s is presented against this framework to create a metaphysical pageantry of symbolism in dress and setting.

Full length. Setting: Harlem is transposed into an undeveloped community manipulated by neocolonial liberals and black opportunists. 11 males (8 black, 3 white), 4 females, (black).

MARY ROHDE

Born in San Antonio, TX on May 17, 1949. B.A. and M.F.A. from Trinity University. She is an actress and member of the Dallas Theater Center's resident company. Also an instructor in Trinity University's Graduate School of Drama. Recipient: Rockefeller Playwriting Fellowship; American Theater Critics Association, Best New Play produced outside of New York, 1978–79.

Address: 3636 Turtle Creek, Dallas, TX 75219

Agent: Bridget Aschenberg, c/o I.C.M.,
40 West 57th St., New York, NY 10019
(212) 556-5720

TITLE • AVAILABILITY • PRODUCTIONS

Ladybug, Ladybug, Fly Away Home: manuscript*; Dallas Theater Center, TX; Trinity University, TX

*contact agent

SYNOPSIS

Ladybug, Ladybug, Fly Away Home: "In the Lovely Lady Beauty Shop of Polly, Texas, the author centers an ammonia-scented little universe where mirth, mystery and vicious gossip blend. Customers under the dryers, cantankerous and overly curious, regale and pry, set the suffocating tone of the tiny town where watching and telling is a preoccupation. Out of well-understood and faithfully-drawn characters, crackling comedy springs, immediate and honest. But tucked into the fun are hints that something's wrong and that it's being covered up." . . . Otis Guernsey, **The Best New Plays of 1978–1979.**

Full length. Setting: a duplex, one side the home of Mama Alice Kayro, the other side her beauty shop — The Lovely Lady. 2 males, 7 females.

ALAN ROLAND

Born in Brooklyn, NY on June 20, 1930. Educated at Antioch College, B.A.; Adelphi U., Clinical Psychology Ph.D.; National Psychological Association for Psychoanalysis — psychoanalytic training. Writing in the field of drama includes plays, librettos, and psychoanalytic drama criticism. Has also organized and coordinated interdisciplinary seminars on The Psychoanalytic Dimension in Avant-Garde Drama and The Psychological Dimension in Modern Film Classics.

Address: 274 West 11th St., New York, NY
   10014 (212) 982-2410

TITLE • AVAILABILITY • PRODUCTIONS

Mr. Stefan (three acts): manuscript*

The War of the Sons of Light (Composer: Ami Maayani): manuscript + (Libretto for Opera-Oratorio)

Mr. Stefan (one act): manuscript*; Berkshire Theatre Winter Workshop, MA

Hold-Up (one act): manuscript*; S. Berkshire Arts, Action Theatre, MA; Bergen County Players, NJ

Ahmed's Razor (An opera-dance-drama) (Choreographer: Anna Sokolow, Composer: Ami Maayani): manuscript*

   *contact author
   + contact: Israel Music Institute, Tel-Aviv, Israel

SYNOPSES

Hold-Up: A black owner of an art gallery struggling to survive the recession is held up by a white hood. No money is to be had, but the fast-speaking, suave owner entices the thief to stay until he finally goes off with several prints. This plan is interrupted and almost spoiled by the unexpected entrance of a suburban housewife, resting from her shopping. As the thief finally leaves with the pictures, the owner hides more in a closet and quickly phones the local TV news station that he has had a major art theft.

One act. Setting: an art gallery with graphics on the walls. 2 males, 1 female.

Mr. Stefan: An eccentric Soviet scientist, who is always inventing the wrong thing at the wrong time in the wrong place, is sent by the powers-that-be, on a rest-cure cruise with an eminent psychiatrist to straighten out his noggin and put him in step with the bureaucracy. Mr. Stefan, however, 'stefanizes" the psychiatrist who turns out to be equally eccentric at heart. The threat of Siberia for each does not prevent them from soaring off into ethereal solutions for mankind's problems.

R

SHELDON ROSEN

Born in the Bronx, NY on August 26, 1943. B.A. from University of Rochester in Psychology. M.S. from Syracuse U. in Telecommunications (The Sheldon Leonard-Danny Thomas Fellowship at Syracuse). Playwright-in-Residence at The National Art Centre, 1976–77; Playwright-in-Residence, Stratford Festival, 1979; Chairman of the Guild of Canadian Playwrights, 1979–80. Recipient: Canada Council Playwriting Grant, 1972, 1976–77, 1978; Canadian Author's Association Award, 1980.

Address: 460 Palmerston Blvd., Toronto, Ontario
   M6G 2P1 (416) 532-7594 or (416) 626-5464
   (Service)

Agent: Susan Schulman, 165 West End Ave., New York, NY 10022 (212) 877-2216

TITLE • AVAILABILITY • PRODUCTIONS

Love Mouse: Playwright's Canada, 8 York St., Toronto, Ontario M5J 1R2, $3.50; Toronto Learning Resources Centre; Poor Alex Theatre, Toronto

Meyer's Room: in **A Collection of Canadian Plays,** Simon & Pierre Publishers, P.O. Box 280, Adelaide St. Postal Station, Toronto 1, Ontario; Poor Alex Theatre, Toronto; C.B.C. Radio, Toronto

The Wonderful World of William Bends, who is not quite himself today: Playwright's Canada, $3.50; Tarragon Theatre, Toronto

Stag King: manuscript*; Tarragon Theatre, Toronto

The Box: West Coast Plays, P.O. Box 7206, Berkeley, CA 94707; Vancouver East Cultural Centre; Factory Theatre Lab., Toronto

Frugal Repast: Playwright's Canada, $3.50; Vancouver East Cultural Centre

The Grand Hysteric: Playwright's Canada, $3.50; Vancouver East Cultural Centre

Alice in Wonderland: manuscript*; PNE Coliseum, Vancouver

Waiting to Go: manuscript*

Ned and Jack: Playwright's Canada, $4.95; Vancouver East Cultural Centre; Stratford Festival, Stratford, Ontario

Dwelling (mime play): manuscript*; City Stage, Vancouver

Impact (mime play): manuscript*; Arts Club, Vancouver

Souvenirs: manuscript*; Toronto Free Theatre, Toronto

   *contact author

SYNOPSES

Ned and Jack: John Barrymore climbs fourteen floors of fire escape to break into playwright Edward Sheldon's apartment to find out why his best friend didn't make it to the opening of his **Hamlet.** The play is a late-night encounter between two dynamic figures from the 1920's New York theatre world, at a point when their personal and professional lives were in crisis.

Full length. Setting: penthouse bedroom overlooking Central Park. 3 males.

Stag King: A family play adapted from an 18th Century Italian fairy tale by Carlo Gozzi. Through black magic and manipulation, the King is transformed into an enchanted stag and hunted down, only to be rescued by a powerful magician.

Full length. Setting: multi-sets of castle, court yard an various parts of a nearby forest. 10 males, 2 females, doubling.

Waiting To Go: A young commercial artist's life is changed by a chance meeting with a Czechoslavakian janitor in the men's room at Lincoln Center during a matinee performance of **The Nutcracker.**

One act that lasts as long as the music to Act 1 of **The Nutcracker.** Setting: a men's room. 3 males.

JAMES L. ROSENBERG

Born Sheridan, WY on May 19, 1921. A.B., University of Denver. Has taught at the English Department, Kansas State University; Theatre Department, Tulane University. Visiting Professor of Drama, University of Birmingham (England). Currently Professor of Playwriting and Director of Graduate Studies, Drama Department, Carnegie-Mellon University. Translator: **Sir Gawain and the Green Knight** (verse translation), Rinehart; **The Chinese Wall,** by Max Frisch (translated from the German), Hill and Wang; **The Wicked Cooks,** by Gunter Grass (translated from the German), in **New Theatre of Europe: II,** Dell; **Three Plays by Max Frisch** (translated from the German) Hill and Wang; author of **A Primer of Kinetics** (poems), The Swallow Press. Recipient: MCA Writing Fellowship, Universal Studios; Fulbright Fellowship to England, 1968–69; Public Committee for the Humanities for TV script on John Kane; Commission from Iron Clad Agreement.

Address: 3230 Beechwood Blvd., Pittsburgh, PA 15217 (412) 421-6247

TITLE • AVAILABILITY • PRODUCTIONS

The Death and Life of Sneaky Fitch: Dramatists Play Service, 440 Park Avenue South, New York, NY 10016, $3.95; numerous school, college, theatre group productions, Off Off Broadway

Table Stakes (one act): Studio Theatre, Carnegie-Mellon Univ., PA

Voices (one act): Studio Theatre, Carnegie-Mellon Univ., PA

The Processing Room: manuscript*

Cells: manuscript*

Mel Says to Give You His Best: Dramatists Play Service, $1.25; American College Theatre Festival; Pennsylvania State University

Good Breeding: manuscript*

Gladys: manuscript*; Carnegie-Mellon University, PA; Chatham College

The Aspern Papers (adaptation): manuscript*; Chatham College; The Mattress Factory

Jeeves, By Jove! (adaptation): manuscript*

Kane: manuscript*; WQED-TV, PA

My Dear Sisters: manuscript*; The Iron Clad Agreement, Pittsburgh, PA

   *contact author

SYNOPSES

The Death and Life of Sneaky Fitch: To the ambitious little town of Gopher Gulch, Sneaky Fitch is an abrasive disgrace — a no-good, drunken, brawling nuisance. When he falls ill there is a sigh of relief, and when he apparently dies (thanks to some suspicious "medicine" administered by the departing Doc Burch) there are few tears. But when Sneaky rises from his coffin the picture changes, for no one dares confront a man who has come back from the dead. Capitalizing on his "invincibility" Sneaky soon takes over as sheriff, mayor and town banker — not to mention being the man who faces down Rackham, the fastest gun in the West. In short, where he was formerly unbearable he is now insufferable. But mortality (thanks to the reappearance of Doc Burch) suddenly returns, and once the truth is out it's curtains for Sneaky — this time for keeps — and all ends as boisterously and happily as you might wish.

Setting: exterior. 10 males, 3 females.

Good Breeding: A Brechtian Farce. Eberhard Funk, bourgeois to the marrow, middle-aged, and married to the twenty-year-old Millie, has failed in his effort to perpetuate the Funk line. In line with sound business practice, he decides to advertise in the newspaper for a person to fill the

R

James L. Rosenberg (cont'd)

post of honor in his place. Among the applicants (all of them deemed unsuitable) is Roger, Millie's secret beloved, who appears in various disguises, all of them unsuccessful, until at last, appearing as himself, he is joyously and even insistently selected by Eberhard, who virtually forces the two young people into the bedroom together and concludes the play with a veritable war-dance of triumph, screaming: "I've won! I've won!" The shades of Machiavelli, Moliere, and Brecht are invoked from time to time in this mildly grotesque comedy.

Setting: interior. 5 males, 2 females.

The Processing Room: In an Orwellian world of the future, where wars and pollution have forced society to literally go underground, French and Eva live together in a subterranean garbage-disposal plant, slaves to a system they ony dimly comprehend and do not even know how to question. A new man, Springer, is assigned to work with them; eager and optimistic, he inspires Eva with hope for a brighter future through correspondence school education, and when, eventually, the growing relationship between Springer and Eva arouses French's jealousy, there is a fight in which Springer is killed. In this upside-down world, blacks have replaced whites as the wealthy, educated, dominant race, and when the supervisors of the processing room — two well-dressed African blacks with Oxford accents — hear of the killing, they solve the problem by disposing of Springer's body with the rest of the garbage. In the play's final scene, a new man, eager to make good, arrives to replace and the cycle continues.

Setting: interior. 5 males, 1 female.

ROBERT S. ROSS

Born in Winthrop, MA on January 21, 1938. Educated at Boston University, B.A., cum laude; San Francisco State University, M.A.; currently concluding Ph.D. program at the University of Southern California. In addition to his doctoral studies and writing for the stage, he is currently teaching classes in Theatre at the University of Southern California. Recipient: Story College Creative Award for **Death of the Colonel;** Fellowship for Doctoral Program in Theater History, USC; Shubert Fellowship in Playwriting at San Francisco State U.

Address: 341 Diamond St., Laguna Beach, CA 92651

Agent: Audrey Wood, International Creative Management, 40 West 57th St., New York, NY 10019 (212) 556-5600

TITLE • AVAILABILITY • PRODUCTIONS

A Queen Can Lay Eggs (formerly **The Ghost Violets**): manuscript*; O'Neill Theater Center's National Playwrights Conference, CT; Trinity Methodist Church Theatre, San Francisco, CA

Ishtar: manuscript*; O'Neill Theater Center's National Playwrights Conference, CT

Promise of the Raining Aged: manuscript*; The Gallery Players Playhouse, Venice, CA

   *contact author

SYNOPSES

A Queen Can Lay Eggs: An aging professor, Baratnal, disillusioned, disgruntled, and lost, is torn between the sociological norm of accepted moralities, and the new consciousness of the 1960s. Baratnal has been involved for many years in a mutually-destructive homosexual relationship with a colleague. A new graduate student enters the picture, creating a triangle of conflict leading to an explosive rift among all three parties; but the experience enables Baratnal to gain inner peace and an objective perspective on his life.

Full length. Setting: the livingroom of Baratnal's "furnished apartment." 3 males, 1 female.

Robert Ross (cont'd)

Ishtar: A tenuous family relationship is disrupted when the son brings home a young girl of questionable repute. During her stay she inadvertently brings to the forefront the dissatisfactions, frustrations, illusions, and disappointments that exist in the family relationships. They discover that they have chosen their hell by pretending that they are victims of circumstance who cannot change their nature. This allows each a sense of previously unexperienced freedom and points them toward a more healthy and constructive future as a family unit.

Full length. Setting: an adjoining kitchen and family room. 2 males, 2 females.

Promise of the Raining Aged: The play tells the story of a middle-class black youth torn between the demands and needs of his white buddies, his father, the white girl he grows to love, and an old black man who attempts to help him. It treats in a sensitive and human way the growth of a heterosexual relationship between a black and a white without overt racial overtones or sexual sensationalism. The story is told through the eyes of an aging black who has found a kind of peace that by 1960 seemed no longer possible for a much newer generation, whether it was white or black. It concentrates on the development and collapse of relationships among young people for whom the future is uncertain and the past unclear. Their struggle is a positive affirmation of human values and the dreams of youth.

Full length. Setting: a deteriorating games-souvenir shop at the end of the boardwalk in Revere Beach, Massachusetts. 7 males, 3 females.

ENID RUDD

Born in Newark, NJ. Graduated American Academy of Dramatic Arts. Studied at the American Theatre Wing and at the H.B. Studio. Member, Herbert Berghof Playwrighting Foundation. TV credits: **Hollywood Television Theatre** — K.C.E.T., **The Ashes of Mrs. Reasoner,** a full-length play. On the TV staff for **One Life to Live** and **Edge of Night.** Recipient: Best Play, 1977, Actors Theatre of Louisville, **Does Anybody Here Do the Peabody?**

Address: 13 Glenside Dr., West Orange, NJ
07052

TITLE • AVAILABILITY • PRODUCTIONS

Peterpat: Samuel French, 25 West 45th St., New York, NY 10036, $2.50; Longacre Theatre; European productions

Marriage Gambol: manuscript*; summer and dinner theatres

The Ashes of Mrs. Reasoner: manuscript*; Paramus Playhouse, NJ

What Do I Do About Hemingway: manuscript*; Walden, NY

Does Anybody Here Do the Peabody?: manuscript*; T. Schreiber Theater, NYC; Actors Theatre of Louisville, KY

A Step Out of Line: manuscript*; H.B. Studio, NYC

*contact author

SYNOPSES

Does Anybody Here Do the Peabody?: With music from the thirties and talent as good as anybody, Polly Raisen wants something more than middle-class morality, disappointed ambitions and playing the piano in Woolworths for the rest of her life. At the critical moment a savior appears. Barney is hep, Hollywood, hateful and full of hope. But he offers Polly a most unbelievable and bizarre possibility. An entirely new career in show "biz." Polly's dilemma reflected in the suspicious eyes of her daughter, sister and mother dances her to conclusive deci-

R

Enid Rudd (cont'd)

sions. Her response to the title question sets the tragic-comic tone of her life. Does anybody here do the Peabody?

Full length. Setting: dining room and alcove of a middle-class flat during the thirties. 3 males, 6 females.

What Do I Do about Hemingway?: A member of the hip generation in search of freedom and relief hides herself away in an abandoned oil tank. Her relentless pursuer is Martin Max who seeks to supply all her needs with an offer of love, compassion and a steady job as a Good Humor salesman. Her aspiring family is torn between wanting her safe and their own ambitions for her realized. They all grow up and out in the strangest way and the hippies aren't too far from life after all.

Full length. Setting: exterior of an abandoned oil tank; bedroom of an upper-income country home. 6 males, 5 females.

ROBERT WALLACE RUSSELL

B.A. Philosophy, University of Southern California. Original screenplays, five Hollywood features and many non-theatrical films. Co-librettist, **Take Me Along** and **Flora The Red Menace.**

Address: 345 West 58th St., New York, NY 10019

TITLE • AVAILABILITY • PRODUCTIONS

Washington Shall Hang: Theodore Gaus' Sons, 30 Prince St., Brooklyn, NY 11201, $5.75; The Players Club, NYC

Queen Lear (adaptation): manuscript*

    *contact author

SYNOPSIS

Washington Shall Hang: Through the cunning of John Andre, Henry Clinton and Benedict Arnold, George Washington has been captured and the American Revolution has collapsed. Washington is court-martialled before a court composed of his three enemies, who are now viscounts in the new American peerage. The presiding officer is Prince Frederick Duke of York, 18-year-old second son of George III and his papa's Viceroy in the Kingdom of America. Peggy Arnold, young Horatio Nelson and Banastre Tarleton are historical principals.

Full length. Setting: a warehouse room with furniture. 7 males, 3 females.

LEO RUTMAN

Born New York City on September 23, 1938. Educated at Hofstra University, B.A.; graduate work at Columbia, Brandeis and Yale Universities in Drama. Recently completed novel and screenplay. Lecturer in English, Hunter College and Fordham University; lecturer in Theater Department, Lehman College. "There are still many young American playwrights with the gifts to blast this theater out of its formulas . . . Leo Rutman is one of them." — Robert Brustein, **The Third Theater Revisited.** Novel, **Five Good Boys,** Viking Press, 1981–82. Recipient: Columbia University Sam S. Shubert Playwriting Award; Brandeis University Playwright in Residence Award; Yale University, Joseph E. Levine Film Fellowship.

Address: 945 West End Ave., New York, NY 10025

Agent: Phillip Spitzer, 111-25 76th Ave., Forest Hills, NY 11375 (212) 263-7592

TITLE • AVAILABILITY • PRODUCTIONS

They Got Jack: Yale/Theater*; The New Theater, NYC

Interlude at a Shoe Shine Stand: manuscript*; Columbia University, NYC

Jesus Is a Junkie: manuscript*; 13th Street Theater, NYC

Where is Che Guevara?: manuscript*; The Actors Studio, NYC

Gott Ist Tot! Killed along with James Bond in a Four Car Collision on the Los Angeles Freeway: manuscript*

America in Heat: manuscript*

The Life and Death of Rogue Robbie Kilkenny: manuscript*

Night Whispers: manuscript*

A Night Wind: manuscript*

The World is Mine at Six o'Clock Tonight (rock musical): manuscript*

Twenty Years After the Man in the Iron Mask: manuscript*; Theater for the New City, NYC

Leon Trotsky: manuscript*

*contact author

SYNOPSES

Leon Trotsky: Trotsky, now living in Mexico, awaiting assassination by Stalin, looks back on his life. The play is an examination of the young revolutionary, the architect of the Russian Revolution, the hero of the Civil War victory over the White Russians and the loser to Stalin in the struggle for power after Lenin's death. It also examines his personal life, his failure as a father to his son and daughter and his two marriages. All the action is in flashback as Trotsky awaits death.

Full length. Setting: one set using a raked stage to suggest the descent into Trotsky's past. 9 males, 3 females.

Gott Is Tot! Killed along with James Bond in a Four Car Collision on the Los Angeles Freeway: An ad agency's latest client is Adolf Hitler, who will run against Paul Newman for the presidency . . . and win. Other agency clients are James Bond and God. A phantasmagoric burlesque style is used to look at mod fascism in operation.

Full length. Setting: an imaginative representation of an ad agency/mental institution. 9 males, 3 females.

R/S

Leo Rutman (cont'd)

A Night Wind: A murder that took place thirty years ago on the streets of New York propels a playwright to write a film in an attempt to discover who is the actual murderer. The resolution of the play revolves around what the playwright must do when he cannot resolve a situation with his own art. The movie within a play uses '40s music and other stylistic effects to recreate the past.

Full length. Cast of 12 doubling and tripling in various roles.

BERNARD SABATH

Coach for Professional Writers Workshop, Medill School of Journalism, Northwestern University (Chicago campus) since 1965. Recipient: Sergel Prize, 1975; Jacksonville University, 1975; Des Moines Community Playhouse, 1975; Colonial Players, 1975; Stanley Drama, 1969; Humboldt (Calif.) State, 1968; California State Theatre at San Diego, 1963; Blue Masque Contemporary Series, 1963; Baton Rouge Theatre, 1962; Stevens Award for Serious Drama at Dramatists' Alliance, 1961; University of Nebraska Theatre, 1961. TV for CBS Drama Workshop. Radio for BBC. Member of Playwrights at Tanglewood for Boston University, 1968. OADR, 1967; Midwest Playwrights Lab, 1979.

Agent: Robert A. Freedman, Brandt & Brandt,
  1500 Broadway, New York, NY 10036
  (212) 840-5760

TITLE • AVAILABILITY • PRODUCTIONS

The Summer Demons: unavailable; Wilmington Drama League, DE

Eclipse Day: unavailable; IASTA, Off Broadway

The Man Who Lost the River: manuscript*; Virginia Museum Theatre; reading, Hartford Stage Company, CT

A Happy New Year to the Whole World except Alexander Graham Bell: manuscript*; Jacksonville Summer Repertory Theatre, FL

The Boys in Autumn: manuscript*; optioned

Daughter of the Giant: manuscript*; optioned

Moscow Lights: manuscript*; American Conservatory Theatre, CA

    *contact agent

SYNOPSES

The Man Who Lost the River: A comedy with fantasy element. In 1910, the final spring of Sam Clemens' life, a pompous young publisher's representative comes to ask the author to write one final fictional boy — a creation to stand beside Tom and Huck. The old man, grown bitter through loneliness and loss, protests that boyhood and humor no longer interest him. Meanwhile, a thieving and dirty runaway youth lurks about the house — ghost or real? — tantalizing Clemens, drawing the old man back to long-ago optimism and creative force. He tricks the youngster into an unexpected destiny, then sits down to write, just as Halley's comet comes to collect him. "A beautiful play ... vivid, exciting theatre." — **Richmond News Leader.**

Full length. Composite set: livingroom/office. 5 males, 5 females.

Bernard Sabath (cont'd)

A Happy New Year to the Whole World except Alexander Graham Bell: A comedy about the American age of invention. Time, 1877 — a crucial moment for young (thirty) A.G. Bell who needs financing for final work and demonstration on the telephone. He approaches Sam Clemens, forty, known to be invention prone. Clemens, burned on several investments already, needs a major one to enable him to stay home and write rather than traveling the country to lecture in order to support a costly lifestyle. The meeting with Bell is a conflict between two stubborn geniuses. Clemens finally does not invest, but soon becomes the first private "subscriber" to the telephone. He trumpets his dissatisfaction with Bell to the world. Bell eventually comes demanding an apology. Other characters include Clemens' wife Livy; a high school lad deep in inventing; an investment-rich haberdashery clerk and his malapropping wife. "An intriguing play ... bright flights of fancy ... stimulating theatre." **Jacksonville Journal.**

Full length. Unit set. 8 males, 3 females.

HOWARD SACKLER+

Born in New York City on December 19, 1929. Educated at Brooklyn College. Director, Caedmon Records, 1953–68. Has directed films, television and for stage. Recipient: Rockefeller Grant; Bittauer Foundation; Maxwell Anderson Award; Sergel Award; Pulitzer Prize; New York Drama Critics Circle Award; Tony Award.

Attorney: c/o Jay Harris, 120 East 56th Street, New York, NY 10022 (212) 758-0800

TITLE • AVAILABILITY • PRODUCTIONS

Urie Acosta: not available; Berkeley, CA

Mr. Welk and Jersey Jim: not available; New York City

The Yellow Loves: not available; Chicago, IL

A Few Inquiries: Dial Press, 1 Dag Hammarskjold Plaza, 245 East 47th St., New York, NY 10017; Boston, MA

The Nine O'Clock Mail: Samuel French, 25 West 45th St., New York, NY 10036, Call for information; Boston, MA

The Pastime of Monsieur Robert: manuscript*; London

Sarah: manuscript*

Skippy: Best Short Plays, 1971, Chilton Press, Chilton Way, Radnor, PA 19089, $10.50

The Great White Hope: Samuel French, $2.50; Arena Stage, Washington, DC; Broadway

Semmelweiss: manuscript*; Studio Arena Theater, Buffalo, NY; Washington, DC

Goodbye Fidel: manuscript*; Broadway

*contact attorney

S

FRED SAIDY

Born in Los Angeles, CA on February 17, 1907. Graduated N.Y.U. (Journalism). Sports Editor, **Manitou** (Colorado) **Springs Journal,** Columnist and writer of verse (**N.Y. World, Tribune, Saturday Review),** Contributor to **New York Times.** Screenplays for Red Skelton, Lucille Ball, et al. Librettist of five Broadway musicals. Staff writer for NBC television, editor of magazine **Broadway.** Appearances on TV as panelist and bridge expert. Recipient: Antoinette Perry Award for Best Musical, 1947; George Jean Nathan Award for Best Musical Book of 1947. Nominated by Screen Writer's Guild for Best Musical Screenplay 1968. **Finian's Rainbow** cited by Brooks Atkinson as "setting the American musical 50 years ahead."

Address: 467 South Arnaz Drive, Los Angeles, CA 90048

Agent: Herman Meltzler, 551 Fifth Ave., New York, NY 10017 (212) 682-3476

TITLE • AVAILABILITY • PRODUCTIONS

Librettos for:

Bloomer Girl (music—Harold Arlen): Tams Witmark Record Library, 757 Third Avenue, New York, NY 10017 (212) 688-2525; Broadway

Finian's Rainbow (music—Burton Lane): Tams Witmark; Broadway

Flahooley (music—Sammy Fain): manuscript*; Broadway

Jamaica (music—Harold Arlen): Tams-Witmark; Broadway

Happiest Girl (music—Offenbach): Tams-Witmark; Broadway

All above: Lyrics by E.Y. Harburg

The Greeks Had a Cure for it: manuscript*

 Angelina (music, John Jacob Loeb): manuscript*

   *contact author

SYNOPSES

The Greeks Had a Cure for It: A paraphrased updated version of Aristophane's **Lysistrata,** tailored to a cast of 10 and minimum scenery, with a score by Offenbach (music) and Harburg (lyrics). Suited for college and amateur productions. Leads: 3 males, 2 females, and chorus.

Flahooley: Revised version of story laid in toy factory, presenting theme of scarcity in the midst of plenty, in comical satire terms. It takes place in the world's largest toy factory and the toys are a prominent feature of the action. Interwoven with the live cast — a boy and girl duo, a comic tycoon, a board of directors and some Arabs who have come to have their magic lamp repaired — are puppets, which play dialogue and singing scenes with the principals.

Angelina: A romantic comedy about Little Italy, circa 1922, treating its love of opera and the paradoxical emergence of the squealing bobby-soxers. Enrico Caruso's voice is featured plus a middle-aged romance and a young romance.

ARTHUR SAINER

Born in New York City on September 12, 1924. B.A., Washington Square College, New York University; M.A., Graduate Faculty of Philosophy, Columbia University. **Village Voice** drama critic. Conducted playwriting workshops at Bennington, Hunter, Adelphi, Post Colleges and Wesleyan U. **The Radical Theatre Notebook,** an exploration of experimental theatre in the U.S., published by Avon in 1975. Has directed four of his own plays. Recipient: playwriting grant from Office of Advanced Drama Research; John Golden playwriting award; Ford Foundation grant.

Address: 565 West End Ave., New York, NY 10024

TITLE • AVAILABILITY • PRODUCTIONS

The Bitch of Waverly Place: manuscript*; Judson Poets' Theatre, NYC; Bridge Theatre

The Game of the Eye: manuscript*; Sarah Lawrence College, NY

The Day Speaks but Cannot Weep: manuscript*; Sarah Lawrence College, NY; La Mama, NYC

The Blind Angel: manuscript*; Bridge Theatre

Untitled Chase: manuscript*; Washington Square Park; Astor Place Playhouse, NYC

God Wants What Men Want: manuscript*; Bridge Theatre

The Bomb Flower: manuscript*; Bridge Theatre

The Children's Army Is Late: manuscript*; C. W. Post College; Theater for the New City, NYC

Noses: manuscript*; Theatre Genesis, NYC

Om, A Sharing Service: The Radical Theatre Notebook, Avon Books, 250 West 55th St., New York, NY 10019, $2.65; Arlington Street Church

The Thing Itself: Playwrights for Tomorrow, Vol. 2, University of Minnesota Press, Minneapolis, MN 55455, $5.50 cloth, $1.95 paper; revision available in manuscript; Firehouse Theater; Theater for the New City, NYC; Florida State University

Boat Sun Cavern: manuscript*; Bennington College; Theatre for the New City, NYC

China Takes Eleven Hours: manuscript*

Van Gogh: manuscript*; La Mama, NYC

I Hear It Kissing Me, Ladies retitled **11 Piece Quiet:** manuscript*; Unit Theatre

1 Piece Smash: The Scene/2, available at Drama Book Shop, 150 West 52nd St., New York, NY 10019, $3.50; Open Space; WGBH-TV; Quaigh Theatre, NYC

Images of the Coming Dead: manuscript*; Open Space; Theatre for the New City, NYC

The Celebration: Jooz/Guns/Movies/The Abyss: manuscript*; Theater for the New City, NYC; WBAI-FM; video excerpts on French Educational TV

The Spring Offensive: The Radical Theatre Notebook; Bridge Collective at Super Nova; Ohio State

Go Children Slowly: manuscript*; Cubiculo Theatre, NYC; Odyssey Theatre, NYC

Charley Chestnut Rides the I.R.T.: manuscript*; Theater for the New City, NYC

Day Old Bread: The Worst Good Time I Ever Had: manuscript*; Theater for the New City, NYC

After the Baal-Shem Tov: manuscript*; Theater for the New City, NYC

Carol in Winter Sunlight: manuscript*; Theatre for the New City, NYC

Witnesses: manuscript*; Open Space

Sunday Childhood Journey's to Nobody at Home: manuscript*; Theatre for the New City, NYC

   *contact author

S

Arthur Sainer (cont'd)
SYNOPSES

The Celebration: Jooz/Guns/Movies/The Abyss: An epic and sometimes comic history of the Jews, shifting back and forth from Biblical times (Abraham and Isaac, Moses, Pharaoh and Mrs. Pharaoh, Jonah) to the nineteenth and twentieth centuries: a Polish village, the Lower East Side, the Warsaw Ghetto, contemporary Manhattan. Focuses on Jim, a writer, his estranged wife Lillian, a demonic movie producer with whom Jim works, and Grampa who comes from the old world and becomes a butcher on the Lower East Side. There are a number of original songs.

Full length. Fluid, abstract set recommended. Numerous male and female roles, requiring doubling.

Charley Chestnut Rides the I.R.T.: Structured like a piece of popular entertainment: songs, puppets, parodies of movies. Charley's a subway conductor, night shift on the I.R.T. Typical night: Charley's fight with middle-aged scavenger who wants Charley's **Daily News;** silent dialogue with blonde in whisky ad; Graffiti Kid who sprays car and sometimes passengers . . . Typical day at home: Mary doing housework, Ella doing homework. But a visit to the doctor — and Charley gets the death warrant. Rare blood disease? We're never told. How long? Months. What's Charley feeling? Cheated. Through poker-playing scenes with his buddies at the local garage, family scenes and strange subway encounters, grotesque, sometimes comic scenes, we see Charley struggling to regain control of his life or at least understand what's happening. At one point there's a musical recreation of the '39 World's Fair, when Charley and Mary were young lovers.

Full length. Setting: subway car, kitchen, garage and open area for street, etc. Numerous male and female roles, requiring doubling.

The Children's Army is Late: Story of David, experimental filmmaker, his wife Carol, daughter Kate and their dog Demeter, living in a rural area, domestic life set against re-enactment of myths and legends that involve Hector and Achilles, the Goddess Diana, the Drowned Man, and against other strange figures: Man with the Suitcase, comic figures of Mushky and Milly. David wants to do documentary footage about an old man, but the first old man he finds dies, and the second old man, a Mr. Edison, dies after David has done much talking with and filming of him. The dog Demeter uncovers the dead Edison who then takes David on a fantastic tour of the Chamber of the Dead. Includes a number of lyrical songs, as well as comic songs like "The 8th Street Rag."

Full length. Open space recommended. Numerous male and female parts, requiring doubling.

EDWARD SAKAMOTO

Born in Honolulu, HI on April 4, 1940. B.A. in English from the U. of Hawaii, postgraduate studies in Journalism, U. of Southern California. Newspaperman, Theater critic, member of Los Angeles Drama Critics' Circle, 1970–72. Work included in **Talk Story,** anthology of Hawaii's local writers, 1978. Recipient: Three Copley Newspapers Ring of Truth Awards for news editing, 1971–73; Rockefeller Grant for Playwriting, 1978; Rockefeller Grant, 1981–82.

Address: 1017 Ridge Crest St., Monterey Park, CA 91754

TITLE • AVAILABILITY • PRODUCTIONS

Yellow Is My Favorite Color: manuscript*; East West Players, L.A., CA; Asian American Theater, San Francisco, CA

That's the Way the Fortune Cookie Crumbles: manuscript*; East West Players, L.A., CA

Voices in the Shadows: manuscript*; East West Players, L.A., CA; Asian American Theater, San Francisco, CA

Edward Sakamoto (cont'd)

Aala Park: manuscript*; East West Players, L.A., CA

Manoa Valley: manuscript*; East West Players, L.A., CA

   *contact author

SYNOPSES

Yellow Is My Favorite Color: The comic mis-adventures of a third generation Japanese-American are explored from age eight to forty (by an adult actor) in a multi-media presentation of reality and fantasy.

Full length. Setting: one abstract set with screen for film clips and/or slides. 4 males, 4 females, playing 16 roles.

Voices in the Shadows: Drama focuses on a Japanese-American family across three generations. The climax comes in the father's confrontation with his daughter's boyfriend and the circumstances behind the daughter's suicide.

Full length. Setting: a livingroom. 6 males, 2 females.

Manoa Valley: Described by critics as Chekhovian in flavor, the play is set in Honolulu in 1959 and delves into the changing times in the year of statehood when a Hawaii-Japanese family's traditions are under siege as the schism between East and West is bridged.

Full length. Setting: backyard patio. 5 males, 5 females.

FRANK SALISBURY

Born in Fort Worth, TX on March 2, 1930 and now a resident of Southern California. He has written for nighttime television **(Schlitz Playhouse, Science Fiction Theatre)** and for the past ten years for the following daytime TV serials, **Search for Tomorrow, Somerset, General Hospital, Edge of Night, As the World Turns** and **The Guiding Light.** He has translated one novel, **Les Ogres,** from the French. Recipient: nominated for a L.A. Drama Critics Circle Award, 1975.

Address: 3631 Dixie Canyon Place, Sherman Oaks, CA 91423

Agent: Jerome Siegel Associates, 8733 Sunset Blvd., Los Angeles, CA 90069 (213) 652-6033

TITLE • AVAILABILITY • PRODUCTIONS

The Bonner Method: manuscript*

There in the Shade: (two one-act plays): manuscript*; Readings

The Seagulls of 1933: manuscript*; Actors Alley Theatre, Sherman Oaks, CA

The Ice-Cream Sunday: manuscript*; Actors Alley, CA; Cast Theatre, Los Angeles, CA

Venice: manuscript*; Group Repertory Theatre, N. Hollywood, CA

   *contact agent

SYNOPSES

The Seagulls of 1933: A comedy. Takes place on the terrace and private beach of a villa in the South of France. Present day. Concerns the antics of a group of Americans on the French Riviera as they pursue their natural bents to sometimes hopeless warps.

Full length. 4 males, 5 females.

S

Frank Salisbury (cont'd)

The Ice-Cream Sunday: Set on the grounds of the Massenet estate in Southern California. Present day. A comedy of confused identities that occur at a birthday party.

Full length. 3 males, 5 females.

Venice: The play deals with an alcoholic woman, her husband and son over a two-day period.

Full length drama. Setting: back yard of a rented house in Venice, CA. 3 males, 3 females.

GERTRUDE SAMUELS

Born Manchester, England; U.S. Citizen. Formerly journalist/author/photographer on **The New York Times Sunday Magazine;** then editor on the **Magazine;** above career after earlier stints on the **New York Post, Time,** and **Newsweek.** Also contributed articles to many periodicals, including **Look, National Geographic, Redbook, The Nation, Saturday Evening Post,** etc. Foreign correspondent, covering wars in Korea and Israel. Special consultant for a time to UNICEF. Fiction: **Of David & Eva** (New American Library, 1979); **Adam's Daughter** (Crowell, 1977); **The People vs. Baby** (Doubleday, 1965); **Run, Shelley, Run!** (Crowell, 1974); **Mottele — A Partisan Odyssey** (Harper and Row, 1976). Non-fiction: **B-G: Fighter of Goliaths** (Crowell, 1961); **The Secret of Gonen** (Avon, 1969). Working on new novel, on prison parole, for Crowell. For NBC-TV and CBS-TV, she has done adaptations of **Run, Shelley, Run!** and **Adam's Daughter.** Recipient: George Polk Award of Long Island University, 1955; Overseas Press Club citation, 1956; Page One Award, New York Newspaper Guild, 1959, 1965; Spirit of Achievement Award from Women's Division, Albert Einstein College of Medicine, Yeshiva University, 1960.

Address: 75 Central Park West, New York, NY 10023

Agent: Ben Kamsler, H.N. Swanson, Inc., 8523 Sunset Blvd., Los Angeles, CA 90069
(213) 652-5385

TITLE • AVAILABILITY • PRODUCTIONS

Judah the Maccabee & Me: DeKalb College Literary Arts Journal, Clarkston, GA*; The Lambs, NYC

The Corrupters (adapted from her novel, **The People vs. Baby**): **Best Short Plays of 1969;** Chilton Book Co., 201 King of Prussia Rd., Radnor, PA 19089, $6.95; The Actors Studio, NYC; W.P.A. Theatre, NYC

The Assignment: manuscript*; The Actors Studio, NYC; Manchester Library Theatre, Manchester, England; Oslo Radio (in Norwegian)

Kibbutz (a musical play): work in progress

Reckonings (trilogy of short dramas): manuscript*; Concord Hotel, NY; Gene Frankel Theatre Workshop, NYC

The Reckoning: manuscript*; Actors Studio, NYC

*contact agent

SYNOPSES

The Assignment: Political espionage play on an American newspaperman's hunt for the "Angel of Death" — Joseph Mengele, the No. 1 war criminal, devil of Auschwitz. The story focuses on two cousins who survived the concentration camps; one lives in England, the other became a New York journalist. When the cousin in England "disappears," the American publisher gives Hank

Gertrude Samuels (cont'd)

Rubens, the main character, the "assignment" of crossing the Atlantic to find out what's happened . . . becomes a good friend, then lover of a businessman's daughter . . . and it's growing evident that suspicious things are happening around that grandiose home. The trail leads the young people to Germany (in the second act) . . . a trail of vengeance, in the form of a mystery-thriller.

Full length. Setting: gracious livingroom, Manchester, England; then playing areas to denote in Germany, a church, editor's office, factory anteroom, judge's bench facing audience for the trial scene. 7 males, 2 females.

The Corrupters: One-hour straight drama of social realism, portraying the life and problems of the female addict, young people, essentially non-criminal but caught up in the law courts, prison life, prostitution and the street itself. Adapted from the playwright's documentary novel, **The People vs. Baby,** which the National Council on Crime and Delinquency described as "unusually incisive, sensitive and understanding."

Setting: done on levels and playing areas, to denote Girl's Term Court, judge's bench; cell block at Eastern State Prison; the Lincoln Room in the prison; Angelo's Candy Store; back to Court. 8 males, 8 females.

HERB SCHAPIRO

M.A., ABD: New York University. Has written for TV (for PBS): **In the Face of Justice; Whatever Happened to the Little Red Schoolhouse?** Film Documentaries: **Stages of a Summer; Island in Time; In and Out of the Inner City.** Teaching, Theater Arts and Writing: The New School, CUNY, Rutgers, NYU/Writer-in-the-Schools Project (Arts Council/National Endowment); Writer-in-Residence, ESAA/HEW Arts Council Project. Directing: Summer theater; Prison and School Equity tour; inner-city arts, street theater, film projects; writing, acting workshops. Recipient: Obie; Drama Desk Awards; Tony Nomination (all for **The Me Nobody Knows);** Stanley Drama Award; Actors Studio Work-in-Progress Grant; New York State Arts Council Younger Audience Play Commission; NY and New Jersey Humanities Grants.

Address: 415 East 52nd St., New York, NY 10022 (212) 935-1532

TITLE • AVAILABILITY • PRODUCTIONS

Survivors: manuscript*; Actors Studio, NYC

The Big Game: manuscript*; Actors Studio, NYC

A Little Something Before You Go: manuscript*; Actors Studio, NYC: St. Clement's, NYC

Kill the One-Eyed Man: manuscript*; Provincetown Playhouse, NYC

Where Does it Hurt and How Can We Help You? and **Underwear:** manuscript*

The Me Nobody Knows (original idea, adaptation, add'l. lyrics): inquire at Samuel French, Inc., 25 West 45th St., New York, NY 10036; Broadway; National tour; many foreign countries

Teddy (book & lyrics): manuscript*

Leading Lady (book & lyrics): manuscript*

Don't Cry, Child, Your Father's in America: manuscript*; Henry St. Playhouse, NYC

Ainsky: A Living History of One Man in His Time and Ours: manuscript*; Emelin Theatre

*contact author

S

Herb Schapiro (cont'd)
SYNOPSES

A Little Something Before You Go: A woman gives a dinner in memory of her recently deceased husband, inviting friends and landlords, creditors and strangers, in a wild attempt to fill something of the vacuum she feels. An absurdist farce based on the fanciful possibility that all kinds of people can yet sit down at the same table together, out of spite, weariness, pride, whatever, perhaps just because it's so dark and nasty outside.

Two acts. One set — livingroom of an old NYC brownstone apartment. 6 males, 4 females.

Leading Lady (musical): Based on events in the life of Victoria Woodhull, seeing her as a great performer on various stages of the American scene, one of our first superstars — of sex, business, religion, politics . . .

Two acts. Scenes — from medicine show to political convention, etc. Principals: 3 males, 2 females, chorus.

Teddy (musical): A satirical fable on Nixonism and other problems in the age of Aquarius. Main character: a bear (Teddy) of Chaplinesque humanity, who awakes after a bad dream in midwinter to discover that the woods are gone, goes in company of his Bert Lahrian Ranger to New York (Wall Street, etc.) to find out why and save his people.

Two sets. Settings — the North Woods and Wall Street. 6 males, 2 females, chorus.

EDAN SCHAPPERT

Born in Tuckahoe, NY, April 12, 1934. Educated at University of Washington, Seattle, B.A., Graduate Work at University of Hawaii and San Francisco State College. Studied in New York at Cooper Union, Gene Frankel Theatre Workshop, the New School, and National Academy of Television Arts and Sciences. Radio scripts purchased by Corporation for Public Broadcasting's **Earplay** Project. Recipient: Honorable Mention Awards from Broadcast Ministry of Connecticut and Connecticut Public Television competition for **The Holiday Spirit** and **The Trouble Maker.** Full-length drama **The Big Shot** first-prize winner in Northeastern University play script contest. Spring, 1976.

Address: 141 East 33rd St., New York, NY 10016

TITLE • AVAILABILITY • PRODUCTIONS

Celebrate Me!: manuscript*; Playbox Theatre, NYC; Riverdale Showcase Theatre, NY

The Ice Cubes: Drama Book Shop, 150 West 52nd St., New York, NY 10019, $4.00; New York Theatre Ensemble, NYC; Folk City Showcase, NYC; Corp. for Public Broadcasting

Water Strike!: manuscript*; NY Theatre Ensemble, NY

The Trouble Maker: manuscript*; Playbox Theatre, NYC

The Pandas: manuscript*; Riverdale Showcase, NY

Regret Me Not: manuscript*; Folk City Showcase, NY

The Big Shot: manuscript*; Northeastern Univ., Boston, MA

Cocktail Party: manuscript*

The Holiday Spirit: manuscript*

Abstract of a Present Day: manuscript*

Hairy Tales of Evolution: manuscript*

Will o'The W.A.S.P.: manuscript*

Oh What Food We Morsels Be: manuscript*

    *contact author

Edan Schappert (cont'd)

SYNOPSES

Regret Me Not: Four fantasies dealing satirically with the age-old problem of lack of communication. The plays have humor that is suited to all age levels. Produced nationally for radio broadcast by Corporation for Public Broadcasting, the collection includes "The Onion and the Strawberry Seed," "The Birds," "The Pandas," and "The Ice Cubes." Reviewed for trade papers by Stuart H. Benedict, "... the plays are imaginative, charming without ever being cutesy and allegorical without descending to the didactic. A sheer delight."

60 minutes. Minimal sets and props. 1 male, 1 female.

The Big Shot: Adult drama depicting personality development of a young man with the country's current political climate providing the backdrop.

Full length. Minimal sets. 5 males, 3 females.

JOAN SCHENKAR

Born in Seattle, WA on August 15, 1942. Bennington College, B.A. Advanced degrees in literature and aesthetics from University of California at Berkeley and S.U.N.Y. at Stony Brook. Playwright-in-Residence at Joseph Chaikin's experimental group The Winter Project; Ludwik Flauszen's workshop on Words, Polish Lab Theatre; Cummington Community for the Arts; Florida Studio Theatre. Professional musician and college teacher. Recipient: CAPS Grant.

Address: 21-34 45th Avenue, Long Island City, NY 11101 (212) 361-0375

TITLE • AVAILABILITY • PRODUCTIONS

The Next Thing: manuscript*; La Mama, Los Angeles, CA

Cabin Fever: manuscript*; La Mama, Los Angeles, CA; New York Shakespeare Festival, NYC

Last Words: manuscript*; Studio 17, NYC; Florida Studio Theatre

Signs of Life: The Women's Project, **Performing Arts Journal** Publications, P.O. Box 858, Peter Stuyvesant Station, N.Y., NY 10009, $6.95; American Place Theatre, NYC

The Last of Hitler: manuscript*

   *contact author

S

JAMES SCHEVILL

Born in Berkeley, CA on June 10, 1920. Harvard
University, B.S. 1942. Served in the U.S. Army,
1942–1946. Member of the Faculty, California
College of Arts and Crafts, Oakland; San Francisco State College; since 1969, Professor of
English, Brown University. Recipient: National
Theatre Competition Prize, 1945; Dramatists
Alliance Contest prize, 1948; Fund for the Ad-
vancement of Education Fellowship, 1953; Phe-
lan Biography Competition prize, 1954; Phelan
Playwriting Competition prize, 1958; Ford grant
for work with Joan Littlewood's Theatre Workshop, 1960; Rockefeller grant, 1964; William
Carlos Williams Award, 1965; Roadstead Foundation award, 1966; Governor's Award in the
Arts, Rhode Island, 1974.

Address: 17 Keene St., Providence, RI 02906

Agent: Bertha Case, 345 West 58th St., New York, NY 10019 (212) 541-9451

TITLE • AVAILABILITY • PRODUCTIONS

Everyman's History of Love (one act): **Ramparts Magazine*** (incomplete version); California
    College of Arts and Crafts, Oakland, CA

High Sinners, Low Angels (musical comedy): Bern Porter Books, San Francisco, CA (out of
    print)*; Theatre San Francisco, CA

The Bloody Tenet: Religious Drama I, Meridian Books, 1301 Ave. of the Americas, New York,
    NY 10019, $1.95; Central Congregational Church, Providence, RI: The Actor's Workshop,
    San Francisco, CA

The Black President: manuscript*

The Master (one act): **Playwrights for Tomorrow,** Vol. 1, Univ. of Minnesota Press, Minneapolis,
    MN 55455, $1.95; The Actor's Workshop, San Francisco, CA; The Guthrie Theatre,
    Minneapolis; various productions

The Space Fan (companion one act to **The Master): Playwrights for Tomorrow,** Vol I;
    The Guthrie Theater, Minneapolis, MN

Lovecraft's Follies (music by Richard Cumming): The Swallow Press, Chicago, IL (out of
    print)*; Trinity Square Repertory Co., Providence, RI; Cafe Theatre, Philadelphia, PA

Voices of Mass and Capital A (Play for voices with music by Andrew Imbrie): Friendship
    Press, New York (out of print)*; San Francisco Poetry Festival, CA

Liberty Is the Color of Night: manuscript*

Oppenheimer's Chair (one act): manuscript*; Brown University Theatre, RI; Magic Theatre,
    Berkeley, CA

The Death of Anton Webern (radio play): **Violence and Glory: Poems 1962-68,** The
    Swallow Press, $3.50 (paperback); The Roadstead Foundation, Fish Creek, WI; B.B.C.,
    London

This Is Not True (new short opera libretto from **Everyman's History of Love,** music by Paul
    McIntyre): manuscript*; University of Minnesota, MN

The Pilots (one act): **Breakout: In Search of New Theatrical Environments,** The Swallow
    Press, $10.00 (hard cover), $3.50 (paperback); Brown University Theatre, RI; La Mama
    Theatre Club, NYC

The Ushers (music by Gerald Shapiro): manuscript*; Brown University Theatre at Brown,
    University Art Festival, RI

The Violence and Glory of Barney Stetson (one act): manuscript*; also slightly different
    version in **Violence and Glory;** Brown University Theatre; La Mama Theatre Club, NYC

Emperor Norton Lives!: manuscript*; Babcock Theatre, University of Utah

James Schevill (cont'd)

Fay Wray Meets King Kong (one act): **Wastepaper Theatre Anthology,** The Pourboire Press, P.O. Box 315, Woods Hole, MA 02543; Wastepaper Theatre, Providence, RI

Sunset and Evening Stance or Mr. Krapp's New Tapes (one act): **Wastepaper Theatre Anthology;** Wastepaper Theatre, Providence, RI

The Telephone Murderer (one act): **Wastepaper Theatre Anthology;** Wastepaper Theatre, Providence, RI

Naked in the Garden (one act; music by James Schevill): manuscript*; Rhode Island School of Design Theatre, RI

Cathedral of Ice (music by Richard Cumming): The Pourboire Press, $3.00 (paperback); Trinity Square Repertory Co., RI

Year After Year: manuscript*; Wastepaper Theatre, Providence, RI

Mother O, or the Last American Mother: manuscript*

Alice in the American Wonderland (music by James Schevill): manuscript*; tour of schools in New England by Looking Glass Theatre, RI

The Dark Voice: manuscript*; Wastepaper Theatre, RI

Emperor Norton (music, Jerome V. Rosen): manuscript*; Magic Theatre, San Francisco, CA

Dungyard: manuscript*; Brown University, Providence, RI

   *contact agent

SYNOPSES

The Master: The play concerns an American "Master" training a female disciple in the nature of American Power. The comic, savage interrogation moves back and forth through key events of American History ending in a ritualistic eagle dance and marriage ceremony where the roles are reversed and the woman assumes her new place of power.

One act. Setting: hardly any required; if desired, an American eagle or flag, etc. may be used. 2 males, 1 female.

Lovecraft's Follies: The story of Stanley Millsage, a much-married, disturbed nuclear physicist. After working on the bomb for The Manhattan Project, he now works for the Marshall Space Center. Caught up in continuous security investigations, Millsage starts to fantasize about the nature of his time, how secret technologies have begun to affect the freedom of an open democratic society. The fantasies he sees spring to life and involve him and his wife with visions of the moon landing, Watergate, Tarzan and the Green Goddess, H.P. Lovecraft, J. Robert Oppenheimer, the invention of the bomb, Oppenheimer's security hearing and a final vision from an Alabama asylum of George Washington and the drifting American ship of state.

Full length. Setting: flexible, mostly indicated by lighting and simple props. Cast of 20 doubling and tripling many roles.

S

MURRAY SCHISGAL+

Born in New York City on November 25, 1926. Attended Long Island University; Brooklyn Law School, L.L.B.; New School for Social Research, B.A. He was a jazz musician, practiced law and then taught English. Recipient: Vernon Rice Award; Outer Circle Critics Award.

Agent: Audrey Wood, c/o International Creative Management, 40 West 57th St., New York, NY 10019 (212) 556-5722

TITLE • AVAILABILITY • PRODUCTIONS

The Typists: Dramatists Play Service, 440 Park Avenue South, New York, NY 10016, $2.50; British Drama League, London; Off Broadway

The Postman: manuscript*; British Drama League, London

A Simple Kind of Love Story: Dramatists Play Service, $2.50 with **The Pushcart Peddlers;** British Drama League, London

Ducks and Lovers: Dramatists Play Service, $2.50; Arts, London

The Tiger: with **The Typists;** Boston, MA; Off Broadway

Knit One, Purl Two: manuscript*; Boston, MA

Luv: Dramatists Play Service, $2.50; London; Broadway

Windows: Dramatists Play Service, $2.50; Los Angeles, CA

The Basement: with **Windows;** New York

Fragments: with **Windows:** New York

Memorial Day: with **Windows:** Baltimore, MD

The Old Jew: with **Windows;** Stockbridge, MA

Jimmy Shine: Dramatists Play Service, $2.50; Broadway

A Way of Life: manuscript*; New York

The Chinese: Dramatists Play Service, $2.50

Dr. Fish: with **The Chinese**

An American Millionaire: Dramatists Play Service, $2.50; Circle in the Square, NYC

All Over Town: Dramatists Play Service, $2.50; Broadway

The Pushcart Peddlers: Dramatists Play Service, $2.50

The Flatulist: with **The Pushcart Peddlers;** Santuary Theater, NYC

Little Johnny: with **The Pushcart Peddlers**

Walter: with **The Pushcart Peddlers;** Santuary Theater, NYC

The Downstairs Boys: manuscript*; Cincinnati Playhouse, OH

A Need for Brussel Sprouts: manuscript*; John Drew Theater, NY

*contact agent

BARBARA SCHNEIDER

Born in Lubeck, Germany on April 23, 1942. Received her training as an actress at the Academy of Arts and Drama in Munich. Has acted in Germany as well as the United States. Member: Playwright's Unit, New York Shakespeare Festival; Dramatists Guild. Articles, Theatre-sketches and poetry published in the **City Star, The Barb, The Womans Poetry Book, Woman to Woman** and Delta Books **Recreations,** among others. Recipient: Susan Smith Blackburn Prize, February 1980; Commission, Actors Theatre of Louisville.

Address: 510 West 110th St., 9C, New York, NY 10025

Agent: Ellen Neuwald, 905 West End Ave., New York, NY 10025 (212) 663-1582

TITLE • AVAILABILITY • PRODUCTIONS

Verdict on the Shooting of a Police Officer: manuscript*; Washington Square Church, NYC

Turtles: manuscript*; Writer's Unit, New York Shakespeare Festival; Capital Repertory, Albany, NY, staged reading

Details Without a Map: manuscript*; O'Neill Theater Center's National Playwrights Conference, CT; Equinox Theatre, Houston, TX

 *contact author or agent

SYNOPSES

Details Without a Map: In a suburb near New York City, a teenage boy has murdered the old woman in the house next door. The only motivation seems to be the $50 he stole to go to the amusement park with his friends. His family is thrown into uncharted territory. How to find causes for this seemingly senseless crime, how to grasp what has happened and why? In the attempt to understand their son, themselves and their world, they do not find many answers. But they begin to question what they see, question it deeply, and change. And — inspite of the tragedy — move forward

Full length. Setting: 2 playing areas: livingroom, boys' area. 1 male, 3 females, 3 teenage boys.

Turtles: A play about William and Dora, a couple, and their struggle to survive in a world of office jobs, promises of promotions and careers in the business-world. They find themselves in absurd, hilarious and most unpleasant situations, ready to give up, ready to give in. But their dreams and their spirit are something to be reckoned with.

Full length. Setting: livingroom and office. 2 males, 1 female.

S

RICHARD SCHOTTER

Born in New York City on February 22, 1944. B.A.,
New York University; M.A., Ph.D (Dramatic
Literature), Columbia University. Has been a
theater critic, an editor of **The Drama Review,** a
trade book editor at Crown Publishers and
Literary Advisor, American Place Theatre,
1971–73. For the past six years, Assistant Pro-
fessor of English, Queens College, CUNY. Editor
The American Place Theatre: Plays. Playwright-
in-Collaboration, Medicine Show Theatre
Ensemble, 1971–73. Recipient: Fulbright
Scholar; CAPS Grant in Playwriting, 1975–76;
Obie Award Nominee, 1973.

Address: 345 West 88th St., New York, NY 10024
(212) 873-3505

Agent: Helen Merrill, 337 West 22nd St., New
York, NY 10011 (212) 924-6314

TITLE • AVAILABILITY • PRODUCTIONS

Medicine Show: An American Entertainment: manuscript*; Theatre at St. Clements, NYC;
The Performing Garage, NYC

Benya the King: manuscript*; Jewish Repertory Theatre, NYC

*contact agent

SYNOPSIS

Benya the King: Benya the King was "inspired" by **Tales of Odessa** by Isaac Babel. It is set in
Odessa around 1912 and is the story of Benya Krik, a scrapman's son who leaves his father's
shop, joins the gang of one-eyed Ephraim Rook, robs the notorious Jew-and-a-half and becomes
the King of the Odessa gangsters.

Full length. Setting: one simple all purpose set. 7 males, 3 females.

JOSEPH SCHRANK

He has worked in film, television and children's
books in addition to plays. His films include **The
Clock, Cabin in the Sky, Song of the Islands, A
Slight Case of Murder, The Magnificent Dope**
and **Bathing Beauty.** For television he has done
**Beauty and the Beast, Cinderella, Hallmark Hall
of Fame.** His children's books include **Seldom
and the Golden Cheese, The Plain Princess and
the Lazy Prince.**

Address: 263 West End Ave., New York, NY
10023 (212) 799-6381

Agent: Bertha Case, 345 West 58th St., New
York, NY 10019 (212) 541-9451

TITLE • AVAILABILITY • PRODUCTIONS

Page Miss Glory: Samuel French, 25 West 45th St., New York, NY 10036, manuscript;
Broadway

Larger than Life: manuscript*; Springfield, MA; Hartford; CT

Pins and Needles: manuscript*; Broadway

Joseph Schrank (cont'd)

Good Hunting: manuscript*; Broadway

The Little Dog Laughed: manuscript*; Boston, MA

Ten O'Clock Scholar: manuscript*

My Aunt Daisy: manuscript*; Westport Country Playhouse, CT

The Magnificent Gourmet: manuscript*; England

Torero: manuscript*

The Plain Princess and the Lazy Prince**; Dramatic Publishing Co., 4150 N. Milwaukee Ave.,
Chicago, IL 60641, $1.00; numerous amateur productions in the USA

Rites of Spring: manuscript*

  *contact agent
  **contact author (amateur rights)

SYNOPSES

The Magnificent Gourmet: A hilarious comedy involving a Food and Wine Society gourmet and a sexy broad in a conflict between the two basic pleasures (and necessities) of life.

Two interior sets. 6 males 3 females.

The Rites of Spring: A comedy about a modern young man's efforts to re-establish contact with nature in an industrialized, over-organized, over-advertised world and its effects on his sex life.

One interior and one exterior set. 4 males, 2 females.

Torero: A musical version of Cyrano de Bergerac laid in Spain of today in which Cyrano is portrayed as the leading toreador of the day. Score by Bernie Wayne.

Multi-settings, 7 males, 3 females.

SANDRA SCOPPETTONE

Born in Morristown, NJ on June 1, 1936. Sandra has written many books; among them are **Suzuki Beane** (picture book, Doubleday, 1961), **Bang Bang You're Dead** (picture book, Harper & Row, 1968), **Trying Hard to Hear You** (novel, Harper & Row, 1974), **The Late Great Me** (novel, Putnam, 1976), **Some Unknown Person** (Putnam), **Happy Endings Are All Alike** (Harper & Row) and **Such Nice People,** (Putnam). She has written for TV and films, including **A Little Bit Like Murder** for ABC's **Wide World of Entertainment,** 1973, **Scarecrow in a Garden of Cucumbers** (independent film, 1972), and **The Inspector of Stairs** (independent film, 1975). She has directed. Recipient, Ludwig Vogelstein Grant, 1973; **Trying Hard to Hear You** won the ALA Award for Best Young Adult Book, 1974; ALA Award, 1979.

Address: 131 Prince St., New York, NY 10012 (212) 777-8439

Agent: Gloria Safier, 667 Madison Ave., New York, NY 10021 (212) 838-4868

TITLE • AVAILABILITY • PRODUCTIONS

The Inspector of Stairs: manuscript*; Assembly Theater; Actors Studio, NYC

Are You Prepared to be a United States Marine?: manuscript*; Actors Studio, NYC;
Cubiculo Theater, NYC

S

Sandra Scoppettone (cont'd)

Home Again, Home Again, Jiggity Jig!: manuscript*; Actors Studio, NYC: Tosos, NM

Stuck: manuscript*; O'Neill Theater Center's National Playwrights Conference, CT; Open Space Theater, NYC

*contact agent

SYNOPSIS

Stuck: Two couples, one in their early forties, the other older (he has retired), review their lives through humorous fantasy only to discover that nothing changes. The one pre-occupation they all seem to share is sex.

Full length. Setting: two sets. Each set is a porch on a Victorian type house in a small town. The same basic set can be used for both. 2 males, 3 females.

JOHN SCOTT

Born in Bellaire, OH on July 20, 1937. Educated at South Carolina State College, B.A.; Bowling Green State University, M.A., Ph.D. Teaches playwriting, dramatic theory, and directs at Bowling Green State University where he is resident playwright in the Theatre Department.

Address: 2228 Glenwood Ave., Toledo, OH 43620 (419) 241-1929

Agent: Viki McLaughlin-Cowell, Buttonwood Road, Peekskill, NY 10566 (914) 739-7577

TITLE • AVAILABILITY • PRODUCTIONS

Ride a Black Horse: manuscript*; O'Neill Theater Center's National Playwrights Conference, CT; Negro Ensemble Company, NYC

Karma: manuscript*; Silvera Writer's Workshop, NYC; Urban Arts Theatre

The Good Ship Credit: manuscript*; Silvera Writer's Workshop, NYC; Arts Consortium, NY

Shades: manuscript*; Silvera Writer's Workshop, NYC; Bowling Green University, OH

The Zaire Mark: manuscript*; Bowling Green University, OH

The Alligator Man: manuscript*; N.Y. Theatre Ensemble, NYC; Bowling Green U., OH

Time Turns Black: manuscript*; Bowling Green U., OH; Silvera Writer's Workshop, NYC

Black Sermon Rock: manuscript*; Bowling Green U., OH

After Work: manuscript*; Bowling Green U., OH

I Talk with the Spirits: manuscript*; Bowling Green U., OH

Shadow and Act: manuscript*; Bowling Green U., OH

Ovet and Tevo: manuscript*; Spectrum Productions, MS

Pieces of a Man: manuscript*; WGTE-TV, Toledo, OH

*contact author or agent

SYNOPSES

Karma: Karma, a black writer-activist in her mid-thirties, gropes through the conflicting vagaries of pursuing love with her man while fighting the demands of her junkie ex-husband, a militant colleague, and a protective mother. Her life and newly developing love for Ron are threatened by

John Scott (cont'd)

assaults from drug pushers and family demands. This woman's play examines the problems of black women particularly, who must maintain their femininity while struggling to develop the toughness required to survive in a milieu that demands competitive strength.

Full length. Setting: modern apartment with kitchen area in a city. 4 males, 4 females.

Shades: Interracial romance is the connecting theme and is examined through two couples who must look at the economic, career, social, and family pressures that their respective romances cause. First, the black male/white female relationship is seen through A.J. Matinee, an unemployed actor, and his blond lover, Serene. They battle A.J.'s ex-wife, an egotistical friend, and an effete director. Next, the black female/white male relationship is seen through Melba, a lonely schoolteacher, and her Jewish intellectual lover. This duo must face Melba's brother, a Vietnam emotional casualty, and the respective mothers. A blind chorus of street passers-by liven the atmosphere until the chilling conclusion when the lovers are blinded by the vengeance of their antagonists.

Full length (connected one acts). Setting: urban street; apartment interior. 5 males (3 black, 2 white), 5 females (3 black, 2 white).

ANTHONY SCULLY

Born in Hartford, CT on May 28, 1942. Grew up in Washington, DC. Attended Gonzaga High School. Graduated from Boston College, 1966; Yale School of Drama, 1969. Was a member of the Jesuit order for some years during the Sixties.

Address: 318 West 101 St., #7, New York, NY 10025 (212) 864-4346

Agent: Esther Sherman, William Morris Agency, 1350 Avenue of the Americas, New York, NY 10019 (212) 586-5100

TITLE • AVAILABILITY • PRODUCTIONS

The Great Chinese Revolution: not available; Yale Repertory Company, CT

Once More: not available; Morse College Theatre, Yale University, CT

All Through the House: not available; Manhattan Theatre Club, NYC

Little Black Sheep: manuscript*; Beaumont Theatre, Lincoln Center, NYC

Dracula, King of the Night: manuscript*; Palace of Fine Arts, San Francisco, CA

Quasimodo (music, Larry Grossman; lyrics, Hal Hackady): manuscript*

   *contact author

SYNOPSIS

Little Black Sheep: The play, a black comedy, takes place in New Haven in the residence of the Jesuits who are studying at Yale on the day of Robert Kennedy's death in June of 1968. It is about the breakdown of one kind of belief and the beginnings of another.

Full length. Setting: one unit set. 7 males, 1 female.

S

JOHN SEDLAK

Born Perth Amboy, NJ on February 27, 1942. Education: Masters degree in Playwriting, Catholic University, Washington, DC, 1972; Law degree, Georgetown University Law Center, Washington, DC 1974; worked at Lorton Reformatory under a playwriting grant from The National Endowment for the Arts. Served as Playwright-in-Residence at New Playwrights Theatre, Washington, DC, currently, Playwright-in-Residence, Theater Wagon, Staunton, VA. Intrested in: acting; writing film scripts.

Address: Theater Wagon, Box 167-F, Route 5, Staunton, VA 24401 (703) 248-1868

TITLE • AVAILABILITY • PRODUCTIONS

Cornerstone: manuscript*; Hartke Theatre, Catholic University

Lonnie, James, Bernhardt, and Zoowolski (one act): manuscript*; O'Neill Theater Center's National Playwrights Conference, CT

Gus & Co. (one act): manuscript*

Musing: manuscript*; Courtyard Playhouse, NYC

Fox Against the Fence: manuscript*; New Playwrights Theatre, Washington, DC

A Few Good Men: manuscript*

*contact author

SYNOPSES

Fox Against the Fence: Two dreams in which the characters of the first act are reincarnated in the second act as new characters fulfilling the karma left them by their earlier lives. James, a young, black pool hustler and petty criminal and his bumbling partner, Lonnie, try to derail a nightmare in which James is standing trial for the murder of Lonnie. The courtroom resembles a comedy review when the duo is forced to perform a degrading Jim Crow routine while recreating their past. The murderer acknowledges his act and is released from the dream. In the second act, the murderer comes back as victim. An avant garde theatre company lures a lone actor to an audition where they have begun an improvisation about a revolutionary group torn apart by inner dissention. While carrng on this improv, the company loses control, turns on its director and slays him a bit too realistically.

Two acts. Ensemble: 6 males, 2 females; black protagonists, 5 blacks, 3 whites. 1 unit set.

A Few Good Men: a tragicomedy about three misfit American servicemen held as P.O.W.s in a Vietnamese rain forest so remote that both they and their captors are unaware the war has ended.

Full length. Setting: one unit set. 6 males (1 black).

RICHARD SEFF

Born in New York City. Educated at New York University. Studied acting two years with Stella Adler. Richard, after eighteen years as a successful theatrical agent, now writes and acts exclusively.

Address: 399 East 72nd St., New York, NY 10021

Agent: Leo Bookman, William Morris Agency
1350 Avenue of the Americas, New York, NY 10019 (212) 586-5100

TITLE • AVAILABILITY • PRODUCTIONS

The Whole Ninth Floor: manuscript*; Playhouse-on-the-Mall, Paramus, NJ

Paris Is Out: Samuel French, 25 West 45th St., New York, NY 10036, $2.50; Playhouse-on-the-Mall, Paramus, NJ; Brooks Atkinson Theater, Broadway

Consenting Adults: manuscript*; Squaw Valley Community of Writers Festival — A.C.T.

Endangered Species: manuscript*

Masquerade (music, Gilbert Becaud, lyrics, Jason Darrow): manuscript*

The Homing Pigeon: manuscript*

Shine (music, Roger Anderson; lyrics, Lee Goldsmith; co-author, Richard Altman): manuscript*

   *contact agent

SYNOPSIS

Consenting Adults: Kitty Milan, a charming executive secretary with a sense of humor about the impending ending of her most recent emotional disaster, invites her old college friend Elliot Hedges to share a weekend in her expensive East Hampton rented house. Elliot, a homosexual, who is about to end an eight-year relationship of his own, forces Kitty to face some truths about herself, as well as facing some of his own. His friend Peter Newman arrives, as do an odd couple, Juleen and Henry Bauer, to complete the quintet of people engaged in varyingly successful battles for control.

Full length. Setting: a smart Long Island livingroom in an expensive summer rental. 3 males, 2 females.

LINDA SEGAL

Born in Davenport, IA on January 15, 1937. B.F.A., Goodman Theatre; M.F.A., Brandeis University. As an actress, she has appeared at the Cincinnati Playhouse in the Park; the Hartford Stage Company; Olney Theatre, Maryland; San Francisco Shakespeare Festival; O'Neill Theater Center's National Playwrights Conference among other regional and stock theaters. On Broadway she appeared in **Da** and **The Student Gypsy.** She worked for two years as an improvisational performer Off Broadway with **The Second City** and as an original member of the revue, **The Stewed Prunes.** Recipient: Shubert Fellow of Playwriting, Brandeis, 1975–77.

Address: 55 Pineapple Street, Brooklyn, NY 11201 (212) 852-4215/(212) 840-1234, service.

Linda Segal (cont'd)
TITLE • AVAILABILITY • PRODUCTIONS

Patchwork: manuscript*; Brandeis University, MA

Moving Day: manuscript*; Cubiculo Theatre, NYC; WCVB-TV, Boston, MA

Corner, 28th and Bank: manuscript*; Brandeis University, MA; Cubiculo Theatre, NYC

Feldshuh & Brackett: manuscript*; Brandeis University, MA

Speakeasy: manuscript*; Actors Studio, NYC: Ensemble Studio Theatre, reading, NYC

Valentine: manuscript*; Actors Studio, NYC

   *contact author

NEIL SELDEN

Born in New York City on March 20, 1931. His plays and musicals, plus a quartet of film scripts, are augmented by a soon to be published novel, two books of fiction and numerous short stories and plays for young readers. Recipient: Audrey Wood Award, 1972; Wisconsin Library Poetry Award, 1953.

Address: 21 Pine Drive, Roosevelt, NJ 08555
   (609) 448-4492

Agent: Steve Weiss, William Morris Agency,
   151 El Camino, Beverly Hills, CA 90212
   (213) 274-7451

TITLE • AVAILABILITY • PRODUCTIONS

The Wall: manuscript*

Say Farewell to the Squirrels: manuscript*

Marvin (with M. Imbrie): manuscript*

A Responsible Spider (with M. Imbrie): manuscript*

Someone's Comin' Hungry (with M. Imbrie): manuscript*; Pocket Theatre, NYC

A Girl Like Norman Mailer (with M. Imbrie): manuscript*

The Feeling Shop (with M. Imbrie): manuscript*; Actors Studio Workshop, NYC; Ensemble Studio Theatre Workshop, NYC

Car (with M. Imbrie): manuscript*; Berlin Festival; American Conservatory Theatre, San Francisco, CA

Raincheck (with M. Imbrie): manuscript*; Berlin Festival; Ham & Clove Repertory, NYC

Gino (with M. Imbrie): manuscript*; Journey Theatre, NYC

Ocean in a Teacup: manuscript*; Rainy Nite House, NYC; Satsang Theatre, NYC

Clearing (with M. Imbrie): manuscript*; Huntington Theatre Workshop, NY; Actors Studio Workshop, NYC

Sam Dead: manuscript*; Assembly Theatre Workshop, NY

Mary Magdalen: manuscript*; Satsang Theatre, NYC

Priest and Prostitute: manuscript*; Satsang Theatre, NYC

Mr. Shandy (with M. Imbrie): manuscript*; Roundabout Theatre, NYC; Actors Studio Workshop, NYC

The Policeman's Wife (with M. Imbrie): manuscript*

Leaves for a Sunday Afternoon (with M. Imbrie): manuscript*

   *contact agent

SYNOPSES

Car and Raincheck: Two lonely men encounter each other over the sale of a used car and come close to friendship; but their inability to reach out and communicate has comic and dangerous consequences which force them apart. A frankfurter street vendor refuses to recognize the boyhood friend, now very successful, who once lured him into the rape of a girl the vendor later married. The vendor is forced to admit his identity and confront the friend.

Full length. Setting: bare stage with or without a representational car. 2 males.

The Feeling Shop: Three women who live together are informed that the State is sending them a man for purposes of procreation in a time when men are nearly non-existent. When the man arrives, they find that he is very old and wants only to destroy himself. The State will not let him die unless he creates new life. The three women struggle to infuse life into the man. He impregnates the youngest woman and falls in love with the eldest. A child is born and the State reneges on its promise to let him die.

Full length. Setting: an interior of a basement. 1 male, 7 females.

Ocean in a Teacup (musical): The personality of a Bengali guru brings new vision to the disciples whose lives are interwoven with his: a widow demanding punishment for a thief; a communist student-organizer; the estranged mother and father of a juvenile delinquent; an alcoholic poet; a woman in love with a married schoolteacher. Based on the biography of Sri Anukulchandra Chakravorty.

Full length. Setting: bare stage. 7 males, 3 females.

BRUCE SERLEN

Born in Kew Gardens, NY on April 26, 1947. B.A., in English and General Literature, Harpur College (SUNY, Binghamton), 1968. M.A., Speech and Theatre Arts, Hunter College (CUNY), 1973. Participated in a Canadian-American Playwrights Exchange held in Montreal, 1979. Recipient: John Golden Award for Playwriting, 1971, 1972 — for work in the Hunter College graduate theater program; Commission from Actors Theatre of Louisville.

Address: 600 West 111 Street, #4B,
New York, NY 10025

TITLE • AVAILABILITY • PRODUCTIONS

Doomed Love: manuscript*; Back Alley Theatre, Washington, DC

St. James Park: manuscript*; American Shakespeare Theatre, New Play Series, Stratford, CT

Icarus Nine: manuscript*; Circle Theatre, NYC; Clark Center (Playwrights Horizons), NYC

Washer Women: The Cycle: manuscript*; Back Alley Theatre, Washington, DC

The Steak Palace: manuscript*; The Open Space in Soho, NYC

Fenders: manuscript*; Theatre at St. Clement's, NYC

The Consoling Virgin: manuscript*; The Actors Studio, NYC; Theatre for the New City, NYC

The City at 4 A.M.: manuscript*; The Actors Studio, NYC

Demeter's Lost Daughter: manuscript*; Theatre at St. Clement's, NYC

Bishop Street: manuscript*; The Actors Studio, NYC; The White Barn, CT

Second-Story Sunlight: manuscript*; The Actors Studio, NYC

Deep River: manuscript*

Graceland: manuscript*

S

Bruce Serlen (cont'd)

Genuine Red Snapper: manuscript*

The Sit-Up Set-Up (part of **Admissions**): manuscript*; Actors Theatre of Louisville, KY

  *contact author

SYNOPSES

Deep River: The conflict between two brothers erupts when the older of the two leaves his wife to live with another woman who happens to be black.

Full length. Setting: one interior. 3 males, 1 female.

Graceland: The equilibrium in a Manhattan West Side "people's" church is disrupted when one of the would-be directors becomes entangled with the young man caretaker and the girl he has picked up for the night.

Full length. Setting: one interior. 3 males, 1 female.

Genuine Red Snapper: A desperate comedy where a young woman leaves her live-in boyfriend to find her true vocation, ending up in pursuit of a rampant fish scandal. Set in a variety of New York locales from Soho to Central Park West.

Full length. Setting: a number of easily adaptable sets. 2 males, 2 females.

NTOZAKE SHANGE

Born in New Jersey on October 18, 1948. B.A., with honors in American Studies, Barnard College, 1970. M.A., American Studies, University of Southern California, 1973. She has taught at C.C.N.Y., Mills College, Medgar Evers College, Sonoma State College and the University of California. Has written **Sassafrass** (novella), **Nappy Edges** and **Three Pieces.** Recipient: Obie Award; Outer Critics Circle Award; Three Audelco Awards; Pushcart Prize.

Address: 164 Perry St., New York, NY 10014

Agent: David M. Franklin Associates, Suite 1290, South, Omni International, Atlanta, GA 30303 (404) 688-2233

TITLE • AVAILABILITY • PRODUCTIONS

For Colored Girls Who Have Considered Suicide/When the Rainbow is Enuf: Samuel French, 25 West 45th St., New York, NY 10036, $5.95; The Bacchanal, Berkeley, CA; Henry Street Settlement, NYC

A Photograph: A Still Life with Shadows/A Photograph: A Study In Cruelty: not available; New York Shakespeare Festival, NYC

A Photograph: Lovers in Motion: St. Martin's Press, 175 Fifth Ave., New York, NY 10010; Equinox Theatre, Houston, TX

Where the Mississippi Meets the Amazon (a cabaret): manuscript*; New York Shakespeare Festival, NYC

†**Magic Spell #7:** Samuel French, St. Martin's Press; New York Shakespeare Festival, NYC

Boogie Woogie Landscapes: St. Martin's Press; Symphony Space Theatre, NYC; Kennedy Center, Washington, DC

Mother Courage: manuscript*; New York Shakespeare Festival, NYC

  *contact agent
  †Lincoln Center, Theatre on Film & Tape

ADELE EDLING SHANK

Born in Minnesota on April 9, 1940. B.A. and M.A. in Playwriting from U. of California, Davis, 1967. Has written articles on contemporary avant-garde theater published in **The Drama Review** and European journals. Entries for the Oxford Companion to the Theatre and Teatro del Novecento. Translated with Everard d'Harnon-court, Arrabal's **The Architect and the Emperor of Assyria,** published by Grove Press. Recipient: Co-winner of the Actors Theatre of Louisville Great American Play Contest, 1979; Rockefeller Playwrights-in-Residence Grant, 1981.

Address: 42A Chalcot Road, London, NW1 8LS
(01) 722-1158

Agent: Michael Imison, Dr. Jan Van Loewen, Ltd., 81-83 Shaftesbury Ave., London, WIV 8BX, (01) 437-5546

TITLE • AVAILABILITY • PRODUCTIONS

Fox & Co.: manuscript*; U. of California

Sunset/Sunrise: West Coast Plays, P.O. Box 7206, Berkeley, CA 94707, $4.95; Actors Theatre of Louisville, KY; Los Angeles Free Public Theatre, CA

Winterplay: manuscript*; American Place Theatre, NYC; Magic Theatre, San Francisco, CA

Stuck: manuscript*

*contact author or agent

SYNOPSES

Fox & Co.: A contemporary version of Jonson's **Volpone** set in the headquarters of a multi-national corporation. Elliot T. Fox is the conservative president of the corporation while Foxy, his alter ego, is a self-indulgent hedonist. Assisted by his faithful secretary, Miss Jewel, he manipulates his co-workers but is finally outwitted by Miss Jewel and his disintegrating schizophrenic personality is revealed.

Full length. Setting: corporate headquarters, non-realistic. 7 males, 4 females.

Sunset/Sunrise: A hyperreal comedy set in the backyard of a middle class suburban California home. It is the home of James and Louise who live there with their daughter, Anne, who believes she is allergic to everything except plastic and does not leave her room. She partakes in family life via closed circuit TV. Their son, Josh, left home six months ago, but got only as far as his car, which is parked beside the house. The play begins on a Saturday afternoon as family and friends arrive for a swim and a barbecue dinner and ends at dawn on Sunday morning when James and Louise break years of silence.

Full length. Setting: realistic backyard with patio, barbecue, car and part of the house rooms seen through sliding doors. 6 males, 8 females.

Winterplay: The second in a series of California plays, this hyperreal comedy is set inside the house of **Sunset/Sunrise** and finds the same family on the previous Christmas Day. An older son returns home for the day bringing his lover to meet the family. The play follows the family through the trials of Christmas presents and dinner where they are joined by their daughter, Anne, wearing a special protective suit. Late in the evening, inspired by his older brother's independence, Josh moves out of the house to live in his car.

Full length. Setting: combination family room-dining room-kitchen. 4 males, 4 females.

S

JACK SHARKEY

Born, Chicago, IL on May 6, 1931. B.A. in English
in Creative Writing, St. Mary's College, Winona,
MN, 1953. Member of Nu Delta Chapter of Alpha
Psi Omega (national dramatic fraternity). Novels
include **Murder, Maestro, Please: Death for Auld
Lang Syne; It's Magic, You Dope; The Programmed People; The Crispin Affair.** Short stories and
humor articles variously in **The Magazine of Fantasy and Science Fiction, Galaxy, Alfred Hitchcock's Mystery Magazine, Playboy, Dude, Gent,
Fantastic, Amazing, Worlds Beyond.** He now
writes exclusively for dinner theatre and all
amateur and community groups, specializing in
"family-style" comedy. Principal Playwright of
Garden Grove's Village Green, culture center for
the Visual Arts in Southern California. Recipient:

Best Editorial of 1967 award from American Association of Industrial Editors; Key to the City of
Garden Grove.

Agent: Samuel French, 25 West 45th St., New York, NY 10036, (212) 582-4700

TITLE • AVAILABILITY • PRODUCTIONS

Here Lies Jeremy Troy: Samuel French, 25 West 45th St., New York, NY 10036, $2.50; Lake-
wood Theater, Skowhegan, ME; Forrest Theater, Philadelphia, PA

M Is for the Million: Samuel French, $2.50; Brookfield Players, WI

Kiss or Make Up: Samuel French, $2.50; Brookfield Players, WI

How Green Was My Brownie (Support Your Local Elf): Samuel French, $2.50; St. Jude Players,
South Holland, IL

A Gentleman and a Scoundrel: Samuel French, $2.50; Pheasant Run Playhouse, St. Charles,
IL

Meanwhile, Back on the Couch: Samuel French, $2.50; Abbey Playhouse, Philadelphia, PA

Spinoff: Samuel French, $2.50; Limestone Valley Theater, Cockeysville, MD

Roomies: Samuel French, $2.50; Limestone Valley Theatre, Cockeysville, MD

Who's on First? Samuel French, $2.50; Country Club Comedy Playhouse, Mt. Prospect, IL

What a Spot! (musical co-written with Dave Reiser): Samuel French, $2.50; Country Club
Comedy Playhouse, Mt. Prospect, IL

Saving Grace: Samuel French, $2.50; Limestone Valley, MD

The Creature Creeps!: Samuel French, $2.50; St. Jude Players, IL

Take a Number, Darling: Samuel French, $2.50; Country Club Comedy Playhouse, IL

The Murder Room: Samuel French, $2.50; Marian St. Theatre, Sydney, Australia

Dream Lover: Samuel French, $2.50; Cleveland, OH; Edwards Air Force Base, CA

Pushover (musical co-written with Ken Easton): Samuel French, $2.50; Palatine, IL

Hope for the Best (musical co-written with Dave Reiser): Samuel French, $2.50; Country Club
Comedy Playhouse, IL

Rich is Better: Samuel French, $2.50; Pittsburgh, PA

Once Is Enough: Samuel French, $2.50; Florida

Tournabout (with Ken Easton): Samuel French, $2.50; Palatine, IL

Turkey In the Straw: Samuel French, $2.50

Double Exposure: Samuel French, $2.50; Cleveland, OH

Missing Link: Samuel French, $2.50; Westminster Playhouse, CA

"Not the Count of Monte Cristo?!" (musical with Dave Reiser): Samuel French, $2.50

Operetta! (musical with Dave Reiser): Samuel French, $2.50; Chapman College, Orange, CA

My Son the Astronaut: Samuel French, $2.50

Woman Overboard (musical with Dave Reiser): Samuel French, $2.50

The Clone People: Samuel French, $2.50; Long Beach, CA

Return of the Maniac: Samuel French, $2.50

June Groom: Samuel French, $2.50; Cabrillo Playhouse, San Clemente, CA

A Turn for the Nurse: Samuel French, $2.50

Honestly, Now!: Samuel French, $2.50; Gem Theatre, Garden Grove, CA

The Picture of Dorian Gray (with Dave Reiser): Samuel French, $2.50

Play On!: Samuel French, $2.50

Slow Down, Sweet Chariot (with Dave Reiser): Samuel French, $2.50; Strawberry Bowl, Garden Grove, CA

Par for the Corpse: Samuel French, $2.50; Irvine Community Theatre, Irvine, CA

But Why Bump Off Barnaby?: Samuel French, $2.50; Gem Theatre, Garden Grove, CA

SYNOPSES

Slow Down, Sweet Chariot: A musical comedy about a woman who, dying on the brink of her daughter's wedding, learns that her proposed son-in-law is a rat and refuses to accompany her angel to heaven until she can get her daughter into the arms of her true love.

Full length. Setting: one interior set. 4 males, 7 females.

Double Exposure: A super-macho movie star who moonlights as the author of kiddie books, faces losing both careers when his producer and his publisher meet on Oscar Night.

Full length. Setting: one interior set. 4 males, 3 females.

Turkey in the Straw: A troupe of Broadway-bound players, stuck in a real turkey in the straw-hat circuit, scheme to rewrite and save their show behind the back of its author-producer. The musical-within-this-musical, "Space Enough for All," is hilariously dreadful — a ghastly treatise on tolerance for outer-space aliens.

Full length. Setting: various semi-sets. 9 males, 7 females.

WALLACE SHAWN

Born in New York City, 1943. Taught English in India, 1965–66; student of Philosophy, Politics, and Economics at Magdalen College, Oxford, including study with G. J. Warnock, 1966–68; taught Latin at the Church of the Heavenly Rest Day School in Manhattan, 1968–70; student of acting with Katharine Sergava at the H.B. Studio, 1971; shipping clerk in New York's Garment District, 1974; xerox machine operator at Hamilton Copy Center, Sixth Avenue, New York, 1976. Recently completed libretto for short opera by brother Allen Shawn, **In the Dark,** performed at the Lenox Arts Center, directed by the author. Recipient: Obie, 1975, for **Our Late Night.**

Agent: Audrey Wood, ICM, 40 West 57th St., New York, NY 10019 (212) 556-5722

TITLE • AVAILABILITY • PRODUCTIONS

Four Meals in May: manuscript*

The Old Man: manuscript*

Wallace Shawn (cont'd)

The Hotel Play: manuscript*

Play in Seven Scenes: manuscript*

The Hospital Play: manuscript*

Our Late Night: manuscript*; Andre Gregory's Manhattan Project, NYC; New York Shakespeare Festival, NYC

Three Short Plays: manuscript*; Workshop, New York Shakespeare Festival, NYC; Joint Stock Theatre Group, London

The Mandrake (adaptation): manuscript*; New York Shakespeare Festival, NYC

Marie and Bruce: manuscript*; New York Shakespeare Festival, NYC

My Dinner with Andre: manuscript*; Royal Court Theater, London

*contact agent

SYNOPSES

The Hotel Play: A hotel in the tropics. 42 males, 20 females.

Play in Seven Scenes: A family lives in the mountains. A doctor visits them. 2 males, 3 females.

The Hospital Play: The play takes place in a hospital. 10 males, 11 females.

MARSHA SHEINESS

Born in Corpus Christi, TX on November 20, 1940. Educated at Del Mar College, Baylor University, Southern Methodist University, North Texas State College, Los Angeles City College, Los Angeles State College. Screenplay, **Have a Nice Weekend,** also **The Electric Company** and an illustrated book, **Two Swallows in No Time** (Chelsea House) and for TV, **The Doctors.** Recipient: Exxon Award; **Dramatics Magazine** One-Act Play competition; National Endowment for the Arts, 1979–80; Commission from **Earplay;** Commission from Actor's Theater of Louisville.

Address: 315 West 19th St., New York, NY 10011

Agent: Charles Hunt, c/o Fifi Oscard Agency, 19 West 44th St., New York, NY 10036 (212) 764-1100

TITLE • AVAILABILITY • PRODUCTIONS

Pancho Pancho (ten minutes): manuscript*; The Little Room, NYC; Angels Company Theater, Los Angeles, CA

Clair and the Chair: manuscript*; Playwrights Horizons, NYC

Dealer's Choice: manuscript*; Playwrights Horizons, NYC

Stop the Parade: manuscript*; Playwrights Horizons, NYC

Monkey Monkey Bottle of Beer, How Many Monkey's Have We Here?: Samuel French, 25 West 45th St., New York, NY 10036, $2.50; The New Theater, NYC; Cincinnati Playhouse, OH

Professor George: Samuel French, $1.25; O'Neill Theater Center's National Playwrights Conference, CT; University of North Carolina, Chapel Hill

The Spelling Bee: Samuel French, $2.50; O'Neill Theater Center's National Playwrights Conference, CT; Playwrights Horizons, NYC

Floaters: manuscript*

Marsha Sheiness (cont'd)

Reception: manuscript*

Bernie and the Beast: manuscript*

Best All 'Round: manuscript*

 *contact agent

SYNOPSES

Dealer's Choice: Con-artist, Jack, and his friends, Michael and Jerry, find employment with a psychic who astonishes them all by being "for real." "She has a great sense of how far one can go with the fantastic in an everyday situation" — Michael Feingold, **Village Voice.** "Sheiness is going to be a talent to reckon with . . . " — William Barber, **Long Island Press.**

Full length. Setting: Sarah's house, a hotel room. 4 males, 2 females.

Stop the Parade: A penetrating satire set around the turn of the century, in a small western town. Wayne Bonner, sheriff, finds out that his woman, Roy Ann, is leaving him because she wants more out of life. Through a comedy of errors, a con woman, two would-be detectives, a female impersonator and his benefactor, a nice guy, and a greedy business man find themselves unwilling deputies pledged to help Wayne stop the parade of women led by Roy Ann.

Full length. Setting: a hotel lobby; a saloon; the street. 8 males, 2 females.

The Spelling Bee: A taut, suspenseful comedy that builds to a shocking climax as *Steve, *Nina, *Bart, and *Ralph compete in the National Championship run-offs for the best speller in the country. Each child's mother is determined that her kid will win, while the Quizzer, Freddie Stans, is hopeful that this show will be his chance to "Make it."

*The children are played by adults. They must be played simply without trying to "act" like children, for the meaning of the play to be clear. Full length. Setting: an old auditorium. 4 males, 4 females.

SAMUEL SHEM

Born in Fayetteville, NC on August 6, 1944. B.A., Harvard, magna cum laude; Ph.D., Oxford University, England; M.D., Harvard Medical School, cum laude. Novel, **The House of God** (Richard Marek/Putnam), Dell, paperback and **Follies,** (Richard Marek/Putnam). United Artists film, **The House of God.** Practicing Psychiatrist. Co-Chairman, P.E.N. New England. Recipient: Rhodes Scholarship, 1966–69.

Address: 75 Bellevue St., Newton, MA 02158

Agent: Robert Freedman, Brandt & Brandt,
 1501 Broadway, New York, NY 10036
 (212) 840-5760

TITLE • AVAILABILITY • PRODUCTIONS

Room for One Woman: Samuel French, 25 West 45th St., New York, NY 10036, $2.50;
 Impossible Ragtime Theatre, NYC

Napoleon's Dinner: Samuel French, $2.50; Impossible Ragtime Theatre, NYC

George and Martha: manuscript*

Freudian Lovesong: manuscript*

The Hollywood Messiah: manuscript*

 *contact agent

S

Samuel Shem (cont'd)

SYNOPSES

George and Martha: George, on his twenty-sixth birthday, finds that his modern-day life in Boston is repeating the love-life of the young George Washington. A comedy.

Full length. Setting: 5 playing areas. 3 males, 3 females.

Freudian Lovesong: A comedy about shrinks in love.

Full length. Setting: 7 playing areas. 4 males, 3 females.

The Hollywood Messiah: Set at poolside in Beverly Hills, this is the story of a New York rabbi who travels to Hollywood convinced that a young stand-up comic (who calls himself "The Hollywood Messiah") is the real Messiah that the Jews have been awaiting for two thousand years. A comedy.

Full length. Setting: one playing area. 3 males, 3 females.

SAM SHEPARD

Born in Fort Sheridan, IL on November 5, 1943. Has had numerous odd jobs as waiter, musician, etc. Book of short stories, **Hawk Moon.** Breeds Appaloosa horses at his California home. Presently acting in such films as **Days of Heaven, Resurrection, The Raggedy Man.** Recipient: seven Obies; Pulitzer Prize; Rockefeller Grant; Guggenheim Grant; OADR Grant; Yale University Fellowship.

Agent: Lois Berman, 250 West 57th St., New York, NY 10019 (212) 581-0670/1

TITLE • AVAILABILITY • PRODUCTIONS

Cowboys: Theatre Genesis, NYC

Rock Garden: Samuel French, 25 West 45th St., New York, NY 10036, $5.95; Theatre Genesis, NYC

Up to Thursday: Cherry Lane Theater, NYC

Dog: *; La Mama ETC, NYC

Rocking Chair: *; La Mama ETC, NYC

Chicago: Urizen Books, 66 West Broadway, New York, NY 10007, $6.95; Theatre Genesis, NYC

Melodrama Play: with **Chicago;** La Mama ETC, NYC; Martinique, NYC

Icarus's Mother; with **Chicago;** Caffe Cino, NYC: Open Space, London

4-H Club: Samuel French, $6.95; Cherry Lane, NYC

Fourteen Hundred Thousand: with **Chicago;** Firehouse Theatre, MN

Red Cross: with **Chicago;** Provincetown Playhouse, NYC; Judson Poet's Theatre, NYC

La Turista: Four Two Act Plays, Urizen, $6.95; American Place Theatre, NYC; Theatre Upstairs, London

Cowboys #2; with **Rock Garden;** Old Reliable, NYC: Mark Taper Forum, Los Angeles, CA

Forensic and the Navigators: Urizen, $7.95; Theatre Genesis, NYC; Astor Place Theater, NYC

Holy Ghostly: with **Forensic and the Navigators;** La Mama ETC, NYC; Kings Head, London

S

The Unseen Hand: with **Forensic and the Navigators;** La Mama, ETC, NYC; Astor Place Theater, NYC

Operation Sidewinder: with **La Turista;** Vivian Beaumont Theater, NYC

Shaved Splits: with **Forensic and the Navigators;** La Mama ETC, NYC

Mad Dog Blues: Samuel French, $5.95; Theatre Genesis, NYC

Cowboy Mouth (with Patty Smith); with **Mad Dog Blues;** St. Clement's Church, NYC; Transverse Theatre, Edinburgh, Scotland

Terminal: *; Open Theatre, NYC

Back Bog Beast Bait: with **Forensic and the Navigators;** American Place Theater, NYC

The Tooth of Crime: with **La Turista;** Open Space, London; Performing Garage, NYC

Geography of a Horse Dreamer: with **La Turista;** The Upstairs, Royal Court, London

Little Ocean: *; Hempstead Theatre Club

Nightwalk: *; Open Theatre, NYC

Action: with **Rock Garden;** Magic Theater, San Francisco, CA

Killer's Head: with **Rock Garden;** Magic Theater, CA; American Place Theater, NYC

Blue Bitch: *

Suicide In B-Flat: Samuel French, manuscript, $6.50; Yale Repertory Theatre

Man Fly

Sad Lament of Pecos Bill on the Eve of Killing His Wife: *

Buried Child: Dramatists Play Service, 440 Park Avenue South, New York, NY 10016, $2.50; Theatre for the New City, NYC

Jackson's Dance (with Jacques Levy); Long Wharf Theatre, CT

Angel City: with **Mad Dog Blues;** McCarter Theatre, Princeton, NJ

Seduced: Dramatists Play Service, $2.50; Trinity Square Repertory Co., Providence, RI

The Curse of the Starving Class: with **Mad Dog Blues;** Magic Theater, CA; New York Shakespeare Festival, NYC

†Tongues (with Joseph Chaikin): **Sam Shepard: Seven Plays,** Bantam Books, 666 Fifth Ave., New York, NY 10019 (price not set); New York Shakespeare Festival, NYC

Savage/Love: with **Tongues;** New York Shakespeare Festival, NYC

True West: with **Tongues;** Magic Theater, CA; New York Shakespeare Festival, NYC

*contact agent
†Lincoln Center, Theatre on Film & Tape

S

MARTIN SHERMAN

Born in Philadelphia, PA. Graduate of Boston University's Division of Theatre Arts. Playwright-in-Residence, Mills College, Oakland. Member of The Ensemble Studio Theatre. For television, wrote CBS special **Don't Call Me Mama Anymore;** for the BBC, **Movements.** Recipient: residency grant, Wurlitzer Foundation of New Mexico, 1973; National Endowment for the Arts Fellowship, 1980.

Address: 344 West 12th St., New York, NY 10014; 35 Leinster Square, London W2, England

Agent: Charles Hunt, c/o Fifi Oscard Associates, 19 West 44th St., New York, NY 10036 (212) 764-1100/Margaret Ramsay, 14A Goodwins Court, London CW2, England

TITLE • AVAILABILITY • PRODUCTIONS

A Solitary Thing (music by Stanley Silverman): manuscript*; Mills College, Oakland, CA

Fat Tuesday: manuscript*; Actors Studio, NYC

Next Year in Jerusalem: manuscript*; HB Playwrights Foundation, NYC

The Night Before Paris: manuscript*; Traverse Theatre, Edinburgh; Actors Studio, NYC

Things Went Badly in Westphalia: The Best Short Plays of 1970, Chilton Book Co., 201 King of Prussia Rd., Radnor, PA 19089, $7.50; University of Connecticut

Delta Lady (in collaboration with Drey Shepperd): manuscript*

Passing By: manuscript*; Stables Theatre, Australia; Almost Free Theater, London; Playwrights Horizons, NYC

Soaps: manuscript*; Playwrights Horizons, NYC

Cracks: manuscript*; O'Neill Theater Center's National Playwrights Conference, CT; The Changing Scene, Denver, CO; Theatre de Lys, NYC

Rio Grande: manuscript*; Playwrights Horizons, NYC

Bent: Samuel French, 25 West 45th St., New York, NY 10036, $2.50; O'Neill Theater Center's National Playwrights Conference, CT; Royal Court London; Broadway

    *contact agent

SYNOPSES

Passing By: The progress of a love affair which opens with a casual pickup in a New York cinema, is cemented over several weeks when the lovers are marooned together by hepatitis, and ends when they are pulled apart by their incompatible professional ambition. Both characters are men. "Much of it is funny, some of it moving . . . brilliantly achieves its objectives" — **London Times.**

Long one act. Setting: studio apartment in New York, with side scenes in a movie theatre, a wine store, and Central Park.

Cracks: A comic whodunit about the mysterious death of a rock star.

Two acts. Setting: rock star's home in Southern California. 5 males, 4 females.

LARRY SHUE

Born in New Orleans, LA on July 23, 1946. B.F.A. in Theatre Arts (cum laude) from Illinois Wesleyan University. Member of The Agenda, improv comedy group, Hollywood. Actor-in-Residence, Milwaukee Repertory Co. since 1977. Playwright-in-Residence, Milwaukee Repertory Theatre since 1979. Recipient: Best Actor in a Musical and Best Actor in a Non-Musical from Atlanta Circle of Drama Critics; Eddie Fox Award in Special Services Entertainment, Fort Lee, VA.

Address: c/o Milwaukee Repertory Theatre, 929 N. Water St., Milwaukee, WI 53202
(414) 276-2101   (home)

TITLE • AVAILABILITY • PRODUCTIONS

Siliasocles: not available; Illinois Wesleyan U.

My Emperor's New Clothes: manuscript*; Illinois Wesleyan U; Dartmouth College

Grandma Duck is Dead: manuscript*; Milwaukee Repertory Theatre, WI; Greer Garson Theatre, Santa Fe, NM

The Nerd: manuscript*; Milwaukee Repertory Theatre, WI

   *contact author

SYNOPSES

Grandma Duck Is Dead: Set in a Midwest college dorm in June, 1968, it is the story of a bunch of guys who choose to drown out the distant drums of Viet Nam by engaging in constant, sometimes desperate, silliness. Many and elaborate are their voices and routines, and hilarity reigns until an experiment in hypnosis nearly ends in tragedy.

One act. Setting: a college dormitory room. 4 males, 1 female.

My Emperor's New Clothes: A musical play for children, adapted from the story by Hans Christian Andersen. This popular version is set in the kingdom of Mango-Chutney, where the Emperor is busy giving everything a new name. In addition to the familiar tale of two weavers making fools of a prideful populace, there is a love story between the Emperor's marriageable daughter and the Royal Army, which consists of one man. There are songs, chases, mistaken identities and many moments of audience participation.

One act. Setting: two sets, a town square and a palace interior. 4 males, 2 females.

The Nerd: "A 34-year-old architect, the original Mr. Nice Guy, is celebrating his birthday with his girlfriend, his best friend, a stuffy client, his wife and bratty son. The architect has problems, his girlfriend has taken a job as a weather girl at a TV station, the IRS is auditing him, the client doesn't like his designs, but those difficulties seem minor when The Nerd, Rick Steadman, shows up at his door . . . A stupid, insensitive social misfit, Steadman wreaks havoc on the architect's life, giving the supreme test to the architect's patience and human kindness." Damien Jacques, **Milwaukee Journal.**

Full length. Setting: a livingroom. 5 males, 2 females.

S

MICHAEL SHURTLEFF

Born in Oslo, Norway on July 3. B.A., Lawrence
University, WI; M.F.A., Yale University School of
Drama. Casting director for fifty Broadway
shows and the film versions of **The Sound of
Music, Jesus Christ Superstar, 1776, All The
Way Home** etc. Author of novel, **Happy New Year
Gregorio** and novella, **The Lady Is a Tramp,
Geraldine** (New World Writing). Taught How to
Audition classes for ten years in NYC and now
teaching Audition and Scene Study workshops
in Hollywood. Author of **Audition** (Walker, hard-
cover; Bantam, paperback). Director of film, **Call
Me By My Rightful Name.** Recipient: Metropoli-
tan New York Short Play Contest, 1977; Best
Short Plays of 1979, (**Sailing**).

Address: 6619 Cahuenga Terrace, Los Angeles,
CA 90068 (213) 469-8745/462-6565

Agent: Lewis Chambers, 663 Fifth Avenue, Suite 614, New York, NY 10022 (212) 753-4493

TITLE • AVAILABILITY • PRODUCTIONS

A Fine Summer Night: manuscript*; Corner Loft Theatre, NYC

Who Are You?: manuscript*; Corner Loft Theatre, NYC: University Place Theatre, NYC

Take Very Good Care of Yourself: manuscript*; Fifth Avenue Theatre, NYC

Lock the Door Behind You: manuscript*; New York Theatre Ensemble, NYC

Coming to Terms: manuscript*; Corner Loft Theatre, NYC; Cast Theatre, Hollywood, CA

Driving Yourself Crazy: manuscript*; Corner Loft Theatre, NYC: University Place Theatre, NYC

Tell Me You Don't Love Me Charlie Moon: manuscript*; Corner Loft Theatre, NYC;
Night Flight Theatre, Hollywood, CA

Woman to Woman (4 short acts): manuscript*; Corner Loft Theatre, NYC; 30th St.
Theatre, NYC

Sailing: Samuel French, 25 West 45th St., New York, NY 10036, $1.25; Corner Loft
Theatre, NYC: Night Flight Theatre, Hollywood, CA

Getting into Death: manuscript*; Night Flight Theatre, Hollywood, CA

Spirit Your Wife Away to the Woods: manuscript*; Night Flight Theatre, Hollywood, CA

Call Me By My Rightful Name: Dramatists Play Service, 440 Park Avenue South, New York, NY
10016, $2.50; One Sheridan Square, NYC

Up To Snuff: manuscript*; Beverly Hills Playhouse, Beverly Hills, CA

*contact agent

SYNOPSES

A Fine Summer Night: A romantic sophisticated comedy about four people on an island; a summer night on the deck of a fine house overlooking the ocean and the romantic entanglements between two older and two younger couples.

Full length. Setting: a single setting with an inset. 2 males, 2 females.

Coming to Terms: A romantic comedy about a New York couple approaching forty and finding
their marriage failing, they turn to younger lovers.

Full length. Setting: multiple single setting of various New York locales. 3 males, 2 females.

Woman to Woman: One-act plays about women's relationships to women, to be performed only
by women. **A Garden Full of Snow, Getting into Death, During the War** and **When the Sun Goes
Down.** Comedy dramas.

All plays can be done by 2 females except the latter which has 3.

SEYMOUR SIMCKES

Born in Saratoga Springs, NY. B.A., magna cum laude, Phi Beta Kappa, Harvard College; B.J.E., Hebrew Teachers College; M.F.A., Stanford University; Ph.D., Harvard University. Two novels, **Seven Days of Mourning** and **The Comatose Kids.** Two films, **The Last Temptation of Christ** and **The Human Windmill.** Teacher, translator and short story writer. Recipient: Wallace Stegner Writing Fellowship; National Endowment for the Arts, 1967–68; Littauer Foundation Grant, 1970–71; National Endowment for the Arts Literature Award, 1979.

Address: 157 Mansfield St., New Haven, CT 06511

TITLE • AVAILABILITY • PRODUCTIONS

Seven Days of Mourning: manuscript*; Theatre Company of Boston, MA: Circle in the Square, NYC

Ten Best Martyrs of the Year: manuscript*; Theater For The New City, NYC

Bum Sunday: manuscript*; Ensemble Studio Theatre, NYC

   *contact author

LYDIA SIMMONS

Born in Ripley, MS on August 19, 1933. B.S., Mississippi State College for Women; M.A., Ph.D., New York University. Has done scripts for Cable Channel C in New York; wrote for the University of Michigan Quarterly **Review;** article in **Other Stages.** Recipient: One-act play award, Barn Theatre, 1976; Columbia University Grant, 1978; National Endowment for the Arts Grant, 1979.

Address: 115 East 39th St., New York, NY 10016 (212) 661-2925

TITLE • AVAILABILITY • PRODUCTIONS

Beggars in the Church: manuscript*; Pembroke University, NC

King: manuscript*

House on the Island: manuscript*

The Secretaries: manuscript*; Barn Theatre, NJ; New York Theatre Ensemble, NYC

Wabash Cannon Ball: manuscript*; New York Theatre Ensemble, NYC

Big Tits: manuscript*; Reading, Open Eye, NYC & 13th St. Theatre, NYC

The Office: manuscript*

Mother: manuscript*; Joseph Jefferson Theatre, NYC

Satisfaction Guaranteed: manuscript*

Death of a Baptist in a Small Southern Town: manuscript*

And Love Me All the Time: manuscript*; Cable TV, NYC

S

Lydia Simmons (cont'd)

Boys & Girls Together: manuscript*

A Brief Vacation: manuscript*

Homelife: manuscript*; Cable TV, NYC

Necessary Murders: manuscript*; Reading, 13th St. Theatre, NYC

Sans Everything: manuscript*; Theatre Projects, NYC

When Other Friendships: manuscript*

It Wouldn't Be You: manuscript*

The Companion: manuscript*

The Loving: manuscript*

Permutations Perceptions and Unspoken Agreements: manuscript*

Repetitions: manuscript*; Reading, 13th St., Theatre, NYC

Dr. Miner: manuscript*

   *contact author

SYNOPSES

Sans Everything: A play about three women in a mental institution, and what they do when they realize that no one, in or out of the hospital, gives a damn about whether they stay in or get out, live or die. What does a person do when all alternatives are dreadful? What does one do when living is itself a pain? One woman leaves, not knowing what the future brings. Life is there and must be lived.

Full length. Setting: cell area of a mental institution. 7 males, 9 females.

The Secretaries: A play about victimization and its effects on both victim and victimizer, about the connection between sexuality and power, sexuality and violence. Two long-suffering secretaries, on one final evening, divest their powerful boss of both wife and mistress. Through their sacrificing subservience, they establish control over him, even as they make it appear that he is, as always, in complete command of his women and his world.

One act. Setting: the president's office. 1 male, 2 female.

NEIL SIMON

Born in the Bronx, NY on July 4, 1927. He attended New York University and served in the United States Army Air Force. He started his career writing sketches for **The Phil Silvers Show.** Recipient: Shubert Award, 1968; Special Tony award, 1975. The only playwright to have four plays simulanteously on Broadway.

Address: c/o Dramatists Guild, 234 West 44th St., New York, NY 10036 (212) 398-9366

TITLE • AVAILABILITY • PRODUCTIONS

Catch A Star (sketches written with Danny Simon); Broadway

New Faces of 1956 (sketches written with Danny Simon); Broadway

Come Blow Your Horn: Samuel French, 25 West 45th St., New York, NY 10036, $2.50; Broadway

Adventures of Marco Polo (book with William Friedberg): Samuel French, $2.50

Heidi (book with William Friedberg): Samuel French, $2.50

Little Me (lyrics by Carolyn Leigh, music by Cy Coleman); Tams-Witmark, 757 Third Ave., New York, NY 10017; Broadway

Barefoot in the Park: Samuel French, $2.50; Broadway

The Odd Couple: Samuel French, $2.50; Broadway

Sweet Charity (music by Cy Coleman, lyrics by Dorothy Fields); Tams-Witmark; Broadway

The Star Spangled Girl: Dramatists Play Service, 440 Park Avenue South, New York, NY 10016, $2.20; Broadway

Promises, Promises (music by Burt Bacharach, lyrics by Hal David); Tams-Witmark; Broadway

Plaza Suite: Samuel French, $2.50; Broadway

The Last of the Red Hot Lovers: Samuel French, $2.50; Broadway

The Gingerbread Lady: Samuel French, $2.50; Broadway

The Prisoner of Second Avenue: Samuel French, $2.50; Broadway

The Sunshine Boys: Samuel French, $2.50; Broadway

The Good Doctor: Samuel French, $2.50; Broadway

God's Favorite: Samuel French, $2.50; Broadway

California Suite: Samuel French, $2.50; Broadway

Chapter Two: Samuel French, $2.50; Broadway

They're Playing Our Song: Samuel French, $2.50; Broadway

I Ought to Be in Pictures: *; Broadway

Fools: manuscript*; Boston, MA; Broadway

BERNARD SLADE

Born in St. Catharines, Ontario, Canada on May 2, 1930. Educated in England. Has written over 100 TV shows for three American networks, the Canadian Broadcasting Corporation and the BBC. His career started with ten years as an actor. He is married (Jill) and has two children, Laurel and Christopher. Recipient: Academy Award nomination for Best Screenplay; Tony nomination, Writers Guild nomination and Drama Desk Award for **Same Time, Next Year.**

Address: 345 N. Saltair, Los Angeles, CA 90049

Agent: Jack Hutto, 110 West 57th St., New York NY 10011 (212) 581-5610

TITLE • AVAILABILITY • PRODUCTIONS

Simon Says Get Married: manuscript*; Crest Theatre, Toronto

A Very Close Family: manuscript*; Manitoba Theatre Centre, Winnipeg

Fling!: Samuel French, 25 West 45th St., New York, NY 10036, $2.50

Same Time, Next Year: Samuel French, $2.50; Broadway; Paris

Tribute: Samuel French, $2.50; Broadway; Paris

Romantic Comedy: Samuel French, $2.50; Broadway

*contact agent

S

EARL HOBSON SMITH

Born in Thayer, MO on September 4, 1898. Educated at the University of Kentucky A.B. Alviene School of the Theater, New York, NY and Columbia University M.A. He taught speech and Theatre Arts for quite a number of years at Lincoln Memorial University as Director of the department. Mr. Smith is a Doctor of Literature. He is a member of the Dramatists Guild, the American Theater Association, and the American National Theater and Academy.

Address: Rt. 2, Box 114, Speedwell, TN 37870
(615) 562-2858

TITLE • AVAILABILITY • PRODUCTIONS

Stephen Foster: Dramatists Play Service, 440 Park Ave. South, New York, NY 10016, $1.25; Cain Park Theater, Cleveland, OH; Minn. Centennial Show Boat, Minneapolis, MN

The Long Way Home: New River Historical Society. P.O. Box 711, Radford, VA; Ingles Amphitheater, VA

The Trail of the Lonesome Pine: June Tolliver Theater, Big Stone Gap, VA

The Little Shepherd of Kingdom Come: manuscript*; Little Shepherd Theater, Whitesburg, KY

Farewell to Valley Forge: manuscript*; Freedom's Foundation Theater, Valley Forge, PA

Daniel Boone: manuscript*; Indian Fort Theater, Beara, KY

Abraham Lincoln's Love Affairs: manuscript*; Lincoln Memorial Univ. Theater

The Tennessee River Story: manuscript*; Lincoln Memorial University Theater

Abraham Lincoln's State of the Union: manuscript*

Kiss Me Again: manuscript*

*contact author

GLENN ALLEN SMITH

Born in El Centro, CA on April 29, 1935. A.B. in Latin-American Studies, U.C.L.A.; M.A. in Drama, Baylor U. Has written Libretto for the opera, **The Top Loading Lover.** Recipient: Playwriting Residency at the Dallas Theater Center, 1979, under Rockefeller Foundation Grant; Helene Wurlitzer Foundation.

Address: 4408 Amherst, Dallas, TX 75225
(214) 691-7048

TITLE • AVAILABILITY • PRODUCTIONS

Sister: manuscript*; Dallas Theater Center, TX; Off Off Broadway

A Home Away From: manuscript*; Off Broadway

Curious in L.A.: manuscript*; Dallas Theater Center, TX; Theatre Suburbia, Houston, TX

Glenn Allen Smith (cont'd)

Manny (book & lyrics): manuscript*; Dallas Theater Center, TX; Redlands Theatre Festival, CA

Barnaby Sweet: manuscript*; St. Nicholas Theater, Chicago, IL; U. of Wisconsin

Glory!: manuscript*; New Playwrights Foundation, L.A., CA

Sort of a Love Song: manuscript*; Cricket Theatre, Minn., MN

Years in the Making: manuscript*; Dallas Theater Center, TX; U. of New Orleans, LA

Land of Fire: manuscript*; Dallas Theater Center, TX

    *contact author

MARC P. SMITH

Born in Worcester, MA on January 6, 1934. B.A., Clark University, Major in International Relations. Chief writer for the American Forces, Korea Network, 1957–58. One of the co-founders of the National Playwrights Conference. Charter playwright, O'Neill Theater Center's National Playwrights Conference, New York co-ordinator for first three years. Film writer for Army Pictorial Center, **Encyclopedia Britannica** Films, Inc., Eastern Educational TV and Cambist Films, Inc. Founder and executive producer, Worcester Foothills Theatre Company.

Address: c/o Worcester Foothills Theatre, P.O. Box 236, Worcester, MA 01602 (617) 754-0546

Agent: Paul B. Berkowsky, 1540 Broadway, New York, NY 10036 (212) 354-4722

TITLE • AVAILABILITY • PRODUCTIONS

The Shelter: manuscript*; O'Neill Theater Center's National Playwrights Conference, CT

Lamentation on a High Hill: manuscript*; O'Neill Theater Center's National Playwrights Conference, CT; Off Off Broadway

Storeyville 1 (musical): manuscript*; Worcester, MA

Be a Sport: manuscript*; Worcester, MA

The Brewster Papers: manuscript*; Worcester Foothills Theatre

The Unrest Cure: manuscript*; Worcester Foothills Theatre

The Last Great Nipmuc: manuscript*; Worcester Foothills Theatre

Time: 1940: manuscript*; Worcester Foothills Theatre; Los Angeles, CA

Be a Sport (musical version): manuscript*; Worcester Foothills Theatre

Viva Vaudeville: manuscript*; Worcester Foothills Theatre

Memo from a Mad Producer (musical): manuscript*; Worcester Foothills Theatre

    *contact author

SYNOPSES

Storeyville 1 (music and lyrics, Ernest McCarty): A musical docudrama portraying the life cycle of the musical jazz modes that made Storeyville, the red light district of New Orleans, synonymous with the lusty, gusty sound of a burgeoning new country.

Full length. Setting: unit set. 3 males, 3 females plus a suggested number of dancers.

The Brewster Papers: A full year before the shot heard 'round the world was fired in Concord, an

Marc P. Smith (cont'd)

area west of Concord had pulled away from British rule. Here is a fictionalized account of some of the people caught up in those events who risked loss of land and all rights and then faced death for the ideals that were to crystalize later as the tenets of the American Revolution.

Full length. Setting: one interior. 3 males, 3 females.

Time: 1940: The Holliman family of Worcester, MA face the course of national and world events leading to World War II. This will be the last full year of peace the United States will have for some thirty-five years and the Hollimans instinctively know the world they have known is ending. Their stories are told in flashbacks and through the songs of that era.

Full length. Setting: one interior. 4 males, 2 females.

ROBERT KIMMEL SMITH

Born in Brooklyn, NY on July 31, 1930. Attended Brooklyn College. After many years in advertising, began writing full time in 1970. **Chocolate Fever,** a children's book, was published in 1972. A comic novel, **Sadie Shapiro's Knitting Book,** published in 1973, has been published in fourteen countries and six languages. For the past several years, he has been developing new comedy programs for CBS. Married, with two children, he still makes his home in his native Brooklyn. His wife, Claire, is a well-known literary agent. Mr. Smith's chief regret is that he cannot play tennis as well as he cooks. Recipient: ANDY Award (advertising), 1967; OPIE Award (Best Comic Novel), 1973; Massachusetts Children's Book Award, 1980.

Address: 210 Rugby Rd., Brooklyn, NY 11226

Agent: Lois Berman, 250 West 57th St., New York, NY 10019 (212) 581-0670

TITLE • AVAILABILITY • PRODUCTIONS

A Little Singing (one act): manuscript*; O'Neill Theater Center's National Playwrights Conference, CT; Washington Theater Club; Manhattan Theatre Club, NYC

Up in Smoke (one act): manuscript*; Berkshire Theater Festival/Winter Workshop, MA

A Little Dancing (one act): **Best Short Plays of 1975,** Chilton Book Co., 201 King of Prussia Rd., Radnor, PA 19089, $10.00

SYNOPSES

A Little Singing: A two-character play that pits a white, middle-aged, Jewish businessman against a young, black Internal Revenue Service tax examiner. The men discover that they have more in common than it first appears, and that even a tax collector can have a heart. This is a warm, human comedy of the inevitability of love and taxes.

One hour. Setting: an IRS office. 2 males.

Up in Smoke: An absurdist (?) comedy of man vs. bureaucracy in which a young poet reports a smokey chimney violation to the authorities and ends up being fed into the furnace himself. Written in 1972, it is a comment upon Watergate.

Playing time: 50 minutes with laughs, 30 minutes without. Setting: a municipal office. 4 leads: young man, young woman, 2 middle-aged male officials. 4 supporting roles (with doubling): 3 men (young or old) and 1 woman.

Robert Kimmel Smith (cont'd)

A Little Dancing: A middle-class morality play about Mom and marijuana. A young man, Paul Levy, introduces his mother to the pleasures (?) of marijuana, much against his will. While under the influence, Mrs. Levy reveals family secrets to her son — secrets Paul would have been better off not knowing. At the end of the play, Paul must choose between loyalty to his mother, or personal freedom and escape. The play is fast, funny, warm and touching.

One hour. Setting a "finished" basement. 1 male (20's), 1 female (50's).

STEVEN SOMKIN

Born in New York City in 1941. He studied Philosophy at Carleton College, B.A.; Medicine at Tufts University School of Medicine, M.D.; Playwriting at the New School. He has been a member of the New Dramatists and the Harold Clurman writers/directors unit at The Actors Studio.

Address: 230 Riverside Drive, New York, NY 10025 (212) 663-5787

TITLE • AVAILABILITY • PRODUCTIONS

A Mild Case of Death: manuscript*

Dear John: manuscript*; WPA Theatre, NYC

Invitation to a Wine-Tasting: manuscript*

The Sophisticated Seductress: manuscript*

To Marianne with Love: manuscript*

Kara's Monument: manuscript*

The Promotion of Artaud Wistaar: manuscript*; New Dramatists, NYC

Sing "Melancholy Baby"!: not available; Warren Robertson Theatre Workshop

The American Oasis: manuscript*; New Dramatists, NYC

Lust: not available; New Dramatists, NYC

Nine Tenths of the Flaw: manuscript*; New Dramtists, NYC

A Time for Teens and Libertines: manuscript*

Beyond Consent: manuscript*; 4th Friday Playwrights, NYC

    *contact author

SYNOPSIS

Beyond Consent: A forty-year-old pediatrician comes to terms with strong sexual desires, unexpectedly released by a premature heart attack, that focus initially on an adolescent patient (herself a rape victim) and then on a young mother.

Full length. Setting: a doctor's office. 2 males, 4 females.

S

JERRY SPINDEL

Jerry Spindel was born in New Jersey in 1944 and educated at Antioch College and Harvard University. He has taught high school English and worked as a journalist and research librarian. His fiction has appeared in **Midstream** and **The Carleton Miscellany.**

Address: 15 Saxon Terrace, Newton Highlands, MA 02161 (617) 244-6164

TITLE • AVAILABILITY • PRODUCTIONS

O Canada: manuscript*; Playhouse Workshop, WNAC-TV, Boston, MA

Respects: manuscript*; O'Neill Theater Center's National Playwrights Conference, CT; Mark Twain Masquers, Hartford, CT

War and Peace: A Bedroom Farce: manuscript*; Playwrights Platform (reading)

*contact author

SYNOPSIS

Respects: A former patient shows up at the home of his psychiatrist on the evening of his funeral and requests, then demands, that the grieving family turn over to him the file the doctor kept during their consultation. "A biting, madcap play" — **Newsweek.**

One-act comedy/drama. Setting: a living room. 3 males, 2 females.

FRANCIS H. STANTON

Born in Norway, ME. Graduated from Harvard University, A.B., Music Major. Several hundred songs recorded by most of the major recording artists. Wrote the songs for Paramount Picture **Framed,** 1975, theme song **A Romantic Guy, I** for long-running **Bob Cummings TV Show.** Has had at least one number one song in fifteen countries. Has been music publisher for thirty years. Recipient: Special popular music awards from ASCAP; Three awards from ASCAP for "Outstanding Country Songs."

Address: 2315 Foxhaven Dr., Franklin, TN 37064 (615) 373-8506

TITLE • AVAILABILITY • PRODUCTIONS

Look Where I'm At (musical): manuscript*; Off Broadway, Theatre 4, NYC

The Boy Who Made Magic (musical): manuscript*; Hayloft Theatre, Manassas, VA

*contact author

SYNOPSIS

The Boy Who Made Magic: The story is of Jan, the boy from a mountain village in Central Europe

Francis H. Stanton (cont'd)

who leaves home to seek fame and fortune as a magician. After losing several jobs, he stumbles upon a group of Strolling Players. Jan is taken on as apprentice to the ailing magician of the troupe. Upon the magician's sudden death, Jan is thrust on the stage to perform in his place. The audience gasps and applauds Jan's illusions. Later, he abandons his cohorts and his love and becomes world-famous, only to find he needs more solid relationships to live with himself. He "vanishes" (his best trick of all) and returns to his roots, having learned that "happiness comes from within."

The cast includes 5 males and 5 females. 4 of the males and 2 of the females double. The doubling enhances rather than detracts from the show. One set.

BARRIE STAVIS

Born in New York City on June 16, 1906. Attended Columbia University. Co-founder and member of the Board of Directors of New Stages; Co-founder, United States Institute of Theatre Technology, member of the Board of Directors, 1961–64 and 1969–72. Visiting Fellow, Institute for the Arts and Humanistic Studies, Pennsylvania State University. Has lectured and/or conducted seminars on playwriting at U. of Wisconsin; U. of Minnesota; U. of Delaware; Brigham Young U.; Pennsylvania State U.; Syracuse U.; U. of Kansas; U. of Oregon; The Swedish Dramatic Institute, etc. Has written for magazines; for TV; also novels; operas, **Joe Hill** and **Galileo Galilei.** Recipient: Yaddo Fellowship; National Theatre Conference, (two times).

Address: 70 East 96th Street, New York, NY 10028

Attorney: Benjamin Zinkin, Cohn, Grossberg and Zinkin, 505 Park Ave., New York, NY 10022 (212) 688-6940

TITLE • AVAILABILITY • PRODUCTIONS

The Sun and I: not available; New York; San Francisco, CA

Refuge: Haven Press, 65 East 96 St., New York, NY 10028, $1.50; London; Madrid

Lamp at Midnight: Haven Press, $2.25; New York, Bristol Old Vic, England

The Man Who Never Died: Dramatists Play Service, 440 Park Avenue South, New York, NY 10016, $2.50; Leipzig, Germany; New York

Harpers Ferry: Haven Press, $7.95; Guthrie Theatre, MN; Milwaukee, WI

Coat of Many Colors: Haven Press, $7.95; Provo, UT

Lamp at Midnight (one-hour version): Haven Press, $1.50; Chicago, New York

Harpers Ferry (75-minute version): manuscript*; University Park, PA

The Raw Edge of Victory: manuscript*; Midland, TX

    *contact attorney

SYNOPSIS

The Raw Edge of Victory: The play deals with George Washington and the Revolutionary War, covering the period of 1776 to 1783. It examines war, revolution and peace; the ambiguities of armed conflict. It also explores the movement from a colony to a nation, from a subject to a citizen.

Full length. Setting: basic unit set. 18 males, 2 females.

S

DANIEL A. STEIN

Born in Cincinnati, OH on February 6, 1943. B.A., Columbia College, NYC; M.F.A., Yale School of Drama; D.F.A., Yale School of Drama. Taught Drama at the U. of California, Irvine and then became a free lance playwright. Has written mixed media shows for Speed Art Museum. Teaches a course on how to write historical drama. Recipient: Eudora Welty Americana Award for the PBS-TV production of **The Trial of Moke.**

Address: c/o Milwaukee Repertory Co., 929 N. Water St., Milwaukee, WI 53202 (414) 273-7121

TITLE • AVAILABILITY • PRODUCTIONS

Kentucky!: manuscript*; Actors Theatre of Louisville, KY

Farewells (one-woman show): manuscript*; South Coast Repertory Theater

Just Between Us (one-woman show): manuscript*; Actors Theatre of Louisville, KY

The Trial of the Moke: manuscript*; Milwaukee Repertory Theatre, WI

An Independent Woman (one-woman show): manuscript*; Actors Theatre of Louisville, KY

Stark Mad in White Satin: manuscript*; Milwaukee Repertory Theatre, WI

Metric Madness: manuscript*; Seattle Repertory Theatre, WA

　　*contact author

SYNOPSES

The Trial of the Moke: Based upon the actual historic event, this is a drama about Henry Flipper, the first black man to graduate from West Point. Flipper becomes an officer at Ft. Davis, TX and is subsequently court-martialed on a charge of theft. The play deals with his attempts to come to terms with his identity as a black.

Full length. Setting: unit set with flashbacks done with lighting. 12 males, 2 females, and about 8 non-speaking roles.

Metric Madness: A children's play which entertains while teaching the Metric system. The play is fast moving and presentational, starting with robots on another planet who come to earth to teach the Metric system.

Long one act. Setting: minimal set pieces required. 2 males, 4 females.

Stark Mad in White Satin: A tribute to the plays and players of the 19th century. Anecdotes and histories of such actors as: Edwin Booth, Charlotte Cushman, Joe Jefferson, Adah Menken, Lola Montez, Edwin Forrest, Augustin Daly and Clara Morris. Long one act. Setting: no sets or props required. 1 male, 1 female.

JOSEPH STEIN

Born New York, NY. Educated: CCNY, B.S.S.; Columbia University, M.S.A. Wrote for numerous radio and television programs including **Henry Morgan Show, Tallulah Bankhead Show, NBC All Stars; Your Show of Shows; The Sid Caesar Show,** etc. Wrote screenplays of **Enter Laughing** and **Fiddler on the Roof.** Recipient: Newspaper Guild Award; Drama Critics Circle Award; Tony Award, **Fiddler on the Roof.**

Address: 250 West 57th St., New York, NY 10019 (212) 246-9709

Agent: Shirley Bernstein, c/o Paramuse Artists, 1414 Ave. of the Americas, New York, NY 10019 (212) 758-5055

TITLE • AVAILABILITY • PRODUCTIONS

Mrs. Gibbons Boys: Samuel French, 25 West 45th St., New York, NY 10036, manuscript; Broadway, London

Plain and Fancy (musical): Samuel French, $2.50; Broadway; London; numerous stock performances

Mr. Wonderful (musical): Music Theatre Int'l., 119 West 51st St., New York, NY 10019; Broadway

Take Me Along (musical): Trans-Witmark, 757 Third Ave., New York, NY 10017; Broadway; stock

Juno (musical): Mr. Talbert, Wm. Morris Agency, 1350 Ave. of Americas, New York, NY 10019; Broadway

Enter Laughing: Samuel French, $2.50; Broadway; Los Angeles

The Body Beautiful (musical): Samuel French, $2.50; Broadway

†**Fiddler on the Roof** (musical): Music Theatre Int'l., Crown Publishing Co., 419 Park Ave. South, New York, NY 10016, $4.95; Broadway; 22 foreign productions; stock, etc.

Zorba (musical): Trans-Witmark; Random House, 201 E. 50th St., New York, NY 10022, $4.50; Broadway; Los Angeles; seven foreign productions

So Long, 174th Street (musical): *; Broadway

King of Hearts: Kippy's Productions, 144 W. 52nd St., New York, NY 10020; Broadway

Carmelina: Paramuse Artists, 1414 Ave. of the Americas, New York, NY 10019; Broadway

*contact agent
†Lincoln Center, Theatre on Film & Tape

MARK STEIN

Born in Washington, DC on May 18, 1951. B.A., University of Wisconsin, 1973. Recipient: University of Wisconsin George B. Hill Award for Fiction, 1972 and 1973; National Endowment for the Arts, Playwright-in-Residence, New Playwrights Theatre; Blum-Kovler Foundation Grant, New Playwrights Theatre, 1981.

Address: 2059 N. Woodstock St., #205, Arlington, VA 22207 (703) 522-0274

Agent: Jonathan Sand, Writers & Artists Agency, 162 West 56th St., New York, NY 10019 (212) 246-9029

S

Mark Stein (cont'd)

TITLE • AVAILABILITY • PRODUCTIONS

Pinnacle: manuscript*; New Playwrights Theatre, Washington, DC; Performance Community, Chicago, IL

Booking the Nile Circuit: manuscript*; Players Company, Baltimore, MD; Children's Radio Theatre, WPFW, Washington, DC

Does the Name Pavlov Ring a Bell?: manuscript*; WGMS, Washington, DC

Breaking the Sweet Glass: manuscript*; New Playwrights Theatre, Washington, DC

Mr. Wilson's Peace of Mind: manuscript*; Quaigh Theatre, NYC; Yale Cabaret, New Haven, CT

Smoke: manuscript*; Quaigh Theatre, NYC

The Amsterdam Avenue Theater Presents/Direct from Death Row/The Scottsboro Boys: manuscript*; New Playwrights Theatre, Washington, DC

*contact agent

SYNOPSES

Pinnacle: A comedy focusing on four women who work in the pattern room of a needlepoint-kit factory. A retiring 1930s radical is being replaced by a young woman who happens to have been a 1960s radical. Along with a bungling but cheerful Bronx native and the beleagured supervisor, the four women confront the patterns in their daily rituals.

Full length. Setting: a sad excuse for an office. 2 males, 4 females.

The Amsterdam Avenue Theater Presents/Direct from Death Row/The Scottsboro Boys: Three weeks after the release of the first four of the nine Scottsboro Boys in 1937, they appeared in a Harlem vaudeville show. This play is a fictionalized account of that show. The vaudeville acts depict the Scottsboro Case. Interspersed between these acts are flashback scenes depicting the previous three week's struggle among a civil rights leader, a representative of the Communist Party and the vaudeville impressario, for control of the newly released celebrities.

Full length. Setting: a vaudeville theater in Harlem. 6 males, 2 females.

HERSCHEL STEINHARDT

Born May 21. Studied at Wayne State University, New School for Social Research, Hunter College. He worked as a newsboy, theater usher and cook before moving to New York to write plays. Worked with the Federal Theater Project and as a press representative for the Displaced Persons Program.

Address: P.O. Box 163, Lathrup Village, MI 48076 or 18216 Maryland, Southfield, MI 48075 (313) 569-0037

Agent: Bertha Klausner, International Literary Agency, 71 Park Avenue, New York, NY 10016 (212) 685-2642

TITLE • AVAILABILITY • PRODUCTIONS

Sons of Men: Bookman-Twayne**, $4.95; NBC-TV

A Star in Heaven: New Voices, NY**, $3.95; Concept-East, Detroit, MI

Man on Earth: manuscript**

Song of the Street: manuscript**; Paul Robeson Theatre, Detroit, MI

The Power of the Dog: manuscript**

Herschel Steinhardt (cont'd)

Before the Morning: manuscript**

No One Walks Alone: manuscript*; American Jewish Committee, Europe; South America

Voice of the Bell: manuscript*; Citizens Committee for Displaced Persons, NYC

Six Men Seated in a Subway: manuscript*; Henry St. Playhouse, NYC

The Wind & The Rain: manuscript*; Wayne State University, Detroit, MI

God's in His Heaven: manuscript*; Wayne State University, Detroit, MI

The Lieutenant, The Boy & The Dog: Impressario Magazine*

The Scotsman & The German Farmer: Young Israel Viewpoint*

    *contact author
    **contact agent

SYNOPSES

The Power of the Dog: A country peddler comes into possession of a valuable painting. Cheated by an antique dealer, he steals the work only to find that he is trapped. He cannot sell it, nor can he return it — to do so would only enrich the man who cheated him. Moral: there is a bit of larceny in everyone.

Full length. Setting: three simple sets. 8 males, 3 females.

Man on Earth: A middle-aged man, a failure in his profession, finds that he has to start all over again in order to support his two children. While the setting takes place in a real estate office, it shows the keen competition and double-dealing in the business world.

Full length. Setting: an office. 6 males, 3 females.

ALLEN STERNFIELD

Born in Worcester, MA on January 14, 1930. Now resident of Boston and a product of the Boston school system. He was a professional trumpet player. Co-founder and Artistic Director of Playwrights' Platform in Boston. Playwright-in-Residence, University of North Carolina, 1973.

Address: 51 Brackett St., Brighton, MA 02135
    (617) 787-3606

Agent: Ann Woodward, 31 Revere St., Boston, MA 02151 (617) 523-0237

TITLE • AVAILABILITY • PRODUCTIONS

The Advance Man: manuscript*; Playwrights' Platform, Boston, MA

Benito: manuscript*; A.C.T. of San Francisco, CA; Playwrights' Platform, Boston, MA

Hide and Seek (formerly titled **Statement):** Dramatic Publishing Co., 86 East Randolph St., Chicago, IL 60601, $1.00; Playwrights' Platform

Holmes and Moriarty (one act): manuscript*; O'Neill Theater Center's National Playwrights Conference, CT; Carolina Playmakers, NC

Wild Man of Borneo: manuscript*; Cubiculo Theatre, NYC

Circa 1933: manuscript*; Playwrights' Platform, Boston, MA

Hall of Fame: manuscript*

S

Allen Sternfield (cont'd)

Exegesis: manuscript*

The Music Festival: manuscript*; Wakefield Trycycle; London, England

The Emperor Waltz: manuscript*; Playwrights' Platform, Boston, MA

Legality of Food: manuscript*

Midchannel: manuscript*

Stalingrad II: manuscript*

Kramers Golden Ambulance: manuscript*

  *contact author

SYNOPSES

Holmes and Moriarty: A comedy in which those arch rivals attend the baseball games together. "Holmes and Moriarty is aggressively funny, one of the true great nut comedies." Mike Steele, **Minneapolis Tribune.**

One act. Setting: Holmes' rooms on Baker Street and the box in a baseball park. 5 males, 1 female.

The Advance Man: Alf Shafter, the advance man for O'Brien's Circus, comes to Fairview, USA. He spreads corruption and draws out corruption from the townspeople. He is eventually martyred and murdered by his own weakness but not before he selects a new advance man to carry out his work.

Full length. Setting: multiple — a circus, hotel lobby, hotel room and a parlor. 5 males, 3 females.

Stalingrad II: A young man living amidst urban blight imagines himself to be an aide to General Von Paulus in the closing days of the Battle of Stalingrad. The sights and sounds around him take on a grim reality until he can no longer distinguish one battle from the other and he surrenders to the Russians as well as to his own madness.

Full length. Setting: a furnished room. 3 males, 3 females. Special sound effects.

MILAN STITT

Educated at Albion College. B.A. in English from U. of Michigan, M.F.A., Yale School of Drama. Has lectured and taught at many colleges, written screenplays and TV plays. Member of Dramatists Guild, Authors League of America, P.E.N. and Writers Guild of America, East. Recipient: Minor Avery Hopwood Playwriting Award; Major Avery Hopwood Playwriting Award; NEA Playwriting Grant; CAPS Award. He is resident playwright at the Circle Repertory Company.

Address: 42925 Whitestone Court, Northville, MI 48167

Agent: Helen Merrill, 337 W. 22nd St., New York, NY 10011 (212) 924-6314

TITLE • AVAILABILITY • PRODUCTIONS

Towers of Achievement: not available; U. of Michigan

The First "R": not available; Morgan Junior High School, Wallingford, CT

Take a Little Chance: not available; U. of Michigan

In the Pursuit: not available; Hofbrau Haus, New Haven, CT

Edie's Home: not available; Triad Playwrights Co.; WBAI, NYC

The Runner Stumbles: Dramatists Play Service, 440 Park Avenue South, New York, NY 10016, $2.50; Berkshire Theatre Festival; Manhattan Theatre Club, NYC; Broadway

Back in the Race: Dramatists Play Service, $2.50; Circle Repertory Co., NYC: BoarsHead Theatre, MI

RICHARD STOCKTON

Ohio born (1932), California trained, and New York oriented (since 1959). Teaching Assistant for Playwrights' Unit at UCLA and Graduate Fellow in Playwriting at State University of Iowa. Wrote the first drama staged in the Off Off Broadway cabaret theatre movement (Phase 2 on Bleecker St.). First American playwright to have a world premiere at The Abbey in Dublin. Has also written for television, radio, commercial film, children's theatre and outdoor drama. Television credits include **The United States Steel Hour, The Great Adventure,** and anthology dramas for various series on CBC, BBC, and ETV. Recipient: The Samuel Goldwyn Award for Creative Writing; The Samuel French National Playwriting Competition; The Alden Award of the Dramatists' Alliance; The Bellows Prize; H. K. Smith Sr. Memorial Playwriting Award; Players Workshop National Playwriting Contest; Commission to write a bicentennial play for Winston-Salem.

Address: 261 Broadway, #2B, New York, NY 10017 (212) 732-3079 (home)/(212) 398-3354 (service)

TITLE • AVAILABILITY • PRODUCTIONS

The Casket Maker (one act): **Cimarron Review** (2), U. of Oklahoma; manuscript*; Phase 2 NYC; Theatre Cleveland, OH

The House Shall Tremble: manuscript*; UCLA; Chino Prison; U. of Iowa

A Fabulous Tale: Best Short Plays 1956–1958*; Tokyo English Theatre; UCLA

The Litter of Flowers: manuscript*; Little Theatre of Jacksonville

The Weed Bouquet: manuscript*; The Playwrights' Showcase, New Orleans, LA

Love Among the Platypi (*collaboration): manuscript*; Bucks County Playhouse, PA; Green Hills Theatre

One World at a Time: manuscript*; The Lambs Club, NYC; University of Oregon

Till the Day Break: manuscript*; Old Salem Corporation, Winston-Salem

Prisoner of the Crown (**collaboration): manuscript*; The Abbey, Dublin; Milwaukee Repertory; Virginia Museum Theatre

    *with Peggy Plimmer
    **with Richard T. Herd
    *contact author

SYNOPSES

Prisoner of the Crown: A highly theatricalized roast of the British Government and Courts for the royal rape administered in 1916 to Sir Roger Casement — Irish patriot, accused homosexual, and last knight of the realm hanged for high treason. A timeless (and timely!) examination of the official line that "national security" justifies any and all violations of civil liberties and individual rights. This spurious assertion is hounded through the periwigged precincts of the Old Bailey

Richard Stockton (cont'd)

with equal mixture of hilarity, history, hysteria, and contemporary irony. Requires a company of 14 versatile male actors who double over 50 roles while roaming from a basic courtroom setting to a dozen suggestive locations — backward, forward, and sideways in time. (WARNING: This play was uniformly despised by the orthodox London critics who covered the Abbey premiere.)

Love Among the Platypi: This romantic comedy (with a fantasy kicker) concerns a pretty, likable, New York girl who has inherited a peculiar power directly from the Greek sorceress, Circe (who transformed Ulysses' sailors into swine on the voyage home from Troy). Unfortunately for the various predatory men who pursue her, she has no control over the power. When they behave like swine — ZAP! She shares her accumulation of docile housepets with a zany spinster upstairs and the Bronx Zoo. The plot is complicated by investigators from the Bureau of Missing Persons, a nice young man (whom she would like to keep that way), and a paternal professor of Ancient Mythology who finds her case curiously familiar. If there is a serious message in this...it couldn't be helped.

One set: a brownstone livingroom in Greenwich Village. 2 females, 5 males.

One World at a Time: A comedy-drama about the leading 19th-century American iconoclast, humanist, and agnostic — Robert Ingersoll. This play explores in very human terms the terrible cost of candor to the most outspoken man of his day. It dramatizes the extraordinary courage of one individual who would not put a padlock on his tongue, nor shackles on his brain for any man — any bigot — any cause — or any reason — not even to be President of the United States. This is a true story — rich with native wit, robust humor, and love of family — which just **happens** to be about the man described by one biographer as "the breath of brimstone in your grandmother's closet!"

Setting: a law rookery in Peoria (sparsely furnished at the start, then more lavish later) and the livingroom of a fashionable townhouse on Manhattan's Gramercy Park. 1 female, 8 males.

SAMUEL SUSSMAN

Born in New York City on September 29, 1913. Educated at City College of New York, B.S.; Brooklyn College, M.S. in Education. Retired from New York City public schools where he served as Assistant Principal. Courses in playwriting at Gene Frankel Workshop and at Actor's Studio with Lee Strasberg.

Address: 444 Neptune Ave., Brooklyn, NY 11224 (212) 996-3230

Agent: Bertha Klausner, 71 Park Ave., New York, NY 10016 (212) 685-2642

TITLE • AVAILABILITY • PRODUCTIONS

A Prelude to Hamlet: manuscript*; Salt City Playhouse, Syracuse, NY; Troupe Theatre, NYC

The Button Pusher: manuscript**
   *contact agent
   **contact author

SYNOPSES

A Prelude to Hamlet: The play deals with the events leading up to Shakespeare's **Hamlet.** It explains the duality in Hamlet's nature by revealing the influences that shaped him — the father's taste for war, the intellectual and moral leanings of his mother and uncle. The play thus becomes a tug of war over the direction of Hamlet's future. The King's mounting acts of violence compel Gertrude and Claudius to take counter measures. Ultimately, out of desperation, they kill the King.

Samuel Sussman (cont'd)

Though set in the past, it is a modern play. Its anti-war sentiment and its discussion of the ideal state are pertinent today. The ending is ironic. ("We're safe." "Now Hamlet can come home.") We know that Hamlet's return (in Shakespeare's play) will lead to the death of Claudius and Gertrude.

Full length. Setting: a room in the palace of Elsinore. 10 males, 3 females.

The Button Pusher: The play is set in Hollywood in 1931, a few years after the changeover from silent movies to the talkies. Amy Love, an actress, separated from her husband for four years, finds herself pregnant. How she gets out of her predicament is the subject of this comedy. The title characterizes Frank Arrowette, a writer, who loves to manipulate people's lives.

Full length. Setting: livingroom in Amy's house. 4 males, 3 females.

JEFFREY SWEET

Born in Boston, MA on May 3, 1950. M.A. and B.F.A., New York University (Film). Composer, lyricist, journalist, short story writer. Author of **Something Wonderful Right Away.** Has had works published in **Newsday, L.A. Times, Ellery Queen, Gallery** etc. Regular contributor to **The Dramatists Guild Quarterly.** Founder of New York Writers Bloc, a playwrights forum. Has taught workshops in playwriting and improvisation at the Goodman Theatre, Victory Gardens Theatre and The Dramatists Guild. Author of one of **Best Detective Stories of 1974.** Recipient: **Scholastic Magazine** Award, 1967; OADR Grant, 1970; Award for criticism, **Harper's,** 1970; Corporation for Public Broadcasting, 1973; Society of Midland Authors Award, 1978; NEA Creative Writing Fellowship, 1979; Commission Grant, National Radio Theatre of Chicago, 1980.

Address: 500 West End Avenue, 3G, New York, NY 10024 (212) 724-7512

Agent: Susan Schulman, 165 West End Avenue, New York, NY 10024 (212) 877-2216

TITLE • AVAILABILITY • PRODUCTIONS

Winging It!: not available; Milwaukee Repertory Theatre, WI: St. Clements, NYC

Hitch: not available; Los Angeles, CA (showcase)

Wicked John and the Devil: not available; **Earplay;** Manhattan Theatre Club, NYC

Narrow Escape: manuscript*; Los Angeles, CA (showcase)

Porch: Samuel French, 25 West 45th St., New York, NY 10036, $1.50; Arena Stage, Washington, DC; Encompass Theatre, NY

Chords: not available

Neighbors (with David Warrack): manuscript*; Aquarius Theater, Ontario

Stops Along the Way: Best Short Plays of 1981, Chilton Book Co., Chilton Way, Radnor, PA 19089; Actors Alley, Los Angeles, CA; Lincoln Center, NYC

Parental Guidance: manuscript**; Actors Studio, NYC; Victory Gardens Theatre, Chicago, IL

The Unreasonable Man: manuscript*; Victory Gardens Theatre, Chicago, IL

After the Fact: Samuel French, $1.50; Victory Gardens Theatre, Chicago, IL

Narrow Escape: manuscript*; Los Angeles, CA

Holding Patterns (with Stephen Johnson, Sandra Hastie, Christine Plapp, Tom Toce): manuscript*; Theatre Express, Pittsburgh, PA

    *contact author
    **contact agent

S

Jeffrey Sweet (cont'd)

SYNOPSES

Porch and **After the Fact:** Father, daughter and her former lover come to terms on a midwestern front porch; preceded by a prologue about a father's run-in with a local reporter. "Written with subtlety and an increasingly compelling emotion". Richard Eder, **New York Times.**

One act, 90 minutes. Setting: suggestion of a front porch. 2 males, 1 female.

Parental Guidance (formerly **Hard Feelings**): Love and violence in a seedy motel on Ventura Boulevard. "It's easy to see why directors may be drawn to his work. The sensibility is human without getting maudlin, and as straightforward as it is careful about naturalistic detail". Linda Winer, **Chicago Tribune.**

Full length. Setting: lobby of a motel. 5 males, 2 females.

The Unreasonable Man (formerly **Ties**): A guest director at a small college finds himself at the focal point of a romantic tangle. "The play we've been waiting for this season. The genuine article, a drama of solid craft and sensitive artistry." Richard Christiansen, **Chicago Tribune.**

Full length. Setting: unit set suggesting a variety of locations. 6 males, 2 females.

PETER SWET

Born Queens, NY, September 25, 1942. B.A., University of Dayton, OH. Past Playwright-in-Residence, Impossible Ragtime Theatre, NY. Member, Dramatists Guild and Writers Guild of America. Presently writes for **Sesame Street** in addition to being primary writer for the comedy team of Stiller and Meara and has spent several seasons as script writer for NBC-TV's serial, **Another World.** Recipient: Emmy nomination **(Another World);** MacDowell Colony Grant, 1980; Stanley Foundation Production Grant.

Address: P.O. Box 108, Westhampton, NY 11977
(516) 325-1134

TITLE • AVAILABILITY • PRODUCTIONS

The Interview: Dramatists Play Service, 440 Park Avenue South, New York, NY 10016, $1.25; Gene Frankel Workshop, NYC; Mercer Arts Center, NYC

Debris: manuscript*; Gene Frankel Workshop, NYC; Theatre in Space

Rondelay: manuscript*; Impossible Ragtime Theatre, NYC

Insurance!: manuscript*

Satisfaction: manuscript*

*contact author

SYNOPSES

Satisfaction: A free-wheeling bedroom farce set off by a bored married couple's efforts to catch up with the "Me" Generation's imperative of self-fulfillment. They turn to other romantic interests in hopes of finding the answer, but instead become embroiled in a series of unasked for adventures involving mishaps, foul-ups, mistaken identity, secrets and — yes — some time honored Feydeau door slamming, ultimately leading to surprising revelations in a whirlwind wrap up that leaves all concerned on a more or less permanent detour in their quest for satisfaction.

Full length. Setting: apartment interior with isolated settings. 5 males, 4 females.

Insurance!: An unsuspecting insurance investigator is summoned to the surrealistic inner sanc-

Peter Swet (cont'd)

tum of a billionaire industrialist for what he assumes will be a routine investigation. The industrialist has purposes of his own, however, and a battle of wits and wills ensues as the investigator slowly unravels a series of seeming enigmas to discover himself inescapably faced with what can only be the moral decision of his lifetime.

One act: Setting: an inner office (surrealistically, a sanctum sanctorum). 2 males.

Rondelay: "Ten people take part in a chain letter romance . . . (with) . . . a bed as centerpiece, swinging like a turntable from Central Park to a suite at the Pierre. The bed is almost always occupied, but the play is even more about parting than loving. The fascination is all in the variation. 'Ronde' and 'Ronde' it goes . . . a breezy modernization of the original." — Mel Gussow, **New York Times,** writing on Impossible Ragtime Theatre's Equity Showcase of **Rondelay,** a new play taken from Schnitzler's **La Ronde.**

Full length. 9 settings: centered about a revolving bed (4 in Act One, 5 in Act Two). 6 males, 4 females.

BRIAN TAGGERT

Educated at Glendale College and transferred to Royal Scottish Academy of Music and Drama. Scholarship after first year. Received DDA: equivalent to American B.A. Started writing episodic television (**Emergency, Adam 12),** moved on to **Movie of the Week, Mark of Zorro, The Spell, Night Cries;** motion picture, **The Fright.** Recipient: Los Angeles Dramatists Award, 1976.

Address: 7507 Sunset Blvd., Suite 1, Los
Angeles, CA 90046 (213) 273-6116

Agent: Bloom-Levy-Shore and Associates,
8816 Burton Way, Beverly Hills, CA 90212
(213) 858-7741

TITLE • AVAILABILITY • PRODUCTIONS

When Last I Saw the Lemmings: manuscript*; Matrix Theater, Hollywood, CA

A Valley Full of Needles: manuscript*

Last Things: manuscript*

*contact author

SYNOPSES

A Valley Full of Needles: Caustically comedic evolving into violence. Hamish, perennial student, returns home for his mother's funeral. His loutish father has remarried a woman not much older than Hamish. Hamish has returned not so much for the funeral as to re-establish ties with his younger brother, Devon, whom he fears will have all the individuality stamped out of him as a result of being raised by "John Wayne on a cattle drive." A hostile ugly secret taints the household that only Hamish and his father know and can work out. A sardonic, barbed exchange gives way to violence and a lesson on giving and taking . . . love and responsibility.

Full length. Setting: livingroom, diningroom. 4 characters.

Last Things: A thriller based in an old folks home where people are disenfranchised, treated like children, fed like animals and almost totally ignored. But beware of the seemingly insignificant. They can band together and create a power force. They do, and the result is a microcosm of power; the struggles, politics and chicanery necessary for survival. Despots underestimate the will to survive and guerillas have sprouted up in the most unlikely spots. In **Last Things** an underlying humor aids this thrust and leavens the anger.

Full length. Setting: living room, dining room. 7 characters.

T

STANLEY TAIKEFF

Born in Brooklyn, New York on April 27, 1940. Received M.A. in Theatre from Hunter College, CUNY. He has published poetry in **Voices of Brooklyn, Manhattan Review, Bitterroot, Writer's Notes & Quotes, Poetry Parade, Hyacinths & Biscuits** and other literary magazines. Short stories published in **Abyss,** Volumes 1 and 2, and **One: A Magazine of Fiction.** Articles published in **Dramatists Guild Quarterly** and **Writers Guild of America West Newsletter.** Has read his poetry and prose at Atelier's East, New York City. Member, New Dramatists. Recipient: Shubert Playwriting Fellowship; John Golden Award; poetry prize, Terre Haute Poets' Study Club Award; O.A.D.R. grant.

Address: 3A Second Place, Brooklyn, NY 11231

TITLE • AVAILABILITY • PRODUCTIONS

Denoument: manuscript*; Playwrights Opportunity Theatre; Thirteenth St. Theatre, NYC

Solo Recital: Dramatics Magazine, Vol. XLV, No. 6, March 1974*; Little Theater, 65th St., YMCA, NYC; Madrid Community School, Madrid, IA

Into That Good Night: manuscript*; Little Theater, 65th St. YMCA, NYC

The Afflictions of Marlene: manuscript*; Little Theater, 65th St. YMCA, NYC

Andy Grunnt: manuscript*

The Stamp Family: manuscript*

Don Juan of Flatbush: manuscript*; Missouri Repertory Theater; Corner Theatre, Baltimore, MD

The Sugar Bowl: manuscript*; O'Neill Theater Center's National Playwrights Conference, CT; New Dramatists, NYC

Ah, Eurydice: manuscript*; Dramatists Play Service, 440 Park Avenue South, New York, NY 10016, $1.25; Shelter/West Company, NYC; various others

A Cock to Asclepius: manuscript*; New Dramatists, NYC

In the Modern Style: manuscript*; Joseph Jefferson Theatre Company, NYC: New Dramatists, NYC

Duet for Parents: manuscript*; New Dramatists, NYC

Brigitte Berger: manuscript*; New Dramatists, NYC

Last Ferry to Thebes: manuscript*; New Dramatists, NYC

*contact author

SYNOPSES

The Sugar Bowl: The Sugar Bowl, a one-time popular candy store in Brooklyn is the "home" for Zeke Zuckerman, a thirty-year-old man searching for meaning in a world that has slipped by him. During the course of the play, he taunts Moe, the owner of the store, about his past and tries to pick up the threads of his youth with his childhood pals, who drop into the store. After his friends reject him, Zeke turns to Moe in despair and it is only then that a reconciliation between the two is achieved.

Full length. Setting: a candy store. 9 males, 1 female.

A Cock to Asclepius: A comedy-drama about Socrates and his wife, Xanthippe on the day of the philosopher's execution. The play fuses myth, legend, poetry, fact and fiction in an attempt to arrive at the truth about their marriage and struggles.

Full length. Setting: a prison cell. 9 males, 3 females.

Last Ferry to Thebes: Variations on the classical theme of Oedipus and Jocasta.

Full length. Setting: Oedipus' summer house on the Aegean. 3 males, 5 females.

TED TALLY

Born Winston-Salem, NC on April 9, 1952. Educated in North Carolina public schools, B.A. from Yale (cum laude) and M.F.A. Yale School of Drama. Taught Playwriting at both. Co-authored (with Dale Burg), **Couples Only** for CBS-TV. Feature filmscripts include **Empire,** a screenplay for Orion Pictures and a new (untitled) script for United Artists. Recipient: Authors Award, Carolina Dramatic Assoc. 1969; Betty Smith Prize in Playwriting, 1969; Theron Rockwell Field Prize, 1977; Molly Kazan Award, 1977; John Golden Fellowship, 1976–77; CBS Foundation Fellowship, 1977–78; CAPS Fellowship, 1978–79; Drama-Logue Award for Outstanding Achievement in Theatre, 1980.

Address: 152 East 83rd St., New York, NY 10028

Agent: Helen Merrill, 337 West 22nd St., New York, NY 10011 (212) 924-6314

TITLE • AVAILABILITY • PRODUCTIONS

Night Mail: manuscript*; Yale Cabaret; CT; Body Politic, Chicago, IL

Clews: manuscript*; Yale University, CT

We've Got to Stop Meeting Like This: manuscript*; West Park Theatre, NYC

Terra Nova: manuscript*; Yale Repertory, CT; Mark Taper Forum, Los Angeles, CA

Hooters: Dramatists Play Service, 440 Park Avenue South, New York, NY 10016, $2.50; Playwrights Horizons, NYC; Empty Space, Seattle, WA

Coming Attractions: Dramatists Play Service, $2.50; Phoenix Theatre, NYC, staged reading; Playwrights Horizons, NYC

    *contact agent

JULES TASCA

Born in Philadelphia, PA on December 10, 1938. Educated at Pennsylvania State University, B.A.; Villanova University, Villanova, PA, M.A., Drama. Associate Professor at Gwynedd Mercy College, Gwynedd Valley, PA. Major duties include — Chairman of the Drama Dept., Teach courses in Theater, Directing, Playwriting, Drama Form, Creative Writing, Speech, Shakespeare, English Literature, and Cinema. Also taught on a part-time basis at the following colleges: Beaver College, Glenside, PA; Villanova University, Villanova, PA; PA State University, Ogontz Campus, Abington, PA. Co-authored **Hal Linden Special** on CBS-TV. Recipient: Joseph Jefferson Award nomination for Outstanding Achievement in Chicago Area Theatre for the Best New Play, **The Mind With The Dirty Man,** 1972–73. Contributor

to Howard Teichman's biography, **George S. Kaufman — An Intimate Portrait.** Listed in **Who's Who in the East,** 1976–77.

Address: 313 Heston Ave., Norristown, PA 19401 (215) 539-9284

Agent: Hayden Griffin, 160 East 48th St., New York, NY 10017 (212) 688-9283

T

Jules Tasca (cont'd)

TITLE • AVAILABILITY • PRODUCTIONS

Tear Along the Dotted Line: The Dramatic Publishing Co., 4150 N. Milwaukee Avenue, Chicago, IL 60641, $2.00; Valley Players, Gwynedd Valley, PA

Subject to Change: Samuel French, 25 West 45th St., New York, NY 10036, $2.50; Pheasant Run Playhouse, Chicago, IL

Tadpole: Dramatists Play Service, 440 Park Avenue South, New York, NY 10016, $2.50, Mark Taper Forum, Los Angeles, CA

The Mind with the Dirty Man: Samuel French, $2.50; Mark Taper Forum, Los Angeles, CA; Huntington Hartford Theatre, CA

Chip Off Olympus: Samuel French, $2.50; Triangle Theatre, NYC

Nip 'n Tuck: manuscript*

5 One Act Plays by Mark Twain (adaptation): Samuel French, $2.50; Valley Players, PA

Party of the First Part: manuscript*

One Act by Art Smythe, Full Length Play by Joe Jones: manuscript*

Romeo & Juliet Are Lovers: manuscript*; Mark Taper Forum, LA (reading)

Alive and Kicking: manuscript*; Gwynedd Valley, PA

The Last Damned Witch in Salem: manuscript*

Goody One Shoe: manuscript*

   *contact agent

SYNOPSES

Tadpole: Jimmy (The Arm) Younkers, after many successful prior years of big-league pitching stardom, and extravagant living, has decided to "hold out" on signing the reduced contract resulting from his failing record of recent seasons. But while Jimmy's athletic powers are waning, his destructive lifestyle has yet to run its course. Having walked out on his wife and children, he continues to pursue romantic assignations with ladies near and far; he borrows money he knows he will never repay; he indulges every impulse and has no hesitation in dragging others down with him; and, in general, he refuses to admit that the days of glory are over. But, throughout, he remains cocky, irreverent and unfailingly funny, as he moves through a series of events in which humor, human frailty and ultimate poignance are blended with rare theatrical skill.

This biting, acerbic comedy combines zany humor, remarkable characterizations and telling comments on contemporary American society as it explores the plight of a big-league baseball pitcher, who has lost his throwing arm but not his driving ego.

Setting: middle-class home, interior. 5 males, 2 females.

Chip Off Olympus: Set in Los Angeles, the cradle of movieland, the play concerns a funny bizarre family who, all in their separate ways, attempt to find something in life that will give them an illusion of greatness. Dora, the mother; saves memorabilia from the movies — Bogart's trench coat from "Casablanca", John Wayne's helmet from "Sands of Iwo Jima", etc. Augie tries to become a famous writer at his family's expense. Natalie becomes a religious fanatic and runs around giving family possessions away, and develops a stigmata which spreads as her fanaticism reaches fever pitch. Michael is a doctor who has developed a no-fail heart valve, but whose marriage slips out from under him. A funny and thought provoking evening as all the LaDona's illusions come crashing down at the conclusion.

Setting: Beverly Hills home interior. 2 males, 3 females, 2 extra males.

The Mind with the Dirty Man: Small town leader, Wayne Stone, is the head of the local film review board. He and his prudish colleagues strive to keep smutty movies out of their small community. Hilarity ensues when Stone's underground filmmaker son returns to take over the local movie house to exhibit his X-rated movies, his latest — **The Shoe Fetish.** This only starts the comedy — Wayne and his wife, Alma, next find out that only son, Clayton, plans to marry the porno queen star of the film right there in town in front of the movie house on opening night under the search lights. These and other events are jocularly resolved in an outrageous turnabout, laugh packed, ending that makes its point about the hypocrisy of conventional American mores.

Setting: interior of middle class home. 3 males, 4 females.

RONALD TAVEL

Master's Degree in Philosphy and Elizabethan Literature. Wrote novel, **Street of Stairs.** Worked two years as Andy Warhol's scenarist. Founded and named the Theatre of the Ridiculous movement. Literary advisor for **Scripts Magazine,** contributor to the Sub-plot Theatre (in the American Place Complex), founding member of the New York Theatre Strategy. Playwright-in-Residence at The Play-House of the Ridiculous, The Theatre of the Lost Continent, The Actors Studio, The Yale Divinity School, Williamstown Theatre Second Company, New Playwrights' Theatre of Washington. Recipient: Obie Award, 1969, 1973; APT grant in Playwriting, 1970; Rockefeller Foundation Stipend in Playwriting, 1972, 1978; Creative Artists Public Service Program grant, 1972, 1974; Guggenheim Fellowship,

1973; National Endowment for the Arts Fellowship, 1974-75; The New York State Council on the Arts Younger Audience Play Commission; ZBS Foundation, AIR stipend, 1976.

Address: 438 West Broadway, Apt. 1, New York, NY 10012 (212) 226-4725

Agent: Helen Merrill, 337 West 22nd St., New York, NY 10011 (212) 924-6314

TITLE • AVAILABILITY • PRODUCTIONS

Christina's World (verse play): **Writing at Wyoming*** 1958 (one act); **Chicago Review,** Vol. 16 No. 1, 1963 (complete play)

Tarzan of the Flicks: Blacklist No. 6* (1965), excerpts; Goddard College, Plainfield, VT

Screen Test (one act): Play-House of the Ridiculous; Queens College, NYC; Columbia University, NYC

The Life of Juanita Castro (one act): **Tri-Quarterly*** No. 6 (1966); Coda Galleries, NY; St. Marks Playhouse, NYC; Rutgers University, NJ

Vinyl (one act): **Clyde,** Vol. 2, No. 2*; **Cine Diary** No. 12 (Tokyo, Japan, 1967), in Japanese; Caffe Cino, NYC

Kitchenette (one act): **Partisan Review*** (Spring 1967); Play-House of the Ridiculous, NYC; No Exit Cafe, Chicago, IL; Massachusetts Institute of Technology, MA

Shower (one act): **The Young American Writers,** edited by Richard Kostelanetz, Funk & Wagnalls, Inc., 666 Fifth Ave., New York, NY 10019 (out of print); Coda Galleries; St. Marks Playhouse, NYC; The Extension

The Life of Lady Godiva (one act): **Theatre of the Ridiculous, Performing Arts Journal,** 92 St. Marks Place, New York, NY 10009, $4.95; Play-House of the Ridiculous, NYC; University of Notre-Dame; various others productions

Indira Gandhi's Daring Device (one act): manuscript*; Play-House of the Ridiculous, NYC; Rutgers University, NJ; Columbia University, NY

Gorilla Queen: The Off Off Broadway Book, Bobbs-Merrill, 4 West 58th St., New York, NY 10019, $10.00; Judson Memorial Church; Martinique Theatre, NY

Canticle of the Nightingale (one act musical play): manuscript*; performed in Sweden and Denmark; Manhattan Theatre Club, NY

Cleobis and Bito (one act oratorio): manuscript*; The Extension

Arenas of Lutetia: Experiments in Prose, edited by Eugene Wildman, The Swallow Press, Chicago, IL*; Judson Memorial Church, NYC

Boy on the Straight-Back Chair: Word Plays, Performing Arts Journal, $6.95; American Place Theatre, NYC; Smithsonian Institute, DC

Vinyl Visits an FM Station (one act): **TDR, The Drama Review,** Vol. 14, No. 4 (1970); The Playwrights Unit; Greyfriars Theatre Society, Pasadena, CA; Theatre of the Lost Continent, NYC

T

Ronald Tavel (cont'd)

Secrets of the Citizens Correction Committee (one act): **Scripts** No. 3, January 1972; Theatre at Saint Clement's, NYC

Playbirth (one act): manuscript*; Theatre for the New City, NYC

My Foetus Lived on Amboy Street (play for voices): manuscript*; Recorded by the ZBS Foundation, Fort Edward, NY

The Clown's Tail (play for younger audiences): manuscript*; Cherry Lane Theatre, NYC

Mr. Tavel Writes a Play for Mr. Weiss (one act): manuscript*

Gazelle Boy: manuscript*; subject of the course Theology and Drama, Yale University Divinity School, CT; O'Neill Theater Center's National Playwrights Conference, CT

Bigfoot: manuscript*; American Place Theatre, NYC; Theatre Genesis; Yale University Drama School, CT

How She Became Queen of Greece: manuscript*; Theatre Genesis, NYC

The Last Days of British Honduras: manuscript*; New York Shakespeare Festival, NYC

A History of Modern Florida: manuscript*; Westbeth, NYC

The Ovens of Anita Orange Juice: manuscript*; Williamstown Theatre, MA; Westbeth Theatre Center, NYC

The Nutcracker in the Land of Nuts: manuscript*; La Mama, NYC

*contact agent

SYNOPSES

Boy on the Straight-Back Chair: A country-rock musical set in a small western town of the early 1960s. While the townspeople pretend to know nothing about it, a charming young man sets about to systematically murder off his numerous female admirers.

Full length. Setting: one very simple and inexpensive set. 5 males, 9 females plus musicians.

The Life of Lady Godiva: A rowdy and bawdy musical comedy-drama. Traveling through an indefinable historical era, Lady Godiva manages to make her historic ride. One of the most performed plays to come out of the Theatre of the Ridiculous movement.

One long act. Setting: one all-purpose set. 4 males, 2 females.

The Nutcracker in the Land of Nuts: A musical retelling of Hoffman's holiday story in which the Nutcracker sets about to find the magical nut whose kernel will cure his mistress of a growing case of "weremousehood."

Full length. Setting: one or two flexible sets. Approximately 12 actors.

HIRAM TAYLOR

Born Mobile, AL on February 29, 1952. B.S., Syracuse University. Director, producer, writer — children's theatre programs. Special Foreign Studies Abroad Program, playwriting, for six months in Amsterdam, Nederlands. Artistic Director, The Tayman-Welsh Theatre Company, NYC. Recipient: First Place, Bultman Playwriting Award 1974.

Address: 40 First Ave., Apt. 14-C, New York, NY 10009 (212) 228-1272

TITLE • AVAILABILITY • PRODUCTIONS

The Penniless Prince: manuscript*; Mobile Theatre Guild Children's Tour, AL

Dishpan Hands: manuscript*; Mobile Theatre Guild Children's Tour, AL

Members: manuscript*; Syracuse University, NY; Direct Theatre, NYC

Thief in the Night: manuscript*; Syracuse University, NY; Jacob Obracstrat Theatre (Amsterdam, Nederlands)

Mobile: manuscript*; N.A.A.S. Script Development Workshop

Movie Buff: manuscript*; N.A.A.S. Script Development Workshop; Actor's Playhouse, NYC

Cocktails and Hors d'Oeuvres: manuscript*; Cherry Lane Theatre, NYC

Teasers: manuscript*; Quaigh Theatre, NYC

Bumps and Grinds: manuscript*; The Journey Co., NYC

Fifth Avenue: manuscript*; Actor's Playhouse, NYC

Opening Night: manuscript*; Celebrity Centre, NY

Duet: manuscript*

    *contact author

SYNOPSES

Fifth Avenue: A thriller. A young woman is held captive on a rock in Central Park by a killer who is blowing up the Plaza Hotel.

Full length. Setting: one set, an exterior. 1 male, 1 female.

Opening Night: A comedy. Charlotte, a famous actress, refuses to go on until she has figured out the difference in her own personality and the personality of the character she is playing.

Full length. Setting: one set. 2 males, 1 female.

Duet: Musical comedy. Two friends from a small town become famous in the recording industry. She, as a disco queen and he, as a punk rock star. Their careers climax when they make a duet album together.

Full length. Setting: no real set. 1 male, 1 female.

HOWARD M. TEICHMANN

Born in Chicago, IL, January 22, 1916. Educated at University of Wisconsin, B.A. Graduate work at University of Wisconsin. Writing credits include: Orson Welles' **The Mercury Theatre of the Air;** Senior Editor of the Office of War Information, Overseas Branch office; Expert Consultant in radio on staff of Lt. Gen. Brehon Somervell. TV credits include: **Showtime USA,** and the first television special for Ford's 50th Anniversary. Books: **George S. Kaufman — An Intimate Portrait** (Atheneum, 1972); **Smart Aleck — The Wit, World and Life of Alexander Woollcott** (William Morrow & Co., 1976); **Alice — The Life and Times of Alice Roosevelt Longworth,** (Prentice-Hall, 1979).

Address: 863 Park Ave., New York, NY 10021

Agent: Candida Donadio, 111 West 57th St., New York, NY 10019 (212) 757-5076

T

Howard Teichmann (cont'd)

TITLE • AVAILABILITY • PRODUCTIONS

The Solid Gold Cadillac (co-author, with George S. Kaufman): Dramatists Play Service, 440 Park Avenue South, New York, NY 10016, $2.50; Broadway

Miss Lonelyhearts: Dramatists Play Service, $2.50; Broadway

The Girls in 509: Samuel French, 25 West 45th St., New York, NY 10036, $2.50; Broadway

A Rainy Day in Newark: Samuel French, $2.50; Broadway

Smart Aleck: Alexander Woollcott at 8:40: manuscript*; American Place Theatre, NYC

　　*contact agent

SYNOPSES

The Solid Gold Cadillac: A satiric comedy, poking fun at Big Business in government.

No sets, four drops. 11 males, 6 females.

Miss Lonelyhearts: Adaptation of the Nathanael West novel. A comic-tragic work about a young newspaper reporter and his inescapable search for higher values.

Setting: no conventional sets; furniture representing newspaper office, bar, apartment, and farm. 6 males, 7 females.

The Girls in 509: A comedic spoof of both major political parties in the United States. A pair of hermit ladies have holed up in a midtown New York hotel and face eviction after many years, not knowing what the political climate of the country is.

Setting: hotel room. 9 males, 3 females.

MEGAN TERRY

Born in Seattle, WA on July 22, 1932. B.Ed. from U. of Washington; Certificates in Directing, Design and Acting from Banff School of Fine Arts; Graduate work at U. of Alberta and Yale. She was a founding member of New York's Open Theatre. She was Adjunct Professor of Theatre at the U. of Nebraska; lectured and gave playwriting seminars at more than 200 universities and theaters; on the playwriting faculty of Squaw Valley Community of Writers. She is the Playwright-in-Residence at the Omaha Magic Theatre. Recipient: Guggenheim Grant, 1977; NEA Literature Grant; two Rockefeller Grants; two OADR Grants; CAPS Grant; Obie Award for the Best Play; Stanley Drama Award; ABC Award for Writing for the Camera; two first place prizes for National Radio Play Awards.

Address: 2309 Hanscom Blvd., Omaha, NE 68105

Agent: Elisabeth Marton, 96 Fifth Avenue, New York, NY 10011 (212) 255-1908

TITLE • AVAILABILITY • PRODUCTIONS

Beach Grass: manuscript*; Cornish Theatre, Seattle, WA

Seascape: manuscript*; Cornish Theatre, Seattle, WA

Go Out and Move the Car: manuscript*; Cornish Theatre, Seattle, WA

The Dirt Boat: manuscript*; KING-TV, Seattle, WA

New York Comedy: Two: manuscript*; Saratoga Gallery Theatre, NY

Ex-Miss Copper Queen on a Set of Pills: Samuel French, 25 West 45th St., New York, NY 10036, $2.50; Cherry Lane Theatre, NYC

When My Girlhood Was Still All Flowers: manuscript*; Open Theatre, NYC

Eat at Joe's: manuscript*; Open Theatre, NYC

The Gloaming, Oh My Darling: with **Viet Rock;** Firehouse Theatre, MN; The Company Theatre, L.A., CA

Calm Down Mother: Samuel French, $1.25; Open Theatre, NYC; Sheridan Square Playhouse, NYC

Keep Tightly Closed in a Cool Dry Place: with **Viet Rock;** Sheridan Square Playhouse, NYC; Edinburgh Festival

The Magic Realists: Samuel French, $2.50; LaMama, NYC

Viet Rock: Samuel French, $3.95; LaMama, NYC: Yale, New Haven, CT

Comings and Goings: with **Viet Rock;** LaMama, NYC: Edinburgh Festival

Jack — Jack: manuscript*; Firehouse Theatre, MN; Nancy, France

The Key Is at the Bottom: manuscript*; Mark Taper Forum, CA

Changes: manuscript*; LaMama, NYC

Massachusetts Trust: Omaha Magic Theatre Press, 1417 Farnam St., Omaha, NB, $5.00; Brandeis U., MA

Home: Or Future Soap: Samuel French, $2.50; PBS-TV; London

The People vs Ranchman: with **Ex-Miss Copper Queen . . .;** Fortune Theatre, NYC: Kingston Mines, Chicago, IL

Sanibel and Captiva: with **The Magic Realists;** WGBH Radio

The Tommy Allen Show: Omaha Magic Theatre Press; Actor's Studio, NYC: Omaha Magic Theatre

One More Little Drinkie: with **The Magic Realists;** PBS-TV

Approaching Simone: Samuel French, $2.50; Boston U., MA; LaMama, NYC

American Wedding Ritual: Omaha Magic Theatre Press, $1.00; **Earplay**

Choose a Spot on the Floor: manuscript*; Omaha Magic Theatre, NB

Grooving: manuscript*; Brooklyn Academy of Music, NY

Susan Peretz at the Manhattan Theatre Club: manuscript*; New York Strategy Festival

Saint Hydro-Clemency: manuscript*; St. Clement's Theatre, NYC

Nightwalk (with Sam Shepard and Jean-Claude van Itallie): Bobbs-Merrill Co., 4 W. 58th St., New York, NY 10019, $10.00; Open Theatre, NYC; World Tour

We Can Feed Everybody Here: manuscript*; Westbeth Feminist's Collective, NYC

The Narco Linguini Bust: manuscript*; Omaha Magic Theatre, NB

Babes in the Bighouse: Omaha Magic Theatre Press, $5.00; Omaha Magic Theatre, NB; Foot of the Mountain, Minneapolis, MN

The Pioneer: Omaha Magic Theatre Press, $2.00; Theatre Genesis, NYC: Omaha Magic Theatre, NB

Hothouse: Samuel French, $2.50; Circle Repertory Co., NYC; Matrix Theatre, L.A., CA

Mother Jones and the Traveling Family Circus: manuscript*; Mark Taper Forum, CA

100,000 Horror Stories of the Plains: Omaha Magic Theatre Press, $5.00; Omaha Magic Theatre, NB: U. of South Dakota

Sleazing Toward Athens: manuscript*; U. of Nebraska

Brazil Fado: Omaha Magic Theatre Press, $5.00; Sante Fe Theatre Arts Corp.; Omaha Magic Theatre, NB

T

Megan Terry (cont'd)

American King's English for Queens: Omaha Magic Theatre Press, $5.00; Omaha Magic Theatre, NB; Antioch College, Yellow Springs, OH

Pro Game: Omaha Magic Theatre Press, $2.00; Omaha Magic Theatre, NB; Theatre Genesis, NYC

Fireworks: Omaha Magic Theatre Press, $1.00; Actor's Theatre of Louisville, KY; **Earplay**

Attempted Rescue on Avenue B: Omaha Magic Theatre Press, $5.00; Chicago Theatre Strategy, IL

Goona-Goona: Omaha Magic Theatre Press, $5.00; Omaha Magic Theatre, NB

Couplings and Groupings: Samuel French, $1.70; University of Nebraska

Two Pages a Day: The Drama Review, N.Y. University Press, University Place, New York, NY, $3.00

Willa-Willie-Bill's Dope Garden: Omaha Magic Theatre Press, $1.50

*contact agent

SYNOPSES

Approaching Simone: A musical-transformation biography of the life of the great French philosopher, Simone Weil.

Full length. Setting: open stage. Any number of players.

Goona-Goona: An intense, slap-stick, Punch and Judy bitter comedy about spouse and child abuse. With music.

Full length. Setting: one set. From 6 to 12 actors, any sex or age.

Hothouse: War stories from a woman's point of view. Set in Seattle, just after the Korean War, the play deals with the relationships of grandmother, daughter and granddaughter and the men and wars in their lives.

Full length. Setting: one set. 4 males, 4 females.

STEVE TESICH +

Born in Titovo Uzice, Yugoslavia. B.A., Indiana University; M.A. in Russian Literature, Columbia University. Has recently done the screenplays for **Breaking Away, Four Friends, Eyewitness, The World According to Garp.** Recipient: Oscar, 1980.

Agent: Sam Cohn, International Creative Management, 40 West 57th St., New York, NY 10019 (212) 556-5600

TITLE • AVAILABILITY • PRODUCTIONS

The Predators: manuscript*; ACDA Workshop

Lake of the Woods: manuscript*; American Place Theatre, NYC

Nourish the Beast: Samuel French, 25 West 45th St., New York, NY 10036, $2.50; American Place Theatre, NYC

Gorky: Samuel French, $2.50; American Place Theatre, NYC

Steve Tesich (cont'd)

The Carpenters: Dramatists Play Service, 440 Park Avenue South, New York, NY 10016, $2.50; American Place Theatre, NYC

The Passing Game: Samuel French, $2.50; American Place Theatre, NYC

Touching Bottom includes **The Road, A Life, Baptismal:** Samuel French, $2.50; American Place Theatre, NYC

Division Street: manuscript*; Mark Taper Forum, Los Angeles, CA; Broadway

    *contact agent

THOM THOMAS

Born in Lawrence, PA on August 31, 1940. Attended the Pittsburgh Playhouse School of the Theatre; B.F.A., Carnegie Mellon University, 1966. Artistic Director, Pittsburgh Playhouse, Rabbit Run Summer Theatre, Odd Chair Playhouse and Pittsburgh Civic Light Opera. Has directed over 150 plays and musicals in regional theater and summer stock. Recipient: M.C.A. Fellow; Shubert Fellow; Ford Foundation Grant; National Endowment for the Arts Grant; Cameron Overseas Grant; American Conservatory Theatre Fellowship in Directing; Man of the Year in Theatre (Pittsburgh Jaycees).

Address: 301 West 45th St., New York, NY 10036

Agent: Janet Roberts, William Morris Agency, 1350 Avenue of the Americas, New York, NY 10019 (212) 586-5100

TITLE • AVAILABILITY • PRODUCTIONS

The Interview: Samuel French, 25 West 45th St., New York, NY 10036, $2.50; Pittsburgh Playhouse, PA; Academy Festival Theatre, Lake Forest, IL

The Ball Game: manuscript*; Playwrights Horizons, NYC: Open Space, London

Approaching Zero (adaptation, **Gas Trilogy):** manuscript*; LaMama ETC, NYC

Without Apologies: manuscript*; No Smoking Playhouse, NYC

    *contact agent

SYNOPSES

The Interview: A young American reporter is permitted an exclusive interview with a very famous man.

Full length. Setting: a sand garden in a Roman villa. 3 males.

The Ball Game: While the city of Pittsburgh goes mad because the Pirates have won the World Series, a family, who live in a high-rise apartment overlooking the violence and the frenzy, begin to react in strange and bizarre ways.

Full length. Setting: living room of a middle class family. 3 males, 3 females.

Approaching Zero: This is a new adaptation of Georg Kaiser's **Gas Trilogy.** The nine-hour trilogy has been compressed into an hour and a half. It tells about the Rise and Fall of an ambitious and unscrupulous family beginning at the turn of the century and ending with the final holocaust in the not too distant future.

Full length without intermission. Setting: bare stage. 4 males, 3 females, all but one male play a variety of roles.

T

FREDI TOWBIN

Born in New York City. B.A., Bard College; M.F.A.
Columbia University School of the Arts, 1972.
Established TV comedy writer (**Eight Is Enough,
Love Boat, Advice to the Lovelorn**) etc.
Playwright-in-Residence, Colonnades Theatre
Lab. Author of Off Off Broadway essay, **Burns-
Mantle Best Plays** series (5 recent volumes).
Former **Mademoiselle** magazine Guest Editor;
syndicated Hearst columnist and head public
relations writer, Columbia Records. Member of
Playwrights Unit, Actors Studio. Finalist, Great
American Play Competition, Actors Theatre of
Louisville, Samuel French Play Competition.
Recipient: MacDowell Colony; Ossabaw Colony;
Millay Colony.

Address: 10919 1/2 Hartsook Street, North
   Hollywood, CA 91601

Agent: Gary Kessler, ICM, 8899 Beverly Blvd., Los Angeles, CA 90048 (213) 550-4338

TITLE • AVAILABILITY • PRODUCTIONS

Bed & Breakfast: manuscript*; Joseph Jefferson Theatre Co., N.Y.C.; White Barn Theatre,
   Westport, CT

What! and Leave Bloomingdale's! (co-author): manuscript*; Joseph Jefferson Theatre; ANTA
   Theatre, Los Angeles, CA

"Jules and Jim" Is Playing in this Godforsaken Town: not available; Experimental Theatre
   Workshop, Columbia University, NYC

DMZ Political Cabaret: manuscript*; Mercer Arts Center, NYC; WNET-TV

Love in a Pub: manuscript*

Those Nice C. Watters: manuscript*; Joseph Jefferson, NYC

   *contact agent

SYNOPSES

Bed & Breakfast: "Bed & Breakfast, a near relative to **Annie Hall,** is a comedy which makes you
cry, a love story which makes you laugh. It is a study in human relations which makes you
recognize — in every attempt at connection between the immensely real man and woman who are
the sole characters — your own fears, your own regrets, your own ability to give as much as you
take . . . More touching than Neil Simon but just as funny!!". **Soho News**

Full length. Setting: set split stage. 1 male, 1 female.

What! and Leave Bloomingdale's!: A twice-divorced psychologist and his never-married girlfriend
love each other but not their different lifestyles. He lives on the West Side near Zabars; she on the
East, near Bloomingdale's. To do?

Those Nice C. Watters: Two elderly sisters meet for their usual Wednesday lunch at Chock Full
O'Nuts. Confronted by a lively young couple, one sister realizes — in the nick of time — that life
is for the living.

DAVID TRAINER

Born in Hartford, Connecticut, in 1947. Attended the University of Pennsylvania and Columbia University. Recipient: Wesleyan-O'Neill Fellowship.

Address: 114 West 81st St., Apt. 2R, New York, NY 10024

Agent: Gilbert Parker, c/o William Morris Agency, 1350 Avenue of the Americas, New York, NY 10019 (212) 586-5100

TITLE • AVAILABILITY • PRODUCTIONS

The Undertaking: Random House, Inc.,* 201 East 50th St., New York, NY 10022 (out of print); Playwrights Unit, NYC

Thief: with **The Undertaking;** O'Neill Theater Center's National Playwrights Conference, CT

The Pig: Random House, Inc.*

The Acquisition: manuscript*; American Place Theater, NYC

The Dance Next Door: manuscript*; Mark Taper Forum; New Theater for Now, Los Angeles, CA

Cafeteria Style Lunch: manuscript*; Mark Taper Forum; New Theater for Now, Los Angeles, CA

Mr. Curator's Proposal: The Best Short Plays of 1975, Chilton Book Co.,, 201 King of Prussia Rd., Radnor, PA 19089, $8.95

Alone in the Dark: manuscript*; Ark Theatre Co., NYC

*contact agent

CLIFFORD TURKNETT

Born in Cisco, TX on August 5, 1946. B.S., University of Wyoming, Theater, 1972. When he is not writing, he is acting. He is a professional actor with stage and film credits.

Address: 15039 Dickens Street, #3, Sherman Oaks, CA 91403 (213) 990-3343

TITLE • AVAILABILITY • PRODUCTIONS

Daddy's Duet: manuscript*; O'Neill Theater Center's National Playwrights Conference, CT; Mark Taper Forum Lab, Los Angeles, CA

Trail's End: manuscript*

T

Clifford Turknett (cont'd)

Night Lights: manuscript*

   *contact author

SYNOPSES

Daddy's Duet: Nelson and Stanley, two parentless, rootless, alienated young men, enter the waiting room of a hospital maternity ward late at night and confront Charles, an expectant father. The confrontation dredges up old memories and resentments. Charles' fear of love and account-ability provokes an aggressive attack from Nelson and Stanley who test him for the role of fatherhood.

One act. Setting: waiting room of a maternity ward. 3 males, 1 female.

Trail's End: Three men stop at the Trail's End bar and confront Jack, the proprietor, who makes it difficult for them to leave.

Full length. Setting: a highway bar. 4 males.

Night Lights: A contemporary comedy set in Los Angeles. Related thematically, each act focuses on different characters and situations.

Full length. Setting: three interior sets. 3 males, 3 females.

DENNIS LANCE TURNER

Born in San Francisco, CA on June 1, 1942. B.A., University of Washington, 1965; Yale School of Drama, M.F.A., 1968. Instructor in Theatre at Hunter College; University of Hartford; St. Joseph College; Bowling Green University. Dialogue writer, **Love of Life,** CBS, 1974. Former Executive Director, CSC Repertory, NYC. Management Consultant, F.E.D.A.P.T.; New York State Council on the Arts.

Address: 114 Garfield Place, Brooklyn, NY 11215

Agent: Earl Graham, 317 West 45th St., New York, NY 10036 (212) 489-8288

TITLE • AVAILABILITY • PRODUCTIONS

The Rapists: manuscript*; University of Washington; Off Off Broadway

Charlie Was Here and Now He's Gone: manuscript*; Eastside Playhouse, NYC: New Dramatists, NYC

Give My Regards to Broadway: manuscript*; New Dramatists, NYC; PAF Playhouse, Long Island, NY

Nell: manuscript*; Lyric Theatre, NYC; No Smoking Playhouse, NYC

   *contact agent

SYNOPSIS

Give My Regards to Broadway: A middle-aged playwright, once popular, finds himself involved in a vanity production of his latest play. By isolating himself in luxury, he has forgotten that conflict with others is a lifeline to his talent. Through confrontation with his over-protective lover and with his agent, he relives his past glory while desperately searching for the means to break from his self-imposed exile.

Full length. Setting: library of a large suburban home. 4 males.

KNOX TURNER

Born in Salem, MA on June 6, 1949. Attended Proctor Academy, NH; Franklin & Marshall College, PA, A.B., 1971. Was recreational therapist, Hospital Neuro-Psiquiatrico, Honduras; educator, York County, PA; Senior Literature Program Specialist, National Endowment for the Arts, 1974–79; Playwrights Projects consultant for NEA Theatre Program, 1980.

Address: 1847 Biltmore St., N.W., #B,
Washington, DC 20009 (202) 667-3424

TITLE • AVAILABILITY • PRODUCTIONS

Current as a Sometime Thing: manuscript*; American Society of Theatre Arts, Wash., DC; Direct Theatre, NY

Anniversary: manuscript*; New Playwrights' Theatre of Washington, DC

Geranium: manuscript*; Quaigh Theatre, NY

Labyrinth: manuscript*

*contact author

SYNOPSES

Current as a Sometime Thing: Set in rural Pennsylvania after Hurricane Agnes flooded the Susquehanna River, a down-on-his-luck electrician struggles to right a life gone sour in a world grown increasingly complex. His only companion is a callow 20-year-old, trapped in a farmhouse basement undergoing renovation.

One act. Setting: farmhouse basement. 2 males.

Geranium: Zemmie, 80, retreats to the attic of her home and feigns senility to get exactly what she wants out of life. It is a play largely about promises and, ultimately, why and how we keep them.

One act. Setting: an attic. 2 males, 1 female.

Labyrinth: Daedalus, Crete's master architect at the peak of Minoan culture, comes to realize the ethical and professional compromises he must make both as a family man and architect for the privilege of working in the most arts-supportive empire of that time. Here two families — one apprenticed, the other divine, and both wholly dependent on each other — collide in a sober world of practical survival.

Full length. Setting: one multi-purpose set. 6 males, 2 females.

U

YALE UDOFF

Born in Brooklyn, New York on March 29, 1935. Educated at Michigan State University, B.A. In addition to the theater, Mr. Udoff has written film criticism (**Film Quarterly, Film Comment**) and also writes for film and television. Some of his TV credits include: **C.B.S. Playhouse, ABC Movie of the Week (Hitchhike).** He wrote the original screenplay, **Bad Timing/A Sensual Obsession,** directed by Nicholas Roeg. Recipient: Stanley Drama Award for **The Little Gentleman** and **The Club;** Charles MacArthur Playwriting Award for **Magritte Skies.**

Address: Suite #22, 8217 Beverly Blvd., Los Angeles, CA 90048

Agent: Shapiro-Lichtman, 2049 Century Park East, Los Angeles, CA 90067 (213) 550-8545
Douglas Rae, 28 Charing Cross Road, London W.C.2 (01) 836-3903

TITLE • AVAILABILITY • PRODUCTIONS

The Little Gentleman (one act): **Best Short Plays of 1971,** Chilton Book Co., 201 King of Prussia Rd., Radnor, PA 19089, $7.50 (hard cover); Avon Books, 250 West 55th St., New York, NY 10019, $3.95 (paperback)

The Club (one act): manuscript*

Shade (one act): manuscript*; Paris, France; New York University

The Academy of Desire (one act): manuscript*; American Conservatory Theatre, San Francisco, CA; Circle Repertory Co., NYC

His Master's Voice (one act): manuscript*

The Rose Critic (one act): manuscript*

Dust to Dust (one act): manuscript*; Actors Studio, Los Angeles, CA

A Gun Play: Samuel French, 25 West 45th St., New York, NY 10036, $2.50; Vol. 8, **Playwrights for Tomorrow,** Univ. of Minn. Press; Hartford Stage Company, Hartford, CT; Cherry Lane Theater, NYC

Magritte Skies: manuscript*; O'Neill Theater Center's National Playwrights Conference, CT Playwrights Horizons, NYC

Fault Line: manuscript*; Squaw Valley Writers Conference, CA

The Example: manuscript*

   *contact agent

SYNOPSES

The Little Gentleman: A Jewish family has a baby who speaks with a clipped British accent (played by an adult actor sitting in a baby carriage).

One act. Setting: kitchen of an upper-middle-class apartment building. 1 male, 3 females.

The Club: Three old Jewish men are in hostile and comic combat with an old Italian in a strange steamroom as all wait for the agreement they've entered into to come to fruition.

One act. Setting: steamroom. 5 males, 1 female.

Fault Line: On a lonely island, a family and their guests gather for the weekend when, suddenly, the world around them starts to crumble. Back on the mainland (which they're unable to make contact with), either war or revolution has broken out; the island itself is rocked and shaken by a series of tremors. Animals start to talk to men. Mozart hovers in the background. Into this situation comes an unexpected stranger, a man of considerable mystery. Soon the stranger is dead (murder? suicide?), and now the lives of everyone on the island begin, like the world around them, to shatter and come apart.

Full length. Setting: various rooms of a large mansion, outdoor terrace, a cliff, and hints of various exterior areas. 6 males, 3 females.

ROBERT UNGER

Graduate, Yale Drama School, 1951. Teacher, Creative Writing, Nassau Community College (five years). Teacher, Communications, CUNY (five years). Director, Repertory of Original Works Inc. (five years). Writes poetry, plays, films. Current film development of play **Bohikee Creek;** volume of unpublished poetry. Recipient: Rockefeller Grant in Creative Writing, 1967 (for play **Chronicles of Bohikee Creek);** First Prize, Broadway Theater League of Indiana, 1971 (for play **Behind The Dunes).**

Address: 25 West 81st St., New York, NY
 10024 (212) 724-7003

TITLE • AVAILABILITY • PRODUCTIONS

Tomorrow (one act): manuscript*; Off Broadway; Master Institute Theater; Theater Alliance

Chronicles of Bohikee Creek: manuscript; Off Broadway, Stage 73, NYC; Actors Studio, NYC; Free Southern Theater

C.C. Ryder in "Behind The Dunes": manuscript; Nassau Community College, NY

Ward 8 Macabre: manuscript*; Nassau Community College, NY

Mendola's Rose: manuscript*; Studio Theatre, NY; currently under option

Wally's Garage: manuscript

Empty Closets: manuscript*

 *contact author

SYNOPSES

Mendola's Rose: He sells flowers on his "Mobile Flowery." She sells life.

Full length. Setting: one set, three areas, all props, no walls. 1 male (mid-60s), 1 female (mid-50s).

C.C. Ryder in "Behind The Dunes": Four people looking for some answers, among other things.

Full length. Setting: one exterior. 2 males (1 black, 1 white), 2 females (1 black, 1 white).

Ward 8 Macabre: Poses the old question who's really sane — those inside, or outside?

Full length. Setting: one set. 15-character play with music. A family, ages 7 through 70.

V

JEAN-CLAUDE VAN ITALLIE

Lecturer in Playwriting, Princeton University. Has previously taught at Yale and the New School in New York City. Was Playwright-of-the-Ensemble of Open Theater 1963–70. Has written screenplays and for public affairs TV. Recipient: Vernon Rice Drama Desk Award, 1967; Obie Award; Guggenheim Fellowship; Ford Foundation Grant; Rockefeller Grant; CAPS Grant.

Address: Box L, Charlemont, MA 01339

Agent: Janet Roberts, William Morris Agency, 1350 Avenue of the Americas, New York, NY 10019 (212) 586-5100

TITLE • AVAILABILITY • PRODUCTIONS

Almost Like Being: Dramatists Play Service, 440 Park Avenue South, New York, NY 10016, $2.50; La Mama ETC, NYC; Open Theater, NYC

Where Is de Queen?: with **Almost Like Being;** Firehouse Theatre, Minn., MN

I'm Really Here: with **Almost Like Being;** La Mama ETC, NYC; Open Theater, NYC

The Hunter and the Bird: with **Almost Like Being;** La Mama ETC, NYC; Open Theater, NYC

War: with **Almost Like Being;** La Mama ETC, NYC; Open Theater, NYC

Eat Cake: Dramatists Play Service, $2.50; Changing Scene, Denver, CO

Harold: with **Eat Cake;** Theater for the New City, NYC

Take a Deep Breath: with **Eat Cake;** DMZ, Village Vanguard, NYC

Photographs: Mary and Howard: with **Eat Cake;** Mark Taper Forum, CA

Thoughts on the Instant of Greeting a Friend on the Street: with **Eat Cake;** St. Mark's Playhouse, NYC

The Girl and the Soldier: with **Eat Cake;** Cafe LaMama, NYC

Rosary: with **Eat Cake**

America, Hurrah (Interview, TV, Motel): Dramatists Play Service, $2.50; Pocket Theater, NYC; Royal Court Theatre, London

†The Serpent: Dramatists Play Service, $2.50; Teatro Degli Arte, Rome

The King of the United States: Dramatists Play Service, $2.50; Exchange Theatre, NYC

Mystery Play (non-musical version of **The King of the United States):** Dramatists Play Service, $2.50; Cherry Lane Theater, NYC

The Seagull (new English version): Dramatists Play Service, $2.50; Manhattan Theatre Club, NYC; McCarter Theater, NJ

The Fable: Dramatists Play Service, $2.50; Lenox Arts Festival, MA; Westbeth Theater, NYC

The Cherry Orchard: Dramatists Play Service, $2.50; Beaumont Theater, NYC

The Three Sisters: Dramatists Play Service, $2.50;

Uncle Vanya: Dramatists Play Service, $2.50;

Bag Lady: Dramatists Play Service, $1.25

†Lincoln Center, Theatre on Film & Tape

SYNOPSES

The Fable: Is a fairy-tale told in poetry and music. It requires 8 actors of various sexes. There are two "improvisational" scenes while the rest of the play is fully written. It is an attempt to write a "fairy-tale for our times," with the images used being the images that seemed strongest when writing. It works well. It is an exciting piece, I hope, for director and actors too.

Jean-Claude van Itallie (cont'd)

The Seagull: is simply Anton Chekov's play **The Seagull** but it is a version which, I know you will agree upon reading, is clearer than any other available. It tries to stick to the spirit of Chekov without Victorianisms or becomng colloquial. I hope that its main virtue is clarity. It reads quickly and simply, a virtue I am proud of, and my spiritual friend Chekov is too.

W. EDWIN VER BECKE

Born on July 22, 1912, W. Edwin Ver Becke has spent over fifty years in the creative arts. He was once teacher at the University of Minnesota and active in the early Little Theatre movement. He was Founder-Director of the Sausalito Little Theatre, San Francisco Community Theatre, and the Laguna Beach Drama Readers. In 1951, A.N.T.A. published his manual, **Little Theatre Structure.** He is also a lecturer, poet, a painter having taken awards and shown his work in leading museums and galleries. His plays have been seen at Little Theatre productions and the Playwrights Theater in Hollywood. His work has been published in **Christian Science Monitor, Hemispheres, School Arts, V.V.V., Eros, Circle** and numerous avant garde magazines. He is a specialist in short avant garde plays. As an artist he has designed stage sets. Recipient: Citation, Maxwell Anderson Awards.

Address: 840 8th Avenue, Capitol Apt., 6M, New York, NY 10019 (212) 586-8470

TITLE • AVAILABILITY • PRODUCTIONS

Flight of the Sea Gull: manuscript*

Picnic Ground: manuscript*

Dark Corridor: manuscript*

Crystal Chandelier: manuscript*

Ten Brief Plays: manuscript*; Stanford University, CA

Four to Go (four related plays): manuscript*

Adventures in Futility (three avant garde plays): manuscript*

Seminar: manuscript*; American Playwrights Theater, CA

Love Is the Way (musical-lyrics and book): manuscript*

Rubirosa Moth: manuscript*

The Doll: manuscript*

Come into the House of Jane: manuscript*

Bernies Ballroom: manuscript*

A Lady Called Judas: manuscript*

I Will Call You Sarah: manuscript*

Mud: manuscript in progress

Tragedy of Oscar Wilde: manuscript*; Rutgers University, NJ

Lucifer in the Boneyard: manuscript*

*contact author

V

W. Edwin Ver Becke (cont'd)
SYNOPSES

The Doll: Jenny is retarded, forced since childhood to live in a sort of slum attic, watched over by police-case worker Miss Mercy. Three acts relate her loves, torture, education, leading to suicide of parents and self and final freedom of Miss Mercy.

7 scenes. Setting: one set with staircase. 4 males, 4 females, chorus.

I Will Call You Sarah: Everyone in this family seems insane or love starved. The mother, Sarah, runs a dilapidated New York house (theatre district). Faggie, her queer son, is outrageous. Sarah, ex-follies girl, teaches dancing and keeps her aged father. Faggie's roommate, Brownie, is finally seduced by Sarah. The daughter of Sarah is most interesting in her failing love affair with a silk merchant. She seems the only normal person in the odd family.

3 acts. Setting: one set wth staircase. 4 males, 2 females, incidentals.

Crystal Chandelier: Bessie, Negro spiritualist, psychic, hears voices in the chandelier. She is caretaker of ancient St. Augustine estate; guardian to its three sister-residents. Dolly, child bride, is thwarted in her marriage. The plot revolves about Bessie trying to save the estate from a no-good wastrel and to keep her three girls safe in the old home.

3 acts. Setting: one set with staircase. 4 females, 6 males.

VINCENT VIAGGIO

Born in Brooklyn, NY on March 10, 1950. B.A., English Literature, City College of New York, 1972; M.A., Creative Writing, City College of New York, 1976. He has written two screenplays and had poetry published. Lyricist and co-composer of over thirty songs.

Address: 121 North Broadway, #32 A, White Plains, NY 10603 (914) 948-5497

TITLE • AVAILABILITY • PRODUCTIONS

The Man Who Was Dracula: manuscript*; St. Gregory's Church, NYC; Nat Horne Theatre, NYC

Midnight Mass: manuscript*; Theatre Matrix, NYC

Wall, Prize, Redemption: A Trilogy: manuscript*; Circle Repertory Company, NYC; Westbeth Title Theatre, NYC

Beals & Becker (a cabaret): manuscript*; Theatre Matrix, NYC; Sylvette's Cafe, NYC

A Queen's Folly: manuscript*; New York Renaissance Faire, Sterling Forest, NY; Straussberg Inn, PA

Papalina: manuscript*; Theatre Matrix, NYC

The Final Episode: manuscript*; Theatre Matrix, NYC: Cable TV; Global Village, NYC

Squirrels: manuscript*; Theatre Matrix, NYC: Circle Repertory Company, NYC

A Parent Primer: manuscript*; Theatre Matrix, NYC

It's a Cinch/The Root of Employment: manuscript*; Bond St. Theatre, NYC: Theatre Matrix, NYC

   *contact author

SYNOPSES

Midnight Mass: A comic thriller about a young woman who entices her former professional killer boyfriend to murder her rich husband, not knowing the husband has already commissioned her boyfriend to kill her.

Full length, 1½ hours. Setting: one interior. 2 males, 1 female.

The Man Who Was Dracula: A dramatic fictional tribute to Bela Lugosi, not another Dracula play. It depicts a final attempt by the drug ridden, impoverished, once-proud classical actor to return to the Shakespearean stage.

Full length. Setting: interior. 8 males, 2 females.

Papalina: An ecclesiastical drama about the rise and fall of a legendary and controversial woman pope in the ninth century, dramatised through game-like scenes narrated by a crazed papal jester.

Full length. Setting: one set. 17 males, 2 females.

GORE VIDAL

Born in West Point, NY on October 3, 1925. Educated at Phillips Exeter Academy, NH. Has written for TV; **Omnibus, Studio One, Philco Playhouse,** etc. Novels: **The City and The Pillar, Messiah, 1876, Washington, D.C.** etc. Films: **Suddenly Last Summer, Lefthanded Gun, Myra Breckenridge** etc. Also several books of essays. Founder of newspaper, **The Hyde Park Townsman.** Ran as the Democratic-Liberal candidate for Congress.

Agent: Owen Laster, William Morris Agency, 1350 Avenue of the Americas, New York, NY 10019 (212) 586-5100

TITLE • AVAILABILITY • PRODUCTIONS

Visit to a Small Planet: Dramatists Play Service, 440 Park Avenue South, New York, NY 10016, $2.50; Broadway

The Best Man: Dramatists Play Service, $2.50; Broadway

On the March to the Sea: manuscript*; Hyde Park, NY; Frankfurt, Germany

Romulus (adaptation): Dramatists Play Service, $2.50; Broadway

Weekend: Dramatists Play Service, $2.50; Broadway

An Evening with Richard Nixon and . . .: manuscript*; Broadway

   *contact agent

V

PAULA A. VOGEL

Born in Washington, DC on November 16, 1951.
Founder of the Bryn Mawr Drop-Out Society.
Other undergraduate education in theater at
Catholic University, 1972–74; Ph.D. program at
Cornell in Dramatic Literature, Playwriting.
Faculty member at Cornell, taught and designed
course, "Madwomen on Stage." Member of the
Theatre Arts Faculty there. Executive member of
Women's Studies, 1977–78. Worked as staff
member, American Place Theatre, 1978–79. Con-
ducted playwriting workshops at McGill Univer-
sity and St. Elizabeth's Hospital. Has written
critical essays on theater and a novel. Recipient:
Heerbes-McCalmon Playwriting Award, 1975
and 1976; American College Theater Festival
Award for the Best New Play; ANTA-West Award,
1978; National Endowment for the Arts Playwrit-

ing Fellowship, 1979–80; Commission from Actors Theatre of Louisville.

Address: 42 Grove Street, #13, New York, NY 10014

Agent: Helen Merrill, 337 West 22nd St., New York, NY 10011 (212) 924-6314

TITLE • AVAILABILITY • PRODUCTIONS

Meg: Samuel French, 25 West 45th St., New York, NY 10036, $2.50; Cornell University, NY;
    Toneel Academie, Netherlands

Desdemona: manuscript*

The Last Pat Epstein Show Before the Reruns: manuscript*

Apple-Brown Betty: manuscript*; Actors Theatre of Louisville, KY

The Oldest Profession: manuscript*

Bertha in Blue: manuscript*

Dribble: manuscript*

    *contact agent

SYNOPSES

Meg: Margaret More Roper the daughter of Sir Thomas More, discovers through her marriage to
the comic village idiot that her personal power becomes increasingly limited in the More
household. As Sir Thomas travels the celebrated route into history, Margaret, educated in Latin
and Greek and sheltered by her father, learns to travel the sobering journey into the diminished
roles of wife and mother.

Full length. Setting: several platform levels suggested. 3 males, 2 females.

Bertha in Blue: An elderly Russian Jew from the Catskills returns for the first time in over fifty
years to the New York City of his youth. He visits the spot of a once flourishing Yiddish theater
which has long since been converted into a porno movie house. Confused, he mistakes the blue
movie actress for the famous actress Bertha Kalish, and attempts to save her from a life of white
slavery.

One act. Setting: exterior and interior of porno movie house. 3 males.

The Oldest Profession: Five elderly women sit on a bench in New York City and discuss food, the
economy, the weather . . . and their business affairs. We learn that the women are the oldest prostitutes in New York; the Upper West Side has been their district for over forty-five years. The
women construct strategies to carry on the trade as their number decreases, the "market"
changes and as the regular customers become infirm. There is a power struggle for the position
of madam; by the end, the youngest one, Vera, sits alone on the bench in the sun.

One act. Setting: a bench near 72nd Street and Broadway. 5 females.

JOHN VON HARTZ

Born in Baltimore, Maryland on January 18, 1933. Graduated Middlebury College, B.A. Newspaper reporter for the **Berkshire Eagle,** Pittsfield, Massachusetts. Writer/Editor for **Time-Life Books,** Time Inc. When not writing for a living, John has worked at all sorts of odd jobs from loader in a pea cannery in Washington State to building superintendent in New York City. Member of the New Dramatists Committee, Inc. Recipient: National Endowment for the Arts, Creative Writing Fellowship, 1978; Guggenheim Fellowship, 1981–82.

Address: 111 East 2nd St., New York, NY 10009
   (212) 982-7932

Agent: Biff Liff, William Morris Agency, 1350
   Avenue of the Americas, New York, NY 10019
   (212) 586-5100

TITLE • AVAILABILITY • PRODUCTIONS

Down on the Farm: manuscript*; New Dramatists, NYC

Home/Work: manuscript*; Astor Place Theater, NYC; Triangle Theater, NYC

The Beach Children: manuscript*; New Dramatists, NYC

A Little Wine with Lunch: manuscript*; No Smoking Playhouse, NYC

Mothers and Daughters: manuscript*; No Smoking Playhouse, NYC

Off-Season: manuscript*; No Smoking Playhouse, NYC

   *contact author

SYNOPSES

Home/Work: In the first of these two one-acts, **Home Is Where You Hang Yourself,** a thirty-three-year-old man hangs himself in front of his parents' TV every time the New York Mets lose a game. The state of mind that drives him to do this is explored when his sister brings home her latest boyfriend.

Setting: living room with noose. 2 males, 2 females.

In the second half of this evening, **The New Man,** a new employee throws a typewriter through the window of a New York publishing house, touching off a series of self-confessions, misunderstandings, and sexual rejuvenations among the staff. **"Home/Work** introduces a new playwright with an original comic talent for the theater." — Mel Gussow, **New York Times.**

Setting: modern office in skyscraper. 4 males, 2 females.

A Little Wine with Lunch: A comedy revue about the reactions of people enjoying a glass of wine with the noontime meal. A secretry convinces her boss that making love on the subway isn't that important to their relationship. A lad shares a loving cup with his dog. A newlywed disgraces herself while showing slides of her first — but her husband's second — honeymoon. A convicted politician laments the fact that he will soon be free to go home to his wife.

Full evening. Setting: none, done in cabaret style. 2 males, 2 females.

Mothers and Daughters: Three generations of women contend for their lot — and each other — in this highly charged comedy/drama. "The play has an endearing protagonist and a theme — mothers and daughters who are "blood sisters and best friends" as well as rivals — that strikes a chord of universality." Mel Gussow, **N.Y. Times**

Full length. Setting: a livingroom. 2 males, 3 females.

V/W

KURT VONNEGUT, JR.

Born in Indianapolis, IN on November 11, 1922. Parents Kurt and Edith (Lieber) Vonnegut. Student at Cornell University (1940–42), University of Chicago (1945–47). Managing Editor of Cornell **Sun** in 1942; reporter on the Chicago City News Bureau in 1946; public relations with General Electric Co.; free lance writer; teacher at Hopefield School, Sandwich, Massachusetts; lecturer at Writers Workshop, University of Iowa. Served with Infantry in Austria; decorated with Purple Heart. Author of (novels) **Player Piano, Sirens of Titan, Mother Night, Cat's Cradle, God Bless You, Mr. Rosewater, Slaughterhouse-Five, Breakfast of Champions, Welcome to the Monkey House, Slapstick, Jailbird** (essays, speeches and articles, published in 1976), **Wampeters, Foma & Granfalloons,** and (TV play)

Between Time and Timbuktu. Member of the American Academy of Arts and Sciences. Recipient: Guggenheim Fellowship. Adaptations of his books **(Player Piano, Sirens of Titan, God Bless You, Mr. Rosewater** and **Cats Cradle)** have been made into plays.

Address: c/o Donald C. Farber, 600 Madison Avenue, New York, NY 10022

Attorney: Donald C. Farber, Counsel to Conboy, Hewitt, O'Brien & Boardman, (address above). (212) 758-8000

TITLE • AVAILABILITY • PRODUCTIONS

Happy Birthday, Wanda June: Samuel French, 25 West 45th St., New York, NY 10036, $2.50; Theatre de Lys, NYC; Edison Theatre, Broadway

JEFF WANSHEL

Born in a shallow depression outside Muscle Shoals, AL, educated at Wesleyan University, Middletown, CT and the Yale Drama School, Wanshel has been represented on four occasions at the O'Neill Theater Center's National Playwrights Conference and has been in frequent residence at the Albee Foundation. He has also attended, amongst others, Yaddo and the McDowell Colony. In 1975, he collaborated with Director Larry Arrick and the National Theatre of the Deaf on **Parade.** He adapted Thurber's **The Greatest Man in the World** for PBS series, **The Great American Short story.** He spent half the period, 1970–75, outside the country. In India, he took courses in self-discipline and broadmindedness; one he failed and in the other received an incomplete. A bitter, reclusive

man, prematurely bald as the result of an unhappy love affair, Wanshel's plays are popular with those driven mad by grief. Recipient: Audrey Wood Fellowship; Ray Stark Fellowship; CAPS Grant; Rockefeller Award in Playwriting.

Agent: Audrey Wood, International Creative Management, 40 West 57th St., New York, NY 10019 (212) 556-5600

TITLE • AVAILABILITY • PRODUCTIONS

The Rhesus Umbrella: Dramatists Play Service, 440 Park Avenue South, New York, NY 10016, $2.50; Yale Repertory Theatre, CT

The Disintegration of James Cherry: Dramatists Play Service, $2.50; O'Neill Theater Center's National Playwrights Conference, CT; Lincoln Center, NYC

auto-destruct: with **The Rhesus Umbrella;** O'Neill Theater Center's National Playwrights Conference, CT; Magic Theatre, San Francisco, CA

The General Brutus: manuscript*; O'Neill Theater Center's National Playwrights Conference, CT; **Earplay**

Fog and Mismanagement: manuscript*; University of Rhode Island; Circle Repertory Company, NYC

Isadora Duncan Sleeps with the Russian Navy: Dramatists Play Service, $2.50; O'Neill Theater Center's National Playwrights Conference, CT; University of North Carolina, Chapel Hill, NC

The Wild Goose: manuscript*; Magic Theatre, San Francisco, CA

Holeville: manuscript*; Dodger Theatre, Brooklyn Academy of Music, NYC

*contact agent

SYNOPSES

The Disintegration of James Cherry: The story of a "nice young man to whom the most ingeniously awful things keep happening." The dialogue is strange and quietly wonderful: "If the stickleback catches you, the stickleback will kill you. There is a stickleback loose somewhere in the afternoon." "Wanshel gets the quick, long-echoing epistemological laugh of the born comic writer . . . funny, vivid, and subtle." — **Newsweek.**

Full length; two acts. Setting: one set (modular). Approximately 7 males, 5 females.

auto-destruct: He robbed the Bank of Mexico and married a gas station attendant. "The Marx Brothers meet Franz Kafka in Old Mexico! It has to be seen to be believed — has the mind bending quality of back-to-back shaggy dog stories . . . insane, weird, and consistently funny . . . " — **Berkeley Gazette.**

Full length (but short); one act. Setting: a car. 7 to 9 males, 1 optional female.

Isadora Duncan Sleeps with the Russian Navy: A biographical vaudeville retelling the life of the dance eccentric. A base for experimentation and theatrical extravagance, composed of fifty vignettes like shifting images in a kaleidoscope. "A dramatized comic strip . . . hoops of legend, farce and fantasy . . . adroit, entertaining, and funny." — **New York Times.**

Full length; one act. Setting: one set or none (Europe and America). Approximately 65 roles, including Rodin, Anna Pavlova, Diaghilev, Stanislavsky, Lenin, Whitman, Billy Sunday, Sol Hurok, the Daredevil Sailors of the Cruiser Aurora, and Death; at least 7 males, 3 females, 2 optional children.

BRENDAN NOEL WARD

Born in New York City on December 26, 1947. B.A., Hunter College; M.A., Cornell; M.F.A., Iowa. Theodor Mommsen Fellow, Balliol College, Oxford; Teaching Fellow, Cornell; University Fellow, C.U.N.Y. Playwright-in-Residence Iowa Repertory; Mark Taper Forum; Vandam Theatre Company; LARR, Los Angeles. Currently Associate Producer, New Horizons Entertainment, Inc.; Creative Director and President, First Harvest Productions. Screenwriting Instructor, Yale University. Screenplay, **A Woman Apart,** CBS. Residencies at Yaddo; Millay Colony; Ossabaw; Albee Colony. Recipient: Shubert Grant, 1972–'73–'74; American College Theater Festival, Region 7 winner; CAPS Grant; Dramatists Guild Grant.

W

Brendan Noel Ward (cont'd)

Address: Manhattan Plaza, 400 West 43rd St., FF, New York, NY 10036 (212) 279-6906

Agent: Chasman, Landau Associates, 6725 Sunset Blvd., Suite 506, Hollywood, CA 90028 (213) 463-1156

TITLE • AVAILABILITY • PRODUCTIONS

Knots: manuscript*; Iowa City, IA; Dublin Theatre Festival

Divine Revelation Never Ending Whiskey: manuscript*; Iowa City, IA

Vietnam Ladies About Their Business: manuscript*; Iowa City, IA

Coralville, U.S.A.: manuscript*; Coralville, IA

When We Were Very Young: manuscript*; Moline, IL

Mrs. Old and the Unicorn: manuscript*; Kansas City, MO; Wilkes Barre, PA

The Great Potato Famine (with Dan Wray): manuscript*; Mark Taper Forum, CA

Partial Disabilities: manuscript*; Direct Theatre, NYC

Dungalore (with Dan Wray): manuscript*; Sheridan Square Theatre, NYC

Dancers: manuscript*; Vandam Theatre, NYC; Dublin Theatre Festival

Washington at Valley Forge (with Peter Stampfel and Dan Wray): manuscript*; La Mama, Hollywood, CA

The History of the Saints: Faith, Hope and Charity (three plays): manuscript*

*contact agent

SYNOPSES

Knots: Using a language inspired by R.D. Laing, **Knots** is a dramatization of the process whereby we come to possess a deterministic outlook on the world and a thwarted capacity to love.

One act. Avant garde piece with optional video elements. 2 males, 1 female.

Dancers: A photo-realist drama of Irish immigrant family life before the process of Americanization destroyed it. The play presents the quiet tragedy of Anne and Bill, and their neighbor, the ex-nun, Rose, whose religious and cultural traditions are shown to be incestuous. The incest theme is carried into the next generation when a relationship between Bill and his daughter Sara is consummated resulting in the dissolution of the family.

Full length. Setting: a Hell's Kitchen tenement. 2 males (1 adult, 1 boy), 3 females.

The History of the Saints: Faith, Hope and Charity: This is the story of a great American family through two generations. It examines the relationship between individual virtue, the demands of society, the force of history and national identity.

Three-play cycle in a poetic-realist style, designed to be performed in repertory and utilizing a chorus. 7 males, 8 females. Sound track, video and filmed sequences used in tandem. A total environment piece within a realist framework.

DALE WASSERMAN

Born in Rhinelander, WI on November 2, 1917. He has written for TV: Kraft Television Theater, Studio One, Playhouse 90, Dupont Show of the Month, Matinee Theatre etc. Screenplays: **World Strangers, The Vikings, Two Faces to Go, Quick Before it Melts, Mr. Buddwing, A Walk with Love and Death, Man of La Mancha, Conquest, Survivors, Scheherazade** and others. Member: Writers Guild of America, East; Dramatists Guild; ALA; Academy of Motion Picture Arts and Sciences; French Society of Authors and Composers; Spanish Society of Authors. Founder and Artistic Director of Midwest Playwrights Lab. Founding member and trustee of the O'Neill Theater Center; Trustee and play selector of National Repertory Theatre. Recipient: Top Television Play of the Year, 1954; Writers Guild Award; Writers Guild of America (twice); Emmy Award (twice); Tony Award; New York Critics Circle Award; Outer Circle Critics Award; Saturday Review Citation; Variety Award; Spanish Pavilion Award; Joseph Jefferson Award; Honorary Doctorate in Humane Letters, U. of Wisconsin, 1980.

Attorney: c/o Becker & London, 15 Columbus Circle, New York, NY 10023 (212) 541-7070

TITLE • AVAILABILITY • PRODUCTIONS

Living the Life (with Bruce Geller & Jack Urbont): not available; Phoenix Theatre, NYC

Pencil of God: manuscript*; Karamu Theatre, Cleveland, OH

998: manuscript*; Professional Theatre, Hollywood, CA

One Flew Over the Cuckoo's Nest (adaptation): Samuel French, 25 West 45th St., New York, NY 10036, $2.50; Broadway

Man of La Mancha: Tams-Witmark, Inc., 757 Third Avenue, New York, NY 10017; Goodspeed Opera House, E. Haddam, CT; Broadway

Play with Fire: manuscript*; Westwood Playhouse, Los Angeles, CA

Great Big River (with Jack Urbont & Michael Colby): manuscript*; Five Flags Theatre, Dubuque, IA

    *contact attorney

WENDY WASSERSTEIN

Born in Brooklyn, NY on October 18, 1950. B.A. from Mount Holyoke College, M.A. from City College of NY and attended Yale Drama School. Adapted her play, **Uncommon Women and Others** for **Theatre In America.** Also adapted John Cheever's, **The Sorrows of Gin** for **Great Performances,** WNET. Member of the Steering Committee, Women's Committee of The Dramatists Guild, 1980–81. Film with Christopher Durang, **House of Husbands.**

Address: c/o Gordis, 15 West 81st St., New York, NY 10024

Agent: Arlene Donovan, I.C.M., 40 West 57th St., New York, NY 10019 (212) 556-5600

Wendy Wasserstein (cont'd)

TITLE • AVAILABILITY • PRODUCTIONS

Any Woman Can't: manuscript*; Playwrights Horizons, NYC

Montpelier, Pazazz: manuscript*; Playwrights Horizons, NYC

When Dinah Shore Ruled the Earth (with Chris Durang): manuscript*; Yale Cabaret, New Haven, CT

Uncommon Women and Others: Dramatists Play Service, 440 Park Avenue South, New York, NY 10016, $2.50; O'Neill Theater Center's National Playwrights Conference, CT; Playwrights Horizons, NYC

Isn't It Romantic: manuscript*; Phoenix Theatre, NYC

   *contact author

SYNOPSIS

Uncommon Women and Others: Five women of a Seven Sisters school meet eight years later to discuss their choices and reflect on their college life.

Full length. Setting: one set. 9 females.

GORDON R. WATKINS

Attended the Juilliard School of Music, Katherine Dunham School of Dance, Hunter College (M.A.) and New School for Social Research (Film directing). He has acted on T.V. and served as a Producer, Director and Writer. Recipient: 1956, Anne M. Gannett Scholarship from American Federation of Music Clubs; 1954–60, Juilliard School of Music Scholarship; 1968–69, John Golden Fellowship for Graduate Study of Directing and Playwriting; 1971, National Association of Television Program Executives' Award for Excellence in the Performing Arts; 1972, Ohio State Award for Excellence in Television Production.

Address: 675 Lincoln Ave., 17H, Brooklyn, NY 11208 (212) 827-7491/371-2855

TITLE • AVAILABILITY • PRODUCTIONS

Tinkerman to the Promised Land: manuscript*; NYC; Washington, DC; Newark, NJ

A Lion Roams the Street: manuscript*; Burlington, VT, NYC, Newark, NJ

Man in the Middle: manuscript*; Hunter Playwrights' Workshop; Little Theatre, West Side YMCA, NYC

Ballad of Santa's Happy Helpers: manuscript*; Orange, NJ (ESAA)

Too Late: manuscript*; The Toussaint Group Inc.; Cliffside Park, NJ; Orange, NJ (ESAA)

Sojourner Truth: manuscript*

The Sacrifice: manuscript*; NYC

Cages: manuscript*; NYC; Wilmington, DE

   *All manuscripts obtainable from: Mr. Gordon Watkins, The Toussaint Group, Inc., 420 East 51st St., New York, NY 10022 (212) 371-2855

SYNOPSES

Man in the Middle: William "Bear" Walker, ex-gang member, returns to his old neighborhood as a welfare investigator. He is attacked by the local gang, sold out by his old friend, rejected by the

Gordon R. Watkins (cont'd)

people he wants to help — and undercut by the establishment he represents. As Walker fights to combat the decaying conditions of the ghetto and the indifference of the authorities to them, he turns from peaceful methods to protest and is finally forced to violence.

Setting: Mrs. Thomas' apartment, Amanda's apartment, steps, lot, Welfare office. 15 males, 5 females, community residents, welfare workers and police.

Sojourner Truth: About 1797 in New York State, a black child was born into the immeasurable indignities and hardships of American slavery. Desperate and frightened, she sought consolation in personal dialogues with God throughout her early life. One morning after a conversation with her God, the slave called Isabelle started on a journey for her people and became Sojourner Truth, legendary pioneer in the fight for the abolition of slavery, women's rights, humane labor practices and prison reform.

Setting: 1805–1860. No realistic setting required. 5 black males, 7 white males, 4 black females, 5 white females.

Cages: The major action takes place in a New York bar where unsuspecting patrons are manipulated and sometimes forced to become go-go dancers by an ominous bartender. The play deals with the external and internal barriers that are used to separate us, so that we are easily controlled and frustrated in our attempts to bring about positive change. The forceful articulation of minority dreams and frustrations is punctuated by the sensitive presentation of the burdens of loneliness and desperation so many of us bear. The play suggests that we must learn true compassion to change the society.

Full length. Setting: contemporary bar. 3 black males, 3 white males, 1 black female, 2 white females.

JOHN WEIDMAN

Born in New York City on September 25, 1946. Educated at Harvard College, B.A. 1968; Yale Law School, J.D. 1974; contributing editor, **The National Lampoon** Magazine, 1970–74; associate editor, 1974–76. First play, **Pacific Overtures,** produced 1976.

Address: 19 West 76th St., New York, NY 10023

Agent: Robert Freedman, 1501 Broadway, New York, NY (212) 840-5760

TITLE • AVAILABILITY • PRODUCTIONS

†**Pacific Overtures** (musical, music and lyrics by Stephen Sondheim): Dodd Mead & Co., 791 Madison Ave., New York, NY 10016; Winter Garden Theater, NYC

Pacific Overtures (play version, completed prior to decision to develop material as a musical, about the opening of Japan, 1853): manuscript*

*contact agent
†Lincoln Center, Theatre on Film & Tape

W

LESLIE WEINER

University of Virginia, B.A. Hunter College, M.F.A

Address: 666 Fifth Ave., New York, NY 10019
(212) 765-0700

Agent: Bret Adams, 36 East 61st St., New York, NY 10021 (212) 752-7864

TITLE • AVAILABILITY • PRODUCTIONS

In the Counting House: manuscript*; Biltmore Theatre, NYC

Are You Now or Have You Ever Been Blue?: manuscript*; Berkshire Theater Festival, Stockbridge, MA

An Evening with the Poet-Senator: manuscript*; Playhouse Theater, NYC

How the '70's Began: manuscript*; Hunter Playwrights, NYC

Nouveau Jersey: manuscript*

Milo's Venus: manuscript*; Hunter Playwrights, NYC

Close Relations: manuscript*; Manhattan Punch Line, NYC

   *contact author

SYNOPSIS

Close Relations: A play in two parts. In part I, a sixty-year-old son visits his eighty-nine-year-old father. Though neither is aware of it, this is their last visit together. In part II, the son welcomes his thirty-two-year-old daughter back to New York after she has spent six years in the midwest. Three generations of a vivid family.

Setting: a livingroom, an office. 2 males, 1 female.

MICHAEL WELLER

Born in New York, September 26, 1942. Attended Stockbridge School, Windham College, Brandeis University and the University of Manchester, England. Has done film scripts for Milos Forman, **Hair** and **Ragtime.** Recipient: Drama Desk Award for **Moonchildren;** American Theatre Critics Citation for **Loose Ends;** Rockefeller Award; CAPS Grant.

Address: 215 East 5th St, New York, NY 10003

Agent: Rosenstone/Wender, 3 East 48th St., New York, NY 10017 (212) 832-8330

Michael Weller (cont'd)

TITLE • AVAILABILITY • PRODUCTIONS

Fred (adaptation): manuscript*; Hi Charlie, Brandeis U.

'Cello Days at Dixon's Place: manuscript*; Loeb Theatre, (experimental annex)

How Hóho Rose and Fell: manuscript*; N.U.S. Festival, Exeter Other Space

Three Cockolds (adaptation): manuscript*; Manchester Repertory Theatre

The Making of Theodore Thomas; Citizen (adaptation): manuscript*; Stepney Institute, London

The Happy Valley: manuscript*; Edinburgh Festival

More Than You Deserve: manuscript*; New York Shakespeare Festival

23 Years Later: manuscript*; Mark Taper Forum, CA; Ensemble Studio Theatre, NY

The Greatest Little Show on Earth: manuscript*

The Bodybuilders: Off Broadway Plays-2, Penguin Books, Inc., 625 Madison Ave., New York, NY 10022; Open Space Theatre, London; Traverse Theatre, Edinburgh

Now There's Just the Three of Us: Off Broadway Plays-2; Open Space Theatre, London; Traverse Theatre, Edinburgh

Tira: Faber & Faber, Ltd. 3 Queen Square, London, W.C. 1, England; Open Space Theatre, London; WPA Theatre, NYC

Grant's Movie: Faber & Faber Ltd.; Open Space Theatre, London

Moonchildren: Samuel French, 25 West 45th St., New York, NY 10036, $2.50; Royal Court Theatre, London; Arena Stage, Washington, DC

Fishing: Samuel French, $2.50; New York Shakespeare Festival; New End, London

Split: Samuel French, $2.00; Ensemble Studio Theatre, NY; Second Stage Theatre, NYC

Loose Ends: Samuel French, $2.50; Arena Stage, Washington, DC; Circle-in-the-Square, NYC

Dwarfman: manuscript*; Goodman Theatre, Chicago, IL

*contact agent

RICHARD ERROL WESLEY

Born in Newark, NJ on July 11, 1945. B.F.A. in Drama from Howard University, 1967. Member, New Lafayette Theatre, 1969–73. Current member of Advisory Board of Frank Silvera Writer's Workshop of New York. Has written movies, **Uptown Saturday Night.** Recipient: Drama Desk Award, 1972, **The Black Terror;** Audelco Award for Outstanding Playwriting, 1974; NAACP Image Award, 1974, **Uptown Saturday Night;** Rockefeller Grant, 1973.

Address: 221 Montclair Ave., Upper Montclair, NJ 07043

Agent: Rosenstone/Wender, 3 East 48th St., New York, NY 10017 (212) 832-8330

TITLE • AVAILABILITY • PRODUCTIONS

The Black Terror: The New Lafayette Presents, Anchor Books, 245 Park Ave., New York, NY 10017, $3.95; New York Shakespeare Festival, NYC

Gettin' It Together: Dramatists Play Service, 440 Park Avenue South, New York, NY 10016, $2.50; New York Shakespeare Festival, NYC

Richard Errol Wesley (cont'd)

Strike Heaven on the Face: manuscript*; Phoenix Repertory Theatre, NYC

Goin' thru Changes: manuscript*; O'Neill Theater Center's National Playwrights Conference, CT; Billie Holiday Theatre, NYC

The Past Is the Past: with **Gettin' It Together;** O'Neill Theater Center's National Playwrights Conference, CT; Billie Holiday Theatre, NYC

The Sirens: Dramatists Play Service, $2.50; Manhattan Theatre Club, NYC

†**The Mighty Gents** (formerly **The Last Street Play):** Dramatists Play Service, $2.50; O'Neill Theater Center's National Playwrights Conference, CT; Broadway

On the Road to Babylon (music & lyrics, Peter Link): manuscript*; Milwaukee Repertory Company, WI

    *contact agent
    †Lincoln Center, Theatre on Film & Tape

HUGH WHEELER

Born in London, England on March 19, 1916. B.A. in English from the University of London. Served in the U.S. Army, WW II. Has written many novels, some under pseudonyms. Also done screenplays: **A Little Night Music; Travels with My Aunt; Something for Everyone; Cabaret; Nijinski.** Recipient: Edgar Allen Poe Award; Tony Award; Drama Critics Circle Award; Drama Desk Award.

Agent: Lazarow & Company, 119 West 57th St., New York, NY 10019 (212) 586-5930

TITLE • AVAILABILITY • PRODUCTIONS

Big Fish, Little Fish: Dramatists Play Service, 440 Park Avenue South, New York, NY 10016, manuscript; Broadway; London

Look: We've Come Through!: Dramatists Play Service, $2.50; Broadway

We Have Always Lived in the Castle (adaptation): Dramatists Play Service, $2.50; Broadway

A Little Night Music (adaptation): Music Theatre International, 119 West 57th St., New York, NY 10019; Broadway

Irene (with Joseph Stein, adaptation): Tams-Witmark, 757 Third Avenue, New York, NY 10017;Broadway

Candide: Music Theatre International; Broadway

Pacific Overtures: Dodd Mead & Co., 79 Madison Ave., New York, NY 10017; Broadway

Sweeney Todd: Music Theatre International; Broadway

RON WHYTE

Born in Black Eagle, Montana. M.F.A. in Playwriting from Yale School of Drama; Master of Divinity, Union Theological Seminary. Playwright-in-Residence, The Actors Studio; Coordinator, Playwrights and Directors Pilot Project at The Actors Studio. Panelist, New York State Council on the Arts. Panelist, National Endowment for the Arts. Consultant, Dept. of Health, Education and Welfare. Former Associate Editor, Arts, **The Soho Weekly News.** Author of **The Flower That Finally Grew.** Co-author, **The Story of Film.** Screenplays, **The Happiness Cage, Pigeons** and **The Parents.** Recipient: Rockefeller Playwriting Grant; Joseph Jefferson Awards (four times); **Time** Magazine, Ten Best Plays of the Year; American Place Theatre Grant; Joseph E. Levine Fellowship; ABC Fellowship in Playwriting; William Morris Fellowship; Shubert Fellowship.

Address: 317 West 99th St., New York, NY 10025 (212) 666-6051

Agent: Helen Merrill, 337 West 22nd St., New York, NY 10011 (212) 924-6314

TITLE • AVAILABILITY • PRODUCTIONS

The Final Extinction of Alexander Pope: manuscript*; Postus-Teatret, Denmark

Disability: A Comedy: manuscript*; Mark Taper Forum Lab, L.A., CA; Arena Stage, Wash., DC

The Hunchback of Notre Dame: manuscript*; American Stage Festival, Milford, NH

Counter/Cultures: 1967: not available; Birmingham Festival Theatre, AL

Funeral March for a One-Man Band: manuscript*; St. Nicholas Theater Co., Chicago, IL; Westbeth Theater Center, NYC

Welcome to Andromeda: Samuel French, 25 West 45th St., New York, NY 10036, $2.50; Cherry Lane Theatre, NYC; Actors Theatre of Louisville, Louisville, KY

Horatio: manuscript*; Arena Stage, Wash. DC; American Conservatory Theatre, San Francisco, CA

American Shrapnel: manuscript*; American Shakespeare Theatre, Stratford, CT

Revelations: manuscript*

Emil and Nell: manuscript*

Andromeda: 2: manuscript*; The Actors Studio, NYC

*contact agent

W

SALLY DIXON WIENER

Born Burlington, IA on September 18, 1926. B.A. U. of Arizona. Barnard College, 1945–46. Later studied Playwriting at The New School. Has also studied composing. Former newspaper reporter on dailies in Tucson and Salt Lake City and White Plains and for the **New York Times.** Occasional reporting and articles for **The Dramatists Guild Quarterly** and **Newsletter.** Recipient: Winner, City of Carmel's Second Festival of Firsts Playwriting Competition, for **Show Me a Hero.**

Address: 40 Tunstall Road, Scarsdale, NY 10583

Agent: Robert Freedman, Brandt & Brandt,
1501 Broadway, New York, NY 10036
(212) 840-5760

TITLE • AVAILABILITY • PRODUCTIONS

Marjorie Daw (one-act musical): manuscript and score*; Library and Museum of the Performing Arts, Lincoln Center, NYC; Theatre at Noon, St. Peter's Center, NYC

Telemachus, Friend (one-act musical): Samuel French, 25 West 45th St., New York, NY 10036; Theatre at Noon, St. Peter's Gate, NYC; Baruch College, NYC

The Blue Magi (one-act musical): manuscript and score*; Theatre at Noon, St. Peter's, NYC; The Lambs Gate, NYC

The Pimienta Pancakes (one-act, with music): manuscript and score*; Theatre Off Park, NYC; Double Image Theatre, NYC

Flyin' Turtles (musical): manuscript and score*; Western New Mexico University, Silver City, NM

Schatzie (musical): manuscript*

Show Me a Hero: manuscript*; Sunset Center, Carmel, CA; Equity Showcase at St. Malachy's Theatrespace, NYC

Mlle. Olympe Zabriske (musical): manuscript*

The Second Adam: manuscript*

The Second Battle of Baltimore: manuscript*

   *contact agent

SYNOPSES

Show Me a Hero: Three generations of a Colorado farm family come to terms with themselves over the Vietnam death of a son when a conscientious objector falls in love with a young widow visiting the farm with her young son.

Full length. Setting: one set, includes a portion of farmhouse parlor, the kitchen-dining area and a small outside porch. Incidental country western music score with script. 4 males, (including young boy), 3 females.

Marjorie Daw: Adapted from Thomas Bailey Aldrich's short story. Basically an exchange of letters between two young men, friends, one of whom, John Flemming, is laid up with a broken leg in the family brownstone in the New York summer of 1872, and the other of whom, Edward Delaney, is vacationing with his ailing father in a farmhouse in New Hampshire. Delaney, to divert his friend Flemming, writes him about the wealthy Dresden shepherdess heiress just across the road — Marjorie Daw. When Aldrich's famous story first appeared in 1873 in **Atlantic Magazine** it caused a stir in literary circles and a revival of interest in the short-story form, to which his peculiar contribution was the surprise ending.

One act, one-hour musical. Setting: area-staged, and the more simply the better. 7 males, 3 females.

The Blue Magi: Adapted from O. Henry's "The Gift of the Magi." A bluesy-jazzy contemporary treatment of the famous Christmas story in which the young man sells his watch to buy his wife

Sally Dixon Wiener (cont'd)

combs for her hair, which she in turn cuts to sell in order to buy him a fob-chain for his watch.

One act, 45-minute musical. Setting: storefront indications of Mme. Sophronie's shop, The Crowning Glory, Hair Goods of All Kinds; "The Gift of the Magi" antique shop, and the front stoop of the brownstone and the parlor-floor-front room in which the young couple live. 3 males, 2 females.

C. E. WILKINSON

Born in Boston, MA on June 22, 1948. B.A., S.U.N.Y., Old Westbury, LI; M.F.A., Sarah Lawrence College. Poems published in **The Paris Review, Mississippi Review, Chelsea, Nimrod** and other magazines; **For Neruda/For Chile,** Beacon Press; **An Anthology of Women Poets,** Dremen Press. Member of Dramatists Guild. Associate Director, 1971–78 and Artistic Director, 1978 for the Kuku Ryku Theatre Lab. Recipient: Millay Colony residency, 1979.

Address: Thwale House, 1319 Third Ave., New York, NY 10021

Agent: Howard Morhaim, Morhaim Agency, 330 West 101st St., New York, NY 10028 (212) 865-8189

TITLE • AVAILABILITY • PRODUCTIONS

Mr. Cripple Kicks the Bucket: manuscript*; Kuku Ryku Theatre Lab, NYC

Island (with S. Jones): Wm. Finley, 36 West 20th St., New York, NY 10011; Byrd Hoffman School, NYC; The Theatre Project, Baltimore, MD

Going Home (with S. Jones & S. Weiser): Wm. Finley; University of Michigan Experimental Theatre Festival, MI; Performing Garage, NYC

Briar Rose (with S. Weiser): Wm. Finley; New Theatre Festival, Baltimore, MD; Munich Theatre Festival

She Only Beats Her Dogs to Death Because She Is Unhappy: manuscript**; Kuku Ryku Theatre Lab, NYC

Sacco & Vanzetti Meet Julius & Ethel Rosenberg!!: manuscript*; Kuku Ryku Theatre Lab, NYC

    *contact agent
    **contact author

SYNOPSES

Sacco & Vanzetti Meet Julius & Ethel Rosenberg!!: A Monty Pythonesque vaudeville in which Marilyn Monroe, Tania, Jonathan Livingston Seagull, Chairman Mao, Che Guevara and William Randolph Hearst's mistress (among others, including the title characters) romp and terrorize one another for various lousy but cheerily self-righteous reasons. A bizarre, tap-dancing, fun-filled travesty of tragedy, replete with odd documentary speeches. Thus, while the stage actions of the historically-named characters bear little or no resemblance to those of their counterparts in the real world, they do say some of the same things, and usually with the wrong mouths. Forewarned is forearmed.

Full length. Setting: twin electric chairs with Christmas tree lights, Dr. TV narration booth with fish tank and working monitor, slide screen. 10-11 males, 7 females.

She Only Beats Her Dogs to Death Because She Is Unhappy: A soap opera black comedy about deception and self-deception. The conflict between self-absorbed artist Peter, his schizy-rich teen tenant Emma and luscious Amanda Opal, Miss Emma's visiting "nurse," occurs as they

C. E. Wilkinson (cont'd)

make and break alliances, inflict and suffer pain, all the while spouting elaborate ethical justifications which are breath-takingly false. In the end, the only one who perhaps deserves to escape danger manages not to escape.

Full length. Setting: writers room filled with books and garbage; staircase leading to garret.

Mr. Cripple Kicks the Bucket: A surrealistic black comedy which documents the struggle of the viciously effective Mother Organza and ninny-nice Sister Swallow, two nursing Sisters of Charity, over the treatment of Mr. Cripple, the oldest and sickest patient in the world. Meanwhile, poor dreamy Mr. Cripple struggles for himself.

One act. Setting: a hospital room with bed and window. 1 male, 2 females.

JUNE VANLEER WILLIAMS

Born in Cleveland, OH, on June 24. Case-Western Reserve, B.A.; Stanford University, PJF. Two volumes of poetry, **Moments in Repose** and **Will the Real You Please Stand Up.** Coordinated Karamu House's Golden Anniversary, 1965. Journalist, actress, playwright, casting director. Lectured at University of the Americas; University of Mexico; Cuyahoga Community College; Cleveland State University. Member of Actors Equity; Screen Actors Guild (has Broadway and film credits under stage-name of Jay Vanleer); Overseas Press Club; Dramatists Guild; Authors League of America. Was in U.S. Air Force as Public Information Specialist during Korean Conflict. Is Editorial Assistant to W.O. Walker of Call and Post and Book Review Editor. Recipient: The Ohio State Bar Association's Jour-

nalism Award (for the best story of the year to aid jurisprudence, in two categories: Individual and for the Newspaper), 1969; Professional Journalism Fellowship from Stanford University, 1970; Bel-Air Civic Award; Ursuline Alumnae Award; "Personal Poetry" Certificate from WHMC, Germantown, Maryland.

Address: 2196 East 79th St., Cleveland, OH 44103 (216) 721-7079

TITLE • AVAILABILITY • PRODUCTIONS

The Face of Job: manuscript*; Martinique Theatre, NYC

The Eyes of the Lofty: manuscript*; Karamu House, OH

Two Wandering Sons of Ham (musical): manuscript*

The Meek Don't Inherit: manuscript*

A Bit of Almsgiving: manuscript*

  *contact author

SYNOPSES

A Bit of Almsgiving: A self-centered and egotistical woman is released from a swank detoxification center and persuades her husband to return her to her mother's and sister's residence, where she proceeds to wreak havoc.

4 males, 6 females.

The Eyes of the Lofty: The pathetic story of a retired vaudevillian who is forced to make his home with his son and daughter-in-law. The antagonism and problems that arise between the father and his daughter-in-law results in his being suspected of her murder.

One act. Setting: shows portions of the livingroom and kitchen. 4 males, 2 females.

June Vanleer Williams (cont'd)

Two Wandering Sons of Ham: A story depicting the life and times of Bert Williams, first black man in the Ziegfield Follies, and his side-kick, George Walker. Musical numbers of the productions they put on during their career interspersed with the racial set-backs and how they were surmounted.

Full length. Large-scale musical settings. Large cast of 10 principals and huge chorus.

SAMM-ART WILLIAMS+

Born in Burgaw, NC in 1946. Attended Morgan State College in Baltimore, MD, graduating in 1968. Lived in Philadelphia and worked with the Freedom Theater. Moved to New York and joined the Negro Ensemble Company as an actor and a member of its Playwrights Workshop. Recipient: John Glassner Playwriting Award for **Home;** North Carolina Governor's Award.

Agent: Flora Roberts, 65 East 55th St.,
  New York, NY 10022 (212) 355-4165

TITLE • AVAILABILITY • PRODUCTIONS

Kamilla: manuscript*

Do Unto Others: manuscript*

Welcome to Black River: manuscript*; Negro Ensemble Co., NYC

The Coming: manuscript*; Negro Ensemble Co., NYC

A Love Play: manuscript*; Negro Ensemble Co., NYC

The Frost of Renaissance: manuscript*; Theatre of the Riverside Church, NYC

Brass Birds Don't Sing: manuscript*; Stage 73, NYC

†Home: Dramatists Play Service, 440 Park Avenue South, New York, NY 10016, $2.50; Negro Ensemble Co., NYC; Broadway

The Sixteenth Round: manuscript*; Negro Ensemble Co., NYC

  *contact agent
  †Lincoln Center, Theatre on Film & Tape

W

TENNESSEE WILLIAMS

Born in Columbus, MS on March 26, 1911. Attended the University of Missouri, Washington University, St. Louis, and University of Iowa. Recipient: two Rockefeller Fellowships; four New York Drama Critics Circle Awards; two Pulitzer Prizes; Gold Medal from American Academy of Arts & Letters and The National Institute of Arts & Letters; Donaldson Award; Entertainment Hall of Fame; Medal of Honor by the National Arts Club; the Theatre Hall of Fame; Kennedy Center Honors Award.

Agent: Mitch Douglas, c/o I.C.M., 40 West 57th St., New York, NY 10019 (212) 556-5600

TITLE • AVAILABILITY • PRODUCTIONS

This Property Is Condemned: Dramatists Play Service, 440 Park Avenue South, New York, NY 10016, $3.95, in **27 Wagons Full of Cotton;** New York; London

The Purification: in **27 Wagons Full of Cotton;** Dallas, TX;

The Last of My Solid Gold Watches: in **27 Wagons Full of Cotton;** Los Angeles, CA

Auto-Da-Fe: in **27 Wagons Full of Cotton;** New York

The Strange Kind of Romance: in **27 Wagons Full of Cotton;** London

†27 Wagons Full of Cotton: New Orleans, LA; NYC

The Lady of Larkspur Lotion: in **27 Wagons Full of Cotton;** N.Y.; London

Hello from Bertha: in **27 Wagons Full of Cotton;** Bromley; Kent

Portrait of a Madonna: in **27 Wagons Full of Cotton;** Los Angeles, CA; N.Y.

Lord Byron's Love Letter: in **27 Wagons Full of Cotton;** New York

The Long Goodbye: in **27 Wagons Full of Cotton;** New York

Something Unspoken: in **27 Wagons Full of Cotton;** New York; London

Talk to Me Like the Rain and Let Me Listen: in **27 Wagons Full of Cotton;** Westport, CT; New York

Moony's Kid Don't Cry: Dramatists Play Service, $2.25, in **American Blues;** Los Angeles, CA; New York

†Camino Real: in **American Blues;** New York

The Case of the Crushed Petunias: in **American Blues;** Cleveland, OH; New York

The Dark Room: in **American Blues;** London

The Long Stay Cut Short: in **American Blues;** London

Battle of Angels: Dramatists Play Service, $2.50; Off Broadway

The Glass Menagerie: Dramatists Play Service, $2.50; Cleveland, OH; New York

A Streetcar Named Desire: Dramatists Play Service, $2.50; Broadway

Summer & Smoke: Dramatists Play Service, $2.50; Dallas, TX; New York

The Rose Tattoo: Dramatists Play Service, $2.50; New York; London

†Cat on a Hot Tin Roof: Dramatists Play Service, $2.50; Broadway

I Rise in Flame, Cried the Phoenix: Dramatists Play Service, $1.00; New York; London

Sweet Bird of Youth: Dramatists Play Service, $2.50; Florida; New York

Suddenly Last Summer: Dramatists Play Service, $2.50; Off Broadway

The Fugitive Kind (formerly **Orpheus Descending**): Dramatists Play Service, $2.50; Broadway

A Perfect Analysis Given by a Parrot: Dramatists Play Service, $1.00; New York

W

The Night of the Iguana: Dramatists Play Service, $2.50; Broadway

Period of Adjustment: Dramatists Play Service, $2.50; Miami, FL; Broadway

The Milk Train Doesn't Stop Here Anymore: Dramatists Play Service, $2.50; Broadway; Spoleto, Italy

Slapstick Tragedy (The Mutilated & The Gnadiges Fraulein): Dramatists Play Service, $1.25; New York

The Seven Descents of Myrtle: Dramatists Play Service, $2.50; Broadway

Out Cry: Dramatists Play Service, manuscript; Chicago; Broadway

Two-Character Play (revised edition of **Outcry**): Dramatists Play Service, $3.45

In the Bar of a Tokyo Hotel: Dramatists Play Service, $2.50; New York; London

I Can't Imagine Tomorrow: Dramatists Play Service, $4.45; WNET

Small Craft Warnings: Dramatists Play Service, $2.95; Off Broadway

The Frosted Glass Coffin: Dramatists Play Service, $4.45

Stairs to the Roof: Inquire at Samuel French, 25 West 45th St., New York, NY 10036; Pasadena, CA

You Touched Me (with Donald Windham): Inquire at Samuel French; Cleveland, OH; Broadway

Eccentricities of a Nightingale: Dramatists Play Service, $2.50; WNET; numerous productions

Confessional: New Directions, No. 287, 80 Eighth Avenue, New York, NY 10011, paper $2.95; Maine

At Liberty: New York

The Red Devil Battery Sign: *; Boston, MA; Vienna

Demolition Downtown: Esquire Magazine*; London

Vieux Carré: Dramatists Play Service, $3.95; Broadway; London

A Lovely Sunday for Creve Coeur: Dramatists Play Service, $2.50; American Spoletto Festival; Hudson Guild Theatre, NYC

Kirche, Kutchen Und Kinder: manuscript*; Off Broadway

Life Boat Drill: manuscript*; Off Broadway

Clothes for a Summer Hotel: Dramatists Play Service, $2.50; Broadway

†Will Mr. Merriwether Return From Memphis?: manuscript*; Florida Keys Performing Center

Of Masks Outrageous and Austere: manuscript*

Something Cloudy, Something Clear: manuscript*; Jean Cocteau Repertory, NYC

A House Not Meant to Stand: manuscript*; Goodman Theatre, Chicago, IL

*contact agent
†Lincoln Center, Theatre on Film & Tape

DORIC WILSON

Born in Los Angeles, CA on February 24, 1939.
Raised in the Columbia Basin of Washington
state. Came to NYC in 1958. Pioneer of the Off
Off Broadway movement. The first playwright at
the Caffe Cino with his play, **And He Made a Her,**
1961. A playwright/director/producer, he was an
original member of the Barr-Wilder-Albee
Playwright's Unit and Circle Repertory Theater.
In 1972, he formed TOSOS Theatre Co., the first
theatre to deal seriously with investigating the
gay experience. His play, **Forever After** won the
San Francisco's Cable Car Award for Best Play
80/81. Member of the Dramatist Guild, The Gay
Theatre Alliance and The Evette Society.

Address: 115 Bedford St., Basement, New York,
NY 10014 (212) 243-3440

Agent: Terry Helbing, c/o JH Press, P.O. Box 294, Village Station, New York, NY 10014
(212) 255-4713

TITLE • AVAILABILITY • PRODUCTIONS

And He Made a Her: manuscript*; Caffe Cino, NYC; Cherry Lane Theatre, NYC

Babel, Banel, Little Tower: manuscript*; Caffe Cino, NYC

Now She Dances!: manuscript*; Caffe Cino, NYC; Stable Theatre, Detroit, MI

Pretty People: manuscript*; Caffe Cino, NYC; Angel St. Theatre, London, England

In Absence: manuscript*; Gotham Art Theater, NYC; Ensemble Project, NYC

Now She Dances!: JH Press, P.O. Box 294, Village Station, New York, NY 10014, $3.95;
TOSOS Theatre Co., NYC; Common Ground II Festival, Fordham U., NYC

The West Street Gang: Sea Horse Press, 307 W. 11th St., New York, NY 10003, $5.95;
TOSOS Theatre Co., NYC; Theatre Rhinoceros, San Francisco, CA

A Perfect Relationship: Sea Horse Press, $5.95; The Glines, NYC; American Rep., Amsterdam,
Holland

Turnabout (under pseudonymn Howard Aldon): manuscript*; Richland Players, WA

Forever After: JH Press, $3.95; The Glines, NYC; Theatre Rhinoceros, San Francisco, CA

Surprise: manuscript*

Street Theatre: JH Press, $3.95; Theatre Rhinoceros, San Francisco, CA

Ad Hoc Committee: manuscript*

A Genius of Sorts: manuscript*

*contact agent

SYNOPSES

A Perfect Relationship: A domestic comedy, satirizing the new machismo in gay male lifestyles:
Ward is into backroom bars, Greg is into lifting weights, Barry is into leather, Muriel is into Tom,
Hank and Richard — who is into photographing it all until Barry moves in with his plants and
Hank loses his cover, Tom loses his cool, Ward and Greg lose their lease and Muriel loses her pa-
tience.

Full length. Setting: Manhattan apartment. 4 males, 1 female.

Surprise: A "straight" comedy of manners, investigating the mid-life, mid-career, mid-
relationships at a suitably subdued surprise fortieth birthday party Peggy throws for Ellen. Scott,
Peggy's ex-lover arrives instead.

Full length. Setting: Peggy's apartment. 4 males, 4 females.

Forever After: The Muses of comedy and tragedy climb down from the theater's proscenium to interrupt, influence and aggravate what the lovers assumed to be the happy forever after conclusion of their play.

Full length. Setting: a livingroom framed by a proscenium. 4 males (Two drags)

LANFORD WILSON

Born in Lebanon, MO on April 13, 1937. Playwright-in-Residence at Circle Repertory Company since 1969. Recipient: Rockefeller Grant, 1967, 1971; Guggenheim Grant, 1970; Vernon Rice Drama Desk Award, 1967, **The Rimers of Eldritch;** Obie Award, Outer Circle Critics Award, New York Drama Critics Award (all 1973) for **The Hot l Baltimore;** Obie Award, 1975 for **The Mound Builders;** Christopher Award, 1974 for TV play, **The Migrants;** Pulitzer Prize, Theater Club Inc. Medal, Brandeis University Creative Arts Award, New York Drama Critics Circle Award (all 1980 for **Talley's Folly).**

Address: Sag Harbor, NY 11963

Agent: Ms. Bridget Aschenberg, I.C.M., 40 West 57th St., New York, NY 10019 (212) 556-5720

TITLE • AVAILABILITY • PRODUCTIONS

So Long at the Fair: manuscript*; Caffe Cino, NYC

Home Free!: Balm in Gilead, Hill & Wang, 19 Union Square, New York, NY 10003, $3.95
Caffe Cino, NYC

No Trespassing: manuscript*; Caffe Cino, NYC

The Madness of Lady Bright: Dramatists Play Service, $3.95; Caffe Cino, NYC

Balm in Gilead: with **Home Free!;** La Mama E.T.C., NYC

Ludlow Fair: with **Home Free!;** Caffe Cino, NYC

This is Rill Speaking: Dramatists Play Service, $3.95; Caffe Cino, NYC

The Sand Castle: Dramatists Play Service, $2.50; Caffe Cino, NYC

Sex Is Between Two People: manuscript*; Caffe Cino, NYC

Days Ahead: Hill & Wang; Caffe Cino, NYC

Sa-Hurt?: manuscript*

Wandering: with **Days Ahead;** Caffe Cino, NYC

Rimers of Eldritch: Dramatists Play Service, $2.50; La Mama E.T.C., NYC

Untitled Play: manuscript*; Judson Poet's Theatre, NYC

The Gingham Dog: Dramatists Play Service, $2.50; Washington Theatre Club, Washington, DC; Broadway

Serenading Louie: Dramatists Play Service, $2.50; Washington Theatre Club, Washington, DC

Lemon Sky: Dramatists Play Service, $2.50; O'Neill Theater Center's National Playwrights Conference, CT; Buffalo Arena Theatre, NY

One Arm (adaptation): manuscript*

Sextet (Yes): with **The Sand Castle;** Circle Repertory Company, NYC

Stoop: with **The Sand Castle;** Channel 13, NYC

The Great Nebula in Orion: Dramatists Play Service, $2.50; Circle Repertory Company, NYC

W

Lanford Wilson (cont'd)

The Family Continues: with **Great Nebula . . .;** Circle Repertory Company, NYC

Victory on Mrs. Dandywine's Island: with **Great Nebula . . .;** Circle Repertory Company, NYC

Ikke, Ikke, Nye, Nye, Nye: with **Great Nebula . . .;** Circle Repertory Company, NYC

The Hot l Baltimore: Dramatists Play Service, $3.95; Circle Repertory Company, NYC

The Mound Builders: Dramatists Play Service, $3.95; Circle Repertory Company, NYC

Brontosaurus: Dramatists Play Service, $1.25; Circle Repertory Company, NYC

†Talley's Folly: Dramatists Play Service, $4.95; Circle Repertory Company, NYC; Broadway

†Fifth of July: Dramatists Play Service, $2.50; Circle Repertory Company, NYC; Broadway

A Tale Told: manuscript*; Circle Repertory Company, NYC

    *contact agent
    *†Lincoln Center, Theatre on Film & Tape

SHIMON WINCELBERG

Born in Kiel, Germany on September 26, 1924. Attended the High School of Music and Art, NY; Providence College, RI; Manhattan Technical Institute, NY. W.W. II, Combat Intelligence, 106th Infantry, Okinawa Campaign. Lecturer, American Studies, Medical College, Niigata, Japan, 1945. His writings have appeared in **The New Yorker; Commentary; The New Leader; Punch; Harper's Bazaar;** also represented in **The Best American Short Stories; The Best American Plays; Best Short Plays; On American Literature.** Co-author (with Anita M. Wincelberg), **The Samurai of Vishograd,** Jewish Publication Society. Recipient: Writers Guild of American Award for year's best-written TV script (3 times); "Special Award," Mystery Writers of America; British Arts Council Grant.

Attorney: Leonard Korobkin, Esq., 1801 Avenue of the Stars, Suite 310, Los Angeles, CA 90067
    (213)277-8200

TITLE • AVAILABILITY • PRODUCTIONS

Kataki: Samuel French, 25 West 45th St., New York, NY 10036, $2.50; Kraft Theatre, TV; Broadway; touring productions

Resort-76 (from **A Cat in the Ghetto** by R. Bryks): manuscript*; Royal Dramatic Theatre, Stockholm; Aarhus Theatre, Denmark; the Whole Theatre Company, NJ

Hidalgo (based on stories of Israel Zangwill): manuscript*

The Samurai of Vishograd: manuscript*

    *contact attorney

SYNOPSES

Kataki: The tragicomic encounter of a callow G.I., frightened and indignant upon finding himself marooned with a tough, resourceful Japanese peasant-soldier during the latter days of World War II.

Three acts. Setting: one set. 2 males (one must be either Oriental or an expert mime).

Hidalgo: In the style of Restoration Comedy, a musical about the near-disastrous fiscal and romantic involvements between a splendidly arrogant beggar and con-man of aristocratic Sephar-

Shimon Wincelberg (cont'd)

dic origins, his daughter and his immigrant disciple, and a powerful but bewildered family of German Jews. The play also involves the Prince Regent and the Jewish bare-knuckles boxing champion of England. Music, Bernard Herrmann; Lyrics, Diane Lampert.

Two acts. Setting: eleven sets. 8 males, 4 females. 6 bit parts. 10-15 extras (dancers).

Resort 76: A dark comedy about the surrealistic maneuverings which ensue amongst an ill-assorted group of Jewish internees in a Polish ghetto during WW II, when one of them suddenly gets his hands on the means of survival — a cat. (". . . a humor which ranges the full gamut from the macabrest jokes to the most exquisite of ironies, from situations of lunatic comedy to bursts of brutal scorn.") — Svenska Dagbladet, Stockholm . . . "a trenchant drama . . . wry and harrowing." — **New York Times**

Full length. Setting: one set. 7 males, 3 females.

AUBREY WISBERG

Mr. Wisberg has written over forty motion pictures. His published books are: **Bushman at Large, This Is the Life!, Patrol Boat 999.** Recipient: Winner International Unit Award for film **The Burning Cross.**

Address: 23 East 74th St., (The Volney), New York, NY 10021 (212) 794-1640

Agent: In New York: Jay Garon, 415 Central Park West, New York, NY 10025
(212) 866-3654-2
In Hollywood, CA: Ilse Lahn, Kohner-Levy Agency, 9169 Sunset Blvd., Los Angeles, CA 90069 (213) 550-1060

TITLE • AVAILABILITY • PRODUCTIONS

Second Floor Front: manuscript*; College of the Mainland Theatre, TX; Arena Theatre, Texas City, TX

An Evening at Home: manuscript*; Hollywood productions

A Quiet Place by the Sea: manuscript*

What Will the Neighbors Say!: manuscript*

The Amateur Sinner: manuscript*

The Three Arabian Knights (lyrics by Johnny Mercer; music by Franz Steineinger): manuscript*

Love That Girl!: manuscript*

*contact New York agent

SYNOPSES

The Three Arabian Knights: Sinbad, Ali Baba and Aladdin are thrown together by Fate and the unscrupulous Caliph of Baghdad. To save their lives from royal condemnation, the three heroes agree to perform several impossible tasks. The tasks ironically contribute to the Caliph's destruction, but not until the dramatic, comedic and romantic adventures met by the comrades write a new colorful chapter for the Arabian Nights.

What Will the Neighbors Say!: A primitive personality from an obstinately undeveloped Third World country finds himself unexpectedly thrown into the maelstrom of sophisticated social and political chicanery on an unanticipated visit to the United States. He resorts to a personal basic philosophy to contend with his problem, that is unusual enough to sow the seeds of World War III.

The Amateur Sinner: A worldly vagabond of charm and intellect, if of no material fortune, wanders

Aubrey Wisberg (cont'd)

into an obscure French village where, with the aid of a new friend, they turn a somnolent and self-centered little bucolic community upside down. The consequences send waves washing against consternated officialdom in Paris itself.

RUTH WOLFF

Smith College, B.A., Yale University School of Drama. Films: **The Abdication** starring Liv Ullmann and Peter Finch; **The Incredible Sarah** (the life of Sarah Bernhardt) starring Glenda Jackson. Novel: **The Abdication.** Articles: **"We Open In Florence," New York Times Magazine; "The Aesthetic of Violence," Ms. Magazine.** Recipient: Rockefeller Grant, 1967; Kennedy Center Commission to write Bicentennial Play, **Eden Again.**

Address: 45 East 89th St., New York, NY 10028

Agent: Audrey Wood, International Creative Management, 40 West 57th St., New York, NY 10019 (212) 556-5722

TITLE • AVAILABILITY • PRODUCTIONS

Folly Cove: manuscript*; O'Neill Theater Center's National Playwrights Conference, CT

Still Life with Apples: manuscript*; O'Neill Theater Center's National Playwrights Conference, CT; Radio Broadcast, CA

Arabic Two: manuscript*; New Theatre; Greenwich Players

Eleanor of Aquitaine: manuscript*; Playwrights Horizons, NYC

The Abdication: The New Women's Theatre, Vintage Press, 201 East 50th St., New York, NY 10022, $5.95; Bristol Old Vic, England; Il Gruppo Arte Drammatica, Italy

George and Frederic: manuscript*; Playwrights Horizons, NYC

Empress of China: manuscript*; Playwrights Horizons, NYC

Eden Again: manuscript*

Sarah in America: manuscript*; Kennedy Center, Washington, DC

*contact agent

SYNOPSES

George and Frederic: A play with music by Laurence Rosenthal and Frederic Chopin. About the love affair between George Sand and Frederic Chopin, illustrating, through Sand's life, the complexities of freedom and the "liberated" life.

Full length. Setting: piano on a bare stage. Then, simply suggested, various settings. 4 males, 3 females.

Arabic Two: The curtain rises on a young couple's livingroom and they bid the audience, "Welcome to a divorce!" Since we all were at their wedding, the beginning of their marriage, they invite us back to witness the end. Does he have another love? Does she? They play out their emotions in fact and fantasy, revealing the complexity of their involvement with each other and the mysterious bond of the marriage tie.

Two acts. Setting: livingroom. 1 male, 1 female.

The Abdication: In 1655, Christina of Sweden abdicated her throne and went to Rome where she converted to Catholicism and fell in love with her confessor, Cardinal Decio Azzolino. The play begins with her arrival at the Vatican and her first encounter with the Cardinal. Her growing love

W

Ruth Wolff (cont'd)

for him alternates with flashbacks into her youth and young womanhood in Sweden, leading to the emotional breakdown which resulted in her giving up the crown.

Two acts. Setting: one multi-purpose space suggesting a room in the Vatican into which fade various scenes from the Swedish court. 6 males, 4 females.

HERMAN WOUK

Born in New York City on May 27, 1915. B.A. from Columbia U. Was a radio script writer for leading comedians, 1936–41. Served in the U.S. Navy, 1941–46. Has written many novels: **Aurora Dawn; The City Boy; The Caine Mutiny; Marjorie Morningstar; Youngblood Hawke; Don't Stop the Carnival; The Winds of War; War and Remembrance;** Non-fiction: **This Is My God.** Recipient: Pulitzer Prize **(The Caine Mutiny);** Hon. L.H.D., Yeshiva U.; Hon. D. Lit., Clark U.; Columbia U., Medal of Excellence; D. Lit. (Hon.), American International College; Alexander Hamilton Medal, Columbia University, NY, 1980.

Agent: BSW Literary Agency, 3255 N St., N.W., Washington, DC 20007 (202) 342-0275

TITLE • AVAILABILITY • PRODUCTIONS

The Traitor: Samuel French, 25 West 45th St., New York, NY 10036, $2.50; Broadway

The Caine Mutiny Court-Martial: Samuel French, $2.50; Granada Theater, Santa Barbara, CA; Broadway

Nature's Way: Samuel French, $2.50; Broadway

SYNOPSIS

The Traitor: The title figure is not a Communist, but a thoughtful young atomic scientist, with no high regard for Marxism, who sincerely believes that the best way to stop the coming of war is to let the Russians in on the secret of the atom bomb. With both sides possessing such a terrible weapon, he feels that they would have to get together to work out a way to avoid the mutual suicide of a new world struggle. When trapped by Naval Intelligence, he sees the error of his path and helps in the trapping the chief Russian secret agent.

Full length. Setting: livingroom of an apartment. 15 males, 3 females.

ELIZABETH WRAY

Born in Rochester, NY on January 15, 1950. B.A. in English, Mills College, 1970; M.F.A. in Writing, Columbia University, 1976. Poems published in: **Partisan Review, New Letters, Kayak, Epoch** and many others. Worked for four years as an editor and radio producer for **Black Box Magazine, Watershed Tapes** (series of contemporary poets reading their own work on cassette tapes), **The Poem That Never Ends,** a series of programs on contemporary U.S. poetry for public radio. Currently Playwright-in-Residence, Julian Theatre, San Francisco, CA

Address: 100 Delores St., #3, San Francisco, CA 94103

W

Elizabeth Wray (cont'd)

TITLE • AVAILABILITY • PRODUCTIONS

Knitting: not available; Mill Valley Center for the Performing Arts, CA

Nightstone: not available; U. of Montana, MT

Corners: not available; Washington Project for the Arts, Wash., D.C.

Memory Motel: Chrysalis, March 1981, manuscript*

Broken Borders: manuscript*; American Place Theatre, Women's Project Series, NYC; Bay Area Playwrights Festival 3, San Francisco, CA

Rock Island: manuscript*

Double Shift: manuscript*; Indiana State University, Evansville, IN

Cold Pipes: manuscript*

Mobile Homes: manuscript*; Julian Theatre, San Francisco, CA

Cold Storage: manuscript*; Eureka Theatre, San Francisco, CA

*contact author

SYNOPSES

Rock Island: The time is 1936 in the Dust Bowl, on a Rock Island Railroad right-of-way along the Oklahoma-Arkansas border. Five American "types" (former IWW man, would-be starlet, itinerant female soapboxer, former ringmaster with P.T. Barnum, newspaperman from Trenton) wait to hop a train west. They become involved with each other as a drama unravels involving the discovery, capture and escape of the former IWW man, who has dynamited a border post set up to collect revenues from itinerant farmers.

Full length. 4 males, 3 females.

Broken Borders: An episodic play in twelve scenes, following the journey of a woman over the decimated landscape of an unspecified war. It explores the anonymity of modern war and the difficulty any person has in choosing sides or taking action.

Long one act (90 minutes). Setting: minimal suggestions of a one room apartment, a trench, a railroad station, a road, a border post, a look-out post. 23 speaking characters played by an ensemble of 8 actors, 4 males, 4 females; 3 non-speaking extras.

Mobile Homes: Three American Scenes: The action follows a thirty-year-old waitress and former rock singer, Ava, who decides to leave her home and family in Baltimore where her life has come to a standstill and travel across the country to make an audition set up for her at a club in San Francisco. The play is about taking responsibility for one's own actions, about the pain of leaving home, the limbo of being on the road and the difficult joy of beginning again.

Setting: Three locations, **Porch,** the front porch of a Baltimore row house; **Border,** a cafe/gas station on the Texas-New Mexico border; **Car,** near a Dodge van, San Francisco. 4 males, 2 females.

ELIZABETH WYATT

Born in Hove, England on June 17, 1944. Graduated from Boston University, Philosophy, and then entered the theater as the best means of ethical self-expression. Recipient: Office of Advanced Drama Research Award.

Address: 33 Woodland Road, Brookline, MA 02167 (617) 232-8673

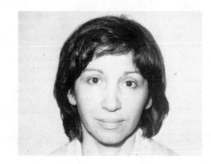

TITLE • AVAILABILITY • PRODUCTIONS

The Assassination of Robert F. Kennedy as Performed by Wives of Our Armed Forces: manuscript*; Loeb Experimental Theater, Harvard, MA

Spaced: manuscript*; Newbury Street Theater, Boston, MA

The Finishing Touch: manuscript*; Playwrights Platform, Boston, MA

Mobiles: manuscript*; Playwrights Platform, Boston, MA

Getting Through: manuscript*; Cubiculo Theatre, NYC; N.E.T. Work Theater, NYC

Spring Fever: manuscript*; Nucleo Eclettico Theater, Boston, MA

The Natural Philosophy of Love: manuscript*; Mobius Experimental Theater Co., Boston, MA

Poets' Corner: manuscript*; Peoples Theater, Cambridge, MA (workshop)

The Chinese Box: manuscript*; (tentatively scheduled for) Syracuse Stage, NY

Two Mothers: manuscript*; Reading, Forum for Italian Playwrights, NYC

Tremors Caused by Being Born: manuscript*

  *contact author

SYNOPSES

Poets' Corner: Three suburban women meet for a poetry workshop in an effort to further their writing careers. One of their sons, a twelve-year-old, is writing a paper on Hiroshima and protesting the distance which separates his mother from the rest of the world. He provokes her to attack him, and then she realizes that the violence they talk about is very close to home.

Long one act. 3 females, 1 boy.

Tremors Caused By Being Born: Two mothers meet in the intimacy of a maternity ward after giving birth to baby boys. One baby is wanted, the other is wanted on condition . . . In trying to help Ruth go to school and still keep her baby, Flo offers her a home and offers to look after her child. The fact that Ruth is an established homemaker and Flo is a wanderer does not stop them planning a life together until reality steps in.

Full length. 2 males, 3 females.

Y

WAKAKO YAMAUCHI

Born in Westmorland, CA on October 25, 1942. Has had short stories published in: **Aiiieeeee,** an anthology of Asian American Writers; **Amerasia Journal; Solo, Women on Woman Alone** anthology; **Yardbird Reader,** anthology of third world writers. **And the Soul Shall Dance** was produced on **Hollywood Television Theater.** Recipient: Rockefeller Playwright-in-Residence Grant, 1977, 1979; Rockefeller Foundation Award, 1980; American Theater Critics Association Award for outstanding play, 1976–77, not produced in New York.

Address: 15922 Halldale Ave., Gardena, CA 90247

Agent: Elly Shusham, William Morris Agency, 151 El Camino Drive, Beverly Hills, CA 90212 (213) 274-7451

TITLE • AVAILABILITY • PRODUCTIONS

And the Soul Shall Dance: manuscript*; East/West Players, L.A., CA; Pan Asian Repertory, NY

The Music Lessons: manuscript**; New York Shakespeare Festival, NYC

Shirley Temple, Hot-Cha-Cha: manuscript**

12-1-A: manuscript**

Not a Through Street: manuscript*

  *contact author
  **contact agent

SYNOPSES

And the Soul Shall Dance: A play about two immigrant families struggling for survival during the depression years and how one adapts and the other does not.

Full length. Setting: interior and exterior of a farmhouse. 2 males, 4 females.

The Music Lessons: A play about a transient laborer who comes to work on a widow's farm and finds both the widow and her daughter falling in love with him.

Full length. Setting: farm kitchen, interior of a cabin, pool-hall. 5 males, 3 females.

12-1-A; A play about a family of Japanese Americans who are incarcerated (along with 110,000 other Japanese and Japanese Americans) in the American concentration camps of World War II and how they make their choices in that limited situation.

Full length. Setting: interior of a barracks. 8 males, 4 females.

SUSAN YANKOWITZ

Born in Newark, NJ on February 20. Educated at Sarah Lawrence College and Yale School of Drama. **Silent Witness,** a novel, May 1976, Knopf; **The Prison Game,** teleplay, **Visions,** KCET-TV, Los Angeles, Fall 1976; **Milk & Honey,** musical teleplay, **Visions,** 1977, also **The Forerunner: Charlotte Perkins Gilman** (PBS-TV) and screenplay **Silent Witness.** Teacher of Playwriting and Dramatic Literature at Quinnipiac College; Southern Connecticut State College; Harvard; Bronx Community College. Playwright-in-Residence at The Academy Theatre, Atlanta, Georgia; the Provisional Theatre, Los Angeles, California; the Magic Theatre, Omaha, Nebraska. Recipient: Guggenheim Fellowship in Playwriting, 1975; CAPS Award in Playwriting, 1974; Rockefeller Foundation Grant, 1973–74; National Endowment for the Arts Creative Writing Fellowship, 1972–3; MacDowell Colony Fellowship, 1971; Vernon Rice Drama Desk Award for Most Promising Playwright 1969–70; Joseph E. Levine Fellowship in Screenwriting, 1968–69; NEA Creative Writing Grant, 1979–80.

Address: 205 West 89th St., New York, NY 10024

Agent: Gloria Loomis, A. Watkins Agency, 77 Park Ave., New York, NY 10016 (212) 532-0080

TITLE • AVAILABILITY • PRODUCTIONS

True Romances: manuscript*; Mark Taper Forum Lab, Los Angeles, CA;

Still Life: manuscript*; Interart Theatre, NYC

The America Piece: manuscript*; Provisional Theatre, Los Angeles, CA; Theatre Festival, Nancy, France; U.S. tour

Wooden Nickels: manuscript*; Theatre for the New City, NYC

Acts of Love: manuscript*; Academy Theatre, Atlanta, GA

A Series of Monologues: manuscript*; in **The Wicked Women Revue** and **?!,** at Theatre for the New City, The Little Church Around the Corner, NYC

Terminal: Three Works by the Open Theatre, Drama Book Specialists, 150 West 52nd St., New York, NY 10019, $12.50; **Scripts,** Vol. 1, October 1971 (out of print); Open Theatre, NYC; Roundhouse, London

Boxes: Playwrights for Tomorrow, Vol. 11, Univ. of Minnesota Press, 2307 University Ave., SE, Minneapolis, MN 55414, $3.45 (paperback); Magic Theatre, Berkeley, CA; Bronx Community College, NY

Positions: manuscript*; in **Up!** at Westbeth Cabaret, NYC

Slaughterhouse Play: Yale/Theatre, Summer 1969; **New American Plays,** Vol. 4, Hill & Wang, 19 Union Sq., New York, NY 10003; New York Shakespeare Festival, NYC

Basics: manuscript*; in **Tabula Rasa,** Brooklyn Academy of Music, NY

Nightmare: manuscript*; Yale University, New Haven, CT

Sideshow: manuscript*; National Theatre of the Deaf tour

Transplant: manuscript*; Magic Theatre, Omaha, NB

The Ha-Ha Play: Scripts, Vol. 10, October 1972 (out of print)*; Cubiculo Theatre, NYC

The Lamb: manuscript*; Cubiculo Theatre, NYC

Rats' Alley (radio play): manuscript*; WGBH radio

That Old Rock-a-Bye: manuscript*; Cooper Square Theatre, NYC

The Cage: manuscript*; Omar Khayyam Cafe, NYC

Qui Est Anna Marks!: manuscript*; TEP, Paris, France

    *contact author

Susan Yankowitz (cont'd)

SYNOPSES

Boxes: A play about city living, about the various ways in which people box themselves in. The piece is written for an ensemble company. Much of the action is physical and meant to be improvised by the group that performs the piece. The size of the company may range from 6 to 10, flexible genders.

Setting: modest and simple; a bare stage with modular constructions which serve as houses, theatre boxes, podiums, etc.

Slaughterhouse Play: Deals with the cyclical nature of violence, using the metaphor of racial struggle. White people own and operate a slaughterhouse in which black people are butchered for meat.

Score by Bob Dennis. Setting: a combination slaughterhouse, butcher shop, livingroom and street. A large cast — about 20 persons — is required, plus musicians. If an inter-racial company is not available, masks may be used.

SAUL ZACHARY

Born in Brooklyn, NY on September 12, 1934. B.A., Brooklyn College; M.A., Smith College. Co-founder and former Artistic Director of Playwrights Platform, Boston, MA. Has directed, taught Theater at Smith College and the University of South Florida and also written short stories and for TV. Recipient: Dubuque Fine Arts Society, National One-Act Playwriting Contest, 1981; National Endowment for the Arts Fellowship in Playwriting, 1979; Mass. Arts and Humanities Foundation Fellowship, 1975; P.E.N. American Center Grant, 1975; U.S.F. Research Council Award, 1970 and 1969; M.C.A. Creative Writing Fellowship, 1967; CBS-TV Writing Grant Award, 1960.

Address: 338 West 19th St., New York, NY 10011
    (212) 989-0948

TITLE • AVAILABILITY • PRODUCTIONS

One Long Day: manuscript*; Brooklyn College, NY

A Stomach Full of Echoes: manuscript*; Gene Frankel Theatre, NYC: M.A.D.D. Company, Tampa, FL

Shapes of Midnight: manuscript*; U. of South Florida

Glass: The Grecourt Review, Smith College, Northampton, MA 01060; $1.25; U. of South Florida; Playwrights' Platform, Boston, MA

The Color of Heat: The Grecourt Review, $1.25; Playwrights' Platform, Boston, MA; Impossible Ragtime Theatre, NYC

Ground Zero: manuscript*; Playwrights' Platform, Boston, MA

A Likeness to Life: manuscript*; Playwrights' Platform, Boston, MA; N.Y. Theatre Ensemble, NYC

Nocturne: manuscript*; New York Shakespeare Festival, NYC; The Production Company, NYC

Spectre: manuscript*; The Actors Studio, NYC

The Here and the Now: manuscript*

Letter to the World: manuscript*

Spots: manuscript*; Dubuque Fine Arts Players, Dubuque, IA

    *contact author

MARC ALAN ZAGOREN

Born in Perth Amboy, NJ on April 25, 1940. B.A. University of Michigan, M.F.A. Yale Univ., Playwright-in-Residence, Drake University, North Carolina School of the Arts and State University of New York. He has written such films as: **Chasing Rainbows, Synda Areson.** In collaboration with David S. Meranze, he wrote the films **Dutch Treat** and **Second Fiddle,** as well as for C.B.S. TV series, **Ivan the Terrible** and **Gilbert.** Associate Professor, Fairleigh Dickinson University, Rutherford, NJ. Recipient: Jule and Avery Hopwood Award; NEA Creative Writing Fellowship; New Jersey State Council on the Arts Award.

Address: 5 Roosevelt Place, Montclair, NJ
07042 (201) 746-7711

Agent: Joyce Ketay, 320 West 90th St.,
New York, NY 10024 (212) 799-2398

TITLE • AVAILABILITY • PRODUCTIONS

Knight of the Twelfth Saucer: Best Short Plays, Chilton Book Co., Radnor, Pa. 19089; Actors Studio, NYC; Lincoln Center, NYC

Gilbert (in collaboration with David S. Meranze): manuscript*; CBS; Lincoln Center, NYC

The Signorina: manuscript*; The New York Cultural Center; staged reading: reading, Circle-in-the-Square, NYC

Curtains (in collaboration with David S. Meranze): manuscript*; currently optioned

Swan Song (in collaboration with David S. Meranze): manuscript*

Henry's Day: manuscript*; staged reading, The Shubert Theatre, Los Angeles, CA

Dalliance: manuscript*; North Carolina School of the Arts; State U. of NY

Princess Grace and the Fazzaris: manuscript*; New Jersey Theatre Forum, staged reading; Williamstown Theatre Festival, MA

White Jazz (in collaboration with Michael Moriarty): manuscript*

Grand Finale: manuscript*; American Theater Experiment

Moonlight and Love Songs: manuscript*

   *contact agent

SYNOPSES

The Signorina: A comedy about a shy, young veterinarian who lives in New York City and is so taken with the lifestyle of an artistic and seemingly charming young couple that he tries to pattern his life after theirs.

Full length. Setting: a garden in Manhattan's West Nineties. 3 males, 2 females.

Henry's Day: A small town high school principal locks himself in his garage the day a local holiday is declared honoring his retirement, because he is suddenly aware that his life has not added up the way he wanted it to. Farce comedy.

Full length. Setting: the backyard and garage of a four-family house in New Jersey. 8 males, 7 females.

Dalliance: A serious comedy about a group of people who all feel they have reached a turning point in their lives and desperately want to make a new beginning. A play about the early middle age of the generation that grew up in post-World War II America.

Full length. Setting: the deck and adjacent area of a dazzling suburban house. 5 males, 5 females.

Z

CURTIS ZAHN

Born in Detroit, MI on November 12, 1912. Educated at University of California at Berkeley; San Francisco State College, (Cinema); Actors Studio, Playwrights Lab; Herbert Berghoff. Associate Editor, **Trace** magazine. Guest Editor, **Coastline** quarterly. Collected short stories, **American Contemporary, New Directions.** His plays are in the Curtis Zahn Collection at Boston University and Lincoln Center Libraries. Recipient: Dylan Thomas Award, for poetry; Old Globe Theater, six awards including Overall Excellency; Eugene Field Society, Poetry.

Address: 1352 Miller Drive, Los Angeles, CA
90069 (213) 656-4896

TITLE • AVAILABILITY • PRODUCTIONS

Five-Four-Three-Two-One: Poetry & Drama, Magazine*; Donnell Library, NYC; Poetry, Los Angeles, CA

An Albino Kind of Logic: First Stage, Purdue University, Lafayette, IN 47907*; Globe Theatre, San Diego, CA; Century Playhouse, Los Angeles, CA

In a Name, Nothing: manuscript*

Reactivated Man: Library of the Performing Arts, Lincoln Center, New York, NY 10023*; Edw. Ludlum Theatre, Los Angeles, CA; Angry Arts Festival, (nine theatres in L.A. county)

Conditioned Reflex: First Stage*; Theatre de Lys, NYC: Barter Theater, VA

Under-Ground: manuscript*; White Barn Theatre, CT; Academy Theater, GA

Genesis & Exodus of Operation A-132: manuscript*

Purgation: manuscript*

Transistorized Electric Butterknife: manuscript*

Con-Fron-Ta-Tion: manuscript*; New Playwrights Theatre, Los Angeles, CA; Actors Studio West, Los Angeles, CA

Respectfully, CX-49-D: manuscript*

Origin of the Species: manuscript*

Landscape w/Figures: manuscript*; Theatre Rapport, Los Angeles, CA

Seascape w/Figures: manuscript, Lincoln Center Library*

*contact author

SYNOPSES

Reactivated Man: A husband/father has an overactive conscience and cannot function in the normal environment — too honest, too unselfish. Won't take jobs that aid military offense; won't kill ants or mice, won't even sell real estate (parasitic). His wife has heard about an illegal, maverick group of ex-doctors who perform abortive operations on the brain to remove the conscience. After the operation, he has become reactionary, aggressive, and wholly selfish. His wife is horrified. Now liberated from all responsibility, the protagonist grabs the (willing) nurse, refuses to pay the bill and drives off. But before doing so, he seizes the jar containing his "conscience" and tosses it to his wife, telling her "this will be something for the children to remember me by."

Long one act. Setting: an abandoned adobe ruin by the seashore. 3 males, 2 females.

The Genesis & Exodus of Operation A-132: We are in Decentralia, Minor — a hypothetical nation somewhere in the underprivileged world. The general has convinced the natives that they should spend their impoverishment on armaments and blackmail the world. Secretly, two countries have poured nuclear hardware into Decentralia unbeknown to the other. The general and his scientist alter ego are alone on Operation X, a hilltop, where his control panel awaits any whim to destroy the world. The scientist tries to dissuade the general. American captives (experts and techni-

Curtis Zahn (cont'd)

cians) are brought to him. One of the captives is an ex-Peace Corps dropout., He is a pacifist and also disenchanted with all of the quarrelling nations. In the end, he, the general, and the scientist are alone where, at any moment, the general may push the button. The general tosses his revolver to the ground. They can kill him. The scientist refuses because he is amoral and philosophizes that this would only give the world temporary peace. The ex-Peace Corp man will not use the gun because Pacifism means no one has the right to take a life, even if it would save another — or millions. At final curtain, nothing has been resolved — or has something been illuminated?

Full length. Setting: two sets if prologue is used. 5 males, 4 females.

JOHN RANDOLPH ZAPOR

Born in DuBois, PA on June 26, 1944. Attended Indiana University of PA and Elizabeth Town College, B.A. in Communications. Currently employed, Office of Employment Security for PA. Has written over two hundred features for newspapers, trade publications, including **Dramatists Guild Quarterly, Future,** etc. Served on the Executive Board, Indiana Players, as well as the advisory boards of several foundations. Recipient: Outstanding Young Man of America, 1979; Citations for Community Service, PA State Senate and Legislature, 1979; Nominee, Governor's Award for Service to the Arts.

Address: 105 Elmington Drive, Indiana, PA 15701

TITLE • AVAILABILITY • PRODUCTIONS

Whatever You Call It (musical; book and lyrics; with Mike Shaffer): manuscript*; Berlin International Theatre, West Berlin

All Stop (one act; with M. Shaffer): manuscript*; Norwalk Community Theater

All the Way across Town (one act; with M. Shaffer): manuscript*; Norwalk Community Theater

Requiem for a President (with M. Shaffer): manuscript*; Readers' Theater, Indiana U. of PA

An Island We Imagined: manuscript*; Readers' Theater, Indiana U. of PA

Climate of Noon: manuscript*; Indiana U. of PA

Night of the Body Count: manuscript*; Indiana U. of PA

Mister Jordon (juvenile market): Eldridge Publishing Co., Franklin, Ohio 45005, 85¢; Staged: WIN (experimental program in motivation — as teaching device).

They Burned the Church While I Was Gone: manuscript*

Chimera (musical; book and lyrics; composer – James Crozier): manuscript*; Indiana U. of PA

Among Your Clowns: manuscript*

Tin Man: manuscript*

   *contact author

SYNOPSES

Among Your Clowns: Viet Nam is past tense but Jimmy has to pull himself together., He remembers it all: his abortive shot at draft dodging . . . political activism . . . Toronto . . . his buddies . . . and the girls. He reprises his life with all of them at the mercy of his imagination. An archeological expedition, a magical mystery tour of the politicized/doped up/fragmented sixties.

Setting: one multi-level, several locations, primarily indicated by lighting shifts. 4 males (3 white, 1 black), 3 females (2 white, 1 black).

John Randolph Zapor (cont'd)

They Burned the Church While I Was Gone: The midway of a small carnival on the eve of a solar eclipse. A nightmare mixture of naturalism and the surreal, the lives of several carnival workers lived in the unspoken belief that the eclipse makes these last hours the eve of something new in all their lives. A very adult piece.

Setting: the carnival grounds, multi-level, multi-unit. 7 males, 5 females, 3 children, assorted townspeople, etc. Optimum cast of 20, minimum of 17.

DICK D. ZIGUN

Born in Bridgeport, CT on May 11, 1953. B.A., Drama, Bennington College; M.F.A., Yale School of Drama, Playwriting, 1978. Has worked at Yale Rep; American Place Theatre; Research Assistant to Richard Gilman; Theatre for the New City; **Playbill** Magazine. Performance Art: **The Letter to Sara; The Carnival Booth; Eat My Criticism?; Deposit.** Member, New Dramatists. Recipient: Shubert Fellowships, 1975–76, 1976–77; Eugene O'Neill Scholar, 1977–78; Molly Kazan Prize, 1977–78; Columbia Pictures Grant; Playwright-in-Residence, Mark Taper Forum.

Address: 34 Watts St., #4, New York, NY 10013
(212) 226-1677

Agent: Helen Merrill, 337 West 22nd St., New York, NY 10011 (212) 924-6314

TITLE • AVAILABILITY • PRODUCTIONS

Lather: not available; Bennington College, VT

Equal Rights: manuscript*; Bennington College, VT; Yale Club, NYC

Vermont Medicine Show: manuscript*; Bennington College, VT

Huey's Legacy: manuscript**; Yale Drama School, CT

His Master's Voice: manuscript**; Yale Cabaret, CT

The Letter to Sara: manuscript*; P.S. #1, NYC

Three Unnatural Acts: manuscript**; Yale School of Drama, CT; Mark Taper Forum, CA

Wonderland, U.S.A.: manuscript**; Mark Taper Forum Workshop, CA

  *contact author
  **contact agent

SYNOPSES

Wonderland, U.S.A.: A "remake" of Lewis Carroll's **Alice's Adventures in Wonderland.** This play moves the story into the context of an American amusement park.

Full length. Setting: sculptural set conceptualization is contained within the script — making use of a wall of doors, a neon sign and white gloved hands suspended on wires which fall from above. 5 males, 4 females; includes a ventriloquist, deaf actress, eleven-year-old black girl, muscle man, Asian midget, Jewish comic, sex goddess, Hispanic tapdancer and fat white man with tattoos.

Three Unnatural Acts: A theatrical response to the lives of Karen Ann Quinlan, Charles Lindbergh and Son of Sam. "Zigun's free-floating imagination . . . weds expressionism with the American comic book . . . the klutzy Bruno Hauptmann . . . kidnaps the Lindbergh baby, who is an egg. He drops the egg as a symbolic, accidental murder. His execution is staged by having his feet plunged into the aquarium and his hand in an electric toaster. That should give you some idea of the Zigun style" . . . **Los Angeles Times.**

Full length. Setting: sculptural set using slide projections and numerous toy objects. 1 female, 1 young girl, 1 male.

His Master's Voice: A melodrama. This is the story of a ventriloquist, Max, who upon the death of vaudeville, sets out to kill Thomas A. Edison.

One hour. Setting: minimal, two ventriloquial dummies. 4 or 5 males, one a ventriloquist, 1 or 2 females.

PAUL ZINDEL+

Born in Staten Island, New York on May 15, 1936. Majored in Chemistry at Wagner College, B.S. 1958; M.Sc., 1959. Four novels for young adults (Harper & Row): **The Pigman; My Darling, My Hamburger; I Never Loved Your Mind; Pardon Me, You're Stepping On My Eyeball.** Childrens' book (Harper & Row): **I Love my Mother.** Author of screenplays for: Up The Sandbox; Mame. Recipient: Ford Foundation Grant. The following awards for **The Effect of Gamma Rays On Man-In-The-Moon Marigolds:** New York Drama Critic's Award for Best American Play; Obie Award; Pulitzer Prize (drama). Los Angeles Drama Critic's Award for Best American Play **(And Miss Reardon Drinks A Little).**

Contact: Golberg, Michael & Co., 1888 Century Park East, Suite 1815, Los Angeles, CA 90067 (213) 552-9600

TITLE • AVAILABILITY • PRODUCTIONS

Dimensions of a Peacock: manuscript*; NYC

Euthanasia: manuscript*; NYC

The Endless Hearts: manuscript*; NYC

The Pigman: Dramatists Play Service, 440 Park Avenue South, New York, NY 10016, $2.50

A Dream of Swallows: Jan Hus House, NYC

The Effect of Gamma Rays on Man In the Moon Marigolds: Dramatists Play Service, $2.50; Alley Theatre, Houston, TX; Mercer-O'Casey Theatre, NYC

And Miss Reardon Drinks A Little: Dramatists Play Service, $2.50; Mark Taper Forum, Los Angeles, CA; Broadway

Let Me Hear You Whisper: Dramatists Play Service, $2.50; WNET-TV

The Ladies Should Be In Bed: with **Let Me Hear You Whisper**

The Secret Affairs of Mildred Wild: Dramatists Play Service, $2.50; Broadway

Ladies at the Alamo: Dramatists Play Service, $2.50; Actors' Studio, NYC; Broadway

*contact attorney

A

à/Townsend Brewster
Aala Park/Edward Sakamoto
* Abdication, The/Ruth Wolff
* A-Birthing At Nubbin Ridge/Lanny Flaherty
Abraham Lincoln's Love Affairs/Earl H. Smith
Abraham Lincoln's State of the Union/Earl H. Smith
Absinthe/Joseph Hart
Absolute Power Over Movie Stars/Robert Patrick
Absolutely Everything/Rose L. Goldemberg
Abstract Of A Present Day/Edan Schappert
Academy, The/Mario Fratti
Academy Of Desire, The/Yale Udoff
Acife And Pendabis/Daniel W. Owens
Acorns In Moondust/Louis LaRusso II
Acquisition, The/David Trainer
Acrobats/Israel Horovitz
Across the River and Into the Jungle/Arthur Kopit
Act, The/George Furth
Act, The/Sallie Bingham
Action/Sam Shepard
* Actors, The/Lezley Havard
Actors Exercise/John Pyros
Actors Nightmare, The/Christopher Durang
Acts Of Love/Susan Yankowitz
Adam/Lonnie Carter
Adam And Eve/Sy Reiter
Ad Hoc Committee, The/Doric Wilson
Adjustment, The/Albert Bermel
Adolf Hitler Show, The/Sam A. Eisenstein
Adora/Jean Reavey
Adorable Dodo, The/Benjamin Bradford
* Advance Man, The/Allen Sternfield
Advantage Of Dope, The/Oyamo
Adventure of Eddie Greshaw, The/Eddie Lawrence
* Adventure Of The Clouded Crystal, The/Tim Kelly
Adventures In Futility/W. Edwin Ver Becke
Adventures Of Karagoz, The/Charles Ludlam
Adventures Of Marco Polo/Neil Simon
Adventures Of Peter Cottontail, The/R. Eugene Jackson
* Adversary, The/Barry Berg
Affair, The/Helen Duberstein
Afflictions Of Marlene, The/Stanley Taikeff
African Star/John Jiler
Afrindi Aspect, The/Silas Jones
* Afterglow/M.H. Appleman
Aftermath/Gus Edwards
* Afternoons In Vegas/Jack Gilhooley
After The Baal-Shem Tov/Arthur Sainer
After The Fact/Jeffrey Sweet
After The Fall/Arthur Miller
After The Season/Corinne Jacker

After Work/John Scott
Against The Law/Mark Leib
Agnes Of God/John Pielmeier
Agreement, The/Joseph Lizardi
A-Haunting We Will Go/Tim Kelly
Ah, Eurydice!/Stanley Taikeff
Ahmed's Razor/Alan Roland
Ah! Wine/Leonard Melfi
Ain't Doin' Nothin' But Singin' My Song/Johnny Brandon
Ain't It Awful About Marie Antoinette?/James Prideaux
Airline/Tim Kelly
A Is For Alpha/Elyse Nass
Ajuba & The Magic Gourd/S. Garrett Robinson
Akosula Of The First And Final Day/Ray Aranha
Alchemist's Book, The/Kathy Hurley
Alchemy Da Vinci/Louis Phillips
Alexis Is Fallen/Ossie Davis
Alfred Dies/Israel Horovitz
Alfred The Great/Israel Horovitz
Alias Smedley Pewtree/Tim Kelly
Alice In The American Wonderland/James Schevill
Alice In Wonder/Conrad Bishop
Alice In Wonder/Ossie Davis
Alice In Wonderland/Sheldon Rosen
Alice's Adventures In Wonderland/Tim Kelly
Alice Through A Glass Lightly/Tom Eyen
Alice Through The Looking Glass/Sy Reiter
Alice Wake Up!/Conrad Bishop
Alinsky/Herb Schapiro
Alive!/Leonard Melfi
Alive And Kicking/Jules Tasca
All Honorable Men/Michael J. Chepiga
* Alligator Man/Jack A. Kaplan
Alligator Man, The/John Scott
Allison/Sally Ordway
All My Sons/Arthur Miller
All Over/Edward Albee
All Over Town/Murray Schisgal
All Runners, Come/James Childs
All Stop/John R. Zapor
All Summer Long/Robert Anderson
All The Way Across Town/John R. Zapor
All Through The House/Anthony Scully
All Together Now/Jeffrey Kindley
Alma's Rules/Richard Lees
Almost Like Being/Jean-Claude van Itallie
Almost On A Runway/Donna de Matteo
Alone In The Dark/David Trainer
Always Marry A Bachelor/Tim Kelly
* Amateur Sinner, The/Aubrey Wisberg
Amator, Amator/Townsend Brewster
* Amazing Activity Of Charley Contare And The Ninety-eight Street Gang, The/Roy London
· Ambassador/Anna Marie Barlow
Amen Corner, The/James Baldwin
America & Its People/Peter Copani

America Hurrah/Jean-Claude van Itallie
America In Heat/Leo Rutman
* American Buffalo/David Mamet
* American Chestnut/Bill Bozzone
American Clock, The/Arthur Miller
American Dream, The/Edward Albee
American Flag Ritual, The/Ed Bullins
* American Gothic/Mark Eichman
American Hamburger League,
The/Norman Kline
* American Hystery/David K. Heefner
* American Iceberg, The/Albert Evans
* American Imagination, The/Richard
Foreman
American Kaleidescope/Jean Reavey
American King's English For
Queens/Megan Terry
* American Oasis, The/Steven Somkin
American Primitive/William Gibson
American Shrapnel/Ron Whyte
American War Women, The/Roma Greth
American Wedding Ritual/Megan Terry
America Piece, The/Susan Yankowitz
America Was/Jack Heifner
Americommedia/Michael Christofer
Amertyl/Arthur Jasspe
Among Adults/Jeffrey Kindley
* Among Your Clowns/John R. Zapor
* Amsterdam Avenue Theater
Presents/Direct From Death Row/The
Scottsboro Boys, The/Mark Stein
A, My Name Is Alice/Joseph T. Pintauro
Anabiosis/Charles Gordone
An Act Of Kindness/Joseph Julian
An Albino Kind Of Logic/Curtis Zahn
An American Millionaire/Murray Schisgal
An American Sunset/James Prideaux
Ananais, Jr./Townsend Brewster
* An Audible Sigh/Lee Kalcheim
An Awfully Big Adventure/Thomas M.
Fontana
And/Robert Gordon
And He Made A Her/Doric Wilson
And Love Me All The Time/Lydia Simmons
And Miss Reardon Drinks A Little/Paul
Zindel
Androcles And The Lion/Michael Colby
Androgyne/F.V.Hunt
Andromeda/Townsend Brewster
Andromeda:2/Ron Whyte
. . . And The Boy Who Came To Leave/Lee
Kalcheim
* And The Soul Shall Dance/Wakako
Yamauchi
And Things That Go Bump In The
Night/Terrence McNally
And Where She Stops Nobody
Knows/Oliver Hailey
Andy Grunnt/Stanley Taikeff
* An Echo Of Bells/Charles Frink
An Enemy Of The People/Arthur Miller
An Even Exchange/Elaine G. Denholtz
An Evening At Home/Aubrey Wisberg
* An Evening In Our Century/Drury Pifer
An Evening Of Courteline/Eddie Lawrence
An Evening With The Avenger/T. C. Miller
An Evening With The Poet-Senator/Leslie

Weiner
An Evening With Richard Nixon/Gore
Vidal
An Exploratory Operation/Jonathan Levy
Angel City/Sam Shepard
Angelface/Richard Foreman
Angel, Honey, Baby, Darling,
Dear. . ./Robert Patrick
Angelina/Fred Saidy
Angel In The House/Drury Pifer
Angel On My Shoulder/Stephen Levi
Angels In Agony/Robert Patrick
An Hour With Poe: Out of Space, Out of
Time/Robert Kornfeld
Animal/Oliver Hailey
Animal Lovers/Donna de Matteo
Animals/Eddie Lawrence
* Animals Are Passing From Our
Lives/Robert H. Eisele
An Independent Woman/Daniel A. Stein
An Interview With F.Scott Fitzgerald/Paul
Hunter
An Island We Imagined/John R. Zapor
* Anne In The Camps/Patricia Goldstone
Annie Laurie/J. Lawrence & R.E. Lee
Anniversary/Knox Turner
* Anniversary, The/Mario Fratti
Anniversary Waltz/Jerome Chodorov
Annunciation, The/Maria I. Fornes
* An Old Family Recipe/Jack A. Kaplan
Anonymous Lover, The/Townsend
Brewster
An Opposite Attraction/Stephen Levi
Another Aida/A.R. Gurney, Jr.
Another Morning Rising/J.E. Franklin
Another Part Of The Forest/Lillian
Hellman
Another Quiet Evening At Home/Lonnie
Carter
Another Side Of Tomorrow/Lee Hunkins
Another Time/Michael Colby
Answer Is Two, The/Eugene McKinney
Anthony In The Desert/Wallace Hamilton
Anthropologists, The/Benjamin Bradford
An Unscheduled Appearance/Frederick
Bailey
Anyone Can Whistle/Arthur Laurents
Any Woman Can't/Wendy Wasserstein
Aphrodite/The Witch Play/E. Macer-Story
Appalachia Sounding/Romulus Linney
Apple A/Mike Firth
Apple, The/Jack Gelber
Apple-Brown Betty/Paula A. Vogel
Apple Pie/Myrna Lamb
Apples In Eden/Rose L. Goldemberg
Approaching Chimera/Allan Havis
* Approaching Simone/Megan Terry
* Approaching Zero/Thom Thomas
Apricot Cranberry Mince-Meat Peach
Pie/Robert W. Martin
* Arabic Two/Ruth Wolff
Arbor, The/Jonathan Ringkamp
Arbuckle's Rape/Louis Phillips
Archbishop's Ceiling, The/Arthur Miller
Archie's Comeback/Norman Beim
Arenas Of Lutetia/Ronald Tavel
Aretha In The Ice Palace or The Fully

Guaranteed Fuck-Me Doll/Tom Eyen
Are You Now Or Have You Ever Been
  Blue?/Leslie Weiner
Are You Prepared To Be a United States
  Marine/Sandra Scoppettone
* Arizona/F.V.Hunt
Ark Of Safety/Howard Richardson
Arm Yourself And Harm Yourself/Imamu
  A. Baraka
Arnold Bliss Show, The/Robert Patrick
* Around The Corner From The White
  House/Don Flynn
Around The World In 80 Days/A.R. Gurney,
  Jr.
Arrangement In Rose And
  Silver/Townsend Brewster
Arrival/Richard Lees
Arthur Ashe And I/Townsend Brewster
Arthur, King Of England/R. Eugene
  Jackson
* Artichoke/Joanna M. Glass
* Artists, The/Anna M. Barlow
* Art Of Dining, The/Tina Howe
Art Of Love, The/Robert Kornfeld
Arts And Letters/Jonathan Levy
As Above, So Below/Richard Olson
Ashes Of Mrs. Reasoner, The/Enid Rudd
As I Lay Dying, A Victim Of Spring/Leslie
  Lee
* As On A Darkling Plain/John McLiam
Aspern Papers, The/James L. Rosenberg
Assassination Of Robert F. Kennedy As
  Performed By Wives Of Our Armed
  Forces, The/Elizabeth Wyatt
* Assignment, The/Gertrude Samuels
As The Twig/Allen Boretz
* As To The Meaning of Words/Mark
  Eichman
Asylum/Arthur Kopit
* Asylum/Jerome McDonough
As You Can See/Steve Carter
At Last A Meeting Of Minds Takes
  Place/Crispin Larangeira
At Liberty/Tennessee Williams
Attempted Rescue On Avenue B/Megan
  Terry
At The Bus Stop/Kathy Hurley
At The End Of Long Island/Richard Lees
At The Gate/David Lifson
* At The Grand/Luther Davis
Augusta/Larry Ketron
Auntie Mame/J.Lawrence & R.E. Lee
* Aunts Of Antioch City/Nathan N.Barrett
Aurora/Maria I. Fornes
Australia Play/Sally Ordway
Autobiography Of Morgan Lefay,
  The/E.Macer-Story
Auto-Da-Fe/Tennessee Williams
* auto-destruct/Jeff Wanshel
Autograph Hound, The/James Prideaux
Autumn Garden, The/Lillian Hellman
Autumn's Laughter/Tobi Louis
* Avenue A Anthology/John Chodes
Avenue B/Jack Gilhooley
* Avenue Of Dream/Elyse Nass
* Avocado Kid or Zen In The Art Of

Guacamole, The/Philip K. Gotanda
* Axe Of Creation/Helen Duberstein

B

Baba Chops/Charles Gordone
Baba Goya/Steve Tesich
Babel, Babel, Little Tower/Doric Wilson
Babes In The Bighouse/Megan Terry
Baby/Drury Pifer
Baby Death, SOS And Other Anxiety
  Pieces For The Contemporary American
  Stage/Sharon S. Martin
* Baby Kids, The/Leonard Melfi
Baby With The Bath Water/Christopher
  Durang
Bacchae Rock, The/John Pyros
Back Bog Beast Bait/Sam Shepard
* Back County Crimes/Lanie Robertson
Backdoor Of Heaven/Jean Riley
Back In The Race/Milan Stitt
Backwards/Elyse Nass
* Bad Habits/Terrence McNally
Bad Place To Get Your Head, A/Robert
  Patrick
Bag Lady/Jean-Claude van Itallie
Bag Of Flies/Venable Herndon
Baker-Maker/Nathan N. Barrett
Balance Of Payments/Robert Lord
Ball/John Jiler
Ballad Of Brooklyn/Myrna Lamb
Ballad Of John Ogilvie, The/Ernest Ferlita
Ballad Of Santa's Happy Helpers/Gordon
  R. Watkins
Ballad Of The Sad Cafe, The/Edward
  Albee
Ballet Behind The Bridge, A/Lennox Brown
* Ballet In A Bear Pit, A/Lennox Brown
* Ball Game, The/Thom Thomas
Balloons And Other Ironies/Benjamin
  Bradford
Balloon Shot/Joe Manchester
* Ballroom In St. Patrick's Cathedral,
  The/Louis Phillips
Balls/Paul Foster
Balls: A Jock Comedy/John Kirk
Balm In Gilead/Lanford Wilson
Bang?/Ken Eulo
Bank Street Breakfast/Robert Patrick
* Banners/Anthony Damato
Banquet, The/Louis Phillips
Baptism, The/Imamu A. Baraka
Baptismal/Steve Tesich
Ba-Ra-Ka/Imamu A. Baraka
* Barbarians, The/Oyamo
Barbary Shore/Jack Gelber
Barbecue Pit, The/Donna de Matteo
Barefoot Antelope, The/David S. Milton
Barefoot Ballerina, The/Martha A. Fuentes
Barefoot In The Park/Neil Simon
* Bargainin' Thing/Daniel W. Owens
Barnaby Sweet/Glenn A. Smith
Barrel Of Monkeys/Tim Kelly
Baseball Play/Steve Metcalfe

Basement, The/Lennox Brown
Basement, The/Murray Schisgal
Basics/Susan Yankowitz
Basic Training Of Pavlo Hummel/David Rabe
Batman Bops The Book Bandits/John Pyros
Bats Of Portobello, The/Jerome Chodorov
Battle Cry/Paul Mroczka
Battle Hymn/Michael Blankfort
Battle Of Angels/Tennessee Williams
* Battle Of Valor, The/Norman Beim
Beach Children, The/John Von Hartz
Beach Club, The/Ludmilla Bollow
* Beaches/Paul Mroczka
Beach Grass/Megan Terry
Beals & Becker/Vincent Viaggio
Be A Sport/Marc P. Smith
Beau Johnny/Tim Kelly
Beautiful!/Leonard Melfi
Beautiful Mariposa, The/Eddie Lawrence
Beauty & The Beast/R. Eugene Jackson
Beauty/Truth/Lonnie Carter
Because I Said So/Myrna Lamb
Beclch/Rochelle Owens
Becoming Persons/Lennox Brown
Bed And Breakfast/Fredi Towbin
Bed Of Rose's/Dot DeCamp
Bedroom, The/M.H. Appleman
Before The Morning/Herschel Steinhardt
Before The Rain/Anthony Damato
* Beggar's Choice/Kathleen Betsko
Beggars In The Church/Lydia Simmons
Begone, Begonia/C.H. Keeney
Believers, The/Roma Greth
Bella Figura/Jonathan Ringkamp
* Belonging Place, A/C. Robert Jones
Bench, The/James Prideaux
Benedictus/Johnny Brandon
Benefit Of A Doubt/Edward J. Clinton
Benito/Allen Sternfield
Bent/Martin Sherman
* Benya The King/Richard Schotter
Bernie And The Beast/Marsha Sheiness
Bernie's Ballroom/W.Edwin Ver Becke
Berserkers, The/Warren Kliewer
* Bertha In Blue/Paula A. Vogel
Best All "Round"/Marsha Sheiness
Best Is Yet To Be, The/M.H. Appleman
Best Man, The/Gore Vidal
Best of Everybody, The/Bernard M. Kahn
Best Of Friends/James Elward
Betrayals/Mario Fratti
Betrothed, The/Jerome McDonough
Between Now And Then/Leslie Lee
Between The Dark & The Daylight/Ludmilla Bollow
* Beyond Consent/Steven Somkin
* Beyond Here Are Monsters/James Nicholson
Beyond Therapy/Christopher Durang
Bibi Robinson/Anthony Damato
* Bicicletta/Lonnie Carter
Bicycle Man, The/Edward J. Moore
Bicycle Riders, The/Anna M. Barlow
Big Alabama Wonder, The/Franklyn

MacGregor
* Big Apple Messenger/Shannon K. Kelley
Big Deal, The/Ossie Davis
Big Fish, Little Fish/Hugh Wheeler
Bigfoot/Ronald Tavel
Big Game, The/Herb Schapiro
Big Gate, The/Albert Evans
Big Hotel/Charles Ludlam
Big House, The/Lonnie Carter
Big Man, The Legend Of John Henry/Dianne Lampert
* Big Sell, The/Paul Mroczka
* Big Shot, The/Edan Schappert
Big Story, The/Lee Falk
Big Sur/Frank Gagliano
Big Tits/Lydia Simmons
Bilby's Doll/Sheppard Kerman
Billy/Seth Glassman
* Billy God/Harold Heifetz
Billy Irish/Thomas Babe
* Billy Noname/Johnny Brandon
Biograph, The/Lonnie Carter
Birdbath/Leonard Melfi
Bird Cage, The/Arthur Laurents
Bird In The Bush, A/Warren Kliewer
Bird Seed/Sharon S. Martin
Birds Of Passage/Benjamin Bradford
Birmingham/Rochelle H. Dubois
Birth And After Birth/Tina Howe
Birthday/Mario Fratti
Birthday/Jolene Goldenthal
Birth Of Venus, The/Frank M. Mosier
Bishop Street/Bruce Serlen
Bistro Car On The CNR, A/D.R. Andersen
Bitch Of Kynossema, The/Conrad Bishop
Bitch Of Waverly Place, The/Arthur Sainer
* Bit Of Almsgiving, A/June V. Williams
Bits And Pieces/Corinne Jacker
Bitter Exchange, A/Frederick Bailey
Black And Whitey/Howard Pflanzer
Black Angel/Michael Christofer
Black Antigone/William Hairston
Black-Belt Bertram/Townsend Brewster
Black Body Blues/Gus Edwards
Black Dog/Conrad Bishop
Black English/Louis Rivers
Black Girl/J.E.Franklin
Black Heat/Joseph Lizardi
Black Jesus/Ken Eulo
Black Mass/Imamu A. Baraka
* Black Medea/Ernest Ferlita
Black On White/Jack R. Guss
Black Pictures/Louis Rivers
Black Power Chant/Imamu A. Baraka
Black President, The/James Schevill
Black Princess, The/Kathy Hurley
Black Sermon Rock/John Scott
Black Sheep, The/Don Flynn
Black Terror, The/Richard E. Wesley
Black Thoughts On A Bright Monday/Gloria Gonzalez
Blakes Design/Kenneth H. Brown
Blanderbets, The/Jean Reavey
Blanko/Sam Havens
* Bleachers, The/Willard Manus
Blind Angel, The/Arthur Sainer

Blind Home Coming Near/Shannon K.
Kelley
Blind Junkie, The/Peter Copani
Blinking Heart, The/Lonnie Carter
Bliss Or A Psycho-Bedellic Attack/Peter
Copani
Block Party, The/Joseph Lizardi
Blood Brothers/Victor Power
Bloodletting/Susan Rivers
Blood Promise Of A Shopping Plaza,
The/Lennox Brown
* bloodrite, the/Owa
Bloodrites/Imamu A. Baraka
Blood, Sweat And Stanley Poole/James
Goldman
Bloody Tenet, The/James Schevill
Bloomer Girl/Fred Saidy
Bloom Is Off The Rose, The/A. Petrides &
D. Kagan
Bluebeard/Charles Ludlam
Bluebeard Had A Wife/Tim Kelly
Blue Bitch/Sam Shepard
Blue Collars/Joseph Lizardi
* Blue Magi, The/Sally D. Wiener
Blue Period Of Merv And Louise
Sandstrom, The/Raymond Platt
Blues Deduction, The/E.Macer-Story
Blues For Mr. Charlie/James Baldwin
* Blues Smile, The/Lennox Brown
Blvd DeParis/Richard Foreman
Bo/Amlin Gray
Boa Constrictor, The/Benjamin Bradford
Boarder & Mrs. Rifkin, The/Alan Havis
Board Of Education/Imamu A. Baraka
Boardwalk (With 2 Houses)/Mark Eisman
Boat Sun Cavern/Arthur Sainer
Boccaccio Rhythm Theater, The/T.C.
Miller
Body & The Wheel, The/William Gibson
Body Beautiful, The/Joseph Stein
Bodybuilders, The/Michael Weller
Bogey's Back/Paul Foster
Bolo/Robert W. Martin
Bomb Flower, The/Arthur Sainer
Bone Of Contention/Dot DeCamp
Bonner Method, The/Frank Salisbury
* Bonus, The/Maxwell Glanville
Bonus March/Wallace Hamilton
* Bon Voyage/Edward Mabley
Boogey Man, The/Edward Clinton
Boogie Woogie Landscapes/Ntozake
Shange
* Booji/B. Molette & C. Molette
Bookcase, The/Richard Olson
Booking The Nile Circuit/Mark Stein
Book Of Lambert, The/Leslie Lee
Book Of Murder, The/Ron Cowen
Book Of Splendor:Pt 1/Richard Foreman
Book Of Splendor:Pt 2/Richard Foreman
Booth Brothers, The/Warren Kliewer
Borders/Charles Eastman
Boris, Beware/Howard Pflanzer
Born Yesterday/Garson Kanin
* Bosoms And Neglect/John Guare
Bosses/Mario Fratti
Boston Proper/J.J. Coyle
Botticelli/Terrence McNally

Bottoms Up/F.V. Hunt
Bough Break, The/James Childs
Bouquet For Lorraine/Louis Rivers
Bourgeois Blues/Larry Loonin
Box/Edward Albee
Box, The/Daniel W. Owens
Box, The/Sheldon Rosen
Boxes/Valerie Harris
* Boxes/Susan Yankowitz
Boxing Day/Billy Bozzone
* Boy On The Straight-Back Chair/Ronald
Tavel
Boys & Girls Together/Lydia Simmons
Boys In Autumn, The/Bernard Sabath
Boys In The Band, The/Mart Crowley
Boy Tarzan Appears In A Clearing/Imamu
A. Baraka
* Boy Who Made Magic, The/Francis H.
Stanton
Brain, The/Helen Duberstein
Brambles On The Sheepskin/Ramon
Delgado
Brass Birds Don't Sing/Samm-Art Williams
Brass Ring/Peggy Phillips
Brazil Fado/Megan Terry
* Bread/David S. Milton
Break A Leg/Ira Levin
Breakfast, Lunch, And Dinner/Corinne
Jacker
Breaking The Sweet Glass/Mark Stein
Break In The Skin, A/Ronald Ribman
Breakout, The/OyamO
Break Up/Ernest A. Joselovitz
Breech Baby, The/Leonard Melfi
Breeding Ground/Edward M. Cohen
Breeze From The Gulf, A/Mart Crowley
Brer Rabbit's Big Secret/R. Eugene
Jackson
* Brewster Papers, The/Marc P. Smith
Briar Rose/C.E.Wilkinson
Bridal Dinner, The/A.R. Gurney, Jr.
Bridal Party, The/A.R. Gurney, Jr.
Bride Of Frankenstein/Tim Kelly
Bridge, The/Oscar Brand
Bridge, The/Mario Fratti
Bridge, The/Robert Kornfeld
* Bridge At Belharbour, The/Janet L. Neipris
Bridgehead, The/Frederick Bailey
Brief And Violent Reign Of Absalom,
The/James D. Pendleton
Brief Vacation, A/Lydia Simmons
Brig, The/Kenneth H. Brown
* Bright And Golden Land, The/Harry
Granick
* Bright Wings/Lloyd Gold
Brigitte Berger/Stanley Taikeff
Bringing It All Back Home/Terrence
McNally
Bringing Mother Down/Lanie Robertson
Brink Of Glory, The/Peggy Phillips
Brixton Recovery, The/Jack Gilhooley
* Broken Borders/Elizabeth Wray
Broken Lease, The/Helen Duberstein
Brontosaurus/Lanford Wilson
Brooklyn Bridge Is Falling Down/Joseph
Hart
Brothel, The/Mario Fratti

* Brother Champ/Michael Kassin
Brother Of Dragons/Ramon Delgado
Brothers O'Toole, The/Tim Kelly
Broussard Bunch, The/J.E. Franklin
Brownstone/Israel Horovitz
* Brownsville Raid, The/Charles Fuller
Brutesong/Frederick A. Raborg, Jr.
* Bubba/Sam Havens
Bubble, The/Ernest A. Joselovitz
* Buddy Pals/Neil Cuthbert
Buffoons/David Lifson
Bugs/Benjamin Bradford
Bugs And Other Animals/Mark Eichman
Builder, The/C.H. Keeney
Bullet Headed Birds/Philip K. Gotanda
Bull Fight Cow/Allen Davis III
Bumper Snickers/R. Eugene Jackson
Bumper To Bumper/Sam Havens
Bumps And Grinds/Hiram Taylor
Bum Sunday/Seymour Simckes
Bungalow/Joseph G. Gottfried
Bunny Boy/Wallace Hamilton
Bunny Hop/Jean Reavey
Burial Of Esposito/Ronald Ribman
Buried Child/Sam Shepard
Burning Man, The/Tim Kelly
Burning Of The Lepers, The/Wallace
Hamilton
Burning Sky, The/Lennox Brown
* Bury My Knee At Wounded Groin/Carl
Larsen
Business Of Relations/Larry Loonin
Bus Play And Slipt/Daniel W. Owens
Bust, The/Benjamin R. Barber
* Busy Bee Good Food All Night
Delicious/Charles Eastman
Butcher Shop, The/Myrna Lamb
Butler Carries The Sun Away, The/Stanley
Nelson
Butler Did It, The/Tim Kelly
* Butterfaces/Leonard Melfi
* Butterfingers Angel, Mary And Joseph,
Herod The Nut, And The Slaughter Of
12 Hit Carols In A Pear Tree,
The/William Gibson
* Button Pusher, The/Samuel Sussman
But What Have You Done For Me
Lately?/Myrna Lamb
But Why Bump Off Barnaby?/Jack
Sharkey
Buzzards, The/Mars Hill
Byron/Kathy Hurley
Byron/Jack Larson

C

Cabin Fever/Joan Schenkar
* Cabrona/Cynthia Buchanan
Cacciatore I: Charlie And Vito/Joseph T.
Pintauro
Cacciatore II: Flywheel And Anna/Joseph
T. Pintauro
Cacciatore III: Uncle Zepp/Joseph T.
Pintauro
Cactus Flower/Abe Burrows

Cafe Con Leche/Gloria Gonzalez
* Cafe Society/D.R. Andersen
* Cafeteria Style Lunch/David Trainer
Cage, The/Mario Fratti
Cage, The/Mars Hill
Cage, The/Lee Hunkins
Cage, The/Susan Yankowitz
Caged/Mark Berman
Caged/Mark Eichman
* Cages/Gordon R. Watkins
Caine Mutiny Court-Martial, The/Herman
Wouk
* Cakes With The Wine/Edward M. Cohen
California Suite/Neil Simon
Calliope/M.H. Appleman
Call Me By My Rightful Name/Michael
Shurtleff
Call On Kuprin, A/J. Lawrence & R.E. Lee
Calm Down Mother/Megan Terry
Camille/Barbara Field
Camille/Charles Ludlam
Camino Real/Tennessee Williams
* Campion/William Griffin
* Canadian Gothic-American
Modern/Joanna M. Glass
Can-Can/Abe Burrows
Candidate, The/Charles Fuller
Candide/Lillian Hellman
Candide/Hugh Wheeler
* Candied House, The/Jack Larson
C & W/Michael Colby
Canned Soul/Sharon S. Martin
Can Of Peas, A/Allen Boretz
Canterville Ghost, The/Tim Kelly
Canticle Of The Nightingale/Ronald Tavel
Can You See A Prince?/Tom Eyen
* Canzada And The Boys/Sam Havens
Caprice/Charles Ludlam
Captain Cook/Aldyth Morris
Captain Fantastic/Tim Kelly
Captain Nemo And His Magical
Marvelous Submarine Machine/Tim
Kelly
Captivity Of Pixie Shedman, The/Romulus
Linney
* Car/N. Selden & M. Imbrie
* Care And Feeding Of Poultry, The/Barbara
Graham
Carlisle Commission, The/Lanie
Robertson
Car Lover, The/Bruce Jay Friedman
Carmelina/Joseph Stein
Carob Trees, The/Jack Larson
Carol In Winter Sunlight/Arthur Sainer
Carolyn/Toni Press
Car Pool/Joanne Koch
Carriage, The/Jolene Goldenthal
Carrie/Jean Nuchtern
Casanova And His Mother/Daniel Lipman
* Casa Rosa/Lucile Bogue
Case Of Peppermint Gum, A/Louis Rivers
Case Of The Crushed Petunias,
The/Tennessee Williams
Case Of The Curious Moonstone, The/Tim
Kelly
Cashmere Love/F.V. Hunt
Casket Maker, The/Richard Stockton

Cask Of Amontillado/Sy Reiter
Casserole/Jack Heifner
Cassiopea/Roma Greth
Castaways, The/D. R. Andersen
Castle Of Otranto, The/R. Eugene Jackson
Castro St./Joel Ensana
Cat And the Cock/Susan Griffin
Catch A Crab/Wendy MacLaughlin
Catch A Star/Neil Simon
Cathedral Of Ice/James Schevill
Cat In A Cage/Howard Richardson
Cat On A Hot Tin Roof/Tennessee
  Williams
Caught/Bernard M. Kahn
Caution: A Love Story/Tom Eyen
Cavalier, The/Robert H. Eisele
Cave, The/Tim Kelly
Cavorting With The Whartons/Mars Hill
C.C. Pyle And The Bunyon Derby/Michael
  Christofer
* C.C. Ryder In "Behind The Dunes"/Robert
  Unger
Cedars Mark The Campground/Lanny
  Flaherty
Celebrate America/Nancy Henderson
Celebrate Me!/Edan Schappert
Celebration/Mars Hill
* Celebration, The: Jooz/Guns/Movies/The
  Abyss/Arthur Sainer
Cellar, The/George Freek
'Cello Days At Dixon's Place/Michael
  Weller
Cells/James L. Rosenberg
Cenci Myth, The/Larry Loonin
Centipede/Carl Larsen
Ceremony Of Innocence/Ronald Ribman
Challah and Raspberries/June Calender
Chamber Music/Arthur Kopit
Chamber #8/Crispin Larangeira
Chambers/Paul S. Lim
Change Of Mind/Jonathan Ringkamp
Changes/Megan Terry
Changes: A Love Story/George Hammer
Chapel/Wendy MacLaughlin
Chapter Two/Neil Simon
Character Lines/Larry Ketron
Characters In A Play/Vernon Hinkle
Charade/Jolene Goldenthal
Charcoals And Pastels/Benjamin Bradford
Charles & Tribulations/Theodore Gross
Charles Fuller Presents The Dynamic
  Jerry Bland & His Blandelles With The
  Fabulous Miss Marva Jane/Charles
  Fuller
* Charley Chestnut Rides The I.R.T./Arthur
  Sainer
Charley's Charmers/Tim Kelly
* Charlie The Chicken/Jonathan Levy
Charlie Was Here And Now He's
  Gone/Dennis L. Turner
Charlotte Sweet/Michael Colby
Chattering Illiterates, The/Robert Patrick
* Cheaters/Michael Jacobs
Cheesecake/Robert Patrick
Che Guevara/Mario Fratti
* Cherry, Larry, Sandy, Doris, Jean,
  Paul/Jack Larson

Cherry Orchard, The/Jean-Claude van
  Itallie
Cherry Soda Water/The Gulf Of
  Crimson/Stephen Levi
Chessman/Norman Beim
Chicago/Sam Shepard
Chief Rathebe/Townsend Brewster
* Chieftains/James Childs
* Childe Byron/Romulus Linney
* Children/A.R. Gurney, Jr.
Children At The White House/David Lifson
Children Of A Lesser God/Mark Medoff
Children Of The Land/Toni Press
* Children's Army Is Late, The/Arthur Sainer
Children's Hour, The/Lillian Hellman
Children's Religious One Acts/Mark
  Edwards
Chile, 1973/Mario Fratti
Chimera/John R. Zapor
China Takes Eleven Hours/Arthur Sainer
Chinese, The/Murray Schisgal
Chinese Box, The/Elizabeth Wyatt
Chinese Caper, The/Sally Ordway
Chinese Friend, The/Mario Fratti
Chinese Restaurant Syndrome/Corinne
  Jacker
Chinese Screen, The/China C. Pendarvis
* Chinese Viewing Pavilion, The/Gus
  Kaikkonen
Chipmunk Heaven/Jack A. Kaplan
* Chip Off Olympus/Jules Tasca
Chisler's Paradise/Antoni Gronowicz
* Chocolate Cake/Mary Gallagher
Chocolat Volatil/Townsend Brewster
Choices/Pete Copani
Choices/Joseph G. Gottfried
Choir Practice/Romulus Linney
Choose A Spot On The Floor/Megan Terry
Chords/Jeffrey Sweet
Choreography Of Love, The/Townsend
  Brewster
Chorus Line, A/James Kirkwood
Chosen Room, A/John Pielmeier
* Christchild/J.E. Franklin
Christina's World/Ronald Tavel
Christine Fonnegra/Frank M. Mosier
Christmas Carol, A/Barbara Field
Christmas Carol, A/Israel Horovitz
Christmas Carol, A/Charles Ludlam
Christmas Carol, A/Jerome McDonough
Chronicles Of Bohikee Creek/Robert
  Unger
Chuck/Jack Larson
Chucky's Hunch/Rochelle Owens
Cinder-Ella/R. Eugene Jackson
Cinderella Revisited/Tom Eyen
* Cindy/Johny Brandon
* Cindy/Maxwell Glanville
Cinnamon Rolls/June Calender
Cinque/Leonard Melfi
Circa 1933/Allen Sternfield
Circle, The/Paul Mroczka
Circumstance/Benjamin Bradford
* Circus Animals' Desertion, The/Patricia
  Goldstone
Circus Lady/Jason Miller
Circus Once, The/Vernon Hinkle

Citizen Number One/Lucile Bogue
City At 4 A.M., The/Bruce Serlen
City Has Lost Its Angels, The/J. Lawrence & R.E. Lee
City Life/Elyse Nass
* City Mouse. . .Country Mouse/Charles Horine
Claire And The Chair/Marsha Sheiness
Clair-Obscur/Israel Horovitz
Clara's Ole Man/Ed Bullins
Clara's Play/John Olive
Classical Spirit, The/William Griffin
Classical Therapy/Richard Foreman
Clay's Rebellion/Ossie Davis
Clean/Daniel W. Owens
Cleaning House/Robert Patrick
Cleaning Women, The/George Hammer
Clean Sweep, A/Lennox Brown
* Clearing/N. Selden & M. Imbrie
Clearing In The Woods, A/Arthur Laurents
Cleavages/Lee Goldsmith
Clementina/Robert Kornfeld
Cleobis And Bito/Ronald Tavel
Cleopatra/Richard Henrickson
Clews/Ted Tally
Climate Of Noon/John R. Zapor
* Clocks, The/Carl Larsen
Clone People, The/Jack Sharkey
* Close Relations/Leslie Weiner
Closet Drama/Howard Pflanzer
· * Close Ties/Elizabeth Diggs
Closing The Halls Where Once Fatima Stood/Lanie Robertson
Clothes For A Summer Hotel/Tennessee Williams
Clown, The/C. Robert Jones
Clowns' Corner Concert, The/Ray Aranha
Clown's Tail, The/Ronald Tavel
* Club, The/Yale Udoff
Club Cotton/Joe T. Ford
* Coal Diamond, The/Shirley M. Lauro
Coat Of Many Colors/Barrie Stavis
* Cock May Crow, The/John McLiam
Cocktail Party/Edan Schappert
* Cocktails And Hor D'Oeuvres/Hiram Taylor
Cocktail Sip, The/Townsend Brewster
* Cock To Asclepius, A/Stanley Taikeff
Coconut Folk-Singer/Rochelle Owens
Code 99/Benjamin Bradford
Coffin, The/Mario Fratti
Cold Christmas/Anna M. Barlow
Cold Pipes/Elizabeth Wray
Cold Storage/Ronald Ribman
Cold Storage/Elizabeth Wray
Collection Of Short Plays, A/Jerome Kass
Colonel Is An Emigre, The/Eddie Lawrence
Colonial Dudes, The/Martin B. Duberman
Color Of Heat, The/Saul Zachary
Colors Of Conscience/Antoni Gronowicz
Columbia, Gem Of The Ocean/Imamu A. Baraka
Comeback, The/Jack Gilhooley
Comeback, The/A.R. Gurney, Jr.
Comeback, The/Israel Horovitz
* Comeback Act, The/Myrna Lamb

Come Blow Your Horn/Neil Simon
Come Into The House Of Jane/W. Edwin Ver Becke
Come Marching Home/Robert Anderson
Come Next Tuesday/Frank D. Gilroy
Come On Strong/Garson Kanin
Comes A Time/Crispin Larangeira
* Comes Tomorrow/George Hammer
Come Up And See My Casserole/Frank M. Mosier
Coming, The/Samm-Art Williams
Coming Attractions/Ted Tally
* Coming Of Age/Barbara Field
* Coming Out/Joanne Koch
Comings And Goings/Megan Terry
* Coming To Terms/Michael Shurtleff
* Commedia World Of Lafcadio Bean, The/Frank Gagliano
Commentaries On "The Tibetian Book Of The Dead"/Lanie Robertson
Commitment, The/Joseph Lizardi
Commitments And Other Alternatives/Norman Kline
* Common Garden Variety/Jane Chambers
Communion In Dark Sun, A/Lennox Brown
Community Of Two/Jerome Chodorov
Companion, The/Lydia Simmons
Company/George Furth
Competitors, The/Jack Gilhooley
* Complaint Department Closes At Five, The/Edward M. Cohen
Complete Works Of Kalkbrenner, The/Townsend Brewster
Concentric Circles/Benjamin Bradford
Concert Grande/Owa
Conditioned Reflex/Curtis Zahn
Conerico Was Here To Stay/Frank Gagliano
Confession, The/D.L. Coburn
Confessional/Tennessee Williams
* Confessions Of A Female Disorder/Susan Miller
Confdence Man, The/Ray E. Fox
Conflict Of Interest/Jay Broad
Con-fron-ta-tion/Curtis Zahn
Congo Square/Frank Gagliano
Connection, The/Jack Gelber
Conpersonas/Paul S. Lim
Conquest Of Everest/Arthur Kopit
Conquest of Helen, The/Leonard L. Perlmutter
Conquest Of The Universe/When Queens Collide/Charles Ludlam
Consanguine/Lanny Flaherty
* Consenting Adults/Richard Seff
Conservation Menace, The/Robert Patrick
Consoling Virgin, The/Bruce Serlen
Contemporary Flesh, The/William Griffin
* Contest, The/Shirley M. Lauro
Continental Divide/Oliver Hailey
* Continual And Repeated Murder Of George, The/Allen Boretz
Contract, The/Joseph Lizardi
Contretemps/Lanny Flaherty
Convention Of Tuba Players Convenes In Fat City, A/Louis Phillips
Conversation/Allen Boretz

Conversation Piece/Benjamin Bradford
Conversion, The/Lennox Brown
Conversion Of Aaron Weiss, The/Mark
  Medoff
Convertible Teacher, The/Tim Kelly
Coocooshay/Robert Auletta
Cop, The/Howard Pflanzer
Cophetua/S. Garrett Robinson
Copout!/Helen Duberstein
Cop-Out/John Guare
Cops/Terry C. Fox
Cops & Robbers/Leslie Lee
Cop Shop/Robert Lord
Coralville, U.S.A./Brendan N. Ward
Corn/Charles Ludlam
* Cornelius, The Last/Robert W. Martin
Corner, The/Ed Bullins
Cornered/Robert Patrick
Corner Of God/Louis C. Adelman
Corners/Elizabeth Wray
Cornerstone/John Sedlak
Corner, 28th And Bank/Linda Segal
Coronation, The/Joel Ensana
Coronation Of The Black Queen,
  The/Imamu A. Baraka
* Corridor, The/Diane Kagan
* Corrupters, The/Gertrude Samuels
Cosmo And Company/Crispin Larangeira
Costume Ball, The/Norman Beim
Counter/Cultures: 1967/Ron Whyte
* Counterpart Cure, The/Jeffrey Kindley
Counting The Ways/Edward Albee
Country Boy/Sallie Bingham
Country Gothic/Tim Kelly
* Couple Of The Year/Sam Havens
* Couples/Joseph Lizardi
Couplings And Groupings/Megan Terry
Courage & Rose/Eric M. Lord
Court/Tom Eyen
Cousin's Castle/Joseph T. Pintauro
Cowboy And The Legend, The/Benjamin
  Bradford
Cowboy Mouth/Sam Shepard
Cowboy Pictures/Larry Ketron
* Cowboys/Paul Mroczka
Cowboys/Sam Shepard
Cowboys #2/Sam Shepard
Coyote Hotel/Frederick Bailey
Crabs/Sally Ordway
Crabs In A Bucket/Louis Rivers
* Crab Quadrille/Myrna Lamb
Crack/Crispin Larangeira
* Cracks/Martin Sherman
Cracks In The Grand Old Manse/Jean
  Reavey
Crawling Arnold/Jules Feiffer
Crazy, Mixed-up Island Of Dr. Moreau/Tim
  Kelly
* Crazy Niggers/OyamO
Crazy Paper Caper, The/J. Eugene
  Jackson
Cream Cheese/Lonnie Carter
Creation, The/J. E. Franklin
Creation Of The World & Other Business,
  The/Arthur Miller
Creature Creeps!, The/Jack Sharkey
Creedmore/Ray Aranha

Creeps By Night/Tim Kelly
Creepy Castle Hassle, The/R. Eugene
  Jackson
Cretan Bull, The/Kenneth H. Brown
Crime, The/Michael Blankfort
* Crimes Of The Heart/Beth Henley
Crisscross/Oliver Hailey
Crisscrosscreeks/Lanny Flaherty
Critics Choice/Ira Levin
Crocodile Smile, The/J. Lawrence &
  R.E. Lee
Crop Rotation/James Nicholson
Cross Country/Susan Miller
Cross-Eyed Bear, The/Eugene McKinney
Crossroad, The/Rose L. Goldemberg
* Crown Of Thorn/Wendy MacLaughlin
Crucible, The/Arthur Miller
* Cruising Speed 500 MPH/Anna M. Barlow
Cry Louder Than A Black Cat/Elyse Nass
Cry Of A Summer Night/Tobi Louis
Cry Of Players, A/William Gibson
Cry Of The Banshee/Tim Kelly
* Crystal Chandelier/W. Edwin Ver Becke
Cuban Thing, The/Jack Gelber
Cuba Si!/Terrence McNally
Curfew!/Jane Chambers
Curing Of Eddie Stoker, The/Lanie
  Robertson
Curious In L.A./Glenn A. Smith
* Current As A Sometime Thing/Knox
  Turner
Curse Of The Langston House, The/Maria
  I. Fornes
Curse Of The Starving Class/Sam Shepard
Curtain Call/Roma Greth
Curtain Call, Mr. Aldridge Sir/Ossie Davis
Curtain Call, Mr. Aldridge Sir!!/William
  Hairston
* Curtains/Gloria Gonzalez
Curtains/Marc A. Zagoren
Custer/Robert E. Ingham
Cut Of The Axe/Sheppard Kerman
Cut Out The Lights And Call The Law/J. E.
  Franklin
* Cut-Ups & Cut-Outs/Nathan N. Barrett
cyklops I/Owa

D

* daBones Of Babylon/A.E.O. Goldman
Daddy/Ed Bullins
Daddy/A Commotion Of Zebras/Susan
  Miller
Daddy Beautiful, Hot Pants And Little
  Blue Jewel/Robert Riche
Daddy's Boys/Michael Jacobs
* Daddy's Duet/Clifford Turknett
Daddy's Girl/Elizabeth Diggs
Daisy At The Dance/Frederick A. Raborg, Jr.
* Dalliance/Marc A. Zagoren
* Dame Lorraine/Steve Carter
* Damien/Aldyth Morris
Damien Letter/Aldyth Morris
Damned Thing, The/Martin Halpern
* Damon's Song/William F. Brown

Dance And The Railroad, The/David H. Hwang
Dance Next Door, The/David Trainer
* Dance On A Country Grave/Kelly Hamilton
Dance On Saturday Night, The/Stephen Levi
* Dancers/Brendan N. Ward
Dance To A Nosepicker's Drum/Maxwell Glanville
Dancin' To Calliope/Jack Gilhooley
Daniel Boone/Thomas Babe
Daniel Boone/Earl H. Smith
Danse Macabre #2/George Freek
Dante/Imamu A. Baraka
Daphne In Cottage D/Stephen Levi
Dark Ages/Kevin O'Morrison
Dark And The Day, The/Sheppard Kerman
Dark Corner Of An Empty Room, The/Norman Beim
Dark Corridor/W. Edwin Ver Becke
Dark Corridor, The/Richard Reich
Dark Deeds At Swan's Place/Tim Kelly
Dark Moon And The Full, The/Joseph Hart
* Darkness, Fierce Winds/James Childs
* Dark Night Of The Soul, A/Robert Eisele
Dark Night Of The Theatre/Lanie Robertson
Dark Of The Moon/Howard Richardson
Dark Pony/Mamet David
Dark Room, The/Tennessee Williams
Dark Voice, The/James Schevill
Darwin High-Point/Stanley Disney
Das Lusitania Songspiel/Christopher Durang
Date, The/Joel Ensana
Daughter Of A Traveling Lady/Peter Dee
Daughter Of The Giant/Bernard Sabath
Daughters Of Abraham/Thomas G. Dunn
Daughters Of Lot, The/Warren Kliewer
David & Jonathan/Norman Beim
David Show, The/A. R. Gurney, Jr.
* Davis J/Lloyd Gold
Dawn Man, The/Leonard L. Perlmutter
Daydreams/Crispin Larangeira
Day For Surprises, A/John Guare
* Day In The Life, A/Richard France
Day In The Port Authority, A/Gloria Gonzalez
Day Of Grace, A/Charles Frink
Day Old Bread: The Worst Good Time I Ever Had/Arthur Sainer
Days Ahead/Lanford Wilson
Days And Nights Of An Ice Cream Princess/Sandra Bertrand
Days Between, The/Robert Anderson
* Day Six/Martin Halpern
Day Speaks But Cannot Weep, The/Arthur Sainer
Days To Come/Lillian Hellman
* Day The Marching Band Went Wild, The/Mark Berman
Day The Whores Came Out To Play Tennis, The/Arthur Kopit
Dead And Never Called Me Mother/Robert Lord
* Deadly Nightshade/Jane Chambers
* Dead Man's Bluff/Mario Fratti

Dead Stars/Louis Phillips
* Dealers' Choice/Marsha Sheiness
Dear Carmine DeSapio/Leonard Melfi
Dear Ignatius, Dear Isabel/Ernest Ferlita
Dear John/Steven Somkin
Dear Mr. Giordano/Donna de Matteo
Dearo Family/Priscilla B. Dewey
Dear Whitey/John Pyros
Dear World/J. Lawrence & R.E. Lee
* Death And Life Of Sneaky Fitch, The/James L. Rosenberg
Death Comes To Us All, Mary Agnes/Christopher Durang
Death In The Rose Arbor, A/Sandra Bertrand
Deathlist/Ed Bullins
Death Of A Baptist In A Small Southern Town/Lydia Simmons
Death Of Anton Webern, The/James Schevill
Death Of A Salesman/Arthur Miller
Death Of Bernard, The/Believer, The/Israel Horovitz
Death Of Bessie Smith, The/Edward Albee
Death Of Eagles, The/Harding Lemay
Death Of King Phillip, The/Romulus Linney
Death Of Malcolm X, The/Imamu A. Baraka
Death Of Martha Washington, Jr., The/David K. Heefner
Deathtrap/Ira Levin
Debris/Peter Swet
Deceitful Marriage, The/Tim Kelly
* December In New York/Joseph Lizardi
December Wedge/Ross MacLean
Decision/Leonard L. Perlmutter
Decision, The/Lanie Robertson
Deed From The King Of Spain, A/James Baldwin
* Deepest Hunger, The/Willard Manus
Deep Heat/Sharon S. Martin
* Deep River/Bruce Serlen
Defender, The/James D. Pendleton
Degenerate, The/Frank M. Mosier
Deja Vu/Charles Leipart
Delicate Balance, A/Edward Albee
Deli's Fable/Susan Dworkin
Delly's Oracle/Benjamin R. Barber
Delta/Robert Pine
Delta Lady/Martin Sherman
Demented World Of Tom Eyen, The/Tom Eyen
Demeter's Lost Daughter/Bruce Serlen
Democracy/Romulus Linney
Demolition Downtown/Tennessee Williams
Denim Lecture/Susan Miller
Dennis And Rex/Shannon K. Kelley
Denoument/Stanley Taikeff
'Dentity Crisis/Christopher Durang
Departemento De Soltero/Richard Reich
Departure, The/Joel Ensana
* Der Lumpentanzer/Frank M. Mosier
Der Ring Gott Farblonjet/Charles Ludlam
* Descendants/Jack Gilhooley
Desdemona/Paula A. Vogel

APPENDIX

Desert, The/Janet L. Neipris
* Deserter, The/Norman Beim
Desiderata/E. Macer-Story
Design For A Stained Glass Window/Howard Richardson
Desolate Place Near A Deep Hole, A/Sally Ordway
Dessie/Conrad Bishop
* Details Without A Map/Barbara Schneider
Detours/Elyse Nass
Devices/Kenneth H.Brown
Devil In The Grass/Peter Dee
Devil Mas'/Lennox Brown
* Devour The Snow/Abe Polsky
Diaghilev & Nijinsky/Robert Patrick
Dialect Determinism/Ed Bullins
Dianna Paxton, Dancer/June Calender
Dick And Jane/Jules Feiffer
Different Drummer, A/Eugene McKinney
Dilly/J. Lawrence & R.E. Lee
Dilly, The/Raymond Platt
Dimensions Of A Peacock/Paul Zindel
Dinner Party, The/Richard Olson
Dinny & The Witches/William Gibson
* Dinosaur Door, The/Barbara Garson
Dirge/Jerome McDonough
Dirt Boat, The/Megan Terry
Dirtiest Show In Town, The/Tom Eyen
Dirty Dove, The/Jean Riley
Dirty Old Man, The/Avra Petrides
Dirty Work In High Places/Tim Kelly
Disability: A Comedy/Ron Whyte
Discrimination For Everybody/Edward Mabley
Disfiguration/Leonard Melfi
Dishpan Hands/Hiram Taylor
Disintegration Of Della Longstreet, The/Norman Beim
* Disintegration Of James Cherry, The/Jeff Wanshel
Disposable Woman, The/Frederic Hunter
Distant Relations/Sheppard Kerman
* Disturbing Death Of Ernie Melia, The/Patricia Goldstone
Divine Revelation Never Ending Whisky/Brendan N. Ward
Division Street/Steve Tesich
DMZ Political Cabaret/Fredi Towbin
* Does Anybody Here Do The Peabody?/Enid Rudd
Does The Name Pavlov Ring A Bell?/Mark Stein
Dog/Sam Shepard
Dog Ran Away, The/Jonathan Ringkamp
Dog That Was, The/Aldyth Morris
Do I Hear A Waltz?/Arthur Laurents
Doillies/Benjamin Bradford
Doing A Good One For The Red Man/Mark Medoff
* Doll, The/W. Edwin Ver Becke
* Dolls, The/Lee Hunkins
Domestic Issues/Corinne Jacker
Donald Duck/T. C. Miller
Don Juan In Texas/Arthur Kopit
Don Juan Of Flatbush/Stanley Taikeff
* Donnegan's Crusade/Charles Frink

Don't Cry, Child, Your Father's In America/Herb Schapiro
Don't Drink The Water/Woody Allen
* Don't Go Gentle Into The Night/Faizul B. Khan
Don't Tell My Mother I'm Living In Sin/Victor Power
Don't You Know It's Raining/Richard France
Doomed Love/Bruce Serlen
* Doomsday Conspiracy, The/Leonard L. Perlmutter
Doorbell, The/Mario Fratti
* Doors/Benjamin R. Barber
Do Re Mi/Garson Kanin
* Double Exposure/Jack Sharkey
Double Feature/Joseph Julian
Double Fraktur L, A/Benjamin Bradford
Double Play/Gloria Gonzalez
* Doubleplay/Edward Mabley
Double Shift/Elizabeth Wray
Dough/F. V. Hunt
Do Unto Others/Samm-Art Williams
Down/Elyse Nass
* Down At Maggie Macomber's/J.J. Coyle
* Down By the Gravois (Under The Anheuser-Busch)/James Nicholson
Down On The Farm/John Von Hartz
Downstairs Boys, The/Murray Schisgal
* Downstairs Dragon, The/John Finch
Down Under/McCrea Imbrie
Dracula, King Of The Night/Anthony Scully
Dracula, The Vampire Play/Tim Kelly
Dragon Of The Six Resemblances, The/Aldyth Morris
Dramatic Instincts/Frederic Hunter
Drat! The Cat!/Ira Levin
* Dr. B. S. Black/B. & C. Molette
Dr. Cook's Garden/Ira Levin
Dr. Denton's Secret/Joseph G. Gottfried
* Dreambelly/Conrad Bishop
Dream Lover/Joel Ensana
Dream Lover/Jack Sharkey
Dreams/Norman Beim
* Dreams And Victims/Charles Frink
Dreams Of Glory/Frank D. Gilroy
Dream Of Swallows, A/Paul Zindel
Dream Tantras/Richard Foreman
Dressed In Clean Clothes/Louis C. Adelman
Dreyfus In Rehearsal/Garson Kanin
Dr. Fish/Murray Schisgal
Dr. Hero/Israel Horovitz
Dribble/Paula A. Vogel
Drive-In/Richard Olson
Driving Yourself Crazy/Michael Shurtleff
* Dr. Jekyll And Mr. Hyde/James P. Marvin
Dr. Kheal/Maria I. Fornes
Dr. Miner/Lydia Simmons
Dr. Selavy's Magic Theater/Richard Foreman
* Drums Carry A Far Distance/Lucille Bogue
* Dr. Zastro's Sanatorium For The Ailments Of Women — Mental, Physical & Sexual/Ludmilla Bollow

* **Duchess Of Santiago, The**/Frank M. Mosier
Ducks And Lovers/Murray Schisgal
Duck Variations, The/David Mamet
Duet/David S. Milton
Duet/Hiram Taylor
Duet For Parents/Stanley Taikeff
Duet For Solo Voice/David S. Milton
Dumas & Son/Jerome Chodorov
Dumping Ground/Elizabeth Diggs
Dune Road/Joseph G. Gottfried
Dungalore/Brendan N. Ward
Dungmen Are Coming, The/Elaine G. Denholtz
Dungyard/James Schevill
Duplex, The/Ed Bullins
* **During The War**/Michael Shurtleff
Dust To Dust/Yale Udoff
Dutchman/Imamu A. Baraka
Dwarfman/Michael Weller
Dwelling/Sheldon Rosen

E

Eagle & The Rock, The/Frank M. Mosier
* **Early Bird**/John Jiler
Earthworms/Albert Innaurato
Easy Money/Leonard L. Perlmutter
Eat At Joe's/Megan Terry
Eat Cake/Jean-Claude van Itallie
Ebur And Ebony/Townsend Brewster
Eccentricities Of A Nightingale/Tennessee Williams
Echoes/N. Richard Nash
Eclipse/Mars Hill
Eclipse/J. Lawrence & R.E. Lee
Eclipse Day/Bernard Sabath
Ecologists, The/Townsend Brewster
Eddie In The Doorway/Neal Black
* **Eden**/Steve Carter
Eden/Jerome McDonough
Eden Again/Ruth Wolff
Eden Rose, The/Robert Anderson
Edge Of The Knife/Henry Gilfond
Edie's Home/Milan Stitt
Edifying Further Elaborations On The Mentality Of A Chore/Sharon S. Martin
* **Edna**/Vernon Hinkle
Education Of Hyman Kaplan, The/Oscar Brand
Effect Of Gamma Rays On Man-In-The-Moon Marigolds, The/Paul Zindel
Egad, The Woman In White/Tim Kelly
Egwuwu/Owa
Eider Down/Lanny Flaherty
Eighth Planet, The/Silas Jones
* **Einstein And The Polar Bear**/Tom Griffin
* **Elagabalus**/Martin B. Duberman
El Capitan/Barbara Field/
* **Elderly Gentleman Seeks**/Barbara Graham
* **Eldorado Dream**/Jean Reavey
Eleanor Of Aquitaine/Ruth Wolff
Election Night/Joseph Hart

Electra/Robert Montgomery
Electric Map, The/Martin B. Duberman
Electronic Nigger, The/Ed Bullins
Elegy To A Down Queen/Leslie Lee
Elena/Jonathan Ringkamp
Eleonora Duse/Mario Fratti
Elevator, The/Ken Eulo
Elevator Escapade, The/Leonard Melfi
El Exejente/Stanley Nelson
El Hermano/Romulus Linney
* **Elizabeth I**/Paul Foster
* **Elizabeth Stuart Company, The**/Jean Nuchtern
El Macho/Joseph Lizardi
El Tigre de Payare/Lanie Robertson
Elusive Angel, The/Jack Gilhooley
Emanons/Stanley Nelson
* **Emeritus**/David Lifson
Emil And Nell/Ron Whyte
* **Emily Tillington**/Daniel W. Owens
Emily Tis Thee I Love/Roy London
Eminent Domain/Percy Granger
Emma Instigated Me/Rochelle Owens
Emma Ponafidine/Louisa Burns-Bisogno
Emperor Norton/James Schevill
Emperor Norton Lives!/James Schevill
Emperor Of Late Night Radio, The/T.C. Miller
Emperor Waltz, The/Allen Sternfield
Empress Of China/Ruth Wolff
Empty Closets/Robert Unger
Enchanted Cottage, The/Percy Granger
Enchanted Pig, The/Charles Ludlam
Enclave, The/Arthur Laurents
Endangered Species/Richard Seff
Endless Hearts, The/Paul Zindel
* **End Of Innocence**/Edmund Morris
* **End Of The Teflon-Coated Life, The**/June Calender
Enemy, The/J.E. Franklin
Engagement In San Domingue/Nathan N. Barrett
Eunuchs Of The Forbidden City/Charles Ludlam
Enter Laughing/Joseph Stein
Enter Pharoah Nussbaum/Tim Kelly
Entertaining Innumerable Reflections On The Subject At Hand/Sharon S. Martin
Entertainment, The/Raymond Platt
Entrepreneurs Of Avenue B/Jack Gilhooley
* **Envoi Messages, The**/Louis Phillips
Envoys/Richard France
Equal Rights/Dick D. Zigun
* **Eris**/Lee Falk
* **Ernest Is The West**/Peter Ramsey
* **Erotic Behavior Upstate**/Leonard Melfi
* **Escape, The**/Victor Power
Escape To Freedom/Ossie Davis
Eskimos Have Landed, The/Tim Kelly
Establishment, The/Norman Beim
* **Estate, The**/Ray Aranha
* **Esther**/C.K. Mack
* **Etchings In Firelight**/C. Robert Jones
Eubie/Johnny Brandon
* **Eulogy Of Jacob Herman Garfinkle,**

The/Jerome Kass
Eunuchs Of The Forbidden City/Charles Ludlam
Euthanasia/Paul Zindel
* **Evdoxia Smith On The Moon**/Avra Petrides
Evelyn Brown/Maria I. Fornes
* **Evening Star**/Howard Richardson
Events From the Life Of Ted Snyder/Jay Broad
Everlasting Reich, The/Susan Griffin
Ever So Humble/Warren Kliewer
Everyman And Roach/Jonathan Ringkamp
Everyman's History Of Love/James Schevill
Everything In The Garden/Edward Albee
Everything's Jim Dandy/Tim Kelly
Evidence/Richard Foreman
Example, The/Yale Udoff
* **Except For Susie Finkle**/Joe Manchester
Exegesis/Allen Sternfield
Ex-expatriate, The/Donna de Matteo
Exhausting The Possibilities/Larry Loonin
* **Exhibition**/Janet L. Neipris
Ex-Miss Copper Queen On A Set Of Pills/Megan Terry
Exotic Arms/Howard Pflanzer
Exotic Places/Ronald Ribman
Experimental Death Unit I/Imamu A. Baraka
Experiment In Lust, An/Ross MacLean
Exlainers, The/Jules Feiffer
Expo 99/Robert Auletta
* **Expressionist, The**/Eddie Lawrence
Expresso & Brioche/F.V. Hunt
Eye Of The Gull/Jane Chambers
Eye Of The Storm/David Lifson
Eyes Of The Harem/Maria I. Fornes
* **Eyes Of The Lofty, The**/June V. Williams

F

* **Fable, The**/Jean-Claude van Itallie
Fables/Jerome McDonough
Fabulous Jennie, The/Ramon L. Delgado
* **Fabulous Jeromes, The**/Ramon L. Delgado
Fabulous Miss Marie, The/Ed Bullins
Fabulous Tale, A/Richard Stockton
Face Of Job, The/June V. Williams
* **Faces**/Norman Kline
Factory Ping Pong/Larry Loonin
Fading Hours/Lee Hunkins
Fading Of Miss Dru, The/Kathy Hurley
Fairy Godmother, The/Stephen Levi
Fall Of The House of Usher, The/Tim Kelly
Fam & Yam/Edward Albee
Familiar Pattern/David Lifson
Familiar Stranger, The/J. Lawrence & R.E. Lee
Families/Conrad Bishop
Family/Sallie Bingham
Family, The/Mario Fratti
Family Affair/James Goldman
Family Bar, The/Robert Patrick
Family Continues, The/Lanford Wilson
Family Devotions/David H. Hwang

* **Family, Family**/Sally Ordway
Family Game, The/Eugene McKinney
Family House/C.K. Mack
Family Portrait, A/Robert Lord
* **Family Rites**/Alan Havis
Family Room, The/Joseph Lizardi
* **Family Weather**/Albert Bermel
Fancies/Crispin Larangeira
Fantasies At The Frick/Leonard Melfi
Fantasy/Tobi Louis
* **Fantod, The**/Amlin Gray
Farewells/Daniel A. Stein
Farewell To Valley Forge/Earl H. Smith
* **Farm Bill, The**/Susan Dworkin
Farmers Almanac/Rochelle Owens
Far Rockaway/Frank D. Gilroy
Farvorfen Vinkel/David Lifson
Fate, Fortune And Final Solutions/Wallace Dace
* **Father And Son**/Sam A. Eisenstein
* **Father Dreams**/Mary Gallagher
Fathers/Jack R. Guss
Fathers & Sons/Thomas Babe
Fathers And Sons/Richard France
* **Father's Day**/Oliver Hailey
Father Uxbridge Wants To Marry/Frank Gagliano
Fat Tuesday/Martin Sherman
* **Fault Line**/Yale Udoff
Fay Wray Meets King Kong/James Schevill
Feast, The/Toni Press
* **Feathered Serpent, The**/Edward Mabley
Feathertop/Richard France
Federation Of United Colored Kinsmen/Michael Kassin
Fedra Of the Canyon/Lucile Bogue
* **Feedback**/Albert Evans
* **Feel Free**/Charlotte Kraft & Nancy Henderson
* **Feeling Shop, The**/N. Selden & M. Imbrie
Fefu And Her Friends/Maria I. Fornes
Feiffer's People/Jules Feiffer
Feldshuh & Brackett/Linda Segal
Felicia & The Magic Pinks/R. Eugene Jackson
Female Flower/Robert Patrick
Fences/Rose L. Goldemberg
Fence War, The/Benjamin Bradford
Fenders/Bruce Serlen
Ferdinand & The Dirty Knight/R. Eugene Jackson
Ferryboat/Anna M. Barlow
Ferryboat/Leonard Melfi
Fetching The Tree/E. Macer-Story
* **Feuerbach's Wife**/Drury Pifer
* **Few Good Men, A**/John Sedlak
Few Inquiries, A/Howard Sackler
Fiddler On The Roof/Joseph Stein
* **Fifth Avenue**/Hiram Taylor
Fifth Of July, The/Lanford Wilson
Fifth Season, The/Sylvia Regan
Figaro/Mark Leib
"Fight Like Hell 'Til You Get To Heaven"/Janet McReynolds
Figures From Giacometti/George Freek
Filial Pieties/George Freek

Filiation/Jerome McDonough
* Filigree People/Peter Dee
* Film Club, The/Merritt Abrash
Film Festival/Sally Ordway
* Final Act, The/Howard Pflanzer
Finale/James Elward
Final Episode, The/Vincent Viaggio
Final Exams/Ken Eulo
Final Extinction Of Alexander Pope,
The/Ron Whyte
* Final Voyage Of Aphrodite, The/Diane
Kagan
* Fine Summer Night, A/Michael Shurtleff
Fingernails Blue As Flowers/Ronald
Ribman
Finian's Rainbow/Fred Saidy
Finishing Touch, The/Elizabeth Wyatt
Finishing Touches/Jean Kerr
Finnegans Wake/David K. Heefner
Fire At Luna Park/Theodore Gross
Firekeeper/Mark Medoff
Fireworks/Megan Terry
First Book Of Kings/Frank M. Mosier
First Breeze Of Summer, The/Leslie Lee
First Day Of Us, The/Peter Copani
First Impressions/Abe Burrows
First In Way/Mars Hill
First Love/Charles Fuller
First Mistake/Norman Beim
* First Monday In October/J. Lawrence &
R.E. Lee
First Offenders/Bruce J. Friedman
First One Asleep, Whistle/Oliver Hailey
First "R", The/Milan Stitt
First Thirty/Neil Cuthbert
First Word And The Last, The/Richard
France
Fish, The/Drury Pifer
Fishing/Michael Weller
Fishing Contest/Thomas G. Dunn
Five-Four-Three-Two-One/Curtis Zahn
5 One Act Plays By Mark Twain/Jules
Tasca
Five One Act Plays In English/Mario Fratti
Five P.M./Jolene Goldenthal
Five Thousand Feet High/Helen
Duberstein
Fix!/Mark Eisman
Flag Bearer, The/Wallace Dace
* Flahooley/Fred Saidy
* Flatbush Football Golem, The/David
Lifson
Flat Monotone, A/Paul Mroczka
Flatulist, The/Murray Schisgal
Fledermas/Garson Kanin
Fledgling, The/Judith Morley
* Flesh, Flash And Frank Harris/Paul S. Lim
Flight/Wallace Dace
Flight Of The Dodo/Ramon L. Delgado
Flight Of The Sea Gull/W. Edwin Ver
Becke
* Flight Three Five Nine/C.H. Keeney
Fling!/Bernard Slade
Floaters/Marsha Sheiness
Floating Lightbulb, The/Woody Allen
Flotsam/Joel Ensana
* Flounder Complex, The/Anthony Damato

Flower Girl, The/Leonard Melfi
Flux/Susan Miller
Fly Away Home/Mary Gallagher
Fly From The Wrath/Tobi Louis
* Flying Elephant, The/Allen Boretz
Flying Horses/Janet L. Neipris
Flyin' Turtles/Sally D. Wiener
* FOB/David H. Hwang
Fog/Robert Patrick
Fog And Mismanagement/Jeff Wanshel
* Fog Drifts In The Spring/Lennox Brown
Foggia/Helen Duberstein
Follies/James Goldman
Folly Cove/Ruth Wolff
* Food/Ross MacLean
Food, The Music Of Love/Rochelle H.
Dubois
* Fool Of Hearts/Gus Kaikkonen
Fools/Neil Simon
Footloose & Fancy 3/Ray E. Fox
For An Eggshell/Kathy Hurley
For Any Evil/Maxwell Glanville
For Colored Girls Who Have Considered
Sucide/When The Rainbow Is
Enuf/Ntozake Shange
Forensic & The Navigators/Sam Shepard
Foreplay-Doorplay/Robert Auletta
* Forever After/Doric Wilson
Forgotten Lover, The/Susan Dworkin
Forgotten Treasure, The/Kathy Hurley
For Heaven's Sake!/Helen Kromer
For Left-Handed Piano With
Obbligato/George Freek
Former Gotham Girl, A/Gloria Gonzalez
Former One-On-One Basketball Champion,
The/Israel Horovitz
For The Love Of Mike/C.H. Keeney
* For The Use Of The Hall/Oliver Hailey
48 Spring Street/Ken Eulo
Forward Together/Antoni Gronowicz
Founding Father/Amlin Gray
Four Corners/Helen Duberstein
Four Fs, The/Robert W. Martin
4-H Club/Sam Shepard
* Four Lanes To Jersey/Roma Greth
Four Meals In May/Wallace Shawn
4 Noh Plays/Tom Eyen
* Four Of A Kind/John Nassivera
Four On A Garden/Abe Burrows
Four Play/Ross MacLean
Fourteen Hundred Thousand/Sam Shepard
Fourth For The Eighth, A/William Griffin
Fourth Son/Aldyth Morris
Four To Go/W. Edwin VerBecke
Four Women/J.E. Franklin
* Fox Against The Fence/John Sedlak
* Fox & Co./Adele E. Shank
Fox, Hound & Huntress/Lance Lee
Fragments/Murray Schisgal
Frank Buck Can't Make It/David Freeman
Frankenstein//Tim Kelly
* Frankenstein Affair, The/Ken Eulo
Frankensteins Are Back In Town, The/Tim
Kelly
Frankenstein Slept Here/Tim Kelly
Franklin Street/Ruth Goetz
Fred/Michael Weller

Free And Clear/Robert Anderson
Freedom Trail!/Lucile Bogue
Free! Free! Free!/Sally Ordway
Freek Advise, The/John Pyros
French Touch, The/Jerome Chodorov
Frequency, The/Larry Ketron
* Freudian Lovesong/Samuel Shem
Friday Bench, The/Mario Fratti
Friday Night/James Elward
Friend Of The Family/Wallace Hamilton
Friends/Lee Kalcheim
Friends/Crispin Larangeira
Friends And Monsters/Leonard Melfi
Friendship Centre/Robert Lord
Friends Indeed!/David Cohen
Friends Of My Heart, The/Franklyn
   MacGregor
Fritz Was Here/J.E. Franklin
Frizzly Hen, The/Anna M. Barlow
Froegle Dictum, The/Mark Medoff
From A Dark Land/Harding Lemay
From A To Z/Woody Allen
* From Now On/Anthony Inneo
From Now On/William Packard
From Our Point Of View/Kathy Hurley
From Sea To Shining Sea/R. Eugene
   Jackson
Frosted Glass Coffin, The/Tennessee
   Williams
Frost Fire, The/Leonard Melfi
Frost of Renaissance, The/Samm-Art
   Williams
Frozen/Elaine G. Denholtz
Frugal Repast/Sheldon Rosen
Frustrata, The Dirty Little Girl With The
   Paper Rose Stuck In Her Head,
   Is Demented/Tom Eyen
F.S. Perls Memorial Dream Theater,
   The/T. C. Miller
Fugitive Kind, The/Tennessee Williams
Fugue On A Funny House/Ray Aranha
* Funeral, The/William Packard
Funeral March For A One-Man Band/Ron
   Whyte
FUNNYLINGUS/Owa
Fun Zone/Jack Larson
Further Wonders Of The Divil In
   Massachusetts/David K. Heefner
Futz/Rochelle Owens

G

Galilee/Susan Dworkin
Gambits/Lance Lee
Game/Benjamin Bradford
Game Of Billiards, A/Rochelle Owens
Game Of Kings And Queens, A/Benjamin
   Bradford
Game Of The Eye, The/Arthur Sainer
Gaming/Allen Boretz
Gandhiji/Rose L. Goldemberg
Gang's All Here, The/J. Lawrence &
   R.E. Lee
* Garden Full Of Snow, A/Michael Shurtleff

Garden In Los Angeles, A/Robert H. Eisele
Garden Of Eden, The/Owa
Gazelle Boy/Ronald Tavel
Gemini/Albert Innaurato
Gemini/Arthur Kopit
Gene & Jean/R. Cowen & D. Lipman
* Gene And Jeanne/Arthur Jasspe
General Brutus, The/Jeff Wanshel
General Seeger/Ira Levin
* Genesis & Exodus Of Operation
   A-132/Curtis Zahn
Geneva Crossroads/Charlotte Kraft
Genius Of Sorts, A/Doric Wilson
Gentleman And A Scoundrel, A/Jack
   Sharkey
Gentleman Caller/Ed Bullins
* Genuine Red Snapper/Bruce Serlen
Geographies Of Northern Provinces/Lanie
   Robertson
Geography Of A Horse Dreamer/Sam
   Shepard
Geometric Progressions/Benjamin
   Bradford
* George And Frederic/Ruth Wolff
* George And Martha/Samuel Shem
* Geranium/Knox Turner
Gertrude Stein And Other Great Men/Tom
   Eyen
* Get On Board, Little Children/Nancy
   Henderson
Getting Along Famously/Michael Jacobs
Getting Into Death/Michael Shurtleff
Getting It On In Hollywood/Bob Barry
Getting Mama Married/Stephen Levi
Getting Through/Elizabeth Wyatt
Gettin' It Together/Richard E. Wesley
Ghost Dance/Joseph Hart
Ghosts/Louis Rivers
Ghost Story, A/John Pielmeier
Ghost Town/Albert Evans
Giants In The Earth, The/Kenneth Bernard
Gift, The/Mario Fratti
Gift And The Giving, The/Tim Kelly
Gift Of The Magi/David Lifson
Gift Of The Magi/John Olive
Gift Of The Magi/Sy Reiter
Gift Of Time, A/Garson Kanin
Gilbert/Marc A. Zagoren
* Gimmick, The/Joseph Julian
Gimpy/David Lifson
Gin Game, The/D.L. Coburn
Gingerbread Lady, The/Neil Simon
Gingham Dog, The/Lanford Wilson
Gino/N. Seldon & M. Imbrie
Girl And The Soldier, The/Jean-Claude van
   Itallie
Girl Beneath The Tulip Tree,
   The/Townsend Brewster
Girl In Pink Tights/Jerome Chodorov
Girl In The Freudian Slip, The/William F.
   Brown
* Girl In The Window, A/Allen Boretz
Girl Like Norman Mailer, A/N. Selden
   & M. Imbrie
Girls Are The Funniest/Richard Reich
* Girls In 509, The/Howard M. Teichmann
* Girls Most Likely To Succeed, The/

D.R. Andersen
Girls Of Summer/N. Richard Nash
Giveaway/Conrad Bishop
* Give My Regards To Broadway/Dennis L.
  Turner
Give My Regards To Off-Off-
  Broadway/Tom Eyen
Glad Tidings/Edward Mabley
Gladys/James L. Rosenberg
* Gladys Mazurky/Betsy J. Robinson
Glass/Frederick A. Raborg, Jr.
Glass/Saul Zachary
Glass Menagerie, The/Tennessee Williams
* Glenn Miller Died For Our Sins/Robert
  Pine
Glitter And Spit/Robert Lord
Gloaming, Oh My Darling, The/Megan
  Terry
Glory!/Glenn A. Smith
* Glory! Hallelujah!/Anna M. Barlow
Glory Hallelujah/Robert Kornfeld
Glory Of A Name, The/James Childs
Goalie, The/Louis Phillips
Goats, The/Benjamin Bradford
Goats/Robert H. Eisele
Go Children Slowly/Arthur Sainer
God Bless/Jules Feiffer
Goddess In The Junkyard/Charles Frink
God Have Mercy On The June-Bug/Louis
  Phillips
* God Play, The/E.K. Kerr
God Save The King/Felix Doherty
God's Favorite/Neil Simon
God's Got No Beard/Robert H. Eisele
God's In His Heaven/Herschel Steinhardt
God Wants What Men Want/Arthur Sainer
Goethe With Shades/A.E.O. Goldman
Goin'a Buffalo/Ed Bullins
* Going Co-op/Barbara Garson
Going Home/C.E. Wilkinson
Going Over/Robert Gordon
Goin' Thru Changes/Richard E. Wesley
Golda/William Gibson
Gold Coast Of Times Square, The/Lennox
  Brown
* Golddiggers Of 1633/Lee Goldsmith
Golden Age, The/A.R. Gurney, Jr.
Goldena Medina, The/Harry Granick
Golden Animal, The/Robert Patrick
Golden Boy/William Gibson
Golden Circle, The/Robert Patrick
Golden Dreams/Michael Colby
Golden Ducks Of Summer, The/Louis
  LaRusso II
Golden Fleece, The/A.R. Gurney, Jr.
Golden Fleecing, A/R. Eugene Jackson
* Golden Gate Bridge, The/Ludmilla Bollow
* Golden Land, The/George Hammer
Golden Pyramids Of Ohama, The/Rochelle
  H. Dubois
* Golden Sorrow, A/Peggy Phillips
Goldilocks/Jean Kerr
Golem, The/Sylvia Regan
Goners/Conrad Bishop
* Good Breeding/James L. Rosenberg
Goodbye, Cruel World/Stephen Levi
Goodbye, Dan Bailey/Kenneth Bernard

Goodbye Fidel/Howard Sackler
* Goodbye Freddy/Elizabeth Diggs
Goodbye, Howard/Romulus Linney
Goodbye, I Guess/Michael Blankfort
Goodbye People, The/Herb Gardner
Good Days, Bad Days/Benjamin Bradford
Good Doctor, The/Neil Simon
Good Girl Is Hard To Find, A/Imamu A.
  Baraka
Good Help Is Hard To Find/Arthur Kopit
Good Hunting/Joseph Schrank
Goodly Creatures/William Gibson
Good Parts, The/Israel Horovitz
Good Ship Credit, The/John Scott
Good Soup, The/Garson Kanin
Good Times Are Here Again/Crispin
  Larangeira
Goody One Shoe/Jules Tasca
* Goona-Goona/Megan Terry
Gordone Is A Muthah/Charles Gordone
Gorgeous Piece, A/Edward M. Cohen
Gorilla Queen/Ronald Tavel
Gorky/Steve Tesich
Go Stare At The Moon/Martha A. Fuentes
* Gott Ist Tot! Killed Along With James
  Bond In A Four Car Collision On The
  Los Angeles Freeway/Leo Rutman
Go Out And Move The Car/Megan Terry
Governor, The/Franklyn MacGregor
Governor's House, The/Lennox Brown
* Graceland/Bruce Serlen
Grand Exit/Joel Ensana
Grand Finale/Marc A. Zagoren
Grand Hysteric, The/Sheldon Rosen
Grandma Duck Is Dead/Larry Shue
Grand Tarot, The/Charles Ludlam
Grand Tenement/November 22nd/Tom
  Eyen
Grant's Movie/Michael Weller
* Grave Undertaking, A/Lloyd Gold
* Grease/Jim Jacobs
Great All-American Musical Disaster,
  The/Tim Kelly
Great American Succer Family, The/Peter
  Copani
* Great American Success, The/Richard
  Henrickson
Great American Quiz Show Scandal,
  The/Louis Phillips
Great Big Coca Cola Swamp In The
  Sky/Jay Broad
Great Big River/Dale Wasserman
Great Chinese Revolution, The/Anthony
  Scully
* Greatest Day Of The Century, The/Roma
  Greth
Greatest Little Show On Earth,
  The/Michael Weller
Great Goodness Of Life/Imamu A. Baraka
Great Labor Day Classic, The/Israel
  Horovitz
Great Nebula In Orion, The/Lanford
  Wilson
Great Potato Famine, The/Brendan N.
  Ward
* Great Solo Town/Thomas Babe
Great To Be Alive/Sylvia Regan

Great 200th Anniversary H-Bomb Crisis,
The/Robert Riche
Great Waltz/Jerome Chodorov
Great White Hope, The/Howard Sackler
* Greeks Had A Cure For It, The/Fred Saidy
Green Archer, The/Tim Kelly
* Green Grows The Holly/Felix Doherty
Green Pond/Robert Montgomery
Green Room, The/Kenneth H. Brown
* Greenroom, The/Robert Eisele
Greet Tomorrow/David Lifson
Gregorius The Great/Jonathan Ringkamp
Greta/Antoni Gronowicz
Gringo Planet/Frederick Bailey
Grooving/Megan Terry
Ground Lies Fallow/Jonathan Ringkamp
Ground Zero/Saul Zachary
Grownups/Jules Feiffer
* G.R. Point/David A. Berry
* Guava Lagoon/John Jiler
Guess What's Coming To Dinner/J.E.
Franklin
Guess Who's Not Coming To
Dinner/Norman Beim
* Guess Work/Robert Auletta
Guest Of Honor, The/Howard Pflanzer
Guilty, The/Harry Granick
Gun Play, A/Yale Udoff
Gus & Co./John Sedlak
Guttman Ordinary Scale, The/Martin B.
Duberman
Guys And Dolls/Abe Burrows
Gypsy/Arthur Laurents

H

* Hagar's Children/Ernest A. Joselovitz
Hage, The Sexual History/Robert Auletta
Ha-Ha Play, The/Susan Yankowitz
Haircut, The/Norman Beim
* Haircut, The/Judith Morley
* Hair Products/Sharon S. Martin
Hairy Tales Of Evolution/Edan Schappert
Half Horse, Half Cockeyed
Alligator/Warren Kliewer
Half Past Wednesday/Anna M. Barlow
Halfway/Roma Greth
Halfway To Somewhere/Conrad Bishop
Hallelujah!/James Elward
Hallelujah, Baby!/Arthur Laurents
Hall Of Fame/Allen Sternfield
Halloween/Leonard Melfi
Halloween Bandit, The/Mark Medoff
Halloween Hermit/Robert Patrick
Halloween Mask/David S. Milton
Halloween 2050 A.D./Joel Ensana
Ham And Borscht/Judith Morley
Hamburger/Frank B. Ford
Hamhocks/S. Garrett Robinson
Hamster Of Happiness, The/Charles
Eastman
Handful Of Fire/N. Richard Nash
* Hand-Me-Downs, The/J. E. Franklin

Handsel And Gretal Meet The Ghost Of J.
Edgar Hoover/E. Macer-Story
Hanging Of Emanuel, The/Israel Horovitz
Hangin' Loose/R. Eugene Jackson
* Hannah: A Parable In Music/Helen
Kromer
Hansel And Gretel/Neville Aurelius
Happenings/Larry Loonin
Happiest Girl/Fred Saidy
Happiest Man Alive, The/Jerome Chodorov
Happily Never After/Tim Kelly
* Happiness Cage, The/Dennis J. Reardon
* Happy Bar, The/Kenneth H. Brown
Happy Birthday, Wanda June/Kurt
Vonnegut, Jr.
Happy Dollar/Lee Falk
* Happy New Year To The Whole World
Except Alexander Graham Bell,
A/Bernard Sabath
Happy Time, The/N. Richard Nash
Happy Valley, The/Michael Weller
Hard Way, The/Allen Boretz
Harlequinades For Mourners/Townsend
Brewster
Harlequin And Company/Michael Colby
Harold/Jean-Claude van Itallie
Harper's Bizarre!/Ludmilla Bollow
Harpers Ferry/Barrie Stavis
Harrison Of The Mounted/Arthur Jasspe
Harrison Progressive School, The/Stanley
Nelson
* Harry & Thelma In The Woods/Stan
Lachow
* Harry Kelly/Harold Heifetz
Harry, Noon And Night/Ronald Ribman
* Harry Outside/Corinne Jacker
Harvest Moon Ball, The/Charles Leipart
Hatchet Club/Paul S. Lim
Haunted Host, The/Robert Patrick
Have A Heart/Robert F. Joseph
Having Fun In The Bathroom/Leonard
Melfi
Hawkshaw The Detective/Tim Kelly
* Haymarket/Joanne Koch
Head/Drury Pifer
Head Of Hair, The/Allen Davis III
* Headsets/Shannon K. Kelley
* Heart Of The Lotus/Martin Halpern
* Heart Of The Tiger/C. Robert Jones
Heartsong/Arthur Laurents
Heaven Mother, The/Roma Greth
* heaven must be a very complicated
place/Owa
Hedda Gabler/Joe T. Ford
Hedge Of Serpents/Ramon L. Delgado
Heidi/Neil Simon
!Heimskringla!/Paul Foster
Heinz/Allan Havis
Heiress, The/Ruth Goetz
Helen/Johnny Brandon
Helen/James Childs
Helen's Hand/Raymond Platt
Hello From Bertha/Tennessee Williams
Hello, I Love You/Barry Berg
Hello, Thank You, And Goodbye/Louis
LaRusso II

Hells Of Dante, The/Harry Granick
Help, I Am/Robert Patrick
Helper, The/Ed Bullins
Helping Hands/Benjamin Bradford
Hemingway Play, The/Frederic Hunter
* Henry's Day/Marc A. Zagoren
Here And The Now, The/Saul Zachary
Here Come The Butterflies/Allen Boretz
Here Lies Jeremy Troy/Jack Sharkey
Here Wait/Roy London
Hero, The/Arthur Kopit
Herod First/Albert Bermel
Heroes & Butterflies/Robert Lord
Hero Of The Jungle/Ross MacLean
He/She: Pizza Pie/Lanie Robertson
Hessian Corporal, The/Paul Foster
He Wants Shih!/Rochelle Owens
Heyday/Herbert Appleman
Hey Out There, Is There Anyone Out
    There?/Elanie G. Denholtz
* Hey, Rube/Janet McReynolds
Hey You, Light Man!/Oliver Hailey
* Hidalgo/Shimon Wincelberg
Hidden River, The/Ruth Goetz
* Hide And Seek/Lezley Havard
Hide And Seek/Allen Sternfield
Hide-And-Seek Odyssey Of Madeleine
    Gimple, The/Frank Gagliano
High As A Kite/Robert Lord
* Highchairs, The/Elaine G. Denholtz
High Sinners, Low Angels/James Schevill
High Structure Falls Further, A/Benjamin
    Bradford
High Time/A. Petrides & D. Kagan
Hillbilly Liberation/OyamO
Hills Send Off Echoes, The/Ernest Ferlita
Hippie As A Lark/Robert Patrick
Hirsch Lekert/David Lifson
His First Step/OyamO
His Master's Voice/Yale Udoff
* His Master's Voice/Dick D. Zigun
* History Of The American Film,
    A/Christopher Durang
* History Of The Saints: Faith, Hope And
    Charity, The/Brendan N. Ward
Hitch/Jeffrey Sweet
* Hitler In Landsberg/Wallace Dace
Ho! Ho! Ho!/Ruth Gordon
* Hoja!/Frank B. Ford
Holding On/Ernest A. Joselovitz
Holding Pattern/Jeffrey Sweet
Hold Me!/Jules Feiffer
Hold-Up, The/Jean Nuchtern
* Hold-Up/Alan Roland
Holeville/Jeff Wanshel
Holiday Spirit, The/Edan Schappert
* Holly-Haven/Robert F. Joseph
* Hollywood Messiah, The/Samuel Shem
* Holmes And Moriarty/Allen Sternfield
Holy Communion/Joseph T. Pintauro
Holy Ghostly/Sam Shepard
Holy Ghosts/Romulus Linney
* Holy Places/Gail Kriegel
Holzmann/Lonnie Carter
Home/Samm-Art Williams
Home Again, Home Again, Jiggity

Jig!/Sandra Scoppettone
Home Again, Kathleen/Thomas Babe
Home And The River/Benjamin Bradford
* Home At Six/Lee Falk
Home Away From, A/Glenn A. Smith
Home Boy/Ed Bullins
Home Fires/John Guare
Home Free!/Lanford Wilson
Homefront Blues/Jack Gilhooley
* Home-Grown Dilemma/Jean Reavey
Home Is A Long Way/Lennox Brown
Homelife/Lydia Simmons
Home Of The Brave/Arthur Laurents
Home On The Range/Imamu A. Baraka
Home: or Future Soap/Megan Terry
* Homerica/Paul S. Lim
* Home/Work/John Von Hartz
Homing Pigeon, The/Richard Seff
Homo/Rochelle Owens
Honestly, Now!/Jack Sharkey
Honest-To-God Schnozzola, The/Israel
    Horovitz
Honeymoon, The/Louis LaRusso II
Honors At Dawn/Arthur Miller
Hooded Gnome, The/Frederick Bailey
Hooks & i's/Allen Davis III
Hooper Law, The/Harry Granick
Hoop-La/Robert Patrick
Hooray For Hollywood/Mark Edwards
Hooters/Ted Tally
Hop/Israel Horovitz
Hope For The Best/Jack Sharkey
Hopscotch & The 75th/Israel Horovitz
Horatio/Ron Whyte
Horn Of Plenty/Leonard Melfi
Horror Show, The/Barry Berg
Horse Opera/Leonard Melfi
Horse Story, A/Donna de Matteo
* Hospital Play, The/Wallace Shawn
Hostess, The/Sally Ordway
Hostile Terrain/Paul Hunter
Hot Corner, The/Allen Boretz
Hotel China/Richard Foreman
Hotel Eros/J. J. Coyle
Hotel Europe/Helen Duberstein
Hotel For Criminals/Richard Foreman
* Hotel Play, The/Wallace Shawn
* Hothouse/Megan Terry
* Hot Ice/Charles Ludlam
Hot I Baltimore, The/Lanford Wilson
* Hot Pink Blues/Nancy Henderson
Hound Of The Baskervilles, The/Tim Kelly
House And Field/Mars Hill
Houseboat In Kashmir/J. Lawrence &
    R.E. Lee
Housekeeper, The/James Prideaux
House Not Meant To Stand, A/Tennessee
    Williams
* House of Bedlam, The/Kenneth Arnold
House Of Blue Leaves/John Guare
House Of Cards/Theodore Gross
House Of Emotions/Rochelle H. Dubois
* House Of Sleeping Beauties, The/David H.
    Hwang
House On Lake Geneva, The/Paul Foster
House On Prince Edward Street,

The/Wallace Dace
House On The Island/Lydia Simmons
House Party/Ed Bullins
House Shall Tremble, The/Richard Stockton
House Without Windows/Richard Reich
How Can You Tell The Good Guys From The Bad Guys?/Warren Kliewer
How Do You Do/Ed Bullins
How Do You Live With Love?/Paul Hunter
How Green Was My Brownie/Jack Sharkey
* **How He Became A Writer**/Harding Lemay
How Hoho Rose And Fell/Michael Weller
How I Came To Be Here Tonite/Robert Patrick
* **How I Got That Story**/Amlin Gray
How She Became Queen Of Greece/Ronald Tavel
How The '70's Began/Leslie Weiner
How The West Was Fun/Townsend Brewster
How To Get Rid of A Housemother/Tim Kelly
How To Manual, A/John Pyros
How To Rob A Bank/David Lifson
How To Say Goodbye/Mary Gallagher
How To Steal An Election/Oscar Brand
How To Steal An Election/William F. Brown
How To Succeed In Business Without Really Trying/Abe Burrows
How To Work Your Way Through College On A Credit Card/C.H. Keeney
How We Danced While We Burned/Kenneth Bernard
Huey's Legacy/Dick D. Zigun
Hunchback Of Notre-Dame, The/Ron Whyte
Hungry Mother Mountain/Harold Heifetz
Hunter And Bird, The/Jean-Claude van Itallie
Hurrah For The Bridge/Paul Foster
* **Hurrah For The Fun**/Charles Horine
Hurrah For Us/David Lifson
Husband-In-Law/Sheppard Kerman
* **Huzzy**/Mars Hill
Hymen And Carbuncle/Robert Patrick
Hypocrites, Frauds And Cheats/Warren Kliewer
Hypocritical Satellites, The/J. Kline Hobbs

I

I Am Lucy Terry/Ed Bullins
I Am Trying To Tell You Something/Robert Patrick
I. . .As In Identity/Lucile Bogue
I Came To New York To Write/Robert Patrick
I Can't Find It Anywhere/Oliver Hailey
I Can't Imagine Tomorrow/Tennessee Williams
Icarus Nine/Bruce Serlen
Icarus's Mother/Sam Shepard
Ice/Michael Christofer

* **Ice-Cream Sunday, The**/Frank Salisbury
Ice Cubes, The/Edan Schappert
* **Ice Game**/Valerie Harris
Ida-Eyed/Richard Foreman
Ida The Indomitable/Norman Beim
Ideal State, The/Benjamin Bradford
Idiots Karamazov, The/C. Durang & A. Innaurato
Idol Makers, The/Stephen D. Parks
Idomeneus/Townsend Brewster
I Don't Know Where You're Coming From At All!/Shirley M. Lauro
I'd Rather Sit Alone On A Pumpkin/Barry Berg
If God Wouldn't Eat With A German/Jonathan Ringkamp
* **If I'm Dead, Start Without Me**/Vernon Hinkle
If Sherlock Holmes Were A Woman/Tim Kelly
I Had A Ball/Jerome Chodorov
I Had 3 Balls But I Lost/Mark Berman
I Have This Friend/Anthony Inneo
I Have To Call My Father/Lennox Brown
I Hear It Kissing Me, Ladies/Arthur Sainer
Ikke, Ikke, Nye, Nye, Nye/Lanford Wilson
I'll Scream If I Want To/Robert Lord
I Lost A Pair Of Gloves Yesterday/Myrna Lamb
Image Of Elmo Doyle, The/Richard France
Images Of The Coming Dead/Arthur Sainer
Imitatin' Us, Imitatin' Us, Imitatin' Death/Daniel W. Owens
Immoralist, The/Ruth Goetz
Immortals, The/Louis Phillips
I'm Not Jewish And I Don't Know Why I'm Screaming/Stan Lachow
Impact/Sheldon Rosen
Improvisation For Actor, Dancer And Musician/Richard Olson
I'm Really Here/Jean-Claude van Itallie
In Absence/Doric Wilson
In A Name, Nothing/Curtis Zahn
Inaugural/Ernest A. Joselovitz
Inbetween/Elyse Nass
In Between The Coming And The Goings/Owa
Incident At Vichy/Arthur Miller
Incidents/Larry Loonin
Incomparable Max, The/J. Lawrence & R.E. Lee
* **Incompetents, The**/T.C. Miller
* **In Connecticut**/Roy London
Incredible Bulk At Bikini Beach, The/Tim Kelly
Incredible Julia, The/Jean Reavey
In-Crowd, The/J.E. Franklin
Indecent Exposure/Robert Patrick
* **Independence Night**/Venable Herndon
Indians/Arthur Kopit
Indian Wants The Bronx, The/Israel Horovitz
Indignities/Frank B. Ford
Indira Gandhi's Daring Device/Ronald Tavel
I Never Sang For My Father/Robert Anderson

I Never Saw Another Butterfly/Albert
Evans
In Fireworks Lie Secret Codes/John Guare
Inheritance, The/Ernest A. Joselovitz
Inheritance, The/Leonard L. Perlmutter
* Inherit The Wind/J. Lawrence & R.E. Lee
Inimitable Education Of Horace Oakley
Anderson III, The/Franklyn MacGregor
Injectors, The/Maxwell Glanville
* In Memoriam/Neville Aurelius
In My Many Names & Days/Charles Fuller
In New England Winter/Ed Bullins
* In Pursuit Of The Sound Of
Hydrogen/Thomas G. Dunn
* Insanity Of Mary Girard, The/Lanie
Robertson
In Separate Chambers/Lanie Robertson
Inside/Norman Beim
Inside Lulu/Ron Cowen
* Insides Of Orchid Price, The/Tobi Louis
* In Sorrow's Room/China C. Pendarvis
Inspector Of Stairs, The/Sandra
Scoppettone
Instructions For A Sandcastle/Benjamin
Bradford
* Insurance/Peter Swet
Insurrection/Imamu A. Baraka
Interlock/Ira Levin
Interlude At A Shoe Shine Stand/Leo
Rutman
Interludes/Alan Havis
Interrogation Room, The/David S. Milton
Interview, The/Joseph T. Pintauro
Interview, The/Peter Swet
* Interview, The/Thom Thomas
In The Bar of A Tokyo Hotel/Tennessee
Williams
In The Boom Boom Room/David Rabe
In The Counting House/Leslie Weiner
* In The Dark/Avra Petrides
In The Deepest Part Of Sleep/Charles
Fuller
In The First Place/William Packard
In The Modern Style/Stanley Taikeff
* In The Name Of The Father/Lezley Havard
In The Presence Of Mine Enemy/Ray E.
Fox
In The Pursuit/Milan Stitt
* In The Rest Room At Rosenblooms/
Ludmilla Bollow
In The Shadow Of The Crematoria/Myrna
Lamb
* In The Voodoo Parlor Of Marie
Leveau/Frank Gagliano
In The Yurt/Sallie Bingham
In The Wine Time/Ed Bullins
Into That Good Night/Stanley Taikeff
Inventory/J.J. Coyle
Inventory/Howard Pflanzer
* Inventory/Betsy J. Robinson
Invisible Man, The/Tim Kelly
* Invitation To A Bear Baiting/Wallace
Hamilton
Invitation To A March/Arthur Laurents
Invitation To A Wine-Tasting/Steven
Somkin
In White America/Oscar Brand & Martin
Duberman

I Ought To Be In Pictures/Neil Simon
Ira Frederick Aldridge/William Hairston
I Remember The House Where I Was
Born/D.R. Andersen
Irene/Hugh Wheeler
I Rise In Flame, Cried The Phoenix/
Tennessee Williams
* Isadora Duncan Sleeps With The Russian
Navy/Jeff Wanshel
Iscariot/Frank M. Mosier
I Shall Return/Louis Garfinkle
* Ishtar/Robert S. Ross
Is It Raining Or Just My Desire?/Susan
Charlotte
Island/Jolene Goldenthal
Island/C.E. Wilkinson
Island Cafe/Steve Metcalfe
Island Of Lost Coeds/Jim Jacobs
Isn't It Romantic/Wendy Wasserstein
* Istanbul/Rochelle Owens
Is That A Fact?/R. Eugene Jackson
Is There Life After High School?/Jeffrey
Kindley
I Talk With The Spirits/John Scott
* Itchy Britches/Nathan N. Barrett
It Has No Choice/Ed Bullins
I Thought I Saw A Snowman/Jolene
Goldenthal
It Isn't Cricket//Robert Lord
It Never Was You/Peggy Phillips
It's A Bird! It's A Plane! It's
Chickenman!/Tim Kelly
It's A Cinch/The Root Of Employ-
ment/Vincent Viaggio
It's A Sin To Tell A Lie/Jason Miller
It's Bigfoot/Tim Kelly
It's Called The Sugar Plum/Israel Horovitz
It's Murder In The Hamptons/Bob Barry
It's Sad, So Sad When An Elf Goes
Bad/Jerome McDonough
It's ShowdownTime/Don Evans
It's To Laugh/Stan Lachow
It's Your Turn Now/Howard Pflanzer
* Ivanhoe/Sy Reiter
Ivory Tower/David Lifson
Ivory Tower, Two Flights Down,
The/Eugene McKinney
I Wanna Go Home/Conrad Bishop
I Went To A Marvelous Party/Norman
Beim
I Will Be Launched/Allen Davis III
I Will Call You Sarah/W. Edwin Ver Becke
It Won't Be Long/Sam A. Eisenstein
I Won't Dance/Oliver Hailey
It Wouldn't Be You/Lydia Simmons
Iz She Izzy Or Iz He Aint'tzy Or Iz They
Both/Lonnie Carter
Izzy/Lonnie Carter

J

* Jabberwock/J. Lawrence & R.E. Lee
Jack And Jill/Leonard Melfi
Jack And The Beanstalk/Thomas G. Dunn

Jack & The Beanstalk/Charles Ludlam
Jack-Jack/Megan Terry
* Jacknife/Steve Metcalfe
Jack N's Awful Demands/Jonathan Levy
Jackson's Dance/Sam Shepard
Jack Swift American Myth/Jonathan
  Ringkamp
Jack's World/Robert W. Martin
* Jack The Ripper/Tim Kelly
* Jacob's Ladder/Barbara Graham
Jade Funerary Suit, The/Townsend
  Brewster
Jamaica/Fred Saidy
Jamestown Diary/R. Eugene Jackson
Jane Heights/James Prideaux
Janis/John Pyros
Jass/John Pielmeier
Jeeves, By Jove/James L. Rosenberg
Jello/Imamu A. Baraka
Jenny And The Revolution/D.R. Andersen
Jenny Kissed Me/Jean Kerr
Jeremy And The Thinking Machine/Janet
  L. Neipris
* Jerusalem Thorn, The/Ramon L. Delgado
* Jesse And The Bandit Queen/David
  Freeman
* Jesse's Land/Ernest A. Joselovitz
Jesus Is A Junkie/Leo Rutman
Jesus Treats/Robert H. Eisele
Je T'aime, Jessica/Stephen Levi
Jew Of Venice, The/Harry Granick
Jigsaw/Jean Reavey
Jillila/Myrna Lamb
Jimmy Shine/Murray Schisgal
* Joan And The Devil/Sy Reiter
Jo Anne!/Ed Bullins
Jocko Or The Monkey's Husband/Tim
  Kelly
Joe: A Dramatic Idiocy/Robert Auletta
Jo-Ella/Judith Morley
John/Toni Press
John Murray Anderson's Almanac/Jean
  Kerr
* Johnnie Will/Victor Power
Johnny Appleseed/Thomas M. Fontana
* Johnny Bull/Kathleen Betsko
Johnny Renaissance/Townsend Brewster
Joined/Daniel W. Owens
Joker In Paradise, A/Jack A. Kaplan
Jonas/Eddie Lawrence
Jones Man, The/Leonard Melfi
* Joslyn Circle, The/Harding Lemay
Journey In July/Wallace Dace
Journey Of The Fifth Horse/Ronald
  Ribman
* Journeys: A Musical Myth/Benjamin R.
  Barber
Journey Tonight, The/Lennox Brown
Joyce Dynel/Robert Patrick
Joyful Noise, A/Oscar Brand
Jud/Barbara Fisher
Judah The Maccabee & Me/Gertrude
  Samuels
Jud & Honoria/Barbara Fisher
Jud & The Oil Slick/Barbara Fisher
* Judas/John W. Kirk
* Judas/Robert Patrick

Judge Not/Elaine G. Denholtz
* Juice Problem, The/OyamO
"Jules And Jim" Is Playing In This
  Godforsaken Town/Fredi Towbin
Jump/Israel Horovitz
Jump!/Charlotte Kraft
Jumping Off Place, The/R. Eugene
  Jackson
June Dawn/Edward Mabley
June Groom/Jack Sharkey
June/Moon/Jack Larson
Junior Miss/Jerome Chodorov
Junk Food/Willard Manus
Junkies Are Full Of Shh/Imamu A. Baraka
Juno/Joseph Stein
* Juno's Swans/E.K. Kerr
* Just Between Us/Anthony Inneo
Just Between Us/Daniel A. Stein
Justice/Terry C. Fox

K

Kama Sutra, The/Tom Eyen
Kamilla/Samm-Art Williams
Kane/James L. Rosenberg
Kara's Monument/Steven Somkin
* Karl And Arthur/Michael Blankfort
Kark Marx Play, The/Rochelle Owens
* Karma/John Scott
* Kataki/Simon Wincelberg
Kate And The Colonel/Mark Edwards
* Keep, The/Mike Firth
Keeping Place, The/Tim Kelly
Keep Tightly Closed In A Cool Dry
  Place/Megan Terry
Kelly/Eddie Lawrence
Kennedy's Children/Robert Patrick
Kentucky!/Daniel A. Stein
Key Is At The Bottom, The/Megan Terry
Kibbutz/Gertrude Samuels
Kicking The Castle Down/Robert Kornfeld
Kid Champion/Thomas Babe
Killdeer, The/Jay Broad
Killer Dove, The/Israel Horovitz
Killers/Paul Mroczka
Killer's Hand/Sam Shepard
* Killer Thing, The/William Packard
Killing Time/Leslie Lee
Kill The One-eyed Man/Herb Schapiro
* Kin/Betsy J. Robinson
* Kinder, Kirche, Kuchen/June Calender
Kindly Observe The People/Barry Berg
King/Lydia Simmons
King Arthur's Knights & Days/Priscilla B.
  Dewey
Kingdom By The Sea/Norman Beim
Kingdom By the Sea, The/Helen
  Duberstein
King For A Day/Frank M. Mosier
* King Humpy/Kenneth Bernard
* King Katherine I/Lucile Bogue
King Of Hearts/Jean Kerr
King Of Hearts/Joseph Stein
King Of Lodz/Thomas G. Dunn
King Of Poland, The/Charles Leipart

King Of Schnorrers/Diane Lampert
King Of The Beach/Ludmilla Bollow
King Of The Golden River/Tim Kelly
* King Of The Hill Is Down, The/William E. Parchman
King Of The United States, The/Jean-Claude van Itallie
King's Servant, The/Felix Doherty
Kirche, Kutchen Und Kinder/Tennessee Williams
Kismet/Luther Davis
Kissinger/Mario Fratti
Kissing Sweet/John Guare
Kiss Me Again/Earl H. Smith
Kiss Or Make Up/Jack Sharkey
* Kiss Them For Me/Luther Davis
Kitchenette/Ronald Tavel
Knight-Mare's Nest, The/Ramon L. Delgado
Knight Of The Twelfth Saucer/Marc A. Zagoren
Knit One, Purl Two/Murray Schisgal
Knitting/Elizabeth Wray
Knock Knock/Conrad Bishop
Knock Knock/Jules Feiffer
Knockout/Louis LaRusso II
* Knots/Brendan N. Ward
Kolyma/Crispin Larangeira
Kontraption/Rochelle Owens
* Kool-Aid's Girl/Robert F. Joseph
Kramer, The/Mark Medoff
Kramer's Golden Ambulance/Allen Sternfield
Krazy Kamp/Tim Kelly
Krewe Of Dionysus, The/Ernest Ferlita
Kuber's Secret/Charlotte Kraft
Kudzu/Jane Chambers

L

* Labyrinth/Knox Turner
Lackawanna Rogues/Louis LaRusso II
Lackland/Bill Bozzone
Ladies At The Alamo/Paul Zindel
Ladies Of The Tower/Tim Kelly
Ladies Should Be In Bed, The/Paul Zindel
Lady And The Clarinet, The/Michael Christofer
* Ladybug, Ladybug, Fly Away Home/Mary Rohde
Lady Called Judas, A/W. Edwin Ver Becke
Lady Dracula/Tim Kelly
Lady From Dubuque, The/Edward Albee
* Ladyhouse Blues/Kevin O'Morrison
Lady, No Lady/Mike Firth
Lady Of Larkspur Lotion, The/Tennessee Williams
Lady Of The Camellias, The/Terrence McNally
* Lady Of The Diamond/Mark Berman
Lady Plum Blossom/Townsend Brewster
Lady Video & The Ecosensor/E. Macer-Story
Lady Who Cried Fox!!, The/Edward Clinton

La Grima Del Diable/Daniel W. Owens
La Justice/Kenneth Bernard
Lake Boat/David Mamet
Lake Of The Woods/Steve Tesich
Lalapalooza Bird, The/Tim Kelly
Lamb, The/Susan Yankowitz
Lamentation On A High Hill/Marc P. Smith
Lamp At Midnight/Barrie Stavis
Lamppost Reunion/Louis LaRusso II
Lana Got Laid In Lebanon/Tom Eyen
Land I Love, The/Peter Copani
Land Of Fire/Glenn A. Smith
* Land Of Lem/S. Garrett Robinson
Landscape Of The Body/John Guare
Landscape W/Figures/Curtis Zahn
* Landscape With Waitress/Robert Pine
Land Where Our Fathers Died/J. J. Coyle
Lantern In The Wind/Tim Kelly
* La Peregrina/Charles Eastman
LaPlotte/Mark Leib
Larger Than Life/Mark Edwards
Larger Than Life/Joseph Schrank
Lark, The/Lillian Hellman
Last Act, The/Jack Gilhooley
Last Available Burial Ground On Manhattan Island, The/Betsy J. Robinson
Last Chalice, The/Joanna M. Glass
Last Chord, The/Charles Gordone
Last Christians, The/Jack Gilhooley
Last Damned Witch In Salem, The/Jules Tasca
* Last Dance Before The Music/Robert Riche
Last Dance For Sybil, A/Ossie Davis
Last Dance In The Sun, A/Lennox Brown
Last Days Of British Honduras, The/Ronald Tavel
* Last Ferry To Thebes/Stanley Taikeff
Last Gasps/Terrence McNally
Last Great Cocktail Party, The/Tom Eyen
Last Great Nipmuc, The/Marc P. Smith
Last Laugh, The/Paul Mroczka
Last Licks/Frank D. Gilroy
Last Minstrel Show, The/Joe T. Ford
Last Moments Of John D. Rockefeller/John Pyros
Last Moments Of W.A.Mozart/John Pyros
Last Of Hitler, The/Joan Schenkar
Last Of Mrs. Lincoln, The/James Prideaux
Last Of My Solid Gold Watches, The/Tennessee Williams
Last Of Sherlock Holmes, The/Tim Kelly
* Last Of The Marx Brothers' Writers, The/Louis Phillips
Last Of The Red Hot Lovers, The/Neil Simon
Last Pat Epstein Show Before The Reruns, The/Paula A. Vogel
Last Respects/Daniel Lipman
* Last Stage Of Labor, The/Edward M. Cohen
Last Summer At Bluefish Cove/Jane Chambers
* Last Supper, A/James D. Pendleton
* Last Things/Brian Taggert
* Last Words/Joan Schenkar

APPENDIX

Late City Edition/Lonnie Carter
Late Drummer Boy, The/Leonard Melfi
Late/Late. . Computer Date!/Ludmilla
  Bollow
Later/Corinne Jacker
Late Show, The/Barbara Field
Late Snow, A/Jane Chambers
Lather/Dick D. Zigun
La Turista/Sam Shepard
Laugh, God!/Jerome Lawrence
Laughing String/Leslie Weiner
Laundry, The/Howard Richardson
* Lawful Mr. Bean, The/C.H. Keeney
Lay Out Letter, The/Charles Fuller
Lazy Baby Susan/Leonard Melfi
Leader/Israel Horovitz
Leading Lady, The/Ruth Gordon
* Leading Lady/Herb Schapiro
* Leaf People, The/Dennis J. Reardon
Lean And Hungry Priest, A/Warren Kliewer
Leaves For A Sunday Afternoon/N. Selden
  & M. Imbrie
Leavin' Cheyenne/Working Her Way
  Down/Percy Granger
Legality Of Food, The/Allen Sternfield
Legend Of The Conway Line/Stanley
  Disney
Lemonade/James Prideaux
Lemonade Joe Rides Again/Tim Kelly
Lemon Sky/Lanford Wilson
Lena And Louie/Leonard Melfi
Leonora/Mark Edwards
* Leonora (The White Crow)/Murray T.
  Bloom
* Leon Trotsky/Leo Rutman
Le Poseur/David Lifson
Leroy And The Ark/Allen Davis III
Let It Bleed/Terrence McNally
Let Me Hear You Whisper/Paul Zindel
Let Me Tell It To You (Dr. Paroo)/Robert
  Patrick
"Let's Hear It For Miss America!"/Gloria
  Gonzalez
* Letters Home/Rose L. Goldemberg
Letter To Sara, The/Dick D. Zigun
Letter To The World/Saul Zachary
Levine/Robert Pine
Liars Die/J.E. Franklin
Liberation/Jerome Kass
Liberation Of Linda Dworkin, The/Norman
  Beim
Liberty Is The Color Of The Night/James
  Schevill
Library, The/John Jiler
Lieutenant, The Boy & The Dog,
  The/Herschel Steinhardt
Life And Death In A Public
  Place/Benjamin Bradford
Life And Death Of Rogue Robbie
  Kilkenny, The/Leo Rutman
Life And/Or Death/Herb Gardner
Life Boat Drill/Tennessee Williams
Life Guard/Louis Phillips
Life In The Day Of, A/Charlotte Kraft
Life In The Theatre, A/David Mamet
Life, Love And Other Minor Matters/Leslie
  Lee

Life Of God,: An Autobiography, The/David
  K. Heefner
Life Of Juanita Castro, The/Ronald Tavel
* Life Of Lady Godiva, The/Ronald Tavel
Life Of The Party, The/A.R. Gurney, Jr.
Life On Dixie Pike/Rochelle H. Dubois
Lifesaver/Conrad Bishop
Life Scenes/Lance Lee
Lifetime Revue/Louis LaRusso II
Light And The Dark Of It, The/Robert
  Gordon
* Lights/Gloria Gonzalez
Lights, Camera, Action/Robert Patrick
Like It Is/Helen Kromer
Likeness To Life, A/Saul Zachary
Lilac Season, The/Louisa Burns-Bisogno
Lily Of The Valley Of The Dolls/Robert
  Patrick
Limb Of Snow/Anna M. Barlow
Line/Israel Horovitz
Lion And The Portugese, The/Susan Rivers
Lion In Winter, The/James Goldman
Lion Roams The Street, A/Gordon R.
  Watkins
Lions Four, Christian's Nothing/Eric M.
  Lord
Listening/Edward Albee
Listen, My Children/Ramon L. Delgado
Listen Professor/Peggy Phillips
Litters Of Flowers, The/Richard Stockton
* Little Bird/Mary Gallagher
* Little Birds Fly, The/Harding Lemay
* Little Black Sheep/Anthony Scully
* Little Dancing, A/Robert K. Smith
Little Deaths, The/Susan Griffin
Little Dog Laughed, The/Joseph Schrank
Little Foxes, The/Lillian Hellman
* Little Gentleman, The/Yale Udoff
Little Girl, Big Town/Townsend Brewster
* Little Going Away Party, A/Sybille
  Pearson
Little Green Bird, The/Jonathan Levy
* Little Holy Water, A/Ramon L. Delgado
Little Johnny/Murray Schisgal
Little Me/Neil Simon
Little More Light Around The Place, A/
  Charles Gordone
Little Murders/Jules Feiffer
Little Night Music, A/Hugh Wheeler
Little Ocean/Sam Shepard
Little Old Hermit Of The Northwest
  Woods, The/E. Macer-Story
Little Red Riding Wolf/R. Eugene Jackson
Little Shepherd Of Kingdom Come, The/
  Earl H. Smith
Little Shop, The/Robert Pine
* Little Singing, A/Robert K. Smith
* Little Something Before You Go, A/Herb
  Schapiro
Little Toy Dog, The/Ramon L. Delgado
Little Travelling Music, A/Rose L.
  Goldemberg
* Little Wine With Lunch, A/John Von Hartz
Live Spelled Backwards/Jerome Lawrence
Live Wire, The/Garson Kanin
Live Woman In The Mines, A/Mark
  Edwards

Living The Life/Dale Wasserman
Lizzie Borden Of Fall River/Tim Kelly
Locket, The/Robert W. Martin
Locking Piece/Louis C. Adelman
Lock The Door Behind You/Michael
  Shurtleff
Loco-Motion, Commotion, Dr. Gorilla And
  Me/Tim Kelly
Lolita/Edward Albee
Lone Canoe/David Mamet
Lonely Places/Norman Beim
Loner/Allen Boretz
Long Goodbye, The/Tennessee Williams
* Long Night's Dying, A/Neville Aurelius
* Long Smoldering, The/Harry Granick
Long Stay Cut Short, The/Tennessee
  Williams
* Long Stretch-Short Haul/Maxwell
  Glanville
Long Way Home, The/Earl H. Smith
Lonnie, James, Bernhardt And
  Zoowolski/John Sedlak
Look At Any Man/Harding Lemay
Look Away, Look Away/Benjamin Bradford
Look Eastward/Townsend Brewster
Look, Ma I'm Dancin'!/J. Lawrence &
  R.E. Lee
Look: We've Come Through!/Hugh
  Wheeler
Look Where I'm At/Francis H. Stanton
Loose Ends/Michael Weller
Lord Byron's Love Letter/Tennessee
  Williams
Losing Things/Benjamin Bradford
Lost In Space And The Mortgage Due/Tim
  Kelly
* Lost Jill, The/Sam A. Eisenstein
Lost Money/Antoni Gronowicz
Lo, The Angel/Nancy Henderson
* Lot's Wife/Joseph Hart
Lotta/Robert Montgomery
Lou Gehrig Did Not Die Of Cancer/Jason
  Miller
Louie And The Elephant/Eddie Lawrence
* Louvain/1915/Barbara Field
Love/Benjamin Bradford
Love: A Game Of Any Length/Robert
  Patrick
* Love Among the Platipy/Richard Stockton
Love & Marriage & Then What?/Paul
  Hunter
Love Course, The/A.R. Gurney, Jr
* Lovecraft's Follies/James Schevill
Love From The Madhouse/Elyse Nass
* Love Games/Elaine G. Denholtz
Love/Hate/Helen Duberstein
Love In A Pub/Fredi Towbin
Love In A Tutu/Neal Black
Love In Buffalo/A.R. Gurney, Jr.
* Love In The Fifth Position/Neal Black
Love Is A Tuna Casserole/Gloria Gonzalez
Love Is Better Than The Next Best
  Thing/C. Robert Jones
Love Is The Way/W. Edwin Ver Becke
Love Lace/Robert Patrick
Love Letters/Rochelle H. Dubois
Loveliest Afternoon Of The Year/John

Guare
Love! Love! Love!/Johnny Brandon
Lovely Sunday For Creve Coeur, A/
  Tennessee Williams
Love Minus/Mary Gallagher
Love Mouse/Sheldon Rosen
Love On A Dark Night/Neal Black
Love One Another/Rose L. Goldemberg
Love Play, A/Samm-Art Williams
Love Revisited/Robert Anderson
Lovers, The/Kenneth Bernard
Lovers And Madmen/Bob Barry
Love Songs For Two Monsters/Jack
  Larson
Love's Tangled Web/Charles Ludlam
Love Suicide At Schofield Barracks,
  The/Romulus Linney
Love That Girl!/Aubrey Wisberg
Love That Waits/David H. Hwang
Loving, The/Lydia Simmons
Loving Kindness/Benjamin Bradford
Lower Drawer, The/Martin Halpern
Lucifer In The Boneyard/W. Edwin
  Ver Becke
Lucky Ones, The/Lucile Bogue
Ludlow Fair/Lanford Wilson
* Ludlow Ladd/Michael Colby
Ludwig & Wagner/Robert Patrick
Lull In The Fighting, A/Robert F. Joseph
Luminosity/A. Petrides & D. Kagan
Luminosity Without Radiance/Diane
  Kagan
Lunch/Benjamin Bradford
Lunch Hour/Jean Kerr
Lunchtime/Leonard Melfi
Lust/Steven Somkin
Luv/Murray Schisgal
Lydie Breeze/John Guare

M

Macbird/Barbara Garson
Mackerel/Israel Horovitz
MacPilate/J.E. Franklin
Madame Cleo Here, At Your Service/
  Warren Kliewer
* Madam Odum/Louis Rivers
Mad Dog Blues/Sam Shepard
Mad Hatter's Psychiatrist, The/Dot
  DeCamp
Madheart/Imamu A. Baraka
Madly In Love/Ruth Goetz
Mad Meg/Robert H. Eisele
Madness Of Lady Bright, The/Lanford
  Wilson
Madonna In The Orchard, The/Paul Foster
Madwoman Of Central Park West,
  The/Arthur Laurents
Ma-Fa/Ernest Ferlita
Mafia/Mario Fratti
Maggie/Lee Hunkins
Magic Drum, The/S. Garrett Robinson
Magic Flute, The/Barbara Field
Magic Realists, The/Megan Terry
Magic Shop, The/Richard France

APPENDIX

Magic Show, The/Bob Randall
Magic Show Of Dr. Ma-Gico/Kenneth
 Bernard
Magic Spell #7/Ntozake Shange
* Magic Time/Jean Nuchtern
* Magnificent Gourmet, The/Joseph
 Schrank
Magritte Skies/Yale Udoff
Mahalia/Don Evans
Maid To Measure/Johnny Brandon
Main-Chance Rag, The/Townsend
 Brewster
Major Milliron Reports/C.H. Keeney
Make A Joyful Noise/Lucile Bogue
Make Haste To Be Kind/Dot DeCamp
Make Like A Dog/Jerome Kass
Making It/Corinne Jacker
Making It!/Frederick A. Raborg, Jr.
Making Of Theodore Thomas, The/Michael
 Weller
Malcolm/Edward Albee
Malcolm: '71/Ed Bullins
* Malice In Wonderland/Mars Hill
Mama And Her Soldiers/Harold Heifetz
Mama Don't Make Me Go To College, My
 Head Hurts/Martha A. Fuentes
Mama's God Of Love/Susan Dworkin
Mame/J. Lawrence & R.E. Lee
* Man Around The House, A/Joseph Julian
Man Called Judas, A/Thomas G. Dunn
Mandala, The/Michael Cristofer
Mandrake, The/Wallace Shawn
Mandrake, The Magician/Lee Falk
* Mandy Lou/C. Robert Jones
Man Fly/Sam Shepard
* Man From Porlock, The/Jack A. Kaplan
Mango/Elyse Nass
Manhattan Trilogy/Anthony Damato
* Manikin/Sandra Bertrand
Man In The Family, The/Mars Hill
* Man In The Middle/Gordon R. Watkins
Man In The Sun/Willard Manus
Manny/Glenn A. Smith
* Manoa Valley/Edward Sakamoto
Man Of La Mancha/Dale Wasserman
* Man On Earth/Herschel Steinhardt
* Man Who Drew Circles, The/Barry Berg
Man Who Dug Fish, The/Ed Bullins
Man Who Had All The Luck, The/Arthur
 Miller
* Man Who Knew John Dillinger, The/Janet
 McReynolds
* Man Who Lost The River, The/Bernard
 Sabath
Man Who Loved Music, The/Howard
 Pflanzer
Man Who Never Died, The/Barrie Stavis
Man Who Raped Kansas, The/Don Flynn
Man Who Stayed By His Negative, The/
 Peter Dee
Man Who Tried To Hate/Robert W. Martin
* Man Who Was Dracula, The/Vincent
 Viaggio
Man With Bags/Israel Horovitz
Man With The Golden Arm, The/Louis C.
 Adelman
* Many Happy Returns/Eric M. Lord

Ma, Pa And Me/Leonard L. Perlmutter
Marathon/Richard Olson
Marching As To War/Rose L. Goldemberg
Marco Polo/Jonathan Levy
Marco Polo Sings A Solo/John Guare
* Marcus Brutus/Paul Foster
Margaret And Kit/Shirley M. Lauro
Marie And Bruce/Wallace Shawn
* Marjorie Daw/Sally D. Wiener
Marked For Murder/C. Robert Jones
Markos: A Vegetarian Fantasy/Kenneth
 Bernard
Mark Twain In The Garden Of Eden/Tim
 Kelly
Marlon Brando Sat Right Here/Louis
 LaRusso II
Marriage, The/William Packard
Marriage Gambol/Enid Rudd
* Marriage Museum, The/Elyse Nass
Marriage Of Bette & Boo, The/Christopher
 Durang
Marriage Of Convenience, A/Norman Beim
Marriage Of Convenience, A/Frederick
 Hunter
Marriage Proposal-Western Style, A/Tim
 Kelly
* Marry Me/Joe T. Ford
Marry Me! Marry Me!/D.R. Andersen
Marsha/Tim Kelly
Martha's Boy/Ludmilla Bollow
Martinique/Peter Dee
Martin Luther: Apostle Of Defiance/John
 Kirk
* Marvelous Adventures Of Tyl, The/
 Jonathan Levy
Marvelous Brown/Diane Kagan
Marvelous Playbill, The/Tim Kelly
* Marvels/Conrad Bishop
Marvin/N. Selden & M. Imbrie
Marx & Angela/Allen Boretz
Mary Jane/Kenneth Bernard
Mary Magdalen/Neil R. Selden
Mary Mary/Jean Kerr
Mary McDougal And The Monk/Joseph T.
 Pintauro
Mascara And Confetti/Townsend Brewster
M*A*S*H/Tim Kelly
Mash Note To An Old Codger/Toni Press
Mask Of Hiroshima, The/Ernest Ferlita
Masquerade/David Lifson
Masquerade/Richard Seff
Massachusetts Trust/Megan Terry
* Masse For The Plagued, A/Sam A.
 Eisenstein
Mass Media/Howard Pflanzer
* Master, The/James Schevill
* Master Class/Jonathan Levy
Master Of The Blue Mineral Mines,
 The/Jonathan Levy
* Master Psychoanalyst, The/Stanley
 Nelson
Match Play/Lee Kalcheim
Materia Medica/Barbara Field
Matinee/Wallace Hamilton
Matinee, The/Bernard M. Kahn
Matinee Ladies/Anne Commire
Matrix/David U. Clarke

* **Matrix**/Barbara Field
Matter Of Time, A/Benjamin Bradford
* **Matters Of Choice**/Don Evans
Matt The Killer/Howard Pflanzer
* **Maude Gonne Says No To The Poet**/Susan Rivers
Max St. Peter McBride/Barbara Fisher
Mayor Of Harlem, The/Ossie Davis
Me And Thee/Charles Horine
* **Meaningful Relationship, A**/Don Flynn
Meanwhile, Back On The Couch/Jack Sharkey
Medal Of Honor Winner, The/Albert Evans
Meddler, U.S.A./C.H. Keeney
Medicine Show: An American Entertainment/Richard Schotter
Medusa Of Forty-Seventh Street/Nancy Henderson
Meek Don't Inherit, The/June V. Williams
Meet/Conrad Bishop
Meeting, The/Anna M. Barlow
Meeting, The/Lennox Brown
Meeting Of The Creditors Of J. Matthew Spengler, The/Michael J. Chepiga
Meeting Place/Robert Lord
* **Meg**/Paula A. Vogel
Megalith/Benjamin Bradford
Melodrama Play/Sam Shepard
Mel Says To Give You His Best/James L. Rosenberg
Members/Hiram Taylor
Memo From A Mad Producer/Marc P. Smith
* **Memoirs Of Charlie Pops, The**/Joseph Hart
Memorial/Tim Kelly
Memorial Day/Sally Ordway
Memorial Day/Murray Schisgal
Memorial To The Honored Dead/Stephen Levi
Memory Bank, The/Martin B. Duberman
Memory Is A Spongecake/Raymond Platt
Memory Motel/Elizabeth Wray
Memory Of Two Mondays, A/Arthur Miller
Memory Shop/Elyse Nass
Me, Myself And You/Anthony Damato
* **Mendola's Rose**/Robert Unger
Me Nobody Knows, The/Herb Schapiro
* **Mention My Name In St. Paul**/Peter Ramsey
Mentor, The/Joanne Koch
Mequasset By The Sea/Jolene Goldenthal
Mercy Drop/Robert Patrick
Mercy Me/Jean Reavey
Mermaid In Lock No. 7, The/Edward Mabley
Merrily We Roll Along!/George Furth
Merry Murders At Montmarie/Tim Kelly
Merry War, The/Rose L. Goldemberg
Message From The Grassroots/Robert Riche
Messiah, The/Martin Halpern
Metaphors/Martin B. Duberman
Metaphysical Cop, The/David S. Milton
* **Metric Madness**/Daniel A. Stein
Meyer's Room/Sheldon Rosen
* **Miami Dig, The**/Susan Dworkin

Michael Field/Rochelle H. Dubois
Michigan, The/Daniel W. Owens
Mickey And Czerwicki Go To Heaven/Terry C. Fox
* **Mickey Mouse Murder Case, The**/Lanie Robertson
Midchannel/Allen Sternfield
Middle Ages, The/A.R. Gurney, Jr.
Middle World, The/Frank D. Gilroy
Midnight Cry, The/Wallace Hamilton
Midnight In Topanga/Frederick Bailey
Midnight Mass/Leonard Melfi
* **Midnight Mass**/Vincent Viaggio
Mighty Gents, The/Richard E. Wesley
Mild Case Of Death, A/Steven Somkin
Mildred/Robert W. Martin
Milk Of Paradise/Sallie Bingham
Milk Train Doesn't Stop Here Anymore, The/Tennessee Williams
Milo's Venus/Leslie Weiner
* **Mind With The Dirty Man, The**/Jules Tasca
* **Mine!**/Jane Chambers
* **Minnesota Moon**/John Olive
* **Minor Scene, A**/Ed Bullins
* **Miracle Of The Magazine Man**/Jerome Kass
Miracle Worker, The/William Gibson
Mirage/Robert Patrick
* **Mirrored Man**/Richard Reich
M Is For The Million/Jack Sharkey
* **Miss Firecracker Contest, The**/Beth Henley
Miss Hamford Beauty Pageant And Battle Of The Bands, The/T.C. Miller
Missing Link/Jack Sharkey
Missing Persons/Stephen Levi
Missing String, The/Robert H. Eisele
Miss Light Goes To War/Stanley Disney
* **Miss Lonelyhearts**/Howard M. Teichmann
Miss Nefertiti Regrets/Tom Eyen
Mister Esteban/Jonathan Ringkamp
Mister Jordon/John R. Zapor
Mister Punch/Conrad Bishop
Mister Shandy/N. Selden & M. Imbrie
Misunderstanding/Daniel W. Owens
Mixed Couples, The/James Prideaux
M.L. Bloom/John Pyros
Mlle. Olympe Zabriske/Sally D. Wiener
Mobile/Hiram Taylor
Mobile Homes/Elizabeth Wray
Mobiles/Elizabeth Wyatt
Mocking Bird/William D. Parchman
Mod Donna/Myrna Lamb
Model Ghetto, The/Howard Pflanzer
Mojo Candy/Thomas Babe
Moke-Eater, The/Kenneth Bernard
* **Molineaux**/John Chodes
Molly/Louis Garfinkle
Molly's Dream/Maria I. Fornes
Momma's Little Angels/Louis LaRusso II
Money/Imamu A. Baraka
Money-Back Guarantee, A/Don Flynn
Money Show, The/Conrad Bishop
Monique/Michael Blankfort
Monkey Monkey Bottle Of Beer, How Many Monkeys Have We Here?/Marsha Sheiness

Monkey Motions/Mars Hill
Monkey Of The Inkpot, The/Helen Duberstein
Monkey Of The Organ Grinder, The/Kenneth Bernard
Monkey Play/Jonathan Levy
Monochrome/Nancy Henderson
Monologia/Myrna Lamb
Monster Soup/Tim Kelly
* Montezuma's Revenge/Allen Davis III
Montgomery Footprints/Ossie Davis
Month Of Fridays, A/Wallace Hamilton
Montpelier Pazazz/Wendy Wasserstein
Montserrat/Lillian Hellman
* Monument, The/Franklyn MacGregor
Mood Indigo/Townsend Brewster
Moon Bridge, The/Benjamin Bradford
Moonchildren/Michael Weller
Moondog/Lucile Bogue
Moon In The Mirror/Lennox Brown
Moonlight And Love Songs/Marc A. Zagoren
Moon Over Deep Bay/Henry Gilfond
Moony's Kid Don't Cry/Tennessee Williams
Moral Facts/T.C. Miller
More Bread And The Circus/Louis Rivers
Mores/Peter Dee
More Than You Deserve/Michael Weller
More War In Store With Peace As Chief Of Police/Lonnie Carter
More You Get The More You Want, The/Johnny Brandon
More You Get, The More You Want, The/Daniel W. Owens
Morgan Yard, The/Kevin O'Morrison
Morning/Israel Horovitz
Morning Star/Sylvia Regan
Morrison/Peterson/Raymond Platt
Moscow Lights/Bernard Sabath
* Moscow Purge Trial, 1938/David S. Milton
Moses/Henry Gilfond
Mother/Lydia Simmons
Mother Ann/Myrna Lamb
Mother Courage/Ntozake Shange
Mother Goose Celebration, A/R. Eugene Jackson
Mother Goose Follies, The/R. Eugene Jackson
Mother Jones/Victor Power
Mother Jones And the Traveling Family Circus/Megan Terry
Mother Mandelbaum: Queen Of The Fences/Barbara Fisher
Mother O, Or The Last American Mother/James Schevill
Motherright/Janet McReynolds
* Mothers And Daughters/John Von Hartz
* Mother's Day/Judith Morley
Mother's Kisses, A/Bruce J. Friedman
Motion Of History, The/Imamu A. Baraka
Mound Builders, The/Lanford Wilson
Mountain Chorus, The/Albert Bermel
* Mountain Fire/Howard Richardson
Mountain Rites/Rochelle Owens
* Mourning Pictures/Honor Moore
Mouse And The Raven, The/Tim Kelly

Mouse in The White House, The/Priscilla B. Dewey
Movie Buff/Hiram Taylor
Movie, Movie On The Wall/Sally Ordway
Moving Day/Linda Segal
Moving On/Gloria Gonzalez
* Moving Violation, The/Sharon S. Martin
* Movin' Mountains/Thomas M. Fontana
Mowgli/Townsend Brewster
* Mr. & Mrs. "A"/Charles Leipart
Mr. & Mrs. Lyle Conger/Joel Ensana
Mr. Biggs/Anna M. Barlow
Mr. Coincidence/Jack A. Kaplan
* Mr. Cripple Kicks The Bucket/C.E. Wilkinson
* Mr. Curator's Proposal/David Trainer
Mr. Dunne & Mr. Dooley/Victor Power
Mr. Happiness/David Mamet
Mr. Opportunity & The Undefeated Rhumba Champ/Charles Leipart
Mr. Optometrist/Stanley Nelson
Mr. Randolph Brown/Louis Rivers
Mrs. Bullfrog/Robert Kornfeld
Mrs. Fiske/David U. Clarke
Mrs. Gibbons Boys/Joseph Stein
Mr. Shandy/N. Selden & M. Imbrie
* Mr. Simian/Sheppard Kerman
Mrs. Middleman's Descent/Martin Halpern
* Mrs. Murray's Farm/Roy London
Mrs. Old And The Unicorn/Brendan N. Ward
* Mrs. Peacock/Stanley Nelson
Mr. Stefan/Alan Roland
Mr. Tavel Writes A Play For Mr. Weiss/Ronald Tavel
Mr. Welk And Jersey Jim/Howard Sackler
Mr. Whittington/Neville Aurelius
Mr. Wilson's Peace Of Mind/Mark Stein
Mr. Wonderful/Joseph Stein
Ms Light And The Centerfold Man/Stanley Disney
Mud/W. Edwin Ver Becke
Muddle/Mark Leib
* Mudnest, The/Victor Power
Multiple Fractures/Ross MacLean
Mummers/Jack Gilhooley
Mummers And Men/David Lifson
Mummer's End/Jack Gilhooley
* Murder Among Friends/Bob Barry
Murder At The Howard Johnson's/R. Clark & S. Bobrick
Murder In The Magnolias/Tim Kelly
Murdermask/Joseph G. Gottfried
Murder Of Einstein, The/Robert Eisele
Murder Of Mrs. Magoo, The/Lanie Robertson
Murder Room, The/Jack Sharkey
* Museum/Tina Howe
* Museum Of Olde Tyme Life, The/Warren Kliewer
Museum Project, A/Barbara Fisher
Musical Chairs/Barry Berg
Musical Festival, The/Allen Sternfield
Music-Hall Sidelights/Jack Heifner
Musicians Of Bremen/Vernon Hinkle
* Music Lessons, The/Wakako Yamauchi
Musing/John Sedlak

* **Mutual Benefit Life**/Robert Patrick
Muzeeka/John Guare
My Aunt Daisy/Joseph Schrank
My Blue Heaven/Jane Chambers
* **My Cup Ranneth Over**/Robert Patrick
My Dear Sisters/James L. Rosenberg
My Dinner With Andre/Wallace Shawn
My Early Years/Charles Leipart
* **My Emperor's New Clothes**/Larry Shue
My Foetus Lived On Amboy Street/
Ronald Tavel
My Life/Corinne Jacker
My Mother, My Father And Me/Lillian
Hellman
My Name Is Bobby/William Packard
My Name Is Sybil Ludington/D.R.
Andersen
My Next Husband Will Be A Beauty/Tom
Eyen
My Sister Eileen/Jerome Chodorov
* **My Sister, My Sister**/Ray Aranha
My Son The Astronaut/Jack Sharkey
Mystery Of Phillis Wheatley, The/Ed
Bullins
Mystery Play/Jean-Claude van Itallie
Mythical-Merry-Go-Round/Susan Charlotte
My Wife Dies At Stonehenge/Conrad
Bishop

N

Naked In The Garden/James Schevill
* **Naked Underneath**/Richard Reich
Name Plate, The/Raymond Platt
Namesake/Amlin Gray
Napoleon's Dinner/Samuel Shem
Narcissus/Roma Greth
Narco Linguini Bust, The/Megan Terry
Narrow Escape/Jeffrey Sweet
Nashville Jamboree/Tim Kelly
Nasty Rumors And Final Remarks/Susan
Miller
Natasha's Theme From The Idiot/Peter
Ramsey
National Guard, The/Robert Auletta
Natives Are Restless, The/Tim Kelly
* **Natives Were Restless, The**/Eddie
Lawrence
Nativity/Robert Lord
Natural Philosophy Of Love, The/Elizabeth
Wyatt
Nature & Purpose Of The Universe, The/
Christopher Durang
Nature Of Violence, The/Ray Aranha
Nature's Way/Herman Wouk
Naughty Naughty/Peter Copani
Navajo House/Tim Kelly
Nearest I'll Get To Heaven, The/Edward M.
Cohen
Nearest Star, The/Jerome McDonough
Necessary Murders/Lydia Simmons
* **Ned And Jack**/Sheldon Rosen
Need For Brussel Sprouts, A/Murray
Schisgal
Needmore/William E. Parchman

Needmore's Mother/William E. Parchman
* **Neffie**/China C. Pendarvis
Neighbors, The/Martha A. Fuentes
Neighbors/Jeffrey Sweet
Neither Kith Nor Kin/Aldyth Morris
* **Nell**/William M. Green & D.L. Turner
Nell Gwyn, The Protestant Whore/Diane
Lampert
Nelson '76/Ross MacLean
Neon Woman, The/Tom Eyen
* **Nerd, The**/Larry Shue
Nest, The/Tina Howe
Nest Among The Stars/Ramon L. Delgado
Never A Snug Harbor/David U. Clarke
* **Nevis Mountain Dew**/Steve Carter
New Day/E. Macer-Story
New Faces Of 1956/Neil Simon
New Faces Of 1968/William F. Brown
New Fire/Ernest Ferlita
New Man, A/Paul Mroczka
News Item/David Lifson
New Woman, The/Benjamin Bradford
* **New Years Day**/June Calender
New York Comedy: Two/Megan Terry
Next/Terrence McNally
Next Contestant, The/Frank D. Gilroy
Next Thing, The/Joan Schenkar
Next Time/Ed Bullins
Next Year In Jerusalem/Martin Sherman
Niagara Falls/Leonard Melfi
Nice Boy For Joanie, A/Judith Morley
Nice Place You Have Here/M.H. Appleman
**Nigger, Nigger Who's The Bad
Nigger**/Daniel W. Owens
Night/Leonard Melfi
Night Before Paris, The/Martin Sherman
Night Class, The/Lennox Brown
Night Club/Kenneth Bernard
Night Fishing In Beverly Hills/Louis C.
Adelman
**Night James Boswell, Esquire, Wrote The
Autobiography Of Dr. Samuel Johnson,
The**/Joe T. Ford
* **Nightlight**/Barry Berg
Night Light/Kenneth H. Brown
* **Night Lights**/Clifford Turknett
Night Mail/Ted Tally
Nightmare/Susan Yankowitz
Night Of The Beast/Ed Bullins
Night Of The Body Count/John R. Zapor
Night Of The Dunce/Frank Gagliano
Night Of The Iguana, The/Tennessee
Williams
Night Of The Moonspell/Edward Mabley
Night Of The No-Moon, The/Leslie Lee
* **Nights Alone**/Valerie Harris
Night School/Michael Kassin
Night Shade/Richard Reich
* **Nightsong**/James D. Pendleton
Nights Passage Into Purple Passion/Louis
Rivers
Nightstone/Elizabeth Wray
Night Sun/Lennox Brown
* **Night Thoreau Spent In Jail, The**/
J. Lawrence & R.E. Lee
Night Thoughts/Corinne Jacker
Nightwalk/Sam Shepard

Nightwalk/Megan Terry
Night Whispers/Leo Rutman
* Night Wind, A/Leo Rutman
Nine/Mario Fratti
Nine As One/OyamO
Nine Hundred Million Chinese/Robert Pine
998/Dale Wasserman
Nine O'Clock Mail, The/Howard Sackler
* Nine Rebels/Sheppard Kerman
Nine Tenths Of The Flaw/Steven Somkin
Ninety-Day Mistress, The/J.J. Coyle
* 96A/Nancy Henderson
Nip 'N Tuck/Jules Tasca
* Nirvana Manor/Judith Morley
* Noah's Ark/Barbara & Carlton Molette
No Better/Robert E. Ingham
Noble's Reward, The/Jerome McDonough
* Nobody Hears A Broken Drum/Jason
Miller
Nocturne/Saul Zachary
No Hard Feelings/Ron Clark & Sam
Bobrick
* Noirhommes, The/Daniel W. Owens
Noisy City Sam/Barbara Fisher
No More Chattanooga Choo Choo/Sally
Ordway
No Mourning After Dark/Michael Kassin
* No Moves Back/Martin Halpern
Noon/Terrence McNally
No One Is Exactly 23/Susan Miller
No One Walks Alone/Herschel Steinhardt
No One Wants To Know/Peter Dee
No One Writes Drawing Room Comedies
Anymore/Stanley Nelson
No Opera In The Op'ry House Tonite/Tim
Kelly
No Place For A Lady/Townsend Brewster
No Place To Be Somebody/Charles
Gordone
Nordland/Richard Reich
Norman, Is That You?/R. Clark &
S. Bobrick
* North Atlantic/Michael Colby
* Nose For A Nose, A/Eddie Lawrence
Noses/Arthur Sainer
Not A Through Street/Wakako Yamauchi
Notes On A Hypothetical Second Coming/
J. Kline Hobbs
Not Far From The Gioconda Tree/Tim
Kelly
Not The Count Of Monte Cristo?/Jack
Sharkey
Nothing But Punks/Jack A. Kaplan
* Nothing Immediate/Shirley M. Lauro
* Nothing Is Forever/Robert W. Martin
Nothing Is Worth Fighting For/Wallace
Dace
No Time/Sallie Bingham
No Time For Sergeants/Ira Levin
Not To The Swift/C.H. Keeney
No Trespassing/Lanford Wilson
Nourish The Beast/Steve Tesich
Nouveau Jersey/Leslie Weiner
No Vacancy/Judith Morley
November People/Roma Greth
No Way!/R. Eugene Jackson
Nowhere To Run/Peter Copani

Now It Makes Sense/Don Flynn
Now She Dances!/Doric Wilson
Now That The Children Are Grown/
Raymond Platt
Now There's Just The Three Of Us/
Michael Weller
* Nutcracker In The Land Of Nuts,
The/Ronald Tavel

O

Oaks Of Mamre, The/James D. Pendleton
Obelisk, The/Ernest Ferlita
Objay Dart For Judith/Drury Pifer
Obscene Verse Of Magdalene Randall-
man, The/James D. Pendleton
Observation Chamber, The/E. Macer-Story
O Canada/Jerry Spindel
Occasion/Ray E. Fox
Occupation/Mars Hill
* Ocean In A Teacup/Neil R. Selden
October Festival/Wallace Dace
Odd Couple, The/Neil Simon
Odd Women, The/Lonnie Carter
Odyssey Of Howard Singleton, The/
William M. Green
Odyssey Of Jeremy Jack, The/Mark
Medoff
Oedipus Again/Alan Havis
Off/Silas Jones
* Offering, The/Gus Edwards
Offering, The/Stephen Levi
Office, The/Maria I. Fornes
Office, The/Lydia Simmons
Office Party, The/Charles Horine
Off-Season/John Von Hartz
Off Season, The/Harding Lemay
Off To Buffalo/Allen Boretz
Off-White/F. V. Hunt
Of Masks Outrageous And Austere/
Tennessee Williams
Of Pickles And Purple Peacocks/Eugene
McKinney
Of Time And The River/Eugene McKinney
Oh, Careless Love!/David Lifson
Oh Dad, Poor Dad, Mamma's Hung You In
The Closet And I'm Feelin' So Sad/
Arthur Kopit
* Oh, What A Beautiful City!/Townsend
Brewster
Oh What Food We Morsels Be/Edan
Schappert
O.K. Certaldo/Rochelle Owens
Old Blues/Jonathan Levy
Old Bones/Steve Tesich
* Oldest Drug Store In New York, The/Arthur
Jasspe
* Oldest Profession, The/Paula A. Vogel
* Old Fashioned/Thomas M. Fontana
Old Folks At Home/Mark Berman
Old Jew, The/Murray Schisgal
Old Man, The/Wallace Shawn
Old Man Joseph And His Family/Romulus
Linney
Old Oak Encounter, The/Jerome

McDonough
Old One-Two, The/A.R. Gurney, Jr.
* **Old Phantoms**/Gus Edwards
Old Skin Flint/C.H. Keeney
Old Smoky/Earl H. Smith
Ole Ball Game, The/Sharon S. Martin
* **Oli Oli Oxen Free**/Charles Eastman
O, Little Town/Jerome McDonough
Olmsted!/Michael Colby
Olympic Park/Myrna Lamb
Om, A Sharing Service/Arthur Sainer
Omega Point, The/William Griffin
Omega's Ninth/Ramon L. Delgado
O My Pretty Quintroon/Townsend
Brewster
Once An Actor/C.H. Keeney
* **Once And For All**/Robert Gordon
Once And For All/William Packard
Once Below A Lighthouse/Ramon L.
Delgado
Once I Put An Ad In The Void/Stanley
Nelson
Once Is Enough/Jack Sharkey
Once More/Anthony Scully
On Cobweb Twine/Anna M. Barlow
**One Act By Art Smythe, Full Length Play
By Joe Jones**/Jules Tasca
One Arm/Lanford Wilson
**One Day In The Life Of Ivan
Denisovich**/Richard France
One Down/Eric M. Lord
One Evening In Thalia/Frederick A.
Raborg, Jr.
One Flew Over The Cuckoo's Nest/Dale
Wasserman
110 In The Shade/N. Richard Nash
**100,001 Horror Stories Of The
Plains**/Megan Terry
* **120 Miles Northeast Of Chicago**/J. Kline
Hobbs
One Last Look/Steve Carter
One Leg Over The Wrong Wall/Albert
Bermel
One Long Day/Saul Zachary
One Man Show/Ruth Goetz
One More Little Drinkie/Megan Terry
One More Waltz With Molly O'Flynn/Peter
Dee
One Night Stand/Herb Gardner
One Person/Robert Patrick
1 Piece Smash/Arthur Sainer
One Shadow Behind/Daniel W. Owens
One Short Day At The Jamboree/Jane
Chambers
* **One World At A Time**/Richard Stockton
Only Game In Town, The/Frank D. Gilroy
Only Good Indian, The/Mario Fratti
Only In America/J. Lawrence & R.E. Lee
* **Only More So**/Joseph Julian
Only Still Life/Bill Bozzone
On Stage Inn/Jean Riley
On Summer Days/Roma Greth
On The Bridge/Howard Pflanzer
On The Brink/M.H. Appleman
On The March To The Sea/Gore Vidal
On The Other Hand/William Packard
On The Road To Babylon/Richard E.

Wesley
On The Rocks/A. Petrides & D. Kagan
**On The Runway Of Life, You Never Know
What's Coming Off Next**/Arthur Kopit
Oooooooops/Robert Patrick
Op/Frank M. Mosier
Open Admissions/Shirley M. Lauro
* **Opening Night**/Hiram Taylor
Open Meeting, The/A.R. Gurney, Jr.
Operation Sidewinder/Sam Shepard
Operetta!/Jack Sharkey
Ophelia Kline/Richard Lees
Oppenheimer's Chair/James Schevill
Opposite End Of The Couch, The/
Frederick Bailey
Opus One-Eleven/Martin Halpern
* **Orbits**/Mark Eisman
Orchestra/Richard Reich
Origin Of The Species/Curtis Zahn
* **Orion's Hound**/Daniel Lipman
Orphan, The/David Rabe
Orphans, The/James Prideaux
Other People's Table, The/Corrine Jacker
Other Side Of The Island, The/Frederick A.
Raborg, Jr.
Other Voices Other Rooms/Anna M.
Barlow
* **O. 2V**/Gail Kriegel
Our Father's Failing/Israel Horovitz
Our First Gobi Fossils/Larry Loonin
Our Hearts Were Young And Gay/Jean
Kerr
Our Late Night/Wallace Shawn
Our Very Own Hole In The Ground/
Bernard M. Kahn
* **Outbreak Of World War I, The**/Merritt
Abrash
Out Cry/Tennessee Williams
Outlanders/Amlin Gray
Out Of Sync/Richard Lees
Out-Of-Town Traffic/Leonard Melfi
Out Of Track/Anna M. Barlow
Out To Lunch/Betsy J. Robinson
Ovens Of Anita Orangejuice, The/Ronald
Tavel
* **Overcoat, The**/Thomas M. Fontana
Overseers, The/Robert Patrick
Over The Glass Mountain/Martha A.
Fuentes
Over Twenty-One/Ruth Gordon
Ovet And Tevo/John Scott
* **Ozone Hour**/Richard Henrickson

P

Pacific Overatures/H. Wheeler &
J. Weidman
Paducah/Sallie Bingham
Pagano/Drury Pifer
Page Miss Glory/Joseph Schrank
Pain(t)/Richard Foreman
Painted School/Antoni Gronowicz
Palm-Leaf Boogie, The/Townsend
Brewster
Palm Sunday/Susan Rivers

Pancho Pancho/Marsha Sheiness
Pandas, The/Edan Schappert
Pandering To The Masses/Richard Foreman
Panes/Rochelle H. Dubois
Panzram's Revenge/Frederic Hunter
Papa For Jeremy Jr., A/Louis Rivers
* Papalina/Vincent Viaggio
Paper Houses/Ludmilla Bollow
Paper Moon/Peggy Phillips
Parable/Ernest A. Joselovitz
Parable Of Abram, A/Michael Kassin
Parabus Objective/Benjamin Bradford
Paradise Gardens East/Frank Gagliano
Paradise Kid, The/Donna de Matteo
Paradise Of Glass/Anthony Damato
Paradise Of Snakes/Felix Doherty
Parakeet Street/Joseph T. Pintauro
Paranoia In The Polo Lounge/T.C. Miller
* Parental Guidance/Jeffrey Sweet
Parent Primer, A/Vincent Viaggio
Par For The Corpse/Jack Sharkey
Paris, France/J. Lawrence & R.E. Lee
Paris Is Out/Richard Seff
Paris Then/Peter Ramsey
Park, The/F. V. Hunt
Park Bench Play, The/Lanie Robertson
Park Your Car In The Harvard Yard/Israel Horovitz
* Parlor Game/Edmund Morris
Partial Disabilities/Brendan N. Ward
Particle Theory/Richard Foreman
Parting At Imsdorf/N. Richard Nash
Party, The/William D. Parchman
Party For Divorce, A/Lee Kalcheim
* Party For Lovers, A/Kevin O'Morrison
Party Of One/Joel Ensana
Party Of The First Part/Jules Tasca
Pas De Deux/Myrna Lamb
Passage In Purgatory/Robert Kornfeld
Passage Through Bohemia, A/Sally Ordway
* Passing By/Martin Sherman
Passing Fancy/Michael Colby
Passing Game, The/Steve Tesich
Passing Through To Exotic Places/Ronald Ribman
Passionate Congressman/Lee Falk
Passione/Albert Innaurato
Passionella/Jules Feiffer
Passion Flowers/William Hairston
Passion Of Frankenstein, The/Robert Kornfeld
Pastime Of Monsieur Robert, The/Howard Sackler
Past Is The Past, The/Richard E. Wesley
* Patagonia/J.J. Coyle
Patchwork/Linda Segal
Path Of The Greater Narwhal, The/Robert Patrick
Patio/Porch/Jack Heifner
Patrick Henry Lake Liquors/Larry Ketron
Patty And Josh/Toni Press
Patty Hearst/Mario Fratti
Patty O'Brien And The Tallest Leprechaun/Dot DeCamp
Pawn, The/Mark Eichman

Pawnee Fork/Mark Edwards
* Payments/Martin B. Duberman
Payoffs/Mark Eisman
Peck/Mars Hill
Pecos Bill And Slue-Foot Sue Meet The Dirty Dan Gang/Tim Kelly
Pendants Delusions/J. Kline Hobbs
* Pele And Hiiaka/Anthony Inneo
Pelican Revisited/Robert W. Martin
Pen/Barbara Field
Pencil Of God/Dale Wasserman
Penelope's House/Susan Rivers
* Penelope's Odyssey/M.H. Appleman
Penniless Prince, The/Hiram Taylor
Penquin Touquet/Richard Foreman
* Penultimate Problem Of Sherlock Holmes, The/John Nassivera
People In The Glass Paperweight, The/Eugene McKinney
* People Of The Empire/Crispin Larangeira
People's Heart, The/Benjamin R. Barber
People vs Ranchman, The/Megan Terry
People vs The People, The/Conrad Bishop
Perdiddle/Lonnie Carter
Perfect Analysis Given By A Parrot, A/Tennessee Williams
* Perfect Gentleman, A/Herbert Appleman
Perfect Party, The/Charles Fuller
Perfect Place For Appeal To Reason, A/Robert F. Joseph
* Perfect Relationship, A/Doric Wilson
Perfect Stranger, The/Neil Cuthbert
* Perfect Stranger, A/James Elward
Performers/Richard Olson
Period Of Adjustment/Tennessee Williams
Permutations, Perceptions And Unspoken Agreements/Lydia Simmons
Personals/Rose L. Goldemberg
Persons, Places 'N Rings/Tobi Louis
* Person To Person/Robert Gordon
Peterpat/Enid Rudd
Peter Sent Me/Robert W. Martin
Petition, The/Don Flynn
Pets/Richard Reich
* Phallacies/John Nassivera
* Phil/F.V. Hunt
Philosophy Of A Fast Half-Back, The/Lennox Brown
Phoebus/A. Petrides & D. Kagan
Phoenix Flies, The/Susan Charlotte
Photograph/James Lapine
Photograph, A/Ntozake Shange
Photograph: Lovers In Motion, A/Ntozake Shange
Photographs: Mary And Howard/Jean-Claude van Itallie
Physician/Charles Horine
* Piaf — A Remembrance/David Cohen
Picking Up Pieces/Susan Dworkin
Pickled Peppers/Norman Beim
Picnic Ground/W. Edwin Ver Becke
* Picnic On The Meuse/Stanley Disney
Picture/Oliver Hailey
Picture Of Dorian Gray, The/Jack Sharkey
Pictures At An Inhibition/Mark Berman
Pieces Of A Man/John Scott
* Pied Piper, The/Priscilla B. Dewey

Pig, The/David Trainer
Pig Bit, The/Israel Horovitz
Pigeons/Harry Granick
Piggy Bank Rag/Edward Mabley
Pig Man, The/Paul Zindel
Pig Pen, The/Ed Bullins
Pilgrimage/Louis Phillips
Pilgrims/James Childs
* Pilgrims Landed Just Down The Road, The/Don Flynn
Pilots, The/James Schevill
Pimienta Pancakes, The/Sally D. Wiener
* Pink Burro, The/Jean Riley
* Pinnacle/Mark Stein
Pinocchio/R. Eugene Jackson
Pins And Needles/Joseph Schrank
Pinter's Revue Sketches/Townsend Brewster
Pioneer, The/Megan Terry
Pirates Or Rackham In Love/Amlin Gray
Pistols In The Park/Eddie Lawrence
Pitfall For A Rational Man/Benjamin Bradford
Pity The Poor Fish/C.H. Keeney
Place + Target/Richard Foreman
Plain And Fancy/Joseph Stein
Plain Princess And The Lazy Prince, The/Joseph Schrank
Plan, The/Stanley Nelson
Planet Fires/Thomas Babe
Playbirth/Ronald Tavel
Play-By-Play/Robert Patrick
Play Dead/Jonathan Ringkamp
* Players On A Beach/Sheppard Kerman
Play For Germs/Israel Horovitz
Playground/Barbara Field
* Play House/Joseph G. Gottfried
Playing Ludwig/Robert Kornfeld
Playing With Strindberg's Fire/Donna de Matteo
* Play In Seven Scenes/Wallace Shawn
Play It Again, Sam/Woody Allen
Play Of Innocence And Change, The/ Jonathan Levy
Play Of Sadness, A/John Pyros
Play Of The Play, The/Ed Bullins
Play On!/Jack Sharkey
Play On Love/Ruth Goetz
Playthings/Sally Ordway
Play With Fire/Dale Wasserman
Play Within, The/Helen Duberstein
Plaza Suite/Neil Simon
* Please Don't Cry And Say "No"/Townsend Brewster
Please Keep Off The Grass/Mark Berman
* Please, No Flowers/Joel Ensana
Pledge Of Allegiance/Wallace Dace
Plot Counter Plot/Michael Christofer
Plotters/Benjamin Bradford
Plot To Assassinate The Chase Manhattan Bank, The/Carl Larsen
Plough And The Stars, The/Edward Mabley
Plumb Loco/Lonnie Carter
* Poe: From His Life And Mind/Stanley Nelson
* Poet And The Prostitute, The/Felix Doherty
Poet And The Rent, The/David Mamet
Poetry Reading, The/Stanley Nelson
Poets, The/Louis LaRusso II
* Poets' Corner/Elizabeth Wyatt
Point Blank/Ossie Davis
* Point Of Departure/James P. Marvin
Points Of Departure/Paul S. Lim
Points Of Departure/Robert Pine
Poised For Violence/Jean Reavey
Poison Tree, The/Ronald Ribman
Police/Imamu A. Baraka
Policeman's Wife, The/N. Selden & M. Imbrie
Politician, The/A.R. Gurney, Jr.
Ponder Heart, The/Jerome Chodorov
Poor Richard/Jean Kerr
Pope Joan/Kenneth Arnold
* Popitch Loves Puccini/Mark Berman
* Porcelain Time/Ron Cowen
* Porch/Jeffrey Sweet
Pork Chops/Willard Manus
Pornographer's Daughter, The/Jonathan Levy
Porno Stars At Home/Leonard Melfi
Portable Hoover, The/Sam A. Eisenstein
Port Authority/Leonard Melfi
Portrait Of A Madonna/Tennessee Williams
Positions/Susan Yankowitz
* Possessor, The/Franklyn MacGregor
Postcards/James Prideaux
Postman, The/Murray Schisgal
Post Mortem/Benjamin Bradford
* Postscript/Merritt Abrash
Pottstown Carnival, The/Roma Greth
Powderroom, The/Joseph Lizardi
Power/Peter Copani
* Power Of The Dog, The/Herschel Steinhardt
Practical Aspects Of Making A President/Stanley Disney
Prague Spring, The/Lee Kalcheim
Praise Song/Townsend Brewster
Prayer For My Daughter, A/Thomas Babe
Precision Machines/Louis Phillips
Predators, The/Steve Tesich
Preggin And Liss/Robert Patrick
* Prelude To Hamlet, A/Samuel Sussman
* Presence Of Mine Enemies/Robert F. Joseph
Presento/Joseph Jullian
Present Tense/Frank D. Gilroy
President And The Psychiatrist, The/Harry Granick
Pretty Penny/Jerome Chodorov
Pretty People/Doric Wilson
Price, The/Arthur Miller
Priest And Prostitute/Neil R. Selden
Primary English Class, The/Israel Horovitz
Prime Time/Priscilla B. Dewey
Prince Of Macy's, The/Gail Kriegel
Prince Of Peasantmania, The/Frank Gagliano
Princess/Benjamin Bradford
Princess Grace And The Fazzaris/Marc A. Zagoren

Princess Rebecca Birnbaum/Jerome Kass
Princess Reluctant, The/Benjamin
 Bradford
Prism Blues/Susan Charlotte
Prisoner Of Second Avenue, The/Neil
 Simon
* Prisoner Of The Crown/Richard Stockton
Private Moments In The Life Of An
 Ordinary Woman/Lucile Bogue
* Prize In The Crackerjack Box, The/William
 Parchman
Problem, The/A.R. Gurney, Jr.
* Processing Room, The/James L.
 Rosenberg
Processional From La Basse, A/Lennox
 Brown
Prodigal In Black Stone/Lennox Brown
Prodigals, The/Don Evans
Prodigal Sister, The/J.E. Franklin
Profection In Black/China C. Pendarvis
Professor Bedlam's Educational Punch &
 Judy Show/Charles Ludlam
Professor George/Marsha Sheiness
Professor Graduates, The/Norman Beim
Pro Game/Megan Terry
Promenade/Maria Irene Fornes
Promenade/Harry Granick
* Promise Of The Raining Aged/Robert S.
 Ross
Promises, Promises/Neil Simon
Promotion Of Artaud Wistaar, The/Steven
 Somkin
Proper And Fine: Fanny Lou Hamer's
 Entourage/Sharon S. Martin
* Protective Custody/Howard Richardson
Proud Flesh/James Nicholson
Prudence In Transit/Stephen Levi
P.S. I Love You/John Pyros
* P.S. Your Cat Is Dead!/James Kirkwood
* Public Good, The/Susan Dworkin
Pull The Covers Over My Head/Don Flynn
Punk In The Country, A/Richard Lees
Puppet, The/James Childs
Puppeteers, The/Helen Duberstein
* Puppet Trip, The/Gloria Gonzalez
Purgation/Curtis Zahn
Purgatorio/Ernest Ferlita
Purification, The/Tennessee Williams
Puritan Night/Ken Eulo
Purlie/Ossie Davis
Purlie Victorious/Ossie Davis
Pushcart Peddlers, The/Murray Schisgal
Pushover/Jack Sharkey
Pussies And Rookies/Leonard Melfi
* Put Them All Together/Anne Commire
* Putting On The Dog/Frederick Bailey
* Pygmalion And Galatea/Norman Beim

Q

Quail Southwest/Larry Ketron
Quality Of Mercy, A/Roma Greth
* Quartet/Peter Dee
Quasimodo/Anthony Scully
* Queen Can Lay Eggs, A/Robert S. Ross

Queen Karen/Jack A. Kaplan
Queen Lear/Robert W. Russell
Queen's Folly, A/Vincent Viaggio
Queen's Will, The/Wallace Hamilton
Questioning Of Nick, The/Arthur Kopit
Qui Est Anna Marks?/Susan Yankowitz
Quiet Evening At Home With the Human
 Race, A/Barry Berg
Quiet Place By The Sea, A/Aubrey
 Wisberg
Quiet Walk, A/Jolene Goldenthal
Quotations From Chairman Mao Tse-
 Tung/Edward Albee

R

* Rabbi, The/Howard Pflanzer
Rabbit, The/Benjamin Bradford
* Rabinowitz Gambit, The/Rose L.
 Goldemberg
Races/Mario Fratti
Radio Station WGOD Is On The Air/Louis
 Phillips
Radish/E. Macer-Story
* Rafferty One By One/Rolf Fjelde
* Rag Doll, The/Allen Davis III
Rag Dolls/R. Eugene Jackson
* Raggedy Andy/D.R. Andersen
* Raggedy Dick And Puss/Tim Kelly
Rain Barrel, The/Wallace Hamilton
Rainbow/Benjamin Bradford
Rainbow Junction/Gail Kriegel
* Raincheck/N. Selden & M. Imbrie
Rainmaker, The/N. Richard Nash
Rainy Day In Newark, A/Howard M.
 Teichmann
Ramon And The Artist/Frederick A.
 Raborg, Jr.
Random Violence/Jane Chambers
Ransom Of Red Chief, The/Clark Gesner
Rape Of Bunny Stuntz, The/A.R. Gurney, Jr.
Rapists, The/Dennis L. Turner
Rascallion/Owa
Rasputin/Lance Lee
* Ratings Sweep, The/Arthur Jasspe
Rat Race, The/Garson Kanin
Rats/Israel Horovitz
Rats' Alley/Susan Yankowitz
Ravelles' Comeback, The/Jack Gilhooley
Raven Rock, The/Leonard Melfi
* Raw Edge Of Victory, The/Barrie Stavis
* Reactivated Man/Curtis Zahn
* Ready For Teddy/Joel Ensana
Real Wife-Beater, The/Elyse Nass
Reason We Eat, The/Israel Horovitz
Rebel Women/Thomas Babe
Recent Killing, A/Imamu A. Baraka
Recepta/Antoni Gronowicz
Reception/Marsha Sheiness
Reckoning, The/Gertrude Samuels
Reckonings/Gertrude Samuels
Recluse, The/Paul Foster
* Reconcilation, The/Albert Evans
Reconciliations In Berlin/Wallace Dace
Recorder, The/Martin B. Duberman

* **Recovery, The**/Albert Bermel
Recruits/David Lifson
Red Burning Light, The/Maria I. Fornes
Red Cross/Sam Shepard
Red Devil Battery Sign, The/Tennessee Williams
Red Dress, The/Richard Reich
Redesther Play, The/Valerie Harris
Red Mountain High/Robert Auletta
Red Pigeon, The/Jack R. Guss
Red Riding Hood And The Big Bad Nuclear Wolf/Charlotte Kraft
Red Riding Hood's Revenge/E. Macer-Story
Red Rover, Red Rover/Oliver Hailey
Red Sky At Morning/Edward Mabley
Red, White and Maddox/Jay Broad
* **Reedee**/Jean Riley
Reflections/Vernon Hinkle
Refrigerators, The/Mario Fratti
Refuge/Barrie Stavis
Refugees/Robert Pine
Refusal, The/Mario Fratti
Refusal/Daniel W. Owens
Regent & The Prune, The/Eric M. Lord
Regina/Lillian Hellman
Region Of The Cross/Henry Gilfond
* **Regret Me Not**/Edan Schappert
Rehearsal/Jack Gelber
Rehearsal For Murder/Ernest A. Joselovitz
Rejections/Owa
Reluctant Mrs. Dracula/Stanley Disney
Remarkable Anna/David U. Clarke
Remarkable Susan/Tim Kelly
Remembering Mr. Maugham/Garson Kanin
Remembering Mrs. Crowley/Jolene Goldenthal
Remington/Ray Aranha
Remote Asylum/Mart Crowley
Renaissance/Lloyd Gold
Renaissance Of Barnabe Barnes, The/Barbara Field
Rendezvous/Benjamin Bradford
Repetitions/Lydia Simmons
Report To The Mayor/Robert Patrick
* **Report To The Stockholders, A**/Kevin O'Morrison
* **Requiem**/Jerome McDonough
Requiem/Kevin O'Morrison
Requiem For A President/John R. Zapor
Reservations/Martin Halpern
* **Resort 76**/Simon Wincelberg
Respectfully, CX-49-D/Curtis Zahn
* **Respects**/Jerry Spindel
Response To A Serpent's Tongue/Susan Charlotte
Responsible Spider, A/McCrae Imbrie
Resurrection Of Bernard Mandlebaum, The/Jerome Kass
Resurrection Of Jackie Cramer, The/Frank Gagliano
Resurrection Of Lady Lester, The/OyamO
Re: The Rosenbergs/Sam A. Eisenstein
Return, The/Mario Fratti
Return Of The Maniac/Jack Sharkey
Return Upriver/Harding Lemay
Reunion/Robert Kornfeld

Reunion/David Mamet
Reunion, The/Frank M. Mosier
Reunion '68/Elyse Nass
Reunion Among Ruins/David K. Heefner
Reunion On Gallows Hill/Tim Kelly
Revelations/Ron Whyte
Revenge Of The Space Pandas Or Binky Rudich And The Two Speed Clock, The/David Mamet
Reverse Psychology/Charles Ludlam
* **Revival**/Lee Hunkins
Revolutionaries Don't Sit In The Orchestra/Gloria Gonzalez
Rhesus Umbrella, The/Jeff Wanshel
Rhoda In Potatoland/Richard Foreman
Rhumba For 8 In 12 E-Z Lessons/George Freek
Rhythm 'N' Blues/William Hairston
Rib Cage/Larry Ketron
Rich And Famous/John Guare
Richest Girl In The World Finds Happiness, The/Robert Patrick
Richest Kid In Town, The/Michael Colby
Rich Is Better/Jack Sharkey
Ride A Black Horse/John Scott
Righting/Ernest A. Joselovitz
Right Of Way/Richard Lees
Rigmarole/Eric M. Lord
Rimers Of Eldritch/Lanford Wilson
Rio Grande/Martin Sherman
Rio Pork/Frederick Bailey
Rip's New Wrinkle/Priscilla B. Dewey
Rise, The/Charles Fuller
* **Rise And Fall Of Cris Cowlin**/Ken Eulo
Rite For Bedtime/Wallace Hamilton
* **Rite Of Passage**/James D. Pendleton
Rite Of Spring/Stanley Nelson
* **Rites Of Passage**/Rose L. Goldemberg
* **Rites Of Spring, The**/Joseph Schrank
* **Ritz, The**/Terrence McNally
* **Rivals**/C. Robert Jones
Riverside Drive, The/Louis C. Adelman
River Street Is Haunted/Louis La Russo II
Road From Camelot, The/Felix Doherty
Roaring Camp/J. Lawrence & R.E. Lee
* **Robbed**/Thomas G. Dunn
Rocco And Raymond/Louis LaRusso II
Rocco, The Rolling Stone/Allen Davis III
Rock Garden/Sam Shepard
Rocking Chair/Sam Shepard
* **Rock Island**/Elizabeth Wray
Rock Of Kosciusko Street, The/William M. Green
* **Rocky Road**/Donna de Matteo
Rocos/Antoni Gronowicz
Roller Coaster, The/Terrence McNally
* **Romance**/Charles Leipart
Roman Guest, The/Mario Fratti
Romantic Comedy/Bernard Slade
Romeo & Juliet Are Lovers/Jules Tasca
Romulus/Gore Vidal
* **Rondelay**/Peter Swet
Room For One Woman/Samuel Shem
Roomies/Jack Sharkey
Room Of Roses/Nathan N. Barrett
Room Service/Allen Boretz

Root Of The Iceplant/Charles Eastman
Rope Walk, The/Rolf Fjelde
* Rosalee Pritchett/Barbara & Carlton
  Molette
Rosary/Jean-Claude van Itallie
Rose Critic, The/Yale Udoff
Roses/Susan Dworkin
Rose Tattoo, The/Tennessee Williams
Rouge Atomique/N. Richard Nash
Rough And Ready/Townsend Brewster
Round The Cherry Tree/Warren Kliewer
* Round Trip/Jean Nuchtern
Route 66/Mark Berman
Rubirosa Moth/W. Edwin Ver Becke
Rumpelstiltskin Is My Name/R. Eugene
  Jackson
Runaway, The/Joseph Lizardi
Runner Stumbles, The/Milan Stitt
Runneth Over Cup, The/Lanie Robertson
Run, Thief, Run!/Joe Manchester
Run To The Sea/Larry Loonin
Rusty And Rico/Leonard Melfi
Ruth And The Rabbi/Stanley Nelson

S

Sabbatai Zevi/Jonathan levy
* Sacco & Vanzetti Meet Julius & Ethel
  Rosenberg!!/C.E. Wilkinson
Sack Of Oak Park, The/Benjamin Bradford
Sacrifice, The/Anthony Damato
Sacrifice, The/Myrna Lamb
Sacrifice, The/Gordon R. Watkins
Sad Lament Of Pecos Bill On The Eve Of
  Killing His Wife/Sam Shepard
* Safe Place, A/C.K. Mack
* Saga/Kelly Hamilton
Sa-Hurt?/Lanford Wilson
Sailing/Michael Shurtleff
* Saint Hugo Of Central Park/Jeffrey
  Kindley
Saint Hydro-Clemency/Megan Terry
Saint Philemon And The Martyr
  Anictetus/Mark Edwards
Saint Salome/Robert H. Eisele
* Sally And Marsha/Sybille Pearson
Salt Lake City Skyline/Thomas Babe
Salvation Army/Robert Patrick
Sam Dead/Neil Selden
Same Time, Next Year/Bernard Slade
Sammi/Ernest A. Joselovitz
Samurai Of Vishograd, The/Shimon
  Wincelberg
Sanctity of Marriage/David Mamet
Sanctuary In The City, A/Gloria Gonzalez
Sand/F.V. Hunt
Sand Box, The/Edward Albee
Sand Castle, The/Lanford Wilson
* Sandra And the Janitor/William Packard
Sandwich, The/Paul Mroczka
San Fernando Valley/Sally Ordway
Sanibel And Captiva/Megan Terry
* Sans Everything/Lydia Simmons
Santacqua/Joanna M. Glass
Sarah/Howard Sackler

Sarah B. Divine!/Tom Eyen
Sarah In America/Ruth Wolff
Sarava/N. Richard Nash
Satchmo/Don Evans
* Satisfaction/Peter Swet
Satisfaction Guaranteed/Lydia Simmons
Saturday Adoption/Ron Cowen
* Saturday Night/Jerome Kass
Satyricon/Paul Foster
* Satyr Play, The/Frank M. Mosier
Savage/Love/Sam Shepard
Save The Children/Joseph Lizardi
Saving Grace/Jack Sharkey
Saxophone For America, A/Mark Berman
Say, Darling/Abe Burrows
Say Farewell To The Squirrels/Neil Selden
Say Hello To Daddy/Ken Eulo
Scabs, The/Louis Rivers
Scapegoat/Elizabeth Diggs
* Scenes From American Life/A.R. Gurney,
  Jr.
Scenes In Isolation/Richard Lees
Scent Of Incense/Lennox Brown
Schatzie/Sally D. Wiener
Schlurp/Stanley Nelson
Schoolhouse On The Lot/Jerome
  Chodorov
School Teacher/Allen Boretz
Scooter Thomas Makes It To The Top Of
  The World/Peter Parnell
* Scoring/Benjamin Bradford
Scotsman & The German Farmer, The/
  Herschel Steinhardt
Scott And Zelda/Paul Hunter
Scraping Bottom/David S. Milton
Scream/Arthur Laurents
Screamers/OyamO
Scream Revolution/Peter Copani
Screen Test/Ronald Tavel
Scuba Duba/Bruce J. Friedman
* Seagull, The/Jean-Claude van Itallie
* Seagulls Of 1933, The/Frank Salisbury
* Sea Horse, The/Edward J. Moore
Sea Mother's Son/Louis LaRusso II
* Sea Of White Horses, A/Peter Dee
Searching Wind, The/Lillian Hellman
Seascape/Edward Albee
Seascape/Megan Terry
Seascape W/Figures/Curtis Zahn
Season In Hell, A/David K. Heefner
Seat Of War/William Griffin
Second Adam, The/Sally D. Wiener
Second Battle Of Baltimore, The/Sally D.
  Wiener
Second Best Bed/Tim Kelly
Second Best Bed/N. Richard Nash
Second Chance/Norman Beim
* Second Chance/Elyse Nass
* Second Chance/Leonard L. Perlmutter
Second Floor Front/Aubrey Wisberg
Second Heaven/Jack A. Kaplan
* Second Scroll, The/Oscar Brand
Second-Story Sunlight/Bruce Serlen
Second Summer, A/Roma Greth
* Secret/Wendy MacLaughlin
Secret Affairs Of Mildred Wild, The/Paul
  Zindel

* **Secretaries, The**/Lydia Simmons
Secret Concubine/Aldyth Morris
* **Secret Life Of Walter Mitty, The**/Joe
Manchester
Secrets Of A Shrinking Universe/A.E.O.
Goldman
**Secrets Of The Citizens Correction
Committee**/Ronald Tavel
Secrets of The Rich/Arthur Kopit
Seduced/Sam Shepard
Seducers, The/Mario Fratti
* **Seduction Duet**/M.H. Appleman
Seeking/Louis Rivers
See Other Side/Robert Patrick
* **See/Saw**/Crispin Larangeira
See The Jaguar/N. Richard Nash
See What I Mean/Joseph Julian
**See What The Lions In The Back Cage
Will Have**/Peter Ramsey
Segments Of A Contemporary Morning/
Benjamin Bradford
Seizure, The/Albert Bermel
Selective Service/Lloyd Gold
Self Destruct/Albert Evans
Semilla/Richard Reich
Seminar/W. Edwin Ver Becke
Semmelweiss/Howard Sackler
**Sentry And The Laughing Ladies,
The**/Sandra Bertrand
Separations/Janet L. Neipris
Sepia Star/Ed Bullins
Serenading Louie/Lanford Wilson
Sermon, The/David Mamet
Serpent, The/Jean-Claude van Itallie
Serving-Girl And The Lady, The/Myrna
Lamb
Seth/Richard Lees
Set It Down With Gold/Frederick Bailey
Set Up For Glory/Howard Pflanzer
Seven Days Hath December/Arthur Jasspe
Seven Days Of Mourning/Seymour
Simckes
Seven Descents Of Myrtle, The/Tennessee
Williams
Seven Loving Women/Richard Olson
* **Seventeen Seconds**/Stanley Disney
* **Seventy-Three Hundred Hamburgers
Later**/George Hammer
Seventy Times Seven/Warren Kliewer
Seven Wives For Dracula/Tim Kelly
* **Several Objects Passing Charley
Greeley**/Carl Larsen
Sex Is Between Two People/Lanford
Wilson
* **Sextet**/Lee Goldsmith
Sextet (Yes)/Lanford Wilson
* **Sexual Perversity In Chicago**/David Mamet
Sex Warfare/Sally Ordway
Shade/Yale Udoff
* **Shades**/John Scott
Shadow And Act/John Scott
Shadow Box, The/Michael Christofer
Shadows/Robert W. Martin
Shakespeare On Shakespeare/Jonathan
Ringkamp
Shame Of Tombstone, The/Tim Kelly
Shanglers, The/Betsy J. Robinson

Shangri-La/J. Lawrence & R.E. Lee
* **Shanty, The**/Faizul B. Khan
Shapes Of Midnight/Saul Zachary
* **Sharing**/Mark Eichman
Shark In The Sky/Robert Kornfeld
Sharper Than A Serpent's Tooth/Rochelle
H. Dubois
Shaved Splits/Sam Shepard
* **Shay**/Anne Commire
* **She Also Dances**/Kenneth Arnold
* **Sheba**/Lee Goldsmith
Sheenie And Shine/John Pyros
Shelter, The/Marc P. Smith
* **She Only Beats Her Dogs To Death
Because She Is Unhappy**/C.E.
Wilkinson
Sherlock Holmes/Tim Kelly
* **Sherlock Holmes And The Adventure Of
The Speckled Band**/Tim Kelly
Sherlock Holmes' First Case/Tim Kelly
Sherlock Meets The Phantom/Tim Kelly
She's Bad Today/A.E.O. Goldman
She Sells Sea Shells/Barbara Field
She Still Stoops To Conquer/Edward
Mabley
Shine/Lee Goldsmith
Shine/Richard Seff
Shirley Basin/Jack Gilhooley
Shirley Temple, Hot-cha-cha/Wakako
Yamauchi
Shirt, The/Leonard Melfi
Shish Kabab/F.V. Hunt
Shooting Gallery/Israel Horovitz
Shoppin'/Richard Lees
Shores Of Pleasure Shores Of Pain/Antoni
Gronowicz
Short And Sweet/J. Lawrence & R.E. Lee
Shortcut To Cheyenne/Stanley Disney
Short Hop To Ohio/Judith Morley
Short Piece For A Naked Tale, A/Owa
Short Play For A Small Theatre, A/Ed
Bullins
Short Stretch At The Galluses, A/Jerome
McDonough
* **Showcase**/Vernon Hinkle
* **Showdown At The Adobe Motel**/Lanny
Flaherty
Shower/Ronald Tavel
* **Show Me A Hero**/Sally D. Wiener
Shrinking Bride, The/Jonathan Levy
Shuffle-Off/Stanley Nelson
Siamese/Lanie Robertson
* **Siamese Connections**/Dennis J. Reardon
Sideshow/Susan Yankowitz
Sidnee Poet Heroical/Imamu A. Baraka
Siege Of Syracuse, The/Martin Halpern
* **Sightlines**/Mark Eisman
Sight Unseen/Townsend Brewster
Sigiliano/Louis LaRusso II
* **Signorina, The**/Marc A. Zagoren
Signs Of Life/Joan Schenkar
Silent Night, Lonely Night/Robert
Anderson
Silent Snow, Secret Snow/Tim Kelly
Siliasocles/Larry Shue
Silk Block, The/Conrad Bishop
Silk Shirt, The/Tim Kelly

Silk Stockings/Abe Burrows
Silver Queen Saloon/Paul Foster
Silver Skies/Robert Patrick
* Silverstein & Co./Susan Miller
* Silver Whispers/James P. Marvin
Silvery Spangly Summer, The/Ludmilla Bollow
* Simas, In Chains!/Frederick A. Raborg, Jr.
Simon Says Get Married/Bernard Slade
Simple Kind Of Love Story, A/Murray Schisgal
Simple Life/Robert E. Ingham
Simultaneous Transmissions/Robert Patrick
Sin And Sorcery/Tobi Louis
* Sing America Sing/Oscar Brand
Singapore Sling/Townsend Brewster
Single Thing In Common, A/William F. Brown
Sing "Melancholy Baby"!/Steven Somkin
* Sing Me Sunshine/Johnny Brandon
Sing To Me Of Far Away Places/Tobi Louis
Sing To Me Through Open Windows/ Arthur Kopit
Sing Your Song, America/Benjamin Bradford
Sin Of Pat Muldoon/John McLiam
Sirens/Lonnie Carter
Sirens, The/Richard E. Wesley
Sister/Glenn A. Smith
Sisterhood Of A Spring Night, The/Lennox Brown
* Sister Mary Ignatius Explains It All For You/Christopher Durang
Sisters of Mercy, The/Patricia Goldstone
Sit-Up Set-Up, The/Bruce Serlen
Six Men Seated In A Subway/Herschel Steinhardt
* Six Passionate Women/Mario Fratti
6 Rms Riv Vu/Bob Randall
Sixteenth Round, The/Samm-Art Williams
Six Toes/Amlin Gray
Sixty Minute Queer Show, The/Kenneth Bernard
Skidding Into Slow Time/Stephen D. Parks
* Skin/David S. Milton
* Skin Deep/Leonard L. Perlmutter
Skip/Israel Horovitz
Skippy/Howard Sackler
Sky-Jack/Charlotte Kraft
Slapstick Tragedy/Tennessee Williams
* Slaughterhouse Play/Susan Yankowitz
Slave, The/Imamu A. Baraka
Slave Ship/Imamu A. Baraka
Sleazing Toward Athens/Megan Terry
Sleep/Jack Gelber
Sleeping Bag, The/Robert Patrick
Sleeping Beauty, The/R. Eugene Jackson
Sleepless Dancer/Anna Brennen
Sleight Of Hand/Barbara Field
Sleight-Of-Hand/John Peilmeier
* Slow Down, Sweet Chariot/Jack Sharkey
Slow Express/Robert W. Martin
* Sluts/Ross MacLean
* Smack!/Drury Pifer

Small Act Of Violence, A/Benjamin Bradford
Small Craft Warnings/Tennessee Williams
Small Winter Crisis, A/Warren Kliewer
Smart Alex/Howard M. Teichmann
Smash, The/Neil Cuthbert
Smaze/Diane Lampert
Smile Of The World, The/Garson Kanin
Smile On The Kewpie Doll, The/Ludmilla Bollow
Smith, Bessie, Death Of The/John Pyros
Smoke/Mark Stein
Smoky Links/Lonnie Carter
Snailer's Smug Larder, The/David U. Clarke
Snapping People/Neil Cuthbert
* Snow And Sand/Anthony Damato
Snowballs And Grapevines/R. Eugene Jackson
Snowbound King, The//Raymond Platt
* Snow Orchid, The/Joseph T. Pintauro
Snow Pressings/Ray Aranha
Snow-Still/Anna Brennen
Snow White/Sandra Bertrand
Snow White And The Seven Solutions/ Charlotte Kraft
Snowhite And The Space Dwarfs/ R. Eugene Jackson
Soaps/Martin Sherman
Soapy Murder Case, The/Tim Kelly
S.O.B./Dot DeCamp
Socks/Joanne Koch
* Soft Shoulders/Avra Petrides
* Soft Touch, The/Neil Cuthbert
* Sojourner Truth/Gordon R. Watkins
Soldiers Of Freedom/Louis Rivers
Soldier's Tale, The/Jack Larson
Soledad Brothers/John Peilmeier
Soledad Tetrad, The/Owa
* Solid Gold Cadillac, The/Howard M. Teichmann
Solitaire/Double Solitaire/Robert Anderson
Solitary In The House, The/Dot DeCamp
Solitary Thing, A/Martin Sherman
Soilitude Forty/Percy Granger
* Solitude, Frenzy And The Revolution/Tobi Louis
So Long At The Fair/Lanford Wilson
So Long, 174th Street/Joseph Stein
Solo Recital//Stanley Taikeff
Some Laugh, Some Cry/Mike Firth
* Some Live, Some Die/Mike Firth
Some Men Are Good At That/Elaine G. Denholtz
* Someone's Comin Hungry/N. Selden & M. Imbrie
Some Say In Ice/J. Lawrence & R.E. Lee
Something About The Albatross/Sandra Bertrand
Something Beautiful/C. Robert Jones
Something Cloudy, Something Clear/ Tennessee Williams
Something Else/Robert Patrick
Something I'll Tell You Tuesday/John Guare
Something That Matters/Don Flynn

Something Unspoken/Tennessee Williams
Sonata For Mott Street/Joseph Hart
Son, Come Home, A/Ed Bullins
S-1/Imamu A. Baraka
* Song For A Nisei Fisherman/Philip K. Gotanda
* Song Of A Nomad Flute/Susan Rivers
Song Of Bernadette/Jean Kerr
Song Of Myself/John Pielmeier
Song Of The Spear/Lennox Brown
Song Of The Street/Herschel Steinhardt
Songs Of Passersby/Conrad Bishop
Song Stories/Conrad Bishop
Son Of Redhead, The/Leonard Melfi
Sons Of Men/Herschel Steinhardt
Son Who Hunted Tigers In Jakarta, The/ Ronald Ribman
Sophia = (Wisdom)/Richard Foreman
* Sophie And Willa/Michael Kassin
Sophisticated Seductress, The/Steven Somkin
So Please Be Kind/Frank D. Gilroy
Sorcerer's Apprentice, The/Wallace Dace
* Sorrows Of Frederick, The/Romulus Linney
Sorrows Of Stephen/Peter Parnell
Sorry/Michael Kassin
Sort Of A Love Song/Glenn A. Smith
Souffle Of Turbot/Raymond Platt
* Sounding Brass/Robert E. Lee
Sounds Of A Triangle/Jean Reavey
Sounds Of Laughter/Tobi Louis
Southern Comfort/Romulus Linney
Souvenirs/Sheldon.Rosen
Spaced/Elizabeth Wyatt
Space Fan, The/James Schevill
Spaceman's Halloween/Charlotte Kraft
Spared/Israel Horovitz
* Sparks Fly Upwards/J. Lawrence & R.E. Lee
Sparrow In Flight/Charles Fuller
Sparrows Of The Field//Ramon L. Delgado
Spartans/Benjamin Bradford
Speakeasy/Linda Segal
Spectre/Saul Zachary
Speed, Bonnie Boat/Nancy Henderson
Spelling Bee, The/C. Robert Jones
* Spelling Bee, The/Marsha Sheiness
* Spermatocidalmania/Robert W. Martin
Sphinx, The/Richard Olson
Spinoff/Jack Sharkey
* Spiritual Rock Incident At Christmas Time/Louis Rivers
Spirit Your Wife Away To,The Woods/ Michael Shurtleff
Spit In The Ocean/Anna M. Barlow
* Splendid Rebels/Ernest A. Joselovitz
Split/Michael Weller
Spots/Saul Zachary
Spring Fever/Elizabeth Wyatt
Spring Journey/Edward Mabley
Spring Offensive, The/Arthur Sainer
Springtime Man, A/Leonard Melfi
Square In The Eye/Jack Gelber

Square Peg, The/Lee Hunkins
Square Roots Of Mother/Nathan N. Barrett
Squirrels/David Mamet
Squirrels/Vincent Viaggio
S.R.O./Ken Eulo
Stag At Eve, The/Robert Riche
Stage Blood/Charles Ludlam
Stage Directions/Israel Horovitz
* Stages/Jerome McDonough
* Stag King/Sheldon Rosen
Stairs To The Roof/Tennessee Williams
* Stalingrad II/Allen Sternfield
Stamp Family, The/Stanley Taikeff
* Standing On My Knees/John Olive
* Stardust/James Nicholson
Star In Heaven, A/Herschel Steinhardt
Star Is Always Loved, The/Peter Copani
Star Is Born Again, A/OyamO
* Stark Mad In White Satin/Daniel A. Stein
Stars And Stripes/Leonard Melfi
Star Spangled Girl, The/Neil Simon
Star Spangled Manor/Dot DeCamp
Starters/Jack Gelber
Star Treatment/Jack Heifner
Starwalk/Robert Patrick
State Office Building Curse/Ed Bullins
Station, The/Jolene Goldenthal
Stationary Wave/Ken Eulo
* Station J/Richard France
* Statues/Janet L. Neipris
Steak Palace, The/Bruce Serlen
Steambath/Bruce J. Friedman
Stephen Foster/Earl H. Smith
Step Out Of Line, A/Enid Rudd
Stevenson/Aldyth Morris
St. Francis/Ludmilla Bollow
Sticks And Bones/David Rabe
Stiletto Or The Crime Of Fashion/Charles Leipart
Still Life/McCrea Imbrie
* Still Life/Susan Rivers
* Still Life/Susan Yankowitz
Still Life With Apples/Ruth Wolff
Still-Love/Robert Patrick
Stimulation/Leonard Melfi
* Stitchers And Starlight Talkers/Kathleen Betsko
St. James Park/Bruce Serlen
Stomach Full Of Echoes, A/Saul Zachary
Stoned Angels, The/Paul Foster
Stones Cry Out, The/Ernest Ferlita
Stoop/Lanford Wilson
Stops/Robert Auletta
Stops Along The Way/Jeffrey Sweet
* Stop The Parade/Marsha Sheiness
* Storeyville I/Marc P. Smith
Stormbound/Larry Ketron
Story/Ross MacLean
Storyville/Ed Bullins
* Straight Up With A Twist/William F. Brown
Strange Kind Of Romance, The/Tennessee Williams
Stranger In A Strange Land, A/Jolene Goldenthal
Strategic Sacrifice/Robert Pine

Streamers/David Rabe
Streetcar Named Desire, A/Tennessee
  Williams
* Street Jesus/Peter Copani
Street Scene/Helen Duberstein
Street Sounds/Ed Bullins
Street Theatre/Doric Wilson
Street Walkers, The/Mars Hill
Strike Heaven On The Face/Richard E.
  Wesley
String-Game, The/Rochelle Owens
* Stuck/Sandra Scoppettone
Stuck/Adele E. Shank
Stuck In The Pictures On A Sunday
  Afternoon/Bill Bozzone
Student Prince/Jerome Chodorov
Studs Edsel/Percy Granger
Stuffed Crocodiles/Michael J. Chepiga
Stuffings/James Prideaux
Subject To Change/James Elward
Subject To Change/Jules Tasca
Subject To Fits/Robert Montgomery
Subject Was Roses, The/Frank D. Gilroy
Suburban Blues/Clifford Turknett
Suburban Tragedy/Jerome Kass
Subway/Frederick Hunter
Subway Sadie/Maxwell Glanville
Subways, Hallways And Rooftops/Stan
  Lachow
Success/Norman Beim
Successful Life Of 3, The/Maria I. Fornes
Suddenly Last Summer/Tennessee
  Williams
Suddenly The Music Starts/Johnny
  Brandon
* Sugar Bowl, The/Stanley Taikeff
Sugar Brown-Divine & May/China C.
  Pendarvis
* Sugar Mill/Venable Herndon
Sugarmouth Sam Don't Dance No
  More/Don Evans
Suicide, The/Mario Fratti
Suicide In B^b/Sam Shepard
Suicides In Limbo/Vernon Hinkle
Summer & Smoke/Tennessee Williams
Summer Camp/Albert Evans
Summer Demons, The/Bernard Sabath
Summer Garden, The/Terrry C. Fox
Summer Reunion/Joseph G. Gottfried
Summer Screen/Lennox Brown
Summer Soldier, The/Peggy Phillips
Summertree/Ron Cowen
Summerville/Joseph Lizardi
Sun And I, The/Barrie Stavis
Sunday/Lennox Brown
Sunday Childhood Journeys To Nobody
  At Home/Arthur Sainer
Sunday Morning/Conrad Bishop
Sunday Runners In The Rain/Israel
  Horovitz
Sunday Shoe, The/Patricia Goldstone
Sunday's Red/Anne Commire
Sunglasses/Leonard Melfi
Sun-like/Jack Larson
Sunset/Louis LaRusso II
Sunset And Evening Stance Or Mr.
  Krapp's New Tapes/James Schevill

* Sunset/Sunrise/Adele E. Shank
Sunshine Blues/Conrad Bishop
Sunshine Boys, The/Neil Simon
Sunstroke/Ronald Ribman
Superkid/R. Eugene Jackson
Super Snooper/R. Eugene Jackson
Supper, The/Lucile Bogue
Supporting Cast, The/George Furth
Sure As You're Born/Helen Kromer
* Surprise!/Kelly Hamilton
Surprise/James Kirkwood
* Surprise/Doric Wilson
Surprise Party, The/Lee Kalcheim
Surrogate Groom, The/Robert F. Joseph
* Survival Games/C.K. Mack
Survivors/Herb Schapiro
Susan Peretz At The Manhattan Theatre
  Club/Megan Terry
Suspended/Drury Pifer
Svelte Anna/Mark Berman
* Svengali/Richard France
S.W.A.K./Sally Ordway
Swan Song/Marc A. Zagoren
Swan Song Of The 11th Dawn/William
  Hairston
Sweeney Todd/Hugh Wheeler
Sweeney Todd, Demon Barber Of The
  Barbary Coast/Tim Kelly
Sweeney Todd, Or The String Of
  Pearls/John Nassivera
Sweet Bird Of Youth/Tennessee Williams
Sweet Charity/Neil Simon
Sweet Dreams/Wild Dreams/June
  Calendar
Sweet Eros/Terrence McNally
Sweet Love Remembered/Ruth Goetz
Sweet Suite/Leonard Melfi
Swiss Family Robinson, The/R. Eugene
  Jackson
* Switzerland/Rolf Fjelde
Sword And Samurai/Aldyth Morris
Swordsmen In Love/Louis LaRusso II
Symposium/T.C. Miller

T

Table Settings/James Lapine
Table Stakes/James L. Rosenberg
* Tadpole/Jules Tasca
Taffy/Anna M. Barlow
* Take A Chance!/Tobi Louis
Take A Deep Breath/Jean-Claude van
  Itallie
Take A Little Chance/Milan Stitt
Take A Number, Darling/Jack Sharkey
Take Any Street/Helen Kromer
Take Me Along/Joseph Stein
Taken In Marriage/Thomas Babe
Take Very Good Care Of Yourself/Michael
  Shurtleff
* Taking Away Of Little Willie, The/Tom
  Griffin
Taking Of Miss Janie, The/Ed Bullins
Tale At Both Ends, A/Mart Crowley
Talent For Murder, A/Jerome Chodorov

Tales Of Pacific N.W./Thomas G. Dunn
Tales Of Robin Hood, The/Louis LaRusso II
Tales Of The Revolution And Other American Fables/Jane Chambers
Tale That Wagged The Dog, The/Tim Kelly
Tale Told, A/Lanford Wilson
Talk To Me Like The Rain And Let Me Listen/Tennessee Williams
Talley's Folly/Lanford Wilson
Tall Green Grass, The/Louis C. Adelman
Tall Stories From The Butcher's Block/ Mark Berman
* Tallulah/William F. Brown
Tameem/Martin Halpern
* Tanglewood/David Cohen
Tango Palace/Maria I. Fornes
Tap Dancing In Molasses/Tim Kelly
Tape/T.C. Miller
Tarantella On A High Wire/George Freek
Tarleton Story, The/Arthur Jasspe
Tarquin Truthbeauty/Robert Patrick
Tarzan Of The Flicks/Ronald Tavel
Taxi Tales/Leonard Melfi
Tea & Sympathy/Robert Anderson
* Teachers Room, The/Howard Pflanzer
Team, The/Lennox Brown
Tear Along The Dotted Line/Jules Tasca
Tears Are For A Very Young Man/Tobi Louis
Teasers/Hiram Taylor
* Teddy/Herb Schapiro
* Teeth/Joanne Koch
Tegaroon/Wallace Hamilton
Telemachus, Friend/Sally D. Wiener
Telephone Murderer, The/James Schevill
Telephone Pole/Jean Reavey
Televisionary/Mark Edwards
Tell Me You Don't Love Me Charlie Moon/ Michael Shurtleff
Tell The Stars/Robert Kornfeld
Temper The Wind/Edward Mabley
Temporarily In Order Or Use It While You Can/Anthony Inneo
Ten Best Martyrs Of The Year/Seymour Simckes
Ten Brief Plays/W. Edwin Ver Becke
Ten Days That Shook The World/Robert E. Lee
* Tennessee/Romulus Linney
Tennessee River Story, The/Earl H. Smith
Tennis Anyone?/F.V. Hunt
Ten O'Clock Scholar/Joseph Schrank
Ten Ton Toys/Jean Reavey
Ten Weeks With The Circus/Tim Kelly
Ten Years Later/Edward Clinton
Terminal/Corinne Jacker
Terminal/Sam Shepard
Terminal/Susan Yankowitz
Terraced Apartment, The/Steve Carter
Terraces/Steve Carter
Terra Nova/Ted Talley
* Terrible Saint, A/Herbert Appleman
Terror By Gaslight/Tim Kelly
Terry By Terry/Mark Leib
Terry Project, The/Honor Moore
Testing Bit, The/Raymond Platt
Tetzel/Frank B. Ford

* Texas/Frank B. Ford
Texas Dry/John Olive
Thanksgiving At Aunt Betty's/Robert Riche
Thanksgotten/Louis LaRusso II
Thank You, Thank You, Doctor/Judith Morley
That All Depends On How The Drop Falls/Owa
That Championship Season/Jason Miller
* That Guggenheim Summer/Joel Ensana
That Merry Gang/William M. Green
That Old Rock-A-Bye/Susan Yankowitz
That's The Way The Fortune Cookie Crumbles/Edward Sakamoto
That Summer-That Fall/Frank D. Gilroy
That's What's Happening, Baby!/Johny Brandon
That They May Win/Arthur Miller
Theatre Games/Jonathan Levy
Theme Is Blackness, The/Ed Bullins
Therapist, The/Robert Pine
There In The Shade/Frank Salisbury
There Must Be A Pony!/James Kirkwood
There's A Wall Between Us, Darling/Sally Ordway
* There She Is, Ms. America/Donna de Matteo
There's No Sugar In Scotch/Leonard Melfi
There Was A Door/Robert W. Martin
These Fallen Angels/Gus Edwards
* These Ruins Are Inhabited/Joe T. Ford
Thespians/Joseph G. Gottfried
* They Burned The Church While I Was Gone/John R. Zapor
They Got Jack/Leo Rutman
They Might Be Giants/James Goldman
They're Playing Our Song/Neil Simon
They Seek A City/Ossie Davis
They Too Arise/Arthur Miller
* They Voted Yes!/Luther Davis
Thicker Than Water/Tobi Louis
Thief/David Trainer
Thief In The Night/Hiram Taylor
Thieves/Herb Gardner
Thing Itself, The/Arthur Sainer
Things Went Badly In Westphalia/Martin Sherman
Thin Lady Fat Man/John Olive
Third Daughter, The/Mario Fratti
* Third Richard, The/John W. Kirk
Thirteen Ways of Looking At A Blackbird/D.R. Andersen
Thirteen Ways Of Looking At Merle/ Townsend Brewster
* Thirtieth Of February/Charlotte Kraft
Thirty Years After/Sam A. Eisenstein
This Big House/Rose L. Goldemberg
This Is Not True/James Schevill
This Is On Me: Dorothy Parker/Thomas M. Fontana
This Is Rill Speaking/Lanford Wilson
* This Piece Of Land/Louis Rivers
This Play Is About Me/Israel Horovitz
This Property Is Condemned/Tennessee Williams
This Scent Of Incense/Lennox Brown

* **This Was Planned To Be A Choral Drama**/J. Kline Hobbs
* **Those Nice C. Watters**/Fredi Towbin
  Though It's Been Said Many Times, Many Ways/Townsend Brewster
  Thoughts On The Instant Of Greeting A Friend On The Street/Jean-Claude van Itallie
  Thousand & One Spells To Cast, A/R. Eugene Jackson
  Thousand Clowns, A/Herb Gardner
  Thread Of Scarlet, A/Howard Richardson
  Three/Crispin Larangeira
* **Three Acts Of Charity**/Peter Ramsey
* **Three Arabian Knights, The**/Aubrey Wisberg
  Three Bags Full/Jerome Chodorov
  3 Black Comedies/Norman Beim
  Three Cockolds/Michael Weller
  Three Colours Of A Dream/Lennox Brown
  Three Darlings, The/C.H. Keeney
  Three Days Before Yesterday/Kevin O'Morrison
  Three Days In The Life Of Clar'bel Light/Stanley Disney
  Three On The Run/Joseph Lizardi
  Three Part Invention/June Calender
  Three People/A.R. Gurney, Jr.
  Three Shepherds And A Lamb/Sy Reiter
  Three Short Plays/Wallace Shawn
  Three Sisters, The/Jean-Claude van Itallie
* **Three Unnatural Acts**/Dick D. Zigun
  Three Wishes For Jamie/Abe Burrows
  Threnody For The Newly Born, A/Townsend Brewster
  Thrombo/Albert Bermel
  Throne In An Autumn Room, The/Lennox Brown
* **Throw Thunder At This House**/J.E. Franklin
* **Thunder Rock**/Oscar Brand
  Thursday Club, The/A.R. Gurney, Jr.
* **Thyestes**/Richard France
  Tidings/Joseph G. Gottfried
  Tiger, The/Murray Schisgal
  Till The Day Break/Richard Stockton
  Time For Singing, A/C. Robert Jones
  Time For Teens And Libertines, A/Steven Somkin
  Time Is A Thief//Tobi Louis
  Time Machine, The/Tim Kelly
* **Time: 1940**/Marc P. Smith
  Time Now/Wallace Hamilton
  Time Of The Cuckoo, The/Arthur Laurents
  Time Of The Promise Green/Martha A. Fuentes
  Timepieces/Paul Mroczka
  Time Shadows/Helen Duberstein
  Time/Space/Lonnie Carter
  Times Square/Leonard Melfi
* **Time Steps**/Gus Kaikkonen
  Time's Up/Lance Lee
* **Time Trial, The**/Jack Gilhooley
  Time Turns Black/John Scott
* **Time Was**/Shannon K. Kelley
  Timid Dragon, The/Tim Kelly
  Tin Cup, The/Richard Reich

Tinkerman To The Promised Land/Gordon R. Watkins
Tin Man/John R. Zapor
Tiny Alice/Edward Albee
Tira/Michael Weller
Titanic/Christopher Durang
To Be A Woman/Robert Kornfeld
To Charlie, With Love/Peggy Phillips
* **Today A Little Extra**/Michael Kassin
  Today We Saw A Turtle/David K. Heefner
* **To Find A Rose**/Priscilla B. Dewey
  Toga! Toga! Toga!/Tim Kelly
* **To Grandmother's House We Go**/Joanna M. Glass
  To Grow A Rose/Robert W. Martin
  To Have And To Have Not/Mars Hill
  Toilet, The/Imamu A. Baraka
* **To Make A Man**/Benjamin Bradford
* **Tom & Mary, Mary & Tom**/John W. Kirk
  To Marianne With Love/Steven Somkin
  Tommy Allen Show, The/Megan Terry
  Tomorrow/Robert Unger
* **Tom Paine**/Paul Foster
  Tom Sawyer/A.R. Gurney, Jr.
  Tom Thumb/Venable Herndon
  To My Eldest And Only Brother/Sharon S. Martin
  Tongues/Sam Shepard
  Tonight In Living Color/A.R. Gurney, Jr.
  Too Late/Gordon R. Watkins
* **Toot**/J.J. Coyle
  Tooth Of The Crime/Sam Shepard
  Top Of The Mark/J. Lawrence & R.E. Lee
* **Torero**/Joseph Schrank
  Tornado/Jack Heifner
  Torrent/Lanny Flaherty
  To See The World In A Drop Of Brine/Townsend Brewster
  To Sit On A Horse/Ray E. Fox
  To Solve A Problem/John Pyros
  To Take Up Eternity Like A Mantle/Sam A. Eisenstein
  Total Immersion Of Madeline Favorini, The/Frank Gagliano
  Total-Recall/Richard Foreman
  Total Recall/Martin Halpern
  Touch And Go/Benjamin Bradford
  Touch And Go/Jean Kerr
* **Touch Black**/Bill Bozzone
  Touching Bottom/Steve Tesich
  Touch Light/Louis C. Adelman
  Touch Of Orpheus, A/Wallace Hamilton
  Tour/Terrence McNally
  Toussaint/Barry Berg
  To Wally Pantoni, I Leave A Credenza/John Guare
  Tower, The/Townsend Brewster
  Towers Of Achievement/Milan Stitt
  Town Crier/Mark Eisman
  Toyland/Louis LaRusso II
  Toys In The Attic/Lillian Hellman
* **Trade A Day**/Henry Gilfond
* **Trade-Offs**/Lonnie Carter
  Tragedy Of Oscar Wilde/W. Edwin Ver Becke
  Trail Of The Lonesome Pine, The/Earl H. Smith

* **Trail's End**/Clifford Turknett
Train Time/Mark Berman
* **Traitor, The**/Herman Wouk
Transatlantic Bridge/Anne Commire
Transceiver/Jerome McDonough
Transcendental Exercises/George Freek
Transfiguration Of Benno Blimpie/Albert Innaurato
* **Transformation Of Aura Rhanes**/Sandra Bertrand
Transformations/George Freek
Transience And Clay/Elyse Nass
Transistorized Electric Butterknife/Curtis Zahn
* **Transitions For A Mime Poem**/Owa
Transplant/Susan Yankowitz
Transplants, The/Wallace Hamilton
* **Trappings**/Charlotte Kraft
Trapshod/A.E.O. Goldman
Travellers/Corinne Jacker
Travel Lightly/Judith Morley
Treadmill To The Goodtime Star/Stanley Disney
Trees/Israel Horovitz
Tremont/Toni Press
* **Tremors Caused By Being Born**/Elizabeth Wyatt
Trespassers/Martin Halpern
Trial Can Be Fun, If You're The Judge, A/Warren Kliewer
Trial Of John D. Lee, The/Charles Horine
Trial Of Judas, The/James D. Pendleton
* **Trial Of Moke, The**/Daniel A. Stein
Trials Of Mrs. Surratt, The/Lanie Robertson
* **Tribal Rites**/Frederick A. Raborg, Jr.
Tribute/Thomas G. Dunn
Tribute/Bernard Slade
Trinidad/Sam A. Eisenstein
Trinity Of Four, The/Lennox Brown
* **Trio For Heartstrings**/Charles Leipart
Triple Play/Joseph Hart
Triple Play/R. Eugene Jackson
Trips/Mark Berman
Triptych/Ernest A. Joselovitz
Trixie True, Teen Detective!/Kelly Hamilton
Troubador, The/David Lifson
Trouble Maker, The/Edan Schappert
True Romances/Susan Yankowitz
True West/Sam Shepard
Tryptich/Oliver Hailey
T-Shirts/Robert Patrick
Tsk, Mary, Tsk/Stanley Nelson
Tune Of The Time, The/Sheppard Kerman
* **Tunes Of Chicken Little, The**/Robert Gordon
Turandot/Jonathan Levy
Turds In Hell/Charles Ludlam
* **Turkey In The Straw**/Jack Sharkey
Turnabout/Jack Sharkey
Turnabout/Doric Wilson
Turn For The Nurse, A/Jack Sharkey
Turnip, The/Lloyd Gold
Turn Of The Century/A.R. Gurney, Jr.
Turnstile/Israel Horovitz
* **Turtles**/Barbara Schneider

Tusitala/Aldyth Morris
Twaddles/Paul Mroczka
'Twas Brilling/Frank D. Gilroy
* **Twelfth Hour, The**/Sylvia Regan
Twelve Dreams/James Lapine
* **12-1-A**/Wakako Yamauchi
27 Wagons Full Of Cotton/Tennessee Williams
* **26501**/Lee Hunkins
23 Pat O'Brien Movies/Bruce J. Friedman
23 Years Later/Michael Weller
Twenty Years After The Man In The Iron Mask/Leo Rutman
Twigs/George Furth
Twilight Dinner, The/Lennox Brown
Twisting Slowly In The Wind/Robert W. Martin
Twit For Twat/Maxwell Glanville
* **Two Avenues Of Reproach**/Jean Reavey
Two Character Play/Tennessee Williams
Two Characters In Search Of An Agreement/Martha A. Fuentes
Two Fools Who Gained A Measure Of Wisdom/Tim Kelly
Two For One/Harry Granick
Two For The Seesaw/William Gibson
Two From Ulysses/F.V. Hunt
Two Gentlemen From Verona/John Guare
Two Girls And A Sailor/Edward M. Cohen
Two If By Sea/Priscilla B. Dewey
Two Marys, The/Warren Kliewer
Two Mothers/Elizabeth Wyatt
Two Pages A Day/Megan Terry
Two-Party System/Myrna Lamb
Two Sisters/Frank M. Mosier
Two Ten/Mars Hill
* **Two Wandering Sons Of Ham**/June V. Williams
Typists, The/Murray Schisgal
Tyranny Of Love/Norman Beim

U

Ultimate Grammar Of Life, The/Mark Medoff
Ulysses In Traction/Albert Innaurato
Umbrella, The/Jack R. Guss
Unamerican Cowboy, The/Charles Eastman
Un Bel Di/Robert Patrick
Uncle, The/David S. Milton
Uncle Eddy/Jay Broad
Uncle Snake/Israel Horovitz
Uncle Vanya/Jean-Claude van Itallie
Uncle Zepp/Joseph T. Pintauro
Uncommon Women and Others/Wendy Wasserstein
* **Under-Ground**/Curtis Zahn
Underground Bird, The/Rose L. Goldemberg
Under Jekyll's Hyde/Tim Kelly
Underlings, The/Thomas M. Fontana
Under MacDougal/James Prideaux
Under One Roof/Helen Kromer
Understudy, The/Ronald Tavel

V

W

Wall, The/Neil Selden
Wall At Higgs Memorial Beach, The/
  Jonathan Ringkamp
Wall, Prize, Redemption: A Trilogy/Vincent
  Viaggio
Wally's Cafe/R. Clark & S. Bobrick
Wally's Garage/Robert Unger
Walter/Murray Schisgal
Wandering/Lanford Wilson
Wanhope Building, The/John Finch
* Wanna/Conrad Bishop
Wanted — Dead Or Alive/Mark Edwards
Wanting/Wallace Hamilton
War/Jean-Claude van Itallie
War And Peace/Jerry Spindel
Warbeck/Louis Phillips
* Ward 8 Macabre/Robert Unger
Warhol Machine, The/Robert Patrick
* Warm Afternoon In Nebraska, A/Louis C.
  Adelman
War Of The Sons Of Light, The/Alan
  Roland
War On Tatem, The/Mark Medoff
War Party, The/Leslie Lee
War Party/Sally Ordway
* War Play/William Packard
Washerwoman, The/Townsend Brewster
Washer Woman: The Cycle/Bruce Serlen
Washington At Valley Forge/Brendan N.
  Ward
Washington Jr./David K. Heefner
Washington Revolting/Lanie Robertson
* Washington Shall Hang/Robert W. Russell
Washington Squares/Elyse Nass
* Watching Over Wally/Raymond Platt
Watchmaker/Alan Havis
Watch On The Rhine/Lillian Hellman
Watch Out Little Boy Or You'll Fall
  In/Wendy MacLaughlin
Watch The Cars And Lights/Leonard Melfi
Water Engine, The/David Mamet
Watergate Classics/Lonnie Carter
* Waterman/Frank B. Ford
* Watermelon Boats/Wendy MacLaughlin
Water Strike!/Edan Schappert
Way Back When/Ray Aranha
Way Of Life, A/Murray Schisgal
Way Of The Wolf, The/Ernest Ferlita
Wayside Motor Inn, The/A.R. Gurney, Jr.
Wayward Angel, The/Eric M. Lord
W.C. Fieldworthy Foiled Again/Tim Kelly
We Agree/Sally Ordway
Web, A/Albert Bermel
We Can Feed Everybody Here/Megan
  Terry
We Commit This Body/Wallace Dace
Wedding Belles And Lumberjacks/Tim
  Kelly
* Wednesday's Children/C. Robert Jones
Wednesday Sharp/Robert Auletta
Weed Bouquet, The/Richard Stockton
Weekend/Gore Vidal
Weep No More For Me/Gus Edwards
We Four/Richard Olson
We Have Always Lived In The Castle/
  Hugh Wheeler

We Hold These Truths/Robert Riche
Welcome To Andromeda/Ron Whyte
Welcome To Black River/Samm-Art
  Williams
Well, The/Sy Reiter
* Well Hung/Robert Lord
* We Never Thought A Wedding/Helen
  Duberstein
We're Here To Help/Toni Press
West Of The Pecos/Tim Kelly
West Side Story/Arthur Laurents
* West Street Gang, The/Doric Wilson
Wet And Dry/Leonard Melfi
We've Got To Stop Meeting Like This/Ted
  Tally
Whales Of August, The/David A. Berry
What! And Leave Bloomingdale's!/Fredi
  Towbin
What Are Friends For?/Townsend
  Brewster
What Are Friends For?/Gus Kaikkonen
What A Spot!/Jack Sharkey
What Can You Say To Mississippi/Ossie
  Davis
What Does A Blind Leopard See?/Lanie
  Robertson
* What Do I Do About Hemingway?/Enid
  Rudd
Whatever This Is — We're All In It
  Together/Tim Kelly
Whatever You Call It/John R. Zapor
What Is Making Gilda So Gray?/Tom Eyen
What Reason Could I Give/Daniel W.
  Owens
What's The Game Now?/Peter Copani
* What's The Matter With Uncle Leo?/
  Martha A. Fuentes
What The Babe Said/Martin Halpern
What Was The Relationship Of The Lone
  Ranger To The Means Of Production/
  Imamu A. Baraka
What Will The Neighbors Say!/Aubrey
  Wisberg
What You Will /Larry Loonin
Wheelbarrow Closers/Louis LaRusso II
W.H.E.N./Elyse Nass
When Dinah Shore Ruled The Earth/
  C. Durang & W. Wasserstein
When I Died My Hair In Venice/Helen
  Duberstein
* When In Rome/Paul Hunter
When Johnny Comes Dancing Home
  Again/Tom Eyen
When Last I Saw The Lemmings/Brian
  Taggert
When Love Is Done/Tobi Louis
When My Girlhood Was Still All
  Flowers/Megan Terry
When Other Friendships/Lydia Simmons
When Princes Could Be Waiters/George
  Hammer
When The Stars Begin To Fall/Lloyd Gold
* When The Sun Goes Down/Michael
  Shurtleff
When We Were Very Young/Thomas Babe
When We Were Very Young/Brendan N.

Ward

When You Comin Back, Red Ryder?/Mark Medoff

When You're By Yourself, You're Alone/ Eugene McKinney

Where Are They??/Daniel W. Owens

* **Where Are You Going, Hollis Jay?**/ Benjamin Bradford

* **Where Credit Is Due**/David Cohen

Where Does It Hurt And How Can We Help You?/Herb Schapiro

* **Where Has Tommy Flowers Gone?**/ Terrence McNally

Where Have All The Flowers Gone?/ Ludmilla Bollow

Where Is Che Guevara/Leo Rutman

Where Is De Queen?/Jean-Claude van Itallie

Where People Gather/Peter Copani

* **Where The Green Bananas Grow**/Allen Davis III

Where The Mississippi Meets The Amazon/Ntozake Shange

Where The Music Is/Anna M. Barlow

Where There's A Will/John Jiler

While Shakespeare Slept/Tim Kelly

* **Whilom**/Lanny Flaherty

Whiskey/Terrence McNally

* **Whispers**/Crispin Larangeira

White Asparagus/Jean Nuchtern

White Cat, The/Mario Fratti

White House Murder Case, The/Jules Feiffer

White Jazz/Marc A. Zagoren

* **White Linen**/Steve Metcalfe

White Pelicans/Jay Broad

Whiteshop, The/S. Garrett Robinson

Whiteskin Game, The/Conrad Bishop

White Whore And The Bit Player, The/Tom Eyen

* **Whizney Land**/John McLiam

Who Are You?/Michael Shurtleff

Who Can Fix The Dragon's Wagon?/R. Eugene Jackson

Who Do You Want, Piere Vidal?/Rochelle Owens

Who Here Has Seen The Color Of The Wind/Louis Phillips

Who is Sally?/A.R. Gurney, Jr.

Who Killed My Bald Sister Sophie?/Tom Eyen

* **Who Killed Richard Cory?**/A.R. Gurney, Jr.

Whole Ninth Floor, The/Richard Seff

Who'll Save The Plowboy?/Frank D. Gilroy

Who Needs Enemies?/Victor Power

Who's Afraid Of Virginia Woolf/Edward Albee

Whose Play?/Albert Bermel

* **Who's Happy Now?**/Oliver Hailey

Who's On First?/Jack Sharkey

Who's There/Conrad Bishop

Who's Who In America/Theodore Gross

Who Wants To Be The Lone Ranger/Lee Kalcheim

Who Won Second Place At Omaha?/Diane Kagan

Why Hanna's Skirt Won't Stay Down/Tom Eyen

* **Why Is That Dumb Son Of A Bitch Down The Street Happier Than I Am?**/Robert Riche

Why Lilly Won't Spin/Nathan N. Barrett

* **Wick And The Tallow, The**/Henry Gilfond

Wicked John And The Devil/Jeffrey Sweet

Widow, The/Marie Irene Fornes

Widow And The Colonel, The/Rochelle Owens

Widow's Blind Date, The/Israel Horovitz

Widow's Might, The/C.H. Keeney

Widow's Walk/Tim Kelly

Widow's Walk/Howard Richardson

* **Wife, The**/Jane Chambers

Wiglaf, A Myth For Actors/Joseph Hart

* **Wilbur And Me**/William F. Brown

Wildcat/N. Richard Nash

Wild Goose, The/Jeff Wanshel

Wild Man Of Borneo/Allen Sternfield

Willa-Willie-Bill's Dope Garden/Megan Terry

Willie/Leslie Lee

Willie C/Ray Aranha

Willie's Weakness/C.H. Keeney

Will Mr. Merriwether Return From Memphis?/Tennessee Williams

Will O' The W.A.S.P./Edan Schappert

Willows For Her Harp/Elyse Nass

Will The Gentlemen In Cabin Six Please Rise To The Occasion/Tom Griffin

Will The Real South Please Rise/J.E. Franklin

* **Wilson In Love**/Charles Horine

Winchester House/Joel Ensana

Wind & The Rain, The/Herschel Steinhardt

Windfall Apples/Roma Greth

Window/Jean Reavey

* **Window And Wall**/Joseph Hart

Windows/Murray Schisgal

Winds Of Change/Barbara Field

* **Wind-up Toys, The**/Sylvia Regan

Wine In Winter/Lennox Brown

Winging It/Jeffrey Sweet

Wings/Arthur Kopit

Winner, The/John Finch

* **Winning**//Benjamin R. Barber

Winston Tastes Good/John Pyros

Winter Is Coming/Lennox Brown

* **Winterplay**/Adele E. Shank

Winter Soldier, The/Frank M. Mosier

Winterspace/Drury Pifer

Winti Train, The/Lennox Brown

Win With Wheeler/Lee Kalcheim

Wisdom Amok/Albert Innaurato

Wisdom Of The Elders/Eric M. Lord

Wish, The/Mario Fratti

* **Witches' Sabbath**/Harry Granick

Witch Who Wouldn't Hang, The/Tim Kelly

With Intent To Commit A Crime/Neville Aurelius

Without Apologies/Thom Thomas

Witness/Terrence McNally

Witnesses, The/Louis Rivers

Witnesses/Arthur Sainer